SELECTED
POETRY AND PROSE
OF
COLERIDGE

SELECTED
POETRY AND PROSE
OF
COLERIDGE

EDITED, WITH AN INTRODUCTION, BY
DONALD A. STAUFFER,
PRINCETON UNIVERSITY

Modern Library College Editions

Distributed by McGraw-Hill, Inc.

Acknowledgment is made to the Clarendon Press for their kind permission to use their edition of *The Complete Poetical Works of Samuel Taylor Coleridge* (edited by E. H. Coleridge, 1912) for the text of all poems in the present volume and to use their edition of *Biographia Literaria* (edited by J. Shawcross, 1907) for the text of that work. Acknowledgment is also made to Harvard University Press for their kind permission to use portions of T. M. Raysor's *Shakespearean Criticism* (1930) as the source of texts for *Romeo and Juliet* and *Hamlet, 1813*. All prose other than that acknowledged above has been based upon the reliable *Coleridge's Works* (edited by W. G. T. Shedd, 1853).

Random House IS THE PUBLISHER OF

THE MODERN LIBRARY

Manufactured in the United States of America

CONTENTS

POETRY

THE SEEDS OF POETRY

PHANTOM MAGIC

CONVERSATION POEMS

INTRODUCTION

BY DONALD A. STAUFFER

"There are such things as fountains in the world."
—Coleridge, Preface to "Christabel"

SHORTLY after Coleridge died in 1834, William Wordsworth called him "the most *wonderful* man that he had ever known—wonderful for the originality of his mind, and the power he possessed of throwing out in profusion grand central truths from which might be evolved the most comprehensive systems." And Charles Lamb, writing in 1834: "His great and dear spirit haunts me. I cannot think a thought, I cannot make a criticism on men or books, without an ineffectual turning and reference to him."

An introduction to Coleridge, like most introductions, should be made through the agency of a friend. Wordsworth and Lamb may be allowed to set the tone here, since they knew him as well as loved him during most of their lives. (Those who prefer the reasons why Coleridge should *not* be remembered or admired may find in bibliographies an ample literature.) When Coleridge chose a name to cover his own periodical essays, he did not adopt the *Tatler* or the *Spectator*, the *Idler* or the *Rambler*, the *Citizen of the World* or the *Hypochondriack*. He chose the *Friend*. There have been less perceptive descriptions of his philosophy and his secret.

As a friend, Coleridge continually sought to communicate. Many of his most startling or useful critical terms are "friendly" words in that they seek this communion or community. "Esemplastic," "coadunate," "fusion," "copula," "union," "intuitive," "organic," "Reason" as he uses it, the great doctrine of the "Imagination" itself—these words as they develop in the pages that follow should show the drift of his mind toward friendship, toward a union that was a communion.

He was a great talker. Perhaps this marks his carelessness of fame, or even his indolence. Perhaps it reveals a fear of solitude, as when he wrote: "The stimulus of conversation suspends the terror that haunts my mind." But perhaps also the flow of talk marks the desire to share thoughts with the warm and the living, to commune with the old familiar faces, and the new ones, rather than with those generations of readers whom a writer personally can never know. Coleridge began to talk at an early age and never left off until he died at sixty-two. The schoolmates at Christ's Hospital flocked to his room to listen; the young William Hazlitt was entranced and exalted at Shrewsbury and Nether Stowey. As a young man of 22, Coleridge preached his social liberalism in a Welsh tavern with such success (he wrote to Southey) "that two great huge fellows of butcher-like appearance danced about the room in enthusiastic agitation. And one of them of his own accord called for a glass of brandy, and drank it off to this, his own toast, 'God save the King! And may he be the last.'"

The talk went on through the years until he had become in his own person a kind of *causerie célèbre*, the Sage of Highgate to whom people made pilgrimages or for whom they gave dinners —Carlyle and Hood and Hunt and Keats and Lockhart and Scott and even the acidulous Francis Jeffrey, with Cooper and Emerson from America. Not all of them liked the torrent of talk, particularly those who preferred to talk themselves. But a man who could hold for decades the austere Wordsworth and the simple Southey and the quirky Lamb, who could moreover transform his nephew Henry Nelson Coleridge into the Boswell who recorded *Table Talk*, is no mere whisperer.

What did he talk about? Everything. Yet essentially his one never-entirely-forgotten subject was relationship—relating parts, or fusing disparates, within a single reality. The ability to see relationships became Coleridge's criterion for recognizing an educated man: "It is the unpremeditated and evidently habitual arrangement of his words, grounded on the habit of foreseeing, in each integral part, or (more plainly) in every sentence, the whole that he then intends to communicate." And in the *Biographia Literaria* he set up (as opposed to Wordsworth's common rustic who speaks simple natural language) his own ideal type, who "chiefly seeks to discover and express those connections of things, or those relative bearings of fact to fact, from which some more or less general law is deducible."

No one in philosophical thought has ever striven more valiantly or unceasingly for one world, a world which was not to be achieved by disregarding its infinite and embarrassing particularities. Wordsworth best described this drive in saying: "There was always a train, a stream, in Coleridge's discourse, always a connection between its parts in his own mind, though one not always perceptible to the minds of others." Though Coleridge's listeners may occasionally have lost themselves (as his readers may lose themselves today) in the Gulf Stream of his mind, a true perspective shows that the stream, though it was wide and without trim boundaries, had a definite and genial current.

To show the difficulty of this search for unity in diversity, let Coleridge be his own accuser, in a passage from the *Anima Poetae* which reveals in its style and images the very faults and qualities he is describing in his thought:

> My illustrations swallow up my thesis. I feel too intensely the omnipresence of all in each, platonically speaking; or, psychologically, my brain-fibres, or the spiritual light which abides in the brain-marrow, as visible light appears to do in sundry rotten mackerel and other *smashy* matters, is of too general an affinity with all things, yet is eternally pursuing the likenesses, or rather, that which is common [between them]. Bring me two things that seem the very same, and then I am quick enough [not only] to show the difference, even to hair-splitting, but to go on from circle to circle till I break against the shore of my hearers' patience, or have my concentricals dashed to nothing by a snore. That is my ordinary mishap.

Or to sum it up positively in a phrase from Charles Lamb: "He had a hunger for eternity."

Such epigraphs as the last two quotations afford a center for the further consideration of Coleridge's "concentricals." In his final image, Coleridge characteristically sees the little world in terms of the great, the mental interchanging with the physical, and describes the movement of his mind as if it were ripples in a lake widening away in circles from the original disturbance. The cause of the disturbance itself, which might be any sudden accident, is not so important as the expanding circles. The effect described presupposes innumerable droplets in fluid relationship, but who cares to count the droplets in a lake? It is their inter-action that produces the beautiful patterns. Coleridge's mind was a capacious reservoir—Professor Lowes calls it "the deep well"—into which he poured everything he read. He read everything and forgot nothing. A schoolfellow at Christ's Hospital, Charles Valentine Le Grice, recalled that when in the late 1780s Edmund Burke issued a pamphlet, conversation-loving friends would throng to Coleridge's room for little suppers: "There was no need of having the book before us. Coleridge had read it in the morning, and in the evening he would repeat whole pages verbatim. Pamphlets swarmed from the press. Coleridge had read them all; and in the evening, with our negus, we had them *viva voce* gloriously."

Coleridge was a chain reader: a footnote in one book would

take him to another, and a passing reference there would lead him to devour a third. Languages and centuries threw up no barriers to his curiosity. And though the most recondite and surprising volumes sank deep down into his mind, he was no mere passive reader. Books, too, he treated as friends, with whom he carried on conversations. Much of the recoverable Coleridge is to be found as marginalia, scribbled in his own books, and in those of his friends, and in volumes—only a genius should be forgiven this particular overpowering drive—borrowed from public libraries. As with his conversations, no one can estimate the effect of these occasional effusions upon contemporary and subsequent thought—these marginal dialogues between STC and breathless authors, these Sibylline leaves that mark the haphazard and fragmentary voice of the oracle.

He was a part of all that he had read. Feeling himself a friend or a peer of all writers—the Church Fathers, the German philosophers, old playwrights, humorists, preachers, scientists, travellers, poets—how could he distinguish their thought from his own? Why should he bother? He did not read without discriminations, as anyone knows who has read his excoriating opinions on Edward Gibbon. But when he sympathized with a writer, he took him to his heart and would repeat him or echo him or transform him into a part of his own thought and writing. The reading in the Coleridgean reservoir has never been plumbed to the bottom, if it ever can be. But it furnished materials for the play of his mind, which can best be described in the image of the fountain in "Kubla Khan" (the image itself is borrowed from a travel book):

> And from this chasm, with ceaseless turmoil seething,
> As if this earth in fast thick pants were breathing,
> A mighty fountain momently was forced;
> Amid whose swift half-intermitted burst
> Huge fragments vaulted like rebounding hail,
> Or chaffy grain beneath the thresher's flail.

What he reshaped and reuttered from the past, Coleridge had fused into his own absorbing mind. John Stuart Mill grants that the Germans anticipated the essentials of the Coleridgean doctrine, but adds: "He has left on the system he inculcated, such traces of himself as cannot fail to be left by any mind of original powers." If the result is plagiarism, then a mathematician plagiarizes when he accepts the quantum theory, or a Christian when he repeats the Lord's Prayer. Coleridge is one of those infrequent figures through whom the current of past thought rushes, narrowing within a single consciousness, and expanding later into other minds. In the first half of the nineteenth century he attracted some of the best thinkers. And in our present century he has adumbrated, or directly inspired, some of the most fruitful and subtle ideas at work in philosophy, in poetic criticism, in semantics, in symbolic logic, in theology. Yet what Mill remarked in 1840 remains true today: "the class of thinkers has scarcely yet arisen by whom he is to be judged." To Mill, "every Englishman of the present day is by implication either a Bethamite or a Coleridgean." The estimate of George Saintsbury, the crotchety historian of criticism, is equally high: in literary criticism Saintsbury ranks Coleridge only with Aristotle and Longinus, and declares that if chairs of literature were to be abolished, he would lead no counterrevolution, provided that the proceeds from the disestablishment were applied to furnish every university student with a copy of the *Biographia Literaria*.

The complete realization of Coleridge's basic thought—the relation of parts to whole when the whole includes all possible experience—is, of course, impossible in any man. Almost unavoidably the whole blurs and minimizes the parts, or the parts confuse the whole. Occasionally Coleridge puts them in perfect balance, as in his illuminating definition of a poem (elsewhere he applies it to a piece of music or a painting) as that species of composition which proposes to itself "such delight from the *whole*, as is compatible with a distinct gratification from each component *part*." Coleridge at his best is both philosopher and poet; he must see infinity in a grain of sand, simultaneously, actually. Ordinarily his thought seems incomplete and difficult because he struggles to make it all-inclusive, and is ill content with any partial pattern. He envisions not only the One, but the All which is at the same time One. He throws wide arches over the cosmos, dangerous as Wotan's rainbow bridge to Valhalla, daring as Milton's highway from hell to the world built over chaos.

Take as an example a recurring pattern in his thought, fairly simple in statement, but reverberating in implications. In his marginal notes on John Donne he sets up the following pentad:

Prothesis.
Christ the Word.

Thesis.	Mesothesis,	Antithesis.
The Scriptures.	The Holy Spirit.	The Church.

Synthesis.
The Preacher.

In his notes on Bunyan's *Pilgrim's Progress* he constructs the same pentad, and remarks that "All things in which the temporal is concerned may be reduced to a pentad." If the movement of time is present primarily in prothesis, mesothesis, and synthesis, the movement of the mind (making its oppositions and distinctions) comes out most clearly in the thesis, mesothesis, and antithesis. A double or triple distinction will not satisfy Coleridge as a description of reality. He needs five points, a magical quincunx, so that two lines may intersect, or two streams merge, or two dreams cross. Time and intellect flow through each other, and each must have its poles. And at the center, as intermediator and unifier, is the Mesothesis, or "the Indifference," or the Holy Spirit.

The thought haunts him. He sets the pentad up again before his *Confessions of an Inquiring Spirit,* with the following explanation: "The Scriptures, the Spirit, and the Church, are co-ordinate; the indispensable conditions and the working causes of the perpetuity and continued renascence and spiritual life of Christ still militant. The Eternal Word, Christ from everlasting, is the Prothesis, or identity;—the Scriptures and the Church are the two poles, or Thesis and Antithesis; and the Preacher in direct line under the Spirit, but likewise the point of junction of the Written Word and the Church, is the Synthesis. This is God's hand in the World." Yet if this is too ethereal, Coleridge is willing to use the same pentad in an analysis of the parts of speech, in which sheer grammar has rarely been treated on a more highly philosophical plane, all the parts of speech streaming from the basic act of consciousness: the prothesis in the noun-verb *I am* which implies identity of being and act.

This extended illustration need not be understood in all its details. It should serve well enough, however, to indicate Coleridge's search for some mediation among multiplicities, some relation that will establish unity.

The search never ceased—in political and scientific and moral and artistic and religious thought. The change in his opinions shows his characteristic drift toward more inclusive realities. He came to be a great admirer of Burke, after his earlier liberal distrust, because he felt that Burke envisioned more of history (including probable future history) than the radical reformers. He abandoned Hartley's mechanistic psychology of association in favor of more vitalistic theories. He gave up Unitarianism for a belief in the Trinity.* He devoted fervent argument to persuad-

Note: Much of his later thought was devoted to an explication of the Trinity, in order to make philosophy more acceptable to a

ing his readers that Bacon's and Plato's systems "are radically one and the same system." The yearning toward this unity of all myriads is well shown in an eloquent passage which happens to come from a lecture on the drama:

> One great principle is common to all the fine arts, a principle which probably is the condition of all consciousness, without which we should feel and imagine only by discontinuous moments, and be plants or brute animals instead of men;—I mean that ever-varying balance, or balancing, of images, notions, or feelings, conceived as in opposition to each other;—in short, the perception of identity and contrariety; the least degree of which constitutes likeness, the greatest absolute difference; but the infinite gradations between these two form all the play and all the interest of our intellectual and moral being, till it leads us to a feeling and an object more awful than it seems to me compatible with even the present subject to utter aloud; though I am most desirous to suggest it. For there alone are all things at once different and the same; there alone, as the principle of all things, does distinction exist unaided by division; there are will and reason, succession of time and unmoving eternity, infinite change and ineffable rest!

In such words as "discontinuous," "opposition," "contrariety," "difference," and "division" and such opposite words as "identity" and "likeness," the passage quoted above suggests Coleridge's struggle to find a principle that would allow him to reconcile unity with variety, the absolute and the individual. He finds a solution in his key-concept of *polarity*, which, in order to establish *poles*, necessarily implies a single object or state of being to possess those poles. Coleridge seizes upon the idea of polarity eagerly, for it allows him to develop a vitalistic concep-

---

Christian, or Christianity to a philosopher. His earlier Unitarianism seemed to him in the end to be marked by folly, ignorance, and "high unreasonableness." The Trinity gave him a better paradigm of reality, since it made allowance for a needful element of mystery, and permitted *relationship*, the fluidity and interplay which established spirit. He applied his trinitarian thinking characteristically to philosophy: "The Hunterian position is a genuine philosophic idea, the negative test of which, as of all ideas, is that it is equi-distant from an *ens logicum* or abstraction, an *ens repraesentativum* or generalization, and an *ens phantasticum* or imaginary thing or *phaenomenon*." He applied it also to biology: "Life itself is neither of these separately, but the copula of all three [reproduction, irritability, and sensibility, the powers of length, surface, and depth]."

tion of life and consciousness as conflict, action, organic growth, creativity. Here again he is his own best speaker, this time in a few sentences from his essay on "Theory of Life," which should be read in full:

> This must be the one great end of Nature, her ultimate production of the highest and most comprehensive individuality. . . . The tendency having been ascertained, what is its most general law? I answer—*polarity*, or the essential dualism of Nature, arising out of its productive unity, and still tending to reaffirm it, either as equilibrium, indifference, or identity. In its *productive* power, of which the product is the only measure, consists its incompatibility with mathematical calculus. For the full applicability of an abstract science ceases, the moment reality begins. Life, then, we consider as the copula, or the unity of thesis and antithesis, position and counterposition,—Life itself being the positive of both.

In following to this point Coleridge's quest for unity, we have drawn illustrations from the fields of theology, literature, grammar, politics, psychology, Baconian science and Platonic philosophy, drama, and biology. Coleridge was myriad-minded, to use his own word for describing Shakespeare. More accurately, his single-minded search led him into myriad fields. Since the destination he longed for was completed reality held in a single view, he took all knowledge as his province, like Francis Bacon whom on the surface he resembled so little and in the depths admired so much.

These disparate fragments should illuminate his doctrine of the Imagination—another form of the "mesothesis" or holy spirit which unites polarities and creates reality. In a famous passage he writes: "The Imagination then I consider either as primary, or secondary. The primary Imagination I hold to be the living power and prime agent of all human perception, and as a repetition in the finite mind of the eternal act of creation in the infinite I AM. The secondary Imagination I consider as an echo of the former, coexisting with the conscious will, yet still as identical with the primary in the *kind* of its agency, and differing only in *degree*, and in the *mode* of its operation. It dissolves, diffuses, dissipates, in order to re-create: or where this process is rendered impossible, yet still at all events it struggles to idealize and to unify. It is essentially *vital*, even as all objects (*as* objects) are essentially fixed and dead."

The terms "primary" and "secondary" are misleading, since Coleridge is not rating them, but simply setting up an order of precedence in time. The first and grounding conception of the Imagination makes it a vital self-consciousness. Within that wide field occurs occasionally that other form of Imagination: voluntary intense creativity, whether of the artist or artisan, inventor or explorer, philosopher or scientist. And with this passage as a base (or better, with Chapters V through XIV of the *Biographia Literaria* from which both passages are drawn), this section may well conclude with the precious paragraph that focuses the whole doctrine of the Imagination on literary criticism proper:

The poet, described in ideal perfection, brings the whole soul of man into activity, with the subordination of its faculties to each other according to their relative worth and dignity. He diffuses a tone and spirit of unity that blends, and (as it were) *fuses,* each into each, by that synthetic and magical power, to which I would exclusively appropriate the name of Imagination. This power, first put in action by the will and understanding, and retained under their irremissive, though gentle and unnoticed, control, *laxis effertur habenis,* reveals itself in the balance or reconcilement of opposite or discordant qualities: of sameness, with difference; of the general with the concrete; the idea with the image; the individual with the representative; the sense of novelty and freshness with old and familiar objects; a more than usual state of emotion with more than usual order; judgment ever awake and steady self-possession with enthusiasm and feeling profound or vehement; and while it blends and harmonizes the natural and the artificial, still subordinates art to nature; the manner to the matter; and our admiration of the poet to our sympathy with the poetry.

The yearning for unity often leads to mysticism, but Coleridge was no mystic. The conception of polarities forbids to men an *undifferentiated* oneness, while the Coleridgean conception of the Imagination as an active re-creative force presupposes material upon which that force works, and which it struggles to transmute and idealize and unify. Coleridge's philosophy rests confidently on a necessary interaction between an inner and an outer world. "All knowledge rests on the coincidence of an object with a subject." Neither subjective nor objective comes first; and indeed, one is known as such by the presence of the other; "both are coinstantaneous and one." Who but the all-inclusive Coleridge, distrusting extremes set up as exclusive answers, would name one son Hartley after the associational mechanistic psychologist and another son Berkeley after the subjective idealist? True to his own ideas, he prudently named still another son Derwent after a lake.

Coleridge's adverse criticism of other thinkers often rests upon his belief that *interaction* between two forces or more is neces-sary for an adequate human notion of reality. He attacks what he calls the Mystic, therefore, because the mystic is a man who "refers to inward feelings and experiences, of which mankind at large are not conscious, as evidences of the truth of any opinion." In the *Biographia Literaria* and elsewhere he demolishes materi-alism and mechanism because they are partial and limited sys-tems. His argument is devastating, but it is balanced by a refuta-tion, similarly based, of Berkeleyan subjectivism. Both are partial. The same belief in a fusing interaction is at work when he points out the weakness in the Cambridge Platonist Henry More, whom he loved: "More had both the philosophic and the poetic genius, supported by immense erudition. But unfortunately the two did not amalgamate. It was not his good fortune to discover, as in the preceding generation William Shakespeare · discovered, a *mordaunt* or common base of both, and in which both the poetic and the philosophical power blended in one." Or to ring the changes again, in terms of general literary criticism: "This is my definition of a *just popular* style: When the author has had his own eye fixed steadily on the *abstract*, yet permits his readers to see only the *concrete*."

In such passages, the "shaping spirit of Imagination" welds the parts of experience. Imagination is active, creative—"for in our life alone does Nature live." (The reverse, of course, is equally true in Coleridge's philosophy: in Nature's life alone do *we* live.) Coleridge modifies other writers' thoughts until they become his own, as when he defines the Platonic idea: "A dis-tinguishable power self-affirmed, and seen in its unity with the Eternal Essence, is, according to Plato, an idea." Again, a reader would hardly guess that Coleridge is describing Wordsworth's early style, though the description might well fit some of Cole-ridge, when he writes: "In the structure of the particular lines and periods, there is a harshness and acerbity connected and combined with images all a-glow, which might recall those prod-ucts of the vegetable world, where gorgeous blossoms rise out of a hard and thorny rind or shell, within which the rich fruit is elaborating."

His very style gives the shape of his thoughts. His frequent italics show the struggle for certainty. His parentheses he defends because they present "the *drama* of reason, the thought growing, instead of a mere *hortus siccus* [dry garden]." The desire to bring everything in and to find relevance and relation in the oddest collocations comes out in his startling description of his own involuted sentences: "My thoughts bustle along like a Surinam toad, with little toads sprouting out of back, side, and belly, vegetating while it crawls." The Imagination is active in the auditor or spectator as well as in the creative artist, so that "The beholder either recognizes it [genius] as a projected form of his own being, that moves before him with a glory round its head, or recoils from it as from a spectre."

The interaction between inner and outer worlds, the "ennobling interchange" for which the Imagination is the organ of perception, is to Coleridge a source of constant wonder. One is so perfectly fitted to the other, like a convex and a concave surface, that each is simultaneously the cause and the realization of its complement. "In looking at objects of nature," Coleridge writes, "I seem rather to be seeking, as it were asking, a symbolic language for something within me." Who is speaking in that sentence? The poet and seer? Or the philosopher and systematizer? Coleridge was both, as his doctrine of the Imagination compels all poets to be both. He was the author who fixed his own eye steadily on the abstract, yet who permitted his readers—at least in his best work—to see the concrete.

So far this argument has scrutinized principally Coleridge's ideas as a philosopher: the friendly need for congeniality, the search for relationships, unity-in-variety held in a single vision, polarity, the relation between self-consciousness and the creative will, the interaction between subjective and objective, the shaping or esemplastic power. The argument might be echoed or parallelled in the mode of poetry, the thinker's intellect transmuted into the poet's eye, the abstract giving way to the concrete in those haunting images of friendly communion and desolate meditation, of soothing nature and frightful phantoms, of wanderers and enchantresses, of garish colors and still points of light, and of a solitary figure, in the shaping mist drawn upward from the ground, staring at the cold moon.

The poet in Coleridge was well aware of the mighty world of eye and ear. Even in his philosophical writing unexpected concrete apparitions are conjured up. Tenuous spiritual relations are presented in terms of landscape. Thus, when he wishes to describe the grounds of poetry which he and Wordsworth will take as their own, merely with difference of emphasis in their approaches, he speaks of "the two cardinal points of poetry" as "faithful adherence to the truth of nature, and the power of giving the interest of novelty by the modifying colours of imagination." Yet he immediately proceeds with a picture-sentence where the eye understands the argument, or illustrates it: "The sudden charm, which accidents of light and shade, which moonlight or sunset diffused over a known and familiar landscape, appeared to represent the practicability of combining both. These are the poetry of nature."

Coleridge cannot be understood, even as a thinker, without full awareness of his tendency to visualize thought. He is not merely rhapsodizing when he writes:

O! what a life is the eye! what a strange and inscrutable essence!

He should be taken literally in this poem, the "Hexameters" addressed to the Wordsworths; and he should be taken literally when he writes in the same poem: "To see is only a language." This language of *seeing* produced his best poems, and must be considered as a distinctive trait in his habit of thinking. Coleridge himself takes us within the magic lantern of his mind when he writes of "Kubla Khan," that strangest of compositions, "if that indeed can be called composition in which all the images rose up before him as *things*, with a parallel production of the correspondent expressions, without any sensation or consciousness of effort."

"Kubla Khan" was composed after the author had taken an anodyne "in consequence of a slight indisposition." Like most human beings, Coleridge went through life slightly indisposed; but his sharper sensitivity and his loftier hopes demanded an excess of anodynes. He took many forms of opium, among which the most important were endless conversation with friends, metaphysical philosophy, enchanted daydreaming, and meditations on the infinite. He used the peculiar gifts of his mind to allay its weaknesses and fears.

The pattern of his poems shows his self-induced therapy. His melancholy lassitude and sense of failure (how often can a Romantic succeed?) appear desperately insuperable in such poems as "Dejection," "The Pains of Sleep," "Limbo," "Work Without Hope," and "The Pang More Sharp Than All." One anodyne is the gay play of language, where Coleridge's intentions surpass his achievement. Another is the summoning up of friends, for which Coleridge created his own form and named it the "Conversation Poem." Professor Harper, in fact, calls this group of poems "Poems of Friendship." Usually their diction is as relaxed as a letter, their stream of freely associated thoughts as desultory as a talk with an intimate, their trust immense. The vast natural world also, with its soothing power and quiet, Coleridge treats as a friend, and such a poem as the "Hymn before Sun-rise, in the Vale of Chamouni" is in essence a Poem of Friendship, with nature offering the consolation and the inspiriting. Through such effusion and communion Coleridge could overcome his fears in solitude.

The greatest opium of all was the daydream. Here intuitions, hopes, and fears that kindle hope, flash into shapes. Intimations are given form and move through stories or allegories. Figures and scenes have the particularity and weighted sense of unstated significance of the figures in visions. Thoughts are seen as things, in coruscating colors; yet outside the central glare everything fades to phantoms, and the transitions are as unnoticed or as unpredictable as in dreams. Few poets experience for long "the somnial magic superinduced on, without suspending, the active powers of the mind." But three times at least—in "The Ancient Mariner," in "Christabel," and in "Kubla Khan"—Coleridge reaches the inexhaustibility of great poetry.

The short-lived fountain of Coleridge's best verse flowed as the result of his association with Wordsworth. It was the luckiest meeting in literary annals. Essentially Coleridge gave Wordsworth a mind, and Wordsworth gave Coleridge a will. Each furnished the other with what every poet must find somewhere: intelligent admiration. Encouraged by each other, they stepped out of the dull draperies of conventional diction that muffled their early verse and found more enterprise in walking naked. Coleridge, who always needed sea anchors to keep him from boxing the compass, found them not only in Wordsworth and cottage life, but in folk poetry and the accentual rhythm of native English verse. The ballad with its simple speech, its pictured action, and its direct drama, offered him a form that cut loose the poet in him from the metaphysician.

But even in his poetry, his dominant idea, the lifelong mystery of an individual searching for unity in a phantasmal cosmos, bubbles up in variants on a repeated image. The Aeolian harp vibrates and thrums at the touch of unseen winds. The Mariner is alone on a wide, wide sea. Christabel is drawn to the huge oak tree in the midnight wood. A pleasure dome is associated with measureless caverns; sunny spots of greenery are enfolded by forests ancient as the hills; Kubla hears from far ancestral voices prophesying war.

Always there is this lonely center of consciousness, with vastness beyond. Resembling Shakespeare's "pity, like a naked newborn babe, striding the blast," Coleridge's is a compulsive image:

The magic image of the magic child.

The child at the center (or the damsel, or the wanderer) is Coleridge, or his shaping imagination. This intuition shapes the image of his secret thought: a living, sometimes frighteningly piteous, focus of consciousness, filled with the desire to concentrate the universe, vast shifting phantom though it is, within that one focus.

Many of Coleridge's best-known distinctions can be seen within the terms of this one image—or is it this one thought? The mesothesis itself, at the center of his pentad, is the magic image. His distinction between the Fancy and the Imagination has proved of little real use to later critics, but Coleridge felt passionately that Fancy mechanically combined dead elements, whereas the living Imagination assimilated, modified, and fused elements into organic unity. Similarly, the distinction between Reason and Understanding becomes Coleridge's own, and not a mere borrowing from Kant, when he feels the Understanding to be a practical power for living and adjusting, but the Reason to be the unchanging light of truth, the Logos itself. The poet in him throws his thoughts again and again into pictures. Reason is "the irradiative power"; it is opposed to "the shaping mist, which the light had drawn upward from the ground, and which that light alone had made visible." And again in 1830:

> Whene'er the mist, that stands 'twixt God and thee,
> Defecates to a pure transparency,
> That intercepts no light and adds no stain—
> There Reason is, and then begins her reign!

Perhaps it was the poet's need for pictures and for thought in terms of personality which led him to exclaim: "Newton *was* a great man, but you must excuse me if I think that it would take many Newtons to make one Milton." From this controlling vision of a warm personal center in a mysterious universe spring the fruitful ideas in his literary criticism: art as creation, art as organism (that is, a living and growing unity) rather than as mechanical combination and proportion and rules, art as discovery. "The poet does not require us to be awake and believe; he solicits us only to yield ourselves to a dream; and this too with our eyes open, and with our judgment ready to awaken us; and meantime, only, not to *dis*believe." From this voyage of discovery into the mind which creates semi-independent of the outer senses, Coleridge returns with subtle modern ideas on semantics, on the relation of words to thoughts, of images to ideas, of system to mystery, reason to riddle. No English critic has larger capacities; and Coleridge could say with more justice than Doctor Johnson that no one had travelled over *his* mind.

The essential Coleridge is the magic image of the magic child. There are other Coleridges: the drug-taker, the political columnist, the helpless man perpetually needing someone to look after him, the father and husband who left so much to be desired, the lover hopelessly attracted to the sister of Wordsworth's wife, the man without the will to finish an undertaking. None of these is the Coleridge that led Wordsworth to pronounce and to repeat: "Coleridge was the only person whose intellect ever astonished me."

Since he spent a lifetime in monopolizing conversation, Coleridge should be allowed once more to have the last words. One of them is a paragraph which in general suggests the secret of the Romantic Movement and which in particular indicates why Coleridge himself should be placed near its fountainhead:

> The Greeks idolized the finite, and therefore were the masters of all grace, elegance, proportion, fancy, dignity, majesty—of whatever, in short, is capable of being definitely conveyed by defined forms or thoughts: the moderns revere the infinite, and affect the indefinite as a vehicle of the infinite;—hence their passions, their obscure hopes and fears, their wandering through the unknown, their grander moral feelings, their more august conception of man as man, their future rather than their past—in a word, their sublimity.

The other passage, "Euthanasia," was committed to writing by Coleridge's nephew on July 10, 1834, fifteen days before his death:

> I am dying, but without expectation of a speedy release. Is it not strange that very recently by-gone images, and scenes of early life, have stolen into my mind, like breezes blown from the spice-islands of Youth and Hope—those two realities of this phantom world! I do not add Love,—for what is Love but Youth and Hope embracing, and so seen as *one*? I say *realities;* for reality is a thing of degrees, from the Iliad to a dream. Yet, in a strict sense, reality is not predicable at all of aught below Heaven. Hooker wished to live to finish his *Ecclesiastical Polity;* so I own I wish life and strength had been spared to me

to complete my Philosophy. For, as God hears me, the originating, continuing, and sustaining wish and design in my heart was to exalt the glory of His name; and, which is the same thing in other words, to promote the improvement of mankind. But *visum aliter Deo*, and His will be done.

It is a good coda, a good death, for it contains so much of his life.

CHRONOLOGY

1772	Samuel Taylor Coleridge born Oct. 21 at Ottery St. Mary in Devonshire
1782-91	At Christ's Hospital in London
1791-93	At Jesus College in Cambridge
1793-94	In the Fifteenth Dragoons
1795	Marries Sarah Fricker
1797	At Nether Stowey, associating with the Wordsworths
1798	Accepts an annuity of 150 pounds from the Wedgwood brothers
1798-99	Travels and studies in Germany
1800	Settles at Greta Hall in Keswick
1804-06	Goes to the Mediterranean (Malta, Naples, Rome) for his health
1808	Gives subscription lecture series (also in 1810-11, 1812, 1813, 1818, 1819)
1809-10	Publishes *The Friend* periodically
1816-34	At Highgate near London under the medical care of James Gillman
1817	*Biographia Literaria* published
1825	*Aids to Reflection* published; yearly pension of 125 pounds from Royal Society of Literature
1830	*Constitution of Church and State* published
1834	Dies July 25.

BIBLIOGRAPHY

Complete Works, ed. by W. G. T. Shedd, 7 vols., New York, Harper, 1853; reissued 1884. The most complete edition, including items not published elsewhere.

Complete Poetical Works, ed. by E. H. Coleridge, 2 vols., Oxford, Clarendon Press, 1912. The best edition of the poetry.

Anima Poetae, ed. by E. H. Coleridge, Boston, Houghton, 1895.

Letters, ed. by E. H. Coleridge, 2 vols., London, Heinemann, 1895.

Unpublished Letters, ed. by E. L. Griggs, 2 vols., London, Constable, 1932; New Haven, Yale, 1933.

Biographia Literaria, ed. by J. Shawcross, 2 vols., Oxford, Clarendon Press, 1907. The best edition.

Coleridge's Shakespearean Criticism, ed. by T. N. Raysor, 2 vols., London, Constable; Cambridge, Harvard, 1930. The most scholarly edition.

Coleridge's Miscellaneous Criticism, ed. by T. N. Raysor, London, Constable, 1936.

Philosophical Lectures . . . Hitherto Unpublished, ed. by Kathleen Coburn, London, Pilot Press, 1949.

Armour, Richard W. and Howes, Raymond F., *Coleridge the Talker,* Ithaca, Cornell, 1940. An excellent introduction to his personality.

Campbell, J. D., *Samuel Taylor Coleridge,* London, Macmillan, 1894. The most complete early biography.

Chambers, E. K., *Samuel Taylor Coleridge,* Oxford, Clarendon Press, 1938. A full manual of biographical facts.

Lowes, John Livingston, *The Road to Xanadu,* Boston and New York, Houghton, 1927. A fascinating and classic source-study of "The Ancient Mariner" and "Kubla Khan."

Muirhead, John H., *Coleridge as Philosopher,* London, Allen & Unwin; New York, Macmillan, 1930. A necessary book for those who wish to develop this subject.

Nethercot, Arthur H., *The Road to Tryermaine,* Chicago, University of Chicago, 1939. A study of the history, background, and purposes of "Christabel."

Richards, I. A., *Coleridge on Imagination,* New York, Harcourt, 1935. Influential in modern conceptions of Coleridge.

Snyder, Alice D., *Coleridge on Logic and Learning,* New Haven,

Yale, 1929; *Coleridge's Treatise on Method*, London, Constable, 1934.

Warren, Robert Penn, *The Rime of the Ancient Mariner*, Reynal and Hitchcock, 1946. Mr. Warren's introductory essay is an interesting example of the new critical approach.

For more detailed bibliographies and for helpful remarks on all important books and articles, consult *The English Romantic Poets: A Review of Research*, New York, Modern Language Association, 1950, particularly "The Romantic Movement" by Ernest Bernbaum, and "Coleridge" by Thomas M. Raysor and René Wellek.

POETRY

THE SEEDS OF POETRY

TO ———

í MIX in life, and labour to seem free,
  With common persons pleas'd and common things,
While every thought and action tends to thee,
  And every impulse from thy influence springs.

[1798?; publ. 1836]

APOLOGIA PRO VITA SUA

THE poet in his lone yet genial hour
Gives to his eyes a magnifying power:
Or rather he emancipates his eyes
From the black shapeless accidents of size—
In unctuous cones of kindling coal,
Or smoke upwreathing from the pipe's trim bole,
    His gifted ken can see
    Phantoms of sublimity.

[1800; publ. 1822]

INSCRIPTION FOR A FOUNTAIN ON A HEATH

THIS Sycamore, oft musical with bees,—
Such tents the Patriarchs loved! O long unharmed
May all its agéd boughs o'er-canopy
The small round basin, which this jutting stone
Keeps pure from falling leaves! Long may the Spring
Quietly as a sleeping infant's breath,
Send up cold waters to the traveller
With soft and even pulse! Nor ever cease
Yon tiny cone of sand its soundless dance,
Which at the bottom, like a Fairy's Page,

1\

3

As merry and no taller, dances still,
Nor wrinkles the smooth surface of the Fount.
Here Twilight is and Coolness: here is moss,
A soft seat, and a deep and ample shade.
Thou may'st toil far and find no second tree.
Drink, Pilgrim, here; Here rest! and if thy heart
Be innocent, here too shalt thou refresh
Thy spirit, listening to some gentle sound,
Or passing gale or hum of murmuring bees!

[1802; publ. 1802]

PHANTOM

ALL look and likeness caught from earth
All accident of kin and birth,
Had pass'd away. There was no trace
Of aught on that illumined face,
Uprais'd beneath the rifted stone
But of one spirit all her own;—
She, she herself, and only she,
Shone through her body visibly.

[1805; publ. 1834]

PSYCHE

THE butterfly the ancient Grecians made
The soul's fair emblem, and its only name—
But of the soul, escaped the slavish trade
Of mortal life!—For in this earthly frame
Ours is the reptile's lot, much toil, much blame,
Manifold motions making little speed,
And to deform and kill the things whereon we feed.

[1808; publ. 1817]

THE KNIGHT'S TOMB

WHERE is the grave of Sir Arthur O'Kellyn?
Where may the grave of that good man be?—

By the side of a spring, on the breast of Helvellyn,
Under the twigs of a young birch tree!
The oak that in summer was sweet to hear,
And rustled its leaves in the fall of the year,
And whistled and roared in the winter alone,
Is gone,—and the birch in its stead is grown.—
The Knight's bones are dust,
And his good sword rust;—   10
His soul is with the saints, I trust.

                              [1817?; publ. 1834]

ON DONNE'S POETRY

With Donne, whose muse on dromedary trots,
Wreathe iron pokers into true-love knots;
Rhyme's sturdy cripple, fancy's maze and clue,
Wit's forge and fire-blast, meaning's press and screw.

                              [1818?; publ. 1836]

EPITAPH

Stop, Christian passer-by!—Stop, child of God,
And read with gentle breast. Beneath this sod
A poet lies, or that which once seem'd he.
O, lift one thought in prayer for S. T. C.;
That he who many a year with toil of breath
Found death in life, may here find life in death!
Mercy for praise—to be forgiven for fame
He ask'd, and hoped, through Christ. Do thou the same!

                              [1833; publ. 1834]

PHANTOM MAGIC

THE RIME OF THE ANCIENT MARINER

IN SEVEN PARTS

Facile credo, plures esse Naturas invisibiles quam visibiles in rerum universitate. Sed horum omnium familiam quis nobis enarrabit? et gradus et cognationes et discrimina et singulorum munera? Quid agunt? quae loca habitant? Harum rerum notitiam semper ambivit ingenium humanum, nunquam attigit. Juvat, interea, non diffiteor, quandoque in animo, tanquam in tabulâ, majoris et melioris mundi imaginem contemplari: ne mens assuefacta hodiernae vitae minutiis se contrahat nimis, et tota subsidat in pusillas cogitationes. Sed veritati interea invigilandum est, modusque servandus, ut certa ab incertis, diem a nocte, distinguamus.—T. BURNET, *Archaeol. Phil.* p. 68.

ARGUMENT

How a Ship having passed the Line was driven by storms to the cold Country towards the South Pole; and how from thence she made her course to the tropical Latitude of the Great Pacific Ocean; and of the strange things that befell; and in what manner the Ancyent Marinere came back to his own Country.

PART I

An ancient Mariner meeteth three Gallants bidden to a wedding-feast, and detaineth one.

IT IS an ancient Mariner,
And he stoppeth one of three.
'By thy long grey beard and glittering eye,
Now wherefore stopp'st thou me?

The Bridegroom's doors are opened wide,
And I am next of kin;
The guests are met, the feast is set:
May'st hear the merry din.'

He holds him with his skinny hand,
'There was a ship,' quoth he.

10

6

'Hold off! unhand me, grey-beard loon!'
Eftsoons his hand dropt he.

The Wedding-Guest is spell-bound by the eye of the old seafaring man, and constrained to hear his tale.

He holds him with his glittering eye—
The Wedding-Guest stood still,
And listens like a three years' child:
The Mariner hath his will.

The Wedding-Guest sat on a stone:
He cannot choose but hear;
And thus spake on that ancient man,
The bright-eyed Mariner.   20

'The ship was cheered, the harbour cleared,
Merrily did we drop
Below the kirk, below the hill,
Below the lighthouse top.

The Mariner tells how the ship sailed southward with a good wind and fair weather, till it reached the line.

The Sun came up upon the left,
Out of the sea came he!
And he shone bright, and on the right
Went down into the sea.

Higher and higher every day,
Till over the mast at noon—'   30
The Wedding-Guest here beat his breast,
For he heard the loud bassoon.

The Wedding-Guest heareth the bridal music; but the Mariner continueth his tale.

The bride hath paced into the hall,
Red as a rose is she;
Nodding their heads before her goes
The merry minstrelsy.

The Wedding-Guest he beat his breast,
Yet he cannot choose but hear;
And thus spake on that ancient man,
The bright-eyed Mariner.   40

The ship driven by a storm toward the south pole.

'And now the STORM-BLAST came, and he
Was tyrannous and strong:
He struck with his o'ertaking wings,
And chased us south along.

With sloping masts and dipping prow,
As who pursued with yell and blow

Still treads the shadow of his foe,
And forward bends his head,
The ship drove fast, loud roared the blast,
And southward aye we fled.   50

And now there came both mist and snow,
And it grew wondrous cold:
And ice, mast-high, came floating by,
As green as emerald.

The land of ice, and of fearful sounds where no living thing was to be seen.

And through the drifts the snowy clifts
Did send a dismal sheen:
Nor shapes of men nor beasts we ken—
The ice was all between.

The ice was here, the ice was there,
The ice was all around: 60
It cracked and growled, and roared and howled,
Like noises in a swound!

Till a great sea-bird, called the Albatross, came through the snow-fog, and was received with great joy and hospitality.

At length did cross an Albatross,
Thorough the fog it came;
As if it had been a Christian soul,
We hailed it in God's name.

It ate the food it ne'er had eat,
And round and round it flew.
The ice did split with a thunder-fit;
The helmsman steered us through!   70

And lo! the Albatross proveth a bird of good omen, and followeth the ship as it returned northward through fog and floating ice.

And a good south wind sprung up behind;
The Albatross did follow,
And every day, for food or play,
Came to the mariner's hollo!

In mist or cloud, on mast or shroud,
It perched for vespers nine;
Whiles all the night, through fog-smoke white,
Glimmered the white Moon-shine.'

The ancient Mariner inhospitably killeth the pious bird of good omen.

'God save thee, ancient Mariner!
From the fiends, that plague thee thus!—   80
Why look'st thou so?'—With my cross-bow
I shot the ALBATROSS.

PART II

The Sun now rose upon the right:
Out of the sea came he,
Still hid in mist, and on the left
Went down into the sea.

And the good south wind still blew behind,
But no sweet bird did follow,
Nor any day for food or play
Came to the mariner's hollo! 90

His shipmates cry out against the ancient Mariner, for killing the bird of good luck.

And I had done a hellish thing,
And it would work 'em woe:
For all averred, I had killed the bird
That made the breeze to blow.
Ah wretch! said they, the bird to slay,
That made the breeze to blow!

But when the fog cleared off, they justify the same, and thus make themselves accomplices in the crime.

Nor dim nor red, like God's own head,
The glorious Sun uprist:
Then all averred, I had killed the bird
That brought the fog and mist. 100
'Twas right, said they, such birds to slay,
That bring the fog and mist.

The fair breeze continues; the ship enters the Pacific Ocean, and sails northward, even till it reaches the Line.

The fair breeze blew, the white foam flew,
The furrow followed free;
We were the first that ever burst
Into that silent sea.

The ship hath been suddenly becalmed.

Down dropt the breeze, the sails dropt down,
'Twas sad as sad could be;
And we did speak only to break
The silence of the sea! 110

All in a hot and copper sky,
The bloody Sun, at noon,
Right up above the mast did stand,
No bigger than the Moon.

Day after day, day after day,
We stuck, nor breath nor motion;

As idle as a painted ship
Upon a painted ocean.

And the Alba-
tross begins to
be avenged.

Water, water, every where,
And all the boards did shrink;   120
Water, water, every where,
Nor any drop to drink.

The very deep did rot: O Christ!
That ever this should be!
Yea, slimy things did crawl with legs
Upon the slimy sea.

About, about, in reel and rout
The death-fires danced at night;
The water, like a witch's oils,
Burnt green, and blue and white.   130

A Spirit had
followed them;
one of the in-
visible inhabi-
tants of this
planet, neither
departed souls

And some in dreams assuréd were
Of the Spirit that plagued us so;
Nine fathom deep he had followed us
From the land of mist and snow.

nor angels; concerning whom the learned Jew, Josephus, and
the Platonic Constantinopolitan, Michael Psellus, may be consulted. They are
very numerous, and there is no climate or element without one or more.

And every tongue, through utter drought,
Was withered at the root;
We could not speak, no more than if
We had been choked with soot.

The shipmates,
in their sore
distress, would
fain throw the
whole guilt on
the ancient

Ah! well a-day! what evil looks
Had I from old and young!   140
Instead of the cross, the Albatross
About my neck was hung.

Mariner: in sign whereof they hang the dead sea-bird round his neck.

PART III

There passed a weary time. Each throat
Was parched, and glazed each eye.
A weary time! a weary time!
How glazed each weary eye,

The ancient
Mariner be-
holdeth a sign

When looking westward, I beheld
A something in the sky.

in the element
afar off.

At first it seemed a little speck,
And then it seemed a mist;   150
It moved and moved, and took at last
A certain shape, I wist.

A speck, a mist, a shape, I wist!
And still it neared and neared:
As if it dodged a water-sprite,
It plunged and tacked and veered.

At its nearer
approach, it
seemeth him
to be a ship;
and at a dear
ransom he
freeth his
speech from
the bonds of
thirst.

With throats unslaked, with black lips baked,
We could nor laugh nor wail;
Through utter drought all dumb we stood!
I bit my arm, I sucked the blood,   160
And cried, A sail! a sail!

A flash of joy;

With throats unslaked, with black lips baked,
Agape they heard me call:
Gramercy! they for joy did grin,
And all at once their breath drew in,
As they were drinking all.

And horror
follows. For
can it be a
ship that
comes onward
without wind
or tide?

See! see! (I cried) she tacks no more!
Hither to work us weal;
Without a breeze, without a tide,
She steadies with upright keel!   170

The western wave was all a-flame.
The day was well nigh done!
Almost upon the western wave
Rested the broad bright Sun;
When that strange shape drove suddenly
Betwixt us and the Sun.

It seemeth
him but the
skeleton of
a ship.

And straight the Sun was flecked with bars,
(Heaven's Mother send us grace!)
As if through a dungeon-grate he peered
With broad and burning face.   180

Alas! (thought I, and my heart beat loud)
How fast she nears and nears!
Are those *her* sails that glance in the Sun,
Like restless gossameres?

And its ribs
are seen as
bars on the
face of the
setting Sun.

Are those *her* ribs through which the Sun
Did peer, as through a grate?
And is that Woman all her crew?
Is that a DEATH? and are there two?
Is DEATH that woman's mate?

The Spectre-
Woman and
her Death-
mate, and no
other on
board the
skeleton ship.

Her lips were red, *her* looks were free,   190
Her locks were yellow as gold:
Her skin was as white as leprosy,
The Night-mare LIFE-IN-DEATH was she,
Who thicks man's blood with cold.

Like vessel,
like crew!

Death and
Life-in-Death
have diced for
the ship's crew,

The naked hulk alongside came,
And the twain were casting dice;
'The game is done! I've won! I've won!'
Quoth she, and whistles thrice.
and she (the latter) winneth the ancient Mariner.

No twilight
within the
courts of the
Sun.

The Sun's rim dips; the stars rush out:
At one stride comes the dark;   200
With far-heard whisper, o'er the sea,
Off shot the spectre-bark.

At the rising
of the Moon,

We listened and looked sideways up!
Fear at my heart, as at a cup,
My life-blood seemed to sip!
The stars were dim, and thick the night,
The steersman's face by his lamp gleamed white;

From the sails the dew did drip—
Till clomb above the eastern bar
The hornéd Moon, with one bright star   210
Within the nether tip.

One after
another,

One after one, by the star-dogged Moon.
Too quick for groan or sigh,
Each turned his face with a ghastly pang,
And cursed me with his eye.

His shipmates
drop down
dead.

Four times fifty living men,
(And I heard nor sigh nor groan)
With heavy thump, a lifeless lump,
They dropped down one by one.

But Life-in-Death begins her work on the ancient Mariner.

The souls did from their bodies fly,—   220
They fled to bliss or woe!
And every soul, it passed me by,
Like the whizz of my cross-bow!

PART IV

The Wedding-Guest feareth that a Spirit is talking to him;

'I fear thee, ancient Mariner!
I fear thy skinny hand!
And thou art long, and lank, and brown,
As is the ribbed sea-sand.[1]

I fear thee and thy glittering eye,
And thy skinny hand, so brown.'—

But the ancient Mariner assureth him of his bodily life, and proceedeth to relate his horrible penance.

Fear not, fear not, thou Wedding-Guest!   230
This body dropt not down.

Alone, alone, all, all alone,
Alone on a wide wide sea!
And never a saint took pity on
My soul in agony.

He despiseth the creatures of the calm,

The many men, so beautiful!
And they all dead did lie:
And a thousand thousand slimy things
Lived on; and so did I.

And envieth that *they* should live, and so many lie dead.

I looked upon the rotting sea,   240
And drew my eyes away;
I looked upon the rotting deck,
And there the dead men lay.

I looked to heaven, and tried to pray,
But or ever a prayer had gusht,
A wicked whisper came, and made
My heart as dry as dust.

I closed my lids, and kept them close,
And the balls like pulses beat;   249

[1] For the last two lines of this stanza, I am indebted to Mr. WORDS-WORTH. It was on a delightful walk from Nether Stowey to Dulverton, with him and his sister, in the Autumn of 1797, that this Poem was planned, and in part composed.

For the sky and the sea, and the sea and the sky
Lay like a load on my weary eye,
And the dead were at my feet.

But the curse
liveth for him
in the eye of
the dead men.

The cold sweat melted from their limbs,
Nor rot nor reek did they:
The look with which they looked on me
Had never passed away.

An orphan's curse would drag to hell
A spirit from on high;
But oh! more horrible than that
Is the curse in a dead man's eye!   260
Seven days, seven nights, I saw that curse,
And yet I could not die.

In his lone-
liness and
fixedness he
yearneth to-
wards the
journeying
Moon, and the
stars that still
sojourn, yet
still move
onward; and
every where
the blue sky
belongs to

The moving Moon went up the sky,
And no where did abide:
Softly she was going up,
And a star or two beside—

Her beams bemocked the sultry main,
Like April hoar-frost spread;
But where the ship's huge shadow lay,
The charméd water burnt alway   270
A still and awful red.

them, and is their appointed rest, and their native country and their own natural
homes, which they enter unannounced, as lords that are certainly expected and
yet there is a silent joy at their arrival.

By the light
of the Moon he
beholdeth
God's crea-
tures of the
great calm.

Beyond the shadow of the ship,
I watched the water-snakes:
They moved in tracks of shining white,
And when they reared, the elfish light
Fell off in hoary flakes.

Within the shadow of the ship
I watched their rich attire:
Blue, glossy green, and velvet black,
They coiled and swam; and every track   280
Was a flash of golden fire.

Their beauty
and their
happiness.

O happy living things! no tongue
Their beauty might declare:
A spring of love gushed from my heart,

He blesseth
them in his
heart.

And I blessed them unaware:
Sure my kind saint took pity on me,
And I blessed them unaware.

The spell
begins to
break.

The self-same moment I could pray;
And from my neck so free
The Albatross fell off, and sank   290
Like lead into the sea.

PART V

Oh sleep! it is a gentle thing,
Beloved from pole to pole!
To Mary Queen the praise be given!
She sent the gentle sleep from Heaven,
That slid into my soul.

By grace of
the holy
Mother, the
ancient
Mariner is
refreshed with
rain.

The silly buckets on the deck,
That had so long remained,
I dreamt that they were filled with dew;
And when I awoke, it rained.   300

My lips were wet, my throat was cold,
My garments all were dank;
Sure I had drunken in my dreams,
And still my body drank.

I moved, and could not feel my limbs:
I was so light—almost
I thought that I had died in sleep,
And was a blesséd ghost.

He heareth
sounds and
seeth strange
sights and
commotions in
the sky and
the element.

And soon I heard a roaring wind:
It did not come anear;   310
But with its sound it shook the sails,
That were so thin and sere.

The upper air burst into life!
And a hundred fire-flags sheen,
To and fro they were hurried about!
And to and fro, and in and out,
The wan stars danced between.

And the coming wind did roar more loud,
And the sails did sigh like sedge;   319

And the rain poured down from one black cloud;
The Moon was at its edge.

The thick black cloud was cleft, and still
The Moon was at its side:
Like waters shot from some high crag,
The lightning fell with never a jag,
A river steep and wide.

The bodies of the ship's crew are inspired [inspirited, S. L.] and the ship moves on.

The loud wind never reached the ship,
Yet now the ship moved on!
Beneath the lightning and the Moon
The dead men gave a groan.   330

They groaned, they stirred, they all uprose,
Nor spake, nor moved their eyes;
It had been strange, even in a dream,
To have seen those dead men rise.

The helmsman steered, the ship moved on;
Yet never a breeze up-blew;
The mariners all 'gan work the ropes,
Where they were wont to do;
They raised their limbs like lifeless tools—
We were a ghastly crew.   340

The body of my brother's son
Stood by me, knee to knee:
The body and I pulled at one rope,
But he said nought to me.

But not by the souls of the men, nor by dæmons of earth or middle air, but by a blessed troop of angelic spirits, sent down by the invocation of the guardian saint.

'I fear thee, ancient Mariner!'
Be calm, thou Wedding-Guest!
'Twas not those souls that fled in pain,
Which to their corses came again,
But a troop of spirits blest:

For when it dawned—they dropped their arms,
And clustered round the mast;   351
Sweet sounds rose slowly through their mouths,
And from their bodies passed.

Around, around, flew each sweet sound,
Then darted to the Sun;

Slowly the sounds came back again,
Now mixed, now one by one.

Sometimes a-dropping from the sky
I heard the sky-lark sing;
Sometimes all little birds that are, 360
How they seemed to fill the sea and air
With their sweet jargoning!

And now 'twas like all instruments,
Now like a lonely flute;
And now it is an angel's song,
That makes the heavens be mute.

It ceased; yet still the sails made on
A pleasant noise till noon,
A noise like of a hidden brook
In the leafy month of June, 370
That to the sleeping woods all night
Singeth a quiet tune.

Till noon we quietly sailed on,
Yet never a breeze did breathe:
Slowly and smoothly went the ship,
Moved onward from beneath.

The lonesome Spirit from the south-pole carries on the ship as far as the Line, in obedience to the angelic troop, but still requireth vengeance.

Under the keel nine fathom deep,
From the land of mist and snow,
The spirit slid: and it was he
That made the ship to go. 380
The sails at noon left off their tune,
And the ship stood still also.

The Sun, right up above the mast,
Had fixed her to the ocean:
But in a minute she 'gan stir,
With a short uneasy motion—
Backwards and forwards half her length
With a short uneasy motion.

Then like a pawing horse let go,
She made a sudden bound: 390
It flung the blood into my head,
And I fell down in a swound.

The Polar
Spirit's fellow-
dæmons, the
invisible in-
habitants of
the element,
take part in
his wrong;
and two of
them relate,
one to the
other, that
penance long
and heavy for
the ancient
Mariner hath
been accorded
to the Polar
Spirit, who
returneth
southward.

How long in that same fit I lay,
I have not to declare;
But ere my living life returned,
I heard and in my soul discerned
Two voices in the air.

'Is it he?' quoth one, 'Is this the man?
By him who died on cross,
With his cruel bow he laid full low   400
The harmless Albatross.

The spirit who bideth by himself
In the land of mist and snow,
He loved the bird that loved the man
Who shot him with his bow.'

The other was a softer voice,
As soft as honey-dew:
Quoth he, "The man hath penance done,
And penance more will do."

PART VI

FIRST VOICE

'But tell me, tell me! speak again,   410
Thy soft response renewing—
What makes that ship drive on so fast?
What is the ocean doing?'

SECOND VOICE

'Still as a slave before his lord,
The ocean hath no blast;
His great bright eye most silently
Up to the Moon is cast—

If he may know which way to go;
For she guides him smooth or grim.
See, brother, see! how graciously   420
She looketh down on him.'

FIRST VOICE

'But why drives on that ship so fast,
Without or wave or wind?'

SECOND VOICE

'The air is cut away before,
And closes from behind.

Fly, brother, fly! more high, more high!
Or we shall be belated:
For slow and slow that ship will go,
When the Mariner's trance is abated.'

I woke, and we were sailing on   430
As in a gentle weather:
'Twas night, calm night, the moon was high;
The dead men stood together.

All stood together on the deck,
For a charnel-dungeon fitter:
All fixed on me their stony eyes,
That in the Moon did glitter.

The pang, the curse, with which they died,
Had never passed away:
I could not draw my eyes from theirs,   440
Nor turn them up to pray.

And now this spell was snapt: once more
I viewed the ocean green,
And looked far forth, yet little saw
Of what had else been seen—

Like one, that on a lonesome road
Doth walk in fear and dread,
And having once turned round walks on,
And turns no more his head;
Because he knows, a frightful fiend   450
Doth close behind him tread.

Marginal notes:

The Mariner hath been cast into a trance; for the angelic power causeth the vessel to drive northward faster than human life could endure.

The supernatural motion is retarded; the Mariner awakes, and his penance begins anew.

The curse is finally expiated.

But soon there breathed a wind on me,
Nor sound nor motion made:
Its path was not upon the sea,
In ripple or in shade.

It raised my hair, it fanned my cheek
Like a meadow-gale of spring—
It mingled strangely with my fears,
Yet it felt like a welcoming.

Swiftly, swiftly flew the ship,   **460**
Yet she sailed softly too:
Sweetly, sweetly blew the breeze—
On me alone it blew.

And the ancient Mariner beholdeth his native country.

Oh! dream of joy! is this indeed
The light-house top I see?
Is this the hill? is this the kirk?
Is this mine own countree?

We drifted o'er the harbour-bar,
And I with sobs did pray—
O let me be awake, my God!   **470**
Or let me sleep alway.

The harbour-bay was clear as glass,
So smoothly it was strewn!
And on the bay the moonlight lay,
And the shadow of the Moon.

The rock shone bright, the kirk no less,
That stands above the rock:
The moonlight steeped in silentness
The steady weathercock.

And the bay was white with silent light,   **480**
Till rising from the same,

The angelic spirits leave the dead bodies,

Full many shapes, that shadows were,
In crimson colours came.

A little distance from the prow

And appear in their own forms of light.

Those crimson shadows were:
I turned my eyes upon the deck—
Oh, Christ! what saw I there!

Each corse lay flat, lifeless and flat,
And, by the holy rood!
A man all light, a seraph-man,   490
On every corse there stood.

This seraph-band, each waved his hand:
It was a heavenly sight!
They stood as signals to the land,
Each one a lovely light;

This seraph-band, each waved his hand,
No voice did they impart—
No voice; but oh! the silence sank
Like music on my heart.

But soon I heard the dash of oars,   500
I heard the Pilot's cheer;
My head was turned perforce away
And I saw a boat appear.

The Pilot and the Pilot's boy,
I heard them coming fast:
Dear Lord in Heaven! it was a joy
The dead men could not blast.

I saw a third—I heard his voice:
It is the Hermit good!
He singeth loud his godly hymns   510
That he makes in the wood.
He'll shrieve my soul, he'll wash away
The Albatross's blood.

PART VII

The Hermit of
the Wood,

This Hermit good lives in that wood
Which slopes down to the sea.
How loudly his sweet voice he rears!
He loves to talk with marineres
That come from a far countree.

He kneels at morn, and noon, and eve—
He hath a cushion plump: 520
It is the moss that wholly hides
The rotted old oak-stump.

The skiff-boat neared: I heard them talk,
'Why, this is strange, I trow!
Where are those lights so many and fair,
That signal made but now?'

Approacheth
the ship with
wonder.

'Strange, by my faith!' the Hermit said—
'And they answered not our cheer!
The planks looked warped! and see those sails,
How thin they are and sere!   530
I never saw aught like to them,
Unless perchance it were

Brown skeletons of leaves that lag
My forest-brook along;
When the ivy-tod is heavy with snow,
And the owlet whoops to the wolf below,
That eats the she-wolf's young.'

'Dear Lord! it hath a fiendish look—
(The Pilot made reply)
I am a-feared'—'Push on, push on!'   540
Said the Hermit cheerily.

The boat came closer to the ship,
But I nor spake nor stirred;
The boat came close beneath the ship,
And straight a sound was heard.

The ship
suddenly
sinketh.

Under the water it rumbled on,
Still louder and more dread:
It reached the ship, it split the bay;
The ship went down like lead.

The ancient
Mariner is
saved in the
Pilot's boat.

Stunned by that loud and dreadful sound,   550
Which sky and ocean smote,
Like one that hath been seven days drowned
My body lay afloat;
But swift as dreams, myself I found
Within the Pilot's boat.

Upon the whirl, where sank the ship,
The boat spun round and round;
And all was still, save that the hill
Was telling of the sound.

I moved my lips—the Pilot shrieked   560
And fell down in a fit;
The holy Hermit raised his eyes,
And prayed where he did sit.

I took the oars: the Pilot's boy,
Who now doth crazy go,
Laughed loud and long, and all the while
His eyes went to and fro.
'Ha! ha!' quoth he, 'full plain I see,
The Devil knows how to row.'

And now, all in my own countree,   570
I stood on the firm land!
The Hermit stepped forth from the boat,
And scarcely he could stand.

The ancient Mariner earnestly entreateth the Hermit to shrieve him; and the penance of life falls on him.

'O shrieve me, shrieve me, holy man!'
The Hermit crossed his brow.
'Say quick,' quoth he, 'I bid thee say—
What manner of man art thou?'

Forthwith this frame of mine was wrenched
With a woful agony,
Which forced me to begin my tale;   580
And then it left me free.

And ever and anon through out his future life an agony constraineth him to travel from land to land;

Since then, at an uncertain hour,
That agony returns:
And till my ghastly tale is told,
This heart within me burns.

I pass, like night, from land to land;
I have strange power of speech;
That moment that his face I see,
I know the man that must hear me:
To him my tale I teach.   590

What loud uproar bursts from that door!
The wedding-guests are there:
But in the garden-bower the bride
And bride-maids singing are:
And hark the little vesper bell,
Which biddeth me to prayer!

O Wedding-Guest! this soul hath been
Alone on a wide wide sea:
So lonely 'twas, that God himself
Scarce seeméd there to be.   600

O sweeter than the marriage-feast,
'Tis sweeter far to me,
To walk together to the kirk
With a goodly company!—

To walk together to the kirk,
And all together pray,
While each to his great Father bends,
Old men, and babes, and loving friends
And youths and maidens gay!

And to teach,
by his own
example, love
and reverence
to all things
that God made
and loveth.

Farewell, farewell! but this I tell   610
To thee, thou Wedding-Guest!
He prayeth well, who loveth well
Both man and bird and beast.

He prayeth best, who loveth best
All things both great and small;
For the dear God who loveth us,
He made and loveth all.

The Mariner, whose eye is bright,
Whose beard with age is hoar,
Is gone: and now the Wedding-Guest   620
Turned from the bridegroom's door.

He went like one that hath been stunned,
And is of sense forlorn:
A sadder and a wiser man,
He rose the morrow morn.
                              [1797-1798; publ. 1798]

CHRISTABEL

PREFACE

THE first part of the following poem was written in the year
1797, at Stowey, in the county of Somerset. The second part.

after my return from Germany, in the year 1800, at Keswick, Cumberland. It is probable that if the poem had been finished at either of the former periods, or if even the first and second part had been published in the year 1800, the impression of its originality would have been much greater than I dare at present expect. But for this I have only my own indolence to blame. The dates are mentioned for the exclusive purpose of precluding charges of plagiarism or servile imitation from myself. For there s amongst us a set of critics, who seem to hold that every possible thought and image is traditional; who have no notion that there are such things as fountains in the world, small as well as great; and who would therefore charitably derive every rill they behold flowing, from a perforation made in some other man's tank. I am confident, however, that as far as the present poem is concerned, the celebrated poets whose writings I might be suspected of having imitated, either in particular passages, or in the tone and the spirit of the whole, would be among the first to vindicate me from the charge, and who, on any striking coincidence, would permit me to address them in this doggerel version of two monkish Latin hexameters.

> 'Tis mine and it is likewise yours;
> But an if this will not do;
> Let it be mine, good friend! for I
> Am the poorer of the two.

I have only to add that the metre of Christabel is not, properly speaking, irregular, though it may seem so from its being founded on a new principle: namely, that of counting in each line the accents, not the syllables. Though the latter may vary from seven to twelve, yet in each line the accents will be found to be only four. Nevertheless, this occasional variation in number of syllables is not introduced wantonly, or for the mere ends of convenience, but in correspondence with some transition in the nature of the imagery or passion.

PART I

> 'Tis the middle of night by the castle clock,
> And the owls have awakened the crowing cock;
> Tu—whit!——Tu—whoo!
> And hark, again! the crowing cock,
> How drowsily it crew.

Sir Leoline, the Baron rich,
Hath a toothless mastiff bitch;
From her kennel beneath the rock
She maketh answer to the clock,
Four for the quarters, and twelve for the hour;   10
Ever and aye, by shine and shower,
Sixteen short howls, not over loud;
Some say, she sees my lady's shroud.

Is the night chilly and dark?
The night is chilly, but not dark.
The thin gray cloud is spread on high,
It covers but not hides the sky.
The moon is behind, and at the full;
And yet she looks both small and dull.
The night is chill, the cloud is gray: 20
'Tis a month before the month of May,
And the Spring comes slowly up this way.

The lovely lady, Christabel,
Whom her father loves so well,
What makes her in the wood so late,
A furlong from the castle gate?
She had dreams all yesternight
Of her own betrothéd knight;
And she in the midnight wood will pray,
For the weal of her lover that's far away.   30

She stole along, she nothing spoke,
The sighs she heaved were soft and low,
And naught was green upon the oak
But moss and rarest mistletoe:
She kneels beneath the huge oak tree,
And in silence prayeth she.

The lady sprang up suddenly,
The lovely lady, Christabel!
It moaned as near, as near can be,
But what it is she cannot tell.—   40
On the other side it seems to be,
Of the huge, broad-breasted, old oak tree.

The night is chill; the forest bare;
Is it the wind that moaneth bleak?

There is not wind enough in the air
To move away the ringlet curl
From the lovely lady's cheek—
There is not wind enough to twirl
The one red leaf, the last of its clan, 50
That dances as often as dance it can,
Hanging so light, and hanging so high,
On the topmost twig that looks up at the sky.

Hush, beating heart of Christabel!
Jesu, Maria, shield her well!
She folded her arms beneath her cloak,
And stole to the other side of the oak.
    What sees she there?

There she sees a damsel bright,
Drest in a silken robe of white,
That shadowy in the moonlight shone: 60
The neck that made that white robe wan,
Her stately neck, and arms were bare;
Her blue-veined feet unsandal'd were,
And wildly glittered here and there
The gems entangled in her hair.
I guess, 'twas frightful there to see
A lady so richly clad as she—
Beautiful exceedingly!

Mary mother, save me now!
(Said Christabel,) And who art thou? 70

The lady strange made answer meet,
And her voice was faint and sweet:—
Have pity on my sore distress,
I scarce can speak for weariness:
Stretch forth thy hand, and have no fear!
Said Christabel, How camest thou here?
And the lady, whose voice was faint and sweet,
Did thus pursue her answer meet:—

My sire is of a noble line,
And my name is Geraldine: 80
Five warriors seized me yestermorn,
Me, even me, a maid forlorn:

They choked my cries with force and fright,
And tied me on a palfrey white.
The palfrey was as fleet as wind,
And they rode furiously behind.

They spurred amain, their steeds were white:
And once we crossed the shade of night.
As sure as Heaven shall rescue me,
I have no thought what men they be;   90
Nor do I know how long it is
(For I have lain entranced I wis)
Since one, the tallest of the five,
Took me from the palfrey's back,
A weary woman, scarce alive.
Some muttered words his comrades spoke:
He placed me underneath this oak;
He swore they would return with haste;
Whither they went I cannot tell—
I thought I heard, some minutes past,   100
Sounds as of a castle bell.
Stretch forth thy hand (thus ended she),
And help a wretched maid to flee.

Then Christabel stretched forth her hand,
And comforted fair Geraldine:
O well, bright dame! may you command
The service of Sir Leoline;
And gladly our stout chivalry
Will he send forth and friends withal
To guide and guard you safe and free   110
Home to your noble father's hall.

She rose: and forth with steps they passed
That strove to be, and were not, fast.
Her gracious stars the lady blest,
And thus spake on sweet Christabel:
All our household are at rest,
The hall as silent as the cell;
Sir Leoline is weak in health,
And may not well awakened be,
But we will move as if in stealth,   120
And I beseech your courtesy,
This night, to share your couch with me.

They crossed the moat, and Christabel
Took the key that fitted well;
A little door she opened straight,
All in the middle of the gate;
The gate that was ironed within and without,
Where an army in battle array had marched out.
The lady sank, belike through pain,
And Christabel with might and main   130
Lifted her up, a weary weight,
Over the threshold of the gate:
Then the lady rose again,
And moved, as she were not in pain.

So free from danger, free from fear,
They crossed the court: right glad they were.
And Christabel devoutly cried
To the lady by her side,
Praise we the Virgin all divine
Who hath rescued thee from thy distress!   140
Alas, alas! said Geraldine,
I cannot speak for weariness.
So free from danger, free from fear,
They crossed the court: right glad they were.

Outside her kennel, the mastiff old
Lay fast asleep, in moonshine cold.
The mastiff old did not awake,
Yet she an angry moan did make!
And what can ail the mastiff bitch?
Never till now she uttered yell   150
Beneath the eye of Christabel.
Perhaps it is the owlet's scritch:
For what can ail the mastiff bitch?

They passed the hall, that echoes still,
Pass as lightly as you will!
The brands were flat, the brands were dying,
Amid their own white ashes lying;
But when the lady passed, there came
A tongue of light, a fit of flame;
And Christabel saw the lady's eye,   160
And nothing else saw she thereby,
Save the boss of the shield of Sir Leoline tall,

Which hung in a murky old niche in the wall.
O softly tread, said Christabel,
My father seldom sleepeth well.

Sweet Christabel her feet doth bare,
And jealous of the listening air
They steal their way from stair to stair,
Now in glimmer, and now in gloom,
And now they pass the Baron's room,   170
As still as death, with stifled breath!
And now have reached her chamber door;
And now doth Geraldine press down
The rushes of the chamber floor.

The moon shines dim in the open air,
And not a moonbeam enters here.
But they without its light can see
The chamber carved so curiously,
Carved with figures strange and sweet,
All made out of the carver's brain,   180
For a lady's chamber meet:
The lamp with twofold silver chain
Is fastened to an angel's feet.

The silver lamp burns dead and dim;
But Christabel the lamp will trim.
She trimmed the lamp, and made it bright,
And left it swinging to and fro,
While Geraldine, in wretched plight,
Sank down upon the floor below.

O weary lady, Geraldine,   190
I pray you, drink this cordial wine!
It is a wine of virtuous powers;
My mother made it of wild flowers.

And will your mother pity me,
Who am a maiden most forlorn?
Christabel answered—Woe is me!
She died the hour that I was born.
I have heard the grey-haired friar tell
How on her death-bed she did say,
That she should hear the castle-bell   200

Strike twelve upon my wedding-day.
O mother dear! that thou wert here!
I would, said Geraldine, she were!

But soon with altered voice, said she—
'Off, wandering mother! Peak and pine!
I have power to bid thee flee.'
Alas! What ails poor Geraldine?
Why stares she with unsettled eye?
Can she the bodiless dead espy?
And why with hollow voice cries she, 210
'Off, woman, off! this hour is mine—
Though thou her guardian spirit be,
Off, woman, off! 'tis given to me.'

Then Christabel knelt by the lady's side,
And raised to heaven her eyes so blue—
Alas! said she, this ghastly ride—
Dear lady! it hath wildered you!
The lady wiped her moist cold brow,
And faintly said, ''tis over now!'

Again the wild-flower wine she drank: 220
Her fair large eyes 'gan glitter bright,
And from the floor whereon she sank,
The lofty lady stood upright:
She was most beautiful to see,
Like a lady of a far countrée.

And thus the lofty lady spake—
'All they who live in the upper sky,
Do love you, holy Christabel!
And you love them, and for their sake
And for the good which me befel, 230
Even I in my degree will try,
Fair maiden, to requite you well.
But now unrobe yourself; for I
Must pray, ere yet in bed I lie.'

Quoth Christabel, So let it be!
And as the lady bade, did she.
Her gentle limbs did she undress,
And lay down in her loveliness.

But through her brain of weal and woe   240
So many thoughts moved to and fro,
That vain it were her lids to close;
So half-way from the bed she rose,
And on her elbow did recline
To look at the lady Geraldine.

Beneath the lamp the lady bowed,
And slowly rolled her eyes around;
Then drawing in her breath aloud,
Like one that shuddered, she unbound
The cincture from beneath her breast:
Her silken robe, and inner vest,   250
Dropt to her feet, and full in view,
Behold! her bosom and half her side——
A sight to dream of, not to tell!
O shield her! shield sweet Christabel!

Yet Geraldine nor speaks nor stirs;
Ah! what a stricken look was hers!
Deep from within she seems half-way
To lift some weight with sick assay,
And eyes the maid and seeks delay;
Then suddenly, as one defied,   260
Collects herself in scorn and pride,
And lay down by the Maiden's side!—
And in her arms the maid she took,
      Ah wel-a-day!
And with low voice and doleful look
These words did say:
'In the touch of this bosom there worketh a spell,
Which is lord of thy utterance, Christabel!
Thou knowest to-night, and wilt know to-morrow,
This mark of my shame, this seal of my sorrow;   270
      But vainly thou warrest,
        For this is alone in
      Thy power to declare,
      That in the dim forest
      Thou heard'st a low moaning,
And found'st a bright lady, surpassingly fair;
And didst bring her home with thee in love and in charity,
To shield her and shelter her from the damp air.'

The Conclusion to Part I

It was a lovely sight to see
The lady Christabel, when she   280
Was praying at the old oak tree.
    Amid the jaggéd shadows
    Of mossy leafless boughs,
    Kneeling in the moonlight,
    To make her gentle vows;
Her slender palms together prest,
Heaving sometimes on her breast;
Her face resigned to bliss or bale—
Her face, oh call it fair not pale,
And both blue eyes more bright than clear,   290
Each about to have a tear.

With open eyes (ah woe is me!)
Asleep, and dreaming fearfully,
Fearfully dreaming, yet, I wis,
Dreaming that alone, which is—
O sorrow and shame! Can this be she,
The lady, who knelt at the old oak tree?
And lo! the worker of these harms,
That holds the maiden in her arms,
Seems to slumber still and mild,   300
As a mother with her child.

A star hath set, a star hath risen,
O Geraldine! since arms of thine
Have been the lovely lady's prison.
O Geraldine! one hour was thine—
Thou'st had thy will! By tairn and rill,
The night-birds all that hour were still.
But now they are jubilant anew,
From cliff and tower, tu—whoo! tu—whoo!
Tu—whoo! tu—whoo! from wood and fell!   310

And see! the lady Christabel
Gathers herself from out her trance;
Her limbs relax, her countenance
Grows sad and soft; the smooth thin lids
Close o'er her eyes; and tears she sheds—

Large tears that leave the lashes bright!
And oft the while she seems to smile
As infants at a sudden light!

Yea, she doth smile, and she doth weep,
Like a youthful hermitess,   320
Beauteous in a wilderness,
Who, praying always, prays in sleep.
And, if she move unquietly,
Perchance, 'tis but the blood so free
Comes back and tingles in her feet.
No doubt, she hath a vision sweet.
What if her guardian spirit 'twere,
What if she knew her mother near?
But this she knows, in joys and woes,
That saints will aid if men will call: 330
For the blue sky bends over all!

PART II

Each matin bell, the Baron saith,
Knells us back to a world of death.
These words Sir Leoline first said,
When he rose and found his lady dead:
These words Sir Leoline will say
Many a morn to his dying day!

And hence the custom and law began
That still at dawn the sacristan,
Who duly pulls the heavy bell,   340
Five and forty beads must tell
Between each stroke—a warning knell,
Which not a soul can choose but hear
From Bratha Head to Wyndermere.

Saith Bracy the bard, So let it knell!
And let the drowsy sacristan
Still count as slowly as he can!
There is no lack of such, I ween,
As well fill up the space between.
In Langdale Pike and Witch's Lair,   350
And Dungeon-ghyll so foully rent,
With ropes of rock and bells of air,

Three sinful sextons' ghosts are pent,
Who all give back, one after t'other,
The death-note to their living brother;
And oft too, by the knell offended,
Just as their one! two! three! is ended,
The devil mocks the doleful tale
With a merry peal from Borodale.

The air is still! through mist and cloud   360
That merry peal comes ringing loud;
And Geraldine shakes off her dread,
And rises lightly from the bed;
Puts on her silken vestments white,
And tricks her hair in lovely plight,
And nothing doubting of her spell
Awakens the lady Christabel.
'Sleep you, sweet lady Christabel?
I trust that you have rested well.'

And Christabel awoke and spied   370
The same who lay down by her side—
O rather say, the same whom she
Raised up beneath the old oak tree!
Nay, fairer yet! and yet more fair!
For she belike hath drunken deep
Of all the blessedness of sleep!
And while she spake, her looks, her air
Such gentle thankfulness declare,
That (so it seemed) her girded vests
Grew tight beneath her heaving breasts.   380
'Sure I have sinn'd!' said Christabel,
'Now heaven be praised if all be well!'
And in low faltering tones, yet sweet,
Did she the lofty lady greet
With such perplexity of mind
As dreams too lively leave behind.

So quickly she rose, and quickly arrayed
Her maiden limbs, and having prayed
That He, who on the cross did groan,
Might wash away her sins unknown,   390
She forthwith led fair Geraldine
To meet her sire, Sir Leoline.

The lovely maid and the lady tall
Are pacing both into the hall,
And pacing on through page and groom,
Enter the Baron's presence-room.

The Baron rose, and while he prest
His gentle daughter to his breast,
With cheerful wonder in his eyes
The lady Geraldine espies,   400
And gave such welcome to the same,
As might beseem so bright a dame!

But when he heard the lady's tale,
And when she told her father's name,
Why waxed Sir Leoline so pale,
Murmuring o'er the name again,
Lord Roland de Vaux of Tryermaine?

Alas! they had been friends in youth;
But whispering tongues can poison truth;
And constancy lives in realms above;   410
And life is thorny; and youth is vain;
And to be wroth with one we love
Doth work like madness in the brain.
And thus it chanced, as I divine,
With Roland and Sir Leoline.
Each spake words of high disdain
And insult to his heart's best brother:
They parted—ne'er to meet again!
But never either found another
To free the hollow heart from paining—   420
They stood aloof, the scars remaining,
Like cliffs which had been rent asunder;
A dreary sea now flows between;—
But neither heat, nor frost, nor thunder,
Shall wholly do away, I ween,
The marks of that which once hath been.

Sir Leoline, a moment's space,
Stood gazing on the damsel's face:
And the youthful Lord of Tryermaine
Came back upon his heart again.   430

O then the Baron forgot his age,
His noble heart swelled high with rage,
He swore by the wounds in Jesu's side
He would proclaim it far and wide,
With trump and solemn heraldry,
That they, who thus had wronged the dame,
Were base as spotted infamy!
'And if they dare deny the same,
My herald shall appoint a week,
And let the recreant traitors seek   440
My tourney court—that there and then
I may dislodge their reptile souls
From the bodies and forms of men!'
He spake: his eye in lightning rolls!
For the lady was ruthlessly seized; and he kenned
In the beautiful lady the child of his friend!
And now the tears were on his face,
And fondly in his arms he took
Fair Geraldine, who met the embrace,
Prolonging it with joyous look.   450
Which when she viewed, a vision fell
Upon the soul of Christabel,
The vision of fear, the touch and pain!
She shrunk and shuddered, and saw again—
(Ah, woe is me! Was it for thee,
Thou gentle maid! such sights to see?)

Again she saw that bosom old,
Again she felt that bosom cold,
And drew in her breath with a hissing sound:
Whereat the Knight turned wildly round,   460
And nothing saw, but his own sweet maid
With eyes upraised, as one that prayed.

The touch, the sight, had passed away,
And in its stead that vision blest,
Which comforted her after-rest
While in the lady's arms she lay,
Had put a rapture in her breast,
And on her lips and o'er her eyes
Spread smiles like light!
                        With new surprise,
'What ails then my belovéd child?'   470

The Baron said—His daughter mild
Made answer, 'All will yet be well!'
I ween, she had no power to tell
Aught else: so mighty was the spell.

Yet he, who saw this Geraldine,
Had deemed her sure a thing divine:
Such sorrow with such grace she blended,
As if she feared she had offended
Sweet Christabel, that gentle maid!
And with such lowly tones she prayed   480
She might be sent without delay
Home to her father's mansion.
                        'Nay!
Nay, by my soul!' said Leoline.
'Ho! Bracy the bard, the charge be thine!
Go thou, with music sweet and loud,
And take two steeds with trappings proud,
And take the youth whom thou lov'st best
To bear thy harp, and learn thy song,
And clothe you both in solemn vest,
And over the mountains haste along,   490
Lest wandering folk, that are abroad,
Detain you on the valley road.

'And when he has crossed the Irthing flood,
My merry bard! he hastes, he hastes
Up Knorren Moor, through Halegarth Wood,
And reaches soon that castle good
Which stands and threatens Scotland's wastes.

'Bard Bracy! bard Bracy! your horses are fleet,
Ye must ride up the hall, your music so sweet,
More loud than your horses' echoing feet!   500
And loud and loud to Lord Roland call,
Thy daughter is safe in Langdale hall!
Thy beautiful daughter is safe and free—
Sir Leoline greets thee thus through me!
He bids thee come without delay
With all thy numerous array
And take thy lovely daughter home:
And he will meet thee on the way
With all his numerous array
White with their panting palfreys' foam: 510

And, by mine honour! I will say,
That I repent me of the day
When I spake words of fierce disdain
To Roland de Vaux of Tryermaine!—
—For since that evil hour hath flown,
Many a summer's sun hath shone;
Yet ne'er found I a friend again
Like Roland de Vaux of Tryermaine.'

The lady fell, and clasped his knees,
Her face upraised, her eyes o'erflowing;   520
And Bracy replied, with faltering voice,
His gracious Hail on all bestowing!—
'Thy words, thou sire of Christabel,
Are sweeter than my harp can tell;
Yet might I gain a boon of thee,
This day my journey should not be,
So strange a dream hath come to me,
That I had vowed with music loud
To clear yon wood from thing unblest,
Warned by a vision in my rest!   530
For in my sleep I saw that dove,
That gentle bird, whom thou dost love,
And call'st by thy own daughter's name—
Sir Leoline! I saw the same
Fluttering, and uttering fearful moan,
Among the green herbs in the forest alone.
Which when I saw and when I heard,
I wonder'd what might ail the bird;
For nothing near it could I see,
Save the grass and green herbs underneath the old tree.   540

'And in my dream methought I went
To search out what might there be found;
And what the sweet bird's trouble meant,
That thus lay fluttering on the ground.
I went and peered, and could descry
No cause for her distressful cry;
But yet for her dear lady's sake
I stooped, methought, the dove to take,
When lo! I saw a bright green snake
Coiled around its wings and neck.   550
Green as the herbs on which it couched,
Close by the dove's its head it crouched;

And with the dove it heaves and stirs,
Swelling its neck as she swelled hers!
I woke; it was the midnight hour,
The clock was echoing in the tower;
But though my slumber was gone by,
This dream it would not pass away—
It seems to live upon my eye!
And thence I vowed this self-same day   56C
With music strong and saintly song
To wander through the forest bare,
Lest aught unholy loiter there.'

Thus Bracy said: the Baron, the while,
Half-listening heard him with a smile;
Then turned to Lady Geraldine,
His eyes made up of wonder and love;
And said in courtly accents fine,
'Sweet maid, Lord Roland's beauteous dove,   570
With arms more strong than harp or song,
Thy sire and I will crush the snake!'
He kissed her forehead as he spake,
And Geraldine in maiden wise
Casting down her large bright eyes,
With blushing cheek and courtesy fine
She turned her from Sir Leoline;
Softly gathering up her train,
That o'er her right arm fell again;
And folded her arms across her chest,
And couched her head upon her breast,   580
And looked askance at Christabel——
Jesu, Maria, shield her well!

A snake's small eye blinks dull and shy;
And the lady's eyes they shrunk in her head,
Each shrunk up to a serpent's eye,
And with somewhat of malice, and more of dread,
At Christabel she looked askance!—
One moment—and the sight was fled!
But Christabel in dizzy trance
Stumbling on the unsteady ground   59u
Shuddered aloud, with a hissing sound;
And Geraldine again turned round,
And like a thing, that sought relief,
Full of wonder and full of grief,

She rolled her large bright eyes divine
Wildly on Sir Leoline.

The maid, alas! her thoughts are gone,
She nothing sees—no sight but one!
The maid, devoid of guile and sin,
I know not how, in fearful wise,   600
So deeply had she drunken in
That look, those shrunken serpent eyes,
That all her features were resigned
To this sole image in her mind:
And passively did imitate
That look of dull and treacherous hate!
And thus she stood, in dizzy trance,
Still picturing that look askance
With forced unconscious sympathy
Full before her father's view——   610
As far as such a look could be
In eyes so innocent and blue!

And when the trance was o'er, the maid
Paused awhile, and inly prayed:
Then falling at the Baron's feet,
'By my mother's soul do I entreat
That thou this woman send away!'
She said: and more she could not say:
For what she knew she could not tell,
O'er-mastered by the mighty spell.   620

Why is thy cheek so wan and wild,
Sir Leoline? Thy only child
Lies at thy feet, thy joy, thy pride,
So fair, so innocent, so mild;
The same, for whom thy lady died!
O by the pangs of her dear mother
Think thou no evil of thy child!
For her, and thee, and for no other,
She prayed the moment ere she died:
Prayed that the babe for whom she died,   630
Might prove her dear lord's joy and pride!
    That prayer her deadly pangs beguiled.
        Sir Leoline!
    And wouldst thou wrong thy only child,
        Her child and thine?

Within the Baron's heart and brain
If thoughts, like these, had any share,
They only swelled his rage and pain,
And did but work confusion there.
His heart was cleft with pain and rage,   640
His cheeks they quivered, his eyes were wild,
Dishonoured thus in his old age;
Dishonoured by his only child,
And all his hospitality
To the wronged daughter of his friend
By more than woman's jealousy
Brought thus to a disgraceful end—
He rolled his eyè with stern regard
Upon the gentle minstrel bard,
And said in tones abrupt, austere—   650
'Why, Bracy! dost thou loiter here?
I bade thee hence!' The bard obeyed;
And turning from his own sweet maid,
The agéd knight, Sir Leoline,
Led forth the lady Geraldine!

THE CONCLUSION TO PART II

A little child, a limber elf,
Singing, dancing to itself,
A fairy thing with red round cheeks,
That always finds, and never seeks,
Makes such a vision to the sight   660
As fills a father's eyes with light;
And pleasures flow in so thick and fast
Upon his heart, that he at last
Must needs express his love's excess
With words of unmeant bitterness.
Perhaps 'tis pretty to force together
Thoughts so all unlike each other;
To mutter and mock a broken charm,
To dally with wrong that does no harm.
Perhaps 'tis tender too and pretty   670
At each wild word to feel within
A sweet recoil of love and pity.
And what, if in a world of sin
(O sorrow and shame should this be true!)
Such giddiness of heart and brain

Comes seldom save from rage and pain,
So talks as it's most used to do.

[1797-1801; publ. 1816]

KUBLA KHAN:

OR, A VISION IN A DREAM. A FRAGMENT.

THE following fragment is here published at the request of a poet of great and deserved celebrity [Lord Byron], and, as far as the Author's own opinions are concerned, rather as a psychological curiosity, than on the ground of any supposed *poetic* merits.

In the summer of the year 1797, the Author, then in ill health, had retired to a lonely farm-house between Porlock and Linton, on the Exmoor confines of Somerset and Devonshire. In consequence of a slight indisposition, an anodyne had been prescribed, from the effects of which he fell asleep in his chair at the moment that he was reading the following sentence, or words of the same substance, in 'Purchas's Pilgrimage': 'Here the Khan Kubla commanded a palace to be built, and a stately garden thereunto. And thus ten miles of fertile ground were inclosed with a wall.' The Author continued for about three hours in a profound sleep, at least of the external senses, during which time he has the most vivid confidence, that he could not have composed less than from two to three hundred lines; if that indeed can be called composition in which all the images rose up before him as *things*, with a parallel production of the correspondent expressions, without any sensation or consciousness of effort. On awaking he appeared to himself to have a distinct recollection of the whole, and taking his pen, ink, and paper, instantly and eagerly wrote down the lines that are here preserved. At this moment he was unfortunately called out by a person on business from Porlock, and detained by him above an hour, and on his return to his room, found, to his no small surprise and mortification, that though he still retained some vague and dim recollection of the general purport of the vision, yet, with the exception of some eight or ten scattered lines and images, all the rest had passed away like the images on the surface of a stream into which a stone has been cast, but, alas! without the after restoration of the latter!

Then all the charm
Is broken--all that phantom-world so fair

Vanishes, and a thousand circlets spread,
And each mis-shape[s] the other. Stay awhile,
Poor youth! who scarcely dar'st lift up thine eyes—
The stream will soon renew its smoothness, soon,
The visions will return! And lo, he stays,
And soon the fragments dim of lovely forms
Come trembling back, unite, and now once more
The pool becomes a mirror.
[From *The Picture; or, the Lover's Resolution*, ll. 91-100.]

Yet from the still surviving recollections in his mind, the Author has frequently purposed to finish for himself what had been originally, as it were, given to him. Σαμερον αδιον ασω: but the to-morrow is yet to come.

As a contrast to this vision, I have annexed a fragment[1] of a very different character, describing with equal fidelity the dream of pain and disease.

KUBLA KHAN

In XANADU did Kubla Khan
A stately pleasure-dome decree:
Where Alph, the sacred river, ran
Through caverns measureless to man
   Down to a sunless sea.
So twice five miles of fertile ground
With walls and towers were girdled round:
And there were gardens bright with sinuous rills,
Where blossomed many an incense-bearing tree;
And here were forests ancient as the hills,   10
Enfolding sunny spots of greenery.

But oh! that deep romantic chasm which slanted
Down the green hill athwart a cedarn cover!
A savage place! as holy and enchanted
As e'er beneath a waning moon was haunted
By woman wailing for her demon-lover!
And from this chasm, with ceaseless turmoil seething,
As if this earth in fast thick pants were breathing,
A mighty fountain momently was forced:
Amid whose swift half-intermitted burst   20

---

[1] *The Pains of Sleep* (p. 82).

Huge fragments vaulted like rebounding hail,
Or chaffy grain beneath the thresher's flail:
And 'mid these dancing rocks at once and ever
It flung up momently the sacred river.
Five miles meandering with a mazy motion
Through wood and dale the sacred river ran,
Then reached the caverns measureless to man,
And sank in tumult to a lifeless ocean:
And 'mid this tumult Kubla heard from far
Ancestral voices prophesying war!   30
    The shadow of the dome of pleasure
    Floated midway on the waves;
    Where was heard the mingled measure
    From the fountain and the caves.
It was a miracle of rare device,
A sunny pleasure-dome with caves of ice!

    A damsel with a dulcimer
    In a vision once I saw:
    It was an Abyssinian maid,
    And on her dulcimer she played,   40
    Singing of Mount Abora.
    Could I revive within me
    Her symphony and song,
    To such a deep delight 'twould win me,
That with music loud and long,
I would build that dome in air,
That sunny dome! those caves of ice!
And all who heard should see them there,
And all should cry, Beware! Beware!
His flashing eyes, his floating hair!   50
Weave a circle round him thrice,
And close your eyes with holy dread,
For he on honey-dew hath fed,
And drunk the milk of Paradise.

                                        [1798; publ. 1816]

LOVE

    ALL thoughts, all passions, all delights,
    Whatever stirs this mortal frame,

All are but ministers of Love,
    And feed his sacred flame.

Oft in my waking dreams do I
Live o'er again that happy hour,
When midway on the mount I lay,
    Beside the ruined tower.

The moonshine, stealing o'er the scene
Had blended with the lights of eve;   10
And she was there, my hope, my joy,
    My own dear Genevieve!

She leant against the arméd man,
The statue of the arméd knight;
She stood and listened to my lay,
    Amid the lingering light.

Few sorrows hath she of her own,
My hope! my joy! my Genevieve!
She loves me best, whene'er I sing
    The songs that make her grieve.   20

I played a soft and doleful air,
I sang an old and moving story—
An old rude song, that suited well
    That ruin wild and hoary.

She listened with a flitting blush,
With downcast eyes and modest grace;
For well she knew, I could not choose
    But gaze upon her face.

I told her of the Knight that wore
Upon his shield a burning brand;   30
And that for ten long years he wooed
    The Lady of the Land.

I told her how he pined: and ah!
The deep, the low, the pleading tone
With which I sang another's love,
    Interpreted my own.

She listened with a flitting blush,
With downcast eyes, and modest grace;
And she forgave me, that I gazed
    Too fondly on her face!   40

But when I told the cruel scorn
That crazed that bold and lovely Knight,
And that he crossed the mountain-woods,
    Nor rested day nor night;

That sometimes from the savage den,
And sometimes from the darksome shade,
And sometimes starting up at once
    In green and sunny glade,—

There came and looked him in the face
An angel beautiful and bright;   50
And that he knew it was a Fiend,
    This miserable Knight!

And that unknowing what he did,
He leaped amid a murderous band,
And saved from outrage worse than death
    The Lady of the Land!

And how she wept, and clasped his knees;
And how she tended him in vain—
And ever strove to expiate
    The scorn that crazed his brain;—   60

And that she nursed him in a cave;
And how his madness went away,
When on the yellow forest-leaves
    A dying man he lay;—

His dying words—but when I reached
That tenderest strain of all the ditty,
My faultering voice and pausing harp
    Disturbed her soul with pity!

All impulses of soul and sense
Had thrilled my guileless Genevieve;   70

The music and the doleful tale,
    The rich and balmy eve;

And hopes, and fears that kindle hope,
An undistinguishable throng,
And gentle wishes long subdued,
    Subdued and cherished long!

She wept with pity and delight,
She blushed with love, and virgin-shame;
And like the murmur of a dream,
    I heard her breathe my name.   80

Her bosom heaved—she stepped aside,
As conscious of my look she stepped—
Then suddenly, with timorous eye
    She fled to me and wept.

She half enclosed me with her arms,
She pressed me with a meek embrace;
And bending back her head, looked up,
    And gazed upon my face.

'Twas partly love, and partly fear,
And partly 'twas a bashful art,   90
That I might rather feel, than see,
    The swelling of her heart.

I calmed her fears, and she was calm,
And told her love with virgin pride;
And so I won my Genevieve,
    My bright and beauteous Bride.

                [1799; publ. 1799]

TIME, REAL AND IMAGINARY

AN ALLEGORY

ON THE wide level of a mountain's head,
  (I knew not where, but 'twas some faery place)
Their pinions, ostrich-like, for sails out-spread,
Two lovely children run an endless race,

A sister and a brother!
This far outstripp'd the other;
Yet ever runs she with reverted face,
And looks and listens for the boy behind:
    For he, alas! is blind!
O'er rough and smooth with even step he passed,   10
And knows not whether he be first or last.

                        [1812?; publ. 1817]

SONG

FROM *ZAPOLYA*

A SUNNY shaft did I behold,
    From sky to earth it slanted:
And poised therein a bird so bold—
    Sweet bird, thou wert enchanted!

He sank, he rose, he twinkled, he trolled
    Within that shaft of sunny mist;
His eyes of fire, his beak of gold,
    All else of amethyst!

And thus he sang: 'Adieu! adieu!
Love's dreams prove seldom true.   10
The blossoms they make no delay:
The sparkling dew-drops will not stay.
    Sweet month of May,
        We must away;
            Far, far away!
                To-day! to-day!'

                        [1815; publ. 1817]

ALICE DU CLOS

OR THE FORKED TONGUE

A BALLAD

'One word with two meanings is the traitor's shield and shaft: and a slit tongue be his blazon!'—*Caucasian Proverb.*

'THE Sun is not yet risen,
But the dawn lies red on the dew:
Lord Julian has stolen from the hunters away,
Is seeking, Lady! for you.
Put on your dress of green,
  Your buskins and your quiver;
Lord Julian is a hasty man,
  Long waiting brook'd he never.
I dare not doubt him, that he means
  To wed you on a day,   10
Your lord and master for to be,
  And you his lady gay.
O Lady! throw your book aside!
I would not that my Lord should chide.'

Thus spake Sir Hugh the vassal knight
  To Alice, child of old Du Clos,
As spotless fair, as airy light
  As that moon-shiny doe,
The gold star on its brow, her sire's ancestral crest!
For ere the lark had left his nest,   20
  She in the garden bower below
Sate loosely wrapt in maiden white,
Her face half drooping from the sight,
  A snow-drop on a tuft of snow!

O close your eyes, and strive to see
The studious maid, with book on knee,—
  Ah! earliest-open'd flower;
While yet with keen unblunted light
The morning star shone opposite
  The lattice of her bower—   30
Alone of all the starry host.

As if in prideful scorn
Of flight and fear he stay'd behind,
  To brave th' advancing morn.

O! Alice could read passing well,
  And she was conning then
Dan Ovid's mazy tale of loves,
  And gods, and beasts, and men.

The vassal's speech, his taunting vein,
It thrill'd like venom thro' her brain;   **40**
  Yet never from the book
She rais'd her head, nor did she deign
  The knight a single look.

'Off, traitor friend! how dar'st thou fix
  Thy wanton gaze on me?
And why, against my earnest suit,
  Does Julian send by thee?

'Go, tell thy Lord, that slow is sure:
  Fair speed his shafts to-day!
I follow here a stronger lure,   **50**
  And chase a gentler prey.'

She said: and with a baleful smile
  The vassal knight reel'd off—
Like a huge billow from a bark
  Toil'd in the deep sea-trough,
That shouldering sideways in mid plunge,
  Is travers'd by a flash.
And staggering onward, leaves the ear
  With dull and distant crash.

And Alice sate with troubled mien   **60**
A moment; for the scoff was keen,
  And thro' her veins did shiver!
Then rose and donn'd her dress of green,
  Her buskins and her quiver.

There stands the flow'ring may-thorn tree!
From thro' the veiling mist you see
  The black and shadowy stem;—
Smit by the sun the mist in glee

Dissolves to lightsome jewelry—
  Each blossom hath its gem!   **70**

With tear-drop glittering to a smile,
The gay maid on the garden-stile
  Mimics the hunter's shout.
'Hip! Florian, hip! To horse, to horse!
  Go, bring the palfrey out.

'My Julian's out with all his clan,
  And, bonny boy, you wis.
Lord Julian is a hasty man,
  Who comes late, comes amiss.'

Now Florian was a stripling squire,   **80**
  A gallant boy of Spain,
That toss'd his head in joy and pride,
Behind his Lady fair to ride,
  But blush'd to hold her train.

The huntress is in her dress of green,—
And forth they go; she with her bow,
  Her buskins and her quiver!—
The squire—no younger e'er was seen—
With restless arm and laughing een,
  He makes his javelin quiver.   **90**

And had not Ellen stay'd the race,
And stopp'd to see, a moment's space,
  The whole great globe of light
Give the last parting kiss-like touch
To the eastern ridge, it lack'd not much,
  They had o'erta'en the knight.

It chanced that up the covert lane,
  Where Julian waiting stood,
A neighbour knight prick'd on to join
  The huntsmen in the wood.   **100**

And with him must Lord Julian go,
  Tho' with an anger'd mind:
Betroth'd not wedded to his bride,
In vain he sought, 'twixt shame and pride,
  Excuse to stay behind.

He bit his lip, he wrung his glove,
He look'd around, he look'd above,
   But pretext none could find or frame.
Alas! alas! and well-a-day!
It grieves me sore to think, to say,   110
That names so seldom meet with Love,
   Yet Love wants courage without a name!

Straight from the forest's skirt the trees
   O'er-branching, made an aisle,
Where hermit old might pace and chaunt
   As in a minster's pile.

From underneath its leafy screen,
   And from the twilight shade,
You pass at once into a green,
   A green and lightsome glade.   120

And there Lord Julian sate on steed;
   Behind him, in a round,
Stood knight and squire, and menial train;
Against the leash the greyhounds strain;
   The horses paw'd the ground.

When up the alley green, Sir Hugh
   Spurr'd in upon the sward,
And mute, without a word, did he
   Fall in behind his lord.

Lord Julian turn'd his steed half round,—   130
   'What! doth not Alice deign
To accept your loving convoy, knight?
Or doth she fear our woodland sleight,
   And join us on the plain?'

With stifled tones the knight replied,
And look'd askance on either side,—
   'Nay, let the hunt proceed!—
The Lady's message that I bear,
I guess would scantly please your ear,
   And less deserves your heed.   140

'You sent betimes. Not yet unbarr'd
   I found the middle door;—

Two stirrers only met my eyes,
    Fair Alice, and one more.

'I came unlook'd for; and, it seem'd,
    In an unwelcome hour;
And found the daughter of Du Clos
    Within the lattic'd bower.

But hush! the rest may wait. If lost,
    No great loss, I divine;   150
And idle words will better suit
    A fair maid's lips than mine.'

'God's wrath! speak out, man,' Julian cried,
    O'ermaster'd by the sudden smart;—
And feigning wrath, sharp, blunt, and rude,
The knight his subtle shift pursued.—
'Scowl not at me; command my skill,
To lure your hawk back, if you will,
    But not a woman's heart.

'"Go! (said she) tell him,—slow is sure;   160
    Fair speed his shafts to-day!
I follow here a stronger lure,
    And chase a gentler prey."

'The game, pardie, was full in sight,
That then did, if I saw aright,
    The fair dame's eyes engage;
For turning, as I took my ways,
I saw them fix'd with steadfast gaze
    Full on her wanton page.'

The last word of the traitor knight   170
    It had but entered Julian's ear,—
From two o'erarching oaks between,
With glist'ning helm-like cap is seen,
    Borne on in giddy cheer,

A youth, that ill his steed can guide,
Yet with reverted face doth ride,
    As answering to a voice,
That seems at once to laugh and chide—

'Not mine, dear mistress,' still he cried,
  ' 'Tis this mad filly's choice.'   180

With sudden bound, beyond the boy,
See! see! that face of hope and joy,
  That regal front! those cheeks aglow!
Thou needed'st but the crescent sheen,
A quiver'd Dian to have been,
  Thou lovely child of old Du Clos!

Dark as a dream Lord Julian stood,
Swift as a dream, from forth the wood,
  Sprang on the plighted Maid!
With fatal aim, and frantic force,   190
The shaft was hurl'd!—a lifeless corse,
Fair Alice from her vaulting horse,
  Lies bleeding on the glade.

                    [1828?; publ. 1834]

LOVE'S APPARITION AND EVANISHMENT

AN ALLEGORIC ROMANCE

LIKE a lone Arab, old and blind,
Some caravan had left behind,
  Who sits beside a ruin'd well,
  Where the shy sand-asps bask and swell;
And now he hangs his agéd head aslant,
And listens for a human sound—in vain!
And now the aid, which Heaven alone can grant,
Upturns his eyeless face from Heaven to gain;—
Even thus, in vacant mood, one sultry hour,
Resting my eye upon a drooping plant,   10
With brow low-bent, within my garden-bower,
I sate upon the couch of camomile;
And—whether 'twas a transient sleep, perchance,
Flitted across the idle brain, the while
I watch'd the sickly calm with aimless scope,
In my own heart; or that, indeed a trance,
Turn'd my eye inward—thee, O genial Hope,
Love's elder sister! thee did I behold,
Drest as a bridesmaid, but all pale and cold,

With roseless cheek, all pale and cold and dim,   20
  Lie lifeless at my feet!
And then came Love, a sylph in bridal trim,
  And stood beside my seat;
She bent, and kiss'd her sister's lips,
  As she was wont to do;—
Alas! 'twas but a chilling breath
Woke just enough of life in death
  To make Hope die anew.

L'ENVOY

In vain we supplicate the Powers above;
There is no resurrection for the Love   30
That, nursed in tenderest care, yet fades away
In the chill'd heart by gradual self-decay.
               [1833; publ. 1834]

CONVERSATION POEMS

THE EOLIAN HARP

COMPOSED AT CLEVEDON, SOMERSETSHIRE

MY PENSIVE Sara! thy soft cheek reclined
Thus on mine arm, most soothing sweet it is
To sit beside our Cot, our Cot o'ergrown
With white-flower'd Jasmin, and the broad-leav'd Myrtle,
(Meet emblems they of Innocence and Love!)
And watch the clouds, that late were rich with light,
Slow saddening round, and mark the star of eve
Serenely brilliant (such should Wisdom be)
Shine opposite! How exquisite the scents
Snatch'd from yon bean-field! and the world *so* hush'd!   **10**
The stilly murmur of the distant Sea
Tells us of silence.
            And that simplest Lute,
Placed length-ways in the clasping casement, hark!
How by the desultory breeze caress'd,
Like some coy maid half yielding to her lover,
It pours such sweet upbraiding, as must needs
Tempt to repeat the wrong! And now, its strings
Boldlier swept, the long sequacious notes
Over delicious surges sink and rise,
Such a soft floating witchery of sound   **20**
As twilight Elfins make, when they at eve
Voyage on gentle gales from Fairy-Land,
Where Melodies round honey-dropping flowers,
Footless and wild, like birds of Paradise,
Nor pause, nor perch, hovering on untam'd wing!
O! the one Life within us and abroad,
Which meets all motion and becomes its soul,
A light in sound, a sound-like power in light,
Rhythm in all thought, and joyance every where—
Methinks, it should have been impossible   **30**
Not to love all things in a world so fill'd;
Where the breeze warbles, and the mute still air
Is Music slumbering on her instrument.

And thus, my Love! as on the midway slope
Of yonder hill I stretch my limbs at noon,
Whilst through my half-clos'd eye-lids I behold
The sunbeams dance, like diamonds, on the main,
And tranquil muse upon tranquillity;
Full many a thought uncall'd and undetain'd,   40
And many idle flitting phantasies,
Traverse my indolent and passive brain,
As wild and various as the random gales
That swell and flutter on this subject Lute!

And what if all of animated nature
Be but organic Harps diversely fram'd,
That tremble into thought, as o'er them sweeps
Plastic and vast, one intellectual breeze,
At once the Soul of each, and God of all?

But thy more serious eye a mild reproof
Darts, O belovéd Woman! nor such thoughts   50
Dim and unhallow'd dost thou not reject,
And biddest me walk humbly with my God.
Meek Daughter in the family of Christ!
Well hast thou said and holily disprais'd
These shapings of the unregenerate mind;
Bubbles that glitter as they rise and break
On vain Philosophy's aye-babbling spring.
For never guiltless may I speak of him,
The Incomprehensible! save when with awe
I praise him, and with Faith that inly *feels;*   60
Who with his saving mercies healéd me,
A sinful and most miserable man,
Wilder'd and dark, and gave me to possess
Peace, and this Cot, and thee, heart-honour'd Maid!
                              [1795; publ. 1796]

REFLECTIONS ON HAVING LEFT A PLACE
OF RETIREMENT

Sermoni propriora.—Hor.

Low was our pretty Cot: our tallest Rose
Peep'd at the chamber-window. We could hear
At silent noon, and eve, and early morn,

The Sea's faint murmur. In the open air
Our Myrtles blossom'd; and across the porch
Thick Jasmins twined: the little landscape round
Was green and woody, and refresh'd the eye.
It was a spot which you might aptly call
The Valley of Seclusion! Once I saw
(Hallowing his Sabbath-day by quietness)   10
A wealthy son of Commerce saunter by,
Bristowa's citizen: methought, it calm'd
His thirst of idle gold, and made him muse
With wiser feelings: for he paus'd, and look'd
With a pleas'd sadness, and gaz'd all around,
Then eyed our Cottage, and gaz'd round again,
And sigh'd, and said, it was a Blesséd Place.
And we *were* bless'd. Oft with patient ear
Long-listening to the viewless sky-lark's note
(Viewless, or haply for a moment seen   20
Gleaming on sunny wings) in whisper'd tones
I've said to my Belovéd, 'Such, sweet Girl!
The inobtrusive song of Happiness,
Unearthly minstrelsy! then only heard
When the Soul seeks to hear; when all is hush'd,
And the Heart listens!'

                    But the time, when first
From that low Dell, steep up the stony Mount
I climb'd with perilous toil and reach'd the top,
Oh! what a goodly scene! *Here* the bleak mount,
The bare bleak mountain speckled thin with sheep;   30
Grey clouds, that shadowing spot the sunny fields;
And river, now with bushy rocks o'er-brow'd,
Now winding bright and full, with naked banks;
And seats, and lawns, the Abbey and the wood,
And cots, and hamlets, and faint city-spire;
The Channel *there*, the Islands and white sails,
Dim coasts, and cloud-like hills, and shoreless Ocean—
It seem'd like Omnipresence! God, methought,
Had built him there a Temple: the whole World
Seem'd *imag'd* in its vast circumference: 40
No *wish* profan'd my overwhelméd heart.
Blest hour! It was a luxury,—to be!

    Ah! quiet Dell! dear Cot, and Mount sublime!
was con⁻ ⁺rain'd to quit you. Was it right,

While my unnumber'd brethren toil'd and bled,
That I should dream away the entrusted hours
On rose-leaf beds, pampering the coward heart
With feelings all too delicate for use?
Sweet is the tear that from some Howard's eye
Drops on the cheek of one he lifts from earth: 50
And he that works me good with unmov'd face,
Does it but half: he chills me while he aids,
My benefactor, not my brother man!
Yet even this, this cold beneficence
Praise, praise it, O my Soul! oft as thou scann'st
The sluggard Pity's vision-weaving tribe!
Who sigh for Wretchedness, yet shun the Wretched,
Nursing in some delicious solitude
Their slothful loves and dainty sympathies!
I therefore go, and join head, heart, and hand,   60
Active and firm, to fight the bloodless fight
Of Science, Freedom, and the Truth in Christ.

Yet oft when after honourable toil
Rests the tir'd mind, and waking loves to dream,
My spirit shall revisit thee, dear Cot!
Thy Jasmin and thy window-peeping Rose,
And Myrtles fearless of the mild sea-air.
And I shall sigh fond wishes—sweet Abode!
Ah!—had none greater! And that all had such!
It might be so—but the time is not yet.   70
Speed it, O Father! Let thy Kingdom come!
                      [1795; publ. 1796]

THIS LIME-TREE BOWER MY PRISON

[ADDRESSED TO CHARLES LAMB, OF THE
INDIA HOUSE, LONDON]

In the June of 1797 some long-expected friends paid a visit to the
author's cottage; and on the morning of their arrival, he met with an
accident, which disabled him from walking during the whole time of
their stay. One evening, when they had left him for a few hours, he
composed the following lines in the garden-bower.

WELL, they are gone, and here must I remain,
This lime-tree bower my prison! I have lost
Beauties and feelings, such as would have been

Most sweet to my remembrance even when age
Had dimm'd mine eyes to blindness! They, meanwhile,
Friends, whom I never more may meet again,
On springy heath, along the hill-top edge,
Wander in gladness, and wind down, perchance,
To that still roaring dell, of which I told;
The roaring dell, o'erwooded, narrow, deep,   10
And only speckled by the mid-day sun;
Where its slim trunk the ash from rock to rock
Flings arching like a bridge;—that branchless ash,
Unsunn'd and damp, whose few poor yellow leaves
Ne'er tremble in the gale, yet tremble still,
Fann'd by the water-fall! and there my friends
Behold the dark green file of long lank weeds,
That all at once (a most fantastic sight!)
Still nod and drip beneath the dripping edge
Of the blue clay-stone.

     Now, my friends emerge   20
Beneath the wide wide Heaven—and view again
The many-steepled tract magnificent
Of hilly fields and meadows, and the sea,
With some fair bark, perhaps, whose sails light up
The slip of smooth clear blue betwixt two Isles
Of purple shadow! Yes! they wander on
In gladness all; but thou, methinks, most glad,
My gentle-hearted Charles! for thou hast pined
And hunger'd after Nature, many a year,
In the great City pent, winning thy way   30
With sad yet patient soul, through evil and pain
And strange calamity! Ah! slowly sink
Behind the western ridge, thou glorious Sun!
Shine in the slant beams of the sinking orb,
Ye purple heath-flowers! richlier burn, ye clouds!
Live in the yellow light, ye distant groves!
And kindle, thou blue Ocean! So my friend
Struck with deep joy may stand, as I have stood,
Silent with swimming sense; yea, gazing round
On the wide landscape, gaze till all doth seem   40
Less gross than bodily; and of such hues
As veil the Almighty Spirit, when yet he makes
Spirits perceive his presence.

     A delight
Comes sudden on my heart, and I am glad

As I myself were there! Nor in this bower,
This little lime-tree bower, have I not mark'd
Much that has sooth'd me. Pale beneath the blaze
Hung the transparent foliage; and I watch'd
Some broad and sunny leaf, and lov'd to see
The shadow of the leaf and stem above   50
Dappling its sunshine! And that walnut-tree
Was richly ting'd, and a deep radiance lay
Full on the ancient ivy, which usurps
Those fronting elms, and now, with blackest mass
Makes their dark branches gleam a lighter hue
Through the late twilight: and though now the bat
Wheels silent by, and not a swallow twitters,
Yet still the solitary humble-bee
Sings in the bean-flower! Henceforth I shall know
That Nature ne'er deserts the wise and pure;   60
No plot so narrow, be but Nature there,
No waste so vacant, but may well employ
Each faculty of sense, and keep the heart
Awake to Love and Beauty! and sometimes
'Tis well to be bereft of promis'd good,
That we may lift the soul, and contemplate
With lively joy the joys we cannot share.
My gentle-hearted Charles! when the last rook
Beat its straight path along the dusky air
Homewards, I blest it! deeming its black wing   70
(Now a dim speck, now vanishing in light)
Had cross'd the mighty Orb's dilated glory,
While thou stood'st gazing; or, when all was still,
Flew creeking o'er thy head, and had a charm
For thee, my gentle-hearted Charles, to whom
No sound is dissonant which tells of Life.

[1797; publ. 1800]

FROST AT MIDNIGHT

THE Frost performs its secret ministry,
Unhelped by any wind. The owlet's cry
Came loud—and hark, again! loud as before.
The inmates of my cottage, all at rest,
Have left me to that solitude, which suits
Abstruser musings: save that at my side

My cradled infant slumbers peacefully.
'Tis calm indeed! so calm, that it disturbs
And vexes meditation with its strange
And extreme silentness. Sea, hill, and wood,   10
This populous village! Sea, and hill, and wood,
With all the numberless goings-on of life,
Inaudible as dreams! the thin blue flame
Lies on my low-burnt fire, and quivers not;
Only that film, which fluttered on the grate,
Still flutters there, the sole unquiet thing.
Methinks, its motion in this hush of nature
Gives it dim sympathies with me who live,
Making it a companionable form,
Whose puny flaps and freaks the idling Spirit   20
By its own moods interprets, every where
Echo or mirror seeking of itself,
And makes a toy of Thought.

                                But O! how oft,
How oft, at school, with most believing mind,
Presageful, have I gazed upon the bars,
To watch that fluttering *stranger!* and as oft
With unclosed lids, already had I dreamt
Of my sweet birth-place, and the old church-tower,
Whose bells, the poor man's only music, rang
From morn to evening, all the hot Fair-day,   30
So sweetly, that they stirred and haunted me
With a wild pleasure, falling on mine ear
Most like articulate sounds of things to come!
So gazed I, till the soothing things, I dreamt,
Lulled me to sleep, and sleep prolonged my dreams!
And so I brooded all the following morn,
Awed by the stern preceptor's face, mine eye
Fixed with mock study on my swimming book:
Save if the door half opened, and I snatched
A hasty glance, and still my heart leaped up,   40
For still I hoped to see the *stranger's* face,
Townsman, or aunt, or sister more beloved,
My play-mate when we both were clothed alike!

    Dear Babe, that sleepest cradled by my side,
Whose gentle breathings, heard in this deep calm,
Fill up the interspersèd vacancies
And momentary pauses of the thought!

My babe so beautiful! it thrills my heart
With tender gladness, thus to look at thee,
And think that thou shalt learn far other lore,   50
And in far other scenes! For I was reared
In the great city, pent 'mid cloisters dim,
And saw nought lovely but the sky and stars.
But *thou*, my babe! shalt wander like a breeze
By lakes and sandy shores, beneath the crags
Of ancient mountain, and beneath the clouds,
Which image in their bulk both lakes and shores
And mountain crags: so shalt thou see and hear
The lovely shapes and sounds intelligible
Of that eternal language, which thy God   60
Utters, who from eternity doth teach
Himself in all, and all things in himself.
Great universal Teacher! he shall mould
Thy spirit, and by giving make it ask.

Therefore all seasons shall be sweet to thee,
Whether the summer clothe the general earth
With greenness, or the redbreast sit and sing
Betwixt the tufts of snow on the bare branch
Of mossy apple-tree, while the night thatch
Smokes in the sun-thaw; whether the eave-drops fall   70
Heard only in the trances of the blast,
Or if the secret ministry of frost
Shall hang them up in silent icicles,
Quietly shining to the quiet Moon.

[1798; publ. 1798]

FEARS IN SOLITUDE

WRITTEN IN APRIL 1798, DURING THE ALARM OF AN INVASION

A GREEN and silent spot, amid the hills,
A small and silent dell! O'er stiller place
No singing sky-lark ever poised himself.
The hills are heathy, save that swelling slope,
Which hath a gay and gorgeous covering on,
All golden with the never-bloomless furze,
Which now blooms most profusely: but the dell,
Bathed by the mist, is fresh and delicate
As vernal corn-field, or the unripe flax,

When, through its half-transparent stalks, at eve,   10
The level sunshine glimmers with green light.
Oh! 'tis a quiet spirit-healing nook!
Which all, methinks, would love; but chiefly he,
The humble man, who, in his youthful years,
Knew just so much of folly, as had made
His early manhood more securely wise!
Here he might lie on fern or withered heath,
While from the singing lark (that sings unseen
The minstrelsy that solitude loves best),
And from the sun, and from the breezy air,   20
Sweet influences trembled o'er his frame;
And he, with many feelings, many thoughts,
Made up a meditative joy, and found
Religious meanings in the forms of Nature!
And so, his senses gradually wrapt
In a half sleep, he dreams of better worlds,
And dreaming hears thee still, O singing lark,
That singest like an angel in the clouds!

My God! it is a melancholy thing
For such a man, who would full fain preserve   30
His soul in calmness, yet perforce must feel
For all his human brethren—O my God!
It weighs upon the heart, that he must think
What uproar and what strife may now be stirring
This way or that way o'er these silent hills—
Invasion, and the thunder and the shout,
And all the crash of onset; fear and rage,
And undetermined conflict—even now,
Even now, perchance, and in his native isle:
Carnage and groans beneath this blessed sun!   40
We have offended, Oh! my countrymen!
We have offended very grievously,
And been most tyrannous. From east to west
A groan of accusation pierces Heaven!
The wretched plead against us; multitudes
Countless and vehement, the sons of God,
Our brethren! Like a cloud that travels on,
Steamed up from Cairo's swamps of pestilence,
Even so, my countrymen! have we gone forth
And borne to distant tribes slavery and pangs,   50
And, deadlier far, our vices, whose deep taint
With slow perdition murders the whole man,

His body and his soul! Meanwhile, at home,
All individual dignity and power
Engulfed in Courts, Committees, Institutions,
Associations and Societies,
A vain, speech-mouthing, speech-reporting Guild,
One Benefit-Club for mutual flattery,
We have drunk up, demure as at a grace,
Pollutions from the brimming cup of wealth;   60
Contemptuous of all honourable rule,
Yet bartering freedom and the poor man's life
For gold, as at a market! The sweet words
Of Christian promise, words that even yet
Might stem destruction, were they wisely preached,
Are muttered o'er by men, whose tones proclaim
How flat and wearisome they feel their trade:
Rank scoffers some, but most too indolent
To deem them falsehoods or to know their truth.
Oh! blasphemous! the Book of Life is made   70
A superstitious instrument, on which
We gabble o'er the oaths we mean to break;
For all must swear—all and in every place,
College and wharf, council and justice-court;
All, all must swear, the briber and the bribed,
Merchant and lawyer, senator and priest,
The rich, the poor, the old man and the young;
All, all make up one scheme of perjury,
That faith doth reel; the very name of God
Sounds like a juggler's charm; and, bold with joy,   80
Forth from his dark and lonely hiding-place,
(Portentous sight!) the owlet Atheism,
Sailing on obscene wings athwart the noon,
Drops his blue-fringéd lids, and holds them close,
And hooting at the glorious sun in Heaven,
Cries out, 'Where is it?'

                    Thankless too for peace,
(Peace long preserved by fleets and perilous seas)
Secure from actual warfare, we have loved
To swell the war-whoop, passionate for war!
Alas! for ages ignorant of all   90
Its ghastlier workings, (famine or blue plague,
Battle, or siege, or flight through wintry snows,)
We, this whole people, have been clamorous

For war and bloodshed; animating sports,
The which we pay for as a thing to talk of,
Spectators and not combatants! No guess
Anticipative of a wrong unfelt,
No speculation on contingency,
However dim and vague, too vague and dim
To yield a justifying cause; and forth,   100
(Stuffed out with big preamble, holy names,
And adjurations of the God in Heaven,)
We send our mandates for the certain death
Of thousands and ten thousands! Boys and girls,
And women, that would groan to see a child
Pull off an insect's leg, all read of war,
The best amusement for our morning meal!
The poor wretch, who has learnt his only prayers
From curses, who knows scarcely words enough
To ask a blessing from his Heavenly Father,   110
Becomes a fluent phraseman, absolute
And technical in victories and defeats,
And all our dainty terms for fratricide;
Terms which we trundle smoothly o'er our tongues
Like mere abstractions, empty sounds to which
We join no feeling and attach no form!
As if the soldier died without a wound;
As if the fibres of this godlike frame
Were gored without a pang; as if the wretch,
Who fell in battle, doing bloody deeds,   120
Passed off to Heaven, translated and not killed;
As though he had no wife to pine for him,
No God to judge him! Therefore, evil days
Are coming on us, O my countrymen!
And what if all-avenging Providence,
Strong and retributive, should make us know
The meaning of our words, force us to feel
The desolation and the agony
Of our fierce doings?

                   Spare us yet awhile,
Father and God! O! spare us yet awhile!   130
Oh! let not English women drag their flight
Fainting beneath the burthen of their babes,
Of the sweet infants, that but yesterday
Laughed at the breast! Sons, brothers, husbands, all

Who ever gazed with fondness on the forms
Which grew up with you round the same fire-side,
And all who ever heard the sabbath-bells
Without the infidel's scorn, make yourselves pure!
Stand forth! be men! repel an impious foe,   140
Impious and false, a light yet cruel race,
Who laugh away all virtue, mingling mirth
With deeds of murder; and still promising
Freedom, themselves too sensual to be free,
Poison life's amities, and cheat the heart
Of faith and quiet hope, and all that soothes,
And all that lifts the spirit! Stand we forth;
Render them back upon the insulted ocean,
And let them toss as idly on its waves
As the vile sea-weed, which some mountain-blast
Swept from our shores! And oh! may we return   150
Not with a drunken triumph, but with fear,
Repenting of the wrongs with which we stung
So fierce a foe to frenzy!

                        I have told,
O Britons! O my brethren! I have told
Most bitter truth, but without bitterness.
Nor deem my zeal or factious or mistimed;
For never can true courage dwell with them,
Who, playing tricks with conscience, dare not look
At their own vices. We have been too long
Dupes of a deep delusion! Some, belike,   160
Groaning with restless enmity, expect
All change from change of constituted power;
As if a Government had been a robe,
On which our vice and wretchedness were tagged
Like fancy-points and fringes, with the robe
Pulled off at pleasure. Fondly these attach
A radical causation to a few
Poor drudges of chastising Providence,
Who borrow all their hues and qualities
From our own folly and rank wickedness,   170
Which gave them birth and nursed them. Others, mean-
    while,
Dote with a mad idolatry; and all
Who will not fall before their images,
And yield them worship, they are enemies
Even of their country!

                    Such have I been deemed.—
But, O dear Britain! O my Mother Isle!
Needs must thou prove a name most dear and holy
To me, a son, a brother, and a friend,
A husband, and a father! who revere
All bonds of natural love, and find them all   180
Within the limits of thy rocky shores.
O native Britain! O my Mother Isle!
How shouldst thou prove aught else but dear and holy
To me, who from thy lakes and mountain-hills,
Thy clouds, thy quiet dales, thy rocks and seas,
Have drunk in all my intellectual life,
All sweet sensations, all ennobling thoughts,
All adoration of the God in nature,
All lovely and all honourable things,
Whatever makes this mortal spirit feel   190
The joy and greatness of its future being?
There lives nor form nor feeling in my soul
Unborrowed from my country! O divine
And beauteous island! thou hast been my sole
And most magnificent temple, in the which
I walk with awe, and sing my stately songs,
Loving the God that made me!—

                              May my fears,
My filial fears, be vain! and may the vaunts
And menace of the vengeful enemy
Pass like the gust, that roared and died away   200
In the distant tree: which heard, and only heard
In this low dell, bowed not the delicate grass.

But now the gentle dew-fall sends abroad
The fruit-like perfume of the golden furze:
The light has left the summit of the hill,
Though still a sunny gleam lies beautiful,
Aslant the ivied beacon. Now farewell,
Farewell, awhile, O soft and silent spot!
On the green sheep-track, up the heathy hill,
Homeward I wind my way; and lo! recalled   210
From bodings that have well-nigh wearied me,
I find myself upon the brow, and pause
Startled! And after lonely sojourning
In such a quiet and surrounded nook,
This burst of prospect, here the shadowy main,

Dim-tinted, there the mighty majesty
Of that huge amphitheatre of rich
And elmy fields, seems like society—
Conversing with the mind, and giving it
A livelier impulse and a dance of thought!   220
And now, belovéd Stowey! I behold
Thy church-tower, and methinks, the four huge elms
Clustering, which mark the mansion of my friend;
And close behind them, hidden from my view,
Is my own lowly cottage, where my babe
And my babe's mother dwell in peace! With light
And quickened footsteps thitherward I tend,
Remembering thee, O green and silent dell!
And grateful, that by nature's quietness
And solitary musings, all my heart   230
Is softened, and made worthy to indulge
Love, and the thoughts that yearn for human kind.
                              [1798; publ. 1798]

THE NIGHTINGALE

A CONVERSATION POEM, APRIL, 1798

No CLOUD, no relique of the sunken day
Distinguishes the West, no long thin slip
Of sullen light, no obscure trembling hues.
Come, we will rest on this old mossy bridge!
You see the glimmer of the stream beneath,
But hear no murmuring: it flows silently,
O'er its soft bed of verdure. All is still,
A balmy night! and though the stars be dim,
Yet let us think upon the vernal showers
That gladden the green earth, and we shall find   10
A pleasure in the dimness of the stars.
And hark! the Nightingale begins its song,
'Most musical, most melancholy' bird!
A melancholy bird? Oh! idle thought!
In Nature there is nothing melancholy.
But some night-wandering man whose heart was pierced
With the remembrance of a grievous wrong.
Or slow distemper, or neglected love,
(And so, poor wretch! filled all things with himself,
And made all gentle sounds tell back the tale   20

Of his own sorrow) he, and such as he,
First named these notes a melancholy strain.
And many a poet echoes the conceit;
Poet who hath been building up the rhyme
When he had better far have stretched his limbs
Beside a brook in mossy forest-dell,
By sun or moon-light, to the influxes
Of shapes and sounds and shifting elements
Surrendering his whole spirit, of his song
And of his fame forgetful! so his fame   30
Should share in Nature's immortality,
A venerable thing! and so his song
Should make all Nature lovelier, and itself
Be loved like Nature! But 'twill not be so;
And youths and maidens most poetical,
Who lose the deepening twilights of the spring
In ball-rooms and hot theatres, they still
Full of meek sympathy must heave their sighs
O'er Philomela's pity-pleading strains.

My Friend, and thou, our Sister! we have learnt   40
A different lore: we may not thus profane
Nature's sweet voices, always full of love
And joyance! 'Tis the merry Nightingale
That crowds, and hurries, and precipitates
With fast thick warble his delicious notes,
As he were fearful that an April night
Would be too short for him to utter forth
His love-chant, and disburthen his full soul
Of all its music!

                        And I know a grove
Of large extent, hard by a castle huge,   50
Which the great lord inhabits not; and so
This grove is wild with tangling underwood,
And the trim walks are broken up, and grass,
Thin grass and king-cups grow within the paths.
But never elsewhere in one place I knew
So many nightingales; and far and near,
In wood and thicket, over the wide grove,
They answer and provoke each other's song,
With skirmish and capricious passagings,
And murmurs musical and swift jug jug,   60
And one low piping sound more sweet than all—

Stirring the air with such a harmony,
That should you close your eyes, you might almost
Forget it was not day! On moonlight bushes,
Whose dewy leaflets are but half-disclosed,
You may perchance behold them on the twigs,
Their bright, bright eyes, their eyes both bright and full,
Glistening, while many a glow-worm in the shade
Lights up her love-torch.

                    A most gentle Maid,
Who dwelleth in her hospitable home   **70**
Hard by the castle, and at latest eve
(Even like a Lady vowed and dedicate
To something more than Nature in the grove)
Glides through the pathways; she knows all their notes,
That gentle Maid! and oft, a moment's space,
What time the moon was lost behind a cloud,
Hath heard a pause of silence; till the moon
Emerging, hath awakened earth and sky
With one sensation, and those wakeful birds
Have all burst forth in choral minstrelsy,   **80**
As if some sudden gale had swept at once
A hundred airy harps! And she hath watched
Many a nightingale perch giddily
On blossomy twig still swinging from the breeze,
And to that motion tune his wanton song
Like tipsy Joy that reels with tossing head.

Farewell, O Warbler! till to-morrow eve,
And you, my friends! farewell, a short farewell!
We have been loitering long and pleasantly,
And now for our dear homes.—That strain again!   **90**
Full fain it would delay me! My dear babe,
Who, capable of no articulate sound,
Mars all things with his imitative lisp,
How he would place his hand beside his ear,
His little hand, the small forefinger up,
And bid us listen! And I deem it wise
To make him Nature's play-mate. He knows well
The evening-star; and once, when he awoke
In most distressful mood (some inward pain
Had made up that strange thing, an infant's dream—)   **100**
I hurried with him to our orchard-plot,
And he beheld the moon, and, hushed at once.

Suspends his sobs, and laughs most silently,
While his fair eyes, that swam with undropped tears,
Did glitter in the yellow moon-beam! Well!—
It is a father's tale: But if that Heaven
Should give me life, his childhood shall grow up
Familiar with these songs, that with the night
He may associate joy.—Once more, farewell,
Sweet Nightingale! once more, my friends! farewell.   110

[1798; publ. 1798]

LINES

WRITTEN IN THE ALBUM AT ELBINGERODE, IN THE HARTZ FOREST

I STOOD on Brocken's sovran height, and saw
Woods crowding upon woods, hills over hills,
A surging scene, and only limited
By the blue distance. Heavily my way
Downward I dragged through fir groves evermore,
Where bright green moss heaves in sepulchral forms
Speckled with sunshine; and, but seldom heard,
The sweet bird's song became a hollow sound;
And the breeze, murmuring indivisibly,
Preserved its solemn murmur most distinct   10
From many a note of many a waterfall,
And the brook's chatter; 'mid whose islet-stones
The dingy kidling with its tinkling bell
Leaped frolicsome, or old romantic goat
Sat, his white beard slow waving. I moved on
In low and languid mood: for I had found
That outward forms, the loftiest, still receive
Their finer influence from the Life within;—
Fair cyphers else: fair, but of import vague
Or unconcerning, where the heart not finds   20
History or prophecy of friend, or child,
Or gentle maid, our first and early love,
Or father, or the venerable name
Of our adoréd country! O thou Queen,
Thou delegated Deity of Earth,
O dear, dear England! how my longing eye
Turned westward, shaping in the steady clouds
Thy sands and high white cliffs!

My native Land!
Filled with the thought of thee this heart was proud,
Yea, mine eye swam with tears: that all the view   30
From sovran Brocken, woods and woody hills,
Floated away, like a departing dream,
Feeble and dim! Stranger, these impulses
Blame thou not lightly; nor will I profane,
With hasty judgment or injurious doubt,
That man's sublimer spirit, who can feel
That God is everywhere! the God who framed
Mankind to be one mighty family,
Himself our Father, and the World our Home.

[1799; publ. 1799]

TO WILLIAM WORDSWORTH

COMPOSED ON THE NIGHT AFTER HIS RECITATION OF A POEM ON THE GROWTH OF AN INDIVIDUAL MIND

FRIEND of the wise! and Teacher of the Good!
Into my heart have I received that Lay
More than historic, that prophetic Lay
Wherein (high theme by thee first sung aright)
Of the foundations and the building up
Of a Human Spirit thou hast dared to tell
What may be told, to the understanding mind
Revealable; and what within the mind
By vital breathings secret as the soul
Of vernal growth, oft quickens in the heart   10
Thoughts all too deep for words!—

Theme hard as high!
Of smiles spontaneous, and mysterious fears
(The first-born they of Reason and twin-birth),
Of tides obedient to external force,
And currents self-determined, as might seem,
Or by some inner Power; of moments awful,
Now in thy inner life, and now abroad,
When power streamed from thee, and thy soul received
The light reflected, as a light bestowed—
Of fancies fair, and milder hours of youth,   20
Hyblean murmurs of poetic thought
Industrious in its joy, in vales and glens

Native or outland, lakes and famous hills!
Or on the lonely high-road, when the stars
Were rising; or by secret mountain-streams,
The guides and the companions of thy way!

Of more than Fancy, of the Social Sense
Distending wide, and man beloved as man,
Where France in all her towns lay vibrating
Like some becalméd bark beneath the burst   30
Of Heaven's immediate thunder, when no cloud
Is visible, or shadow on the main.
For thou wert there, thine own brows garlanded,
Amid the tremor of a realm aglow,
Amid a mighty nation jubilant,
When from the general heart of human kind
Hope sprang forth like a full-born Deity!
——Of that dear Hope afflicted and struck down,
So summoned homeward, thenceforth calm and sure
From the dread watch-tower of man's absolute self,   40
With light unwaning on her eyes, to look
Far on—herself a glory to behold,
The Angel of the vision! Then (last strain)
Of Duty, chosen Laws controlling choice,
Action and joy!—An Orphic song indeed,
A song divine of high and passionate thoughts
To their own music chaunted!

                    O great Bard!
Ere yet that last strain dying awed the air,
With stedfast eye I viewed thee in the choir
Of ever-enduring men. The truly great   50
Have all one age, and from one visible space
Shed influence! They, both in power and act,
Are permanent, and Time is not with them,
Save as it worketh for them, they in it.
Nor less a sacred Roll, than those of old,
And to be placed, as they, with gradual fame
Among the archives of mankind, thy work
Makes audible a linkéd lay of Truth,
Of Truth profound a sweet continuous lay,
Not learnt, but native, her own natural notes!   60
Ah! as I listened with a heart forlorn,
The pulses of my being beat anew:
And even as Life returns upon the drowned,

Life's joy rekindling roused a throng of pains—
Keen pangs of Love, awakening as a babe
Turbulent, with an outcry in the heart;
And fears self-willed, that shunned the eye of Hope;
And Hope that scarce would know itself from Fear;
Sense of past Youth, and Manhood come in vain,
And Genius given, and Knowledge won in vain;   70
And all which I had culled in wood-walks wild,
And all which patient toil had reared, and all,
Commune with thee had opened out—but flowers
Strewed on my corse, and borne upon my bier
In the same coffin, for the self-same grave!

    That way no more! and ill beseems it me,
Who came a welcomer in herald's guise,
Singing of Glory, and Futurity,
To wander back on such unhealthful road,
Plucking the poisons of self-harm! And ill   80
Such intertwine beseems triumphal wreaths
Strew'd before thy advancing!

                    Nor do thou,
Sage Bard! impair the memory of that hour
Of thy communion with my nobler mind
By pity or grief, already felt too long!
Nor let my words import more blame than needs.
The tumult rose and ceased: for Peace is nigh
Where Wisdom's voice has found a listening heart.
Amid the howl of more than wintry storms,
The Halcyon hears the voice of vernal hours   90
Already on the wing.

                Eve following eve,
Dear tranquil time, when the sweet sense of Home
Is sweetest! moments for their own sake hailed
And more desired, more precious, for thy song,
In silence listening, like a devout child,
My soul lay passive, by thy various strain
Driven as in surges now beneath the stars,
With momentary stars of my own birth,
Fair constellated foam, still darting off
Into the darkness; now a tranquil sea,   100
Outspread and bright, yet swelling to the moon.

And when—O Friend! my comforter and guide!
Strong in thyself, and powerful to give strength!—
Thy long sustainéd Song finally closed,
And thy deep voice had ceased—yet thou thyself
Wert still before my eyes, and round us both
That happy vision of belovéd faces—
Scarce conscious, and yet conscious of its close
I sate, my being blended in one thought
(Thought was it? or aspiration? or resolve?)   110
Absorbed, yet hanging still upon the sound—
And when I rose, I found myself in prayer.

[1807; publ. 1817]

LIMBO

DEJECTION: AN ODE

[WRITTEN APRIL 4, 1802]

> Late, late yestreen I saw the new Moon,
> With the old Moon in her arms;
> And I fear, I fear, my Master dear!
> We shall have a deadly storm.
> *Ballad of Sir Patrick Spence.*

I

WELL! If the Bard was weather-wise, who made
  The grand old ballad of Sir Patrick Spence,
  This night, so tranquil now, will not go hence
Unroused by winds, that ply a busier trade
Than those which mould yon cloud in lazy flakes,
Or the dull sobbing draft, that moans and rakes
Upon the strings of this Æolian lute,
    Which better far were mute.
  For lo! the New-moon winter-bright!
  And overspread with phantom light,   **10**
  (With swimming phantom light o'erspread
  But rimmed and circled by a silver thread)
I see the old Moon in her lap, foretelling
  The coming-on of rain and squally blast.
And oh! that even now the gust were swelling,
  And the slant night-shower driving loud and fast!
Those sounds which oft have raised me, whilst they awed,
    And sent my soul abroad,
Might now perhaps their wonted impulse give,
Might startle this dull pain, and make it move and live! **20**

II

A grief without a pang, void, dark, and drear,
  A stifled, drowsy, unimpassioned grief,
  Which finds no natural outlet, no relief,
    In word, or sigh, or tear—
78

O Lady! in this wan and heartless mood,
To other thoughts by yonder throstle woo'd,
  All this long eve, so balmy and serene,
Have I been gazing on the western sky,
  And its peculiar tint of yellow green:
And still I gaze—and with how blank an eye!   30
And those thin clouds above, in flakes and bars,
That give away their motion to the stars;
Those stars, that glide behind them or between,
Now sparkling, now bedimmed, but always seen:
Yon crescent Moon, as fixed as if it grew
In its own cloudless, starless lake of blue;
I see them all so excellently fair,
I see, not feel, how beautiful they are!

III

    My genial spirits fail;
    And what can these avail   40
To lift the smothering weight from off my breast?
    It were a vain endeavour,
    Though I should gaze for ever
On that green light that lingers in the west:
I may not hope from outward forms to win
The passion and the life, whose fountains are within.

IV

O Lady! we receive but what we give,
And in our life alone does Nature live:
Ours is her wedding garment, ours her shroud!
  And would we aught behold, of higher worth,   50
Than that inanimate cold world allowed
To the poor loveless ever-anxious crowd,
  Ah! from the soul itself must issue forth
A light, a glory, a fair luminous cloud
    Enveloping the Earth—
And from the soul itself must there be sent
  A sweet and potent voice, of its own birth,
Of all sweet sounds the life and element!

V

O pure of heart! thou need'st not ask of me
What this strong music in the soul may be!   60

What, and wherein it doth exist,
This light, this glory, this fair luminous mist,
This beautiful and beauty-making power.

Joy, virtuous Lady! Joy that ne'er was given,
Save to the pure, and in their purest hour,
Life, and Life's effluence, cloud at once and shower,
Joy, Lady! is the spirit and the power,
Which wedding Nature to us gives in dower
    A new Earth and new Heaven,
Undreamt of by the sensual and the proud—   70
Joy is the sweet voice, Joy the luminous cloud—
    We in ourselves rejoice!
And thence flows all that charms or ear or sight,
    All melodies the echoes of that voice,
All colours a suffusion from that light.

VI

There was a time when, though my path was rough,
    This joy within me dallied with distress,
And all misfortunes were but as the stuff
    Whence Fancy made me dreams of happiness:
For hope grew round me, like the twining vine,   80
And fruits, and foliage, not my own, seemed mine.
But now afflictions bow me down to earth:
Nor care I that they rob me of my mirth;
    But oh! each visitation
Suspends what nature gave me at my birth,
    My shaping spirit of Imagination.
For not to think of what I needs must feel,
    But to be still and patient, all I can;
And haply by abstruse research to steal
    From my own nature all the natural man—   90
This was my sole resource, my only plan:
Till that which suits a part infects the whole,
And now is almost grown the habit of my soul.

VII

Hence, viper thoughts, that coil around my mind,
    Reality's dark dream!
I turn from you, and listen to the wind,
    Which long has raved unnoticed. What a scream

Of agony by torture lengthened out
That lute sent forth! Thou Wind, that rav'st without,
  Bare crag, or mountain-tairn,[1] or blasted tree,   **100**
Or pine-grove whither woodman never clomb,
Or lonely house, long held the witches home,
  Methinks were fitter instruments for thee,
Mad Lutanist! who in this month of showers,
Of dark-brown gardens, and of peeping flowers,
Mak'st Devils' yule, with worse than wintry song,
The blossoms, buds, and timorous leaves among.
  Thou Actor, perfect in all tragic sounds!
Thou mighty Poet, e'en to frenzy bold!
    What tell'st thou now about?   **110**
  'Tis of the rushing of an host in rout,
  With groans, of trampled men, with smarting wounds—
At once they groan with pain, and shudder with the cold!
But hush! there is a pause of deepest silence!
  And all that noise, as of a rushing crowd,
With groans, and tremulous shudderings—all is over—
  It tells another tale, with sounds less deep and loud!
    A tale of less affright,
    And tempered with delight,
As Otway's self had framed the tender lay,—   **120**
    'Tis of a little child
    Upon a lonesome wild,
Not far from home, but she hath lost her way:
And now moans low in bitter grief and fear,
And now screams loud, and hopes to make her mother hear.

VIII

'Tis midnight, but small thoughts have I of sleep:
Full seldom may my friend such vigils keep!
Visit her, gentle Sleep! with wings of healing,
  And may this storm be but a mountain-birth,
May all the stars hang bright above her dwelling,   **130**
  Silent as though they watched the sleeping Earth!
    With light heart may she rise,

---

[1] Tairn is a small lake, generally if not always applied to the lakes up
in the mountains and which are the feeders of those in the valleys. This
address to the Storm-wind will not appear extravagant to those who
have heard it at night and in a mountainous country.

Gay fancy, cheerful eyes,
Joy lift her spirit, joy attune her voice;
To her may all things live, from pole to pole,
Their life the eddying of her living soul!
  O simple spirit, guided from above,
Dear Lady! friend devoutest of my choice,
Thus mayest thou ever, evermore rejoice.

[1802; publ. 1802]

THE PAINS OF SLEEP

Ere on my bed my limbs I lay,
It hath not been my use to pray
With moving lips or bended knees;
But silently, by slow degrees,
My spirit I to Love compose,
In humble trust mine eye-lids close,
With reverential resignation,
No wish conceiv'd, no thought exprest,
Only a sense of supplication;
A sense o'er all my soul imprest   10
That I am weak, yet not unblest,
Since in me, round me, every where
Eternal Strength and Wisdom are.

But yester-night I prayed aloud
In anguish and in agony,
Up-starting from the fiendish crowd
Of shapes and thoughts that tortured me:
A lurid light, a trampling throng,
Sense of intolerable wrong,
And whom I scorned, those only strong!   20
Thirst of revenge, the powerless will
Still baffled, and yet burning still!
Desire with loathing strangely mixed
On wild or hateful objects fixed.
Fantastic passions! maddening brawl!
And shame and terror over all!
Deeds to be hid which were not hid,
Which all confused I could not know
Whether I suffered, or I did:
For all seemed guilt, remorse or woe,   30

My own or others still the same
Life-stifling fear, soul-stifling shame.

So two nights passed: the night's dismay
Saddened and stunned the coming day.
Sleep, the wide blessing, seemed to me
Distemper's worst calamity.
The third night, when my own loud scream
Had waked me from the fiendish dream,
O'ercome with sufferings strange and wild,
I wept as I had been a child;   **40**
And having thus by tears subdued
My anguish to a milder mood,
Such punishments, I said, were due
To natures deepliest stained with sin,—
For aye entempesting anew
The unfathomable hell within,
The horror of their deeds to view,
To know and loathe, yet wish and do!
Such griefs with such men well agree,
But wherefore, wherefore fall on me?   **50**
To be beloved is all I need,
And whom I love, I love indeed.

                                    [1803; publ. 1816]

LIMBO

*   *   *   *   *

THE sole true Something—This! In Limbo's Den
It frightens Ghosts, as here Ghosts frighten men.
Thence cross'd unseiz'd—and shall some fated hour
Be pulveris'd by Demogorgon's power,
And given as poison to annihilate souls—
Even now it shrinks them—they shrink in as Moles
(Nature's mute monks, live mandrakes of the ground}
Creep back from Light—then listen for its sound;—
See but to dread, and dread they know not why—
The natural alien of their negative eye.   **10**

'Tis a strange place, this Limbo!—not a Place,
Yet name it so;—where Time and weary Space
Fettered from flight, with night-mare sense of fleeing,

Strive for their last crepuscular half-being;—
Lank Space, and scytheless Time with branny hands
Barren and soundless as the measuring sands,
Not mark'd by flit of Shades,—unmeaning they
As moonlight on the dial of the day!
But that is lovely—looks like Human Time,—
An Old Man with a steady look sublime,   20
That stops his earthly task to watch the skies;
But he is blind—a Statue hath such eyes;—
Yet having moonward turn'd his face by chance,
Gazes the orb with moon-like countenance,
With scant white hairs, with foretop bald and high,
He gazes still,—his eyeless face all eye;—
As 'twere an organ full of silent sight,
His whole face seemeth to rejoice in light!
Lip touching lip, all moveless, bust and limb—
He seems to gaze at that which seems to gaze on him!   30
    No such sweet sights doth Limbo den immure,
Wall'd round and made a spirit-jail secure,
By the mere horror of blank Naught-at-all,
Whose circumambiance doth these ghosts enthral.
A lurid thought is growthless, dull Privation,
Yet that is but a Purgatory curse;
Hell knows a fear far worse,
A fear—a future state;—'tis positive Negation!
                              [1817; publ. 1818, 1834]

WORK WITHOUT HOPE

LINES COMPOSED 21ST FEBRUARY 1825

ALL Nature seems at work. Slugs leave their lair—
The bees are stirring—birds are on the wing—
And Winter slumbering in the open air,
Wears on his smiling face a dream of Spring!
And I the while, the sole unbusy thing,
Nor honey make, nor pair, nor build, nor sing.

    Yet well I ken the banks where amaranths blow,
Have traced the fount whence streams of nectar flow.
Bloom, O ye amaranths! bloom for whom ye may,
For me ye bloom not! Glide, rich streams, away!   10
With lips unbrightened, wreathless brow, I stroll:

And would you learn the spells that drowse my soul?
Work without Hope draws nectar in a sieve,
And Hope without an object cannot live.

[1825; publ. 1828]

CONSTANCY TO AN IDEAL OBJECT

Since all that beat about in Nature's range,
Or veer or varnish; why should'st thou remain
The only constant in a world of change,
O yearning Thought! that liv'st but in the brain?
Call to the Hours, that in the distance play,
The faery people of the future day——
Fond Thought! not one of all that shining swarm
Will breathe on thee with life-enkindling breath,
Till when, like strangers shelt'ring from a storm,
Hope and Despair meet in the porch of Death!   10
Yet still thou haunt'st me; and though well I see,
She is not thou, and only thou art she,
Still, still as though some dear embodied Good,
Some living Love before my eyes there stood
With answering look a ready ear to lend,
I mourn to thee and say—'Ah! loveliest friend!
That this the meed of all my toils might be,
To have a home, an English home, and thee!'
Vain repetition! Home and Thou are one.
The peaceful'st cot, the moon shall shine upon,   20
Lulled by the thrush and wakened by the lark,
Without thee were but a becalméd bark,
Whose Helmsman on an ocean waste and wide
Sits mute and pale his mouldering helm beside.

And art thou nothing? Such thou art, as when
The woodman winding westward up the glen
At wintry dawn, where o'er the sheep-track's maze
The viewless snow-mist weaves a glist'ning haze,
Sees full before him, gliding without tread,
An image with a glory round its head;   30
The enamoured rustic worships its fair hues,
Nor knows he makes the shadow, he pursues!

[1826?; publ. 1828]

THE PANG MORE SHARP THAN ALL

AN ALLEGORY

I

HE TOO has flitted from his secret nest,
Hope's last and dearest child without a name!—
Has flitted from me, like the warmthless flame,
That makes false promise of a place of rest
To the tired Pilgrim's still believing mind;—
Or like some Elfin Knight in kingly court,
Who having won all guerdons in his sport,
Glides out of view, and whither none can find!

II

Yes! he hath flitted from me—with what aim,
Or why, I know not! 'Twas a home of bliss,   10
And he was innocent, as the pretty shame
Of babe, that tempts and shuns the menaced kiss,
From its twy-cluster'd hiding place of snow!
Pure as the babe, I ween, and all aglow
As the dear hopes, that swell the mother's breast—
Her eyes down gazing o'er her claspéd charge;—
Yet gay as that twice happy father's kiss,
That well might glance aside, yet never miss,
Where the sweet mark emboss'd so sweet a targe—
Twice wretched he who hath been doubly blest!   20

III

Like a loose blossom on a gusty night
He flitted from me—and has left behind
(As if to them his faith he ne'er did plight)
Of either sex and answerable mind
Two playmates, twin-births of his foster-dame:—
The one a steady lad (Esteem he hight)
And Kindness is the gentler sister's name.
Dim likeness now, though fair she be and good,
Of that bright Boy who hath us all forsook;—
But in his full-eyed aspect when she stood,   30

And while her face reflected every look,
And in reflection kindled—she became
So like Him, that almost she seem'd the same!

IV

Ah! he is gone, and yet will not depart!—
Is with me still, yet I from him exiled!
For still there lives within my secret heart
The magic image of the magic Child,
Which there he made up-grow by his strong art,
As in that crystal orb—wise Merlin's feat,—
The wondrous 'World of Glass,' wherein inisled   40
All long'd-for things their beings did repeat;—
And there he left it, like a Sylph beguiled,
To live and yearn and languish incomplete!

V

Can wit of man a heavier grief reveal?
Can sharper pang from hate or scorn arise?—
Yes! one more sharp there is that deeper lies,
Which fond Esteem but mocks when he would heal.
Yet neither scorn nor hate did it devise,
But sad compassion and atoning zeal!
One pang more blighting-keen than hope betray'd!   50
And this it is my woeful hap to feel,
When, at her Brother's hest, the twin-born Maid
With face averted and unsteady eyes,
Her truant playmate's faded robe puts on;
And inly shrinking from her own disguise
Enacts the faery Boy that's lost and gone.
O worse than all! O pang all pangs above
Is Kindness counterfeiting absent Love!

[1825-1826?; publ. 1834]

BACKGROUND VERSE

SONNET

TO THE RIVER OTTER

DEAR native Brook! wild Streamlet of the West!
    How many various-fated years have past,
    What happy and what mournful hours, since last
I skimm'd the smooth thin stone along thy breast,
Numbering its light leaps! yet so deep imprest
Sink the sweet scenes of childhood, that mine eyes
    I never shut amid the sunny ray,
But straight with all their tints thy waters rise,
    Thy crossing plank, thy marge with willows grey,
And bedded sand that vein'd with various dyes   10
Gleam'd through thy bright transparence! On my way,
    Visions of Childhood! oft have ye beguil'd
Lone manhood's cares, yet waking fondest sighs:
    Ah! that once more I were a careless Child!

[1793?; publ. 1796]

PANTISOCRACY

No MORE my visionary soul shall dwell
On joys that were; no more endure to weigh
The shame and anguish of the evil day,
Wisely forgetful! O'er the ocean swell
Sublime of Hope, I seek the cottag'd dell
Where Virtue calm with careless step may stray,
And dancing to the moonlight roundelay,
The wizard Passions weave an holy spell.
Eyes that have ach'd with Sorrow! Ye shall weep
Tears of doubt-mingled joy, like theirs who start   10
From Precipices of distemper'd sleep,
On which the fierce-eyed Fiends their revels keep,
And see the rising Sun, and feel it dart
New rays of pleasance trembling to the heart.

[1794; publ. 1849]

TO THE AUTHOR OF 'THE ROBBERS'

SCHILLER! that hour I would have wish'd to die,
If thro' the shuddering midnight I had sent
From the dark dungeon of the Tower time-rent
That fearful voice, a famish'd Father's cry—
Lest in some after moment aught more mean
Might stamp me mortal! A triumphant shout
Black Horror scream'd, and all her *goblin* rout
Diminish'd shrunk from the more withering scene!
Ah! Bard tremendous in sublimity!
Could I behold thee in thy loftier mood   10
Wandering at eve with finely-frenzied eye
Beneath some vast old tempest-swinging wood!
Awhile with mute awe gazing I would brood:
Then weep aloud in a wild ecstasy!

                                [1794?; publ. 1796]

TO A YOUNG ASS

ITS MOTHER BEING TETHERED NEAR IT

POOR little Foal of an oppressèd race!
I love the languid patience of thy face:
And oft with gentle hand I give thee bread,
And clap thy ragged coat, and pat thy head.
But what thy dulled spirits hath dismay'd,
That never thou dost sport along the glade?
And (most unlike the nature of things young)
That earthward still thy moveless head is hung?
Do thy prophetic fears anticipate,
Meek Child of Misery! thy future fate?   10
The starving meal, and all the thousand aches
'Which patient Merit of the Unworthy takes'?
Or is thy sad heart thrill'd with filial pain
To see thy wretched mother's shorten'd chain?
And truly, very piteous is *her* lot—
Chain'd to a log within a narrow spot,
Where the close-eaten grass is scarcely seen,
Nhile sweet around her waves the tempting green!

Poor Ass! thy master should have learnt to show
Pity—best taught by fellowship of Woe! 20
For much I fear me that *He* lives like thee,
Half famish'd in a land of Luxury!
How *askingly* its footsteps hither bend?
It seems to say, 'And have I then *one* friend?'
Innocent foal! thou poor despis'd forlorn!
I hail thee *Brother*—spite of the fool's scorn!
And fain would take thee with me, in the Dell
Of Peace and mild Equality to dwell,
Where Toil shall call the charmer Health his bride
And Laughter tickle Plenty's ribless side! 30
How thou wouldst toss thy heels in gamesome play,
And frisk about, as lamb or kitten gay!
Yea! and more musically sweet to me
Thy dissonant harsh bray of joy would be,
Than warbled melodies that soothe to rest
The aching of pale Fashion's vacant breast!

[1794; publ. 1794]

SONNET ON EDMUND BURKE

As LATE I lay in Slumber's shadowy vale,
  With wetted cheek and in a mourner's guise,
  I saw the sainted form of FREEDOM rise:
She spake! not sadder moans the autumnal gale—

'Great Son of Genius! sweet to me thy name,
  Ere in an evil hour with alter'd voice
  Thou bad'st Oppression's hireling crew rejoice
Blasting with wizard spell my laurell'd fame.

'Yet never, BURKE! thou drank'st Corruption's bowl!
  Thee stormy Pity and the cherish'd lure 10
  Of Pomp, and proud Precipitance of soul
Wilder'd with meteor fires. Ah Spirit pure!

'That Error's mist had left thy purgéd eye:
So might I clasp thee with a Mother's joy!'

[1794; publ. 1794]

SONNET TO THE REV. W. L. BOWLES

My HEART has thank'd thee, BOWLES! for those soft strains
  Whose sadness soothes me, like the murmuring
  Of wild-bees in the sunny showers of spring!
For hence not callous to the mourner's pains

Through Youth's gay prime and thornless paths I went:
  And when the mightier Throes of mind began,
  And drove me forth, a thought-bewilder'd man,
Their mild and manliest melancholy lent

A mingled charm, such as the pang consign'd
  To slumber, though the big tear it renew'd;   10
  Bidding a strange mysterious PLEASURE brood
Over the wavy and tumultuous mind,

As the great SPIRIT erst with plastic sweep
Mov'd on the darkness of the unform'd deep.

[1796; publ. 1796]

RELIGIOUS MUSINGS

A DESULTORY POEM, WRITTEN ON THE CHRISTMAS EVE OF 1794

What tho' first,
In years unseason'd, I attun'd the lay
To idle Passion and unreal Woe?
Yet serious Truth her empire o'er my song
Hath now asserted; Falsehood's evil brood,
Vice and deceitful Pleasure, she at once
Excluded, and my Fancy's careless toil
Drew to the better cause!

AKENSIDE, *Pleasures of the Imagination*

ARGUMENT: Introduction. Person of Christ. His prayer on the Cross.
The process of his Doctrines on the mind of the Individual. Character of the Elect. Superstition. Digression to the present War. Origin
and Uses of Government and Property. The present State of Society.
The French Revolution. Millennium. Universal Redemption. Conclusion.

THIS is the time, when most divine to hear,
The voice of Adoration rouses me,
As with a Cherub's trump: and high upborne,
Yea, mingling with the Choir, I seem to view
The vision of the heavenly multitude,
Who hymned the song of Peace o'er Bethlehem's fields!
Yet thou more bright than all the Angel-blaze,
That harbingered thy birth, Thou Man of Woes!
Despiséd Galilaean! For the Great
Invisible (by symbols only seen)   10
With a peculiar and surpassing light
Shines from the visage of the oppressed good man,
When heedless of himself the scourgéd saint
Mourns for the oppressor. Fair the vernal mead,
Fair the high grove, the sea, the sun, the stars;
True impress each of their creating Sire!
Yet nor high grove, nor many-colour'd mead,
Nor the green ocean with his thousand isles,
Nor the starred azure, nor the sovran sun,
E'er with such majesty of portraiture   20
Imaged the supreme beauty uncreate,
As thou, meek Saviour! at the fearful hour
When thy insulted anguish winged the prayer
Harped by Archangels, when they sing of mercy!
Which when the Almighty heard from forth his throne
Diviner light filled Heaven with ecstasy!
Heaven's hymnings paused: and Hell her yawning mouth
Closed a brief moment.

                Lovely was the death
Of Him whose life was Love! Holy with power
He on the thought-benighted Sceptic beamed   30
Manifest Godhead, melting into day
What floating mists of dark idolatry
Broke and misshaped the omnipresent Sire:
And first by Fear uncharmed the drowséd Soul.
Till of its nobler nature it 'gan feel
Dim recollections; and thence soared to Hope.
Strong to believe whate'er of mystic good
The Eternal dooms for His immortal sons.
From Hope and firmer Faith to perfect Love
Attracted and absorbed: and centered there   40
God only to behold, and know, and feel,
Till by exclusive consciousness of God

All self-annihilated it shall make
God its Identity: God all in all!
We and our Father one!

     And blest are they,
Who in this fleshly World, the elect of Heaven,
Their strong eye darting through the deeds of men,
Adore with steadfast unpresuming gaze
Him Nature's essence, mind, and energy!
And gazing, trembling, patiently ascend   50
Treading beneath their feet all visible things
As steps, that upward to their Father's throne
Lead gradual—else nor glorified nor loved.
They nor contempt embosom nor revenge:
For they dare know of what may seem deform
The Supreme Fair sole operant: in whose sight
All things are pure, his strong controlling love
Alike from all educing perfect good.
Their's too celestial courage, inly armed—
Dwarfing Earth's giant brood, what time they muse 60
On their great Father, great beyond compare!
And marching onwards view high o'er their heads
His waving banners of Omnipotence.

Who the Creator love, created Might
Dread not: within their tents no Terrors walk.
For they are holy things before the Lórd
Aye unprofaned, though Earth should league with Hell;
God's altar grasping with an eager hand
Fear, the wild-visag'd, pale, eye-starting wretch,
Sure-refug'd hears his hot pursuing fiends   70
Yell at vain distance. Soon refresh'd from Heaven
He calms the throb and tempest of his heart.
His countenance settles; a soft solemn bliss
Swims in his eye—his swimming eye uprais'd:
And Faith's whole armour glitters on his limbs!
And thus transfigured with a dreadless awe,
A solemn hush of soul, meek he beholds
All things of terrible seeming: yea, unmoved
Views e'en the immitigable ministers
That shower down vengeance on these latter days. 80
For kindling with intenser Deity
From the celestial Mercy-seat they come,
And at the renovating wells of Love

Have fill'd their vials with salutary wrath,
To sickly Nature more medicinal
Than what soft balm the weeping good man pours
Into the lone despoiléd traveller's wounds!

Thus from the Elect, regenerate through faith,
Pass the dark Passions and what thirsty cares
Drink up the spirit, and the dim regards   90
Self-centre. Lo they vanish! or acquire
New names, new features—by supernal grace
Enrobed with Light, and naturalised in Heaven.
As when a shepherd on a vernal morn
Through some thick fog creeps timorous with slow foot,
Darkling he fixes on the immediate road
His downward eye: all else of fairest kind
Hid or deformed. But lo! the bursting Sun!
Touched by the enchantment of that sudden beam
Straight the black vapour melteth, and in globes   100
Of dewy glitter gems each plant and tree;
On every leaf, on every blade it hangs!
Dance glad the new-born intermingling rays,
And wide around the landscape streams with glory!

There is one Mind, one omnipresent Mind,
Omnific. His most holy name is Love.
Truth of subliming import! with the which
Who feeds and saturates his constant soul,
He from his small particular orbit flies
With blest outstarting! From himself he flies,   110
Stands in the sun, and with no partial gaze
Views all creation; and he loves it all,
And blesses it, and calls it very good!
This is indeed to dwell with the Most High!
Cherubs and rapture-trembling Seraphim
Can press no nearer to the Almighty's throne.
But that we roam unconscious, or with hearts
Unfeeling of our universal Sire,
And that in His vast family no Cain
Injures uninjured (in her best-aimed blow   120
Victorious Murder a blind Suicide)
Haply for this some younger Angel now
Looks down on Human Nature: and, behold!
A sea of blood bestrewed with wrecks, where mad

Embattling Interests on each other rush
With unhelmed rage!

         'Tis the sublime of man,
Our noontide Majesty, to know ourselves
Parts and proportions of one wondrous whole!
This fraternises man, this constitutes
Our charities and bearings. But 'tis God   130
Diffused through all, that doth make all one whole;
This the worst superstition, him except
Aught to desire, Supreme Reality!
The plenitude and permanence of bliss!
O Fiends of Superstition! not that oft
The erring Priest hath stained with brother's blood
Your grisly idols, not for this may wrath
Thunder against you from the Holy One!
But o'er some plain that steameth to the sun,
Peopled with Death; or where more hideous Trade   140
Loud-laughing packs his bales of human anguish;
I will raise up a mourning, O ye Fiends!
And curse your spells, that film the eye of Faith,
Hiding the present God; whose presence lost,
The moral world's cohesion, we become
An Anarchy of Spirits! Toy-bewitched,
Made blind by lusts, disherited of soul,
No common centre Man, no common sire
Knoweth! A sordid solitary thing,
Mid countless brethren with a lonely heart   150
Through courts and cities the smooth savage roams
Feeling himself, his own low self the whole;
When he by sacred sympathy might make
The whole one Self! Self, that no alien knows!
Self, far diffused as Fancy's wing can travel!
Self, spreading still! Oblivious of its own,
Yet all of all possessing! This is Faith!
This the Messiah's destined victory!

But first offences needs must come! Even now
(Black Hell laughs horrible—to hear the scoff!)   160
Thee to defend, meek Galilaean! Thee
And thy mild laws of Love unutterable,
Mistrust and Enmity have burst the bands
Of social peace: and listening Treachery lurks

With pious fraud to snare a brother's life;
And childless widows o'er the groaning land
Wail numberless; and orphans weep for bread!
Thee to defend, dear Saviour of Mankind!
Thee, Lamb of God! Thee, blameless Prince of Peace!
From all sides rush the thirsty brood of War!—   170
Austria, and that foul Woman of the North,
The lustful murderess of her wedded lord!
And he, connatural Mind! whom (in their songs
So bards of elder time had haply feigned)
Some Fury fondled in her hate to man,
Bidding her serpent hair in mazy surge
Lick his young face, and at his mouth imbreathe
Horrible sympathy! And leagued with these
Each petty German princeling, nursed in gore!
Soul-hardened barterers of human blood!   180
Death's prime slave-merchants! Scorpion-whips of Fate!
Nor least in savagery of holy zeal,
Apt for the yoke, the race degenerate,
Whom Britain erst had blushed to call her sons!
Thee to defend the Moloch Priest prefers
The prayer of hate, and bellows to the herd,
That Deity, Accomplice Deity
In the fierce jealousy of wakened wrath
Will go forth with our armies and our fleets
To scatter the red ruin on their foes!   190
O blasphemy! to mingle fiendish deeds
With blessedness!

              Lord of unsleeping Love,
From everlasting Thou! We shall not die.
These, even these, in mercy didst thou form,
Teachers of Good through Evil, by brief wrong
Making Truth lovely, and her future might
Magnetic o'er the fixed untrembling heart.

In the primeval age a dateless while
The vacant Shepherd wander'd with his flock,
Pitching his tent where'er the green grass waved.   200
But soon Imagination conjured up
An host of new desires: with busy aim,
Each for himself, Earth's eager children toiled-
So Property began, twy-streaming fount,
Whence Vice and Virtue flow, honey and gall.

Hence the soft couch, and many-coloured robe,
The timbrel, and arched dome and costly feast,
With all the inventive arts, that nursed the soul
To forms of beauty, and by sensual wants
Unsensualised the mind, which in the means 210
Learnt to forget the grossness of the end,
Best pleasured with its own activity.
And hence Disease that withers manhood's arm,
The daggered Envy, spirit-quenching Want,
Warriors, and Lords, and Priests—all the sore ills
That vex and desolate our mortal life.
Wide-wasting ills! yet each the immediate source
Of mightier good. Their keen necessities
To ceaseless action goading human thought
Have made Earth's reasoning animal her Lord; 220
And the pale-featured Sage's trembling hand
Strong as an host of arméd Deities,
Such as the blind Ionian fabled erst.

From Avarice thus, from Luxury and War
Sprang heavenly Science; and from Science Freedom.
O'er waken'd realms Philosophers and Bards
Spread in concentric circles: they whose souls,
Conscious of their high dignities from God,
Brook not Wealth's rivalry! and they, who long
Enamoured with the charms of order, hate 230
The unseemly disproportion: and whoe'er
Turn with mild sorrow from the Victor's car
And the low puppetry of thrones, to muse
On that blest triumph, when the Patriot Sage
Called the red lightnings from the o'er-rushing cloud
And dashed the beauteous terrors on the earth
Smiling majestic. Such a phalanx ne'er
Measured firm paces to the calming sound
Of Spartan flute! These on the fated day,
When, stung to rage by Pity, eloquent men 240
Have roused with pealing voice the unnumbered tribes
That toil and groan and bleed, hungry and blind—
These, hush'd awhile with patient eye serene,
Shall watch the mad careering of the storm;
Then o'er the wild and wavy chaos rush
And tame the outrageous mass, with plastic might
Moulding Confusion to such perfect forms,
As erst were wont,—bright visions of the day!—

To float before them, when, the summer noon,
Beneath some arched romantic rock reclined   **250**
They felt the sea-breeze lift their youthful locks;
Or in the month of blossoms, at mild eve,
Wandering with desultory feet inhaled
The wafted perfumes, and the flocks and woods
And many-tinted streams and setting sun
With all his gorgeous company of clouds
Ecstatic gazed! then homeward as they strayed
Cast the sad eye to earth, and inly mused
Why there was misery in a world so fair.

Ah! far removed from all that glads the sense,   **260**
From all that softens or ennobles Man,
The wretched Many! Bent beneath their loads
They gape at pageant Power, nor recognise
Their cots' transmuted plunder! From the tree
Of Knowledge, ere the vernal sap had risen
Rudely disbranchéd! Blessed Society!
Fitliest depictured by some sun-scorched waste,
Where oft majestic through the tainted noon
The Simoom sails, before whose purple pomp
Who falls not prostrate dies! And where by night,   **270**
Fast by each precious fountain on green herbs
The lion couches: or hyaena dips
Deep in the lucid stream his bloody jaws;
Or serpent plants his vast moon-glittering bulk,
Caught in whose monstrous twine Behemoth yells,
His bones loud-crashing!

                    O ye numberless,
Whom foul Oppression's ruffian gluttony
Drives from Life's plenteous feast! O thou poor Wretch
Who nursed in darkness and made wild by want,
Roamest for prey, yea thy unnatural hand   **280**
Dost lift to deeds of blood! O pale-eyed form,
The victim of seduction, doomed to know
Polluted nights and days of blasphemy;
Who in loathed orgies with lewd wassailers
Must gaily laugh, while thy remembered Home
Gnaws like a viper at thy secret heart!
O agéd Women! ye who weekly catch
The morsel tossed by law-forced charity,
And die so slowly, that none call it murder!

O loathly suppliants! ye, that unreceived   290
Totter heart-broken from the closing gates
Of the full Lazar-house; or, gazing, stand,
Sick with despair! O ye to Glory's field
Forced or ensnared, who, as ye gasp in death,
Bleed with new wounds beneath the vulture's beak!
O thou poor widow, who in dreams dost view
Thy husband's mangled corse, and from short doze
Start'st with a shriek; or in thy half-thatched cot
Waked by the wintry night-storm, wet and cold
Cow'rst o'er thy screaming baby! Rest awhile   300
Children of Wretchedness! More groans must rise,
More blood must stream, or ere your wrongs be full.
Yet is the day of Retribution nigh:
The Lamb of God hath opened the fifth seal:
And upward rush on swiftest wing of fire
The innumerable multitude of wrongs
By man on man inflicted! Rest awhile,
Children of Wretchedness! The hour is nigh
And lo! the Great, the Rich, the Mighty Men,
The Kings and the Chief Captains of the World,   310
With all that fixed on high like stars of Heaven
Shot baleful influence, shall be cast to earth,
Vile and down-trodden, as the untimely fruit
Shook from the fig-tree by a sudden storm.
Even now the storm begins: each gentle name,
Faith and meek Piety, with fearful joy
Tremble far-off—for lo! the Giant Frenzy
Uprooting empires with his whirlwind arm
Mocketh high Heaven; burst hideous from the cell
Where the old Hag, unconquerable, huge,   320
Creation's eyeless drudge, black Ruin, sits
Nursing the impatient earthquake.

                    O return!
Pure Faith! meek Piety! The abhorréd Form
Whose scarlet robe was stiff with earthly pomp,
Who drank iniquity in cups of gold,
Whose names were many and all blasphemous,
Hath met the horrible judgment! Whence that cry?
The mighty army of foul Spirits shrieked
Disherited of earth! For she hath fallen
On whose black front was written Mystery;   330
She that reeled heavily, whose wine was blood;

She that worked whoredom with the Daemon Power,
And from the dark embrace all evil things
Brought forth and nurtured: mitred Atheism!
And patient Folly who on bended knee
Gives back the steel that stabbed him; and pale Fear
Haunted by ghastlier shapings than surround
Moon-blasted Madness when he yells at midnight!
Return pure Faith! return meek Piety!
The kingdoms of the world are yours: each heart   340
Self-governed, the vast family of Love
Raised from the common earth by common toil
Enjoy the equal produce. Such delights
As float to earth, permitted visitants!
When in some hour of solemn jubilee
The massy gates of Paradise are thrown
Wide open, and forth come in fragments wild
Sweet echoes of unearthly melodies,
And odours snatched from beds of Amaranth.
And they, that from the crystal river of life   350
Spring up on freshened wing, ambrosial gales!
The favoured good man in his lonely walk
Perceives them, and his silent spirit drinks
Strange bliss which he shall recognise in heaven.
And such delights, such strange beatitudes
Seize on my young anticipating heart
When that blest future rushes on my view!
For in his own and in his Father's might
The Saviour comes! While as the Thousand Years
Lead up their mystic dance, the Desert shouts!   360
Old Ocean claps his hands! The mighty Dead
Rise to new life, whoe'er from earliest time
With conscious zeal had urged Love's wondrous plan,
Coadjutors of God. To Milton's trump
The high groves of the renovated Earth
Unbosom their glad echoes: inly hushed,
Adoring Newton his serener eye
Raises to heaven: and he of mortal kind
Wisest, he first who marked the ideal tribes
Up the fine fibres through the sentient brain.   370
Lo! Priestley there, patriot, and saint, and sage,
Him, full of years, from his loved native land
Statesmen blood-stained and priests idolatrous
By dark lies maddening the blind multitude

Drove with vain hate. Calm, pitying he retired,
And mused expectant on these promised years.

O Years! the blest pre-eminence of Saints!
Ye sweep athwart my gaze, so heavenly bright,
The wings that veil the adoring Seraphs' eyes,
What time they bend before the Jasper Throne   380
Reflect no lovelier hues! Yet ye depart,
And all beyond is darkness! Heights most strange,
Whence Fancy falls, fluttering her idle wing.
For who of woman born may paint the hour,
When seized in his mid course, the Sun shall wane
Making noon ghastly! Who of woman born
May image in the workings of his thought,
How the black-visaged, red-eyed Fiend outstretched
Beneath the unsteady feet of Nature groans,
In feverous slumbers—destined then to wake,   390
When fiery whirlwinds thunder his dread name
And Angels shout, Destruction! How his arm
The last great Spirit lifting high in air
Shall swear by Him, the ever-living One,
Time is no more!

           Believe thou, O my soul,
Life is a vision shadowy of Truth;
And vice, and anguish, and the wormy grave,
Shapes of a dream! The veiling clouds retire,
And lo! the Throne of the redeeming God
Forth flashing unimaginable day   400
Wraps in one blaze earth, heaven, and deepest hell.

Contemplant Spirits! ye that hover o'er
With untired gaze the immeasurable fount
Ebullient with creative Deity!
And ye of plastic power, that interfused
Roll through the grosser and material mass
In organizing surge! Holies of God!
(And what if Monads of the infinite mind?)
I haply journeying my immortal course
Shall sometime join your mystic choir! Till then   410
I discipline my young and novice thought
In ministeries of heart-stirring song,
And aye on Meditation's heaven-ward wing

Soaring aloft I breathe the empyreal air
Of Love, omnific, omnipresent Love,
Whose day-spring rises glorious in my soul
As the great Sun, when he his influence
Sheds on the frost-bound waters—The glad stream
Flows to the ray and warbles as it flows.

[1794-1796; publ. 1796]

HEXAMETERS

WILLIAM, my teacher, my friend! dear William and dear
   Dorothea!
Smooth out the folds of my letter, and place it on desk or on
   table;
Place it on table or desk; and your right hands loosely half-closing,
Gently sustain them in air, and extending the digit didactic,
Rest it a moment on each of the forks of the five-forkéd left hand,
Twice on the breadth of the thumb, and once on the tip of each
   finger;
Read with a nod of the head in a humouring recitativo;
And, as I live, you will see my hexameters hopping before you.
This is a galloping measure; a hop, and a trot, and a gallop!

All my hexameters fly, like stags pursued by the staghounds,   10
Breathless and panting, and ready to drop, yet flying still on-
   wards,
I would full fain pull in my hard-mouthed runaway hunter;
But our English Spondeans are clumsy yet impotent curb-reins;
And so to make him go slowly, no way left have I but to lame him.

William, my head and my heart! dear Poet that feelest and
   thinkest!
Dorothy, eager of soul, my most affectionate sister!
Many a mile, O! many a wearisome mile are ye distant,
Long, long comfortless roads with no one eye that doth know us.
O! it is all too far to send you mockeries idle:
Yea, and I feel it not right! But O! my friends, my belovéd!   20
Feverish and wakeful I lie,—I am weary of feeling and thinking.

.   .   .   .   .   .

William, my head and my heart! dear William and dear Dorothea!
You have all in each other; but I am lonely, and want you!

[1798-1799; publ. 1851]

ON AN INFANT

WHICH DIED BEFORE BAPTISM

'BE RATHER than be called, a child of God,'
Death whispered! With assenting nod,
Its head upon its mother's breast,
    The Baby bowed, without demur—
Of the kingdom of the Blest
    Possessor, not Inheritor.

[1799; publ. 1834]

HYMN BEFORE SUN-RISE, IN THE VALE OF CHAMOUNI

Besides the Rivers, Arve and Arveiron, which have their sources in the foot of Mont Blanc, five conspicuous torrents rush down its sides; and within a few paces of the Glaciers, the Gentiana Major grows in immense numbers, with its 'flowers of loveliest blue.'

HAST thou a charm to stay the morning-star
In his steep course? So long he seems to pause
On thy bald awful head, O sovran BLANC,
The Arve and Arveiron at thy base
Rave ceaselessly; but thou, most awful Form!
Risest from forth thy silent sea of pines,
How silently! Around thee and above
Deep is the air and dark, substantial, black,
An ebon mass: methinks thou piercest it,
As with a wedge! But when I look again,   10
It is thine own calm home, thy crystal shrine,
Thy habitation from eternity!
O dread and silent Mount! I gazed upon thee,
Till thou, still present to the bodily sense,
Didst vanish from my thought: entranced in prayer
I worshipped the Invisible alone.

Yet, like some sweet beguiling melody,
So sweet, we know not we are listening to it,
Thou, the meanwhile, wast blending with my Thought,
Yea, with my Life and Life's own secret joy: 20

Till the dilating Soul, enrapt, transfused,
Into the mighty vision passing—there
As in her natural form, swelled vast to Heaven!

Awake, my soul! not only passive praise
Thou owest! not alone these swelling tears,
Mute thanks and secret ecstasy! Awake,
Voice of sweet song! Awake, my heart, awake!
Green vales and icy cliffs, all join my Hymn.

Thou first and chief, sole sovereign of the Vale!
O struggling with the darkness all the night,   30
And visited all night by troops of stars,
Or when they climb the sky or when they sink:
Companion of the morning-star at dawn,
Thyself Earth's rosy star, and of the dawn
Co-herald: wake, O wake, and utter praise!
Who sank thy sunless pillars deep in Earth?
Who filled thy countenance with rosy light?
Who made thee parent of perpetual streams?

And you, ye five wild torrents fiercely glad!
Who called you forth from night and utter death,   40
From dark and icy caverns called you forth,
Down those precipitous, black, jaggéd rocks,
For ever shattered and the same for ever?
Who gave you your invulnerable life,
Your strength, your speed, your fury, and your joy,
Unceasing thunder and eternal foam?
And who commanded (and the silence came),
Here let the billows stiffen, and have rest?

Ye Ice-falls! ye that from the mountain's brow
Adown enormous ravines slope amain—   50
Torrents, methinks, that heard a mighty voice,
And stopped at once amid their maddest plunge!
Motionless torrents! silent cataracts!
Who made you glorious as the Gates of Heaven
Beneath the keen full moon? Who bade the sun
Clothe you with rainbows? Who, with living flowers
Of loveliest blue, spread garlands at your feet?—
God! let the torrents, like a shout of nations,
Answer! and let the ice-plains echo, God!
God! sing ye meadow-streams with gladsome voice!   60

Ye pine-groves, with your soft and soul-like sounds!
And they too have a voice, yon piles of snow,
And in their perilous fall shall thunder, God!

   Ye living flowers that skirt the eternal frost!
Ye wild goats sporting round the eagle's nest!
Ye eagles, play-mates of the mountain-storm!
Ye lightnings, the dread arrows of the clouds!
Ye signs and wonders of the element!
Utter forth God, and fill the hills with praise!

   Thou too, hoar Mount! with thy sky-pointing peaks,   70
Oft from whose feet the avalanche, unheard,
Shoots downward, glittering through the pure serene
Into the depth of clouds, that veil thy breast—
Thou too again, stupendous Mountain! thou
That as I raise my head, awhile bowed low
In adoration, upward from thy base
Slow travelling with dim eyes suffused with tears,
Solemnly seemest, like a vapoury cloud,
To rise before me—Rise, O ever rise,
Rise like a cloud of incense from the Earth!   80
Thou kingly Spirit throned among the hills,
Thou dread ambassador from Earth to Heaven,
Great Hierarch! tell thou the silent sky,
And tell the stars, and tell yon rising sun
Earth, with her thousand voices, praises God.

                        [1802; publ. 1802]

A CHILD'S EVENING PRAYER

    Ere on my bed my limbs I lay,
    God grant me grace my prayers to say:
    O God! preserve my mother dear
    In strength and health for many a year;
    And, O! preserve my father too,
    And may I pay him reverence due;
    And may I my best thoughts employ
    To be my parents' hope and joy;
    And O! preserve my brothers both
    From evil doings and from sloth,   10

And may we always love each other
Our friends, our father, and our mother:
And still, O Lord, to me impart
An innocent and grateful heart,
That after my great sleep I may
Awake to thy eternal day! *Amen.*

[1806; publ. 1852]

COLOGNE

In KÖHLN, a town of monks and bones,
And pavements fang'd with murderous stones
And rags, and hags, and hideous wenches;
I counted two and seventy stenches,
All well defined, and several stinks!
Ye Nymphs that reign o'er sewers and sinks,
The river Rhine, it is well known,
Doth wash your city of Cologne;
But tell me, Nymphs, what power divine
Shall henceforth wash the river Rhine?   **10**

[1828; publ. 1834]

PROSE

BIOGRAPHIA LITERARIA:

OR,

Biographical Sketches

OF MY

LITERARY LIFE AND OPINIONS

So wenig er auch bestimmt seyn mag, andere zu belehren, so
wünscht er doch sich denen mitzutheilen, die er sich gleichgesinnt
weiss oder hofft, deren Anzahl aber in der Breite der Welt zerstreut
ist: er wünscht sein Verhältniss zu den ältesten Freunden dadurch
wieder anzuknüpfen, mit neuen es fortzusetzen, und in der letzten
Generation sich wieder andere für seine übrige Lebenszeit zu gewin-
nen. Er wünscht der Jugend die Umwege zu ersparen, auf denen er
sich selbst verirrte.

—GOETHE

TRANSLATION. Little call as he may have to instruct others, he
wishes nevertheless to open out his heart to such as he either knows
or hopes to be of like mind with himself, but who are widely scattered
in the world: he wishes to knit anew his connexions with his oldest
friends, to continue those recently formed, and to win other friends
among the rising generation for the remaining course of his life. He
wishes to spare the young those circuitous paths, on which he himself
had lost his way.

CHAPTER I

*The motives of the present work—Reception of the Author's first publi-
cation—The discipline of his taste at school—The effect of contem-
porary writers on youthful minds—Bowles's sonnets—Comparison
between the Poets before and since Mr. Pope.*

IT HAS been my lot to have had my name introduced, both in
conversation, and in print, more frequently than I find it easy
to explain, whether I consider the fewness, unimportance, and
limited circulation of my writings, or the retirement and distance
in which I have lived, both from the literary and political world.
Most often it has been connected with some charge which I
could not acknowledge, or some principle which I had never

entertained. Nevertheless, had I had no other motive or incitement, the reader would not have been troubled with this exculpation. What my additional purposes were, will be seen in the following pages. It will be found, that the least of what I have written concerns myself personally. I have used the narration chiefly for the purpose of giving a continuity to the work, in part for the sake of the miscellaneous reflections suggested to me by particular events, but still more as introductory to the statement of my principles in Politics, Religion, and Philosophy, and an application of the rules, deduced from philosophical principles, to poetry and criticism. But of the objects, which I proposed to myself, it was not the least important to effect, as far as possible, a settlement of the long continued controversy concerning the true nature of poetic diction; and at the same time to define with the utmost impartiality the real *poetic* character of the poet, by whose writings this controversy was first kindled, and has been since fuelled and fanned.

In 1794, when I had barely passed the verge of manhood, I published a small volume of juvenile poems. They were received with a degree of favor, which, young as I was, I well know was bestowed on them not so much for any positive merit, as because they were considered buds of hope, and promises of better works to come. The critics of that day, the most flattering equally with the severest, concurred in objecting to them obscurity, a general turgidness of diction, and a profusion of new coined double epithets.[1] The first is the fault which a writer is

[1] The authority of Milton and Shakespeare may be usefully pointed out to young authors. In the Comus, and other early Poems of Milton there is a superfluity of double epithets; while in the Paradise Lost we find very few, in the Paradise Regained scarce any. The same remark holds almost equally true of the Love's Labour's Lost, Romeo and Juliet, Venus and Adonis, and Lucrece, compared with the Lear, Macbeth, Othello, and Hamlet of our great Dramatist. The rule for the admission of double epithets seems to be this: either that they should be already denizens of our Language, such as blood-stained, terror-stricken, self-applauding: or when a new epithet, or one found in books only, is hazarded, that it, at least, be one word, not two words made one by mere virtue of the printer's hyphen. A language which, like the English, is almost without cases, is indeed in its very genius unfitted for compounds. If a writer, every time a compounded word suggests itself to him, would seek for some other mode of expressing the same sense, the chances are always greatly in favor of his finding a better word. "Tanquam scopulum sic vites insolens verbum," is the wise advice of Cæsar to the Roman Orators, and the precept applies with double force to the writers in our own language. But it must not be forgotten, that the same Cæsar wrote a grammatical

the least able to detect in his own compositions: and my mind was not then sufficiently disciplined to receive the authority of others, as a substitute for my own conviction. Satisfied that the thoughts, such as they were, could not have been expressed otherwise, or at least more perspicuously, I forgot to enquire, whether the thoughts themselves did not demand a degree of attention unsuitable to the nature and objects of poetry. This remark however applies chiefly, though not exclusively, to the *Religious Musings*. The remainder of the charge I admitted to its full extent, and not without sincere acknowledgments both to my private and public censors for their friendly admonitions. In the after editions, I pruned the double epithets with no sparing hand, and used my best efforts to tame the swell and glitter both of thought and diction; though in truth, these parasite plants of youthful poetry had insinuated themselves into my longer poems with such intricacy of union, that I was often obliged to omit disentangling the weed, from the fear of snapping the flower. From that period to the date of the present work I have published nothing, with my name, which could by any possibility have come before the board of anonymous criticism. Even the three or four poems, printed with the works of a friend, as far as they were censured at all, were charged with the same or similar defects, though I am persuaded not with equal justice: with an EXCESS OF ORNAMENT, in addition to STRAINED AND ELABORATE DICTION. (*Vide the criticisms on the "Ancient Mariner" in the Monthly and Critical Reviews of the first volume of the Lyrical Ballads.*) May I be permitted to add, that, even at the early period of my juvenile poems, I saw and admitted the superiority of an austerer and more natural style, with an insight not less clear, than I at present possess. My judgement was stronger, than were my powers of realizing its dictates; and the faults of my language, though indeed partly owing to a wrong choice of subjects, and the desire of giving a poetic colouring to abstract and metaphysical truths, in which a new world then seemed to open upon me, did yet, in part likewise, originate in unfeigned diffidence of my own comparative talent.—During several years of my youth and early manhood, I reverenced those, who had reintroduced the manly simplicity of the Greek, and of our own elder poets, with such enthusiasm as made the hope seem presumptuous of writing successfully in the same style. Perhaps a similar process has

---

treatise for the purpose of reforming the ordinary language by bringing it to a greater accordance with the principles of Logic or universal Grammar.

happened to others; but my earliest poems were marked by an ease and simplicity, which I have studied, perhaps with inferior success, to impress on my later compositions.

At school I enjoyed the inestimable advantage of a very sensible, though at the same time a very severe master. He[a] early moulded my taste to the preference of Demosthenes to Cicero, of Homer and Theocritus to Virgil, and again of Virgil to Ovid. He habituated me to compare Lucretius, (in such extracts as I then read) Terence, and above all the chaster poems of Catullus, not only with the Roman poets of the, so called, silver and brazen ages; but with even those of the Augustan era: and on grounds of plain sense and universal logic to see and assert the superiority of the former in the truth and nativeness, both of their thoughts and diction. At the same time that we were studying the Greek Tragic Poets, he made us read Shakespeare and Milton as lessons: and they were the lessons too, which required most time and trouble to *bring up*, so as to escape his censure. I learnt from him, that Poetry, even that of the loftiest and, seemingly, that of the wildest odes, had a logic of its own, as severe as that of science; and more difficult, because more subtle, more complex, and dependent on more, and more fugitive causes. In the truly great poets, he would say, there is a reason assignable, not only for every word, but for the position of every word; and I well remember that, availing himself of the synonimes to the Homer of Didymus, he made us attempt to show, with regard to each, *why* it would not have answered the same purpose; and *wherein* consisted the peculiar fitness of the word in the original text.

In our own English compositions, (at least for the last three years of our school education,) he showed no mercy to phrase, metaphor, or image, unsupported by a sound sense, or where the same sense might have been conveyed with equal force and dignity in plainer words. Lute, harp, and lyre, muse, muses, and inspirations, Pegasus, Parnassus, and Hippocrene were all an abomination to him. In fancy I can almost hear him now, exclaiming *"Harp? Harp? Lyre? Pen and ink, boy, you mean! Muse, boy, Muse? Your Nurse's daughter, you mean! Pierian spring? Oh aye! the cloister-pump, I suppose!"* Nay, certain introductions, similes, and examples, were placed by name on a list of interdiction. Among the similes, there was, I remember, that of the Manchineel fruit, as suiting equally well with too many subjects; in which however it yielded the palm at once to the ex-

[a] The Rev. James Bowyer, many years Head Master of the Grammar School, Christ's Hospital.

ample of Alexander and Clytus, which was equally good and apt,
whatever might be the theme. Was it ambition? Alexander and
Clytus!—Flattery? Alexander and Clytus!—Anger? Drunken-
ness? Pride? Friendship? Ingratitude? Late repentance? Still, still
Alexander and Clytus! At length, the praises of agriculture hav-
ing been exemplified in the sagacious observation, that, had
Alexander been holding the plough, he would not have run his
friend Clytus through with a spear, this tried and serviceable
old friend was banished by public edict in secula seculorum. I
have sometimes ventured to think, that a list of this kind, or an
index expurgatorius of certain well known and ever returning
phrases, both introductory, and transitional, including a large
assortment of modest egoisms, and flattering illeisms, &c., &c.,
might be hung up in our law-courts, and both houses of parlia-
ment, with great advantage to the public, as an important saving
of national time, an incalculable relief to his Majesty's ministers,
but above all, as insuring the thanks of country attornies, and
their clients, who have private bills to carry through the house.

Be this as it may, there was one custom of our master's, which
I cannot pass over in silence, because I think it imitable and
worthy of imitation. He would often permit our exercises, under
some pretext of want of time, to accumulate, till each lad had
four or five to be looked over. Then placing the whole number
abreast on his desk, he would ask the writer, why this or that
sentence might not have found as appropriate a place under this
or that other thesis: and if no satisfying answer could be re-
turned, and two faults of the same kind were found in one exer-
cise, the irrevocable verdict followed, the exercise was torn up,
and another on the same subject to be produced, in addition to
the tasks of the day. The reader will, I trust, excuse this tribute
of recollection to a man, whose severities, even now, not seldom
furnish the dreams, by which the blind fancy would fain interpret
to the mind the painful sensations of distempered sleep; but
neither lessen nor dim the deep sense of my moral and intellec-
tual obligations. He sent us to the University excellent Latin and
Greek scholars, and tolerable Hebraists. Yet our classical knowl-
edge was the least of the good gifts, which we derived from his
zealous and conscientious tutorage. He is now gone to his final
reward, full of years, and full of honors, even of those honors,
which were dearest to his heart, as gratefully bestowed by that
school, and still binding him to the interests of that school, in
which he had been himself educated, and to which during his
whole life he was a dedicated thing.

From causes, which this is not the place to investigate, no

models of past times, however perfect, can have the same vivid effect on the youthful mind, as the productions of contemporary genius. The Discipline, my mind had undergone, "Ne falleretur rotundo sono et versuum cursu, concinnis et floribus; sed ut inspiceret quidnam subesset, quæ sedes, quod firmamentum, quis fundus verbis; an figuræ essent mera ornatura et orationis fucus; vel sanguinis e materiæ ipsius corde effluentis rubor quidam nativus et incalescentia genuina;" removed all obstacles to the appreciation of excellence in style without diminishing my delight. That I was thus prepared for the perusal of Mr. Bowles's sonnets and earlier poems, at once increased *their* influence, and *my* enthusiasm. The great works of past ages seem to a young man things of another race, in respect to which his faculties must remain passive and submiss, even as to the stars and mountains. But the writings of a contemporary, perhaps not many years older than himself, surrounded by the same circumstances, and disciplined by the same manners, possess a *reality* for him, and inspire an actual friendship as of a man for a man. His very admiration is the wind which fans and feeds his hope. The poems themselves assume the properties of flesh and blood. To recite, to extol, to contend for them is but the payment of a debt due to one, who exists to receive it.

There are indeed modes of teaching which have produced, and are producing, youths of a very different stamp; modes of teaching, in comparison with which we have been called on to despise our great public schools, and universities

"in whose halls are hung
Armoury of the invincible knights of old"—

modes, by which children are to be metamorphosed into prodigies. And prodigies with a vengeance have I known thus produced! Prodigies of self-conceit, shallowness, arrogance, and infidelity! Instead of storing the memory, during the period when the memory is the predominant faculty, with facts for the after exercise of the judgement; and instead of awakening by the noblest models the fond and unmixed LOVE and ADMIRATION, which is the natural and graceful temper of early youth; *these* nurselings of improved pedagogy are taught to dispute and decide; to suspect all, but their own and their lecturer's wisdom; and to hold nothing sacred from their contempt, but their own contemptible arrogance: boy-graduates in all the technicals, and in all the dirty passions and impudence of anonymous criticism. To such dispositions alone can the admonition of Pliny be requi-

site, "Neque enim debet operibus ejus obesse, quod vivit. An si inter eos, quos nunquam vidimus, floruisset, non solum libros ejus, verum etiam imagines conquireremus, ejusdem nunc honor præsentis, et gratia quasi satietate languescit? At hoc pravum, malignumque est, non admirari hominem admiratione dignissimum, quia videre, complecti, nec laudare tantum, verum etiam amare contingit." *Plin. Epist. Lib.* I.

I had just entered on my seventeenth year, when the sonnets of Mr. Bowles, twenty in number, and just then published in a quarto pamphlet, were first made known and presented to me, by a schoolfellow who had quitted us for the University, and who, during the whole time that he was in our first form (or in our school language a GRECIAN,) had been my patron and protector. I refer to Dr. Middleton, the truly learned, and every way excellent Bishop of Calcutta:

> "Qui laudibus amplis
> Ingenium celebrare meum, calamumque solebat,
> Calcar agens animo validum. Non omnia terræ
> Obruta; vivit amor, vivit dolor; ora negatur
> Dulcia conspicere; at flere et meminisse[3] relictum est."
>
> Petr. Ep., Lib. I, Ep. I.

It was a double pleasure to me, and still remains a tender recollection, that I should have received from a friend so revered the first knowledge of a poet, by whose works, year after year, I was so enthusiastically delighted and inspired. My earliest acquaintances will not have forgotten the undisciplined eagerness and impetuous zeal, with which I laboured to make proselytes, not only of my companions, but of all with whom I conversed, of whatever rank, and in whatever place. As my school finances did not permit me to purchase copies, I made, within less than a year and a half, more than forty transcriptions, as the best presents I could offer to those, who had in any way won my regard. And with almost equal delight did I receive the three or four following publications of the same author.

Though I have seen and known enough of mankind to be well aware, that I shall perhaps stand alone in my creed, and that it will be well, if I subject myself to no worse charge than that of

[3] I am most happy to have the necessity of informing the reader that, since this passage was written, the report of Dr. Middleton's death on his voyage to India has been proved erroneous. He lives and long may he live; for I dare prophecy, that with his life only will his exertions for the temporal and spiritual welfare of his fellow men be limited.

singularity; I am not therefore deterred from avowing, that I regard, and ever have regarded the obligations of intellect among the most sacred of the claims of gratitude. A valuable thought, or a particular train of thoughts, gives me additional pleasure, when I can safely refer and attribute it to the conversation or correspondence of another. My obligations to Mr. Bowles were indeed important, and for radical good. At a very premature age, even before my fifteenth year, I had bewildered myself in metaphysicks, and in theological controversy. Nothing else pleased me. History, and particular facts, lost all interest in my mind. Poetry (though for a school-boy of that age, I was above par in English versification, and had already produced two or three compositions which, I may venture to say, without reference to my age, were somewhat above mediocrity, and which had gained me more credit than the sound, good sense of my old master was at all pleased with,) poetry itself, yea, novels and romances, became insipid to me. In my friendless wanderings on our *leave-days*,[4] (for I was an orphan, and had scarcely any connections in London,) highly was I delighted, if any passenger, especially if he were drest in black, would enter into conversation with me. For I soon found the means of directing it to my favorite subjects

> "Of providence, fore-knowledge, will, and fate,
> Fix'd fate, free will, fore-knowledge absolute,
> And found no end in wandering mazes lost."

This preposterous pursuit was, beyond doubt, injurious both to my natural powers, and to the progress of my education. It would perhaps have been destructive, had it been continued; but from this I was auspiciously withdrawn, partly indeed by an accidental introduction to an amiable family, chiefly however, by the genial influence of a style of poetry, so tender and yet so manly, so natural and real, and yet so dignified and harmonious, as the sonnets &c. of Mr. Bowles! Well were it for me, perhaps, had I never relapsed into the same mental disease; if I had continued to pluck the flower and reap the harvest from the cultivated surface, instead of delving in the unwholesome quicksilver mines of metaphysic depths. But if in after time I have sought a refuge from bodily pain and mismanaged sensibility in abstruse researches, which exercised the strength and subtlety of the understanding without awakening the feelings of the heart; still there

[4] The Christ's Hospital phrase, not for holidays altogether, but for those on which the boys are permitted to go beyond the precincts of the school.

was a long and blessed interval, during which my natural faculties were allowed to expand, and my original tendencies to develope themselves: my fancy, and the love of nature, and the sense of beauty in forms and sounds.

The second advantage, which I owe to my early perusal, and admiration of these poems, (to which let me add, though known to me at a somewhat later period, the Lewsdon Hill of Mr. CROW) bears more immediately on my present subject. Among those with whom I conversed, there were, of course, very many who had formed their taste, and their notions of poetry, from the writings of Mr. Pope and his followers: or to speak more generally, in that school of French poetry, condensed and invigorated by English understanding, which had predominated from the last century. I was not blind to the merits of this school, yet as from inexperience of the world, and consequent want of sympathy with the general subjects of these poems, they gave me little pleasure, I doubtless undervalued the *kind,* and with the presumption of youth withheld from its masters the legitimate name of poets. I saw that the excellence of this kind consisted in just and acute observations on men and manners in an artificial state of society, as its matter and substance: and in the logic of wit, conveyed in smooth and strong epigrammatic couplets, as its *form.* Even when the subject was addressed to the fancy, or the intellect, as in the Rape of the Lock, or the Essay on Man; nay, when it was a consecutive narration, as in that astonishing product of matchless talent and ingenuity, Pope's Translation of the Iliad; still a *point* was looked for at the end of each second line, and the whole was as it were a sorites, or, if I may exchange a logical for a grammatical metaphor, a *conjunction disjunctive,* of epigrams. Meantime the matter and diction seemed to me characterized not so much by poetic thoughts, as by thoughts *translated* into the language of poetry. On this last point, I had occasion to render my own thoughts gradually more and more plain to myself, by frequent amicable disputes concerning Darwin's BOTANIC GARDEN, which, for some years, was greatly extolled, not only by the *reading* public in general, but even by those, whose genius and natural robustness of understanding enabled them afterwards to act foremost in dissipating these "painted mists" that occasionally rise from the marshes at the foot of Parnassus. During my first Cambridge vacation, I assisted a friend in a contribution for a literary society in Devonshire: and in this I remember to have compared Darwin's work to the Russian palace of ice, glittering, cold and transitory. In the same essay too, I assigned sundry reasons, chiefly drawn from a comparison of passages in the Latin poets with the original Greek, from which they were borrowed, for the preference of Collins' odes to those of Gray; and of the simile in Shakespeare

> "How like a younker or a prodigal,
> The skarfed bark puts from her native bay,
> Hugg'd and embraced by the strumpet wind!
> How like the prodigal doth she return,
> With over-weather'd ribs and ragged sails,
> Lean, rent, and beggar'd by the strumpet wind!"

to the imitation in the Bard;

> "Fair laughs the morn, and soft the zephyr blows,
> While proudly riding o'er the azure realm
> In gallant trim the gilded vessel goes,
> YOUTH at the prow and PLEASURE at the helm;
> Regardless of the sweeping whirlwind's sway,
> That hush'd in grim repose, expects its evening prey."

(In which, by the bye, the words "realm" and "sway" are rhymes dearly purchased.) I preferred the original on the ground, that in the imitation it depended wholly on the compositor's putting, or not putting, a *small Capital*, both in this, and in many other passages of the same poet, whether the words should be personifications, or mere abstractions. I mention this, because, in referring various lines in Gray to their original in Shakespeare and Milton; and in the clear perception how completely all the propriety was lost in the transfer; I was, at that early period, led to a conjecture, which, many years afterwards was recalled to me from the same thought having been started in conversation, but far more ably, and developed more fully, by Mr. Wordsworth; namely, that this style of poetry, which I have characterised above, as translations of prose thoughts into poetic language, had been kept up by, if it did not wholly arise from, the custom of writing Latin verses, and the great importance attached to these exercises, in our public schools. Whatever might have been the case in the fifteenth century, when the use of the Latin tongue was so general among learned men, that Erasmus is said to have forgotten his native language; yet in the present day it is not to be supposed, that a youth can *think* in Latin, or that he can have any other reliance on the force or fitness of his phrases, but the authority of the writer from whence he has adopted them. Consequently he must first prepare his thoughts, and then pick out, from Virgil, Horace, Ovid, or perhaps more compendiously from his[5] Gradus, halves and quarters of lines, in which to embody them.

I never object to a certain degree of disputatiousness in a young man from the age of seventeen to that of four or five and twenty, provided I find him always arguing on one side of the question. The controversies, occasioned by my unfeigned zeal for the honor of a favorite contemporary, then known to me only by his works, were of great advantage in the formation and establishment of my taste and critical opinions. In my defence of the lines running into each other, instead of closing at each couplet, and of natural language, neither bookish, nor vulgar, neither redolent of the lamp, nor of the kennel, such as *I will remember thee;* instead of the same thought tricked up in the rag-fair finery of

> "———Thy image on her wing
> Before my FANCY's eye shall MEMORY bring,"

I had continually to adduce the metre and diction of the Greek Poets from Homer to Theocritus inclusive; and still more of our elder English poets from Chaucer to Milton. Nor was this all. But as it was my constant reply to authorities brought against me from later poets of great name, that no authority could avail in opposition to TRUTH, NATURE, LOGIC, and the LAWS of UNIVERSAL GRAMMAR; actuated too by my former passion for metaphysical investigations; I labored at a solid foundation, on which permanently to ground my opinions, in the component faculties of the human mind itself, and their comparative dignity and importance. According to the faculty or source, from which the pleasure given by any poem or passage was derived, I estimated the merit of such poem or passage. As the result of all my reading and meditation, I abstracted two critical aphorisms, deeming them to comprise the conditions and criteria of poetic style; first, that not the poem which we have *read,* but that to which we *return,* with the greatest pleasure, possesses the genuine power, and claims the name of *essential poetry.* Second, that whatever

[5] In the Nutricia of Politian there occurs this line:

"Pura coloratos interstrepit unda lapillos."

Casting my eye on a University prize-poem, I met this line:

"Lactea purpureos interstrepit unda lapillos."

Now look out in the Gradus for *Purus,* and you find as the first synonime, *lacteus;* for *coloratus,* and the first synonime is *purpureus.* I mention this by way of elucidating one of the most ordinary processes in the *ferrumination* of these centos.

lines can be translated into other words of the same language, without diminution of their significance, either in sense, or association, or in any worthy feeling, are so far vicious in their diction. Be it however observed, that I excluded from the list of worthy feelings, the pleasure derived from mere novelty in the reader, and the desire of exciting wonderment at his powers in the author. Oftentimes since then, in pursuing French tragedies, I have fancied two marks of admiration at the end of each line, as hieroglyphics of the author's own admiration at his own cleverness. Our genuine admiration of a great poet is a continuous *under-current* of feeling; it is everywhere present, but seldom anywhere as a separate excitement. I was wont boldly to affirm, that it would be scarcely more difficult to push a stone out from the pyramids with the bare hand, than to alter a word, or the position of a word, in Milton or Shakespeare, (in their most important works at least,) without making the author say something else, or something worse, than he does say. One great distinction, I appeared to myself to see plainly, between, even the characteristic faults of our elder poets, and the false beauty of the moderns. In the former, from DONNE to COWLEY, we find the most fantastic out-of-the-way thoughts, but in the most pure and genuine mother English; in the latter, the most obvious thoughts, in language the most fantastic and arbitrary. Our faulty elder poets sacrificed the passion and passionate flow of poetry, to the subtleties of intellect, and to the starts of wit; the moderns to the glare and glitter of a perpetual, yet broken and heterogeneous imagery, or rather to an amphibious something, made up, half of image, and half of abstract[6] meaning. The one sacrificed the heart to the head; the other both heart and head to point and drapery.

The reader must make himself acquainted with the general style of composition that was at that time deemed poetry, in order to understand and account for the effect produced on me by the SONNETS, the MONODY at MATLOCK, and the HOPE, of Mr. Bowles; for it is peculiar to original genius to become less and less *striking*, in proportion to its success in improving the taste and judgement of its contemporaries. The poems of WEST, indeed, had the merit of chaste and manly diction, but they were cold, and, if I may so express it, only *dead-coloured;* while in the best of Warton's there is a stiffness, which too often gives

[6] I remember a ludicrous instance in the poem of a young trades-man.

"No more will I endure love's pleasing pain,
Or round my heart's leg tie his galling chain."

them the appearance of imitations from the Greek. Whatever relation therefore of cause or impulse Percy's collection of Ballads may bear to the most *popular* poems of the present day; yet in the more sustained and elevated style, of the then living poets, Bowles and Cowper[7] were, to the best of my knowledge, the first who combined natural thoughts with natural diction; the first who reconciled the heart with the head.

It is true, as I have before mentioned, that from diffidence in my own powers, I for a short time adopted a laborious and florid diction, which I myself deemed, if not absolutely vicious, yet of very inferior worth. Gradually, however, my practice conformed to my better judgement; and the compositions of my twenty-fourth and twenty-fifth years (*ex. gr.* the shorter blank verse poems, the lines, which are now adopted in the introductory part of the VISION in the present collection, in Mr. Southey's Joan of Arc, 2nd book, 1st edition, and the Tragedy of REMORSE) are not more below my present ideal in respect of the general tissue of the style than those of the latest date. Their faults were at least a remnant of the former leaven, and among the many who have done me the honor of putting my poems in the same class with those of my betters, the one or two, who have pretended to bring examples of affected simplicity from my volume, have been able to adduce but one instance, and that out of a copy of verses half ludicrous, half splenetic, which I intended, and had myself characterized as *sermoni propiora.*

Every reform, however necessary, will by weak minds be carried to an excess, that itself will need reforming. The reader will excuse me for noticing, that I myself was the first to expose *risu honesto* the three sins of poetry, one or the other of which is the most likely to beset a young writer. So long ago as the publication of the second number of the monthly magazine, under the name of NEHEMIAH HIGGINBOTTOM, I contributed three sonnets, the first of which had for its object to excite a good-natured laugh at the spirit of *doleful egotism,* and at the

---

[7] Cowper's Task was published some time before the Sonnets of Mr. Bowles; but I was not familiar with it till many years afterwards. The vein of satire which runs through that excellent poem, together with the sombre hue of its religious opinions, would probably, *at that time,* have prevented its laying any strong hold on my affections. The love of nature seems to have led Thompson to a chearful religion; and a gloomy religion to have led Cowper to a love of nature. The one would carry his fellow-men along with him into nature; the other flies to nature from his fellow-men. In chastity of diction however, and the harmony of blank verse, Cowper leaves Thompson immeasurably below him; yet still I feel the latter to have been the *born poet.*

recurrence of favorite phrases, with the double defect of being at once trite and licentious. The second, on low, creeping language and thoughts, under the pretence of *simplicity*. And the third, the phrases of which were borrowed entirely from my own poems, on the indiscriminate use of elaborate and swelling language and imagery. The reader will find them in the note[8] below,

SONNET I.

PENSIVE at eve, on the *hard* world I mused,
And *my poor* heart was sad; so at the MOON
I gazed, and sighed, and sighed; for ah how soon
Eve saddens into night! mine eyes perused
With tearful vacancy the *dampy* grass
That wept and glitter'd in the *paly* ray:
And I *did pause me* on my lonely way
And *mused me* on the *wretched ones* that pass
O'er the bleak heath of sorrow. But alas!
Most of *myself* I thought! when it befel,
That the *soothe* spirit of the *breezy* wood
Breath'd in mine ear: "All this is very well,
But much of ONE thing, is for NO thing good."
Oh *my poor heart's* INEXPLICABLE SWELL!

SONNET II.

OH I do love thee, meek SIMPLICITY!
For of thy lays the lulling simpleness
Goes to my heart, and soothes each small distress,
Distress tho' small, yet haply great to me.
'Tis true on Lady Fortune's gentlest pad
I amble on; and yet I know not why
So sad I am! but should a friend and I
Frown, pout and part, then I am *very* sad.
And then with sonnets and with sympathy
My dreamy bosom's mystic woes I pall;
Now of my false friend plaining plaintively,
Now raving at mankind in general;
But whether sad or fierce, 'tis simple all,
All very simple, meek SIMPLICITY!

SONNET III.

AND this reft house is that, the which he built,
Lamented Jack! and here his malt he pil'd,
Cautious in vain! these rats, that squeak so wild,
Squeak not unconscious of their father's guilt.
Did he not see her gleaming thro' the glade!
Belike 'twas she, the maiden all forlorn.
What tho' she milk no cow with crumpled horn,
Yet, *aye* she haunts the dale where *erst* she strav'd:

and will I trust regard them as reprinted for biographical purposes, and not for their poetic merits. So general at that time, and so decided was the opinion concerning the characteristic vices of my style, that a celebrated physician (now, alas! no more) speaking of me in other respects with his usual kindness to a gentleman, who was about to meet me at a dinner party, could not however resist giving him a hint not to mention the "*house that Jack built*" in my presence, for "that I was *as sore as a boil* about that sonnet;" he not knowing, that I was myself the author of it.

CHAPTER II

Supposed irritability of men of Genius—Brought to the test of facts—Causes and Occasions of the charge—Its Injustice.

I HAVE often thought, that it would be neither uninstructive nor unamusing to analyze, and bring forward into distinct consciousness, that complex feeling, with which readers in general take part against the author, in favor of the critic; and the readiness with which they apply to *all* poets the old sarcasm of Horace

> And *aye,* beside her stalks her amorous knight!
> Still on his thighs their wonted brogues are worn.
> And thro' those brogues, still tatter'd and betorn,
> His hindward charms gleam an unearthly white.
> Ah! thus thro' broken clouds at night's high Noon
> Peeps in fair fragments forth the full-orb'd harvest-moon!

The following anecdote will not be wholly out of place here, and may perhaps amuse the reader. An amateur performer in verse expressed to a common friend a strong desire to be introduced to me, but hesitated in accepting my friend's immediate offer, on the score that "he was, he must acknowledge, the author of a confounded severe epigram on my *ancient mariner,* which had given me great pain." I assured my friend that, if the epigram was a good one, it would only increase my desire to become acquainted with the author, and begg'd to hear it recited: when, to my no less surprise than amusement, it proved to be one which I had myself some time before written and inserted in the Morning Post.

To the author of the Ancient Mariner.

> Your poem must eternal be,
> Dear sir! it cannot fail,
> For 'tis incomprehensible,
> And without head or tail.

upon the scribblers of his time: "Genus irritabile vatum." A debility and dimness of the imaginative power, and a consequent necessity of reliance on the immediate impressions of the senses, do, we well know, render the mind liable to superstition and fanaticism. Having a deficient portion of internal and proper warmth, minds of this class seek in the crowd *circum fana* for a warmth in common, which they do not possess singly. Cold and phlegmatic in their own nature, like damp hay, they heat and inflame by co-acervation; or like bees they become restless and irritable through the increased temperature of collected multitudes. Hence the German word for fanaticism, (such at least was its original import,) is derived from the swarming of bees, namely, Schwärmen, Schwärmerei. The passion being in an inverse proportion to the insight, *that* the more vivid, as *this* the less distinct; anger is the inevitable consequence. The absence of all foundation within their own minds for that, which they yet believe both true and indispensable for their safety and happiness, cannot but produce an uneasy state of feeling, an involuntary sense of fear from which nature has no means of rescuing herself but by anger. Experience informs us that the first defence of weak minds is to recriminate.

> "There's no Philosopher but sees,
> That rage and fear are one disease,
> Tho' that may burn, and this may freeze,
> They're both alike the ague."
>
> MAD OX.

But where the ideas are vivid, and there exists an endless power of combining and modifying them, the feelings and affections blend more easily and intimately with these ideal creations than with the objects of the senses; the mind is affected by thoughts, rather than by things; and only then feels the requisite interest even for the most important events and accidents, when by means of meditation they have passed into *thoughts*. The sanity of the mind is between superstition with fanaticism on the one hand, and enthusiasm with indifference and a diseased slowness to action on the other. For the conceptions of the mind may be so vivid and adequate, as to preclude that impulse to the realizing of them, which is strongest and most restless in those, who possess more than mere *talent*, (or the faculty of appropriating and applying the knowledge of others,) yet still want something of the creative, and self-sufficing power of absolute *Genius*. For this reason therefore, they are men of *commanding* genius. While the former rest content between thought and reality, as it were in an intermundium of which their own living spirit supplies the *substance,* and their imagination the ever-varying *form;* the latter must impress their preconceptions on the world without, in order to present them back to their own view with the satisfying degree of clearness, distinctness, and individuality. These in tranquil times are formed to exhibit a perfect poem in palace, or temple, or landscape-garden; or a tale of romance in canals that join sea with sea, or in walls of rock, which, shouldering back the billows, imitate the power, and supply the benevolence of nature to sheltered navies; or in aqueducts that, arching the wide vale from mountain to mountain, give a Palmyra to the desert. But alas! in times of tumult they are the men destined to come forth as the shaping spirit of Ruin, to destroy the wisdom of ages in order to substitute the fancies of a day, and to change kings and kingdoms, as the wind shifts and shapes the clouds.[9] The records of biography seem to confirm this theory. The men of the greatest genius, as far as we can judge from their own works or from the accounts of their contemporaries, appear to have been of calm and tranquil temper in all that related to themselves. In the inward assurance of permanent fame, they seem to have been either indifferent or resigned, with regard to immediate reputation. Through all the works of Chaucer there reigns a chearfulness, a manly hilarity, which makes it almost impossible to doubt a correspondent habit of feeling in the author himself. Shakespeare's evenness and sweetness of temper were almost proverbial in his own age. That this did not arise from ignorance of his own comparative greatness, we have abundant proof in his Sonnets, which could scarcely have been known to Mr. Pope,[10] when he

[9] "Of old things all are over old,
Of good things none are good enough:—
We'll show that we can help to frame
A world of other stuff.

I too will have my kings, that take
From me the sign of life and death:
Kingdoms shall shift about, like clouds,
Obedient to my breath."

WORDSWORTH'S ROB ROY.

[10] Mr. Pope was under the common error of his age, an error far from being sufficiently exploded even at the present day. It consists (as I explained at large, and proved in detail in my public lectures,) in mistaking for the *essentials* of the Greek stage certain rules, which the wise poets imposed upon themselves, in order to render all the remaining parts of the drama consistent with those, that had been forced upon them by circumstances independent of their will; out of which circumstances the drama itself arose. The circumstances in the

asserted, that our great bard "grew immortal in his own despite."
Speaking of one whom he had celebrated, and contrasting the
duration of his works with that of his personal existence, Shakes-
peare adds:

> "Your name from hence immortal life shall have,
> Tho' I once gone to all the world must die;
> The earth can yield me but a common grave,
> When you entombed in men's eyes shall lie.
> Your monument shall be my gentle verse,
> Which eyes not yet created shall o'er-read;
> And *tongues to be* your being shall rehearse,
> When all the breathers of this world are dead:
> You still shall live, such virtue hath my pen,
> Where breath most breathes, e'en in the mouth of men."
>
> SONNET 81st.

I have taken the first that occurred; but Shakespeare's readiness
to praise his rivals, ore pleno, and the confidence of his own
equality with those whom he deemed most worthy of his praise,
are alike manifested in the 86th Sonnet.

> "Was it the proud full sail of his great verse,
> Bound for the praise of all-too-precious you,
> That did my ripe thoughts in my brain inhearse,
> Making their tomb, the womb wherein they grew?
> Was it his spirit, by spirits taught to write
> Above a mortal pitch that struck me dead?
> No, neither he, nor his compeers by night
> Giving him aid, my verse astonished.
> He, nor that affable familiar ghost,

---

time of Shakespeare, which it was equally out of his power to alter,
were different, and such as, in my opinion, allowed a far wider sphere,
and a deeper and more human interest. Critics are too apt to forget,
that *rules* are but means to an end; consequently, where the ends are
different, the rules must be likewise so. We must have ascertained
what the end *is*, before we can determine what the rules *ought* to be.
Judging under this impression, I did not hesitate to declare my full
conviction, that the consummate judgement of Shakespeare, not only
in the general construction, but in all the *detail*, of his dramas, im-
pressed me with greater wonder, than even the might of his genius, or
the depth of his philosophy. The substance of these lectures I hope
soon to publish; and it is but a debt of justice to myself and my
friends to notice, that the first course of lectures, which differed from
the following courses only, by occasionally varying the illustrations of
the same thoughts, was addressed to very numerous, and I need not
add, respectable audiences at the royal institution, before Mr. Schlegel
gave his lectures on the same subjects at Vienna.

Which nightly gulls him with intelligence,
As victors of my silence cannot boast;
I was not sick of any fear from thence!
But when your countenance fill'd up his line,
Then lack'd I matter, that enfeebled mine."

In Spenser, indeed, we trace a mind constitutionally tender, delicate, and, in comparison with his three great compeers, I had almost said, *effeminate;* and this additionally saddened by the unjust persecution of Burleigh, and the severe calamities, which overwhelmed his latter days. These causes have diffused over all his compositions "a melancholy grace," and have drawn forth occasional strains, the more pathetic from their gentleness. But no where do we find the least trace of irritability, and still less of quarrelsome or affected contempt of his censurers.

The same calmness, and even greater self-possession, may be affirmed of Milton, as far as his poems, and poetic character are concerned. He reserved his anger for the enemies of religion, freedom, and his country. My mind is not capable of forming a more august conception, than arises from the contemplation of this great man in his latter days: poor, sick, old, blind, slandered, persecuted,

"Darkness before, and danger's voice behind;—"

in an age in which he was as little understood by the party, *for* whom, as by that, *against* whom he had contended; and among men before whom he strode so far as to *dwarf* himself by the distance; yet still listening to the music of his own thoughts, or if additionally cheered, yet cheered only by the prophetic faith of two or three solitary individuals, he did nevertheless

——"Argue not
Against Heaven's hand or will, nor bate a jot
Of heart or hope; but still bore up and steer'd
Right onward."

From others only do we derive our knowledge that Milton, in his latter day, had his scorners and detractors; and even in his day of youth and hope, that he had enemies would have been unknown to us, had they not been likewise the enemies of his country.

I am well aware, that in advanced stages of literature, when there exist many and excellent models, a high degree of talent, combined with taste and judgement, and employed in works of imagination, will acquire for a man the *name* of a great genius; though even that *analogon* of genius, which, in certain states of society, may even render his writings more popular than the absolute reality could have done, would be sought for in vain in the mind and temper of the author himself. Yet even in instances of this kind, a close examination will often detect, that the irritability, which has been attributed to the author's *genius* as its cause, did really originate in an ill conformation of body, obtuse pain, or constitutional defect of pleasurable sensation. What is charged to the *author*, belongs to the *man*, who would probably have been still more impatient, but for the humanizing influences of the very pursuit, which yet bears the blame of his irritability.

How then are we to explain the easy credence generally given to this charge, if the charge itself be not, as I have endeavoured to show, supported by experience? This seems to me of no very difficult solution. In whatever country literature is widely diffused, there will be many who mistake an intense desire to possess the reputation of poetic genius, for the actual powers, and original tendencies which constitute it. But men, whose dearest wishes are fixed on objects wholly out of their own power, become in all cases more or less impatient and prone to anger. Besides, though it may be paradoxical to assert, that a man can know one thing and believe the opposite, yet assuredly a vain person may have so habitually indulged the wish, and persevered in the attempt, to appear what he is not, as to become himself one of his own proselytes. Still, as this counterfeit and artificial persuasion must differ, even in the person's own feelings, from a real sense of inward power, what can be more natural, than that this difference should betray itself in suspicious and jealous irritability? Even as the flowery sod, which covers a hollow, may be often detected by its shaking and trembling.

But, alas! the multitude of books and the general diffusion of literature, have produced other and more lamentable effects in the world of letters, and such as are abundant to explain, though by no means to justify, the contempt with which the best grounded complaints of injured genius are rejected as frivolous, or entertained as matter of merriment. In the days of Chaucer and Gower, our language might (with due allowance for the imperfections of a simile) be compared to a wilderness of vocal reeds, from which the favorites only of Pan or Apollo could construct even the rude Syrinx; and from this the *constructors* alone could elicit strains of music. But now, partly by the labours of successive poets, and in part by the more artifical state of society and social intercourse, language, mechanized as it were into a barrel-organ, supplies at once both instrument and tune. Thus even the deaf may play, so as to delight the many. Sometimes (for it is with similes, as it is with jests at a wine table, one is sure to suggest another) I have attempted to illustrate the present state of our language, in its relation to literature, by a press-room of larger and smaller stereotype pieces, which, in the present Anglo-Gallican fashion of unconnected, epigrammatic periods, it requires but an ordinary portion of ingenuity to vary indefinitely, and yet still produce something, which, if *not* sense, will be so like it as to do as well. Perhaps better; for it spares the reader the trouble of thinking; prevents vacancy, while it indulges indolence; and secures the memory from all danger of an intellectual plethora. Hence of all trades, literature at present demands the least talent or information; and, of all modes of literature, the manufacturing of poems. The difference indeed between these and the works of genius is not less than between an egg and an egg-shell; yet at a distance they both look alike. Now it is no less remarkable than true, with how little examination works of polite literature are commonly perused, not only by the mass of readers, but by men of first rate ability, till some accident or chance[11]

[11] In the course of one of my Lectures, I had occasion to point out the almost faultless position and choice of words, in Mr. Pope's *original* compositions, particularly in his Satires and moral Essays, for the purpose of comparing them with his translation of Homer, which I do not stand alone in regarding as the main source of our pseudo-poetic diction. And this, by the bye, is an additional confirmation of a remark made, I believe, by Sir Joshua Reynolds, that next to the man who forms and elevates the taste of the public, he that corrupts it, is commonly the greatest genius. Among other passages, I analyzed sentence by sentence, and almost word by word, the popular lines,

"As when the moon, resplendent lamp of light, &c."

much in the same way as has been since done, in an excellent article on Chalmers's British Poets in the Quarterly Review. The impression on the audience in general was sudden and evident: and a number of enlightened and highly educated persons, who at different times afterwards addressed me on the subject, expressed their wonder, that truth so obvious should not have struck them *before;* but at the same time acknowledged (so much had they been accustomed, in reading poetry, to receive pleasure from the separate images and phrases successively, without asking themselves whether the collective meaning was sense or nonsense) that they might in all probability have read the same passage again twenty times with undiminished admiration, and without once reflecting, that "ἄστρα φαεινὴν ἀμφὶ σελήνην φαίνετ' ἀριπρεπέα" (i.e. the stars around, or near the full moon, shine preeminently bright) conveys a just and happy image of a moonlight sky: while it is difficult to determine whether, in the lines,

discussion have roused their attention, and put them on their guard. And hence individuals below mediocrity not less in natural power than in acquired knowledge; nay, bunglers that had failed in the lowest mechanic crafts, and whose presumption is in due proportion to their want of sense and sensibility; men, who being first scribblers from idleness and ignorance, next become libellers from envy and malevolence; have been able to drive a successful trade in the employment of the booksellers, nay, have raised themselves into temporary name and reputation with the public at large, by that most powerful of all adulation, the appeal to the bad and malignant passions of mankind.[12] But as it is the

> "Around *her throne* the vivid planets *roll,*
> And stars *unnumber'd gild* the *glowing pole,*"

the sense or the diction be the more absurd. My answer was; that, though I had derived peculiar advantages from my school discipline, and though my *general* theory of poetry was the same then as now, I had yet experienced the same sensations myself, and felt almost as if I had been newly couched, when, by Mr. Wordsworth's conversation, I had been induced to re-examine with impartial strictness Gray's celebrated elegy. I had long before detected the defects in "the Bard"; but "the Elegy" I had considered as proof against all fair attacks; and to this day I cannot read either without delight, and a portion of enthusiasm. At all events, whatever pleasure I may have lost by the clearer perception of the faults in certain passages, has been more than repaid to me by the additional delight with which I read the remainder.

[13] Especially "in this AGE OF PERSONALITY, this age of literary and political GOSSIPING, when the meanest insects are worshipped with a sort of Egyptian superstition, if only the brainless head be atoned for by the sting of personal malignity in the tail! When the most vapid satires have become the objects of a keen public interest, purely from the number of contemporary characters named in the patch-work notes, (which possess, however, the comparative merit of being more poetical than the text,) and because, to increase the stimulus, the author has sagaciously left his own name for whispers and conjectures! In an age, when even sermons are published with a double appendix stuffed with *names*—in a generation so transformed from the characteristic reserve of Britons, that from the ephemeral sheet of a London newspaper, to the everlasting Scotch Professorial Quarto, almost every publication exhibits or flatters the epidemic distemper; that the very "last year's rebuses" in the Ladies Diary, are answered in a serious elegy "*on my father's death,*" with the name and habitat of the elegaic Oedipus subscribed; and "*other ingenious solutions were likewise given*" to the said *rebuses*—not as heretofore by Crito, Philander, A, B, Y, &c., but by fifty or sixty plain English surnames at full length with their several places of abode! In an age, when a bashful *Phi-*

nature of scorn, envy, and all malignant propensities to require a quick change of objects, such writers are sure, sooner or later, to awake from their dream of vanity to disappointment and neglect with embittered and envenomed feelings. Even during their short-lived success, sensible in spite of themselves on what a shifting foundation it rests, they resent the mere refusal of praise, as a robbery, and at the justest censures kindle at once into violent and undisciplined abuse; till the acute disease changing into chronical, the more deadly as the less violent, they become the fit instruments of literary detraction, and moral slander. They are then no longer to be questioned without exposing the complainant to ridicule, because, forsooth, they are *anonymous* critics, and authorized as "synodical individuals" [13] to speak of themselves plurali majestatico! As if literature formed a caste, like that of the PARAS in Hindostan, who, however maltreated, must not dare to deem themselves wronged! As if that, which in all other cases adds a deeper dye to slander, the circumstance of its being anonymous, here acted only to make the slanderer inviolable! Thus, in *part*, from the accidental tempers of individuals (men of undoubted talent, but not men of genius) tempers rendered yet more irritable by their desire to *appear* men of genius; but still more effectively by the excesses of the mere *counterfeits* both of talent and genius; the number too being so incomparably greater of those who are *thought* to be, than of those who really *are* men of real genius; and in part from the natural, but not therefore the less partial and unjust distinction, made by the public itself between *literary* and all other property;—I believe the prejudice to have arisen, which considers an unusual irascibility concerning the reception of its products as characteristic of genius. It might correct the moral feelings of a numerous class of readers, to suppose a Review set on foot, the object of which should be to criticise all the chief works presented to the public by our ribbon-weavers, calico-printers, cabinet-makers, and china-manufacturers; a Review conducted in the same spirit, and which should take the same freedom with personal character, as our literary journals. They would scarcely, I think, deny their belief,

---

lalethes, or *Phileleutheros* is as rare on the title pages, and among the signatures, of our magazines, as a real name used to be in the days of our shy and notice-shunning grandfathers! When (more exquisite than all) I see an EPIC POEM (spirits of Mars and Mæonides, make ready to welcome your new compeer!) advertised with the special recommendation that the said EPIC POEM contains more than a hundred names of *living* persons."—FRIEND No. 10.

[18] A phrase of Andrew Marvel's.

not only that the "genus irritabile" would be found to include many other *species* besides that of bards; but that the irritability of *trade* would soon reduce the resentment of *poets* into mere shadow-fights (σχιομαχίας) in the comparison. Or is wealth the only rational object of human interest? Or even if this were admitted, has the poet no property in his works? Or is it a rare, or culpable case, that he who serves at the altar of the muses, should be compelled to derive his maintenance from the altar, when too he has perhaps deliberately abandoned the fairest prospects of rank and opulence in order to devote himself, an entire and undistracted man, to the instruction or refinement of his fellow-citizens? Or, should we pass by all higher objects and motives, all disinterested benevolence, and even that ambition of lasting praise which is at once the crutch and ornament, which at once supports and betrays, the infirmity of human virtue; is the character and property of the man, who labours for our intellectual pleasures, less entitled to a share of our fellow feeling, than that of the wine-merchant or milliner? Sensibility indeed, both quick and deep, is not only a characteristic feature, but may be deemed a component part, of genius. But it is not less an essential mark of true genius, that its sensibility is excited by any other cause more powerfully than by its own personal interests; for this plain reason, that the man of genius lives most in the ideal world, in which the present is still constituted by the future or the past; and because his feelings have been habitually associated with thoughts and images, to the number, clearness, and vivacity of which the sensation of *self* is always in an inverse proportion. And yet, should he perchance have occasion to repel some false charge, or to rectify some erroneous censure, nothing is more common than for the many to mistake the general liveliness of his manner and language, *whatever* is the subject, for the effects of peculiar irritation from its accidental relation to himself.[14]

[14] This is one instance among many of deception, by the telling the half of a fact, and omitting the other half, when it is from their mutual counteraction and neutralization, that the *whole* truth arises, as a tertium aliquid different from either. Thus in Dryden's famous line, "Great wit" (which here means genius) "to madness sure is near allied." Now as far as the profound sensibility, which is doubtless *one* of the components of genius, were alone considered, single and unbalanced, it might be fairly described as exposing the individual to ε greater chance of mental derangement; but then a more than usual rapidity of association, a more than usual power of passing from thought to thought, and image to image, is a component equally essential; and in the due modification of each by the other the GENIUS itself consists; so that it would be just as fair to describe the earth, as

For myself, if from my own feelings, or from the less suspicious test of the observations of others, I had been made aware of any literary testiness or jealousy; I trust, that I should have been, however, neither silly nor arrogant enough to have burthened the imperfection on GENIUS. But an experience (and I should not need documents in abundance to prove my words, if I added) a tried experience of twenty years, has taught me, that the original sin of my character consists in a careless indifference to public opinion, and to the attacks of those who influence it; that praise and admiration have become yearly less and less desirable, except as marks of sympathy; nay that it is difficult and distressing to me, to think with any interest even about the sale and profit of my works, important as, in my present circumstances, such considerations must needs be. Yet it never occurred to me to believe or fancy, that the quantum of intellectual power bestowed on me by nature or education was in any way connected with this habit of my feelings; or that it needed any other parents or fosterers than constitutional indolence, aggravated into languor by ill-health; the accumulating embarrassments of procrastination; the mental cowardice, which is the inseparable companion of procrastination, and which makes us anxious to think and converse on any thing rather than on what concerns ourselves; in fine, all those close vexations, whether chargeable on my faults or my fortunes, which leave me but little grief to spare for evils comparatively distant and alien.

Indignation at literary wrongs I leave to men born under happier stars. I cannot *afford it*. But so far from condemning those who can, I deem it a writer's duty, and think it creditable to his heart, to feel and express a resentment proportioned to the grossness of the provocation, and the importance of the object. There is no profession on earth, which requires an attention so early, so long, or so unintermitting as that of poetry; and indeed as that of literary composition in general, if it be such as at all satisfies the demands both of taste and of sound logic. How difficult and delicate a task even the mere mechanism of verse is, may be conjectured from the failure of those, who have attempted poetry late in life. Where then a man has, from his earliest youth, devoted his whole being to an object, which by the admission of all civilized nations in all ages is honorable as a pursuit, and glorious as an attainment; what of all that relates to himself and his family, if only we accept his moral character,

---

in imminent danger of exorbitating, or of falling into the sun, according as the assertor of the absurdity *confined* his attention either to the projectile or to the attractive force exclusively.

can have fairer claims to his protection, or more authorize acts of self-defence, than the elaborate products of his intellect and intellectual industry? Prudence itself would command us to *show*, even if defect or diversion of natural sensibility had prevented us from *feeling*, a due interest and qualified anxiety for the off-spring and representatives of our nobler being. I know it, alas! by woeful experience! I have laid too many eggs in the hot sands of this wilderness, the world, with ostrich carelessness and ostrich oblivion. The greater part indeed have been trod under foot, and are forgotten; but yet no small number have crept forth into life, some to furnish feathers for the caps of others, and still more to plume the shafts in the quivers of my enemies, of them that unprovoked have lain in wait against my soul.

> "Sic vos, non vobis, mellificatis, apes!"

An instance in confirmation of the Note, p. 129, occurs to me as I am correcting this sheet, with the FAITHFUL SHEPHERDESS open before me. Mr. Seward first traces Fletcher's lines;

> "More foul diseases than e'er yet the hot
> Sun bred thro' his burnings, while the dog
> Pursues the raging lion, throwing the fog
> And deadly vapour from his angry breath,
> Filling the lower world with plague and death.—"

To Spenser's Shepherd's Calendar,

> "The rampant lion hunts he fast
> With dogs of noisome breath;
> Whose baleful barking brings, in haste,
> Pyne, plagues, and dreary death!"

He then takes occasion to introduce Homer's simile of the sight of Achilles' shield to Priam compared with the Dog Star, literally thus—
"For this indeed is most splendid, but it was made an evil sign, and brings many a consuming disease to wretched mortals." Nothing can be more simple as a description, or more accurate as a simile; which, (says Mr. S.) is thus *finely* translated by Mr. Pope:

> "Terrific Glory! for his burning breath
> Taints the *red* air with fevers, plagues, and death!"

Now here (not to mention the tremendous bombast) the *Dog Star,* so called, is turned into a *real* Dog, a very odd Dog, a Fire, Fever, Plague, and death-breathing, *red*-air-tainting Dog: and the whole *visual* likeness is lost, while the likeness in the *effects* is rendered absurd by the exaggeration. In Spenser and Fletcher the thought is justifiable; for the images are at least consistent, and it was the intention of the writers to mark the seasons by this allegory of visualized *Puns.*

CHAPTER III

The author's obligations to critics, and the probable occasion—Principles of modern criticism—Mr. Southey's works and character.

To ANONYMOUS critics in reviews, magazines, and news-journals of various name and rank, and to satirists with or without a name in verse or prose, or in verse-text aided by prose-comment, I do seriously believe and profess, that I owe full two thirds of whatever reputation and publicity I happen to possess. For when the name of an individual has occurred so frequently, in so many works, for so great a length of time, the readers of these works (which with a shelf or two of BEAUTIES, ELEGANT EXTRACTS and ANAS, form nine-tenths of the reading public[15]) cannot but be familiar with the name, without distinctly remembering whether it was introduced for an eulogy or for censure. And this becomes the more likely, if (as I believe) the habit of perusing periodical works may be properly added to Averrhoes'[16] catalogue of ANTI-

---

[15] For as to the devotees of the circulating libraries, I dare not compliment their *pass-time*, or rather *kill-time*, with the name of *reading*. Call it rather a sort of beggarly day-dreaming, during which the mind of the dreamer furnishes for itself nothing but laziness, and a little mawkish sensibility; while the whole *materiel* and imagery of the dose is supplied *ab extra* by a sort of mental *camera obscura* manufactured at the printing office, which *pro tempore* fixes, reflects, and transmits the moving phantasms of one man's delirium, so as to people the barrenness of a hundred other brains afflicted with the same trance or suspension of all common sense and all definite purpose. We should therefore transfer this species of *amusement* (if indeed those can be said to retire *a musis*, who were never in their company, or relaxation be attributable to those, whose bows are never bent) from the genus, *reading*, to that comprehensive class characterized by the power of reconciling the two contrary yet co-existing propensities of human nature, namely, indulgence of sloth, and hatred of vacancy. In addition to novels and tales of chivalry in prose or rhyme, (by which last I mean neither rhythm nor metre), this genus comprises as its species, gaming, swinging, or swaying on a chair or gate; spitting over a bridge; smoking; snuff-taking; tête-à-tête quarrels after dinner between husband and wife; conning word by word all the advertisements of a daily newspaper in a public house on a rainy day, &c. &c. &c.

[16] Ex. gr. Pediculos e capillis excerptos in arenam jacere incontusos: eating of unripe fruit; gazing on the clouds, and (in genere) on moveable things suspended in the air; riding among a multitude of

MNEMONICS, or weakeners of the memory. But where this has not been the case, yet the reader will be apt to suspect, that there must be something more than usually strong and extensive in a reputation, that could either require or stand so merciless and long-continued a cannonading. Without any feeling of *anger* therefore (for which indeed, on my own account, I have no pretext) I may yet be allowed to express some degree of *surprize*, that, after having run the critical gauntlet for a certain class of faults which I *had*, nothing having come before the judgement-seat in the interim, I should, year after year, quarter after quarter, month after month (not to mention sundry petty periodicals of still quicker revolution, "or weekly or diurnal") have been, for at least 17 years consecutively dragged forth by them into the foremost ranks of the *proscribed*, and forced to abide the brunt of abuse, for faults directly opposite, and which I certainly had not. How shall I explain this?

Whatever may have been the case with others, I certainly cannot attribute this persecution to personal dislike, or to envy, or to feelings of vindictive animosity. Not to the former, for with the exception of a very few who are my intimate friends, and were so before they were known as authors, I have had little other acquaintance with literary characters, than what may be implied in an accidental introduction, or casual meeting in a mixt company. And, as far as words and looks can be trusted, I must believe that, even in these instances, I had excited no unfriendly disposition.[17] Neither by letter, or in conversation, have

---

camels; frequent laughter; listening to a series of jests and humorous anecdotes, as when (so to modernize the learned Saracen's meaning) one man's droll story of an Irishman occasions another's droll story of a Scotchman, which again, by the same sort of conjunction disjunctive, leads to some étouderie of a Welshman, and that again to some sly hit of a Yorkshireman; the habit of reading tombstones in church-yards, &c. By the bye, this catalogue, strange as it may appear, is not insusceptible of a sound psychological commentary.

[17] Some years ago, a gentleman, the chief writer and conductor of a celebrated review, distinguished by its hostility to Mr. Southey, spent a day or two at Keswick. That he was, without diminution on this account, treated with every hospitable attention by Mr. Southey and myself, I trust I need not say. But one thing I may venture to notice; that at no period of my life do I remember to have received so many, and such high coloured compliments in so short a space of time. He was likewise circumstantially informed by what series of accidents it had happened, that Mr. Wordsworth, Mr. Southey, and I had become neighbours; and how utterly unfounded was the supposition, that we considered ourselves, as belonging to any common school,

I ever had dispute or controversy beyond the common social interchange of opinions. Nay, where I had reason to suppose my convictions fundamentally different, it has been my habit, and I may add, the impulse of my nature, to assign the grounds of my belief, rather than the belief itself; and not to express dissent, till I could establish some points of complete sympathy, some grounds common to both sides, from which to commence its explanation.

---

but that of good sense confirmed by the long-established models of the best times of Greece, Rome, Italy, and England; and still more groundless the notion, that Mr. Southey (for as to myself I have published so little, and that little of so little importance, as to make it ludicrous to mention my name at all) could have been concerned in the formation of a poetic sect with Mr. Wordsworth, when so many of his works had been published not only previously to any acquaintance between them; but before Mr. Wordsworth himself had written anything but in a diction ornate, and uniformly sustained; when too the slightest examination will make it evident, that between those and the after writings of Mr. Southey, there exists no other difference than that of a progressive degree of excellence from progressive development of power, and progressive facility from habit and increase of experience. Yet among the first articles which this man wrote after his return from Keswick, we were characterized as "the School of whining and hypochondriacal poets that haunt the Lakes." In reply to a letter from the same gentleman, in which he had asked me, whether I was in earnest in preferring the style of Hooker to that of Dr. Johnson; and Jeremy Taylor to Burke; I stated, somewhat at large, the comparative excellences and defects, which characterized our best prose writers, from the reformation, to the first half of Charles 2nd; and that of those who had flourished during the present reign, and the preceding one. About twelve months afterwards, a review appeared on the same subject, in the concluding paragraph of which the reviewer asserts, that his chief motive for entering into the discussion was to separate a rational and qualified admiration of our elder writers, from the indiscriminate enthusiasm of a recent school, who praised what they did not understand, and caricatured what they were unable to imitate. And, that no doubt might be left concerning the persons alluded to, the writer annexes the names of Miss BAILIE, W. SOUTHEY, WORDSWORTH and COLERIDGE. For that which follows, I have only hearsay evidence; but yet such as demands my belief; viz. that on being questioned concerning this apparently wanton attack, more especially with regard to Miss Bailie, the writer had stated as his motives, that this lady, when at Edinburgh had declined a proposal of introducing him to her; that Mr. Southey had written against him; and Mr. Wordsworth had talked contemptuously of him; but that as to *Coleridge*, he had noticed him merely because the names of Southey and Wordsworth and Coleridge always went together. But if it were

Still less can I place these attacks to the charge of envy. The few pages which I have published, are of too distant a date; and the extent of their sale a proof too conclusive against their having been popular at any time; to render probable, I had almost said possible, the excitement of envy on *their* account; and the man who should envy me on any *other*, verily he must be *envy-mad!*

Lastly, with as little semblance of reason, could I suspect any animosity towards me from vindictive feelings as the cause. I have before said, that my acquaintance with literary men has been limited and distant; and that I have had neither dispute nor controversy. From my first entrance into life, I have, with few and short intervals, lived either abroad or in retirement. My different essays on subjects of national interest, published at different times, first in the Morning Post and then in the Courier, with my courses of lectures on the principles of criticism as applied to Shakespeare and Milton, constitute my whole publicity; the only occasions on which I *could* offend any member of the republic of letters. With one solitary exception in which my words were first misstated and then wantonly applied to an individual, I could never learn, that I had excited the displeasure of any among my literary contemporaries. Having announced my intention to give a course of lectures on the characteristic merits and defects of English poetry in its different æras; first, from Chaucer to Milton; second, from Dryden inclusive to Thompson; and third, from Cowper to the present day; I changed my plan, and confined my disquisition to the two former æras, that I might furnish no possible pretext for the unthinking to misconstrue, or the malignant to misapply my words, and having stampt their own meaning on them, to pass them as current coin in the marts of garrulity or detraction.

Praises of the unworthy are felt by ardent minds as robberies of the deserving; and it is too true, and too frequent, that Bacon,

---

worth while to mix together, as ingredients, half the anecdotes which I either myself know to be true, or which I have received from men incapable of intentional falsehood, concerning the characters, qualifications, and motives of our anonymous critics, whose decisions are oracles for our reading public, I might safely borrow the words of the apocryphal Daniel, *"Give me leave,* O SOVEREIGN PUBLIC, *and I shall slay this dragon without sword or staff."* For the compound would be as the "Pitch, and fat, and hair which Daniel took, and did seethe them together, and made lumps thereof, and put into the dragon's mouth, and so the dragon burst in sunder; and Daniel said, 'Lo, THESE ARE THE GODS YE WORSHIP.'"

Harrington, Machiavel, and Spinosa, are *not* read, because Hume, Condillac, and Voltaire *are*. But in promiscuous company no prudent man will oppugn the merits of a contemporary in his own supposed department; contenting himself with praising in his turn those whom *he* deems excellent. If I should ever deem it my duty at all to oppose the pretensions of individuals, I would oppose them in books which could be weighed and answered, in which I could evolve the whole of my reasons and feelings, with their requisite limits and modifications; not in irrecoverable conversation, where however strong the reasons might be, the feelings that prompted them would assuredly be attributed by some one or other to envy and discontent. Besides I well know, and I trust, have acted on that knowledge, that it must be the ignorant and injudicious who extol the unworthy; and the eulogies of critics without taste or judgement are the natural reward of authors without feeling or genius. "Sint unicuique sua, præmia."

How then, dismissing, as I do, these three causes, am I to account for attacks, the long continuance and inveteracy of which it would require all three to explain? The solution may seem to have been given, or at least suggested, in a note to a preceding page. *I was in habits of intimacy with Mr. Wordsworth and Mr. Southey!* This, however, transfers, rather than removes the difficulty. Be it, that, by an unconscionable extension of the old adage, "noscitur a socio," my literary friends are never under the water-fall of criticism, but I must be wet through with the spray; yet how came the torrent to descend upon *them?*

First then, with regard to Mr. Southey. I well remember the general reception of his earlier publications: viz. the poems published with Mr. Lovell under the names of Moschus and Bion: the two volumes of poems under his own name, and the Joan of Arc. The censures of the critics by profession are extant, and may be easily referred to:—careless lines, inequality in the merit of the different poems, and (in the lighter works) a predilection for the strange and whimsical; in short, such faults as might have been anticipated in a young and rapid writer, were indeed sufficiently enforced. Nor was there at that time wanting a party spirit to aggravate the defects of a poet, who with all the courage of uncorrupted youth had avowed his zeal for a cause, which he deemed that of liberty, and his abhorrence of oppression by whatever name consecrated. But it was as little objected by others, as dreamt of by the poet himself, that he *preferred* careless and prosaic lines on rule and of forethought, or indeed that he pretended to any other art or theory of poetic diction, besides that which we may all learn from Horace, Quinctilian, the admirable dialogue de Causis Corruptæ Eloquentiæ, or Strada's Prolusions; if indeed natural good sense and the early study of the best models in his own language had not infused the same maxims more securely, and, if I may venture the expression, more vitally. All that could have been fairly deduced was, that in his taste and estimation of writers Mr. Southey agreed far more with Warton, than with Johnson. Nor do I mean to deny, that at all times Mr. Southey was of the same mind with Sir Philip Sidney in preferring an excellent ballad in the *humblest* style of poetry to twenty indifferent poems that strutted in the *highest*. And by what have his works, published since then, been characterized, each more strikingly than the preceding, but by greater splendor, a deeper pathos, profounder reflections, and a more sustained dignity of language and of metre? Distant may the period be, but whenever the time shall come, when all his works shall be collected by some editor worthy to be his biographer, I trust that an excerpta of all the passages, in which his writings, name, and character have been attacked, from the pamphlets and periodical works of the last twenty years, may be an accompaniment. Yet that it would prove medicinal in after times I dare not hope; for as long as there are readers to be delighted with calumny, there will be found reviewers to calumniate. And such readers will become in all probability more numerous, in proportion as a still greater diffusion of literature shall produce an increase of sciolists, and sciolism bring with it petulance and presumption. In times of old, books were as religious oracles; as literature advanced, they next became venerable preceptors; they then descended to the rank of instructive friends; and, as their numbers increased, they sunk still lower to that of entertaining companions; and at present they seem degraded into culprits to hold up their hands at the bar of every self-elected, yet not the less peremptory, judge, who chuses to write from humour or interest, from enmity or arrogance, and to abide the decision (in the words of Jeremy Taylor) "of him that reads in malice, or him that reads after dinner."

The same gradual retrograde movement may be traced, in the relation which the authors themselves have assumed towards their readers. From the lofty address of Bacon: "these are the meditations of Francis of Verulam, which that posterity should be possessed of, he deemed *their* interest:" or from dedication to Monarch or Pontiff, in which the honor given was asserted in equipoise to the patronage acknowledged; from Pindar's

———— ἐπ' ἄλλοι-
-σι δ' ἄλλοι μεγάλοι. τὸ δ' ἔσχατον κορυ-
φοῦται βασιλεῦσι. μηκέτι
πάπταινε πόρσιον.
εἴη σέ τε τοῦτον
ὑψοῦ χρόνον πατεῖν, ἐμέ
τε τοσσάδε νικαφόροις
ὁμιλεῖν, πρόφαντον σοφίᾳ καθ' Ἑλ-
-λανας ἐόντα παντᾷ.—OLYMP. OD. I.

there was a gradual sinking in the etiquette or allowed style of pretension.

Poets and Philosophers, rendered diffident by their very number, addressed themselves to "*learned* readers;" then, aimed to conciliate the graces of "the *candid* reader;" till, the critic still rising as the author sunk, the amateurs of literature collectively were erected into a municipality of judges, and addressed as THE TOWN! And now, finally, all men being supposed able to read, and all readers able to judge, the multitudinous PUBLIC, shaped into personal unity by the magic of abstraction, sits nominal despot on the throne of criticism. But, alas! as in other despotisms, it but echoes the decisions of its invisible ministers, whose intellectual claims to the guardianship of the muses seem, for the greater part, analogous to the physical qualifications which adapt their oriental brethren for the superintendence of the Harem. Thus it is said, that St. Nepomuc was installed the guardian of bridges, because he had fallen over one, and sunk out of sight; thus too St. Cecilia is said to have been first propitiated by musicians, because, having failed in her own attempts, she had taken a dislike to the art, and all its successful professors. But I shall probably have occasion hereafter to deliver my convictions more at large concerning this state of things, and its influences on taste, genius, and morality.

In the "Thalaba," the "Madoc," and still more evidently in the unique[18] "Cid," in the "Kehama," and, as last, so best, the "Don Roderick;" Southey has given abundant proof, "se cogitâsse quám sit magnum dare aliquid in manus hominum, nec persua-

---

[18] I have ventured to call it "unique;" not only because I know no work of the kind in our language (if we except a few chapters of the old translation of Froissart) none, which uniting the charms of romance and history, keeps the imagination so constantly on the wing, and yet leaves so much for after reflection; but likewise, and chiefly, because it is a compilation which, in the various excellencies of translation, selection, and arrangement, required and proves greater genius in the compiler, as living in the present state of society, than in the original composers.

dere sibi posse, non sæpe tractandum quod placere et semper et omnibus cupiat." Plin. Ep., Lib. 7, Ep. 17. But on the other hand, I guess, that Mr. Southey was quite unable to comprehend, wherein could consist the crime or mischief of printing half a dozen or more playful poems; or to speak more generally, compositions which would be enjoyed or passed over, according as the taste and humour of the reader might chance to be; provided they contained nothing immoral. In the present age "perituræ parcere chartæ" is emphatically an unreasonable demand. The merest trifle, he ever sent abroad, had tenfold better claims to its ink and paper, than all the silly criticisms, which prove no more, than that the critic was not one of those, for whom the trifle was written; and than all the grave exhortations to a greater reverence for the public. As if the passive page of a book, by having an epigram or doggrel tale impressed on it, instantly assumed at once loco-motive power and a sort of ubiquity, so as to flutter and buz in the ear of the public to the sore annoyance of the said mysterious personage. But what gives an additional and more ludicrous absurdity to these lamentations is the curious fact, that if in a volume of poetry the critic should find poem or passage which he deems more especially worthless, he is sure to select and reprint it in the review; by which, on his own grounds, he wastes as much more paper than the author, as the copies of a fashionable review are more numerous than those of the original book; in some, and those the most prominent instances, as ten thousand to five hundred. I know nothing that surpasses the vileness of deciding on the merits of a poet or painter, (not by characteristic defects; for where there is genius, *these* always point to his characteristic *beauties;* but) by accidental failures or faulty passages; except the impudence of defending it, as the proper duty, and most instructive part, of criticism. Omit or pass slightly over the expression, grace, and grouping of Raphael's *figures;* but ridicule in *detail* the knitting-needles and broom-twigs, that are to represent trees in his back grounds; and never let him hear the last of his *galli-pots!* Admit that the Allegro and Penseroso of Milton are not *without merit;* but repay yourself for this concession, by reprinting at length the *two poems on the University Carrier!* As a fair specimen of his Sonnets, quote *"A Book was writ of late called Tetrachordon;"* and, as characteristic of his rhythm and metre, cite his literal translation of the first and second psalm! In order to justify yourself, you need only assert, that had you dwelt chiefly on the beauties and excellencies of the poet, the admiration of these might seduce the attention of future writers from the objects of their love and wonder, to an imitation of the few poems and passages in which the poet was most unlike himself.

But till reviews are conducted on far other principles, and with far other motives; till in the place of arbitrary dictation and petulant sneers, the reviewers support their decisions by reference to fixed canons of criticism, previously established and deduced from the nature of man; reflecting minds will pronounce it arrogance in them thus to announce themselves to men of letters, as the guides of their taste and judgement. To the purchaser and mere reader it is, at all events, an injustice. He who tells me that there are *defects* in a new work, tells me nothing which I should not have taken for granted without his information. But he, who points out and elucidates the *beauties* of an original work, does indeed give me interesting information, such as experience would not have authorized me in anticipating. And as to compositions which the authors themselves announce with "Hæc ipsi novimus esse nihil," why should we judge by a different rule two printed works, only because the one author was alive, and the other in his grave? What literary man has not regretted the prudery of Spratt in refusing to let his friend Cowley appear in his slippers and dressing gown? I am not perhaps the only one who has derived an innocent amusement from the riddles, conundrums, tri-syllable lines, &c., &c., of Swift and his correspondents, in hours of languor, when to have read his more finished works would have been useless to myself, and, in some sort, an act of injustice to the author. But I am at a loss to conceive by what perversity of judgement, these relaxations of his genius could be employed to diminish his fame as the writer of "Gulliver's Travels," and the "Tale of a Tub." Had Mr. Southey written twice as many poems of inferior merit, or partial interest, as have enlivened the journals of the day, they would have added to his honor with good and wise men, not merely or principally as proving the versatility of his talents, but as evidences of the purity of that mind, which even in its levities never wrote a line, which it need regret on any moral account.

I have in imagination transferred to the future biographer the duty of contrasting Southey's fixed and well-earned fame, with the abuse and indefatigable hostility of his anonymous critics from his early youth to his ripest manhood. But I cannot think so ill of human nature as not to believe, that these critics have already taken shame to themselves, whether they consider the object of their abuse in his moral or his literary character. For reflect but on the variety and extent of his acquirements! He stands second to no man, either as an historian or as a bibliographer;

and when I regard him as a popular essayist, (for the articles of his compositions in the reviews are for the greater part essays on subjects of deep or curious interest rather than criticisms on particular works[19]) I look in vain for any writer, who has conveyed so much information, from so many and such recondite sources, with so many just and original reflections, in a style so lively and poignant, yet so uniformly classical and perspicuous; no one in short who has combined so much wisdom with so much wit; so much truth and knowledge with so much life and fancy. His prose is always intelligible and always entertaining. In poetry he has attempted almost every species of composition known before, and he has added new ones; and if we except the highest lyric, (in which how few, how very few even of the greatest minds have been fortunate) he has attempted every species successfully: from the political song of the day, thrown off in the playful overflow of honest joy and patriotic exultation, to the wild ballad;[20] from epistolary ease and graceful narrative, to the austere and impetuous moral declamation; from the pastoral claims and wild streaming lights of the "Thalaba," in which sentiment and imagery have given permanence even to the excitement of curiosity; and from the full blaze of the "Kehama," (a gallery of finished pictures in one splendid fancy piece, in which, notwithstanding, the moral grandeur rises gradually above the brilliance of the colouring and the boldness and novelty of the machinery) to the more sober beauties of the Madoc;" and lastly, from the Madoc to his "Roderick," in which, retaining all his former excellencies of a poet eminently inventive and picturesque, he has surpassed himself in language and metre, in the construction of the whole, and in the splendour of particular passages.

Here then shall I conclude? No! The characters of the deceased, like the encomia on tombstones, as they are described with religious tenderness, so are they read, with allowing sympathy indeed, but yet with rational deduction. There are men, who deserve a higher record; men with whose characters it is the interest of their contemporaries, no less than that of posterity, to be made acquainted; while it is yet possible for impartial censure, and even for quick-sighted envy, to cross-examine the tale without offence to the courtesies of humanity; and while the eulogist detected in exaggeration or falsehood must pay the

[19] See the articles on Methodism, in the Quarterly Review: the small volume on the New System of Education, &c.

[20] See the incomparable "Return to Moscow" and the "Old Woman of Berkeley."

full penalty of his baseness in the contempt which brands the
convicted flatterer. Publicly has Mr. Southey been reviled by
men, who, (as I would fain hope for the honor of human nature)
hurled fire-brands against a figure of their own imagination,
publicly have his talents been depreciated, his principles de-
nounced; as publicly do I therefore, who have known him in-
timately, deem it my duty to leave recorded, that it is SOUTHEY'S
almost unexampled felicity, to possess the best gifts of talent and
genius free from all their characteristic defects. To those who
remember the state of our public schools and universities some
twenty years past, it will appear no ordinary praise in any man
to have passed from innocence into virtue, not only free from
all vicious habit, but unstained by one act of intemperance, or
the degradations akin to intemperance. That scheme of head,
heart, and habitual demeanour, which in his early manhood, and
first controversial writings, Milton, claiming the privilege of self-
defence, asserts of himself, and challenges his calumniators to
disprove; this will his school-mates, his fellow-collegians, and
his maturer friends, with a confidence proportioned to the in-
timacy of their knowledge, bear witness to, as again realized
in the life of Robert Southey. But still more striking to those,
who by biography or by their own experience are familiar with
the general habits of genius, will appear the poet's matchless
industry and perseverance in his pursuits; the worthiness and
dignity of those pursuits; his generous submission to tasks of
transitory interest, or such as *his* genius alone could make other-
wise; and that having thus more than satisfied the claims of
affection or prudence, he should yet have made for himself time
and power, to achieve more, and in more various departments
than almost any other writer has done, though employed wholly
on subjects of his own choice and ambition. But as Southey
possesses, and is not possessed by, his genius, even so is he master
even of his virtues. The regular and methodical tenor of his daily
labours, which would be deemed rare in the most mechanical
pursuits, and might be envied by the mere man of business,
loses all semblance of formality in the dignified simplicity of
his manners, in the spring and healthful chearfulness of his spirits.
Always employed, his friends find him always at leisure. No less
punctual in trifles, than stedfast in the performance of highest
duties, he inflicts none of those small pains and discomforts which
irregular men scatter about them, and which in the aggregate
so often become formidable obstacles both to happiness and
utility; while on the contrary he bestows all the pleasures, and
inspires all that ease of mind on those around him or connected

with him, which perfect consistency, and (if such a word might be framed) absolute *reliability*, equally in small as in great concerns, cannot but inspire and bestow: when this too is softened without being weakened by kindness and gentleness. I know few men who so well deserve the character which an antient attributes to Marcus Cato, namely, that he was likest virtue, in as much as he seemed to act aright, not in obedience to any law or outward motive, but by the necessity of a happy nature, which could not act otherwise. As son, brother, husband, father, master, friend, he moves with firm yet light steps, alike unostentatious, and alike exemplary. As a writer, he has uniformly made his talents subservient to the best interests of humanity, of public virtue, and domestic piety; his cause has ever been the cause of pure religion and of liberty, of national independence and of national illumination. When future critics shall weigh out his guerdon of praise and censure, it will be Southey the poet only, that will supply them with the scanty materials for the latter. They will likewise not fail to record, that as no man was ever a more constant friend, never had poet more friends and honorers among the good of all parties; and that quacks in education, quacks in politics, and quacks in criticism were his only enemies.[21]

[21] It is not easy to estimate the effects which the example of a young man as highly distinguished for strict purity of disposition and conduct, as for intellectual power and literary acquirements, may produce on those of the same age with himself, especially on those of similar pursuits and congenial minds. For many years, my opportunities of intercourse with Mr. Southey have been rare, and at long intervals; but I dwell with unabated pleasure on the strong and sudden, yet I trust not fleeting, influence, which my normal being underwent on my acquaintance with him at Oxford, whither I had gone at the commencement of our Cambridge vacation on a visit to an old school-fellow. Not indeed on my moral or religious principles, for *they* had never been contaminated; but in awakening the sense of the duty and dignity of making my actions accord with those principles, both in word and deed. The irregularities only not universal among the young men of my standing, which I always *knew* to be *wrong*, I then learned to feel as *degrading*; learnt to know that an opposite conduct, which was at that time considered by us as the easy virtue of cold and selfish prudence, might originate in the noblest emotions, in views the most disinterested and imaginative. It is not however from grateful recollections only, that I have been impelled thus to leave these my deliberate sentiments on record; but in some sense as a debt of justice to the man, whose name has been so often connected with mine for evil to which he is a stranger. As a specimen I subjoin part of a note, from "the Beauties of the Anti-jacobin," in which, having previously informed

CHAPTER IV

The lyrical ballads with the preface—Mr. Wordsworth's earlier poems —On fancy and imagination—The investigation of the distinction important to the fine arts.

I HAVE wandered far from the object in view, but as I fancied to myself readers who would respect the feelings that had tempted me from the main road; so I dare calculate on not a few, who will warmly sympathize with them. At present it will be sufficient for my purpose, if I have proved, that Mr. Southey's writings no more than my own furnished the original occasion to this fiction of a *new school* of poetry, and to the clamors against its supposed founders and proselytes.

As little do I believe that "Mr. WORDSWORTH's Lyrical Ballads" were in *themselves* the cause. I speak exclusively of the two volumes so entitled. A careful and repeated examination of these confirms me in the belief, that the omission of less than an hundred lines would have precluded nine-tenths of the criticism on this work. I hazard this declaration, however, on the supposition, that the reader has taken it up, as he would have done any other collection of poems purporting to derive their subjects or interests from the incidents of domestic or ordinary life, intermingled with higher strains of meditation which the poet utters in his own person and character; with the proviso, that they were perused without knowledge of, or reference to, the author's peculiar opinions, and that the reader had not had his attention previously directed to those peculiarities. In these,

---

the public that I had been dishonour'd at Cambridge for preaching Deism, at a time when, for my youthful ardour in defense of Christianity, I was decried as a bigot by the proselytes of French Phi- (or to speak more truly, Psi-) losophy, the writer concludes with these words; "since this time he has left his native country, commenced citizen of the world, *left his poor children fatherless, and his wife destitute. Ex his disce his friends*, LAMB *and* SOUTHEY." With severest truth it may be asserted, that it would not be easy to select two men more exemplary in their domestic affections than those whose names were thus printed at full length as in the same rank of morals with a denounced infidel and fugitive, who had left his children *fatherless and his wife destitute!* Is it surprising, that many good men remained longer than perhaps they otherwise would have done, adverse to a party, which encouraged and openly rewarded the authors of such atrocious calumnies? "Qualis es, nescio; sed per quales agis, scio et doleo."

as was actually the case with Mr. Southey's earlier works, the
lines and passages which might have offended the general taste
would have been considered as mere inequalities, and attributed
to inattention, not to perversity of judgement. The men of busi-
ness who had passed their lives chiefly in cities, and who might
therefore be expected to derive the highest pleasure from acute
notices of men and manners conveyed in easy, yet correct and
pointed language; and all those who, reading but little poetry,
are most stimulated with that species of it, which seems most
distant from prose would probably have passed by the volume
altogether. Others more catholic in their taste, and yet habit-
uated to be most pleased when most excited, would have con-
tented themselves with deciding, that the author had been
successful in proportion to the elevation of his style and sub-
ject. Not a few perhaps, might by their admiration of "the lines
written near Tintern Abbey," those "left upon a Seat under a
Yew Tree," the "old Cumberland beggar," and "Ruth," have
been gradually led to peruse with kindred feeling the "Brothers,"
the "Hart-leap Well," and whatever other poems in that col-
lection may be described as holding a middle place between
those written in the highest and those in the humblest style;
as for instance between the "Tintern Abbey," and "the Thorn,"
or the "Simon Lee." Should their taste submit to no further
change, and still remain unreconciled to the colloquial phrases,
or the imitations of them, that are, more or less, scattered through
the class last mentioned; yet even from the small number of
the latter, they would have deemed them but an inconsiderable
subtraction from the merit of the whole work; or, what is some-
times not unpleasing in the publication of a new writer, as serv-
ing to ascertain the natural tendency, and consequently the
proper direction of the author's genius.

In the critical remarks, therefore, prefixed and annexed to
the "Lyrical Ballads," I believe that we may safely rest, as the
true origin of the unexampled opposition which Mr. Words-
worth's writings have been since doomed to encounter. The
humbler passages in the poems themselves were dwelt on and
cited to justify the rejection of the theory. What in and for them-
selves would have been either forgotten or forgiven as imperfec-
tions, or at least comparative failures, provoked direct hostility
when announced as intentional, as the result of choice after full
deliberation. Thus the poems, admitted by *all* as excellent, joined
with those which had pleased the far *greater* number, though
they formed two-thirds of the whole work, instead of being
deemed (as in all right they should have been, even if we take

for granted that the reader judged aright) an atonement for the few exceptions, gave wind and fuel to the animosity against both the poems and the poet. In all perplexity there is a portion of fear, which predisposes the mind to anger. Not able to deny that the author possessed both genius and a powerful intellect, they felt *very positive*, but were not *quite certain*, that he might not be in the right, and they themselves in the wrong; an unquiet state of mind, which seeks alleviation by quarrelling with the occasion of it, and by wondering at the perverseness of the man, who had written a long and argumentative essay to persuade them, that

"Fair is foul, and foul is fair;"

in other words, that they had been all their lives admiring without judgement, and were now about to censure without reason.[22]

[22] In opinions of long continuance, and in which we have never before been molested by a single doubt, to be suddenly *convinced* of an *error*, is almost like being *convicted* of a fault. There is a state of mind, which is the direct antithesis of that, which takes place when we *make a bull. The bull* namely consists in the bringing together two incompatible thoughts, with the *sensation,* but without the *sense,* of their connection. The psychological condition, or that which constitutes the possibility of this state, being such disproportionate vividness of two distant thoughts, as extinguishes or obscures the consciousness of the intermediate images or conceptions, or wholly abstracts the attention from them. Thus in the well known bull, *"I was a fine child, but they changed me;"* the first conception expressed in the word *"I,"* is that of personal identity—*Ego contemplans:* the second expressed in the word *"me,"* is the visual image or object by which the mind represents to itself its past condition, or rather, its personal identity under the form in which it imagined itself previously to have existed, —*Ego contemplatus.* Now the change of one visual image for another involves in itself no absurdity, and becomes absurd only by its immediate juxta-position with the first thought, which is rendered possible by the whole attention being successively absorbed in each singly, so as not to notice the interjacent notion, "changed," which by its incongruity with the first thought, *"I,"* constitutes the bull. Add only, that this process is facilitated by the circumstance of the words *"I"* and *"me,"* being sometimes equivalent, and sometimes having a distinct meaning; sometimes, namely, signifying the act of self-consciousness, sometimes the external image in and by which the mind represents that act to itself, the result and symbol of its individuality. Now suppose the direct contrary state, and you will have a distinct sense of the connection between two conceptions, without that *sensation* of such connection which is supplied by habit. The man *feels* as if he were standing on his head, though he cannot but *see*, that he is truly standing on his feet. This, as a painful sensation, will of course have

That this conjecture is not wide from the mark, I am induced to believe from the noticeable fact, which I can state on my own knowledge, that the same general censure should have been grounded by almost every different person on some different poem. Among those, whose candour and judgement I estimate highly, I distinctly remember six who expressed their objections to the "Lyrical Ballads" almost in the same words, and altogether to the same purport, at the same time admitting, that several of the poems had given them great pleasure; and, strange as it might seem, the composition which one cited as execrable, another quoted as his favorite. I am indeed convinced in my own mind, that could the same experiment have been tried with these volumes, as was made in the well known story of the picture, the result would have been the same; the parts which had been covered by the number of the black spots on the one day, would be found equally *albo* lapide notatæ on the succeeding.

However this may be, it is assuredly hard and unjust to fix the attention on a few separate and insulated poems with as much aversion, as if they had been so many plague-spots on the whole work, instead of passing them over in silence, as so much blank paper, or leaves of a bookseller's catalogue; especially, as no one pretends to have found any immorality or indelicacy; and the poems, therefore, at the worst, could only be regarded as so many light or inferior coins in a roleau of gold, not as so much alloy in a weight of bullion. A friend whose *talents* I hold in the highest respect, but whose *judgement* and strong sound sense I have had almost continued occasion to *revere,* making the usual complaints to me concerning both the style and subjects of Mr. Wordsworth's minor poems; I admitted that there were some few of the tales and incidents, in which I could not myself find a sufficient cause for their having been recorded in metre. I mentioned the "Alice Fell" as an instance; "nay," replied my friend with more than usual quickness of manner, "I cannot agree with you *there!* that, I own, *does* seem to me a remarkably pleasing poem." In the "Lyrical Ballads," (for my experience does not enable me to extend the remark equally unqualified to the two subsequent volumes,) I have heard at different times, and from different individuals every single poem *extolled* and *reprobated,* with the exception of those of loftier kind, which as was before observed, seem to have won universal praise. This fact of itself would have made me diffident in my

---

a tendency to associate itself with the person who occasions it; even as persons, who have been by painful means restored from derangement, are known to feel an involuntary dislike towards their physician.

censures, had not a still stronger ground been furnished by the strange contrast of the heat and long continuance of the opposition, with the nature of the faults stated as justifying it. The seductive faults, the *dulcia vitia* of Cowley, Marini, or Darwin might reasonably be thought capable of corrupting the public judgement for half a century, and require a twenty years' war, campaign after campaign, in order to dethrone the usurper and re-establish the legitimate taste. But that a downright simpleness, under the affectation of simplicity, prosaic words in feeble metre, silly thoughts in childish phrases, and a preference of mean, degrading, or at best trivial associations and characters, should succeed in forming a school of imitators, a company of almost *religious* admirers, and this too among young men of ardent minds, liberal education, and not

"with academic laurels unbestowed;"

and that this bare and bald *counterfeit* of poetry, which is characterized as *below* criticism, should for nearly twenty years have well-nigh *engrossed* criticism, as the main, if not the only, *butt* of review, magazine, pamphlet, poem, and paragraph;—this is indeed matter of wonder! Of yet greater is it, that the contest should still continue as[23] undecided as that between Bacchus

[23] Without however the apprehensions attributed to the *Pagan* reformer of the poetic republic. If we may judge from the preface to the recent collection of his poems, Mr. W. would have answered with Xanthias—

σὺ δ' οὐκ ἔδεισας τὸν ψόφον τῶν ῥημάτων,
καὶ τὰς ἀπειλάς; ΞΑΝ. οὐ μὰ οὐδ' ἐφρόντισα.

And here let me dare hint to the authors of the numerous parodies, and pretended imitations of Mr. Wordsworth's style, that at once to conceal and convey wit and wisdom in the semblance of folly and dulness, as is done in the Clowns and Fools, nay even in the Dogberry, of our Shakespeare, is doubtless a proof of genius, or at all events of satiric talent; but that the attempt to ridicule a silly and childish poem, by writing another still sillier and still more childish, can only prove (if it prove any thing at all) that the parodist is a still greater blockhead than the original writer, and, what is far worse a *malignant* coxcomb to boot. The talent for mimicry seems strongest where the human race are most degraded. The poor, naked, half human savages of New Holland were found excellent mimics: and, in civilized society, minds of the very lowest stamp alone satirize by *copying*. At least the difference, which must blend with and balance the likeness, in order to constitute a just imitation, existing here merely in caricature, detracts from the libeller's heart, without adding an iota to the credit of his understanding.

and the frogs in Aristophanes; when the former descended to the realms of the departed to bring back the spirit of old and genuine poesy.—

X. βρεκεκεκὲξ, κοὰξ, κοάξ.
Δ. ἀλλ' ἐξόλοισθ' αὐτῷ κοάξ.
   οὐδὲν γάρ ἐστ' ἄλλ' ἢ κοάξ.
   οἰμώζετ'· οὐ γάρ μοι μέλει.
X. ἀλλὰ μὴν κεκραξόμεσθά
   γ', ὁπόσον ἡ φάρυγξ ἂν ἡμῶν
   χανδάνῃ, δι' ἡμέρας,
   βρεκεκεκὲξ, κοὰξ, κοάξ!
Δ. τούτῳ γὰρ οὐ νικήσετε.
X. οὐδὲ μὴν ἡμᾶς σὺ πάντως.
Δ. οὐδὲ μὴν ὑμεῖς γε δή μ'
   οὐδέποτε. κεκράξομαι γάρ,
   κἂν με δέῃ, δι' ἡμέρας,
   ἕως ἂν ὑμῶν ἐπικρατήσω τοῦ κοάξ!
X. βρεκεκεκὲξ ΚΟ᾽ΑΞ, ΚΟΑ᾽Ξ!

During the last year of my residence at Cambridge, I became acquainted with Mr. Wordsworth's first publication entitled "Descriptive Sketches;" and seldom, if ever, was the emergence of an original poetic genius above the literary horizon more evidently announced. In the form, style, and manner of the whole poem, and in the structure of the particular lines and periods, there is an harshness and acerbity connected and combined with words and images all a-glow, which might recall those products of the vegetable world, where gorgeous blossoms rise out of the hard and thorny rind and shell, within which the rich fruit was elaborating. The language was not only peculiar and strong, but at times knotty and contorted, as by its own impatient strength; while the novelty and struggling crowd of images, acting in conjunction with the difficulties of the style, demanded always a greater closeness of attention, than poetry, (at all events, than descriptive poetry) has a right to claim. It not seldom therefore justified the complaint of obscurity. In the following extract I have sometimes fancied, that I saw an emblem of the poem itself, and of the author's genius as it was then displayed.

" 'Tis storm; and hid in mist from hour to hour,
All day the floods a deepening murmur pour;
The sky is veiled, and every cheerful sight:
Dark is the region as with coming night;
And yet what frequent bursts of overpowering light!
Triumphant on the bosom of the storm.

Glances the fire-clad eagle's wheeling form;
Eastward, in long perspective glittering, shine
The wood-crowned cliffs that o'er the lake recline;
Wide o'er the Alps a hundred streams unfold,
At once to pillars turn'd that flame with gold;
Behind his sail the peasant strives to shun
The West, that burns like one dilated sun,
Where in a mighty crucible expire
The mountains, glowing hot, like coals of fire."

The poetic PSYCHE, in its process to full developement, undergoes as many changes as its Greek name-sake, the butterfly.[24] And it is remarkable how soon genius clears and purifies itself from the faults and errors of its earliest products; faults which, in its earliest compositions, are the more obtrusive and confluent, because as heterogeneous elements, which had only a temporary use, they constitute the very *ferment*, by which themselves are carried off. Or we may compare them to some diseases, which must work on the humours, and be thrown out on the surface, in order to secure the patient from their future recurrence. I was in my twenty-fourth year, when I had the happiness of knowing Mr. Wordsworth personally, and while memory lasts, I shall hardly forget the sudden effect produced on my mind, by his recitation of a manuscript poem, which still remains unpublished, but of which the stanza, and tone of style, were the same as those of the "Female Vagrant," as originally printed in the first volume of the "Lyrical Ballads." There was here no mark of strained thought, or forced diction, no crowd or turbulence of imagery; and, as the poet hath himself well described in his lines "on re-visiting the Wye," manly reflection, and human associations had given both variety, and an additional interest to natural objects, which in the passion and appetite of the first love they had seemed to him neither to need or permit. The occasional obscurities, which had risen from an imperfect

[24] The fact, that in Greek Psyche is the common name for the soul, and the butterfly, is thus alluded to in the following stanzas from an unpublished poem of the author:

"The butterfly the ancient Grecians made
The soul's fair emblem, and its only name—
But of the soul, escaped the slavish trade
Of mortal life! For in this earthly frame
Ours is the reptile's lot, much toil, much blame,
Manifold motions making little speed,
And to deform and kill the things, whereon we feed."
S. T. C.

controul over the resources of his native language, had almost
wholly disappeared, together with that worse defect of arbitrary
and illogical phrases, at once hackneyed, and fantastic, which
hold so distinguished a place in the *technique* of ordinary poetry,
and will, more or less, alloy the earlier poems of the truest genius,
unless the attention has been specifically directed to their worth-
lessness and incongruity.[25] I did not perceive anything particular
in the mere style of the poem alluded to during its recitation,
except indeed such difference as was not separable from the
thought and manner; and the Spenserian stanza, which always,
more or less, recalls to the reader's mind Spenser's own style,
would doubtless have authorized, in my then opinion, a more
frequent descent to the phrases of ordinary life, than could
without an ill effect have been hazarded in the heroic couplet.
It was not however the freedom from false taste, whether as to
common defects, or to those more properly his own, which
made so unusual an impression on my feelings immediately,
and subsequently on my judgement. It was the union of deep
feeling with profound thought; the fine balance of truth in ob-
serving, with the imaginative faculty in modifying the objects
observed; and above all the original gift of spreading the tone,
the *atmosphere*, and with it the depth and height of the ideal
world around forms, incidents, and situations, of which, for the
common view, custom had bedimmed all the lustre, had dried up
the sparkle and the dew drops. "To find no contradiction in the
union of old and new; to contemplate the ANCIENT of days and
all his works with feelings as fresh, as if all had then sprang

[25] Mr. Wordsworth, even in his two earliest, "the Evening Walk and
the Descriptive Sketches," is more free from this latter defect than
most of the young poets his contemporaries. It may however be exem-
plified, together with the harsh and obscure construction, in which he
more often offended, in the following lines:—

> "'Mid stormy vapours ever driving by,
>   Where ospreys, cormorants, and herons cry;
>   Where hardly given the hopeless waste to cheer,
>   Denied the bread of life, the foodful ear,
>   Dwindles the pear on autumn's latest spray,
>   And *apple sickens* pale in summer's ray;
>   *Ev'n here content has fixed her smiling reign*
>   *With independence, child of high disdain.*"

I hope, I need not say, that I have quoted these lines for no other
purpose than to make my meaning fully understood. It is to be re-
gretted that Mr. Wordsworth has not republished these two poems
entire.

forth at the first creative fiat; characterizes the mind that feels the riddle of the world, and may help to unravel it. To carry on the feelings of childhood into the powers of manhood; to combine the child's sense of wonder and novelty with the appearances, which every day for perhaps forty years had rendered familiar;

'With sun and moon and stars throughout the year,
And man and woman;'

this is the character and privilege of genius, and one of the marks which distinguish genius from talents. And therefore is it the prime merit of genius and its most unequivocal mode of manifestation, so to represent familiar objects as to awaken in the minds of others a kindred feeling concerning them and that freshness of sensation which is the constant accompaniment of mental, no less than of bodily, convalescence. Who has not a thousand times seen snow fall on water? Who has not watched it with a new feeling, from the time that he has read Burns' comparison of sensual pleasure

'To snow that falls upon a river
A moment white—then gone for ever!'

In poems, equally as in philosophic disquisitions, genius produces the strongest impressions of novelty, while it rescues the most admitted truths from the impotence caused by the very circumstance of their universal admission. Truths of all others the most awful and mysterious, yet being at the same time of universal interest, are too often considered as *so* true, that they lose all the life and efficiency of truth, and lie bed-ridden in the dormitory of the soul, side by side with the most despised and exploded errors."—THE FRIEND,[26] p. 76, No. 5.

This excellence, which in all Mr. Wordsworth's writings is more or less predominant, and which constitutes the character of his mind, I no sooner felt, than I sought to understand. Repeated meditations led me first to suspect, (and a more intimate analysis of the human faculties, their appropriate marks, functions, and effects matured my conjecture into full conviction,) that fancy and imagination were two distinct and widely different faculties, instead of being, according to the general belief, either two names with one meaning, or, at furthest, the

[26] As "the Friend" was printed on stampt sheets, and sent only by the post to a very limited number of subscribers, the author has felt less objection to quote from it, though a work of his own. To the public at large indeed it is the same as a volume in manuscript.

lower and higher degree of one and the same power. It is not, I own, easy to conceive a more opposite translation of the Greek *Phantasia* than the Latin Imaginatio; but it is equally true that in all societies there exists an instinct of growth, a certain collective, unconscious good sense working progressively to desynonymize[27] those words originally of the same meaning, which the conflux of dialects had supplied to the more homogeneous languages, as the Greek and German: and which the same cause, joined with accidents of translation from original works of different countries, occasion in mixt languages like our own. The first and most important point to be proved is, that two conceptions perfectly distinct are confused under one and the same word, and (this done) to appropriate that word exclusively to one meaning, and the synonyme (should there be one) to the other. But if (as will be often the case in the arts and sciences) no synonyme exists, we must either invent or borrow a word. In the present instance the appropriation has already begun, and been legitimated in the derivative adjective: Milton had a highly *imaginative*, Cowley a very *fanciful* mind. If therefore I should succeed in establishing the actual existences of two faculties generally different, the nomenclature would be at once determined.

[27] This is effected either by giving to the one word a general, and to the other an exclusive use; as "to put on the back" and "to indorse;" or by an actual distinction of meanings, as "naturalist," and "physician;" or by difference of relation, as "I" and "Me" (each of which the rustics of our different provinces still use in all the cases singular of the first personal pronoun). Even the mere difference, or corruption, in the *pronunciation* of the same word, if it have become general, will produce a new word with a distinct signification; thus "property" and "propriety;" the latter of which, even to the time of Charles II. was the *written* word for all the senses of both. Thus too "mister" and "master," both hasty pronunciations of the same word "magister," "mistress," and "miss," "if" and "give," &c. &c. There is a sort of *minim immortal* among the animalcula infusoria which has not naturally either birth, or death, absolute beginning, or absolute end: for at a certain period a small point appears on its back, which deepens and lengthens till the creature divides into two, and the same process recommences in each of the halves now become integral. This may be a fanciful, but it is by no means a bad emblem of the formation of words, and may facilitate the conception, how immense a nomenclature may be organized from a few simple sounds by rational beings in a social state. For each new application, or excitement of the same sound, will call forth a different sensation, which cannot but affect the pronunciation. The after recollection of the sound, without the same vivid sensation, will modify it still further; till at length all trace of the original likeness is worn away.

To the faculty by which I had characterized Milton, we should confine the term *imagination;* while the other would be contra-distinguished as *fancy*. Now were it once fully ascertained, that this division is no less grounded in nature, than that of delirium from mania, or Otway's

"Lutes, lobsters, seas of milk, and ships of ambe"

from Shakespeare's

"What! have his daughters brought him to this pass?"

or from the preceding apostrophe to the elements; the theory or the fine arts, and of poetry in particular, could not, I thought, but derive some additional and important light. It would in its immediate effects furnish a torch of guidance to the philosophical critic; and ultimately to the poet himself. In energetic minds, truth soon changes by domestication into power; and from direct-ing in the discrimination and appraisal of the product, becomes influencive in the production. To admire on principle, is the only way to imitate without loss of originality.

It has been already hinted, that metaphysics and pyschology have long been my hobby-horse. But to have a hobby-horse, and to be vain of it, are so commonly found together, that they pass almost for the same. I trust therefore, that there will be more good humour than contempt, in the smile with which the reader chastises my self-complacency, if I confess myself uncertain, whether the satisfaction from the perception of a truth new to myself may not have been rendered more poignant by the con-ceit, that it would be equally so to the public. There was a time, certainly, in which I took some little credit to myself, in the belief that I had been the first of my countrymen, who had pointed out the diverse meaning of which the two terms were capable, and analyzed the faculties to which they should be appropriated. Mr. W. Taylor's recent volume of synonymes I have not yet seen;[28] but his specification of the terms in question

[28] I ought to have added, with the exception of a single sheet which I accidentally met with at the printer's. Even from this scanty speci-men, I found it impossible to doubt the talent, or not to admire the ingenuity of the author. That his distinctions were for the greater part unsatisfactory to *my* mind, proves nothing against their accuracy; but it may possibly be serviceable to him, in case of a second edition, if I take this opportunity of suggesting the query; whether he may not have been occasionally misled, by having assumed, as to me he ap-peared to have done, the non-existence of *any* absolute synonymes in our language? Now I cannot but think, that there are many which remain for our posterity to distinguish and appropriate, and which I

has been clearly shown to be both insufficient and erroneous by Mr. Wordsworth in the Preface added to the late collection of his "Lyrical Ballads and other poems." The explanation which Mr. Wordsworth has himself given will be found to differ from mine, chiefly perhaps, as our objects are different. It could scarcely indeed happen otherwise, from the advantage I have enjoyed of frequent conversation with him on a subject to which a poem of his own first directed my attention, and my conclusions concerning which, he had made more lucid to myself by many happy instances drawn from the operation of natural objects on the mind. But it was Mr. Wordsworth's purpose to consider the influences of fancy and imagination as they are manifested in poetry, and from the different effects to conclude their diversity in kind; while it is my object to investigate the seminal principle, and then from the kind to deduce the degree. My friend has drawn a masterly sketch of the branches with their *poetic* fruitage. I wish to add the trunk, and even the roots as far as they lift themselves above ground, and are visible to the naked eye of our common consciousness.

Yet even in this attempt I am aware, that I shall be obliged

---

regard as so much reversionary wealth in our mother-tongue. When two distinct meanings are confounded under one or more words, (and such must be the case, as sure as our knowledge is progressive and of course imperfect) erroneous consequences will be drawn, and what is true in one sense of the word will be affirmed as true in toto. Men of research, startled by the consequences, seek in the things themselves (whether in or out of the mind) for a knowledge of the fact, and having discovered the difference, remove the equivocation either by the substitution of a new word, or by the appropriation of one of the two or more words, that had before been used promiscuously. When this distinction has been so naturalized and of such general currency that the language itself does as it were *think* for us (like the sliding rule which is the mechanic's safe substitute for arithmetical knowledge) we then say, that it is evident to *common sense*. Common sense, therefore, differs in different ages. What was born and christened in the schools passes by degrees into the world at large, and becomes the property of the market and the tea-table. At least I can discover no other meaning of the term, *common sense*, if it is to convey any specific difference from sense and judgement in genere, and where it is not used scholastically for the *universal reason*. Thus in the reign of Charles II. the philosophic world was called to arms by the moral sophisms of Hobbs, and the ablest writers exerted themselves in the detection of an error, which a school-boy would now be able to confute by the mere recollection, that *compulsion* and *obligation* conveyed two ideas perfectly disparate, and that what appertained to the one, had been falsely transferred to the other by a mere confusion of terms.

to draw more largely on the reader's attention, than so immethodical a miscellany can authorize; when in such a work (the *Ecclesiastical Polity*) of such a mind as Hooker's, the judicious author, though no less admirable for the perspicuity than for the port and dignity of his language; and though he wrote for men of learning in a learned age; saw nevertheless occasion to anticipate and guard against "complaints of obscurity," as often as he was about to trace his subject "to the highest well-spring and fountain." Which, (continues he) "because men are not accustomed to, the pains we take are more needful a great deal, than acceptable; and the matters we handle, seem by reason of newness (till the mind grow better acquainted with them) dark and intricate." I would gladly therefore spare both myself and others this labor, if I knew how without it to present an intelligible statement of my poetic creed; not as my *opinions*, which weigh for nothing, but as deductions from established premises conveyed in such a form, as is calculated either to effect a fundamental conviction, or to receive a fundamental confutation. If I may dare once more adopt the words of Hooker, "they, unto whom we shall seem tedious, are in no wise injured by us, because it is in their own hands to spare that labor, which they are not willing to endure." Those at least, let me be permitted to add, who have taken so much pains to render me ridiculous for a perversion of taste, and have supported the charge by attributing strange notions to me on no other authority than their own conjectures, owe it to themselves as well as to me not to refuse their attention to my own statement of the theory, which I *do* acknowledge; or shrink from the trouble of examining the grounds on which I rest it, or the arguments which I offer in its justification.

CHAPTER V

On the law of association—Its history traced from Aristotle to Hartley.

THERE have been men in all ages, who have been impelled as by an instinct to propose their own nature as a problem, and who devote their attempts to its solution. The first step was to construct a table of distinctions, which they seem to have formed on the principle of the absence or presence of the WILL. Our various sensations, perceptions, and movements were classed as active or passive, or as media partaking of both. A still finer distinction was soon established between the voluntary and the spontaneous. In our perceptions we seem to ourselves merely passive to an external power, whether as a mirror reflecting the landscape, or as a blank canvas on which some unknown hand paints it. For it is worthy of notice, that the latter, or the system of idealism may be traced to sources equally remote with the former, or materialism; and Berkeley can boast an ancestry at least as venerable as Gassendi or Hobbs. These conjectures, however, concerning the mode in which our perceptions originated, could not alter the natural difference of *things* and *thoughts*. In the former, the cause appeared wholly external, while in the latter, sometimes our will interfered as the producing or determining cause, and sometimes our nature seemed to act by a mechanism of its own, without any conscious effort of the will, or even against it. Our inward experiences were thus arranged in three separate classes, the passive sense, or what the school-men call the merely receptive quality of the mind; the voluntary; and the spontaneous, which holds the middle place between both. But it is not in human nature to meditate on any mode of action, without enquiring after the law that governs it; and in the explanation of the spontaneous movements of our being, the metaphysician took the lead of the anatomist and natural philosopher. In Egypt, Palestine, Greece, and India the analysis of the mind had reached its noon and manhood, while experimental research was still in its dawn and infancy. For many, very many centuries, it has been difficult to advance a new truth, or even a new error, in the philosophy of the intellect or morals. With regard, however, to the laws that direct the spontaneous movements of thought and the principle of their intellectual mechanism there exists, it has been asserted, an important exception most honorable to the moderns, and in the merit of which our own country claims the largest share. Sir James Mackintosh, (who amid the variety of his talents and attainments is not of less repute for the depth and accuracy of his philosophical enquiries than for the eloquence with which he is said to render their most difficult results perspicuous, and the driest attractive,) affirmed in the lectures, delivered by him in Lincoln's Inn Hall, that the law of association as established in the contemporaneity of the original impressions, formed the basis of all true psychology; and any ontological or metaphysical science, not contained in such (i.e. empirical) psychology, was but a web of abstractions and generalizations. Of this prolific truth, of this great fundamental law, he declared HOBBS to have been the original *discoverer*, while its full application to the whole intellectual system we owed to David Hartley; who stood in the same relation to Hobbs as Newton to Kepler; the law of association being that to the mind, which gravitation is to matter.

Of the former clause in this assertion, as it respects the comparative merits of the ancient metaphysicians, including their commentators, the school-men, and of the modern French and British philosophers from Hobbs to Hume, Hartley, and Condillac, this is not the place to speak. So wide indeed is the chasm between this gentleman's philosophical creed and mine, that so far from being able to join hands, we could scarcely make our voices intelligible to each other: and to *bridge* it over, would require more time, skill, and power than I believe myself to possess. But the latter clause involves for the greater part a mere question of fact and history, and the accuracy of the statement is to be tried by documents rather than reasoning.

First, then, I deny Hobbs's claim in toto: for he had been anticipated by Des Cartes, whose work "De Methodo," preceded Hobbs's "De Natura Humana," by more than a year. But what is of much more importance, Hobbs builds nothing on the principle which he had announced. He does not even announce it, as differing in any respect from the general laws of material motion and impact: nor was it, indeed, possible for him so to do, compatibly with his system, which was exclusively material and mechanical. Far otherwise is it with Des Cartes; greatly as he too in his after writings (and still more egregiously his followers De la Forge, and others) obscured the truth by their attempts to explain it on the theory of nervous fluids, and material configurations. But, in his interesting work, "De Methodo," Des Cartes relates the circumstance which first led him to meditate on this subject, and which since then has been often noticed and employed as an instance and illustration of the law. A child who with its eyes bandaged had lost several of his fingers by amputation, continued to complain for many days successively of pains, now in this joint and now in that, of the very fingers which had been cut off. Des Cartes was led by this incident to reflect on the uncertainty with which we attribute any particular place to any inward pain or uneasiness, and proceeded after long consideration to establish it as a general law; that contemporaneous impressions, whether images or sensations, recal each other mechanically. On this principle, as a ground work, he built up the whole system of human language, as one continued process of association. He showed in what sense not only general terms, but generic images (under the name of abstract ideas) actually existed, and in what consists their nature and power. As one word may become the general exponent of many, so by association a simple image may represent a whole class.

But in truth Hobbs himself makes no claims to any discovery, and introduces this law of association, or (in his own language) discursûs mentalis, as an admitted fact, in the *solution* alone of which, this by causes purely physiological, he arrogates any originality. His system is briefly this; whenever the senses are impinged on by external objects, whether by the rays of light reflected from them, or by effluxes of their finer particles, there results a correspondent motion of the innermost and subtlest organs. This motion constitutes a *representation*, and there remains an *impression* of the same, or a certain disposition to repeat the same motion. Whenever we feel several objects at the same time, the *impressions* that are left, (or in the language of Mr. Hume, the *ideas*, are linked together. Whenever therefore any one of the movements, which constitute a complex impression, is renewed through the senses, the others succeed mechanically. It follows of necessity therefore that Hobbs as well as Hartley and all others who derive association from the connection and interdependence of the supposed matter, the movements of which constitute our thoughts, *must* have reduced all its forms to the one law of time. But even the merit of announcing this law with philosophic precision cannot be fairly conceded to him. For the objects of any two ideas[29] need not

---

[29] I here use the word "idea" in Mr. Hume's sense on account of its general currency amongst the English metaphysicians; though against my own judgement, for I believe that the vague use of this word has been the cause of much error and more confusion. The word, ἰδέα, in its original sense as used by Pindar, Aristophanes, and in the Gospel of St. Matthew, represented the visual abstraction of a distant object, when we see the whole without distinguishing its parts. Plato adopted it as a technical term, and as the antithesis to εἴδωλα, or sensuous images; the transient and perishable emblems, or mental words, of ideas. The ideas themselves he considered as mysterious powers, living, seminal, formative, and exempt from time. In this sense the word became the property of the Platonic school; and it seldom occurs in Aristotle, without some such phrase annexed to it, as according to Plato, or as Plato says. Our English writers to the end of Charles 2nd's reign, or somewhat later, employed it either in the original sense, or platonically, or in a sense nearly correspondent to our present use of the substantive, Ideal, always however opposing it, more or less, to image, whether of present or absent objects. The reader will not be displeased with the following interesting exemplification from Bishop Jeremy Taylor. "St. Lewis the King sent Ivo Bishop of Chartres on an embassy, and he told, that he met a grave and stately matron on the way with a censer of fire in one hand, and a vessel of water in the other; and observing her to have a melancholy, religious, and phantastic deportment and look, he asked her what those symbols meant, and

have co-existed in the same sensation in order to become mutually associable. The same result will follow when one only of the two ideas has been represented by the senses, and the other by the memory.

Long however before either Hobbs or Des Cartes the law of association had been defined, and its important functions set forth by Melanchthon, Ammerbach, and Ludovicus Vives; more especially by the last. Phantasia, it is to be noticed, is employed by Vives to express the mental power of comprehension, or the *active* function of the mind; and imaginatio for the receptivity (vis receptiva) of impressions, or for the *passive* perception. The power of combination he appropriates to the former: "Quæ singula et simpliciter acceperat imaginatio, ea conjungit et disjungit phantasia." And the law by which the thoughts are spontaneously presented follows thus; "quæ simul sunt a phantasia comprehensa, si alterutrum occurrat, solet secum alterum repræsentare." To time therefore he subordinates all the other exciting causes of association. The soul proceeds "a causa ad effectum, ab hoc ad instrumentum, a parte ad totum;" thence to the place, from place to person, and from this to whatever preceded or followed, all as being parts of a total impression, each of which may recal the other. The apparent springs "Saltus vel transitus etiam longissimos," he explains by the same thought having been a component part of two or more total impressions. Thus "ex Scipione venio in cogitationem potentiæ Turcicæ, propter victorias ejus in eâ parte Asiæ in qua regnabat Antiochus."

But from Vives I pass at once to the source of his doctrines, and (as far as we can judge from the remains yet extant of Greek philosophy) as to the first, so to the fullest and most perfect enunciation of the associative principle, viz. to the writings of Aristotle; and of these in particular to the books "De Anima,"

---

what she meant to do with her fire and water; she answered, my purpose is with the fire to burn paradise, and with my water to quench the flames of hell, that men may serve Cod purely for the love of God. But we rarely meet with such spirits which love virtue so metaphysically as *to abstract her from all sensible compositions, and love the purity of the idea.*" Des Cartes having introduced into his philosophy the fanciful hypothesis of *material ideas,* or certain configurations of the brain, which were as so many moulds to the influxes of the external world; Mr. Locke adopted the term, but extended its signification to whatever is the immediate object of the mind's attention or consciousness. Mr. Hume, distinguishing those representations which are accompanied with a sense of a present object, from those reproduced by the mind itself, designated the former by *impressions,* and confined the word *idea* to the latter.

"De Memoria," and that which is entitled in the old translations "Parva Naturalia." In as much as later writers have either deviated from, or added to his doctrines, they appear to me to have introduced either error or groundless supposition.

In the first place it is to be observed, that Aristotle's positions on this subject are unmixed with fiction. The wise Stagyrite speaks of no successive particles propagating motion like billiard balls, (as Hobbs); nor of nervous or animal spirits, where inanimate and irrational solids are thawed down, and distilled, or filtrated by ascension, into living and intelligent fluids, that etch and re-etch engravings on the brain, (as the followers of Des Cartes, and the humoral pathologists in general); nor of an oscillating ether which was to effect the same service for the nerves of the brain considered as solid fibres, as the animal spirits perform for them under the notion of hollow tubes (as *Hartley* teaches)—nor finally, (with yet more recent dreamers) of chemical compositions by elective affinity, or of an electric light at once the immediate object and the ultimate organ of inward vision, which rises to the brain like an Aurora Borealis, and there disporting in various shapes (as the balance of plus and minus, or negative and positive, is destroyed or re-established) images out both past and present. Aristotle delivers a just *theory* without pretending to an *hypothesis;* or in other words a comprehensive survey of the different facts, and of their relations to each other without *supposition,* i.e. a fact *placed under* a number of facts, as their common support and explanation; though in the majority of instances these hypotheses or suppositions better deserve the name of ὑποποιήσεις, or *suffictions.* He uses indeed the word κινήσεις, to express what we call representations or ideas, but he carefully distinguishes them from material motion, designating the latter always by annexing the words ἐν τόπῳ, or κατὰ τόπον. On the contrary, in his treatise "De Anima," he excludes place and motion from all the operations of thought, whether representations or volitions, as attributes utterly and absurdly heterogeneous.

The *general law* of association, or, more accurately, the *common condition* under which all exciting causes act, and in which they may be generalized, according to Aristotle is this. Ideas by having been together acquire a power of recalling each other; or every partial representation awakes the total representation of which it had been a part. In the practical determination of this common principle to particular recollections, he admits five agents or occasioning causes: 1st, connection in time, whether simultaneous, preceding, or successive; 2nd, vicinity or connection in space; 3rd, interdependence or necessary connection, as cause and effect; 4th, likeness: and 5th, contrast. As an additional solution of the occasional seeming chasms in the continuity of reproduction he proves, that movements or ideas possessing one or the other of these five characters had passed through the mind as intermediate links, sufficiently clear to recall other parts of the same total impressions with which they had co-existed, though not vivid enough to excite that degree of attention which is requisite for distinct recollection, or as we may aptly express it, *after-consciousness*. In association then consists the whole mechanism of the reproduction of impressions, in the Aristotelian Psychology. It is the universal law of the *passive* fancy and *mechanical* memory; that which supplies to all other faculties their objects, to all thought the elements of its materials.

In consulting the excellent commentary of St. Thomas Aquinas on the Parva Naturalia of Aristotle, I was struck at once with its close resemblance to Hume's Essay on association. The main thoughts were the same in both, the *order* of the thoughts was the same, and even the illustrations differed only by Hume's occasional substitution of more modern examples. I mentioned the circumstance to several of my literary acquaintances, who admitted the closeness of the resemblance, and that it seemed too great to be explained by mere coincidence; but they thought it improbable that Hume should have held the pages of the angelic Doctor worth turning over. But some time after Mr. Payne, of the King's mews, shewed Sir James Mackintosh some odd volumes of St. Thomas Aquinas, partly perhaps from having heard that Sir James (then Mr.) Mackintosh had in his lectures passed a high encomium on this canonized philosopher, but chiefly from the fact, that the volumes had belonged to Mr. Hume, and had here and there marginal marks and notes of reference in his own hand writing. Among these volumes was that which contains the *Parva Naturalia,* in the old Latin version, swathed and swaddled in the commentary afore mentioned!

It remains then for me, first to state wherein Hartley differs from Aristotle; then, to exhibit the grounds of my conviction, that he differed only to err; and next as the result, to shew, by what influences of the choice and judgement the associative power becomes either memory or fancy; and, in conclusion, to appropriate the remaining offices of the mind to the reason, and the imagination. With my best efforts to be as perspicuous as the nature of language will permit on such a subject, I earnestly solicit the good wishes and friendly patience of my readers, while I thus go "sounding on my dim and perilous way."

CHAPTER VI

That Hartley's system, as far as it differs from that of Aristotle, is neither tenable in theory, nor founded in facts.

OF HARTLEY's hypothetical vibrations in his hypothetical oscillating ether of the nerves, which is the first and most obvious distinction between his system and that of Aristotle, I shall say little. This, with all other similar attempts to render *that* an object of the sight which has no relation to sight, has been already sufficiently exposed by the younger Reimarus, Maasse, &c., as outraging the very axioms of mechanics in a scheme, the merit of which consists in its being mechanical. Whether any other philosophy be possible, but the mechanical; and again, whether the mechanical system can have any claim to be called philosophy; are questions for another place. It is, however, certain, that as long as we deny the former, and affirm the latter, we must bewilder ourselves, whenever we would pierce into the *adyta* or causation; and all that laborious conjecture can do, is to fill up the gaps of fancy. Under that despotism of the eye (the emancipation from which Pythagoras by his *numeral,* and Plato by his *musical* symbols, and both by geometric discipline, aimed at, as the first προπαίδευμα of the mind)—under this strong sensuous influence, we are restless because invisible things are not the objects of vision; and metaphysical systems, for the most part, become popular, not for their truth, but in proportion as they attribute to causes a susceptibility of being *seen,* if only our visual organs were sufficiently powerful.

From a hundred possible confutations let one suffice. According to this system the idea or vibration *a* from the external object A becomes associable with the idea or vibration *m* from the external object M, because the oscillation *a* propagated itself so as to re-produce the oscillation *m*. But the original impression from M was essentially different from the impression A: unless therefore different causes may produce the same effect, the vibration *a* could never produce the vibration *m*: and this therefore could never be the means, by which *a* and *m* are associated. To understand this, the attentive reader need only be reminded, that the ideas are themselves, in Hartley's system, nothing more than their appropriate configurative vibrations. It is a mere delusion of the fancy to conceive the pre-existence of the ideas, in any chain of association, as so many differently coloured billiard-balls in contact, so that when an object, the billiard-stick, strikes the first or white ball, the same motion propagates itself through the red, green, blue, and black, and sets the whole in motion. No! we must suppose the very same force, which *constitutes* the white ball, to *constitute* the red or black; or the idea of a circle to *constitute* the idea of a triangle; which is impossible.

But it may be said, that by the sensations from the objects A and M, the nerves have acquired a disposition to the vibrations *a* and *m*, and therefore *a* need only be repeated in order to re-produce *m*. Now we grant, for a moment, the possibility of such a disposition in a material nerve, which yet seems scarcely less absurd than to say, that a weather-cock had acquired a *habit* of turning to the east, from the wind having been so long in that quarter: for if it be replied, that we must take in the circumstance of *life*, what then becomes of the mechanical philosophy? And what is the *nerve*, but the flint which the wag placed in the pot as the first ingredient of his stone-broth, requiring only salt, turnips, and mutton, for the remainder! But if we waive this, and pre-suppose the actual existence of such a disposition; two cases are possible. Either, every idea has its own nerve and correspondent oscillation, or this is not the case. If the latter be the truth, we should gain nothing by these dispositions; for then, every nerve having several dispositions, when the motion of any other nerve is propagated into it, there will be no ground or cause present, why exactly the oscillation *m* should arise, rather than any other to which it was equally pre-disposed. But if we take the former, and let every idea have a nerve of its own, then every nerve must be capable of propagating its motion into many other nerves; and again, there is no reason assignable, why the vibration *m* should arise, rather than any other ad libitum.

It is fashionable to smile at Hartley's vibrations and vibratiuncles; and his work has been re-edited by Priestley, with the omission of the *material* hypothesis. But Hartley was too great a man, too coherent a thinker, for this to have been done, either consistently or to any wise purpose. For all other parts of his system, as far as they are peculiar to that system, once removed from their mechanical basis, not only lose their main support, but the very motive which led to their adoption. Thus the principle of *contemporaneity*, which Aristotle had made the common *condition* of all the laws of association, Hartley was constrained to represent as being itself the sole *law*. For to what law can the action of *material* atoms be subject, but that of proximity in *place*? And to what law can their *motions* be subjected, but that of *time*? Again, from this results inevitably, that the will, the reason, the judgement, and the understanding, instead of being the determining causes of association, must needs be represented as its *creatures*, and among its mechanical *effects*. Conceive, for instance, a broad stream, winding through a mountainous country with an indefinite number of currents, varying and running into each other according as the gusts chance to blow from the opening of the mountains. The temporary union of several currents in one, so as to form the main current of the moment, would present an accurate image of Hartley's theory of the will.

Had this been really the case, the consequence would have been, that our whole life would be divided between the despotism of outward impressions, and that of senseless and passive memory. Take his law in its highest abstraction and most philosophical form, viz. that every partial representation recalls the total representation of which it was a part; and the law becomes nugatory, were it only for its universality. In practice it would indeed be mere lawlessness. Consider, how immense must be the sphere of a total impression from the top of St. Paul's church; and how rapid and continuous the series of such total impressions. If therefore we suppose the absence of all interference of the will, reason, and judgement, one or other of two consequences must result. Either the ideas, (or relics of such impression,) will exactly imitate the order of the impression itself, which would be absolute *delirium:* or any one part of that impression might recall any other part, and (as from the law of continuity, there must exist in every total impression, some one or more parts, which are components of some other following total impression, and so on ad infinitum) *any* part of *any* impression might recall *any* part of any *other,* without a cause present to determine *what* it should be. For to bring in the will, or reason, as causes of their own cause, that is, as at once causes and effects, can satisfy those only who, in their pretended evidences of a God, having first demanded organization, as the sole cause and ground of intellect, will then coolly demand the pre-existence of intellect, as the cause and ground-work of organization. There is in truth but one state to which this theory applies at all, namely, that of complete lightheadedness; and even to this it applies but partially, because the will and reason are perhaps never wholly suspended.

A case of this kind occurred in a Catholic town in Germany a year or two before my arrival at Göttingen, and had not then ceased to be a frequent subject of conversation. A young woman of four or five and twenty, who could neither read nor write, was seized with a nervous fever; during which, according to the asseverations of all the priests and monks of the neighbourhood, she became *possessed*, and, as it appeared, by a very learned devil. She continued incessantly talking Latin, Greek, and Hebrew, in very pompous tones and with most distinct enunciation. This possession was rendered more probable by the known fact, that she was or had been a heretic. Voltaire humorously advises the devil to decline all acquaintance with medical men; and it would have been more to his reputation, if he had taken this advice in the present instance. The case had attracted the particular attention of a young physician, and by his statement, many eminent physiologists and psychologists visited the town, and cross-examined the case on the spot. Sheets full of her ravings were taken down from her own mouth, and were found to consist of sentences, coherent and intelligible each for itself, but with little or no connection with each other. Of the Hebrew, a small portion only could be traced to the Bible; the remainder seemed to be in the rabbinical dialect. All trick or conspiracy was out of the question. Not only had the young woman ever been a harmless, simple creature; but she was evidently labouring under a nervous fever. In the town, in which she had been resident for many years as a servant in different families, no solution presented itself. The young physician, however, determined to trace her past life step by step; for the patient herself was incapable of returning a rational answer. He at length succeeded in discovering the place, where her parents had lived: travelled thither, found *them* dead, but an uncle surviving; and from him learnt, that the patient had been charitably taken by an old Protestant pastor at nine years old, and had remained with him some years, even till the old man's death. Of this pastor the uncle knew nothing, but that he was a very good man. With great difficulty, and after much search, our young medical philosopher discovered a niece of the pastor's, who had lived with him as his housekeeper, and had inherited his effects. She remembered the girl; related, that her venerable uncle had been too indulgent, and could not bear to hear the girl scolded; that she was willing to have kept her, but that, after her patron's death, the girl herself refused to stay. Anxious enquiries were then, of course, made concerning the pastor's habits; and the solution of the phenomenon was soon obtained. For it appeared, that it had been the old man's custom, for years, to walk up and down a passage of his house into which the kitchen door opened, and to read to himself with a loud voice, out of his favorite books. A considerable number of these were still in the nieces possession. She added, that he was a very learned man and a great Hebraist. Among the books were found a collection of rabbinical writings, together with several of the Greek and Latin fathers; and the physician succeeded in identifying so many passages with those taken down at the young woman's bedside, that no doubt could remain in any rational mind concerning the true origin of the impressions made on her nervous system.

This authenticated case furnishes both proof and instance, that reliques of sensation may exist for an indefinite time in a latent state, in the very same order in which they were originally impressed; and as we cannot rationally suppose the feverish state of the brain to act in any other way than as a stimulus, this fact (and it would not be difficult to adduce several of the same kind) contributes to make it even probable, that all thoughts are in themselves imperishable; and, that if the intelligent faculty should be rendered more comprehensive, it would require only a different and apportioned organization, *the body celestial* instead of *the body terrestrial,* to bring before every human soul the collective experience of its whole past existence. And this, this, perchance, is the dread book of judgement, in whose mysterious hieroglyphics every idle word is recorded! Yea, in the very nature of a living spirit, it may be more possible that heaven and earth should pass away, than that a single act, a single thought, should be loosened or lost from that living chain of causes, to all whose links, conscious or unconscious, the free-will, our only absolute *self,* is co-extensive and co-present. But not now dare I longer discourse of this, waiting for a loftier mood, and a nobler subject, warned from within and from without, that it is profanation to speak of these mysteries[30] τοῖς μηδὲ φαντασθεῖσιν, ὡς καλὸν τὸ τῆς δικαιοσύνης καὶ σωφροσύνης πρόσωπον καὶ ὡς οὔτε ἕσπερος οὔτε ἑῷος οὕτω καλά. Τὸ γὰρ ὁρῶν πρὸς τὸ ὁρώμενον συγγενὲς καὶ ὁμοῖον ποιησάμενον δεῖ ἐπιβάλλειν τῇ θέᾳ. οὐ γὰρ ἂν πώποτε εἶδεν ὀφθαλμὸς ἥλιον, ἡλιοειδὴς μὴ γεγενημένος· οὐδὲ τὸ καλὸν ἂν ἴδοι ψυχή, μὴ καλὴ γενομένη.—PLOTINUS.

[30] "To those to whose imagination it has never been presented, how beautiful is the countenance of justice and wisdom; and that neither the morning nor the evening star are so fair. For in order to direct the view aright, it behoves that the beholder should have made himself congenerous and similar to the object beheld. Never could the eye have beheld the sun, had not its own essence been soliform," (*i.e. pre-configured to light by a similarity of essence with that of light*) "neither can a soul not beautiful attain to an intuition of beauty."

CHAPTER VII

Of the necessary consequences of the Hartleian theory—Of the original mistake or equivocation which procured admission for the theory —Memoria Technica.

WE WILL pass by the utter incompatibility of such a law (if law it may be called, which would itself be the slave of chances) with even that *appearance* of rationality forced upon us by the outward phænomena of human conduct, abstracted from our own consciousness. We will agree to forget this for the moment, in order to fix our attention on that subordination of final to efficient causes in the human being, which flows of necessity from the assumption, that the will and, with the will, all acts of thought and attention are parts and products of this blind mechanism, instead of being distinct powers, whose function it is to controul, determine, and modify the phantasmal chaos of association. The soul becomes a mere ens logicum; for, as a real separable being, it would be more worthless and ludicrous than the Grimalkins in the Cat-harpsichord, described in the Spectator. For these did form a part of the process; but, in Hartley's scheme, the soul is present only to be pinched or *stroked,* while the very squeals or purring are produced by an agency wholly independent and alien. It involves all the difficulties, all the incomprehensibility (if it be not indeed, ὡς ἔμοιγε δοκεῖ, the absurdity), of intercommunion between substances that have no one property in common, without any of the convenient consequences that bribed the judgement to the admission of the *dualistic* hypothesis. Accordingly, this 'caput mortuum' of the Hartleian process has been rejected by his followers, and the consciousness considered as a *result,* as a *tune,* the common product of the breeze and the harp: though this again is the mere remotion of one absurdity to make way for another, equally preposterous. For what is harmony but a mode of relation, the very *esse* of which is *percipi?* An ens rationale, which pre-supposes the power, that by perceiving creates it? The razor's edge becomes a saw to the armed vision; and the delicious melodies of Purcell or Cimarosa might be disjointed stammerings to a hearer, whose partition of time should be a thousand times subtler than ours. But this obstacle too let us imagine ourselves to have surmounted, and "at one bound high overleap all bound!" Yet according to this hypothesis the disquisition, to which I am at present soliciting the reader's attention, may be as truly said to be written by Saint Paul's church, as by *me:* for it is the mere motion of my muscles and nerves; and these again are set in motion from external causes equally passive, which external causes stand themselves in interdependent connection with every thing that exists or has existed. Thus the whole universe co-operates to produce the minutest stroke of every letter, save only that I myself, and I alone, have nothing to do with it, but merely the causeless and *effectless* beholding of it when it is done. Yet scarcely can it be called a beholding; for it is neither an act nor an effect; but an impossible creation of a *something-nothing* out of its very contrary! It is the mere quick-silver plating behind a looking-glass; and in this alone consists the poor worthless I! The sum total of my moral and intellectual intercourse, dissolved into its elements, is reduced to *extension, motion, degrees of velocity,* and those diminished *copies* of configurative motion, which form what we call notions, and notions of notions. Of such philosophy well might Butler say—

> "The metaphysic's but a puppet motion
> That goes with screws, the notion of a notion;
> The copy of a copy and lame draught
> Unnaturally taken from a thought:
> That counterfeits all pantomimic tricks,
> And turns the eyes, like an old crucifix;
> That counterchanges whatsoe'er it calls
> B' another name, and makes it true or false;
> Turns truth to falsehood, falsehood into truth,
> By virtue of the Babylonian's tooth."
>
> MISCELLANEOUS THOUGHTS.

The inventor of the watch, if this doctrine be true, did not in reality invent it; he only looked on, while the blind causes, the only true artists, were unfolding themselves. So must it have been too with my friend ALLSTON, when he sketched his picture of the dead man revived by the bones of the prophet Elijah. So must it have been with Mr. SOUTHEY and LORD BYRON, when the one *fancied* himself composing his "RODERICK," and the other his "CHILDE HAROLD." The same must hold good of all systems of philosophy; of all arts, governments, wars by sea and by land; in short, of all things that ever have been or that ever will be produced. For, according to this system, it is not the affections and passions that are at work, in as far as they are *sensations* or *thoughts.* We only *fancy,* that we act from rational resolves, or prudent motives, or from impulses of anger, love, or generosity. In all these cases the real agent is a *something-nothing-every-thing*, which does all of which we know, and knows nothing of all that itself does.

The existence of an infinite spirit, of an intelligent and holy will, must, on this system, be mere articulated motions of the air. For as the function of the human understanding is no other than merely (to appear to itself) to combine and to apply the phænomena of the association; and as these derive all their reality from the primary sensations; and the sensations again all *their* reality from the impressions ab extra; a God not visible, audible, or tangible, can exist only in the sounds and letters that form his name and attributes. If in *ourselves* there be no such faculties as those of the will, and the scientific reason, we must either have an *innate* idea of them, which would overthrow the whole system; or we can have no idea at all. The process, by which Hume degraded the notion of cause and effect into a blind product of delusion and habit, into the mere sensation of *proceeding* life (nisus vitalis) associated with the images of the memory; this same process must be repeated to the equal degradation of every *fundamental* idea in ethics or theology.

Far, very far am I from burthening with the odium of these consequences the moral characters of those who first formed, or have since adopted the system! It is most noticeable of the excellent and pious Hartley, that, in the proofs of the existence and attributes of God, with which his second volume commences, he makes no reference to the principle or results of the first. Nay, he assumes, as his foundations, ideas which, if we embrace the doctrines of his first volume, can exist no where but in the vibrations of the ethereal medium common to the nerves and to the atmosphere. Indeed the whole of the second volume is, with the fewest possible exceptions, independent of his peculiar system. So true is it, that the faith, which saves and sanctifies, is a collective energy, a total act of the whole moral being; that its living sensorium is in the *heart;* and that no errors of the understanding can be morally arraigned unless they have proceeded from the heart.—But whether they be such, no man can be certain in the case of another, scarcely perhaps even in his own. Hence it follows by inevitable consequence, that man may perchance determine *what* is an heresy;' but God only can know, *who* is a heretic. It does not, however, by any means follow that opinions fundamentally false are harmless. An hundred causes may co-exist to form one complex antidote. Yet the sting of the adder remains venomous, though there are many who have taken up the evil thing; and it hurted them not! Some indeed there seem to have been, in an unfortunate neighbour-nation at least who have embraced this system with a full view of all its moral and religious consequences; some—

> "——— who deem themselves most free,
> When they within this gross and visible sphere
> Chain down the winged thought, scoffing ascent,
> Proud in their meanness; and themselves they cheat
> With noisy emptiness of learned phrase,
> Their subtle fluids, impacts, essences,
> Self-working tools, uncaus'd effects, and all
> Those blind omniscients, those Almighty slaves,
> Untenanting Creation of its God!"

Such men need discipline, not argument; they must be made better men, before they can become wiser.

The attention will be more profitably employed in attempting to discover and expose the paralogisms, by the magic of which such a faith could find admission into minds framed for a nobler creed. These, it appears to me, may be all reduced to one sophism as their common genus; the mistaking the *conditions* of a thing for its *causes* and *essence;* and the process, by which we arrive at the knowledge of a faculty, for the faculty itself. The air I breathe is the *condition* of my life, not its cause. We could never have learnt that we had eyes but by the process of seeing; yet having seen we know that the eyes must have pre-existed in order to render the process of sight possible. Let us cross-examine Hartley's scheme under the guidance of this distinction; and we shall discover, that contemporaneity, (Leibnitz's *Lex Continui,*) is the *limit and condition* of the laws of mind, itself being rather a law of matter, at least of phænomena considered as material. At the utmost, it is to *thought* the same, as the law of gravitation is to loco-motion. In every voluntary movement we first counteract gravitation, in order to avail ourselves of it. It must exist, that there may be a something to be counteracted, and which, by its re-action, may aid the force that is exerted to resist it. Let us consider what we do when we leap. We first resist the gravitating power by an act purely voluntary, and then by another act, voluntary in part, we yield to it in order to light on the spot, which we had previously proposed to ourselves. Now let a man watch his mind while he is composing; or, to take a still more common case, while he is trying to recollect a name; and he will find the process completely analogous. Most of my readers will have observed a small water-insect on the surface of rivulets, which throws a cinque-spotted shadow fringed with prismatic colours on the sunny bottom of the brook; and will have noticed, how the little animal *wins* its way up against the stream, by alternate pulses of active and passive motion, now resisting the current, and now yielding to it in order to gather strength and a momentary *fulcrum* for a further propulsion. This is no unapt emblem of the mind's self-experience in the act of thinking. There are evidently two powers at work, which relatively to each other are active and passive; and this is not possible without an intermediate faculty, which is at once both active and passive. (In philosophical language, we must denominate this intermediate faculty in all its degrees and determinations, the IMAGINATION. But, in common language, and especially on the subject of poetry, we appropriate the name to a superior degree of the faculty, joined to a superior voluntary controul over it.)

Contemporaneity, then, being the common condition of all the laws of association, and a component element in all the materia subjecta, the parts of which are to be associated, must needs be co-present with all. Nothing, therefore, can be more easy than to pass off on an incautious mind this constant companion of each, for the essential substance of all. But if we appeal to our own consciousness, we shall find that even time itself, as the *cause* of a *particular* act of association, is distinct from contemporaneity, as the *condition* of *all* association. Seeing a mackerel, it may happen, that I immediately think of gooseberries, because I at the same time ate mackerel with gooseberries as the sauce. The first syllable of the latter word, being that which had co-existed with the image of the bird so called, I may then think of a goose. In the next moment the image of a swan may arise before me, though I had never seen the two birds together. In the two former instances, I am conscious that their co-existence in *time* was the circumstance, that enabled me to recollect them; and equally conscious am I that the latter was recalled to me by the joint operation of likeness and contrast. So it is with *cause* and *effect;* so too with *order*. So I am able to distinguish whether it was proximity in time, or continuity in space, that occasioned me to recall B. on the mention of A. They cannot be indeed *separated* from contemporaneity; for that would be to separate them from the mind itself. The act of consciousness is indeed identical with *time* considered in its essence. (I mean *time* per se, as contra-distinguished from our *notion* of time; for this is always blended with the idea of space, which, as the *contrary* of time, is therefore its *measure*.) Nevertheless the accident of seeing two objects at the same moment acts as a distinguishable cause from that of having seen them at the same place:

and the true practical general law of association is this; that whatever makes certain parts of a total impression more vivid or distinct than the rest, will determine the mind to recall these in preference to others equally linked together by the common condition of contemporaneity, or (what I deem a more appropriate and philosophical term) of *continuity*. But the will itself by confining and intensifying[31] the attention may arbitrarily give vividness or distinctness to any object whatsoever; and from hence we may deduce the uselessness, if not the absurdity, of certain recent schemes which *promise* an artificial *memory,* but which in reality can only produce a confusion and debasement of the *fancy.* Sound logic, as the habitual subordination of the individual to the species, and of the species to the genus; philosophical knowledge of facts under the relation of cause and effect; a chearful and communicative temper disposing us to notice the similarities and contrasts of things, that we may be able to illustrate the one by the other; a quiet conscience; a condition free from anxieties; sound health, and above all (as far as relates to passive remembrance) a healthy digestion; *these* are the best, these are the only ARTS OF MEMORY.

CHAPTER VIII

The system of DUALISM *introduced by Des Cartes—Refined first by Spinoza and afterwards by Leibnitz into the doctrine of Harmonia præstabilita—Hylozoism—Materialism—Neither of these systems, or any possible theory of association, supplies or supersedes a theory of perception, or explains the formation of the associable.*

To THE best of my knowledge Des Cartes was the first philosopher, who introduced the absolute and essential heterogeneity of the soul as intelligence, and the body as matter. The assumption, and the form of speaking have remained, though the denial of all other properties to matter but that of extension, on which

[31] I am aware, that this word occurs neither in Johnson's Dictionary or in any classical writer. But the word, *"to intend,"* which Newton and others before him employ in this sense, is now so completely appropriated to another meaning, that I could not use it without ambiguity: while to paraphrase the sense, as by *render intense,* would often break up the sentence and destroy that harmony of the position of the words with the logical position of the thoughts, which is a beauty in all composition, and more especially desirable in a close philosophical investigation. I have therefore hazarded the word, *intensify:* though, I confess, it sounds uncouth to my own ear.

denial the whole system of dualism is grounded, has been long exploded. For since impenetrability is intelligible only as a mode of resistance; its admission places the essence of *matter* in an act or power, which it possesses in common with *spirit;* and body and spirit are therefore no longer absolutely heterogeneous, but *may* without any *absurdity* be supposed to be different modes, or degrees in perfection, of a common substratum. To this possibility, however, it was not the fashion to advert. The soul was a *thinking* substance; and body a *space-filling* substance. Yet the apparent action of each on the other pressed heavy on the philosopher on the one hand; and no less heavily on the other hand pressed the evident truth, that the law of causality holds only between homogeneous things, i.e. things having some common property; and cannot extend from one world into another, its opposite. A close analysis evinced it to be no less absurd than the question whether a man's affection for his wife, lay North-east, or South-west of the love he bore towards his child. Leibnitz's doctrine of a pre-established harmony, which he certainly borrowed from Spinoza, who had himself taken the hint from Des Cartes's animal machines, was in its *common* interpretation too strange to survive the inventor—too repugnant to our *common sense;* (which is not indeed entitled to a judicial voice in the courts of scientific philosophy, but whose whispers still exert a strong secret influence). Even Wolf, the admirer and illustrious systematizer of the Leibnitzian doctrine, contents himself with defending the possibility of the idea, but does not adopt it as a part of the edifice.

The hypothesis of Hylozoism on the other side, is the death of all rational physiology, and indeed of all physical science; for that requires a limitation of terms, and cannot consist with the arbitrary power of multiplying attributes by occult qualities. Besides, it answers no purpose; unless, indeed, a difficulty can be solved by multiplying it, or that we can acquire a clearer notion of our soul, by being told that we have a million souls, and that every atom of our bodies has a soul of its own. Far more prudent is it to admit the difficulty once for all, and then let it lie at rest. There is a sediment indeed at the bottom of the vessel, but all the water above it is clear and transparent. The Hylozoist only shakes it up, and renders the whole turbid.

But it is not either the nature of man, or the duty of the philosopher to despair concerning any important problem until, as in the squaring of the circle, the impossibility of a solution has been demonstrated. How the *esse*, assumed as originally distinct from the *scire*, can ever unite itself with it; how *being* can transform itself into a *knowing*, becomes conceivable on one only condition; namely, if it can be shown that the *vis representativa*, or the Sentient, is itself a species of being; i.e. either as a property or attribute, or as an hypostasis or self subsistence. The former is, indeed, the assumption of materialism; a system which could not but be patronized by the philosopher, if only it actually performed what it promises. But how any affection from without can metamorphose itself into perception or will, the materialist has hitherto left, not only as incomprehensible as he found it, but has aggravated it into a comprehensible absurdity. For, grant that an object from without could act upon the conscious *self*, as on a consubstantial object; yet such an affection could only engender something homogeneous with itself. Motion could only propagate motion. Matter has no *Inward*. We remove one surface, but to meet with another. We can but divide a particle into particles; and each atom comprehends in itself the properties of the material universe. Let any reflecting mind make the experiment of explaining to itself the evidence of our sensuous intuitions, from the hypothesis that in any given perception there is a something which has been communicated to it by an impact, or an impression ab extra. In the first place, by the impact on the percepient, or ens representans, not the object itself, but only its action or effect, will pass into the same. Not the iron tongue, but its vibrations, pass into the metal of the bell. Now in our immediate perception, it is not the mere power or act of the object, but the object itself, which is immediately present. We might indeed attempt to explain this result by a chain of *deductions* and *conclusions;* but that, first, the very faculty of deducing and concluding would equally demand an explanation; and secondly, that there exists in fact no such intermediation by logical notions, such as those of cause and effect. It is the object itself, not the product of a syllogism, which is present to our consciousness. Or would we explain this supervention of the object to the sensation, by a productive faculty set in motion by an impulse; still the transition, into the percepient, of the object itself, from which the impulse proceeded, assumes a power that can permeate and wholly possess the soul,

> "And like a God by spiritual art,
> Be all in all, and all in every part."
>   COWLEY.

And how came the *percipient* here? And what is become of the wonder-promising MATTER, that was to perform all these marvels by force of mere figure, weight and motion? The most consistent proceeding of the dogmatic materialist is to fall back into the common rank of *soul-and-bodyists;* to affect the mysterious, and declare the whole process a revelation *given,* and not to be *understood,* which it would be prophane to examine too closely. "Datur non intelligitur." But a revelation unconfirmed by miracles, and a faith not commanded by the conscience, a philosopher may venture to pass by, without suspecting himself of any irreligious tendency.

Thus, as materialism has been generally taught, it is utterly unintelligible, and owes all its proselytes to the propensity so common among men, to mistake distinct images for clear conceptions; and vice versa, to reject as inconceivable whatever from its own nature is unimaginable. But as soon as it becomes intelligible, it ceases to be materialism. In order to explain *thinking,* as a material phænomenon, it is necessary to refine matter into a mere modification of intelligence, with the two-fold function of *appearing* and *perceiving.* Even so did Priestley in his controversy with Price! He stript matter of all its material properties; substituted spiritual powers; and when we expected to find a body, behold! we had nothing but its ghost! the apparition of a defunct substance!

I shall not dilate further on this subject; because it will, (if God grant health and permission), be treated of at large and systematically in a work, which I have many years been preparing, on the PRODUCTIVE LOGOS human and divine; with, and as the introduction to, a full commentary on the Gospel of St. John. To make myself intelligible as far as my present subject requires, it will be sufficient briefly to observe.—1. That all association demands and presupposes the existence of the thoughts and images to be associated.—2. The hypothesis of an external world exactly correspondent to those images or modifications of our own being, which alone, (according to this system), we actually behold, is as thorough idealism as Berkeley's, inasmuch as it equally, (perhaps, in a more perfect degree,) removes all reality and immediateness of perception, and places us in a dream world of phantoms and spectres, the inexplicable swarm and equivocal generation of motions in our own brains.—3. That this hypothesis neither involves the explanation, nor precludes the necessity, of a mechanism and co-adequate forces in the percipient, which at the more than magic touch of the impulse from without is to create anew for itself the correspondent object. The formation of a copy is not solved by the mere pre-existence of an original; the copyist of Raphael's Transfiguration must repeat more or less perfectly the process of Raphael. It would be easy to explain a thought from the image on the retina, and that from the geometry of light, if this very light did not present the very same difficulty. We might as rationally chant the Brahmin creed of the tortoise that supported the bear, that supported the elephant, that supported the world, to the tune of "This is the house that Jack built." The *sic Deo placitum est* we all admit as the sufficient cause, and the divine goodness as the sufficient reason; but an answer to the whence? and why? is no answer to the how? which alone is the physiologist's concern. It is a mere sophisma pigrum, and (as Bacon hath said) the arrogance of pusillanimity, which lifts up the idol of a mortal's fancy and commands us to fall down and worship it, as a work of divine wisdom, an ancile or palladium fallen from heaven. By the very same argument the supporters of the Ptolemaic system might have rebuffed the Newtonian, and pointing to the sky with self-complacent[32] grin have appealed to *common sense*, whether the sun did not move and the earth stand still.

CHAPTER IX

Is philosophy possible as a science, and what are its conditions?—Giordano Bruno—Literary aristocracy, or the existence of a tacit compact among the learned as a privileged order—The author's obligations to the Mystics;—to Immanuel Kant—The difference between the letter and the spirit of Kant's writings, and a vindication of prudence in the teaching of philosophy—Fichte's attempt to complete the critical system—Its partial success and ultimate failure—Obligations to Schelling; and among English writers to Saumarez.

AFTER I had successively studied in the schools of Locke, Berkeley, Leibnitz, and Hartley, and could find in neither of them an abiding place for my reason, I began to ask myself; is a system of philosophy, as different from mere history and historic classification, possible? If possible, what are its necessary conditions? I was for a while disposed to answer the first question in the negative, and to admit that the sole practicable employment for the human mind was to observe, to collect, and to classify. But I soon felt, that human nature itself fought up against this wilful resignation of intellect; and as soon did I find, that the scheme taken with all its consequences and cleared of all inconsistencies, was not less impracticable than contra-natural. Assume in its full extent the position, *nihil in intellectu quod*

---

[32] "And Coxcombs vanquish Berkeley with a grin." *Pope.*

non prius in sensu, without Leibnitz's qualifying *præter ipsum intellectum,* and in the same sense, in which the position was understood by Hartley and Condillac: and what Hume had demonstratively deduced from this concession concerning cause and effect, will apply with equal and crushing force to all the[33] other eleven categorical forms, and the logical functions corresponding to them. How can we make bricks without straw? or build without cement? We learn all things indeed by *occasion* of experience; but the very facts so learnt force us inward on the antecedents, that must be pre-supposed in order to render experience itself possible. The first book of Locke's Essays, (if the supposed error, which it labors to subvert, be not a mere thing of straw, an absurdity which no man ever did, or indeed ever could, believe,) is formed on a σόφισμα ἑτεροζητήσεως, and involves the old mistake of *Cum hoc: ergo, propter hoc.*

The term, Philosophy, defines itself as an affectionate seeking after the truth; but Truth is the correlative of Being. This again is no way conceivable, but by assuming as a postulate, that both are *ab initio,* identical and co-inherent; that intelligence and being are reciprocally each other's substrate. I presumed that this was a possible conception, (*i.e.* that it involved no logical inconsonance,) from the length of time during which the scholastic definition of the *Supreme Being,* as "actus purissimus sine ulla potentialitate," was received in the schools of Theology, both by the Pontifician and the Reformed divines. The early study of Plato and Plotinus, with the commentaries and the THEOLOGIA PLATONICA of the illustrious Florentine; of Proclus, and Gemistius Pletho; and at a later period of the "De Immenso et Innumerabili," and the *"De la causa, principio ed uno,"* of the philosopher of Nola, who could boast of a Sir Philip Sidney and Fulke Greville among his patrons, and whom the idolaters of Rome burnt as an atheist in the year 1660; had all contributed to prepare my mind for the reception and welcoming of the "Cogito quia sum, et sum quia Cogito"; a philosophy of seeming hardihood, but certainly the most ancient, and therefore presumptively the most natural.

Why need I be afraid? Say rather how dare I be ashamed of the Teutonic theosophist, Jacob Behmen? Many indeed, and gross were his delusions; and such as furnish frequent and ample occasion for the triumph of the learned over the poor ignorant *shoemaker,* who had dared think for himself. But while we re-

[33] Videlicet; quantity, quality, relation, and mode, each consisting of three subdivisions. Vide Kritik der reinen Vernunft, pp. 95 and 106. See too the judicious remarks on Locke and Hume.

member that these delusions were such, as might be anticipated from his utter want of all intellectual discipline, and from his ignorance of rational psychology, let it not be forgotten that the latter defect he had in common with the most learned theologians of his age. Neither with books, nor with book-learned men was he conversant. A meek and shy quietist, his intellectual powers were never stimulated into fev'rous energy by crowds of proselytes, or by the ambition of proselytizing. JACOB BEHMEN was an enthusiast, in the strictest sense, as not merely distinguished, but as contra-distinguished, from a fanatic. While I in part translate the following observations from a contemporary writer of the Continent, let me be permitted to premise, that I might have transcribed the substance from memoranda of my own, which were written many years before his pamphlet was given to the world; and that I prefer another's words to my own, partly as a tribute due to priority of publication; but still more from the pleasure of sympathy in a case where *coincidence* only was possible.

Whoever is acquainted with the history of philosophy, during the two or three last centuries, cannot but admit, that there appears to have existed a sort of secret and tacit compact among the learned, not to pass beyond a certain limit in speculative science. The privilege of free thought, so highly extolled, has at no time been held valid in actual practice, except within this limit; and not a single stride beyond it has ever been ventured without bringing obloquy on the transgressor. The few men of genius among the learned class, who actually did overstep this boundary, anxiously avoided the appearance of having so done. Therefore the true depth of science, and the penetration to the inmost centre, from which all the lines of knowledge diverge to their ever distant circumference, was abandoned to the illiterate and the simple, whom unstilled yearning, and an original ebulliency of spirit, had urged to the investigation of the indwelling and living ground of all things. These, then, because their names had never been inrolled in the guilds of the learned, were persecuted by the registered livery-men as interlopers on their rights and priviledges. All without distinction were branded as fanatics and phantasts; not only those, whose wild and exorbitant imaginations had actually engendered only extravagant and grotesque phantasms, and whose productions were, for the most part, poor copies and gross caricatures of genuine inspiration; but the truly inspired likewise, the originals themselves. And this for no other reason, but because they were the *unlearned,* men of humble and obscure occupations. When, and from whom among the literati by profession, have we ever heard the divine doxology repeated, "I thank thee, O Father! Lord of Heaven and Earth! because thou hast hid these things from the wise and prudent, and hast revealed them unto babes." No; the haughty priests of learning not only banished from the schools and marts of science all who had dared draw living waters from the *fountain*, but drove them out of the very temple, which mean time *"the buyers, and sellers, and money-changers"* were suffered to make *"a den of thieves."*

And yet it would not be easy to discover any substantial ground for this contemptuous pride in those literati, who have most distinguished themselves by their scorn of BEHMEN, DE THOYRAS, GEORGE FOX, etc.; unless it be, that *they* could write orthographically, make smooth periods, and had the fashions of authorship almost literally *at their fingers' ends*, while the latter in simplicity of soul, made their words immediate echoes of their feelings. Hence the frequency of those phrases among them, which have been mistaken for pretences to immediate inspiration; as for instance, *"it was delivered unto me;" "I strove not to speak;" "I said, I will be silent;" "but the word was in my heart as a burning fire;" "and I could not forbear."* Hence too the unwillingness to give offence; hence the foresight, and the dread of the clamours, which would be raised against them, so frequently avowed in the writings of these men, and expressed, as was natural, in the words of the only book, with which they were familiar. "Woe is me that I am become a man of strife, and a man of contention,—I love peace: the souls of men are dear unto me: yet because I seek for Light every one of them doth curse me!" O! it requires deeper feeling, and a stronger imagination, than belong to most of those, to whom reasoning and fluent expression have been as a trade learnt in boyhood, to conceive with what *might*, with what inward *strivings* and *commotion*, the perception of a new and vital TRUTH takes possession of an uneducated man of genius. His meditations are almost inevitably employed on the eternal, or the everlasting; for *"the world is not his friend, nor the world's law."* Need we then be surprised, that, under an excitement at once so strong and so unusual, the man's body should sympathize with the struggles of his mind; or that he should at times be so far deluded, as to mistake the tumultuous sensations of his nerves, and the co-existing spectres of his fancy, as parts or symbols of the truths which were opening on him? It has indeed been plausibly observed, that in order to derive any advantage, or to collect any intelligible meaning, from the writings of these ignorant mystics, the reader must bring with him a spirit and judgement superior to that of the writers themselves:

> "And what he brings, what needs he elsewhere seek?"
> PARADISE REGAINED.

—A sophism, which I fully agree with Warburton, is unworthy of Milton; how much more so of the awful person, in whose mouth he has placed it? One assertion I will venture to make, as suggested by my own experience, that there exist folios on the human understanding, and the nature of man, which would have a far juster claim to their high rank and celebrity, if in the whole huge volume there could be found as much fulness of heart and intellect, as burst forth in many a simple page of GEORGE FOX, JACOB BEHMEN, and even of Behmen's commentator, the pious and fervid WILLIAM LAW.

The feeling of gratitude, which I cherish towards these men, has caused me to digress further than I had foreseen or proposed; but to have passed them over in an historical sketch of my literary life and opinions, would have seemed to me like the denial of a debt, the concealment of a boon. For the writings of these mystics acted in no slight degree to prevent my mind from being imprisoned within the outline of any single dogmatic system. They contributed to keep alive the *heart* in the *head;* gave me an indistinct, yet stirring and working presentiment, that all the products of the mere *reflective* faculty partook of DEATH, and were as the rattling twigs and sprays in winter, into which a sap was yet to be propelled from some root to which I had not penetrated, if they were to afford my soul either food or shelter. It they were too often a moving cloud of smoke to me by day, yet they were always a pillar of fire throughout the night, during my wanderings through the wilderness of doubt, and enabled me to skirt, without crossing, the sandy deserts of utter unbelief. That the system is capable of being converted into an irreligious PANTHEISM, I well know. The ETHICS of SPINOZA, may, or may not, be an instance. But at no time could I believe, that *in itself* and *essentially* it is incompatible with religion, natural or revealed: and now I am most thoroughly persuaded of the contrary. The writings of the illustrious sage of Königsberg, the founder of the Critical Philosophy, more than any other work, at once invigorated and disciplined my understanding. The originality, the depth, and the compression of the thoughts; the novelty and subtlety, yet solidity and importance of the distinctions; the adamantine chain of the logic; and I will venture to add (paradox as it will appear to those who have taken their notion of IMMANUEL KANT from Reviewers and Frenchmen) the *clearness* and *evidence,* of the "CRITIQUE OF THE PURE REASON;" of the "JUDGEMENT;" of the "METAPHYSICAL ELEMENTS OF NATURAL PHILOSOPHY;" and of his "RELIGION WITHIN THE BOUNDS OF PURE REASON," took possession of me as with a giant's hand. After fifteen years' familiarity with them, I still read these and all his other productions with undiminished delight and increasing admiration. The few passages that remained obscure to me, after due efforts of thought, (as the chapter on *original apperception,*) and the apparent contradictions which occur, I soon found were hints and insinuations referring to ideas, which KANT either did not think it prudent to avow, or which he considered as consistently *left behind* in a pure analysis, not of human nature in toto, but of the speculative intellect alone. Here therefore he was constrained to commence at the point of *reflection,* or natural consciousness: while in his *moral* system he was permitted to assume a higher ground (the autonomy of the will) as a POSTULATE deducible from the unconditional command, or (in the technical language of his school) the categorical imperative, of the conscience. He had been in imminent danger of persecution during the reign of the late king of Prussia, that strange compound of lawless debauchery and priest-ridden superstition: and it is probable that he had little inclination, in his old age, to act over again the fortunes, and hair-breadth escapes of Wolf. The expulsion of the first among Kant's disciples, who attempted to complete his system, from the university of Jena, with the confiscation and prohibition of the obnoxious work by the joint efforts of the courts of Saxony and Hanover, supplied experimental proof, that the venerable old man's caution was not groundless. In spite therefore of his own declarations, I could never believe, that it was possible for him to have meant no more by his *Noumenon,* or THING IN ITSELF, than his mere words express; or that in his own conception he confined the whole *plastic* power to the forms of the intellect, leaving for the external cause, for the *materiale* of our sensations, a matter without form, which is doubtless inconceivable. I entertained doubts likewise, whether in his own mind he even laid *all* the stress, which he appears to do, on the moral postulates.

An IDEA, in the *highest* sense of that word, cannot be conveyed but by a *symbol;* and, except in geometry, all symbols of necessity involve an apparent contradiction. Φώνησε συνετοίσιν: and for those who could not pierce through this symbolic husk, his writings were not intended. Questions which cannot be fully answered without exposing the respondent to personal danger, are not entitled to a fair answer; and yet to say this openly, would in many cases furnish the very advantage which the adversary is insidiously seeking after. Veracity does not consist in *saying*, but in the intention of *communicating*, truth; and the philosopher who cannot utter the whole truth without conveying falsehood, and at the same time, perhaps, exciting the most malignant passions, is constrained to express himself either *mythically* or equivocally. When Kant therefore was importuned to settle the disputes of his commentators himself, by declaring what he meant, how could he decline the honours of martyrdom with less offence, than by simply replying, "I meant what I said, and at the age of near fourscore, I have something else, and more important to do, than to write a commentary on my own works."

FICHTE's Wissenschaftslehre, or *Lore* of Ultimate Science, was to add the key-stone of the arch: and by commencing with an *act*, instead of a *thing* or *substance*, Fichte assuredly gave the first mortal blow to Spinozism, as taught by Spinoza himself; and supplied the *idea* of a system truly metaphysical, and of a *metaphysique* truly systematic: (i.e. having its spring and principle within itself). But this fundamental idea he overbuilt with a heavy mass of mere *notions*, and psychological acts of arbitrary reflection. Thus his theory degenerated into a crude[34] egoismus,

---

[34] The following burlesque on the Fichtean Egoismus may, perhaps, be amusing to the few who have studied the system, and to those who are unacquainted with it, may convey as tolerable a likeness of Fichte's idealism as can be expected from an avowed caricature.

The categorical imperative, or the annunciation of the new Teutonic God, 'ΕΓΩΕΝΚΑΙΠΑΝ: a dithyrambic Ode, by QUERKOPF VON KLUBSTICK, Grammarian, and Subrector in Gymnasio * * *

"Eu! Dei vices gerens, ipse Divus,
  (*Speak English, Friend!*) the God Imperativus,
Here on this market-cross aloud I cry:
I, I, I! I itself I!
The form and the substance, the what and the why,
The when and the where, and the low and the high,
The inside and outside, the earth and the sky,
I, you, and he, and he, you and I,
All souls and all bodies are I itself I!
          All I itself I!
      (Fools! a truce with this starting!)
          All my I! all my I!
He's a heretic dog who but adds Betty Martin!
Thus cried the God with high imperial tone:
In robe of stiffest state, that scoff'd at beauty,
A pronoun-verb imperative he shone—

a boastful and hyperstoic hostility to NATURE, as lifeless, godless, and altogether unholy: while his *religion* consisted in the assumption of a mere ORDO ORDINANS, which we were permitted *exotericé* to call GOD; and his *ethics* in an ascetic, and almost monkish, mortification of the natural passions and desires.

In Schelling's "NATUR-PHILOSOPHIE," and the "SYSTEM DES TRANSCENDENTALEN IDEALISMUS," I first found a genial coincidence with much that I had toiled out for myself, and a powerful assistance in what I had yet to do.

I have introduced this statement, as appropriate to the narrative nature of this sketch; yet rather in reference to the work which I have announced in a preceding page, than to my present subject. It would be but a mere act of justice to myself, were I to warn my future readers, that an identity of thought, or even similarity of phrase, will not be at all times a certain proof that the passage has been borrowed from Schelling, or that the conceptions were originally learnt from him. In this instance, as in the dramatic lectures of Schlegel to which I have before alluded, from the same motive of self-defence against the charge of plagiarism, many of the most striking resemblances, indeed all the main and fundamental ideas, were born and matured in my mind before I had ever seen a single page of the German Philosopher; and I might indeed affirm with truth, before the more important works of Schelling had been written, or at least made public. Nor is this coincidence at all to be wondered at. We had studied in the same school; been disciplined by the same preparatory philosophy, namely, the writings of Kant; we had both equal obligations to the polar logic and dynamic philosophy of Giordano Bruno; and Schelling has lately, and, as of recent acquisition, avowed that same affectionate reverence for the la-

---

Then substantive and plural-singular grown
He thus spake on! Behold in I alone
(For ethics boast a syntax of their own)
Or if in ye, yet as I doth depute ye,
In O! I, you, the vocative of duty!
I of the world's whole Lexicon the root!
Of the whole universe of touch, sound, sight
The genitive and ablative to boot:
The accusative of wrong, the nom'native of right,
And in all cases the case absolute!
Self-construed, I all other moods decline:
Imperative, from nothing we derive us;
Yet as a super-postulate of mine,
Unconstrued antecedence I assign
To X, Y, Z, the God infinitivus!"

bours of Behmen, and other mystics, which I had formed **at a** much earlier period. The coincidence of SCHELLING's system with certain general ideas of Behmen, he declares to have been *mere* coincidence; while *my* obligations have been more direct. *He* needs give to Behmen only feelings of sympathy; while I owe him a debt of gratitude. God forbid! that I should be suspected of a wish to enter into a rivalry with Schelling for the honours so unequivocally his right, not only as a great and original genius, but as the *founder* of the PHILOSOPHY OF NATURE, and as the most successful *improver* of the Dynamic[35] System which, begun

[35] It would be an act of high and almost criminal injustice to pass over in silence the name of Mr. RICHARD SAUMAREZ, a gentleman equally well known as a medical man and as a philanthropist, but who demands notice on the present occasion as the author of "A new System of Physiology" in two volumes octavo, published 1797; and in 1812 of "An Examination of the natural and artificial Systems of Philosophy which now prevail" in one volume octavo, entitled, "The Principles of physiological and physical Science." The latter work is not quite equal to the former in style or arrangement; and there is a greater necessity of distinguishing the principles of the author's philosophy from his conjectures concerning colour, the atmospheric matter, comets, &c. which, whether just or erroneous, are by no means necessary consequences of that philosophy. Yet even in this department of this volume, which I regard as comparatively the inferior work, the reasonings by which Mr. Saumarez invalidates the immanence of an infinite power in any finite substance are the offspring of no common mind; and the experiment on the expansibility of the air is at least plausible and highly ingenious. But the merit, which will secure both to the book and to the writer a high and honorable name with posterity, consists in the masterly force of reasoning, and the copiousness of induction, with which he has assailed, and (in my opinion) subverted the tyranny of the mechanic system in physiology; established not only the existence of final causes, but their necessity and efficiency in every system that merits the name of philosophical; and, substituting life and progressive power for the contradictory *inert force,* has a right to be known and remembered as the first instaurator of the dynamic philosophy in England. The author's views, as far as concerns himself, are unborrowed and compleatly his own, as he neither possessed nor do his writings discover, the least acquaintance with the works of Kant, in which the germs of the philosophy exist; and his volumes were published many years before the full development of these germs by Schelling. Mr. Saumarez's detection of the Braunonian system was no light or ordinary service at the time; and I scarcely remember in any work on any subject a confutation so thoroughly satisfactory. It is sufficient at this time to have stated the fact; as in the preface to the work, which I have already announced on the Logos, I have exhibited in detail the merits of this writer, and genuine philoso-

by Bruno, was re-introduced (in a more philosophical form, and freed from all its impurities and visionary accompaniments) by KANT; in whom it was the native and necessary growth of his own system. Kant's followers, however, on whom (for the greater part) their master's *cloak* had fallen without, or with a very scanty portion of, his *spirit,* had adopted his dynamic ideas, only as a more refined species of mechanics. With the exception of one or two fundamental ideas, which cannot be with-held from FICHTE, to SCHELLING we owe the completion, and the most important victories, of this revolution in philosophy. To me it will be happiness and honor enough, should I succeed in rendering the system itself intelligible to my countrymen, and in the application of it to the most awful of subjects for the most important of purposes. Whether a work is the offspring of a man's own spirit, and the product of original thinking, will be discovered by those who are its sole legitimate judges, by better tests than the mere reference to dates. For readers in general, let whatever shall be found in this or any future work of mine, that resembles, or coincides with, the doctrines of my German predecessor, though contemporary, be wholly attributed to *him:* provided, that the absence of distinct references to his books, which I could not at all times make with truth as designating citations or thoughts actually *derived* from him; and which, I trust, would, after this general acknowledgement be superfluous; be not charged on me as an ungenerous concealment or intentional plagiarism. I have not indeed (eheu! res angusta domi!) been hitherto able to procure more than two of his books, viz. the 1st volume of his collected Tracts, and his System of Transcendental Idealism; to which, however, I must add a small pamphlet against Fichte, the spirit of which was to *my* feelings painfully incongruous with the principles, and which (with the usual allowance afforded to an antithesis) displayed the love of wisdom rather than the wisdom of love. I regard truth as a divine ventriloquist: I care not from whose mouth the sounds are supposed to proceed, if only the words are audible and intelligible. "Albeit, I must confess to be half in doubt, whether I should bring it forth or no, it being so contrary to the eye of the world, and the world so potent in most men's hearts, that I shall endanger either not to be regarded or not to be understood."

MILTON: *Reason of Church Government.*

And to conclude the subject of citation, with a cluster of cita-

---

pher, who needed only have taken his foundation somewhat deeper and wider to have superseded a considerable part of my labours.

tions, which, as taken from books not in common use, may con-
tribute to the reader's amusement, as a voluntary before a ser-
mon. "Dolet mihi quidem deliciis literarum inescatos subito jam
homines adeo esse, præsertim qui Christianos se profitentur, ut
legere nisi quod ad *delectationem* facit sustineant nihil: unde et
disciplinæ severiores et philosophia ipsa jam fere prorsus etiam a
doctis negliguntur. Quod quidem propositum studiorum, nisi
mature corrigitur, tam magnum rebus incommodum dabit, quam
dedit Barbaries olim. Pertinax res Barbaries est, fateor: sed
minus potest tamen, quam illa mollities et *persuasa prudentia*
literarum, quae si *ratione* caret, sapientiæ virtutisque *specie*
mortales misere circumducit. Succedet igitur, ut arbitror, haud
ita multo post, pro rusticanâ seculi nostri ruditate captatrix illa
communi-loquentia robur animi virilis omne, omnem virtutem
masculam, profligatura, nisi cavetur."

"SIMON GRYNÆUS, candido lectori," prefixed to the Latin
translation of Plato, by Marsilius Ficinus. Lugduni, 1557. A too
prophetic remark, which has been in fulfilment from the year
1680, to the present 1815. N.B. By "persuasa prudentia," Gry-
næus means self-complacent *common sense* as opposed to science
and philosophic reason.

"Est medius ordo, et velut equestris, Ingeniorum quidem
sagacium, et rebus humanis commodorum, non tamen in primam
magnitudinem patentium. Eorum hominum, ut ita dicam, major
annona est. Sedulum esse, nihil temere loqui, assuescere labori,
et imagine prudentiæ & modestiæ tegere angustiores partes cap-
tûs, dum exercitationem et usum, quo isti in civilibus rebus pol-
lent, pro natura et magnitudine ingenii plerique accipiunt."—
BARCLAII ARGENIS, p. 71.

"As therefore physicians are many times forced to leave such
methods of curing as themselves know to be fittest, and being
overruled by the sick man's impatience, are fain to try the best
they can: in like sort, considering how the case doth stand with
this present age, full of tongue and weak of brain, behold we
would (*if our subject permitted it*) yield to the stream thereof.
That way we would be contented to prove our thesis, which be-
ing the worse in itself, notwithstanding is now by reason of com-
mon imbecility the fitter and likelier to be brooked."—HOOKER.

If this fear could be rationally entertained in the controversial
age of Hooker, under the then robust discipline of the scholastic
logic, pardonably may a writer of the present times anticipate a
scanty audience for abstrusest themes, and truths that can neither
be communicated or received without effort of thought, as well
as patience of attention.

"Che s'io non erro al calcular de' punti,
Par ch' *Asinina* Stella a noi predomini,
E 'l Somaro e 'l Castron si sian congiunti.
Il tempo d'Apuleio più non si nomini:
Che se allora un sol huom sembrava un Asino,
Mille Asini a' miei dì rassembran huomini!"
Di Salvatore Rosa Satir. I. l. 10.

CHAPTER X

A chapter of digression and anecdotes, as an interlude preceding that on the nature and genesis of the imagination or plastic power—On pedantry and pedantic expressions—Advice to young authors respecting publication—Various anecdotes of the author's literary life, and the progress of his opinions in religion and politics.

"*Esemplastic. The word is not in Johnson, nor have I met with it elsewhere.*" Neither have I. I constructed it myself from the Greek words, εἰς ἐν πλάττειν, to shape into one; because, having to convey a new sense, I thought that a new term would both aid the recollection of my meaning, and prevent its being confounded with the usual import of the word, imagination. "*But this is pedantry!*" Not necessarily so, I hope. If I am not misinformed, pedantry consists in the use of words unsuitable to the time, place, and company. The language of the market would be in the schools as *pedantic,* though it might not be reprobated by that name, as the language of the schools in the market. The mere man of the world, who insists that no other terms but such as occur in common conversation should be employed in a scientific disquisition, and with no greater precision, is as truly a *pedant* as the man of letters, who either over-rating the acquirements of his auditors, or misled by his own familiarity with technical or scholastic terms, converses at the wine-table with his mind fixed on his musæum or laboratory; even though the latter pedant instead of desiring his wife to *make the tea* should bid her add to the quant. suff. of thea Sinensis the oxyd of hydrogen saturated with caloric. To use the colloquial (and in truth somewhat *vulgar*) metaphor, if the pedant of the cloyster, and the pedant of the lobby, both *smell equally of the shop,* yet the odour from the Russian binding of good old *authentic-looking* folios and quartos is less annoying than the steams from the tavern or bagnio. Nay, though the pedantry of the scholar should betray a little ostentation, yet a well-conditioned mind would more easily, methinks, tolerate the *fox brush* of learned vanity, than the *sans culotterie* of a contemptuous ignorance, that assumes a merit from mutilation in the self-consoling sneer at the pompous incumbrance of tails.

The first lesson of philosophic discipline is to wean the student's attention from the DEGREES of things, which alone form the vocabulary of common life, and to direct it to the KIND abstracted from *degree*. Thus the chemical student is taught not to be startled at disquisitions on the heat in ice, or on latent and fixible light. In such discourse the instructor has no other alternative than either to use old words with new meanings (the plan adopted by Darwin in his Zoonomia;) or to introduce new terms, after the example of Linnæus, and the framers of the present chemical nomenclature. The latter mode is evidently preferable, were it only that the former demands a twofold exertion of thought in one and the same act. For the reader, or hearer, is required not only to learn and bear in mind the new definition; but to unlearn, and keep out of his view, the old and habitual meaning; a far more difficult and perplexing task, and for which the mere *semblance* of eschewing pedantry seems to me an inadequate compensation. Where, indeed, it is in our power to recall an unappropriate term that had without sufficient reason become obsolete, it is doubtless a less evil to restore than to coin anew. Thus to express in one word, all that appertains to the perception, considered as passive, and merely recipient, I have adopted from our elder classics the word *sensuous*; because *sensual* is not at present used, except in a bad sense, or at least as a *moral* distinction; while *sensitive* and *sensible* would each convey a different meaning. Thus too I have followed Hooker, Sanderson, Milton, &c., in designating the *immediateness* of any act or object of knowledge by the word *intuition*, used sometimes subjectively, sometimes objectively, even as we use the word, thought, now as *the* thought, or act of thinking, and now as *a* thought, or the object of our reflection; and we do this without confusion or obscurity. The very words, *objective* and *subjective*, of such constant recurrence in the schools of yore, I have ventured to re-introduce, because I could not so briefly or conveniently by any more familiar terms distinguish the *percipere* from the *percipi*. Lastly, I have cautiously discriminated the terms, THE REASON, and THE UNDERSTANDING, encouraged and confirmed by the authority of our genuine divines and philosophers, before the revolution.

> ———"both life, and sense,
> Fancy, and *understanding*; whence the soul

Reason receives, and REASON is her *being*,
DISCURSIVE or INTUITIVE: discourse[36]
Is oftest yours, the latter most is ours,
Differing but in *degree*, in *kind* the same.

PARADISE LOST, *Book* V.

I say, that I was *confirmed* by authority so venerable: for I had previous and higher motives in my own conviction of the importance, nay, of the necessity of the distinction, as both an indispensable condition and a vital part of all sound speculation in metaphysics, ethical or theological. To establish this distinction was one main object of THE FRIEND; if even in a biography of my own literary life I can with propriety refer to a work, which was printed rather than published, or so published that it had been well for the unfortunate author, if it had remained in manuscript! I have even at this time bitter cause for remembering that, which a number of my subscribers have but a trifling motive for forgetting. This effusion might have been spared; but I would feign flatter myself, that the reader will be less austere than an oriental professor of the bastinado, who during an attempt to extort per argumentum baculinum a full confession from a culprit, interrupted his outcry of pain by reminding him, that it was *"a mere digression!"* All this noise, Sir! is nothing to the point, and no sort of answer to my QUESTIONS! Ah! but, (replied the sufferer,) *it is the most pertinent reply in nature to your blows.*

An imprudent man of common goodness of heart cannot but wish to turn even his imprudences to the benefit of others, as far as this is possible. If therefore any one of the readers of this semi-narrative should be preparing or intending a periodical work, I warn him, in the first place, against trusting in the number of names on his subscription list. For he cannot be certain that the names were put down by sufficient authority; or, should that be ascertained, it still remains to be known, whether they were not extorted by some over zealous friend's importunity; whether the subscriber had not yielded his name, merely from want of courage to answer, no! and with the intention of

[36] But for sundry notes on Shakespeare, &c., and other pieces which have fallen in my way, I should have deemed it unnecessary to observe, that *discourse* here, or elsewhere, does not mean what we *now* call discoursing; but the *discursion* of the *mind*, the processes of generalization and subsumption, of deduction and conclusion. Thus, Philosophy has *hitherto* been DISCURSIVE; while Geometry is *always* and *essentially* INTUITIVE.

dropping the work as soon as possible. One gentleman procured me nearly a hundred names for THE FRIEND, and not only took frequent opportunity to remind me of his success in his canvass, but laboured to impress my mind with the sense of the obligation, I was under to the subscribers; for (as he very pertinently admonished me,) *"fifty-two shillings* a year was a large sum to be bestowed on one individual, where there were so many objects of charity with strong claims to the assistance of the benevolent." Of these hundred patrons ninety threw up the publication before the fourth number, without any notice; though it was well known to them, that in consequence of the distance, and the slowness and irregularity of the conveyance, I was compelled to lay in a stock of *stamped* paper for at least eight weeks beforehand; each sheet of which stood me in five pence previous to its arrival at my printer's; though the subscription money was not to be received till the twenty-first week after the commencement of the work; and lastly, though it was in nine cases out of ten impracticable for me to receive the money for two or three numbers without paying an equal sum for the postage.

In confirmation of my first caveat, I will select one fact among *many.* On my list of subscribers, among a considerable number of names equally flattering, was that of an Earl of Cork, with his address. He might as well have been an Earl of Bottle, for aught I knew of him, who had been content to reverence the peerage in abstracto, rather than in concretis. Of course THE FRIEND was regularly sent as far, if I remember right, as the eighteenth number: i.e. till a fortnight before the subscription was to be paid. And lo! just at this time I received a letter from his Lordship, reproving me in language far more lordly than courteous for my impudence in directing my pamphlets to him, who knew nothing of me or my work! Seventeen or eighteen numbers of which, however, his Lordship was pleased to retain, probably for the culinary or post-culinary conveniences of his servants.

Secondly, I warn all others from the attempt to deviate from the ordinary mode of publishing a work by *the trade.* I thought indeed, that to the purchaser it was indifferent, whether thirty per cent. of the purchase-money went to the booksellers or to the government; and that the convenience of receiving the work by the post at his own door would give the preference to the latter. It is hard, I own, to have been labouring for years, in collecting and arranging the materials; to have spent every shilling that could be spared after the necessaries of life had been furnished, in buying books, or in journies for the purpose of consulting them or of acquiring facts at the fountain head; then to buy the paper, pay for the printing, &c., all at least fifteen per cent. beyond what *the trade* would have paid; and then after all to give thirty per cent. not of the net profits, but of the gross results of the sale, to a man who has merely to give the books shelf or warehouse room, and permit his apprentice to hand them over the counter to those who may ask for them; and this too copy by copy, although if the work be on any philosophical or scientific subject, it may be years before the edition is sold off. All this, I confess, must seem an hardship, and one, to which the products of industry in no other mode of exertion are subject. Yet even this is better, far better, than to attempt in any way to unite the functions of author and publisher. But the most prudent mode is to sell the copy-right, at least of one or more editions, for the most that *the trade* will offer. By few only can a large remuneration be expected; but fifty pounds and ease of mind are of more real advantage to a literary man, than the *chance* of five hundred with the *certainty* of insult and degrading anxieties. I shall have been grievously misunderstood, if this statement should be interpreted as written with the desire of detracting from the character of booksellers or publishers. The individuals did not make the laws and customs of their trade, but, as in every other trade, take them as they find them. Till the evil can be proved to be removable, and without the substitution of an equal or greater inconvenience, it were neither wise or manly even to complain of it. But to use it as a pretext for speaking, or even for thinking, or feeling, unkindly or opprobriously of the tradesmen, as *individuals,* would be something worse than unwise or even than unmanly; it would be immoral and calumnious. My motives point in a far different direction and to far other objects, as will be seen in the conclusion of the chapter.

A learned and exemplary old clergyman, who many years ago went to his reward followed by the regrets and blessings of his flock, published at his own expense two volumes octavo, entitled, a new Theory of Redemption. The work was most severely handled in the Monthly or Critical Review, I forget which; and this unprovoked hostility became the good old man's favorite topic of conversation among his friends. Well! (he used to exclaim,) in the SECOND edition, I shall have an opportunity of exposing both the ignorance and the malignity of the anonymous critic. Two or three years however passed by without any tidings from the bookseller, who had undertaken the printing and publication of the work, and who was perfectly at his ease, as the author was known to be a man of large property. At length the *accounts* were written for; and in the course of a few weeks they were presented by the *rider* for the house, in person. My old friend put on his spectacles, and holding the scroll with no very firm hand, began—*Paper, so much:* O moderate enough—not at all beyond my expectation! *Printing, so much:* well! moderate enough! *Stitching, covers, advertisements, carriage, &c., so much.*—Still nothing amiss. *Selleridge* (for orthography is no necessary part of a bookseller's literary acquirements) £3. 3s. Bless me! only three guineas for the what d'ye call it—the *selleridge?* No more, Sir! replied the rider. Nay, but that is *too* moderate! rejoined my old friend. Only three guineas for *selling* a thousand copies of a work in two volumes? O Sir! (cries the young traveller) you have mistaken the word. There have been none of them *sold;* they have been sent back from London long ago; and this £3. 3s. is for the *cellaridge,* or warehouse-room in our book *cellar.* The work was in consequence preferred from the ominous cellar of the publisher's to the author's garret; and, on presenting a copy to an acquaintance, the old gentleman used to tell the anecdote with great humour and still greater good nature.

With equal lack of worldly knowledge, I was a far more than equal sufferer for it, at the very outset of my authorship. Toward the close of the first year from the time, that in an inauspicious hour I left the friendly cloysters, and the happy grove of quiet, ever honored Jesus College, Cambridge, I was persuaded by sundry Philanthropists and Anti-polemists to set on foot a periodical work, entitled THE WATCHMAN, that, (according to the general motto of the work,) *all might know the truth, and that the truth might make us free!* In order to exempt it from the stamp-tax, and likewise to contribute as little as possible to the supposed guilt of a war against freedom, it was to be published on every eighth day, thirty-two pages, large octavo, closely printed, and price only FOUR-PENCE. Accordingly with a flaming prospectus, *"Knowledge is Power"* &c., *to cry the state of the political atmosphere,* and so forth, I set off on a tour to the North, from Bristol to Sheffield, for the purpose of procuring customers, preaching by the way in most of the great towns, as an hireless volunteer, in a blue coat and white waistcoat, that not a rag of the woman of Babylon might be seen on me. For I was at that time and long after, though a Trinitarian (i.e. ad normam Platonis) in philosophy, yet a zealous Unitarian in Religion; more accurately, I was a *psilanthropist,* one of those who believe our Lord to have been the real son of Joseph, and who

lay the main stress on the resurrection rather than on the cruci-
fixion. O! never can I remember those days with either shame or
regret. For I was most sincere, most disinterested! My opinions
were indeed in many and most important points erroneous; but
my heart was single. Wealth, rank, life itself then seemed cheap
to me, compared with the interests of (what I believed to be)
the truth, and the will of my maker. I cannot even accuse my-
self of having been actuated by vanity; for in the expansion of
my enthusiasm I did not think of *myself* at all.

My campaign commenced at Birmingham; and my first attack
was on a rigid Calvinist, a tallow-chandler by trade. He was a
tall dingy man, in whom length was so predominant over
breadth, that he might almost have been borrowed for a
foundery poker. O that face! a face κατ᾽ ἔμφασιν! I have it before
me at this moment. The lank, black, twine-like hair, *pingui-
nitescent,* cut in a straight line along the black stubble of his thin
gunpowder eye-brows, that looked like a scorched *after-math*
from a last week's shaving. His coat collar behind in perfect
unison, both of colour and lustre, with the coarse yet glib
cordage, that I suppose he called his hair, and which with a
bend inward at the nape of the neck, (the only approach to
flexure in his whole figure,) slunk in behind his waistcoat; while
the countenance lank, dark, very *hard,* and with strong per-
pendicular furrows, gave me a dim notion of some one looking
at me through a *used* gridiron, all soot, grease, and iron! But he
was one of the *thorough-bred,* a true lover of liberty, and, (I
was informed,) had proved to the satisfaction of many, that Mr.
Pitt was one of the horns of the second beast in the Revelations,
that *spoke like a dragon.* A person, to whom one of my letters
of recommendation had been addressed, was my introducer. It
was a new event in my life, my first *stroke* in the new business
I had undertaken of an author, yea, and of an author trading on
his own account. My companion after some imperfect sentences
and a multitude of hums and haas abandoned the cause to his
client; and I commenced an harangue of half an hour to Phile-
leutheros, the tallow-chandler, varying my notes, through the
whole gamut of eloquence, from the ratiocinative to the de-
clamatory, and in the latter from the pathetic to the indignant.
I argued, I described, I promised, I prophesied; and beginning
with the captivity of nations I ended with the near approach of
the millennium, finishing the whole with some of my own verses
describing that glorious state out of *the Religious Musings:*

> "————————————— Such delights
> As float to earth, permitted visitants!

When in some hour of solemn jubilee
The massive gates of Paradise are thrown
Wide open: and forth come in fragments wild
Sweet echoes of unearthly melodies,
And odors snatch'd from beds of Amaranth,
And they, that from the chrystal river of life
Spring up on freshen'd wing, ambrosial gales!"

Religious Musings, l. 356.

My taper man of lights listened with perseverant and praise-worthy patience, though, (as I was afterwards told, on complaining of certain gales that were not altogether ambrosial,) it was a *melting* day with him. And what, Sir, (he said, after a short pause,) might the cost be? *Only* FOUR-PENCE, (O! how I felt the anti-climax, the abysmal bathos of that *four-pence!*) *only four-pence, Sir, each number, to be published on every eighth day.* That comes to a deal of money at the end of a year. And how much, did you say, there was to be for the money? *Thirty-two pages, Sir! large octavo, closely printed.* Thirty and two pages? Bless me! why except what I does in a family way on the Sabbath, that's more than I ever reads, Sir! all the year round. I am as great a one, as any man in Brummagem, Sir! for liberty and truth and all them sort of things, but as to this, (no offence, I hope, Sir!) I must beg to be excused.

So ended my first canvass: from causes that I shall presently mention, I made but one other application in person. This took place at Manchester to a stately and opulent wholesale dealer in cottons. He took my letter of introduction, and, having perused it, measured me from head to foot and again from foot to head, and then asked if I had any bill or invoice of the thing; I presented my prospectus to him; he rapidly skimmed and hummed over the first side, and still more rapidly the second and concluding page; crushed it within his fingers and the palm of his hand; then most deliberately and *significantly* rubbed and smoothed one part against the other; and lastly putting it into his pocket turned his back on me with an *"over-run* with these articles!" and so without another syllable retired into his counting-house. And, I can truly say, to my unspeakable amusement.

This, I have said, was my second and last attempt. On returning baffled from the first, in which I had vainly essayed to repeat the miracle of Orpheus with the Brummagem patriot, I dined with the tradesman who had introduced me to him. After dinner he importuned me to smoke a pipe with him, and two or three other illuminati of the same rank. I objected, both because I was engaged to spend the evening with a minister and his friends, and because I had never smoked except once or twice in my lifetime, and then it was herb tobacco mixed with Oronooko. On the assurance, however, that the tobacco was equally mild, and seeing too that it was of a yellow colour; (not forgetting the lamentable difficulty, I have always experienced, in saying, "No," and in abstaining from what the people about me were doing,) I took half a pipe, filling the lower half of the bowl with salt. I was soon however compelled to resign it, in consequence of a giddiness and distressful feeling in my eyes, which, as I had drunk but a single glass of ale, must, I knew, have been the effect of the tobacco. Soon after, deeming myself recovered, I sallied forth to my engagement; but the walk and the fresh air brought on all the symptoms again, and, I had scarcely entered the minister's drawing-room, and opened a small pacquet of letters, which he had received from Bristol for me; ere I sunk back on the sofa in a sort of swoon rather than sleep. Fortunately I had found just time enough to inform him of the confused state of my feelings, and of the occasion. For here and thus I lay, my face like a wall that is white-washing, *deathy* pale and with the cold drops of perspiration running down it from my forehead, while one after another there dropt in the different gentlemen, who had been invited to meet, and spend the evening with me, to the number of from fifteen to twenty. As the poison of tobacco acts but for a short time, I at length awoke from insensibility, and looked round on the party, my eyes dazzled by the candles which had been lighted in the interim. By way of relieving my embarrassment one of the gentlemen began the conversation, with *"Have you seen a paper to-day, Mr. Coleridge?"* "Sir!" (I replied, rubbing my eyes,) "I am far from convinced, that a Christian is permitted to read either newspapers or any other works of merely political and temporary interest." This remark so ludicrously inapposite to, or rather, incongruous with, the purpose, for which I was known to have visited Birmingham, and to assist me in which they were all then met, produced an involuntary and general burst of laughter; and seldom indeed have I passed so many delightful hours, as I enjoyed in that room from the moment of that laugh to an early hour the next morning. Never, perhaps, in so mixed and numerous a party have I since heard conversation sustained with such animation, enriched with such variety of information, and enlivened with such a flow of anecdote. Both then and afterwards they all joined in dissuading me from proceeding with my scheme; assured me in the most friendly and yet most flattering expressions. that the employment was neither fit for me, nor I fit for the employment. Yet, if I had determined on persevering in it, they promised to exert themselves to the utmost to procure subscribers, and insisted that I should make no more applications in person, but carry on the canvass by proxy. The same hospitable reception, the same dissuasion, and, (that failing), the same kind exertions in my behalf, I met with at Manchester, Derby, Nottingham, Sheffield, indeed, at every place in which I took up my sojourn. I often recall with affectionate pleasure the many respectable men who interested themselves for me, a perfect stranger to them, not a few of whom I can still name among my friends. They will bear witness for me how opposite even then my principles were to those of Jacobinism or even of democracy, and can attest the strict accuracy of the statement which I have left on record in the 10th and 11th numbers of THE FRIEND.

From this rememberable tour I returned with nearly a thousand names on the subscription list of the Watchman; yet more than half convinced, that prudence dictated the abandonment of the scheme. But for this very reason I persevered in it; for I was at that period of my life so compleatly hag-ridden by the fear of being influenced by selfish motives, that to know a mode of conduct to be the dictate of *prudence* was a sort of presumptive proof to my feelings, that the contrary was the dictate of *duty*. Accordingly, I commenced the work, which was announced in London by long bills in letters larger than had ever been seen before, and which, (I have been informed, for I did not see them myself,) eclipsed the glories even of the lottery puffs. But, alas! the publication of the very first number was delayed beyond the day announced for its appearance. In the second number an essay against fast days, with a most censurable application of a text from Isaiah for its motto, lost me near five hundred of my subscribers at one blow. In the two following numbers I made enemies of all my Jacobin and Democratic Patrons; for, disgusted by their infidelity, and their adoption of French morals with French *psilosophy;* and perhaps thinking, that charity ought to begin nearest home; instead of abusing the government and the Aristocrats chiefly or entirely, as had been expected of me, I levelled my attacks at *"modern patriotism,"* and even ventured to declare my belief, that whatever the motives of ministers might have been for the sedition, (or as it was then the fashion to call them, the *gagging*) bills, yet the bills themselves would produce an effect to be desired by all the true friends of freedom, as far as they should contribute to deter men from openly declaiming on subjects, the

principles of which they had never bottomed, and from "plead-
ing to the poor and ignorant, instead of pleading for them." At
the same time I avowed my conviction, that national educa-
tion and a concurring spread of the gospel were the indispen-
sable condition of any true political amelioration. Thus by the
time the seventh number was published, I had the mortification
(but why should I say this, when in truth I cared too little for
any thing that concerned my worldly interests to be at all
mortified about it?) of seeing the preceding numbers exposed
in sundry old iron shops for a penny a piece. At the ninth
number I dropt the work. But from the London publisher I
could not obtain a shilling; he was a ——— and set me at de-
fiance. From other places I procured but little, and after such
delays as rendered that little worth nothing: and I should have
been inevitably thrown into jail by my Bristol printer, who re-
fused to wait even for a month, for a sum between eighty and
ninety pounds, if the money had not been paid for me by a man
by no means affluent, a dear friend, who attached himself to me
from my first arrival at Bristol, who has continued my friend
with a fidelity unconquered by time or even by my own appar-
ent neglect; a friend from whom I never received an advice that
was not wise, nor a remonstrance that was not gentle and
affectionate.

Conscientiously an opponent of the first revolutionary war,
yet with my eyes thoroughly opened to the true character and
impotence of the favorers of revolutionary principles in England,
principles which I held in abhorrence, (for it was part of my
political creed, that whoever ceased to act as an *individual* by
making himself a member of any *society* not sanctioned by his
Government, forfeited the rights of a citizen)—a vehement anti-
ministerialist, but after the invasion of Switzerland, a more vehe-
ment anti-gallican, and still more intensely an anti-jacobin, I
retired to a cottage at Stowey, and provided for my scanty
maintenance by writing verses for a London Morning Paper. I
saw plainly, that literature was not a profession, by which I
could expect to live; for I could not disguise from myself, that,
whatever my talents might or might not be in other respects, yet
they were not of the sort that could enable me to become a
popular writer; and that whatever my opinions might be in
themselves, they were almost equi-distant from all the three
prominent parties, the Pittites, the Foxites, and the Democrats.
Of the unsaleable nature of my writings I had an amusing
memento one morning from our own servant girl. For happen-
ing to rise at an earlier hour than usual, I observed her putting

an extravagant quantity of paper into the grate in order to light the fire, and mildly checked her for her wastefulness; "la, Sir!" (replied poor Nanny) "why, it is only WATCHMEN."

I now devoted myself to poetry and to the study of ethics and psychology; and so profound was my admiration at this time of Hartley's Essay on Man, that I gave his name to my first-born. In addition to the gentleman, my neighbour, whose garden joined on to my little orchard, and the cultivation of whose friendship had been my sole motive in choosing Stowey for my residence, I was so fortunate as to acquire, shortly after my settlement there, an invaluable blessing in the society and neighbourhood of one, to whom I could look up with equal reverence, whether I regarded him as a poet, a philosopher, or a man. His conversation extended to almost all subjects, except physics and politics; with the latter he never troubled himself. Yet neither my retirement nor my utter abstraction from all the disputes of the day could secure me in those jealous times from suspicion and obloquy, which did not stop at me, but extended to my excellent friend, whose perfect innocence was even ad-duced as a proof of his guilt. One of the many busy *sycophants*[37] of that day, (I here use the word sycophant in its original sense, as a wretch who *flatters* the prevailing party by *informing* against his neighbours, under pretence that they are exporters of prohibited *figs* or fancies! for the moral application of the term it matters not which)—one of these sycophantic law-mon-grels, discoursing on the *politics* of the neighbourhood, uttered the following *deep* remark: "As to *Coleridge,* there is not so much harm in *him,* for he is a whirl-brain that talks whatever comes uppermost; but that ——! he is the *dark* traitor. *You never hear* HIM *say a syllable on the subject.*"

Now that the hand of providence has disciplined *all* Europe into sobriety, as men tame wild elephants, by alternate blows and caresses; now that Englishmen of all classes are restored to their old English notions and feelings; it will with difficulty be credited, how great an influence was at that time possessed and exerted by the spirit of secret defamation, (the too constant attendant on party-zeal!) during the restless interim from 1793 to the commencement of the Addington administration, or the year before the truce of Amiens. For by the latter period the minds of the partizans, exhausted by excess of stimulation and humbled by mutual disappointment, had become languid. The same causes, that inclined the nation to peace, disposed the in-

[37] Σύκους φαίνειν, to show or detect figs, the exportation of which from Attica was forbidden by the laws.

dividuals to reconciliation. Both parties had found themselves in the wrong. The one had confessedly mistaken the moral character of the revolution, and the other had miscalculated both its moral and its physical resources. The experiment was made at the price of great, almost, we may say, of humiliating sacrifices; and wise men foresaw that it would fail, at least in its direct and ostensible object. Yet it was purchased cheaply, and realized an object of equal value, and, if possible, of still more vital importance. For it brought about a national una- nimity unexampled in our history since the reign of Elizabeth; and providence, never wanting to a good work when men have done their parts, soon provided a common focus in the cause of Spain, which made us all once more Englishmen by at once gratifying and correcting the predilections of both parties. The sincere reverers of the throne felt the cause of loyalty ennobled by its alliance with that of freedom; while the *honest* zealots of the people could not but admit, that freedom itself assumed a more winning form, humanized by loyalty and consecrated by religious principle. The youthful enthusiasts who, flattered by the morning rainbow of the French revolution, had made a boast of *expatriating* their hopes and fears, now, disciplined by the succeeding storms and sobered by increase of years, had been taught to prize and honour the spirit of nationality as the best safeguard of national independence, and this again as the absolute pre-requisite and necessary basis of popular rights.

If in Spain too disappointment has nipt our too forward ex- pectations, yet all is not destroyed that is checked. The crop was perhaps springing up too rank in the stalk to *kern* well; and there were, doubtless, symptoms of the Gallican *blight* on it. If superstition and despotism have been suffered to let in their wolvish sheep to trample and eat it down even to the surface, yet the roots remain alive, and the second growth may prove all the stronger and healthier for the temporary interrup- tion. At all events, to *us* heaven has been just and gracious. The *people* of England did their best, and have received their rewards. Long may we continue to deserve it! Causes, which it had been too generally the habit of former statesmen to regard as belonging to another world, are now admitted by all ranks to have been the main agents of our success. *"We fought from heaven; the stars in their courses fought against Sisera."* If then unanimity grounded on moral feelings has been among the least equivocal sources of our national glory, that man deserves the esteem of his countrymen, even as patriots, who devotes his life and the utmost efforts of his intellect to the preservation and continuance of that unanimity by the disclosure and establishment of *principles*. For by these all *opinions* must be ultimately tried; and, (as the feelings of men are worthy of regard only as far as they are the representatives of their fixed opinions), on the knowledge of these all unanimity, not accidental and fleeting, must be grounded. Let the scholar, who doubts this assertion, refer only to the speeches and writings of EDMUND BURKE at the commencement of the American war and compare them with his speeches and writings at the commencement of the French revolution. He will find the *principles* exactly the same and the deductions the same; but the practical inferences almost opposite in the one case from those drawn in the other; yet in both equally legitimate and in both equally confirmed by the results. Whence gained he this superiority of foresight? Whence arose the striking *difference*, and in most instances even, the discrepancy between the grounds assigned by *him*, and by those who voted *with* him, on the same questions? How are we to explain the notorious fact, that the speeches and writings of EDMUND BURKE are more interesting at the present day than they were found at the time of their first publication; while those of his illustrious confederates are either forgotten, or exist only to furnish proofs, that the same conclusion, which one man had deduced scientifically, *may* be brought out by another in consequence of errors that luckily chanced to neutralize each other. It would be unhandsome as a conjecture, even were it not, as it actually is, false in point of fact, to attribute this difference to deficiency of talent on the part of Burke's friends, or of experience, or of historical knowledge. The satisfactory solution is, that Edmund Burke possessed and had sedulously sharpened that eye, which sees all things, actions, and events, in relation to the *laws* that determine their existence and circumscribe their possibility. He referred habitually to *principles*. He was a *scientific* statesman; and therefore a *seer*. For every *principle* contains in itself the germs of a prophecy; and, as the prophetic power is the essential privilege of science, so the fulfilment of its oracles supplies the outward and, (to men in general), the *only* test of its claim to the title. Wearisome as Burke's refinements appeared to his parliamentary auditors, yet the cultivated classes throughout Europe have reason to be thankful, that

> "——he went on refining,
> And thought of convincing, while they thought of dining."

Our very sign-boards, (said an illustrious friend to me), give evidence, that there has been a TITIAN in the world. In like manner, not only the debates in parliament, not only our proclamations and state papers, but the essays and leading paragraphs of our journals are so many remembrancers of EDMUND BURKE. Of this the reader may easily convince himself, if either by recollection or reference he will compare the opposition newspapers at the commencement and during the five or six following years of the French revolution with the sentiments, and grounds of argument assumed in the same class of Journals at present, and for some years past.

Whether the spirit of Jacobinism, which the writings of Burke exorcised from the higher and from the literary classes, may not, like the ghost in Hamlet, be heard moving and mining in the underground chambers with an activity the more dangerous because less noisy, may admit of a question. I have given my opinions on this point, and the grounds of them, in my letters to Judge Fletcher occasioned by his CHARGE to the Wexford grand jury, and published in the *Courier*. Be this as it may, the evil spirit of jealousy, and with it the Cerberean whelps of feud and slander, no longer walk their rounds, in cultivated society.

Far different were the days to which these anecdotes have carried me back. The dark guesses of some zealous Quidnunc met with so congenial a soil in the grave alarm of a titled Dogberry of our neighbourhood, that a SPY was actually sent down from the government *pour surveillance* of myself and friend. There must have been not only abundance, but *variety* of these "honorable men" at the disposal of Ministers: for this proved a very honest fellow. After three weeks' truly Indian persever-ance in tracking us, (for we were commonly together,) during all which time seldom were we out of doors, but he contrived to be within hearing, (and all the while utterly unsuspected; how indeed *could* such a suspicion enter our fancies?) he not only rejected Sir Dogberry's request that he would try yet a little longer, but declared to him his belief, that both my friend and myself were as good subjects, for aught he could discover to the contrary, as any in His Majesty's dominions. He had repeat-edly hid himself, he said, for hours together behind a bank at the sea-side, (our favorite seat), and overheard our conversa-tion. At first he fancied, that we were aware of our danger; for he often heard me talk of one *Spy Nozy,* which he was inclined to interpret of himself, and of a remarkable feature belonging to him; but he was speedily convinced that it was the name of a man who had made a book and lived long ago. Our talk ran most upon books, and we were perpetually desiring each other to look at *this,* and to listen to *that;* but he could not catch a word about politics. Once he had joined me on the road; (this occurred, as I was returning home alone from my friend's house, which was about three miles from my own cottage), and, passing himself off as a traveller, he had entered into conversation with me, and talked of purpose in a *democrat* way in order to draw me out. The result, it appears, not only convinced him that I was no friend of Jacobinism; but, (he added), I had "plainly made it out to be such a silly as well as wicked thing, that he felt ashamed though he had only *put it on.*" I distinctly remembered the occurrence, and had mentioned it immediately on my return, repeating what the traveller with his Bardolph nose had said, with my own answer; and so little did I suspect the true object of my "tempter ere accuser," that I expressed with no small pleasure my hope and belief, that the conversation had been of some service to the poor misled malcontent. This incident therefore prevented all doubt as to the truth of the report, which through a friendly medium came to me from the master of the village inn, who had been ordered to entertain the *Government Gentleman* in his best manner, but above all to be silent concerning such a person being in his house. At length he received Sir Dogberry's commands to accompany his guest at the final interview; and, after the absolving suffrage of the *gentleman honored with the confidence of Ministers,* answered, as follows, to the following queries: D. Well, landlord! and what do you know of the person in question? L. I see him often pass by with maister ——, my landlord, (i.e. *the owner of the house*), and sometimes with the new-comers at Holford; but I never said a word to him or he to me. D. But do you not know, that he has distributed papers and hand-bills of a seditious nature among the common people? L. No, your honor! I never heard of such a thing. D. Have you not seen this Mr. Coleridge, or heard of, his haranguing and talking to knots and clusters of the inhabitants?—What are you grinning at, Sir? L. Beg your honor's pardon! but I was only thinking, how they'd have stared at him. If what I have heard be true, your honor! they would not have understood a word he said. When our vicar was here, Dr. L. the master of the great school and Canon of Windsor, there was a great dinner party at maister ———'s; and one of the farmers, that was there, told us that he and the Doctor talked real Hebrew Greek at each other for an hour together after dinner. D. Answer the question, Sir! Does he ever harangue the people? L. I hope your honor an't angry with me. I can say no more than I know. I never saw him talking with any one, but my landlord, and our curate, and the strange gentleman. D. Has he not been seen wandering on the hills towards the Channel, and along the shore, with books and papers in his hand, taking charts and maps of the country? L. Why, as to that, your honor! I own, I have heard; I am sure, I would not wish to say ill of any body; but it is certain, that I have heard—D. Speak out, man! don't be afraid, you are doing your duty to your King and Government. What have you heard? L. Why, folks do say, your honor! as how that he is a *Poet*, and that he is going to put Quantock and all about here in print; and as they be so much together, I suppose that the strange gentleman has some *consarn* in the business.—So ended this formidable inquisition, the latter part of which alone requires explanation, and at the same time entitles the anecdote to a place in my literary life. I had considered it as a defect in the admirable poem of the Task, that the subject, which gives the title to the work, was not, and indeed could not be, carried on beyond the three or four first pages, and that, throughout the poem, the connections are frequently awkward, and the transitions abrupt and arbitrary. I sought for a subject, that should give equal room and freedom for description, incident, and impassioned reflections on men, nature, and society, yet supply in itself a natural connection to the parts, and unity to the whole. Such a subject I conceived myself to have found in a stream, traced from its source in the hills among the yellow-red moss and conical glass-shaped tufts of bent, to the first break or fall, where its drops become audible, and it begins to form a channel; thence to the peat and turf barn, itself built of the same dark squares as it sheltered; to the sheepfold; to the first cultivated plot of ground; to the lonely cottage and its bleak garden won from the heath: to the hamlet, the villages, the market-town, the manufactories, and the seaport. My walks therefore were almost daily on the top of Quantock, and among its sloping combes. With my pencil and memorandum book in my hand, I was *making studies*, as the artists call them, and often moulding my thoughts into verse, with the objects and imagery immediately before my senses. Many circumstances, evil and good, intervened to prevent the completion of the poem, which was to have been entitled "The Brook." Had I finished the work, it was my purpose in the heat of the moment to have dedicated it to our then committee of public safety as containing the charts and maps, with which I was to have supplied the French Government in aid of their plans of invasion. And these too for a tract of coast that, from Clevedon to Minehead, scarcely permits the approach of a fishing-boat!

All my experience from my first entrance into life to the present hour is in favor of the warning maxim, that the man, who opposes in toto the political or religious zealots of his age, is safer from their obloquy than he who differs from them but in one or two points, or perhaps only in degree. By that transfer of the feelings of private life into the discussion of public questions, which is the *queen bee* in the hive of party fanaticism, the partisan has more sympathy with an intemperate Opposite than with a moderate Friend. We now enjoy an intermission, and long may it continue! In addition to far higher and more important merits, our present Bible societies and other numerous associations for national or charitable objects, may serve perhaps to carry off the superfluous activity and fervour of stirring minds in innocent hyperboles and the bustle of management. But the poison-tree is not dead, though the sap may for a season have subsided to its roots. At least let us not be lulled into such a notion of our entire security, as not to keep watch and ward, even on our best feelings. I have seen gross intolerance shewn in support of toleration; sectarian antipathy most obtrusively displayed in the promotion of an undistinguishing comprehension of sects; and acts of cruelty, (I had almost said,) of treachery, committed in furtherance of an object vitally important to the cause of humanity; and all this by men too of naturally kind dispositions and exemplary conduct.

The magic rod of fanaticism is preserved in the very adyta of human nature; and needs only the re-exciting warmth of a master hand to bud forth afresh and produce the old fruits. The horror of the peasants' war in Germany, and the direful effects of the Anabaptists' tenets (which differed only from those of Jacobinism by the substitution of theological for philosophical jargon), struck all Europe for a time with affright. Yet little more than a century was sufficient to obliterate all effective memory of these events. The same principles with similar though less dreadful consequences were again at work from the imprisonment of the first Charles to the restoration of his son. The fanatic maxim of extirpating fanaticism by persecution produced a civil war. The war ended in the victory of the insurgents; but the temper survived, and Milton had abundant grounds for asserting, that "Presbyter was but OLD PRIEST writ large!" One good result, thank heaven! of this zealotry was the re-establishment of the church. And now it might have been hoped, that the mischievous spirit would have been bound for a season, "and a seal set upon him, that he might deceive the nation no more." But no! The ball of persecution was taken up with undimished vigor by the persecuted. The same fanatic principle that, under the solemn oath and covenant, had turned cathedrals into stables, destroyed the rarest trophies of art and ancestral piety, and hunted the brightest ornaments of learning and religion into holes and corners, now marched under episcopal banners, and, having first crowded the prisons of England, emptied its whole vial of wrath on the miserable Covenanters of Scotland. (*Laing's* History of Scotland. —*Walter Scott's* bards, ballads, &c.) A merciful providence at length constrained both parties to join against a common enemy. A wise government followed; and the established church became, and now is, not only the brightest example, but our best and only sure bulwark, of toleration! the true and indispensable bank against a new inundation of persecuting zeal—ESTO PERPETUA!

A long interval of quiet succeeded; or rather, the exhaustion had produced a cold fit of the ague which was symptomatized by indifference among the many, and a tendency to infidelity or scepticism in the educated classes. At length those feelings of disgust and hatred, which for a brief while the multitude had attached to the crimes and absurdities of sectarian and democratic fanaticism, were transferred to the oppressive privileges of the noblesse, and the luxury, intrigues and favoritism of the continental courts. The same principles, dressed in the ostentatious garb of a fashionable philosophy, once more rose triumphant and effected the French revolution. And have we not within the last three or four years had reason to apprehend, that the detestable maxims and correspondent measures of the late French despotism had already bedimmed the public recollections of democratic phrensy; had drawn off to other objects the electric force of the feelings which had massed and upheld those recollections; and that a favorable concurrence of occasions was alone wanting to awaken the thunder and precipitate the lightning from the opposite quarter of the political heaven? (See THE FRIEND, p. 110.)

In part from constitutional indolence, which in the very heyday of hope had kept my enthusiasm in check, but still more from the habits and influences of a classical education and academic pursuits, scarcely had a year elapsed from the commencement of my literary and political adventures before my mind sank into a state of thorough disgust and despondency, both with regard to the disputes and the parties disputant. With more than *poetic* feeling I exclaimed:

"The sensual and the dark rebel in vain,
Slaves by their own compulsion! In mad game
They break their manacles, to wear the *name*
Of freedom, graven on a heavier chain.
O liberty! with profitless endeavour
Have I pursued thee many a weary hour;
But thou nor swell'st the victor's pomp, nor ever
Didst breathe thy soul in forms of human power!
    Alike from all, howe'er they praise thee,
    (Nor prayer nor boastful name delays thee)
    From superstition's harpy minions
    And factious blasphemy's obscener slaves,
    Thou speedest on thy cherub pinions,
The guide of homeless winds and playmate of the waves!"

FRANCE, a Palinodia.

I retired to a cottage in Somersetshire at the foot of Quantock, and devoted my thoughts and studies to the foundations of religion and morals. Here I found myself all afloat. Doubts rushed in; broke upon me *"from the fountains of the great deep,"* and fell *"from the windows of heaven."* The frontal truths of natural religion and the books of Revelation alike contributed to the flood; and it was long ere my ark touched on an Ararat, and rested. The *idea* of the Supreme Being appeared to me to be as necessarily implied in all particular modes of being as the idea of infinite space in all the geometrical figures by which space is limited. I was pleased with the Cartesian opinion, that the idea of God is distinguished from all other ideas by involving its *reality;* but I was not wholly satisfied. I began then to ask myself, what proof I had of the outward *existence* of anything? Of this sheet of paper for instance, as a thing in itself, separate from the phænomenon or image in my perception. I saw, that in the nature of things such proof is impossible; and that of all modes of being, that are not objects of the senses, the existence is *assumed* by a logical necessity arising from the constitution of the mind itself, by the absence of all motive to doubt it, not from any absolute contradiction in the supposition of the contrary. Still the existence of a being, the ground of all existence, was not yet the existence of a moral creator, and governor. "In the position, that all reality is either contained *in* the necessary being as an *attribute,* or exists *through* him, as its *ground,* it remains undecided whether the properties of intelligence and will are to be referred to the Supreme Being in the former or only in the latter sense; as inherent attributes, or only as *consequences* that have existence in other things *through* him. Thus organization, and motion, are regarded, as *from* God, not *in* God. Were the latter the truth, then notwithstanding all the pre-eminence which must be assigned to the ETERNAL FIRST from the sufficiency, unity, and independence of his being, as the dread ground of the universe, his nature would yet fall far short of that, which we are bound to comprehend in the idea of GOD. For, without any knowledge or determining resolve of its own, it would only be a blind necessary ground of other things and other spirits; and thus would be distinguished from the FATE of certain ancient philosophers in no respect, but that of being more definitely and intelligibly described." KANT's *Einzig möglicher Beweisgrund: vermischte Schriften, zweiter Band,* § 102 *and* 103.

For a very long time, indeed, I could not reconcile personality with infinity; and my head was with Spinoza, though my whole heart remained with Paul and John. Yet there had dawned upon me, even before I had met with the Critique of the Pure Reason, a certain guiding light. If the mere intellect could make no certain discovery of a holy and intelligent first cause, it might yet supply a demonstration, that no legitimate argument could be drawn from the intellect *against* its truth. And what is this more than St. Paul's assertion, that by wisdom, (more properly translated by the powers of reasoning) no man ever arrived at the knowledge of God? What more than the sublimest, and probably the oldest, book on earth has taught us,

"Silver and gold man searcheth out:
Bringeth the ore out of the earth, and darkness into light.

But where findeth he wisdom?
Where is the place of understanding?

The abyss crieth; it is not in me!
Ocean echoeth back; not in me!

Whence then cometh wisdom?
Where dwelleth understanding?

Hidden from the eyes of the living:
Kept secret from the fowls of heaven!

Hell and death answer;
We have heard the rumour thereof from afar!

GOD marketh out the road to it;
GOD knoweth its abiding place!

He beholdeth the ends of the earth;
He surveyeth what is beneath the heavens!

And as he weighed out the winds, and measured the sea,
And appointed laws to the rain,
And a path to the thunder,
A path to the flashes of the lightning!

Then did he see it,
And he counted it;
He searched into the depth thereof,
And with a line did he compass it round!

But to man he said,
The fear of the Lord is wisdom for THEE!
And to avoid evil,
That is *thy* understanding."—JOB, CHAP. 28th.

I become convinced, that religion, as both the corner-stone and
the key-stone of morality, must have a *moral* origin; so far at
least, that the evidence of its doctrines could not, like the truths
of abstract science, be wholly independent of the will. It were
therefore to be expected, that its *fundamental* truth would be
such as MIGHT be denied; though only by the fool, and even by
the fool from the madness of the *heart* alone!

The question then concerning our faith in the existence of a
God, not only as the *ground* of the universe by his essence, but
as its maker and judge by his wisdom and holy will, appeared
to stand thus. The sciential *reason*, whose objects are purely
theoretical, remains neutral, as long as its name and semblance
are not usurped by the opponents of the doctrine. But it *then*
becomes an effective ally by exposing the false show of demon-
stration, or by evincing the equal demonstrability of the contrary
from premises equally logical. The *understanding* mean time sug-
gests, the analogy of *experience* facilitates, the belief. Nature
excites and recalls it, as by a perpetual revelation. Our feelings
almost necessitate it; and the law of conscience peremptorily
commands it. The arguments, that at all apply to it, are in its
favor; and there is nothing against it, but its own sublimity. It
could not be intellectually more evident without becoming mor-
ally less effective; without counteracting its own end by sacri-
ficing the *life* of faith to the cold mechanism of a worthless be-
cause compulsory assent. The belief of a God and a future state,
(if a passive acquiescence may be flattered with the name of
belief), does not indeed always beget a good heart; but a good
heart so naturally begets the belief, that the very few exceptions
must be regarded as strange anomalies from strange and unfortu-
nate circumstances.

From these premises I proceeded to draw the following conclusions. First, that having once fully admitted the existence of an infinite yet self-conscious Creator, we are not allowed to ground the irrationality of any other article of faith on arguments which would equally prove that to be irrational, which we had allowed to be *real*. Secondly, that whatever is deducible from the admission of a *self-comprehending* and *creative* spirit may be legitimately used in proof of the *possibility* of any further mystery concerning the divine nature. "*Possibilitatem* mysteriorum (Trinitatis, &c.) contra insultus Infidelium et Hæreticorum a contradictionibus vindico; haud quidem *veritatem*, quæ revelatione solâ stabiliri possit"; says LEIBNITZ in a letter to his Duke. He then adds the following just and important remark. "In vain will tradition or texts of scripture be adduced in support of a doctrine, donec clava impossibilitatis et contradictionis e manibus horum Herculum extorta fuerit. For the heretic will still reply, that texts, the literal sense of which is not so much *above* as directly *against* all reason, must be understood *figuratively*, as Herod is a fox, &c."

These principles I held, *philosophically*, while in respect of revealed religion I remained a zealous Unitarian. I considered the *idea* of the Trinity a fair scholastic inference from the being of God, as a creative intelligence; and that it was therefore entitled to the rank of an *esoteric* doctrine of natural religion: But seeing in the same no practical or moral bearing, I confined it to the schools of philosophy. The admission of the Logos, as *hypostasized* (i.e. neither a mere attribute, or a personification) in no respect removed my doubts concerning the incarnation and the redemption by the cross; which I could neither reconcile *in reason* with the impassiveness of the Divine Being, nor in my moral feelings with the sacred distinction between things and persons, the vicarious payment of a debt and the vicarious expiation of guilt. A more thorough revolution in my philosophic principles, and a deeper insight into my own heart, were yet wanting. Nevertheless, I cannot doubt, that the difference of my metaphysical notions from those of Unitarians in general contributed to my final re-conversion to the whole truth in Christ; even as according to his own confession the books of certain Platonic philosophers (*libri quorundam Platonicorum*) commenced the rescue of St. Augustine's faith from the same error aggravated by the far darker accompaniment of the Manichæan heresy.

While my mind was thus perplexed, by a gracious providence for which I can never be sufficiently grateful, the generous and munificent patronage of Mr. JOSIAH and Mr. THOMAS WEDGEWOOD enabled me to finish my education in Germany. Instead of troubling others with my own crude notions and juvenile compositions, I was thenceforward better employed in attempting to store my own head with the wisdom of others. I made the best use of my time and means; and there is therefore no period of my life on which I can look back with such unmingled satisfaction. After acquiring a tolerable sufficiency in the German language[38] at Ratzeburg, which with my voyage and journey thither I have described in THE FRIEND, I proceeded through Hanover to Göttingen.

Here I regularly attended the lectures on physiology in the morning, and on natural history in the evening, under BLUMENBACH, a name as dear to every Englishman who has studied at that university, as it is venerable to men of science throughout Europe! Eichhorn's lectures on the New Testament were repeated to me from notes by a student from Ratzeburg, a young man of sound learning and indefatigable industry, who is now,

[38] To those, who design to acquire the language of a country in the country itself, it may be useful, if I mention the incalculable advantage which I derived from learning all the words, that could possibly be so learnt, with the objects before me, and without the intermediation of the English terms. It was a regular part of my morning studies for the first six weeks of my residence at Ratzeburg, to accompany the good and kind old pastor, with whom I lived, from the cellar to the roof, through gardens, farmyard, &c., and to call every, the minutest, thing by its German name. Advertisements, farces, jest books, and the conversation of children while I was at play with them, contributed their share to a more home-like acquaintance with the language, than I could have acquired from works of polite literature alone, or even from polite society. There is a passage of *hearty* sound sense in Luther's German letter on interpretation, to the translation of which I shall prefix, for the sake of those who read the German, yet are not likely to have dipt often in the massive folios of this heroic reformer, the simple, sinewy, idiomatic words of the original. "Denn man muss nicht die Buchstaben in der Lateinischen Sprache fragen wie man soll Deutsch reden: sondern man muss die Mutter im Hause, die Kinder auf den Gassen, den gemeinen Mann auf dem Markte, darum fragen: und denselbigen auf das Maul sehen wie sie reden, und darnach dolmetschen. So verstehen sie es denn, und merken dass man Deutsch mit ihnen redet."

TRANSLATION.

For one must not ask the letters in the Latin tongue, how one ought to speak German; but one must ask the mother in the house, the children in the lanes and alleys, the common man in the market, concerning this; yea, and look at the *moves* of their mouths while they are talking, and thereafter interpret. They understand you then, and mark that one talks German with them.

I believe, a professor of the oriental languages at Heidelberg. But my chief efforts were directed towards a grounded knowledge of the German language and literature. From Professor TYCHSEN I received as many lessons in the Gothic of Ulphilas as sufficed to make me acquainted with its grammar, and the radical words of most frequent occurrence; and with the occasional assistance of the same philosophical linguist, I read through[39] OTTFRIED's metrical paraphrase of the gospel, and the most important remains of the THEOTISCAN, or the transitional state of the Teutonic language from the Gothic to the old German of the Swabian period. Of this period (the polished dialect of

[39] This paraphrase, written about the time of Charlemagne, is by no means deficient in occasional passages of considerable poetic merit. There is a flow, and a tender enthusiasm in the following lines (at the conclusion of Chapter V) which, even in the translation will not, I flatter myself, fail to interest the reader. Ottfried is describing the circumstances immediately following the birth of our Lord.

> "She gave with joy her virgin breast;
> She hid it not, she bared the breast,
> Which suckled that divinest babe!
> Blessed, blessed were the breasts
> Which the Saviour infant kiss'd;
> And blessed, blessed was the mother
> Who wrapp'd his limbs in swaddling clothes,
> Singing placed him on her lap,
> Hung o'er him with her looks of love,
> And sooth'd him with a lulling motion.
> Blessed; for she shelter'd him
> From the damp and chilling air;
> Blessed, blessed! for she lay
> With such a babe in one blest bed,
> Close as babes and mothers lie!
> Blessed, blessed evermore,
> With her virgin lips she kiss'd,
> With her arms, and to her breast
> She embraced the babe divine,
> Her babe divine the virgin mother!
> There lives not on this ring of earth
> A mortal, that can sing her praise.
> Mighty mother, virgin pure,
> In the darkness and the night
> For us *she bore* the heavenly Lord!"

Most interesting is it to consider the effect, when the feelings are wrought above the natural pitch by the belief of something mysterious, while all the images are purely natural. Then it is, that religion and poetry strike deepest.

which is analogous to that of our Chaucer, and which leaves the philosophic student in doubt, whether the language has not since then lost more in sweetness and flexibility, than it has gained in condensation and copiousness) I read with sedulous accuracy the MINNESINGER (or singers of love, the provençal poets of the Swabian court) and the metrical romances; and then laboured through sufficient specimens of the *master singers,* their degenerate successors; not however without occasional pleasure from the rude, yet interesting strains of Hans Sachs, the cobbler of Nuremberg. Of this man's genius five folio volumes with double columns are extant in print, and nearly an equal number in manuscript; yet the indefatigable bard takes care to inform his readers, that he never *made a shoe the less,* but had virtuously reared a large family by the labor of his hands.

In Pindar, Chaucer, Dante, Milton, &c., &c., we have instances of the close connection of poetic genius with the love of liberty and of genuine reformation. The *moral* sense at least will not be outraged, if I add to the list the name of this honest shoemaker, (a trade by the bye remarkable for the production of philosophers and poets). His poem entitled the MORNING STAR, was the very first publication that appeared in praise and support of LUTHER; and an excellent hymn of Hans Sachs, which has been deservedly translated into almost all the European languages, was commonly sung in the Protestant churches, whenever the heroic reformer visited them.

In Luther's own German writings, and eminently in his translation of the Bible, the *German* language commenced. I mean the language as it is at present *written;* that which is called the HIGH-GERMAN, as contra-distinguished from the PLATT-TEUTSCH, the dialect of the flat or northern countries, and from the OBER-TEUTSCH, the language of the middle and Southern Germany. The High German is indeed a *lingua communis,* not actually the native language of any province, but the choice and fragrancy of all the dialects. From this cause it is at once the most copious and the most grammatical of all the European tongues.

Within less than a century after Luther's death the German was inundated with pedantic barbarisms. A few volumes of this period I read through from motives of curiosity; for it is not easy to imagine any thing more fantastic, than the very appearance of their pages. Almost every third word is a Latin word with a Germanized ending, the Latin portion being always printed in Roman letters, while in the last syllable the German character is retained.

At length, about the year 1620, OPITZ arose, whose genius more nearly resembled that of Dryden than any other poet, who at present occurs to my recollection. In the opinion of LESSING, the most acute of critics, and of ADELUNG, the first of Lexicographers, Opitz, and the Silesian poets, his followers, not only restored the language, but still remain the models of pure diction. A stranger has no vote on such a question; but after repeated perusal of the work my feelings justified the verdict, and I seemed to have acquired from them a sort of *tact* for what is *genuine* in the style of later writers.

Of the splendid era, which commenced with Gellert, Klopstock, Ramler, Lessing, and their compeers, I need not speak. With the opportunities which I enjoyed, it would have been disgraceful not to have been familiar with their writings; and I have already said as much as the present biographical sketch requires concerning the German philosophers, whose works, for the greater part, I became acquainted with at a far later period.

Soon after my return from Germany I was solicited to undertake the literary and political department in the Morning Post; and I acceded to the proposal on the condition that the paper should thenceforwards be conducted on certain fixed and announced principles, and that I should neither be obliged nor requested to deviate from them in favour of any party or any event. In consequence, that Journal became and for many years continued *anti-ministerial* indeed, yet with a very qualified approbation of the opposition, and with far greater earnestness and zeal both anti-jacobin and anti-gallican. To this hour I cannot find reason to approve of the first war either in its commencement or its conduct. Nor can I understand, with what reason either Mr. Perceval, (whom I am singular enough to regard as the best and wisest minister of this reign), or the present Administration, can be said to have pursued the plans of Mr. PITT. The love of their country, and perseverent hostility to French principles and French ambition are indeed honourable qualities common to them and to their predecessor. But it appears to me as clear as the evidence of the facts can render any question of history, that the successes of the Perceval and of the existing ministry have been owing to their having pursued measures the direct contrary to Mr. Pitt's. Such for instance are the concentration of the national force to one object; the abandonment of the *subsidizing* policy, so far at least as neither to goad nor bribe the continental courts into war, till the convictions of their subjects had rendered it a war of their own seeking; and above all, in their manly and generous reliance on the good sense of the English people, and on that loyalty which is linked to the very[40] heart of the nation by the system of credit and the interdependence of property.

[40] Lord Grenville has lately re-asserted (in the House of Lords) the imminent danger of a revolution in the earlier part of the war against France. I doubt not, that his Lordship is sincere; and it must be flattering to his feelings to believe it. But where are the evidences of the danger, to which a future historian can appeal? Or must he rest on an assertion? Let me be permitted to extract a passage on the subject from THE FRIEND. "I have said that to withstand the arguments of the lawless, the Antijacobins proposed to suspend the law, and by the interposition of a particular statute to eclipse the blessed light of the universal sun, that spies and informers might tyrannize and escape in the ominous darkness. Oh! if these mistaken men, intoxicated and bewildered with the panic of property, which they themselves were the chief agents in exciting, had ever lived in a country where there really existed a general disposition to change and rebellion! Had they ever travelled through Sicily; or through France at the first coming on of the revolution; or even alas! through too many of the provinces of a sister island; they could not but have shrunk from their own declarations concerning the state of feeling and opinion at that time predominant throughout Great Britain. There was a time (Heaven grant that that time may have passed by!) when by crossing a narrow strait, they might have learnt the true symptoms of approaching danger, and have secured themselves from mistaking the meetings and idle rant of such sedition, as shrank appalled from the sight of a constable, for the dire murmuring and strange consternation which precedes the storm or earthquake of national discord. Not only in coffee-houses and public theatres, but even at the tables of the wealthy, they would have heard the advocates of existing Government defend their cause in the language and with the tone of men, who are conscious that they are in a minority. But in England, when the alarm was at its highest, there was not a city, no not a town or village, in which a man suspected of holding democratic principles could move abroad without receiving some unpleasant proof of the hatred, in which his supposed opinions were held by the great majority of the people; and the only instances of popular excess and indignation were on the side of the Government and the Established Church. But why need I appeal to these invidious facts? Turn over the pages of history and seek for a single instance of a revolution having been effected without the concurrence of either the nobles, or the ecclesiastics, or the monied classes, in any country, in which the influences of property had ever been predominant, and where the interests of the proprietors were interlinked! Examine the revolution of the Belgic provinces under Philip 2nd; the civil wars of France in the preceding generation; the history of the American revolution, or the yet more recent events in Sweden and in Spain; and it will be scarcely possible not to perceive that in England from 1791 to the peace of Amiens there were neither tendencies to

Be this as it may, I am persuaded that the Morning Post proved a far more useful ally to the Government in its most important objects, in consequence of its being generally considered as moderately anti-ministerial, than if it had been the avowed eulogist of Mr. Pitt. (The few, whose curiosity or fancy should lead them to turn over the Journals of that date, may find a small proof of this in the frequent charges made by the Morning Chronicle, that such and such essays or leading paragraphs had been sent from the Treasury.) The rapid and unusual increase in the sale of the Morning Post is a sufficient pledge, that genuine impartiality with a respectable portion of literary talent will secure the success of a newspaper without the aid of party or ministerial patronage. But by impartiality I mean an honest and enlightened adherence to a code of intelligible principles previously announced, and faithfully referred to in support of every judgement on men and events; not indiscriminate abuse, not the indulgence of an editor's own malignant passions, and still less, if that be possbile, a determination to make money by flattering the envy and cupidity, the vindictive restlessness and self-conceit of the half-witted vulgar; a determination almost fiendish, but which, I have been informed, has been boastfully avowed by one man, the most notorious of these *mob-sycophants!* From the commencement of the Addington administration to the present day, whatever I have written in THE MORNING POST, or (after that paper was transferred to other proprietors) in the COURIER, has been in defence or furtherance of the measures of Government.

> "Things of this nature scarce survive that night
> That gives them birth; they perish in the sight;

---

confederacy nor actual confederacies, against which the existing laws had not provided sufficient safeguards and an ample punishment. But alas! the panic of property had been struck in the first instance for party purposes; and when it became general, its propagators caught it themselves and ended in believing their own lie; even as our bulls in Borrowdale sometimes run mad with the echo of their own bellowing. The consequences were most injurious. Our attention was concentrated to a monster, which could not survive the convulsions, in which it had been brought forth: even the enlightened Burke himself too often talking and reasoning, as if a perpetual and organized anarchy had been a possible thing! Thus while we were warring against French doctrines, we took little heed whether the means, by which we attempted to overthrow them, were not likely to aid and augment the far more formidable evil of French ambition. Like children we ran away from the yelping of a cur, and took shelter at the heels of a vicious warhorse."

Cast by so far from *after-life,* that there
Can scarcely aught be said, but that *they were!"*
CARTWRIGHT's *Prol. to the Royal Slave.*

Yet in these labours I employed, and, in the belief of partial
friends wasted, the prime and manhood of my intellect. Most
assuredly, they added nothing to my fortune or my reputation.
The industry of the week supplied the necessities of the week.
From government or the friends of government I not only never
received remuneration, or ever expected it; but I was never hon-
oured with a single acknowledgment, or expression of satisfac-
tion. Yet the retrospect is far from painful or matter of regret.
I am not indeed silly enough to take as any thing more than a
violent hyperbole of party debate, Mr. Fox's assertion that the
late war (I trust that the epithet is not prematurely applied)
was a war produced by the MORNING POST; or I should be proud
to have the words inscribed on my tomb. As little do I regard
the circumstance, that I was a specified object of Buonaparte's
resentment during my residence in Italy in consequence of those
essays in the Morning Post during the peace of Amiens. (Of this
I was warned, *directly,* by Baron VON HUMBOLDT, the Prussian
Plenipotentiary, who at that time was the minister of the Prus-
sian court at Rome; and indirectly, through his secretary, by
Cardinal Fesch himself.) Nor do I lay any greater weight on the
confirming fact, that an order for my arrest was sent from Paris,
from which danger I was rescued by the kindness of a noble Bene-
dictine, and the gracious connivance of that good old man, the
present Pope. For the late tyrant's vindictive appetite was omniv-
orous, and preyed equally on a[41] Duc d'Enghien, and the writer
of a newspaper paragraph. Like a true † vulture, Napoleon with an
eye not less telescopic, and with a taste equally coarse in his ravin,
could descend from the most dazzling heights to pounce on the
leveret in the brake, or even on the field-mouse amid the grass.
But I do derive a gratification from the knowledge, that my
essays contributed to introduce the practice of placing the ques-
tions and events of the day in a moral point of view; in giving

[41] I seldom think of the murder of this illustrious Prince without
recollecting the lines of Valerius Flaccus (Argonaut. Lib. I. 30).

"————————————Super ipsius ingens
Instat fama viri, virtusque haud læta Tyranno;
Ergo antire metus, juvenemque exstinguere pergit."

† Θηρᾷ δὲ καὶ τὸν χῆνα καὶ τὴν Δορκάδα,
Καὶ τὸν Λαγωόν, καὶ τὸ τῶν Ταύρων γένος.
PHILE, *de animal. propriet.*

a dignity to particular measures by tracing their policy or im-
policy to permanent principles, and an interest to principles by
the application of them to individual measures. In Mr. Burke's
writings indeed the germs of almost all political truths may be
found. But I dare assume to myself the merit of having first
explicitly defined and analyzed the nature of Jacobinism; and that
in distinguishing the Jacobin from the republican, the democrat,
and the mere demagogue, I both rescued the word from remain-
ing a mere term of abuse, and put on their guard many honest
minds, who even in their heat of zeal against Jacobinism, admit-
ted or supported principles from which the worst parts of that
system may be legitimately deduced. That these are not neces-
sary *practical* results of such principles, we owe to that fortunate
inconsequence of our nature, which permits the heart to rectify
the errors of the understanding. The detailed examination of the
consular Government and its pretended constitution, and the
proof given by me, that it was a consummate despotism in mas-
querade, extorted a recantation even from the Morning Chron-
icle, which had previously extolled this constitution as the
perfection of a wise and regulated liberty. On every great occur-
rence I endeavoured to discover in past history the event, that
most nearly resembled it. I procured, wherever it was possible,
the contemporary historians, memorialists, and pamphleteers.
Then fairly subtracting the points of difference from those of
likeness, as the balance favored the former or the latter, I con-
jectured that the result would be the same or different. In the
series[42] of essays entitled "a comparison of France under Napo-
leon with Rome under the first Cæsars," and in those which fol-
lowed "on the probable final restoration of the Bourbons," I feel
myself authorized to affirm, by the effect produced on many in-
telligent men, that, were the dates wanting, it might have been
suspected that the essays had been written within the last twelve
months. The same plan I pursued at the commencement of the
Spanish revolution, and with the same success, taking the war
of the United Provinces with Philip 2nd. as the ground work

[42] A small selection from the numerous articles furnished by me in
the Morning Post and Courier, chiefly as they regard the sources and
effects of Jacobinism and the connection of certain systems of political
economy with Jacobinical despotism, will form part of "THE FRIEND,"
which I am now completing, and which will be shortly published, for
I can scarcely say re-published, with the numbers arranged in Chap-
ters according to their subjects.

> "Accipe principium rursus, corpusque *coactum*
> Desere; mutata melior procede figura."

of the comparison. I have mentioned this from no motives of vanity, nor even from motives of self-defence, which would justify a certain degree of egotism, especially if it be considered, how often and grossly I have been attacked for sentiments, which I have exerted my best powers to confute and expose, and how grievously these charges acted to my disadvantage while I was in Malta. Or rather they would have done so, if my own feelings had not precluded the wish of a settled establishment in that island. But I have mentioned it from the full persuasion that, armed with the two-fold knowledge of history and the human mind, a man will scarcely err in his judgement concerning the sum total of any future national event, if he have been able to procure the original documents of the past, together with authentic accounts of the present, and if he have a philosophic tact for what is truly important in facts, and in most instances therefore for such facts as the DIGNITY OF HISTORY has excluded from the volumes of our modern compilers, by the courtesy of the age entitled historians.

To have lived in vain must be a painful thought to any man, and especially so to him who has made literature his profession. I should therefore rather condole than be angry with the mind, which could attribute to no worthier feelings, than those of vanity or self-love, the satisfaction which I acknowledged myself to have enjoyed from the republication of my political essays (either whole or as extracts) not only in many of our own provincial papers, but in the federal journals throughout America. I regarded it as some proof of my not having laboured altogether in vain, that from the articles written by me shortly before and at the commencement of the late unhappy war with America, not only the sentiments were adopted, but in some instances the very language, in several of the Massachusetts state-papers.

But no one of these motives nor all conjointly would have impelled me to a statement so uncomfortable to my own feelings, had not my character been repeatedly attacked, by an unjustifiable intrusion on private life as of a man incorrigibly idle, and who, intrusted not only with ample talents, but favored with unusual opportunities of improving them, had nevertheless suffered them to rust away without any efficient exertion, either for his own good or that of his fellow-creatures. Even if the compositions, which I have made public, and that too in a form the most certain of an extensive circulation, though the least flattering to an author's self-love, had been published in books, they would have filled a respectable number of volumes, though every passage of merely temporary interest were omitted. My prose writings have been charged with a disproportionate demand on the attention; with an excess of refinement in the mode of arriving at truths; with beating the ground for that which might have been run down by the eye; with the length and laborious construction of my periods; in short with obscurity and the love of paradox. But my severest critics have not pretended to have found in my compositions triviality, or traces of a mind that shrunk from the toil of thinking. No one has charged me with tricking out in other words the thoughts of others, or with hashing up anew the crambe jam decies cocta of English literature or philosophy. Seldom have I written that in a day, the acquisition or investigation of which had not cost me the previous labour of a month.

But are books the only channel through which the stream of intellectual usefulness can flow? Is the diffusion of truth to be estimated by publications; or publications by the truth, which they diffuse or at least contain? I speak it in the excusable warmth of a mind stung by an accusation, which has not only been advanced in reviews of the widest circulation, not only registered in the bulkiest works of periodical literature, but by frequency of repetition has become an admitted fact in private literary circles, and thoughtlessly repeated by too many who call themselves my friends, and whose own recollections ought to have suggested a contrary testimony. Would that the criterion of a scholar's utility were the number and moral value of the truths, which he has been the means of throwing into the general circulation; or the number and value of the minds, whom by his conversation or letters he has excited into activity, and supplied with the germs of their after-growth! A distinguished rank might not indeed, even then, be awarded to my exertions; but I should dare look forward with confidence to an honorable acquittal. I should dare appeal to the numerous and respectable audiences, which at different times and in different places honored my lecture-rooms with their attendance, whether the points of view from which the subjects treated of were surveyed, whether the grounds of my reasoning were such, as they had heard or read elsewhere, or have since found in previous publications. I can conscientiously declare, that the complete success of the RE-MORSE on the first night of its representation did not give me as great or as heart-felt a pleasure, as the observation that the pit and boxes were crowded with faces familiar to me, though of individuals whose names I did not know, and of whom I knew nothing, but that they had attended one or other of my courses of lectures. It is an excellent though perhaps somewhat vulgar proverb, that there are cases where a man may be as well *"in for a pound as for a penny."* To those, who from ignorance of the serious injury I have received from this rumour of having dreamed away my life to no purpose, injuries which I unwillingly remember at all, much less am disposed to record in a sketch of my literary life; or to those, who from their own feelings, or the gratification they derive from thinking contemptuously of others, would like Job's comforters attribute these complaints, extorted from me by the sense of wrong, to self-conceit or presumptuous vanity, I have already furnished such ample materials, that I shall gain nothing by withholding the remainder. I will not therefore hesitate to ask the consciences of those, who from their long acquaintances with me and with the circumstances are best qualified to decide or be my judges, whether the restitution of the suum cuique would increase or detract from my literary reputation. In this exculpation I hope to be understood as speaking of myself comparatively, and in proportion to the claims, which others are intitled to make on my time or my talents. By what I *have* effected, am I to be judged by my fellow men; what I *could* have done, is a question for my own conscience. On my own account I may perhaps have had sufficient reason to lament my deficiency in self-controul, and the neglect of concentering my powers to the realization of some permanent work. But to verse rather than to prose, if to either, belongs the voice of mourning for

> "Keen pangs of love awakening as a babe
> Turbulent, with an outcry in the heart;
> And fears self-will'd that shunned the eye of hope,
> And hope that scarce would know itself from fear;
> Sense of past youth, and manhood come in vain,
> And genius given and knowledge won in vain;
> And all which I had culled in wood-walks wild,
> And all which patient toil had rear'd, and all
> Commune with thee had open'd out—but flowers
> Strew'd on my corpse, and borne upon my bier,
> In the same coffin, for the self-same grave!"
>
> S. T. C.

These will exist, for the future, I trust, only in the poetic strains, which the feelings at the time called forth. In those only, gentle reader,

> "Affectus animi varios, bellumque sequacis
> Perlegis invidiæ, curasque revolvis inanes,
> Quas humilis tenero stylus olim effudit in ævo.
> Perlegis et lacrymas, et quod pharetratus acutâ

Ille puer puero fecit mihi cuspide vulnus.
OMNIA PAULATIM CONSUMIT LONGIOR ÆTAS,
VIVENDOQUE SIMUL MORIMUR, RAPIMURQUE MANENDO.
Ipse mihi collatus enim non ille videbor;
Frons alia est, moresque alii, nova mentis imago,
Vox aliudque sonat. Jamque observatio vitæ
Multa dedit:—lugere nihil, ferre omnia; jamque
Paulatim lacrymas rerum experientia tersit."

CHAPTER XI

An affectionate exhortation to those who in early life feel themselves disposed to become authors.

IT WAS a favourite remark of the late Mr. Whitbread's, that no man does any thing from a single motive. The separate motives, or rather moods of mind, which produced the preceding reflections and anecdotes have been laid open to the reader in each separate instance. But an interest in the welfare of those, who at the present time may be in circumstances not dissimilar to my own at my first entrance into life, has been the constant accompaniment, and (as it were) the under-song of all my feelings. WHITEHEAD exerting the prerogative of his laureatship addressed to youthful poets a poetic CHARGE, which is perhaps the best, and certainly the most interesting, of his works. With no other privilege than that of sympathy and sincere good wishes, I would address an affectionate exhortation to the youthful literati, grounded on my own experience. It will be but short; for the beginning, middle, and end converge to one charge: NEVER PURSUE LITERATURE AS A TRADE. With the exception of one extraordinary man, I have never known an individual, least of all an individual of genius, healthy or happy without a *profession*, i.e. some *regular* employment, which does not depend on the will of the moment, and which can be carried on so far *mechanically* that an average quantum only of health, spirits, and intellectual exertion are requisite to its faithful discharge. Three hours of leisure, unannoyed by any alien anxiety, and looked forward to with delight as a change and recreation, will suffice to realize in literature a larger product of what is truly *genial*, than weeks of compulsion. Money, and immediate reputation form only an arbitrary and accidental end of literary labor. The *hope* of increasing them by any given exertion will often prove a stimulant to industry; but the *necessity* of acquiring them will in all works of genius convert the stimulant into a *narcotic*. Motives by excess reverse their very nature, and instead of exciting, stun and stupify the mind. For it is one contradistinction of genius from talent, that its predominant end is always comprized in the means; and this is one of the many points, which establish an analogy between genius and virtue. Now though talents may exist without genius, yet as genius cannot exist, certainly not manifest itself, without talents, I would advise every scholar, who feels the genial power working within him, so far to make a division between the two, as that he should devote his *talents* to the acquirement of competence in some known trade or profession, and his genius to objects of his tranquil and unbiassed choice; while the consciousness of being actuated in both alike by the sincere desire to perform his duty, will alike ennoble both. "My dear young friend," (I would say) "suppose yourself established in any honorable occupation. From the manufactory or counting-house, from the law-court, or from having visited your last patient, you return at evening,

> "Dear tranquil time, when the sweet sense of home
> Is sweetest——"

to your family, prepared for its social enjoyments, with the very countenances of your wife and children brightened, and their voice of welcome made doubly welcome, by the knowledge that, as far as *they* are concerned, you have satisfied the demands of the day by the labor of the day. Then, when you retire into your study, in the books on your shelves you revisit so many venerable friends with whom you can converse. Your own spirit scarcely less free from personal anxieties than the great minds, that in those books are still living for you! Even your writing desk with its blank paper and all its other implements will appear as a chain of flowers, capable of linking your feelings as well as thoughts to events and characters past or to come; not a chain of iron, which binds you down to think of the future and the remote by recalling the claims and feelings of the peremptory present. But why should I say *retire?* The habits of active life and daily intercourse with the stir of the world will tend to give you such self-command, that the presence of your family will be no interruption. Nay, the social silence, or undisturbing voices of a wife or sister, will be like a restorative atmosphere, or soft music which moulds a dream without becoming its object. If facts are required to prove the possibility of combining weighty performances in literature with full and independent employment, the works of Cicero and Xenophon among the ancients; of Sir Thomas Moore, Bacon, Baxter, or to refer at once to later and contemporary instances, DARWIN and ROSCOE, are at once decisive of the question.

But all men may not dare promise themselves a sufficiency of self-controul for the imitation of those examples: though strict scrutiny should always be made, whether indolence, restlessness, or a vanity impatient for immediate gratification, have not tampered with the judgement and assumed the vizard of humility for the purposes of self-delusion. Still the church presents to every man of learning and genius a profession, in which he may cherish a rational hope of being able to unite the widest schemes of literary utility with the strictest performance of professional duties. Among the numerous blessings of Christianity, the introduction of an established church makes an especial claim on the gratitude of scholars and philosophers; in England, at least, where the principles of Protestantism have conspired with the freedom of the government to double all its salutary powers by the removal of its abuses.

That not only the maxims, but the grounds of a pure morality, the mere fragments of which

> "—— the lofty grave tragedians taught
> In chorus or iambic, teachers best
> Of moral prudence, with delight received
> In brief sententious precepts;"
>
> PARADISE REGAINED

and that the sublime truths of the divine unity and attributes, which a Plato found most hard to learn and deemed it still more difficult to reveal; that these should have become the almost hereditary property of childhood and poverty, of the hovel and the workshop; that even to the unlettered they sound as *common place,* is a phenomenon, which must withhold all but minds of the most vulgar cast from undervaluing the services even of the pulpit and the reading desk. Yet those, who confine the efficiency of an established church to its *public* offices, can hardly be placed in a much higher rank of intellect. That to every parish throughout the kingdom there is transplanted a germ of civilization; that in the remotest villages there is a nucleus, round which the capabilities of the place may crystallize and brighten; a model sufficiently superior to excite, yet sufficiently near to encourage and facilitate, imitation; *this,* the inobtrusive continuous agency of a Protestant church establishment, *this* it is, which the patriot, and the philanthropist, who would fain unite the love of peace with the faith in the progressive amelioration of mankind, cannot estimate at too high a price. "It cannot be valued with the gold of Ophir, with the precious onyx, or the sapphire. No mention shall be made of coral, or of pearls: for the price of wisdom is above rubies." The clergyman is with his parishioners and among them; he is neither in the cloistered cell, nor in the wilderness, but a neighbour and a family-man, whose education and rank admit him to the mansion of the rich landholder, while his duties make him the frequent visitor of the farm-house and the cottage. He is, or he may become, connected with the families of his parish or its vicinity by marriage. And among the instances of the blindness, or at best of the short-sightedness, which it is the nature of cupidity to inflict, I know few more striking than the clamors of the farmers against church property. Whatever was not paid to the clergyman would inevitably at the next lease be paid to the landholder, while, as the case at present stands, the revenues of the church are in some sort the reversionary property of every family, that may have a member educated for the church, or a daughter that may marry a clergyman. Instead of being *foreclosed* and immovable, it is in fact the only species of landed property, that is essentially moving and circulative. That there exist no inconveniences, who will pretend to assert? But I have yet to expect the proof, that the inconveniences are greater in this than in any other species; or that either the farmers or the clergy would be benefited by forcing the latter to become either *Trullibers* or salaried *placemen.* Nay, I do not hesitate to declare my firm persuasion, that whatever *reason* of discontent the farmers may assign, the true *cause* is this; that they may cheat the *parson,* but cannot cheat the steward; and that they are disappointed, if they should have been able to withhold only two pounds less than the legal claim, having expected to withhold five. At all events, considered relatively to the encouragement of learning and genius, the establishment presents a patronage at once so effective and unburthensome, that it would be impossible to afford the like or equal in any but a Christian and Protestant country. There is scarce a department of human knowledge without some bearing on the various critical, historical, philosophical and moral truths, in which the scholar must be interested as a clergyman; no one pursuit worthy of a man of genius, which may not be followed without incongruity. To give the history of the Bible as a *book*, would be little less than to relate the origin or first excitement of all the literature and science, that we now possess. The very decorum, which the profession imposes, is favorable to the best purposes of genius, and tends to counteract its most frequent defects. Finally, that man must be deficient in sensibility, who would not find an incentive to emulation in the great and burning lights, which in a long series have illustrated the Church of England; who would not hear from within an echo to the voice from their sacred shrines,

"Et Pater Æneas et avunculus excitat Hector."

But, whatever be the profession or trade chosen, the advantages are many and important, compared with the state of a *mere* literary man, who in any degree depends on the sale of his works for the necessaries and comforts of life. In the former a man lives in sympathy with the world, in which he lives. At least he acquires a better and quicker tact for the knowledge of that, with which men in general can sympathize. He learns to manage his genius more prudently and efficaciously. His powers and acquirements gain him likewise more real admiration; for they surpass the legitimate expectations of others. He is something besides an author, and is not therefore considered merely as an author. The hearts of men are open to him, as to one of their own class; and whether he exerts himself or not in the conversational circles of his acquaintance, his silence is not attributed to pride, nor his communicativeness to vanity. To these advantages I will venture to add a superior chance of happiness in domestic life, were it only that it is as natural for the man to be out of the circle of his household during the day, as it is meritorious for the woman to remain for the most part within it. But this subject involves points of consideration so numerous and so delicate, and would not only permit, but require such ample documents from the biography of literary men, that I now merely allude to it *in transitu*. When the same circumstance has occurred at very different times to very different persons, all of whom have some one thing in common; there is reason to suppose that such circumstance is not merely attributable to the *persons* concerned, but is in some measure occasioned by the one point in common to them all. Instead of the vehement and almost slanderous dehortation from marriage, which the *Misogyne*, Boccaccio (*Vita e Costumi di* DANTE, p. 12, 16) addresses to literary men, I would substitute the simple advice: be not *merely* a man of letters! Let literature be an honourable *augmentation* to your arms; but not constitute the coat, or fill the escutcheon!

To objections from conscience I can of course answer in no other way, than by requesting the youthful objector (as I have already done on a former occasion) to ascertain with strict self-examination, whether other influences may not be at work; whether spirits, "*not of health,*" and with whispers "*not from*

heaven," may not be walking in the *twilight* of his consciousness. Let him catalogue his scruples, and reduce them in a distinct intelligible form; let him be certain, that he has read with a docile mind and favourable dispositions the best and most fundamental works on the subject; that he has had both mind and heart opened to the great and illustrious qualities of the many renowned characters, who had doubted like himself, and whose researches had ended in the clear conviction, that their doubts had been groundless, or at least in no proportion to the counter-weight. Happy will it be for such a man, if among his contemporaries elder than himself he should meet with one, who, with similar powers and feelings as acute as his own, had entertained the same scruples; had acted upon them; and who by after-research (when the step was, alas! irretrievable, but for that very reason his research undeniably disinterested) had discovered himself to have quarrelled with received opinions only to embrace errors, to have left the direction tracked out for him on the high road of honorable exertion, only to deviate into a labyrinth, where when he had wandered till his head was giddy, his best good fortune was finally to have found his way out again, too late for prudence though not too late for conscience or for truth! Time spent in such delay is time won: for manhood in the mean-time is advancing, and with it increase of knowledge, strength of judgement, and above all, temperance of feelings. And even if these should effect no change, yet the delay will at least prevent the final approval of the decision from being alloyed by the inward censure of the rashness and vanity, by which it had been precipitated. It would be a sort or irreligion, and scarcely less than a libel on human nature to believe, that there is any established and reputable profession or employment, in which a man may not continue to act with honesty and honor; and doubtless there is likewise none, which may not at times present temptations to the contrary. But woefully will that man find himself mistaken, who imagines that the profession of literature, or (to speak more plainly) the *trade* of authorship, besets its members with fewer or with less insidious temptations, than the church, the law, or the different branches of commerce. But I have treated sufficiently on this unpleasant subject in an early chapter of this volume. I will conclude the present therefore with a short extract from HERDER, whose name I might have added to the illustrious list of those, who have combined the successful pursuit of the Muses, not only with the faithful discharge, but with the highest honors and honorable emoluments, of an established profession. The translation the reader will find in a note

below.[43] "Am sorgfältigsten, meiden Sie die Autorschaft. Zu früh oder unmässig gebraucht, macht sie den Kopf wüste und das Herz leer; wenn sie auch sonst keine üble Folgen gäbe. Ein Mensch, der nur lieset um zu drucken, lieset wahrscheinlich übel; und wer jeden Gedanken, der ihm aufstösst, durch Feder und Presse versendet, hat sie in kurzer Zeit alle versandt, und wird bald ein blosser Diener der Druckerey, ein Buchstabensetzer werden."

HERDER.

CHAPTER XII

A Chapter of requests and premonitions concerning the perusal or omission of the chapter that follows.

IN THE perusal of philosophical works I have been greatly benefited by a resolve, which, in the antithetic form and with the allowed quaintness of an adage or maxim, I have been accustomed to word thus: *"until you understand a writer's ignorance, presume yourself ignorant of his understanding."* This *golden rule* of mine does, I own, resemble those of Pythagoras in its obscurity rather than in its depth. If however the reader will permit me to be my own Hierocles, I trust, that he will find its meaning fully explained by the following instances. I have now before me a treatise of a religious fanatic, full of dreams and supernatural *experiences.* I see clearly the writer's grounds, and their hollowness. I have a complete insight into the causes, which through the medium of his body has acted on his mind; and by application of received and ascertained laws I can satisfactorily explain to my own reason all the strange incidents, which the writer records of himself. And this I can do without suspecting him of any intentional falsehood. As when in broad day-light a

[43] TRANSLATION: "With the greatest possible solicitude avoid authorship. Too early or immoderately employed, it makes the head *waste* and the heart empty; even were there no other worse consequences. A person, who reads only to print, in all probability reads amiss; and he, who sends away through the pen and the press every thought, the moment it occurs to him, will in a short time have sent all away, and will become a mere journeyman of the printing-office, a *compositor.*"

To which I may add from myself, that what medical physiologists affirm of certain secretions applies equally to our thoughts; they too must be taken up again into the circulation, and be again and again re-secreted in order to ensure a healthful vigor, both to the mind and to its intellectual offspring.

man tracks the steps of a traveller, who had lost his way in a fog or by a treacherous moonshine, even so, and with the same tranquil sense of certainty, can I follow the traces of this bewildered visionary. I UNDERSTAND HIS IGNORANCE.

On the other hand, I have been re-perusing with the best energies of my mind the Timæus of PLATO. Whatever I comprehend, impresses me with a reverential sense of the author's genius; but there is a considerable portion of the work, to which I can attach no consistent meaning. In other treatises of the same philosopher, intended for the average comprehensions of men, I have been delighted with the masterly good sense, with the perspicuity of the language, and the aptness of the inductions. I recollect likewise, that numerous passages in this author, which I thoroughly comprehend, were formerly no less unintelligible to me, than the passages now in question. It would, I am aware, be quite *fashionable* to dismiss them at once as Platonic Jargon. But this I cannot do with satisfaction to my own mind, because I have sought in vain for causes adequate to the solution of the assumed inconsistency. I have no insight into the possibility of a man so eminently wise using words with such half-meanings to himself, as must perforce pass into no-meaning to his readers. When in addition to the motives thus suggested by my own reason, I bring into distinct remembrance the number and the series of great men, who after long and zealous study of these works had joined in honoring the name of PLATO with epithets, that almost transcend humanity, I feel, that a contemptuous verdict on my part might argue want of modesty, but would hardly be received by the judicious, as evidence of superior penetration. Therefore, utterly baffled in all my attempts to understand the ignorance of Plato, I CONCLUDE MYSELF IGNORANT OF HIS UNDERSTANDING.

In lieu of the various requests which the anxiety of authorship addresses to the unknown reader, I advance but this one; that he will either pass over the following chapter altogether, or read the whole connectedly. The fairest part of the most beautiful body will appear deformed and monstrous, if dissevered from its place in the organic Whole. Nay, on delicate subjects, where a seemingly trifling difference of more or less may constitute a difference in *kind*, even a *faithful* display of the main and supporting ideas, if yet they are separated from the forms by which they are at once cloathed and modified, may perchance present a skeleton indeed; but a skeleton to alarm and deter. Though I might find numerous precedents, I shall not desire the reader to strip his mind of all prejudices, or to keep all prior systems out of view during his examination of the present. For in truth, such requests appear to me not much unlike the advice given to hypochondriacal patients in Dr. Buchan's domestic medicine; videlicet, to preserve themselves uniformly tranquil and in good spirits. Till I had discovered the art of destroying the memory *a parte post*, without injury to its future operations, and without detriment to the judgement, I should suppress the request as premature; and therefore, however much I may *wish* to be read with an unprejudiced mind, I do not presume to state it as a necessary condition.

The extent of my daring is to suggest one criterion, by which it may be rationally conjectured before-hand, whether or no a reader would lose his time, and perhaps his temper, in the perusal of this, or any other treatise constructed on similar principles. But it would be cruelly misinterpreted, as implying the least disrespect either for the moral or intellectual qualities of the individuals thereby precluded. The criterion is this: if a man receives as fundamental facts, and therefore of course indemonstrable and incapable of further analysis, the general notions of matter, spirit, soul, body, action, passiveness, time, space, cause, and effect, consciousness, perception, memory and habit; if he feels his mind completely at rest concerning all these, and is satisfied, if only he can analyse all other notions into some one or more of these supposed elements with plausible subordination and apt arrangement: to such a mind I would as courteously as possible convey the hint, that for him the chapter was not written.

"Vir bonus es, doctus, prudens; ast *haud tibi spiro*."

For these terms do in truth *include* all the difficulties, which the human mind can propose for solution. Taking them therefore in mass, and unexamined, it requires only a decent apprenticeship in logic, to draw forth their contents in all forms and colours, as the professors of legerdemain at our village fairs pull out ribbon after ribbon from their mouths. And not more difficult is it to reduce them back again to their different genera. But though this analysis is highly useful in rendering our knowledge more distinct, it does not really add to it. It does not increase, though it gives us a greater mastery over, the wealth which we before possessed. For forensic purposes, for all the established professions of society, this is sufficient. But for philosophy in its highest sense as the science of ultimate truths, and therefore scientia scientiarum, this mere analysis of terms is preparative only, though as a preparative discipline indispensable.

Still less dare a favorable perusal be anticipated from the pro-
selytes of that compendious philosophy, which talking of mind
but thinking of brick and mortar, or other images equally ab-
stracted from body, contrives a theory of spirit by nicknaming
matter, and in a few hours can qualify its dullest disciples to
explain the omne scibile by reducing all things to impressions,
ideas, and sensations.

But it is time to tell the truth; though it requires some courage
to avow it in an age and country, in which disquisitions on all
subjects, not privileged to adopt technical terms or scientific sym-
bols, must be addressed to the PUBLIC. I say then, that it is
neither possible or necessary for all men, or for many, to be PHI-
LOSOPHERS. There is a *philosophic* (and inasmuch as it is actual-
ized by an effort of freedom, an *artificial*) *consciousness*, which
lies beneath or (as it were) *behind* the spontaneous conscious-
ness natural to all reflecting beings. As the elder Romans distin-
guished their northern provinces into Cis-Alpine and Trans-Al-
pine, so may we divide all the objects of human knowledge into
those on this side, and those on the other side of the spontaneous
consciousness; citra et trans conscientiam communem. The latter
is exclusively the domain of PURE philosophy, which is therefore
properly entitled *transcendental*, in order to discriminate it at
once, both from mere reflection and *re*-presentation on the one
hand, and on the other from those flights of lawless speculation
which, abandoned by *all* distinct consciousness, because trans-
gressing the bounds and purposes of our intellectual faculties,
are justly condemned, as *transcendent*[44] The first range of hills,

---

[44] This distinction between transcendental and transcendent is ob-
served by our elder divines and philosophers, whenever they express
themselves *scholastically*. Dr. Johnson indeed has confounded the two
words; but his own authorities do not bear him out. Of this celebrated
dictionary I will venture to remark once for all, that I should suspect
the man of a morose disposition who should speak of it without respect
and gratitude as a most instructive and entertaining *book*, and hitherto,
unfortunately, an indispensable book; but I confess, that I should be
surprized at hearing from a philosophic and thorough scholar any but
very qualified praises of it, as a *dictionary*. I am not now alluding to
the number of genuine words omitted; for this is (and perhaps to a
greater extent) true, as Mr. Wakefield has noticed, of our best Greek
Lexicons, and this too after the successive labors of so many giants in
learning. I refer at present both to omissions and commissions of a
more important nature. What these are, me saltem judice, will be
stated at full in THE FRIEND, re-published and completed.

I had never heard of the correspondence between Wakefield and
Fox till I saw the account of it this morning (16th September 1815)

that encircles the scanty vale of human life, is the horizon for the majority of its inhabitants. On *its* ridges the common sun is born and departs. From *them* the stars rise, and touching *them* they vanish. By the many, even this range, the natural limit and bulwark of the vale, is but imperfectly known. Its higher ascents are too often hidden by mists and clouds from uncultivated swamps, which few have courage or curiosity to penetrate. To the multitude below these vapors appear, now as the dark haunts of terrific agents, on which none may intrude with impunity; and now all *a-glow*, with colors not their own, they are gazed at as the splendid palaces of happiness and power. But in all ages there have been a few, who measuring and sounding the rivers of the vale at the feet of their furthest inaccessible falls have learned, that the sources must be far higher and far inward; a few, who even in the level streams have detected elements, which neither the vale itself or the surrounding mountains contained or could supply. How and whence to these thoughts, these strong proba-

---

in the Monthly Review. I was not a little gratified at finding, that Mr. Wakefield had proposed to himself nearly the same plan for a Greek and English Dictionary, which I had formed, and began to execute, now ten years ago. But far, far more grieved am I, that he did not live to compleat it. I cannot but think it a subject of most serious regret, that the same heavy expenditure, which is now employing in the *re-publication* of STEPHANUS augmented, had not been applied to a new Lexicon on a more philosophical plan, with the English, German, and French synonymes as well as the Latin. In almost every instance the precise *individual* meaning might be given in an English or German word; whereas in Latin we must too often be contented with a mere general and *inclusive* term. How indeed can it be otherwise, when we attempt to render the most copious language of the world, the most admirable for the fineness of its distinctions into one of the poorest and most vague languages? Especially when we reflect on the comparative number of the works, still extant, written while the Greek and Latin were living languages. Were I asked what I deemed the greatest and most unmixt benefit, which a wealthy individual, or an association of wealthy individuals, could bestow on their country and on mankind, I should not hesitate to answer, "a philosophical English dictionary; with the Greek, Latin, German, French, Spanish, and Italian synonymes, and with correspondent indexes." That the learned languages might thereby be acquired, better, in half the time, is but a part, and not the most important part, of the advantages which would accrue from such a work. O! if it should be permitted by providence, that without detriment to freedom and independence our government might be enabled to become more than a committee for war and revenue! There was a time, when every thing was to be done by Government. Have we not flown off to the contrary extreme?

bilities, the ascertaining vision, the intuitive knowledge may finally supervene, can be learnt only by the fact. I might oppose to the question the words with which[45] Plotinus supposes NA-TURE to answer a similar difficulty. "Should any one interrogate her, how she works, if graciously she vouchsafe to listen and speak, she will reply, it behoves thee not to disquiet me with interrogatories, but to understand in silence even as I am silent, and work without words."

Likewise in the fifth book of the fifth *Ennead*, speaking of the highest and intuitive knowledge as distinguished from the discursive, or in the language of Wordsworth,

"The vision and the faculty divine;"

he says: "it is not lawful to enquire from whence it sprang, as if it were a thing subject to place and motion, for it neither approached hither, nor again departs from hence to some other place; but it either appears to us or it does not appear. So that we ought not to pursue it with a view of detecting its secret source, but to watch in quiet till it suddenly shines upon us; preparing ourselves for the blessed spectacle as the eye waits patiently for the rising sun." They and they only can acquire the philosophic imagination, the sacred power of self-intuition, who within themselves can interpret and understand the symbol, that the wings of the air-sylph are forming within the skin of the caterpillar; those only, who feel in their own spirits the same instinct, which impels the chrysalis of the horned fly to leave room in its involucrum for antennæ yet to come. They know and feel, that the *potential* works *in* them, even as the *actual* works *on* them! In short, all the organs of sense are framed for a cor-

---

[45] *Ennead*, iii. 1. 8. c. 3. The force of the Greek συνιέναι is imperfectly expressed by "understand;" our own idiomatic phrase *"to go along with me"* comes nearest to it. The passage, that follows, full of profound sense, appears to me evidently corrupt; and in fact no writer more wants, better deserves, or is less likely to obtain, a new and more correct edition—τί οὖν συνιέναι; ὅτι τὸ γενόμενον ἐστι θέαμα ἐμόν, σιώπησις (mallem, θέαμα, ἐμοῦ σιωπώσης), καὶ φύσει γενόμενον θεώρημα, καί μοι γενομένῃ ἐκ θεωρίας τῆς ὡδὶ τὴν φύσιν ἔχειν φιλοθεάμονα ὑπάρχει. (mallem, καὶ μοὶ ἡ γενομένη ἐκ θεωρίας αὐτῆς ὡδὶς) "what then are we to understand? That whatever is produced is an intuition, I silent; and that, which is thus generated, is by its nature a theorem, or form of contemplation; and the birth, which results to me from this contemplation, attains to have a contemplative nature." So Synesius: Ὠδὶς ἱερά, Ἄρρητα γονά. The after comparison of the process of the natura naturans with that of the geometrician is drawn from the very heart of philosophy.

responding world of sense; and we have it. All the organs of spirit are framed for a correspondent world of spirit: though the latter organs are not developed in all alike. But they exist in all, and their first appearance discloses itself in the *moral* being. How else could it be, that even worldings, not wholly debased, will contemplate the man of simple and disinterested goodness with contradictory feelings of pity and respect? "Poor man! he is not made for *this* world." Oh! herein they utter a prophecy of universal fulfilment; for man *must* either rise or sink.

It is the essential mark of the true philosopher to rest satisfied with no imperfect light, as long as the impossibility of attaining a fuller knowledge has not been demonstrated. That the common consciousness itself will furnish proofs by its own direction, that it is connected with master-currents below the surface, I shall merely assume as a postulate pro tempore. This having been granted, though but in expectation of the argument, I can safely deduce from it the equal truth of my former assertion, that philosophy cannot be intelligible to all, even of the most learned and cultivated classes. A system, the first principle of which it is to render the mind intuitive of the *spiritual* in man (i.e. of that which lies *on the other side* of our natural consciousness) must needs have a greater obscurity for those, who have never disciplined and strengthened this ulterior consciousness. It must in truth be a land of darkness, a perfect *Anti-Goshen*, for men to whom the noblest treasures of their own being are reported only through the imperfect translation of lifeless and sightless *notions*. Perhaps, in great part, through words which are but the shadows of notions; even as the notional understanding itself is but the shadowy abstraction of living and actual truth. On the IMMEDIATE, which dwells in every man, and on the original intuition, or absolute affirmation of it, (which is likewise in every man, but does not in every man rise into consciousness) all the *certainty* of our knowledge depends; and this becomes intelligible to no man by the ministry of mere words from without. The medium, by which spirits understand each other, is not the surrounding air; but the *freedom* which they possess in common, as the common ethereal element of their being, the tremulous reciprocations of which propagate themselves even to the inmost of the soul. Where the spirit of a man is not *filled* with the consciousness of freedom (were it only from its restlessness, as of one still struggling in bondage) all spiritual intercourse is interrupted, not only with others, but even with himself. No wonder then, that he remains incomprehensible to himself as well as to others. No wonder, that, in the fearful desert of his consciousness, he wearies himself out with empty words, ∽ which no friendly echo answers, either from his own heart, or the heart of a fellow being; or bewilders himself in the pursuit of *notional* phantoms, the mere refractions from unseen and distant truths through the distorting medium of his own unenlivened and stagnant understanding! To remain unintelligible to such a mind, exclaims Schelling on a like occasion, is honor and a good name before God and man.

The history of philosophy (the same writer observes) contains instances of systems, which for successive generations have remained enigmatic. Such he deems the system of Leibnitz, whom another writer (rashly I think, and invidiously) extols as the *only* philosopher, who was himself deeply convinced of his own doctrines. As hitherto interpreted, however, they have not produced the effect, which Leibnitz himself, in a most instructive passage, describes as the criterion of a true philosophy; namely, that it would at once explain and collect the fragments of truth scattered through systems apparently the most incongruous. The truth, says he, is diffused more widely than is commonly believed; but it is often painted, yet oftener masked, and is sometimes mutilated and sometimes, alas! in close alliance with mischievous errors. The deeper, however, we penetrate into the ground of things, the more truth we discover in the doctrines of the greater number of the philosophical sects. The want of *substantial* reality in the objects of the senses, according to the sceptics; the harmonies or numbers, the prototypes and ideas, to which the Pythagoreans and Platonists reduced all things; the ONE and ALL of Parmenides and Plotinus, without[46] Spinozism; the necessary

[46] This is happily effected in three lines by SYNESIUS, in his Fourth HYMN:

Ἓν καὶ Πάντα—(taken by itself) is *Spinozism.*
Ἓν δ' Ἀπάντων—a mere *anima Mundi.*
Ἓν τε πρὸ πάντων—is mechanical Theism.

But unite all three, and the result is the Theism of Saint Paul and Christianity.

Synesius was censured for his doctrine of the Pre-existence of the Soul; but never, that I can find, arraigned or deemed heretical for his Pantheism, tho' neither Giordano Bruno, or Jacob Behmen ever avowed it more broadly.

Μύστας δὲ Νόος,
Τά τε καὶ τὰ λέγει,
Βυθὸν ἄρρητον
Ἀμφιχορεύων.
Σὺ τὸ τίκτον ἔφυς,

connection of things according to the Stoics, reconcileable with the spontaneity of the other schools; the vital-philosophy of the Cabalists and Hermetists, who assumed the universality of sensation; the substantial forms and entelechies of Aristotle and the schoolmen, together with the mechanical solution of all particular phenomena according to Democritus and the recent philosophers —all these we shall find united in one perspective central point, which shows regularity and a coincidence of all the parts in the very object, which from every other point of view must appear confused and distorted. The spirit of sectarianism has been hitherto our fault, and the cause of our failures. We have imprisoned our own conceptions by the lines, which we have drawn, in order to exclude the conceptions of others. J'ai trouvé que la plupart des sectes ont raison dans une bonne partie de ce qu'elles avancent, mais non pas tant en ce qu'elles nient.

A system, which aims to deduce the memory with all the other functions of intelligence, must of course place its first position from beyond the memory, and anterior to it, otherwise the principle of solution would be itself a part of the problem to be solved. Such a position therefore must in the first instance be demanded, and the first question will be, by what right is it demanded? On this account I think it expedient to make some preliminary remarks on the introduction of POSTULATES in philosophy. The word postulate is borrowed from the science of mathematics. (See Schell. Abhandl. zur Erläuter. des Id. der Wissenschaftslehre.) In geometry the primary construction is not demonstrated, but postulated. This first and most simple construction in space

---

Σὺ τὸ τικτόμενον·
Σὺ τὸ φώτιζον,
Σὺ τὸ λαμπόμενον·
Σὺ τὸ φαινόμενον,
Σὺ τὸ κρυπτόμενον
Ἰδίαις αὐγαῖς.
῍Εν καὶ πάντα,
῍Εν καθ᾽ ἑαυτὸ,
Καὶ διὰ πάντων.

Pantheism is therefore not necessarily irreligious or heretical; tho' it may be taught atheistically. Thus Spinoza would agree with Synesius in calling God Φύσις ἐν Νοεροῖς, the Nature in Intelligences; but he could not subscribe to the preceding Νοῦς καὶ Νοερός, i.e. Himself Intelligence and intelligent.

In this biographical sketch of my literary life I may be excused, if I mention here, that I had translated the eight Hymns of Synesius from the Greek into English Anacreontics before my 15th year.

is the point in motion, or the line. Whether the point is moved in one and the same direction, or whether its direction is continually changed, remains as yet undetermined. But if the direction of the point have been determined, it is either by a point without it, and then there arises the straight line which incloses no space; or the direction of the point is not determined by a point without it, and then it must flow back again on itself, that is, there arises a cyclical line, which does inclose a space. If the straight line be assumed as the positive, the cyclical is then the negation of the straight. It is a line, which at no point strikes out into the straight, but changes its direction continuously. But if the primary line be conceived as undetermined, and the straight line as determined throughout, then the cyclical is the third compounded of both. It is at once undetermined and determined; undetermined through any point without, and determined through itself. Geometry therefore supplies philosophy with the example of a primary intuition, from which every science that lays claim to *evidence* must take its commencement. The mathematician does not begin with a demonstrable proposition, but with an intuition, a practical idea.

But here an important distinction presents itself. Philosophy is employed on objects of the INNER SENSE, and cannot, like geometry, appropriate to every construction a correspondent *outward* intuition. Nevertheless, philosophy, if it is to arrive at evidence, must proceed from the most original construction, and the question then is, what is the most original construction or first productive act for the INNER SENSE. The answer to this question depends on the direction which is given to the INNER SENSE. But in philosophy the INNER SENSE cannot have its direction determined by any outward object. To the original construction of the line I can be compelled by a line drawn before me on the slate or on sand. The stroke thus drawn is indeed not the line itself, but only the image or picture of the line. It is not from it, that we first learn to know the line; but, on the contrary, we bring this stroke to the original line generated by the act of the imagination; otherwise we could not define it as without breadth or thickness. Still however this stroke is the sensuous image of the original or ideal line, and an efficient mean to excite *every* imagination to the intuition of it.

It is demanded then, whether there be found any means in philosophy to determine the direction of the INNER SENSE, as in mathematics it is determinable by its specific image or outward picture. Now the inner sense has its direction determined for the greater part only by an act of freedom. One man's consciousness extends only to the pleasant or unpleasant sensations caused in him by external impressions; another enlarges his inner sense to a consciousness of forms and quantity; a third in addition to the image is conscious of the conception or notion of the thing; a fourth attains to a notion of his notions—he reflects on his own reflections; and thus we may say without impropriety, that the one possesses more or less inner sense, than the other. This more or less betrays already, that philosophy in it first principles must have a practical or moral, as well as a theoretical or speculative side. This difference in degree does not exist in the mathematics. Socrates in Plato shows, that an ignorant slave may 'be brought to understand and of himself to solve the most difficult geometrical problem. Socrates drew the figures for the slave in the sand. The disciples of the critical philosophy could likewise (as was indeed actually done by La Forge and some other followers of Des Cartes) represent the origin of our representations in copperplates; but no one has yet attempted it, and it would be utterly useless. To an Esquimaux or New Zealander our most popular philosophy would be wholly unintelligible. The sense, the inward organ for it, is not yet born in him. So is there many a one among us, yes, and some who think themselves philosophers too, to whom the philosophic organ is entirely wanting. To such a man philosophy is a mere play of words and notions, like a theory of music to the deaf, or like the geometry of light to the blind. The connection of the parts and their logical dependencies may be seen and remembered; but the whole is groundless and hollow, unsustained by living contact, unaccompanied with any realizing intuition which exists by and in the act that affirms its existence, which is known, because it is, and is, because it is known. The words of Plotinus, in the assumed person of nature, hold true of the philosophic energy. Τὸ θεωροῦν μου θεώρημα ποιεῖ, ὥσπερ οἱ γεωμέτραι θεωροῦντες γράφουσιν· ἀλλ' ἐμοῦ μὴ γραφούσης, θεωρούσης δὲ, ὑφίστανται αἱ τῶν σωμάτων γραμμαί. With me the act of contemplation makes the thing contemplated, as the geometricians contemplating describe lines correspondent; but I not describing lines, but simply contemplating, the representative forms of things rise up into existence.

The postulate of philosophy and at the same time the test of philosophic capacity, is no other than the heaven-descended KNOW THYSELF! (E cœlo descendit, Γνῶθι σεαυτόν). And this at once practically and speculatively. For as philosophy is neither a science of the reason or understanding only, nor merely a science of morals, but the science of BEING altogether, its primary ground can be neither merely speculative or merely practical, but both in one. All knowledge rests on the coincidence of an object with a subject. (My readers have been warned in a former chapter that, for their convenience as well as the writer's, the term, subject, is used by me in its scholastic sense as equivalent to mind or sentient being, and as the necessary correlative of object or *quicquid objicitur menti.*) For we can *know* that only which is true: and the truth is universally placed in the coincidence of the thought with the thing, of the representation with the object represented.

Now the sum of all that is merely OBJECTIVE we will henceforth call NATURE, confining the term to its passive and material sense, as comprising all the phænomena by which its existence is made known to us. On the other hand the sum of all that is SUBJECTIVE, we may comprehend in the name of the SELF or INTELLIGENCE. Both conceptions are in necessary antithesis. Intelligence is conceived of as exclusively representative, nature as exclusively represented; the one as conscious, the other as without consciousness. Now in all acts of positive knowledge there is required a reciprocal concurrence of both, namely of the conscious being, and of that which is in itself unconscious. Our problem is to explain this concurrence, its possibility and its necessity.

During the act of knowledge itself, the objective and subjective are so instantly united, that we cannot determine to which of the two the priority belongs. There is here no first, and no second; both are coinstantaneous and one. While I am attempting to explain this intimate coalition, I must suppose it dissolved. I must necessarily set out from the one, to which therefore I give hypothetical antecedence, in order to arrive at the other. But as there are but two factors or elements in the problem, subject and object, and as it is left indeterminate from which of them I should commence, there are two cases equally possible.

1. EITHER THE OBJECTIVE IS TAKEN AS THE FIRST, AND THEN WE HAVE TO ACCOUNT FOR THE SUPERVENTION OF THE SUBJECTIVE, WHICH COALESCES WITH IT.

The notion of the subjective is not contained in the notion of the objective. On the contrary they mutually exclude each other. The subjective therefore must supervene to the objective. The conception of nature does not apparently involve the co-presence of an intelligence making an ideal duplicate of it, i.e. representing it. This desk for instance would (according to our natural notions) be, though there should exist no sentient being to look at it. This then is the problem of natural philosophy. It assumes the objective or unconscious nature as the first, and has therefore to explain how intelligence can supervene to it, or how itself can grow into intelligence. If it should appear, that all enlightened naturalists, without having distinctly proposed the problem to themselves, have yet constantly moved in the line of its solution, it must afford a strong presumption that the problem itself is founded in nature. For if all knowledge has as it were two poles reciprocally required and presupposed, all sciences must proceed from the one or the other, and must tend toward the opposite as far as the equatorial point in which both are reconciled and become identical. The necessary tendence therefore of all natural philosophy is from nature to intelligence; and this, and no other, is the true ground and occasion of the instinctive striving to introduce theory into our views of natural phænomena. The highest perfection of natural philosophy would consist in the perfect spiritualization of all the laws of nature into laws of intuition and intellect. The phænomena (*the material*) must wholly disappear, and the laws alone (*the formal*) must remain. Thence it comes, that in nature itself the more the principle of law breaks forth, the more does the *husk* drop off, the phænomena themselves become more spiritual and at length cease altogether in our consciousness. The optical phænomena are but a geometry, the lines of which are drawn by light, and the materiality of this light itself has already become matter of doubt. In the appearances of magnetism all trace of matter is lost, and of the phænomena of gravitation, which not a few among the most illustrious Newtonians have declared no otherwise comprehensible than as an immediate spiritual influence, there remains nothing but its law, the execution of which on a vast scale is the mechanism of the heavenly motions. The theory of natural philosophy would then be completed, when all nature was demonstrated to be identical in essence with that, which in its highest known power exists in man as intelligence and self-consciousness; when the heavens and the earth shall declare not only the power of their maker, but the glory and the presence of their God, even as he appeared to the great prophet during the vision of the mount in the skirts of his divinity.

This may suffice to show, that even natural science, which commences with the material phænomenon as the reality and substance of things existing, does yet by the necessity of theorizing unconsciously, and as it were instinctively, end in nature as an intelligence; and by this tendency the science of nature becomes finally natural philosophy, the one of the two poles of fundamental science.

2. Or THE SUBJECTIVE IS TAKEN AS THE FIRST, AND THE

PROBLEM THEN IS, HOW THERE SUPERVENES TO IT A COINCIDENT OBJECTIVE.

In the pursuit of these sciences, our success in each depends on an austere and faithful adherence to its own principles, with a careful separation and exclusion of those, which appertain to the opposite science. As the natural philosopher, who directs his views to the objective, avoids above all things the intermixture of the subjective in his knowledge, as for instance, arbitrary suppositions or rather suffictions, occult qualities, spiritual agents, and the substitution of final for efficient causes; so on the other hand, the transcendental or intelligential philosopher is equally anxious to preclude all interpellation of the objective into the subjective principles of his science, as for instance the assumption of impresses or configurations in the brain, correspondent to miniature pictures on the retina painted by rays of light from supposed originals, which are not the immediate and real objects of vision, but deductions from it for the purposes of explanation. This purification of the mind is effected by an absolute and scientific scepticism, to which the mind voluntarily determines itself for the specific purpose of future certainty. Des Cartes who (in his meditations) himself first, at least of the moderns, gave a beautiful example of this voluntary doubt, this self-determined indetermination, happily expresses its utter difference from the scepticism of vanity or irreligion: Nec tamen in eo scepticos imitabar, qui dubitant tantum ut dubitent, et praeter incertitudinem ipsam nihil quaerunt. Nam contra totus in eo eram ut aliquid certi reperirem. DES CARTES, *de Methodo*. Nor is it less distinct in its motives and final aim, than in its proper objects, which are not as in ordinary scepticism the prejudices of education and circumstance, but those original and innate prejudices which nature herself has planted in all men, and which to all but the philosopher are the first principles of knowledge, and the final test of truth.

Now these essential prejudices are all reducible to the one fundamental presumption, THAT THERE EXIST THINGS WITHOUT US. As this on the one hand originates, neither in grounds nor arguments, and yet on the other hand remains proof against all attempts to remove it by grounds or arguments (*naturam furca expellas tamen usque redibit*); on the one hand lays claim to IMMEDIATE certainty as a position at once indemonstrable and irresistible, and yet on the other hand, inasmuch as it refers to something essentially different from ourselves, nay even in opposition to ourselves, leaves it inconceivable how it could possibly become a part of our immediate consciousness (in other words how that, which ex hypothesi is and continues to be extrinsic and alien to our being, should become a modification of our being); the philosopher therefore compels himself to treat this faith as nothing more than a prejudice, innate indeed and connatural, but still a prejudice.

The other position, which not only claims but necessitates the admission of its immediate certainty, equally for the scientific reason of the philosopher as for the common sense of mankind at large, namely, I AM, cannot so properly be intitled a prejudice. It is groundless indeed; but then in the very idea it precludes all ground, and separated from the immediate consciousness loses its whole sense and import. It is groundless; but only because it is itself the ground of all other certainty. Now the apparent contradiction, that the former position, namely, the existence of things without us, which from its nature cannot be immediately certain, should be received as blindly and as independently of all grounds as the existence of our own being, the transcendental philosopher can solve only by the supposition, that the former is unconsciously involved in the latter; that it is not only coherent but identical, and one and the same thing with our own immediate self-consciousness. To demonstrate this identity is the office and object of his philosophy.

If it be said, that this is Idealism, let it be remembered that it is only so far idealism, as it is at the same time, and on that very account, the truest and most binding realism. For wherein does the realism of mankind properly consist? In the assertion that there exists a something without them, what, or how, or where they know not, which occasions the objects of their perception? Oh no! This is neither connatural nor universal. It is what a few have taught and learned in the schools, and which the many repeat without asking themselves concerning their own meaning. The realism common to all mankind is far elder and lies infinitely deeper than this hypothetical explanation of the origin of our perceptions, an explanation skimmed from the mere surface of mechanical philosophy. It is the table itself, which the man of common sense believes himself to see, not the phantom of a table, from which he may argumentatively deduce the reality of a table, which he does not see. If to destroy the reality of all, that we actually behold, be idealism, what can be more egregiously so, than the system of modern metaphysics, which banishes us to a land of shadows, surrounds us with apparitions, and distinguishes truth from illusion only by the majority of those who dream the same dream? "*I* asserted that the world was mad," exclaimed poor Lee, "and the world said, that I was mad, and confound them, they outvoted me."

It is to the true and original realism, that I would direct the attention. This believes and requires neither more nor less, than the object which it beholds or presents to itself, is the real and very object. In this sense, however much we may strive against it, we are all collectively born idealists, and therefore and only therefore are we at the same time realists. But of this the philosophers of the schools know nothing, or despise the faith as the prejudice of the ignorant vulgar, because they live and move in a crowd of phrases and notions from which human nature has long ago vanished. Oh, ye that reverence yourselves, and walk humbly with the divinity in your own hearts, ye are worthy of a better philosophy! Let the dead bury the dead, but do you preserve your human nature, the depth of which was never yet fathomed by a philosophy made up of notions and mere logical entities.

In the third treatise of my *Logosophia,* announced at the end of this volume, I shall give (deo volente) the demonstrations and constructions of the Dynamic Philosophy scientifically arranged. It is, according to my conviction, no other than the system of Pythagoras and of Plato revived and purified from impure mixtures. Doctrina per tot manus tradita tandem in VAPPAM desiit. The science of arithmetic furnishes instances, that a rule may be useful in practical application, and for the particular purpose may be sufficiently authenticated by the result, before it has itself been fully demonstrated. It is enough, if only it be rendered intelligible. This will, I trust, have been effected in the following Theses for those of my readers, who are willing to accompany me through the following Chapter, in which the results will be applied to the deduction of the Imagination, and with it the principles of production and of genial criticism in the fine arts.

THESIS I.

Truth is correlative to being. Knowledge without a correspondent reality is no knowledge; if we know, there must be somewhat known by us. To know is in its very essence a verb active.

THESIS II.

All truth is either mediate, that is, derived from some other truth or truths; or immediate and original. The latter is absolute, and its formula A. A.; the former is of dependent or conditional certainty, and represented in the formula B. A. The certainty, which adheres in A, is attributable to B.

SCHOLIUM. A chain without a staple, from which all the links derived their stability, or a series without a first, has been not inaptly allegorized, as a string of blind men, each holding the skirt of the man before him, reaching far out of sight, but all moving without the least deviation in one straight line. It would be naturally taken for granted, that there was a guide at the head of the file: what if it were answered, No! Sir, the men are without number, and infinite blindness supplies the place of sight?

Equally *inconceivable* is a cycle of equal truths without a common and central principle, which prescribes to each its proper sphere in the system of science. That the absurdity does not so immediately strike us, that it does not seem equally *unimaginable*, is owing to a surreptitious act of the imagination, which, instinctively and without our noticing the same, not only fills up the intervening spaces, and contemplates the *cycle* (of B. C. D. E. F. &c.) as a continuous *circle* (A.) giving to all collectively the unity of their common orbit; but likewise supplies, by a sort of *subintelligitur*, the one central power, which renders the movement harmonious and cyclical.

THESIS III.

We are to seek therefore for some absolute truth capable of communicating to other positions a certainty, which it has not itself borrowed; a truth self-grounded, unconditional and known by its own light. In short, we have to find a somewhat which *is*, simply because it *is*. In order to be such, it must be one which is its own predicate, so far at least that all other nominal predicates must be modes and repetitions of itself. Its existence too must be such, as to preclude the possibility of requiring a cause or antecedent without an absurdity.

THESIS IV.

That there can be one such principle, may be proved a priori; for were there two or more, each must refer to some other, by which its equality is affirmed; consequently neither would be self-established, as the hypothesis demands. And a posteriori, it will be proved by the principle itself when it is discovered, as involving universal antecedents in its very conception.

SCHOLIUM. If we affirm of a board that it is blue, the predicate (blue) is accidental, and not implied in the subject, board. If we affirm of a circle that it is equi-radial, the predicate indeed is implied in the definition of the subject; but the existence of the subject itself is contingent, and supposes both a cause and a percipient. The same reasoning will apply to the indefinite number of supposed indemonstrable truths exempted from the prophane approach of philosophic investigation by the amiable Beattie, and other less eloquent and not more profound inaugurators of common sense on the throne of philosophy; a fruitless attempt, were it only that it is the two-fold function of philosophy to reconcile reason with common sense, and to elevate common sense into reason.

Thesis V.

Such a principle cannot be any THING or OBJECT. Each thing is what it is in consequence of some other thing. An infinite, independent[47] *thing*, is no less a contradiction, than an infinite circle or a sideless triangle. Besides a thing is that, which is capable of being an object of which itself is not the sole percipient. But an object is inconceivable without a subject as its antithesis. Omne perceptum percipientem supponit.

But neither can the principle be found in a subject as a subject, contra-distinguished from an object: for unicuique percipienti aliquid objicitur perceptum. It is to be found therefore neither in object nor subject taken separately, and consequently, as no other third is conceivable, it must be found in that which is neither subject nor object exclusively, but which is the identity of both.

Thesis VI.

This principle, and so characterised, manifests itself in the SUM or I AM; which I shall hereafter indiscriminately express by the words spirit, self, and self-consciousness. In this, and in this alone, object and subject, being and knowing are identical, each involving, and supposing the other. In other words, it is a subject which becomes a subject by the act of constructing itself objectively to itself; but which never is an object except for itself, and only so far as by the very same act it becomes a subject. It may be described therefore as a perpetual self-duplication of one and the same power into object and subject, which presuppose each other, and can exist only as antitheses.

SCHOLIUM. If a man be asked how he *knows* that he is? he can only answer, sum quia sum. But if (the absoluteness of this

---

[47] The impossibility of an absolute thing (substantia unica) as neither genus, species, nor individuum: as well as its utter unfitness for the fundamental position of a philosophic system, will be demonstrated in the critique on Spinozism in the fifth treatise of my Logosophia.

certainty having been admitted) he be again asked, how he, the individual person, came to be, then in relation to the ground of his *existence*, not to the ground of his *knowledge* of that existence, he might reply, sum quia Deus est, or still more philosophically, sum quia in Deo sum.

But if we elevate our conception to the absolute self, the great eternal I AM, then the principle of being, and of knowledge, of idea, and of reality; the ground of existence, and the ground of the knowledge of existence, are absolutely identical, Sum quia sum;[48] I am, because I affirm myself to be; I affirm myself to be, because I am.

Thesis VII.

If then I know myself only through myself, it is contradictory to require any other predicate of self, but that of self-conscious-

[48] It is most worthy of notice, that in the first revelation of himself, not confined to individuals; indeed in the very first revelation of his absolute being, Jehovah at the same time revealed the fundamental truth of all philosophy, which must either commence with the absolute, or have no fixed commencement; that is, cease to be philosophy. I cannot but express my regret, that in the equivocal use of the word *that*, for *in that*, or *because*, our admirable version has rendered the passage susceptible of a degraded interpretation in the mind of common readers or hearers, as if it were a mere reproof to an impertinent question, I am what I am, which might be equally affirmed of himself by any existent being.

The Cartesian Cogito, ergo sum is objectionable, because either the Cogito is used extra Gradum, and then it is involved in the sum and is tautological; or it is taken as a particular mode or dignity, and then it is subordinated to the sum as the species to the genus, or rather as a particular modification to the subject modified; and not pre-ordinated as the arguments seem to require. For Cogito is Sum Cogitans. This is clear by the inevidence of the converse. Cogitat, ergo est is true, because it is a mere application of the logical rule: Quicquid in genere est, est et in specie. Est (cogitans), ergo est. It is a cherry tree; therefore it is a tree. But, est ergo cogitat, is illogical: for quod est in specie, non *necessario* in genere est. It may be true—I hold it to be true, that quicquid vere est, est per veram sui affirmationem; but it is a derivative, not an immediate truth. Here then we have, by anticipation, the distinction between the conditional finite I (which, as known in distinct consciousness by occasion of experience, is called by Kant's followers the empirical I) and the absolute I AM, and likewise the dependence or rather the inherence of the former in the latter; in whom "we live, and move, and have our being," as St. Paul divinely asserts, differing widely from the Theists of the mechanic school (as Sir J. Newton, Locke, &c.) who must say from *whom* we *had* our being, and with it life and the powers of life.

ness. Only in the self-consciousness of a spirit is there the required identity of object and of representation; for herein consists the essence of a spirit, that it is self-representative. If therefore this be the one only immediate truth, in the certainty of which the reality of our collective knowledge is grounded, it must follow that the spirit in all the objects which it views, views only itself. If this could be proved, the immediate reality of all intuitive knowledge would be assured. It has been shown, that a spirit is that, which is its own object, yet not originally an object, but an absolute subject for which all, itself included, may become an object. It must therefore be an ACT; for every object is, as an *object*, dead, fixed, incapable in itself of any action, and necessarily finite. Again the spirit (originally the identity of object and subject) must in some sense dissolve this identity, in order to be conscious of it: fit alter et idem. But this implies an act, and it follows therefore that intelligence or self-consciousness is impossible, except by and in a will. The self-conscious spirit therefore is a will; and freedom must be assumed as a *ground* of philosophy, and can never be deduced from it.

THESIS VIII.

Whatever in its origin is objective, is likewise as such necessarily finite. Therefore, since the spirit is not originally an object, and as the subject exists in antithesis to an object, the spirit cannot originally be finite. But neither can it be a subject without becoming an object, and, as it is originally the identity of both, it can be conceived neither as infinite nor finite exclusively, but as the most original union of both. In the existence, in the reconciling, and the recurrence of this contradiction consists the process and mystery of production and life.

THESIS IX.

This principium commune essendi et cognoscendi, as subsisting in a WILL, or primary ACT of self-duplication, is the mediate or indirect principle of every science; but it is the immediate and direct principle of the ultimate science alone, i.e. of transcendental philosophy alone. For it must be remembered, that all these Theses refer solely to one of the two Polar Sciences, namely, to that which commences with, and rigidly confines itself within, the subjective, leaving the objective (as far as it is exclusively objective) to natural philosophy, which is its opposite pole. In its very idea therefore as a systematic knowledge of our collective KNOWING, (scientia scientiæ) it involves the necessity of some one highest principle or knowing, as at once the source and accompanying form in all particular acts of intellect and perception. This, it has been shown, can be found only in the act and evolution of self-consciousness. We are not investigating an absolute principium essendi; for then, I admit, many valid objections might be started against our theory; but an absolute principium cognoscendi. The result of both the sciences, or their equatorial point, would be the principle of a total and undivided philosophy, as, for prudential reasons, I have chosen to anticipate in the Scholium to Thesis VI. and the note subjoined. In other words, philosophy would pass into religion, and religion become inclusive of philosophy. We begin with the I KNOW MYSELF, in order to end with the absolute I AM. We proceed from the SELF, in order to lose and find all self in GOD.

THESIS X.

The transcendental philosopher does not inquire, what ultimate ground of our knowledge there may lie out of our knowing, but what is the last in our knowing itself, beyond which *we* cannot pass. The principle of our knowing is sought within the sphere of our knowing. It must be something therefore, which can itself be known. It is asserted only, that the act of self-consciousness is for *us* the source and principle of all *our* possible knowledge. Whether abstracted from us there exists any thing higher and beyond this primary self-knowing, which is for us the form of all our knowing, must be decided by the result.

That the self-consciousness is the fixt point, to which for *us* all is morticed and annexed, needs no further proof. But that the self-consciousness may be the modification of a higher form of being, perhaps of a higher consciousness, and this again of a yet higher, and so on in an infinite regressus; in short, that self-consciousness may be itself something explicable into something, which must lie beyond the possibility of our knowledge, because the whole synthesis of our intelligence is first formed in and through the self-consciousness, does not at all concern us as transcendental philosophers. For to us, self-consciousness is not a kind of *being*, but a kind of *knowing*, and that too the highest and farthest that exists for *us*. It may however be shown, and has in part already been shown in pages 242-243, that even when the Objective is assumed as the first, we yet can never pass beyond the principle of self-consciousness. Should we attempt it, we must be driven back from ground to ground, each of which would cease to be a Ground the moment we pressed on it. We must be whirl'd down the gulf of an infinite series. But this would make our reason baffle the end and purpose of all reason, namely, unity and system. Or we must break off the series arbitrarily, and affirm an absolute something that is in and of itself at once cause and effect (*causa sui*), subject and object, or rather the absolute identity of both. But as this is inconceivable, except in a self-consciousness, it follows, that even as natural philosophers we must arrive at the same principle from which as transcendental philosophers we set out; that is, in a self-consciousness in which the principium essendi does not stand to the principium cognoscendi in the relation of cause to effect, but both the one and the other are coinherent and identical. Thus the true system of natural philosophy places the sole reality of things in an ABSOLUTE, which is at once causa sui et effectus, πατὴρ αὐτοπάτωρ υἱὸς ἑαυτοῦ—in the absolute identity of subject and object, which it calls nature, and which in its highest power is nothing else than self-conscious will or intelligence. In this sense the position of Malbranche, that we see all things in God, is a strict philosophical truth; and equally true is the assertion of Hobbs, of Hartley, and of their masters in ancient Greece, that all real knowledge supposes a prior sensation. For sensation itself is but vision nascent, not the cause of intelligence, but intelligence itself revealed as an earlier power in the process of self-construction.

> Μάκαρ, ἵλαθί μοι·
> Πάτερ, ἵλαθί μοι
> Εἰ παρὰ κόσμον,
> Εἰ παρὰ μοῖραν
> Τῶν σῶν ἔθιγον!

Bearing then this in mind, that intelligence is a self-developement, not a quality supervening to a substance, we may abstract from all *degree*, and for the purpose of philosophic construction reduce it to *kind*, under the idea of an indestructible power with two opposite and counteracting forces, which by a metaphor borrowed from astronomy, we may call the centrifugal and centripetal forces. The intelligence in the one tends to *objectize* itself, and in the other to *know* itself in the object. It will be hereafter my business to construct by a series of intuitions the progressive schemes, that must follow from such a power with such forces, till I arrive at the fulness of the *human* intelligence. For my present purpose, I *assume* such a power, as my principle, in order to deduce from it a faculty, the generation, agency, and application of which form the contents of the ensuing chapter.

In a preceding page I have justified the use of technical terms in philosophy, whenever they tend to preclude confusion of thought, and when they assist the memory by the exclusive singleness of their meaning more than they may, for a short time, bewilder the attention by their strangeness. I trust, that I have not extended this privilege beyond the grounds on which I have claimed it; namely, the conveniency of the scholastic phrase to distinguish the kind from all degrees, or rather to express the kind with the abstraction of degree, as for instance multeity instead of multitude; or secondly, for the sake of correspondence in sound in interdependent or antithetical terms, as subject and object; or lastly, to avoid the wearying recurrence of circumlocutions and definitions. Thus I shall venture to use potence, in order to express a specific degree of a power, in imitation of the Algebraists. I have even hazarded the new verb potenziate, with its derivatives, in order to express the combination or transfer of powers. It is with new or unusual terms, as with privileges in courts of justice or legislature; there can be no legitimate *privilege*, where there already exists a positive law adequate to the purpose; and when there is no law in existence, the privilege is to be justified by its accordance with the end, or final cause, of all law. Unusual and new coined words are doubtless an evil; but vagueness, confusion, and imperfect conveyance of our thoughts, are a far greater. Every system, which is under the necessity of using terms not familiarized by the metaphysicks in fashion, will be described as written in an unintelligible style, and the author must expect the charge of having substituted learned jargon for clear conception; while, according to the creed of our modern philosophers, nothing is deemed a clear conception, but what is representable by a distinct image. Thus the *conceivable* is reduced within the bounds of the *picturable*. Hinc patet, quî fiat, ut *cum irrepræsentabile et impossibile* vulgo ejusdem significatûs habeantur, conceptus tam *Continui,* quam *Infiniti,* a plurimis rejiciantur, quippe quorum, *secundum leges cognitionis intuitivæ,* repræsentatio est impossibilis. Quanquam autem harum e non paucis scholis explosarum notionum, præsertim prioris, causam hic non gero, maximi tamen momenti erit monuisse: gravissimo illo errore labi, qui tam perversâ argumentandi ratione utuntur. Quicquid enim *repugnat* legibus intellectus et rationis, utique est impossibile; quod autem, cum rationis puræ sit objectum, legibus cognitionis intuitivæ tantummodo *non subest,* non item. Nam hic dissensus inter facultatem *sensitivam et intellectualem,* (quarum indolem mox exponam,) nihil indigitat, nisi, *quas mens ab intellectu acceptas fert ideas abstractas, illas in concreto exsequi et in Intuitus commutare sæpenumero non posse.* Hæc autem reluctantia *subjectiva* mentitur, ut plurimum, repugnantiam aliquam *objectivam*, et incautos facile fallit, limitibus, quibus *mens humana* circumscribitur, pro iis habitis, quibus *ipsa rerum essentia* continetur[49]—*Kant, de Mundi Sensibilis et Intelligibilis forma et principiis*, 1770.

Critics, who are most ready to bring this charge of pedantry and unintelligibility, are the most apt to overlook the important fact, that, besides the language of words, there is a language of spirits (*sermo interior*) and that the former is only the vehicle of the latter. Consequently their assurance, that they do not understand the philosophic writer, instead of proving any thing against the philosophy, may furnish an equal, and (cæteris paribus) even a stronger presumption against their own philosophic talent.

Great indeed are the obstacles which an English metaphysician has to encounter. Amongst his most respectable and intelli-

---

[49] TRANSLATION: "Hence it is clear, from what cause many reject the notion of the continuous and the infinite. They take, namely, the words irrepresentable and impossible in one and the same meaning; and, according to the forms of sensuous evidence, the notion of the continuous and the infinite is doubtless impossible. I am not now pleading the cause of these laws, which not a few schools have thought proper to explode, especially the former (the law of continuity). But it is of the highest importance to admonish the reader, that those, who adopt so perverted a mode of reasoning, are under a grievous error. Whatever opposes the formal principles of the understanding and the reason is confessedly impossible; but not therefore that, which is therefore not amenable to the forms of *sensuous* evidence, because it is exclusively an object of pure intellect. For this non-coincidence of the sensuous and the intellectual (the nature of which I shall presently lay open) proves nothing more, but that the mind cannot always adequately represent in the concrete, and transform into distinct images, abstract notions derived from the pure intellect. But this contradiction, which is in itself merely subjective (i.e. an incapacity in the nature of man), too often passes for an incongruity or impossibility in the object (i.e. the notions themselves), and seduces the incautious to mistake the limitations of the human faculties for the limits of things, as they really exist."

I take this occasion to observe, that here and elsewhere Kant uses the term intuition, and the verb active (Intueri, *germanice* Anschauen) for which we have unfortunately no correspondent word, exclusively for that which can be represented in space and time. He therefore consistently and rightly denies the possibility of intellectual intuitions. But as I see no adequate reason for this exclusive sense of the term, I have reverted to its wider signification, authorized by our elder theologians and metaphysicians, according to whom the term comprehends all truths known to us without a medium.

gent judges, there will be many who have devoted their atten-
tion exclusively to the concerns and interests of human life, and
who bring with them to the perusal of a philosophic system an
habitual aversion to all speculations, the utility and application
of which are not evident and immediate. To these I would in the
first instance merely oppose an authority, which they themselves
hold venerable, that of Lord Bacon: non inutiles scientiæ existi-
mandæ sunt, quarum in se nullus est usus, si ingenia acuant et
ordinent.

There are others, whose prejudices are still more formidable,
inasmuch as they are grounded in their moral feelings and re-
ligious principles, which had been alarmed and shocked by the
impious and pernicious tenets defended by Hume, Priestley, and
the French fatalists or necessitarians; some of whom had per-
verted metaphysical reasonings to the denial of the mysteries
and indeed of all the peculiar doctrines of Christianity; and
others even to the subversion of all distinction between right and
wrong. I would request such men to consider what an eminent
and successful defender of the Christian faith has observed, that
true metaphysics are nothing else but true divinity, and that in
fact the writers, who have given them such just offence, were
sophists, who had taken advantage of the general neglect into
which the science of logic has unhappily fallen, rather than meta-
physicians, a name indeed which those writers were the first to
explode as unmeaning. Secondly, I would remind them, that as
long as there are men in the world to whom the Γνῶθι σεαυτόν
is an instinct and a command from their own nature, so long will
there be metaphysicians and metaphysical speculations; that false
metaphysics can be effectually counteracted by true metaphysics
alone; and that if the reasoning be clear, solid, and pertinent, the
truth deduced can never be the less valuable on account of the
depth from which it may have been drawn.

A third class profess themselves friendly to metaphysics, and
believe that they are themselves metaphysicians. They have no
objection to system or terminology, provided it be the method
and the nomenclature to which they have been familiarized in
the writings of Locke, Hume, Hartley, Condillac, or perhaps Dr.
Reid, and Professor Stewart. To objections from this cause, it is
a sufficient answer, that one main object of my attempt was to
demonstrate the vagueness or insufficiency of the terms used in
the metaphysical schools of France and Great Britain since the
revolution, and that the errors which I propose to attack cannot
subsist, except as they are concealed behind the mask of a plausi-
ble and indefinite nomenclature.

But the worst and widest impediment still remains. It is the predominance of a popular philosophy, at once the counterfeit and the mortal enemy of all true and manly metaphysical research. It is that corruption, introduced by certain immethodical aphorisming Eclectics, who, dismissing not only all system, but all logical connection, pick and choose whatever is most plausible and showy; who select, whatever words can have some semblance of sense attached to them without the least expenditure of thought; in short whatever may enable men to talk of what they do not understand, with a careful avoidance of every thing that might awaken them to a moment's suspicion of their ignorance. This alas! is an irremediable disease, for it brings with it, not so much an indisposition to any particular system, but an utter loss of taste and faculty for all system and for all philosophy. Like echoes that beget each other amongst the mountains, the praise or blame of such men rolls in vollies long after the report from the original blunderbuss. Sequacitas est potius et coitio quam consensus: et tamen (quod pessimum est) pusillanimitas ista non sine arrogantiâ et fastidio se offert. *Novum Organum*.

I shall now proceed to the nature and genesis of the imagination; but I must first take leave to notice, that after a more accurate perusal of Mr. Wordsworth's remarks on the imagination, in his preface to the new edition of his poems, I find that my conclusions are not so consentient with his as, I confess, I had taken for granted. In an article contributed by me to Mr. Southey's Omniana, on the soul and its organs of sense, are the following sentences. "These (the human faculties) I would arrange under the different senses and powers: as the eye, the ear, the touch, &c.; the imitative power, voluntary and automatic; the imagination, or shaping and modifying power; the fancy, or the aggregative and associative power; the understanding, or the regulative, substantiating and realizing power; the speculative reason, vis theoretica et scientifica, or the power by which we produce or aim to produce unity, necessity, and universality in all our knowledge by means of principles a priori;[50] the will, or

[50] This phrase, *a priori*, is in common, most grossly misunderstood, and an absurdity burdened on it, which it does not deserve. By knowledge, *a priori*, we do not mean, that we can know anything previously to experience, which would be a contradiction in terms; but that having once known it by occasion of experience (that is, something acting upon us from without) we then know, that it must have pre-existed, or the experience itself would have been impossible. By experience only I know, that I have eyes; but then my reason convinces me, that I must have had eyes in order to the experience.

practical reason; the faculty of choice (*Germanice,* Willkür) and (distinct both from the moral will and the choice,) the *sensation* of volition, which I have found reason to include under the head of single and double touch." To this, as far as it relates to the subject in question, namely the words (*the aggregative and associative power*) Mr. Wordsworth's "only objection is that the definition is too general. To aggregate and to associate, to evoke and to combine, belong as well to the imagination as to the fancy." I reply, that if, by the power of evoking and combining, Mr. Wordsworth means the same as, and no more than, I meant by the aggregative and associative, I continue to deny, that it belongs at all to the imagination; and I am disposed to conjecture, that he has mistaken the co-presence of fancy with imagination for the operation of the latter singly. A man may work with two very different tools at the same moment; each has its share in the work, but the work effected by each is distinct and different. But it will probably appear in the next Chapter, that deeming it necessary to go back much further than Mr. Wordsworth's subject required or permitted, I have attached a meaning to both fancy and imagination, which he had not in view, at least while he was writing that preface. He will judge. Would to Heaven, I might meet with many such readers. I will conclude with the words of Bishop Jeremy Taylor: he to whom all things are one, who draweth all things to one, and seeth all things in one, may enjoy true peace and rest of spirit. (*J. Taylor's* VIA PACIS.)

CHAPTER XIII

On the imagination, or esemplastic power.

O Adam, One Almighty is, from whom
All things proceed, and up to him return,
If not depraved from good: created all
Such to perfection, one first nature all,
Indued with various forms, various degrees
Of substance, and, in things that live, of life;
But more refin'd, more spirituous and pure,
As nearer to him plac'd, or nearer tending,
Each in their several active spheres assign'd,
Till body up to spirit work, in bounds
Proportion'd to each kind. So from the root
Springs lighter the green stalk, from thence the **leaves**
More airy: last the bright consummate flower
Spirits odorous breathes. Flowers and their **fruit.**

> Man's nourishment, by gradual scale sublim'd,
> To *vital* spirits aspire: to *animal:*
> To *intellectual!*—give both life and sense,
> Fancy and understanding; whence the soul
> REASON receives, and reason is her *being,*
> Discursive or intuitive.   PAR. LOST. b. V.

"Sane si res corporales nil nisi materiale continerent, verissime dicerentur in fluxu consistere neque habere substantiale quicquam, quemadmodum et Platonici olim recte agnovere.—Hinc igitur, præter purè mathematica et phantasiæ subjecta, collegi quædam metaphysica solâque mente perceptibilia, esse admittenda: et massæ materiali *principium* quoddam superius et, ut sic dicam, *formale* addendum: quandoquidem omnes veritates rerum corporearum ex solis axiomatibus logisticis et geometricis, nempe de magno et parvo, toto et parte, figura et situ, colligi non possint; sed alia de causa et effectu, *actioneque* et *passione,* accedere debeant, quibus ordinis rerum rationes salventur. Id principium rerum, an ἐντελέχειαν an vim appellemus, non refert, modó meminerimus, per solam *Virium* notionem intelligibiliter explicari."

LEIBNITZ: *Op.* T. II. P. II. *p.* 53—T. III. *p.* 321.

Σέβομαι Νοερῶν
Κρυφίαν τάξιν·
Χώρει ΤΙ ΜΕΣΟΝ
Οὐ καταχυθέν.   SYNESII *Hymn.* III. l. 231.

DES CARTES, speaking as a naturalist, and in imitation of Archimedes, said, give me matter and motion and I will construct you the universe. We must of course understand him to have meant: I will render the construction of the universe intelligible. In the same sense the transcendental philosopher says; grant me a nature having two contrary forces, the one of which tends to expand infinitely, while the other strives to apprehend or *find* itself in this infinity, and I will cause the world of intelligences with the whole system of their representations to rise up before you. Every other science presupposes intelligence as already existing and complete: the philosopher contemplates it in its growth, and as it were represents its history to the mind from its birth to its maturity.

The venerable Sage of Koenigsberg has preceded the march of this master-thought as an effective pioneer in his essay on the introduction of negative quantities into philosophy, published 1763. In this he has shown, that instead of assailing the science of mathematics by metaphysics, as Berkeley did in his Analyst, or of sophisticating it, as Wolf did, by the vain attempt of deducing the first principles of geometry from supposed deeper grounds of ontology, it behoved the metaphysician rather to examine whether the only province of knowledge, which man has succeeded in erecting into a pure science, might not furnish materials, or at least hints, for establishing and pacifying the unsettled, warring, and embroiled domain of philosophy. An imitation of the mathematical *method* had indeed been attempted with no better success than attended the essay of David to wear the armour of Saul. Another use however is possible and of far greater promise, namely, the actual application of the positions which had so wonderfully enlarged the discoveries of geometry, mutatis mutandis, to philosophical subjects. Kant having briefly illustrated the utility of such an attempt in the questions of space, motion, and infinitely small quantities, as employed by the mathematician, proceeds to the idea of negative quantities and the transfer of them to metaphysical investigation. Opposites, he well observes, are of two kinds, either logical, that is, such as are absolutely incompatible; or real, without being contradictory. The former he denominates Nihil negativum irrepræsentabile, the connection of which produces nonsense. A body in motion is something—Aliquid cogitabile; but a body, at one and the same time in motion and not in motion, is nothing, or, at most, air articulated into nonsense. But a motory force of a body in one direction, and an equal force of the same body in an opposite direction is not incompatible, and the result, namely, rest, is real and representable. For the purposes of mathematical calculus it is indifferent which force we term negative, and which positive, and consequently we appropriate the latter to that, which happens to be the principal object in our thoughts. Thus if a man's capital be ten and his debts eight, the subtraction will be the same, whether we call the capital negative debt, or the debt negative capital. But in as much as the latter stands practically in reference to the former, we of course represent the sum as $10-8$. It is equally clear that two equal forces acting in opposite directions, both being finite and each distinguished from the other by its direction only, must neutralize or reduce each other to inaction. Now the transcendental philosophy demands; first, that two forces should be conceived which counteract each other by their essential nature; not only not in consequence of the accidental direction of each, but as prior to all direction, nay, as the primary forces from which the conditions of all possible directions are derivative and deducible: secondly, that these forces should be assumed to be both alike infinite, both alike indestructible. The problem will then be to discover the result or product of two such forces, as distinguished from the result of those forces which are finite, and derive their difference solely from the circumstance of their direction. When we have formed a scheme or outline of these two different kinds of force, and of their different results by the process of discursive reasoning, it will then remain for us to elevate the Thesis from notional to actual, by contemplating intuitively this one power with its two inherent indestructible yet counteracting forces, and the results or generations to which their inter-penetration gives existence, in the living principle and in the process of our own self-consciousness. By what instrument this is possible the solution itself will discover, at the same time that it will reveal to and for whom it is possible. Non omnia possumus omnes. There is a philosophic no less than a poetic genius, which is differenced from the highest perfection of talent, not by degree but by kind.

The counteraction then of the two assumed forces does not depend on their meeting from opposite directions; the power which acts in them is indestructible; it is therefore inexhaustibly re-ebullient; and as something must be the result of these two forces, both alike infinite, and both alike indestructible; and as rest or neutralization cannot be this result; no other conception is possible, but that the product must be a tertium aliquid, or finite generation. Consequently this conception is necessary. Now this tertium aliquid can be no other than an inter-penetration of the counteracting powers, partaking of both.

* * * * * *

Thus far had the work been transcribed for the press, when I received the following letter from a friend, whose practical judgement I have had ample reason to estimate and revere, and whose taste and sensibility preclude all the excuses which my self-love might possibly have prompted me to set up in plea against the decision of advisers of equal good sense, but with less tact and feeling.

"Dear C.

"You ask my opinion concerning your Chapter on the Imagination, both as to the impressions it made on myself, and as to those which I think it will make on the PUBLIC, i.e. that part of the public, who, from the title of the work and from its forming a sort of introduction to a volume of poems, are likely to constitute the great majority of your readers.

"As to myself, and stating in the first place the effect on my understanding, your opinions and method of argument were not only so new to me, but so directly the reverse of all I had ever been accustomed to consider as truth, that even if I had compre-

nended your premises sufficiently to have admitted them, and had seen the necessity of your conclusions, I should still have been in that state of mind, which in your note p. 52, 53. you have so ingeniously evolved, as the antithesis to that in which a man is, when he makes a bull. In your own words I should have felt as if I had been standing on my head.

"*The effect on my feelings, on the other hand, I cannot better represent, than by supposing myself to have known only our light airy modern chapels of ease, and then for the first time to have been placed, and left alone, in one of our largest Gothic cathedrals in a gusty moonlight night of autumn. 'Now in glimmer, and now in gloom;' often in palpable darkness not without a chilly sensation of terror; then suddenly emerging into broad yet visionary lights with coloured shadows of fantastic shapes, yet all decked with holy insignia and mystic symbols; and ever and anon coming out full upon pictures and stone-work images of great men, with whose names I was familiar, but which looked upon me with countenances and an expression, the most dissimilar to all I had been in the habit of connecting with those names. Those whom I had been taught to venerate as almost super-human in magnitude of intellect, I found perched in little fretwork niches, as grotesque dwarfs; while the grotesques, in my hitherto belief, stood guarding the high altar with all the characters of Apotheosis. In short, what I had supposed substances were thinned away into shadows, while everywhere shadows were deepened into substances:*

'If substance may be call'd what shadow seem'd,
For each seem'd either!'   MILTON.

"*Yet after all, I could not but repeat the lines which you had quoted from a MS. poem of your own in the* FRIEND, *and applied to a work of Mr. Wordsworth's though with a few of the words altered:*

'————An orphic tale indeed,
A tale *obscure* of high and passionate thoughts
To *a strange* music chaunted!'

"*Be assured, however, that I look forward anxiously to your great book on the* CONSTRUCTIVE PHILOSOPHY, *which you have promised and announced: and that I will do my best to understand it. Only I will not promise to descend into the dark cave of Trophonius with you, there to rub my own eyes, in order to make the sparks and figured flashes, which I am required to see.*

"*So much for myself. But as for the* PUBLIC, *I do not hesitate a moment in advising and urging you to withdraw the Chapter* from the present work, and to reserve it for your announced treatises on the Logos or communicative intellect in Man and Deity. First, because, imperfectly as I understand the present Chapter, I see clearly that you have done too much, and yet not enough. You have been obliged to omit so many links, from the necessity of compression, that what remains, looks (if I may recur to my former illustration) like the fragments of the winding steps of an old ruined tower. Secondly, a still stronger argument (at least one that I am sure will be more forcible with you) is, that your readers will have both right and reason to complain of you. This Chapter, which cannot, when it is printed, amount to so little as an hundred pages, will of necessity greatly increase the expense of the work; and every reader who, like myself, is neither prepared nor perhaps calculated for the study of so abstruse a subject so abstrusely treated, will, as I have before hinted, be almost entitled to accuse you of a sort of imposition on him. For who, he might truly observe, could from your title-page, viz. 𝕸𝖞 𝕷𝖎𝖙𝖊𝖗𝖆𝖗𝖞 𝕷𝖎𝖋𝖊 𝖆𝖓𝖉 𝕺𝖕𝖎𝖓𝖎𝖔𝖓𝖘,' published too as introductory to a volume of miscellaneous poems, have anticipated, or even conjectured, a long treatise on ideal Realism which holds the same relation in abstruseness to Plotinus, as Plotinus does to Plato. It will be well, if already you have not too much of metaphysical disquisition in your work, though as the larger part of the disquisition is historical, it will doubtless be both interesting and instructive to many to whose unprepared minds your speculations on the esemplastic power would be utterly unintelligible. Be assured, if you do publish this Chapter in the present work, you will be reminded of Bishop Berkeley's Siris, announced as an Essay on Tar-water, which beginning with Tar ends with the Trinity, the omne scibile forming the interspace. I say in the present work. In that greater work to which you have devoted so many years, and study so intense and various, it will be in its proper place. Your prospectus will have described and announced both its contents and their nature; and if any persons purchase it, who feel no interest in the subjects of which it treats, they will have themselves only to blame.

"I could add to these arguments one derived from pecuniary motives, and particularly from the probable effects on the sale of your present publication; but they would weigh little with you compared with the preceding. Besides, I have long observed, that arguments drawn from your own personal interests more often act on you as narcotics than as stimulants, and that in money concerns you have some small portion of pig-nature in your moral idiosyncracy, and, like these amiable creatures, must *occasionally be pulled backward from the boat in order to make you enter it. All success attend you, for if hard thinking and hard reading are merits, you have deserved it.*

"Your affectionate, &c."

In consequence of this very judicious letter, which produced complete conviction on my mind, I shall content myself for the present with stating the main result of the Chapter, which I have reserved for that future publication, a detailed prospectus of which the reader will find at the close of the second volume.

The IMAGINATION then, I consider either as primary, or secondary. The primary IMAGINATION I hold to be the living Power and prime Agent of all human Perception, and as a repetition in the finite mind of the eternal act of creation in the infinite I AM. The secondary Imagination I consider as an echo of the former, co-existing with the conscious will, yet still as identical with the primary in the *kind* of its agency, and differing only in *degree*, and in the *mode* of its operation. It dissolves, diffuses, dissipates, in order to re-create; or where this process is rendered impossible, yet still at all events it struggles to idealize and to unify. It is essentially *vital*, even as all objects (*as* objects) are essentially fixed and dead.

FANCY, on the contrary, has no other counters to play with, but fixities and definites. The Fancy is indeed no other than a mode of Memory emancipated from the order of time and space; while it is blended with, and modified by that empirical phenomenon of the will, which we express by the word CHOICE. But equally with the ordinary memory the Fancy must receive all its materials ready made from the law of association.

Whatever more than this, I shall think it fit to declare concerning the powers and privileges of the imagination in the present work, will be found in the critical essay on the uses of the Supernatural in poetry, and the principles that regulate its introduction: which the reader will find prefixed to the poem of 𝔗𝔥𝔢 𝔄𝔫𝔠𝔦𝔢𝔫𝔱 𝔐𝔞𝔯𝔦𝔫𝔢𝔯.

CHAPTER XIV

Occasion of the Lyrical Ballads, and the objects originally proposed— Preface to the second edition—The ensuing controversy, its causes and acrimony—Philosophic definitions of a poem and poetry with scholia.

DURING the first year that Mr. Wordsworth and I were neighbours, our conversations turned frequently on the two cardinal points of poetry, the power of exciting the sympathy of the reader by a faithful adherence to the truth of nature, and the power of giving the interest of novelty by the modifying colors of imagination. The sudden charm, which accidents of light and shade, which moon-light or sun-set diffused over a known and familiar landscape, appeared to represent the practicability of combining both. These are the poetry of nature. The thought suggested itself (to which of us I do not recollect) that a series of poems might be composed of two sorts. In the one, the incidents and agents were to be, in part at least, supernatural; and the excellence aimed at was to consist in the interesting of the affections by the dramatic truth of such emotions, as would naturally accompany such situations, supposing them real. And real in *this* sense they have been to every human being who, from whatever source of delusion, has at any time believed himself under supernatural agency. For the second class, subjects were to be chosen from ordinary life; the characters and incidents were to be such, as will be found in every village and its vicinity, where there is a meditative and feeling mind to seek after them, or to notice them, when they present themselves.

In this idea originated the plan of the "Lyrical Ballads"; in which it was agreed, that my endeavours should be directed to persons and characters supernatural, or at least romantic; yet so as to transfer from our inward nature a human interest and a semblance of truth sufficient to procure for these shadows of imagination that willing suspension of disbelief for the moment, which constitutes poetic faith. Mr. Wordsworth, on the other hand, was to propose to himself as his object, to give the charm of novelty to things of every day, and to excite a feeling analogous to the supernatural, by awakening the mind's attention from the lethargy of custom, and directing it to the loveliness and the wonders of the world before us; an inexhaustible treasure, but for which, in consequence of the film of familiarity and selfish solicitude we have eyes, yet see not, ears that hear not, and hearts that neither feel nor understand.

With this view I wrote "The Ancient Mariner," and was preparing among other poems, "The Dark Ladie," and the "Christabel," in which I should have more nearly realized my ideal, than I had done in my first attempt. But Mr. Wordsworth's industry had proved so much more successful, and the number of his poems so much greater, that my compositions, instead of forming a balance, appeared rather an interpolation of heterogeneous matter. Mr. Wordsworth added two or three poems written in his own character, in the impassioned, lofty, and sustained diction, which is characteristic of his genius. In this form the "Lyrical Ballads" were published; and were presented by him, as an *experiment*, whether subjects, which from their nature rejected the usual ornaments and extra-colloquial style of poems in general, might not be so managed in the language of ordinary life as to produce the pleasureable interest, which it is the peculiar business of poetry to impart. To the second edition he added a preface of considerable length; in which, notwithstanding some passages of apparently a contrary import, he was understood to contend for the extension of this style to poetry of all kinds, and to reject as vicious and indefensible all phrases and forms of style that were not included in what he (unfortunately, I think, adopting an equivocal expression) called the language of *real* life. From this preface, prefixed to poems in which it was impossible to deny the presence of original genius, however mistaken its direction might be deemed, arose the whole long-continued controversy. For from the conjunction of perceived power with supposed heresy I explain the inveteracy and in some instances, I grieve to say, the acrimonious passions, with which the controversy has been conducted by the assailants.

Had Mr. Wordsworth's poems been the silly, the childish things, which they were for a long time described as being; had they been really distinguished from the compositions of other poets merely by meanness of language and inanity of thought; had they indeed contained nothing more than what is found in the parodies and pretended imitations of them; they must have sunk at once, a dead weight, into the slough of oblivion, and have dragged the preface along with them. But year after year increased the number of Mr. Wordsworth's admirers. They were found too not in the lower classes of the reading public, but chiefly among young men of strong sensibility and meditative minds; and their admiration (inflamed perhaps in some degree by opposition) was distinguished by its intensity, I might almost say, by its *religious* fervor. These facts, and the intellectual energy of the author, which was more or less consciously felt, where it was outwardly and even boisterously denied, meeting with sentiments of aversion to his opinions, and of alarm at their consequences, produced an eddy of criticism, which would of itself have borne up the poems by the violence with which it whirled them round and round. With many parts of this preface, in the sense attributed to them, and which the words undoubtedly seem to authorize, I never concurred; but on the contrary objected to them as erroneous in principle, and as contradictory (in appearance at least) both to other parts of the same preface, and to the author's own practice in the greater number of the poems themselves. Mr. Wordsworth in his recent collection has, I find, degraded this prefatory disquisition to the end of his second volume, to be read or not at the reader's choice. But he has not, as far as I can discover, announced any change in his poetic creed. At all events, considering it as the source of a controversy, in which I have been honored more than I deserve by the frequent conjunction of my name with his, I think it expedient to declare once for all, in what points I coincide with his opinions, and in what points I altogether differ. But in order to render myself intelligible I must previously, in as few words as possible, explain my ideas, first, of a POEM; and secondly, of POETRY itself, in *kind*, and in *essence*.

The office of philosophical *disquisition* consists in just *distinction;* while it is the privilege of the philosopher to preserve himself constantly aware, that distinction is not division. In order to obtain adequate notions of any truth, we must intellectually separate its distinguishable parts; and this is the technical *process* of philosophy. But having so done, we must then restore them in our conceptions to the unity, in which they actually co-exist; and this is the *result* of philosophy. A poem contains the same elements as a prose composition; the difference therefore must consist in a different combination of them, in consequence of a different object being proposed. According to the difference of the object will be the difference of the combination. It is possible, that the object may be merely to facilitate the recollection of any given facts or observations by artificial arrangement; and the composition will be a poem, merely because it is distinguished from prose by metre, or by rhyme, or by both conjointly. In this, the lowest sense, a man might attribute the name of a poem to the well-known enumeration of the days in the several months;

> "Thirty days hath September,
> April, June, and November," &c.

and others of the same class and purpose. And as a particular pleasure is found in anticipating the recurrence of sounds and quantities, all compositions that have this charm superadded, whatever be their contents, *may* be entitled poems.

So much for the superficial *form*. A difference of object and contents supplies an additional ground of distinction. The immediate purpose may be the communication of truths; either of truth absolute and demonstrable, as in works of science; or of facts experienced and recorded, as in history. Pleasure, and that of the highest and most permanent kind, may *result* from the *attainment* of the end; but it is not itself the immediate end. In other works the communication of pleasure may be the immediate purpose; and though truth, either moral or intellectual, ought to be the *ultimate* end, yet this will distinguish the character of the author, not the class to which the work belongs. Blest indeed is that state of society, in which the immediate purpose would be baffled by the perversion of the proper ultimate end; in which no charm of diction or imagery could exempt the Bathyllus even of an Anacreon, or the Alexis of Virgil, from disgust and aversion!

But the communication of pleasure may be the immediate object of a work not metrically composed; and that object may have been in a high degree attained, as in novels and romances. Would then the mere superaddition of metre, with or without rhyme, entitle *these* to the name of poems? The answer is, that nothing can permanently please, which does not contain in itself the reason why it is so, and not otherwise. If metre be superadded, all other parts must be made consonant with it. They must be such, as to justify the perpetual and distinct attention to each part, which an exact correspondent recurrence of accent and sound are calculated to excite. The final definition then, so deduced, may be thus worded. A poem is that species of composition, which is opposed to works of science, by proposing for its *immediate* object pleasure, not truth; and from all other species (having *this* object in common with it) it is discriminated by proposing to itself such delight from the *whole,* as is compatible with a distinct gratification from each component *part.*

Controversy is not seldom excited in consequence of the disputants attaching each a different meaning to the same word; and in few instances has this been more striking, than in disputes concerning the present subject. If a man chooses to call every composition a poem, which is rhyme, or measure, or both, I must leave his opinion uncontroverted. The distinction is at least competent to characterize the writer's intention. If it were subjoined, that the whole is likewise entertaining or affecting, as a tale, or as a series of interesting reflections, I of course admit this as another fit ingredient of a poem, and an additional merit. But if the definition sought for be that of a *legitimate* poem, I answer, it must be one, the parts of which mutually support and explain each other; all in their proportion harmonizing with, and supporting the purpose and known influences of metrical arrangement. The philosophic critics of all ages coincide with the ultimate judgement of all countries, in equally denying the praises of a just poem, on the one hand, to a series of striking lines or distiches, each of which, absorbing the whole attention of the reader to itself, disjoins it from its context, and makes it a separate whole, instead of an harmonizing part; and on the other hand, to an unsustained composition, from which the reader collects rapidly the general result, unattracted by the component parts. The reader should be carried forward, not merely or chiefly by the mechanical impulse of curiosity, or by a restless desire to arrive at the final solution; but by the pleasureable activity of mind excited by the attractions of the journey itself. Like the motion of a serpent, which the Egyptians made the emblem of intellectual power; or like the path of sound through the air; at every step he pauses and half recedes, and from the retrogressive movement collects the force which again carries him onward. "Præcipitandus est *liber* spiritus," says Petronius Arbiter most happily. The epithet, *liber*, here balances the preceding verb; and it is not easy to conceive more meaning condensed in fewer words.

But if this should be admitted as a satisfactory character of a poem, we have still to seek for a definition of poetry. The writings of PLATO, and Bishop TAYLOR, and the "Theoria Sacra" of BURNET, furnish undeniable proofs that poetry of the highest kind may exist without metre, and even without the contra-distinguishing objects of a poem. The first chapter of Isaiah (indeed a very large portion of the whole book) is poetry in the most emphatic sense; yet it would be not less irrational than strange to assert, that pleasure, and not truth, was the immediate object of the prophet. In short, whatever *specific* import we attach to the word, poetry, there will be found involved in it, as a necessary consequence, that a poem of any length neither can be, or ought to be, all poetry. Yet if an harmonious whole is to be produced, the remaining parts must be preserved *in keeping* with the poetry; and this can be no otherwise effected than by such a studied selection and artificial arrangement, as will partake of *one*, though not a *peculiar* property of poetry. And this again can be no other than the property of exciting a more continuous and equal attention than the language of prose aims at, whether colloquial or written.

My own conclusions on the nature of poetry, in the strictest use of the word, have been in part anticipated in the preceding disquisition on the fancy and imagination. What is poetry? is so nearly the same question with, what is a poet? that the answer to the one is involved in the solution of the other. For it is a distinction resulting from the poetic genius itself, which sustains and modifies the images, thoughts, and emotions of the poet's own mind.

The poet, described in *ideal* perfection, brings the whole soul of man into activity, with the subordination of its faculties to each other, according to their relative worth and dignity. He diffuses a tone and spirit of unity, that blends, and (as it were) *fuses,* each into each, by that synthetic and magical power, to which we have exclusively appropriated the name of imagination. This power, first put in action by the will and understanding, and retained under their irremissive, though gentle and unnoticed, controul (*laxis effertur habenis*) reveals itself in the balance or reconciliation of opposite or discordant qualities: of sameness, with difference; of the general, with the concrete; the idea, with the image; the individual, with the representative; the sense of novelty and freshness, with old and familiar objects; a more than usual state of emotion, with more than usual order; judgement ever awake and steady self-possession, with enthusiasm and feeling profound or vehement; and while it blends and harmonizes the natural and the artificial, still subordinates art to nature; the manner to the matter; and our admiration of the poet to our sympathy with the poetry. "Doubtless," as Sir John Davies observes of the soul (and his words may with slight alteration be applied, and even more appropriately, to the poetic IMAGINATION)

"Doubtless this could not be, but that she turns
    Bodies to spirit by sublimation strange,
As fire converts to fire the things it burns,
    As we our food into our nature change.

From their gross matter she abstracts their forms,
    And draws a kind of quintessence from things;
Which to her proper nature she transforms,
    To bear them light on her celestial wings.

Thus does she, when from individual states
    She doth abstract the universal kinds;
Which then re-clothed in divers names and fates
    Steal access through our senses to our minds."

Finally, GOOD SENSE is the BODY of poetic genius, FANCY its DRAPERY, MOTION its LIFE, and IMAGINATION the SOUL that is everywhere, and in each; and forms all into one graceful and intelligent whole.

CHAPTER XV

The specific symptoms of poetic power elucidated in a critical analysis of Shakespeare's Venus and Adonis, and Lucrece.

IN THE application of these principles to purposes of practical criticism as employed in the appraisal of works more or less imperfect, I have endeavoured to discover what the qualities in a poem are, which may be deemed promises and specific symptoms of poetic power, as distinguished from general talent determined to poetic composition by accidental motives, by an act of the will, rather than by the inspiration of a genial and productive nature. In this investigation, I could not, I thought, do better, than keep before me the earliest work of the greatest genius, that perhaps human nature has yet produced, our *myriad-minded* [51] Shakespeare. I mean the "Venus and Adonis," and the "Lucrece"; works which give at once strong promises of the strength, and yet obvious proofs of the immaturity, of his genius. From these I abstracted the following marks, as characteristics of original poetic genius in general.

1. In the "Venus and Adonis," the first and most obvious excellence is the perfect sweetness of the versification; its adaptation to the subject; and the power displayed in varying the march of the words without passing into a loftier and more majestic rhythm than was demanded by the thoughts, or permitted by the propriety of preserving a sense of melody predominant. The delight in richness and sweetness of sound, even to a faulty excess, if it be evidently original, and not the result of an easily imitable mechanism, I regard as a highly favourable promise in the compositions of a young man. "The man that hath not music in his soul" can indeed never be a genuine poet. Imagery (even taken from nature, much more when transplanted from books, as travels, voyages, and works of natural history); affecting incidents; just thoughts; interesting personal or domestic feelings; and with these the art of their combination or intertexture in the form of a poem; may all by incessant effort be acquired as a trade, by a man of talents and much reading, who, as I once before observed, has mistaken an intense desire of poetic reputa-

[51] 'Ανὴρ μυριόνους, a phrase which I have borrowed from a Greek monk, who applies it to a Patriarch of Constantinople. I might have said, that I have *reclaimed*, rather than borrowed it: for it seems to belong to Shakespeare, "de jure singulari, et ex privilegio naturæ."

tion for a natural poetic genius; the love of the arbitrary end for a possession of the peculiar means. But the sense of musical delight, with the power of producing it, is a gift of imagination; and this together with the power of reducing multitude into unity of effect, and modifying a series of thoughts by some one predominant thought or feeling, may be cultivated and improved, but can never be learned. It is in these that "poeta nascitur non fit."

2. A second promise of genius is the choice of subjects very remote from the private interests and circumstances of the writer himself. At least I have found, that where the subject is taken immediately from the author's personal sensations and experiences, the excellence of a particular poem is but an equivocal mark, and often a fallacious pledge, of genuine poetic power. We may perhaps remember the tale of the statuary, who had acquired considerable reputation for the legs of his goddesses, though the rest of the statue accorded but indifferently with ideal beauty; till his wife, elated by her husband's praises, modestly acknowledged that she herself had been his constant model. In the "Venus and Adonis" this proof of poetic power exists even to excess. It is throughout as if a superior spirit more intuitive, more intimately conscious, even than the characters themselves, not only of every outward look and act, but of the flux and reflux of the mind in all its subtlest thoughts and feelings, were placing the whole before our view; himself meanwhile unparticipating in the passions, and actuated only by that pleasureable excitement, which had resulted from the energetic fervor of his own spirit in so vividly exhibiting, what it had so accurately and profoundly contemplated. I think, I should have conjectured from these poems, that even then the great instinct, which impelled the poet to the drama, was secretly working in him, prompting him by a series and never broken chain of imagery, always vivid and, because unbroken, often minute; by the highest effort of the picturesque in words, of which words are capable, higher perhaps than was ever realized by any other poet, even Dante not excepted; to provide a substitute for that visual language, that constant intervention and running comment by tone, look and gesture, which in his dramatic works he was entitled to expect from the players. His "Venus and Adonis" seem at once the characters themselves, and the whole representation of those characters by the most consummate actors. You seem to be told nothing, but to see and hear everything. Hence it is, that from the perpetual activity of attention required on the part of the reader; from the rapid flow, the quick change, and the play-

ful nature of the thoughts and images; and above all from the alienation, and, if I may hazard such an expression, the utter *aloofness* of the poet's own feelings, from those of which he is at once the painter and the analyst; that though the very subject cannot but detract from the pleasure of a delicate mind, yet never was poem less dangerous on a moral account. Instead of doing as Ariosto, and as, still more offensively, Wieland has done, instead of degrading and deforming passion into appetite, the trials of love into the struggles of concupiscence; Shakespeare has here represented the animal impulse itself, so as to preclude all sympathy with it, by dissipating the reader's notice among the thousand outward images, and now beautiful, now fanciful circumstances, which form its dresses and its scenery; or by diverting our attention from the main subject by those frequent witty or profound reflections, which the poet's ever active mind has deduced from, or connected with, the imagery and the incidents. The reader is forced into too much action to sympathize with the merely passive of our nature. As little can a mind thus roused and awakened be brooded on by mean and indistinct emotion, as the low, lazy mist can creep upon the surface of a lake, while a strong gale is driving it onward in waves and billows.

3. It has been before observed that images, however beautiful, though faithfully copied from nature, and as accurately represented in words, do not of themselves characterize the poet. They become proofs of original genius only as far as they are modified by a predominant passion; or by associated thoughts or images awakened by that passion; or when they have the effect of reducing multitude to unity, or succession to an instant; or lastly, when a human and intellectual life is transferred to them from the poet's own spirit,

"Which shoots its being through earth, sea, and air."

In the two following lines for instance, there is nothing objectionable, nothing which would preclude them from forming, in their proper place, part of a descriptive poem:

"Behold yon row of pines, that shorn and bow'd
Bend from the sea-blast, seen at twilight eve."

But with a small alteration of rhythm, the same words would be equally in their place in a book of topography, or in a descriptive tour. The same image will rise into semblance of poetry if thus conveyed:

"Yon row of bleak and visionary pines,
By twilight glimpse discerned, mark! how they flee
From the fierce sea-blast, all their tresses wild
Streaming before them."

I have given this as an illustration, by no means as an instance, of that particular excellence which I had in view, and in which Shakespeare even in his earliest, as in his latest, works surpasses all other poets. It is by this, that he still gives a dignity and a passion to the objects which he presents. Unaided by any previous excitement, they burst upon us at once in life and in power.

"Full many a glorious morning have I seen
Flatter the mountain tops with sovereign eye."

Shakespeare, Sonnet 33rd.

"Not mine own fears, nor the prophetic soul
Of the wide world dreaming on things to come—

* * * * * * *
* * * * * * *

The mortal moon hath her eclipse endur'd,
And the sad augurs mock their own presage;
Incertainties now crown themselves assur'd,
And Peace proclaims olives of endless age.
Now with the drops of this most balmy time
My Love looks fresh, and DEATH to me subscribes!
Since spite of him, I'll live in this poor rhyme,
While he insults o'er dull and speechless tribes.
And thou in this shalt find thy monument,
When tyrants' crests, and tombs of brass are spent."

Sonnet 107.

As of higher worth, so doubtless still more characteristic of poetic genius does the imagery become, when it moulds and colors itself to the circumstances, passion, or character, present and foremost in the mind. For unrivalled instances of this excellence, the reader's own memory will refer him to the LEAR, OTHELLO, in short to which not of the *"great, ever living, dead man's"* dramatic works? "Inopem me copia fecit." How true it is to nature, he has himself finely expressed in the instance of love in Sonnet 98.

"From you have I been absent in the spring,
When proud pied April drest in all its trim
Hath put a spirit of youth in every thing,
That heavy Saturn laugh'd and leap'd with him,
Yet nor the lays of birds, nor the sweet smell

> Of different flowers in odour and in hue,
> Could make me any summer's story tell,
> Or from their proud lap pluck them, where they grew:
> Nor did I wonder at the lilies white,
> Nor praise the deep vermilion in the rose;
> They were, tho' sweet, but figures of delight,
> Drawn after you, you pattern of all those.
> Yet seem'd it winter still, and, you away,
> *As with your shadow I with these did play!*"

Scarcely less sure, or if a less valuable, not less indispensable mark

> Γονίμου μὲν ποιητοῦ————
> ————ὅστις ῥῆμα γενναῖον λάκοι,

will the imagery supply, when, with more than the power of the painter, the poet gives us the liveliest image of succession with the feeling of simultaneousness!

> "With this, he breaketh from the sweet embrace
> Of those fair arms, that held him to her heart,
> And homeward through the dark lawns runs apace:
> *Look! how a bright star shooteth from the sky,*
> *So glides he in the night from Venus' eye.*"

4. The last character I shall mention, which would prove indeed but little, except as taken conjointly with the former; yet without which the former could scarce exist in a high degree, and (even if this were possible) would give promises only of transitory flashes and a meteoric power; is DEPTH, and ENERGY of THOUGHT. No man was ever yet a great poet, without being at the same time a profound philosopher. For poetry is the blossom and the fragrancy of all human knowledge, human thoughts, human passions, emotions, language. In Shakespeare's *poems* the creative power and the intellectual energy wrestle as in a war embrace. Each in its excess of strength seems to threaten the extinction of the other. At length in the DRAMA they were reconciled, and fought each with its shield before the breast of the other. Or like two rapid streams, that, at their first meeting within narrow and rocky banks, mutually strive to repel each other and intermix reluctantly and in tumult; but soon finding a wider channel and more yielding shores blend, and dilate, and flow on in one current and with one voice. The "Venus and Adonis" did not perhaps allow the display of the deeper passions. But the story of Lucretia seems to favor and even demand their intensest workings. And yet we find in *Shakespeare's* management of the tale neither pathos, nor any other *dramatic* quality. There

is the same minute and faithful imagery as in the former poem, in the same vivid colors, inspirited by the same impetuous vigor of thought, and diverging and contracting with the same activity of the assimilative and of the modifying faculties; and with a yet larger display, a yet wider range of knowledge and reflection; and lastly, with the same perfect dominion, often *domination*, over the whole world of language. What then shall we say? even this; that Shakespeare, no mere child of nature; no automaton of genius; no passive vehicle of inspiration possessed by the spirit, not possessing it; first studied patiently, meditated deeply, understood minutely, till knowledge, become habitual and intuitive, wedded itself to his habitual feelings, and at length gave birth to that stupendous power, by which he stands alone, with no equal or second in his own class; to that power which seated him on one of the two glory-smitten summits of the poetic mountain, with Milton as his compeer, not rival. While the former darts himself forth, and passes into all the forms of human character and passion, the one Proteus of the fire and the flood; the other attracts all forms and things to himself, into the unity of his own IDEAL. All things and modes of action shape themselves anew in the being of MILTON; while SHAKESPEARE becomes all things, yet for ever remaining himself. O what great men hast thou not produced, England! my country! truly indeed—

> "Must *we* be free or die, who speak the tongue,
> Which SHAKESPEARE spake; the faith and morals hold,
> Which MILTON held. In every thing we are sprung
> Of earth's first blood, have titles manifold!"
>
> WORDSWORTH.

CHAPTER XVI

Striking points of difference between the Poets of the present age and those of the 15th and 16th centuries—Wish expressed for the union of the characteristic merits of both.

CHRISTENDOM, from its first settlement on feudal rights, has been so far one great body, however imperfectly organized, that a similar spirit will be found in each period to have been acting in all its members. The study of Shakespeare's *poems* (I do not include his dramatic works, eminently as they too deserve that title) led me to a more careful examination of the contemporary poets both in this and in other countries. But my attention was especially fixed on those of Italy, from the birth to the death of

Shakespeare; that being the country in which the fine arts had been most sedulously, and hitherto most successfully cultivated. Abstracted from the degrees and peculiarities of individual genius, the properties common to the good writers of each period seem to establish one striking point of difference between the poetry of the fifteenth and sixteenth centuries, and that of the present age. The remark may perhaps be extended to the sister art of painting. At least the latter will serve to illustrate the former. In the present age the poet (I would wish to be understood as speaking generally, and without allusion to individual names) seems to propose to himself as his main object, and as that which is the most characteristic of his art, new and striking IMAGES; with INCIDENTS that interest the affections or excite the curiosity. Both his characters and his descriptions he renders, as much as possible, specific and individual, even to a degree of portraiture. In his diction and metre, on the other hand, he is comparatively careless. The measure is either constructed on no previous system, and acknowledges no justifying principle but that of the writer's convenience; or else some mechanical movement is adopted, of which one couplet or stanza is so far an adequate specimen, as that the occasional differences appear evidently to arise from accident, or the qualities of the language itself, not from meditation and an intelligent purpose. And the language from Pope's "Translation of Homer" to Darwin's "Temple of Nature," may, notwithstanding some illustrious exceptions, be too faithfully characterized, as claiming to be poetical for no better reason, than that it would be intolerable in conversation or in prose. Though alas! even our prose writings, nay even the style of our more set discourses, strive to be in the fashion, and trick themselves out in the soiled and over-worn finery of the meretricious muse. It is true that of late a great improvement in this respect is observable in our most popular writers. But it is equally true, that this recurrence to plain sense and genuine mother English is far from being general; and that the composition of our novels, magazines, public harangues, &c., is commonly as trivial in thought, and yet enigmatic in expression, as if ECHO and SPHINX had laid their heads together to construct it. Nay, even of those who have most rescued themselves from this contagion, I should plead inwardly guilty to the charge of duplicity or cowardice, if I withheld my conviction, that few have guarded the purity of their native tongue with that jealous care, which the sublime Dante in his tract "De la nobile volgare eloquenza" declares to be the first duty of a poet. For language is the armoury of the human mind; and at once contains the trophies of

its past, and the weapons of its future conquests. "Animadverte, quam sit ab improprietate verborum pronum hominibus prolabi in errores circa res!" HOBBES: *Exam. et Exmend. hod. Math.*—"Sat vero, in hâc vitæ brevitate et naturæ obscuritate, rerum est, quibus cognoscendis tempus impendatur, ut confusis et multivocis sermonibus intelligendis illud consumere non opus sit. Eheu! quantas strages paravere verba nubila, quæ tot dicunt, ut nihil dicant—nubes potius, e quibus et in rebus politicis et in ecclesiâ turbines et tonitrua erumpunt! Et proinde recte dictum putamus a Platone in Gorgia: ὃς ἂν τὰ ὀνόματα εἰδῇ, εἴσεται καὶ τὰ πράγματα: et ab Epicteto, ἀρχὴ παιδεύσεως ἡ τῶν ὀνομάτων ἐπίσκεψις: et prudentissime Galenus scribit, ἡ τῶν ὀνομάτων χρῆσις ταραχθεῖσα καὶ τὴν τῶν πραγμάτων ἐπιταράττει γνῶσιν, Egregie vero J. C. Scaliger, in Lib. I. de Plantis: Est *primum,* inquit, *sapientis officium, bene sentire, ut sibi vivat: proximum, bene loqui, ut patriæ vivat.*" SENNERTUS *de Puls: Differentiâ.*

Something analogous to the materials and structure of modern poetry I seem to have noticed (but here I beg to be understood as speaking with the utmost diffidence) in our common landscape painters. Their foregrounds and intermediate distances are comparatively unattractive: while the main interest of the landscape is thrown into the background, where mountains and torrents and castles forbid the eye to proceed, and nothing tempts it to trace its way back again. But in the works of the great Italian and Flemish masters, the front and middle objects of the landscape are the most obvious and determinate, the interest gradually dies away in the background, and the charm and peculiar worth of the picture consists, not so much in the specific objects which it conveys to the understanding in a visual language formed by the substitution of figures for words, as in the beauty and harmony of the colors, lines and expression, with which the objects are represented. Hence novelty of subject was rather avoided than sought for. Superior excellence in the manner of treating the same subjects was the trial and test of the artist's merit.

Not otherwise is it with the more polished poets of the 15th and 16th century, especially with those of Italy. The imagery is almost always general: sun, moon, flowers, breezes, murmuring streams, warbling songsters, delicious shades, lovely damsels cruel as fair, nymphs, naiads, and goddesses, are the materials which are common to all, and which each shaped and arranged according to his judgement or fancy, little solicitous to add or to particularize. If we make an honourable exception in favour of some English poets, the thoughts too are as little novel as the images; and the fable of their narrative poems, for the most part drawn from mythology, or sources of equal notoriety, derive their chief attractions from the manner of treating them; from impassioned flow, or picturesque arrangement. In opposition to the present age, and perhaps in as faulty an extreme, they placed the essence of poetry in the *art*. The excellence, at which they aimed, consisted in the exquisite polish of the diction, combined with perfect simplicity. This, their prime object, they attained by the avoidance of every word, which a *gentleman* would *not* use in dignified conversation, and of every word and phrase, which none but a *learned* man *would* use; by the studied position of words and phrases, so that not only each part should be melodious in itself, but contribute to the harmony of the whole, each note referring and conducing to the melody of all the foregoing and following words of the same period or stanza; and lastly with equal labor, the greater because unbetrayed, by the variation and various harmonies of their metrical movement. Their measures, however, were not indebted for their variety to the introduction of new metres, such as have been attempted of late in the "Alonzo and Imogen," and others borrowed from the German, having in their very mechanism a specific overpowering tune, to which the generous reader humours his voice and emphasis, with more indulgence to the author than attention to the meaning or quantity of the words; but which, to an ear familiar with the *numerous* sounds of the Greek and Roman poets, has an effect not unlike that of galloping over a paved road in a German stage-waggon without springs. On the contrary, our elder bards both of Italy and England produced a far greater as well as more charming variety by countless modifications and subtle balances of sound in the common metres of their country. A lasting and enviable reputation awaits that man of genius, who should attempt and realize a union; who should recall the high finish, the appropriateness, the facility, the delicate proportion, and above all, the perfusive and omnipresent grace, which have preserved, as in a shrine of precious amber, the "Sparrow" of Catullus, the "Swallow," the "Grasshopper," and all the other little loves of Anacreon: and which, with bright, though diminished glories, revisited the youth and early manhood of Christian Europe, in the vales of [52]

[52] These thoughts were suggested to me during the perusal of the Madrigals of GIOVAMBATISTA STROZZI published in Florence (nella Stamperia del Sermartelli) 1st May 1593, by his sons Lorenzo and Filippo Strozzi, with a dedication to their deceased paternal uncle, "Signor Leone Strozzi, Generale delle battaglie di Santa Chiesa." As I do not remember to have seen either the poems or their author mentioned in any English work, or have found them in any of the common

collections of Italian poetry; and as the little work is of rare occurrence, I will transcribe a few specimens. I have seldom met with compositions that possessed, to my feelings, more of that satisfying *entireness*, that complete adequateness of the manner to the matter which so charms us in Anacreon, join'd with the tenderness, and more than the *delicacy* of Catullus. Trifles as they are, they were probably elaborated with great care; yet in the perusal we refer them to a spontaneous energy rather than to voluntary effort. To a cultivated taste there is a delight in *perfection* for its own sake, independent of the material in which it is manifested, that none but a cultivated taste can understand or appreciate.

After what I have advanced, it would appear presumption to offer a translation; even if the attempt were not discouraged by the different genius of the English mind and language, which demands a denser body of thought as the condition of a high polish, than the Italian. I cannot but deem it likewise an advantage in the Italian tongue, in many other respects inferior to our own, that the language of poetry is more distinct from that of prose than with us. From the earlier appearance and established primacy of the Tuscan poets, concurring with the number of independent states, and the diversity of written dialects, the Italians have gained a poetic idiom, as the Greeks before them had obtained it from the same causes with greater and more various discriminations—ex. gr. the ionic for their heroic verses; the attic for their iambic; and the two modes of the doric, the lyric or sacerdotal, and the pastoral, the distinctions of which were doubtless more obvious to the Greeks themselves than they are to us.

I will venture to add one other observation before I proceed to the transcription. I am aware, that the sentiments which I have avowed concerning the points of difference between the poetry of the present age, and that of the period between 1500 and 1650, are the reverse of the opinion commonly entertained. I was conversing on this subject with a friend, when the servant, a worthy and sensible woman, coming in, I placed before her two engravings, the one a pinky-colored plate of the day, the other a masterly etching by Salvator Rosa from one of his own pictures. On pressing her to tell us, which she preferred, after a little blushing and flutter of feeling, she replied—"Why, that, Sir! to be sure!" (pointing to the *ware* from the Fleet-street print shops); "it's so *neat* and elegant. T'other is such a *scratchy* slovenly thing." An artist, whose writings are scarcely less valuable than his works, and to whose authority more deference will be willingly paid, than I could even wish should be shown to mine, has told us, and from his own experience too, that good taste must be *acquired*, and like all other good things, is the result of thought, and the submissive study of the best models. If it be asked, "But what shall I deem such?" the answer is; *presume* those to be the best, the *reputation* of which has been matured into *fame* by the consent of ages. For wisdom always has a final majority, if not by conviction, yet by acquiescence. In addition to Sir J. Reynolds I may mention Harris of Salisbury; who in one of his philosophical disquisitions has written on the means of acquiring a just taste with the precision of Aristotle, and the elegance of Quintilian.

"MADRIGALE.

Gelido suo ruscel chiaro, e tranquillo
M'insegnò Amor di state a mezzo'l giorno;
Ardean le selve, ardean le piagge, e i colli.
Ond 'io, ch' a più gran gielo ardo e sfavillo,
Subito corsi; ma sì puro adorno
Girsene il vidi, che turbar no'l volli:
Sol mi specchiava, e'n dolce ombrosa sponda
Mi stava intento al mormorar dell' onda.

MADRIGALE.

Aure, dell' angoscioso viver mio
Refrigerio soave,
E dolce sì, che più non mi par grave
Nè l' arder, nè l' morir, anz' il desio;
Deh voi'l ghiaccio, e le nubi, e'l tempo rio
Discacciatene omai, che l' onda chiara,
E l' ombra non men cara
A scherzare, e cantar per suoi boschetti,
E prati Festa et Allegrezza alletti.

MADRIGALE.

Pacifiche, ma spesso in amorosa
Guerra co'fiori, e l' erba
Alla stagione acerba
Verdi Insegne del giglio, e della rosa,
Movete, Aure, pian pian; che tregua ò posa,
Se non pace, io ritrove;
E so ben dove:—Oh vago, e mansueto
Sguardo, oh labbra d'ambrosia, oh rider lieto!

MADRIGALE.

Hor come un Scoglio stassi,
Hor come un Rio se'n fugge,
Ed hor crud' Orsa rugge,
Hor canta Angelo pio: ma che non fassi?
E che non fammi, O Sassi,
O Rivi, o Belue, o Dii, questa mia vaga
Non so, se Ninfa, ò Maga,
Non so, se Donna, ò Dea,
Non so, se dolce ò rea?

MADRIGALE.

Piangendo mi baciaste,
E ridendo il negaste:
In doglia hebbivi pia,

n festa hebbivi ria:
Nacque Gioia di pianti,
Dolor di riso: O amanti
Miseri, habbiate insieme
Ognor Paura e Speme.

MADRIGALE.

Bel Fior, tu mi rimembri
La rugiadosa guancia del bel viso;
E sì vera l'assembri,
Che'n te sovente, come in lei m'affiso:
Et hor del vago riso,
Hor del sereno sguardo
Io pur cieco risguardo. Ma qual fugge,
O Rosa, il mattin lieve?
E chi te, come neve,
E'l mio cor teco, e la mia vita strugge?

MADRIGALE.

Anna mia, Anna dolce, oh sempre nuovc
E più chiaro concento,
Quanto dolcezza sento
In sol Anna dicendo? Io mi pur pruovo,
Nè quì tra noi ritruovo,
Nè tra cieli armonia,
Che del bel nome suo più dolce sia:
Altro il Cielo, altro Amore,
Altro non suona l'Ecco del mio core.

MADRIGALE.

Hor che'l prato, e la selva si scolora,
Al tuo sereno ombroso
Muovine, alto Riposo;
Deh ch' io riposi una sol notte, un hora
Han le fere, gli augelli, ognun talora
Ha qualche pace; io quando,
Lasso! non vonne errando,
E non piango, e non grido? e qual pur forte?
Ma poichè non sent' egli, odine Morte.

MADRIGALE.

Risi e piansi d'Amor; nè però mai
Se non in fiamma, ò 'n onda, ò 'n vento scrissi:
Spesso mercè trovai
Crudel; sempre in me morto, in altri vissi:
Hor da' più scuri Abissi al ciel m'alzai,
Hor ne pur caddi giuso;
Stanco al fin qui son chiuso."

Arno, and the groves of Isis and of Cam; and who with these should combine the keener interest, deeper pathos, manlier reflection, and the fresher and more various imagery, which give a value and a name that will not pass away to the poets who have done honor to our own times, and to those of our immediate predecessors.

CHAPTER XVII

Examination of the tenets peculiar to Mr. Wordsworth—Rustic life (above all, low and rustic life) especially unfavorable to the formation of a human diction—The best parts of language the product of philosophers, not of clowns or shepherds—Poetry essentially ideal and generic—The language of Milton as much the language of real life, yea, incomparably more so than that of the cottager.

AS FAR then as Mr. Wordsworth in his preface contended, and most ably contended, for a reformation in our poetic diction, as far as he has evinced the truth of passion, and the *dramatic* propriety of those figures and metaphors in the original poets, which, stripped of their justifying reasons, and converted into mere artifices of connection or ornament, constitute the characteristic falsity in the poetic style of the moderns; and as far as he has, with equal acuteness and clearness pointed out the process by which this change was effected, and the resemblances between that state into which the reader's mind is thrown by the pleasureable confusion of thought from an unaccustomed train of words and images; and that state which is induced by the natural language of empassioned feeling; he undertook a useful task, and deserves all praise, both for the attempt and for the execution. The provocations to this remonstrance in behalf of truth and nature were still of perpetual recurrence before and after the publication of this preface. I cannot likewise but add, that the comparison of such poems of merit, as have been given to the public within the last ten or twelve years, with the majority of those produced previously to the appearance of that preface, leave no doubt on my mind, that Mr. Wordsworth is fully justified in believing his efforts to have been by no means ineffectual. Not only in the verses of those who have professed their admiration of his genius, but even of those who have distinguished themselves by hostility to his theory, and depreciation of his writings, are the impressions of his principles plainly visible. It is possible, that with these principles others may have been blended, which are not equally evident; and some which are unsteady and subvertible from the narrowness or imperfection of their basis. But it is more than possible, that these errors of defect or exaggeration, by kindling and feeding the controversy, may have conduced not only to the wider propagation of the accompanying truths, but that, by their frequent presentation to the mind in an excited state, they may have won for them a more permanent and practical result. A man will borrow a part from his opponent the more easily, if he feels himself justified in continuing to reject a part. While there remain important points in which he can still feel himself in the right, in which he still finds firm footing for continued resistance, he will gradually adopt those opinions, which were the least remote from his own convictions, as not less congruous with his own theory than with that which he reprobates. In like manner with a kind of instinctive prudence, he will abandon by little and little his weakest posts, till at length he seems to forget that they had ever belonged to him, or affects to consider them at most as accidental and "petty annexments," the removal of which leaves the citadel unhurt and unendangered.

My own differences from certain supposed parts of Mr. Wordsworth's theory ground themselves on the assumption, that his words had been rightly interpreted, as purporting that the proper diction for poetry in general consists altogether in a language taken, with due exceptions, from the mouths of men in real life, a language which actually constitutes the natural conversation of men under the influence of natural feelings. My objection is, first, that in *any* sense this rule is applicable only to *certain* classes of poetry; secondly, that even to these classes it is not applicable, except in such a sense, as hath never by any one (as far as I know or have read) been denied or doubted; and lastly, that as far as, and in that degree in which it is *practicable*, yet as a *rule* it is useless, if not injurious, and therefore either need not, or ought not to be practised. The poet informs his reader, that he had generally chosen *low and rustic* life; but not *as* low and rustic, or in order to repeat that pleasure of doubtful moral effect, which persons of elevated rank and of superior refinement oftentimes derive from a happy *imitation* of the rude unpolished manners and discourse of their inferiors. For the pleasure so derived may be traced to three exciting causes. The first is the naturalness, in *fact*, of the things represented. The second is the apparent naturalness of the *representation*, as raised and qualified by an imperceptible infusion of the author's own knowledge and talent, which infusion does, indeed, constitute it an *imitation* as distinguished from a mere *copy*. The third cause may be found in the reader's conscious feeling of his superiority awakened by the contrast presented to him; even as for the same purpose the kings and great barons of yore retained sometimes *actual* clowns and fools, but more frequently shrewd and witty fellows in that *character*. These, however, were not Mr. Wordsworth's objects. *He* chose low and rustic life, "because in that condition the essential passions of the heart find a better soil, in which they can attain their maturity, are less under restraint, and speak a plainer and more emphatic language; because in that condition of life our elementary feelings coexist in a state of greater simplicity, and consequently may be more accurately contemplated, and more forcibly communicated; because the manners of rural life germinate from those elementary feelings; and from the necessary character of rural occupations are more easily comprehended, and are more durable; and lastly, because in that condition the passions of men are incorporated with the beautiful and permanent forms of nature."

Now it is clear to me, that in the most interesting of the poems, in which the author is more or less dramatic, as "the Brothers," "Michael," "Ruth," "the Mad Mother," &c., the persons introduced are by no means taken *from low or rustic life* in the common acceptation of those words; and it is not less clear, that the sentiments and language, as far as they can be conceived to have been really transferred from the minds and conversation of such persons, are attributable to causes and circumstances not necessarily connected with "their occupations and abode." The thoughts, feelings, language, and manners of the shepherd-farmers in the vales of Cumberland and Westmoreland, as far as they are actually adopted in those poems, may be accounted for from causes, which will and do produce the same results in *every* state of life, whether in town or country. As the two principal I rank that INDEPENDENCE, which raises a man above servitude, or daily toil for the profit of others, yet not above the necessity of industry and a frugal simplicity of domestic life; and the accompanying unambitious, but solid and religious, EDUCATION, which has rendered few books familiar, but the Bible, and the liturgy or hymn book. To this latter cause, indeed, which is so far *accidental,* that it is the blessing of particular countries and a particular age, not the product of particular places or employments, the poet owes the show of probability, that his personages might really feel, think, and talk with any tolerable resemblance to his representation. It is an excellent remark of Dr. Henry More's, (Enthusiasmus triumphatus, Sec. XXXV.), that "a man of confined education, but of good parts, by constant reading of the Bible will naturally form a more winning and commanding rhetoric than those that are learned; the intermixture of tongues and of artificial phrases debasing *their* style."

It is, moreover, to be considered that to the formation of healthy feelings, and a reflecting mind, *negations* involve impediments not less formidable than sophistication and vicious intermixture. I am convinced, that for the human soul to prosper in rustic life a certain vantage-ground is pre-requisite. It is not every man that is likely to be improved by a country life or by country labors. Education, or original sensibility, or both, must pre-exist, if the changes, forms, and incidents of nature are to prove a sufficient stimulant. And where these are not sufficient, the mind contracts and hardens by want of stimulants: and the man becomes selfish, sensual, gross, and hard-hearted. Let the management of the POOR LAWS in Liverpool, Manchester, or Bristol be compared with the ordinary dispensation of the poor rates in agricultural villages, where the *farmers* are the overseers and guardians of the poor. If my own experience have not been particularly unfortunate, as well as that of the many respectable country clergymen with whom I have conversed on the subject, the result would engender more than scepticism concerning the desireable influences of low and rustic life in and for itself. Whatever may be concluded on the other side, from the stronger local attachments and enterprising spirit of the Swiss, and other mountaineers, applies to a particular mode of pastoral life, under forms of property that permit and beget manners truly republican, not to rustic life in general, or to the absence of artificial cultivation. On the contrary the mountaineers, whose manners have been so often eulogized, are in general better educated and greater readers than men of equal rank elsewhere. But where this is not the case, as among the peasantry of North Wales, the ancient mountains, with all their terrors and all their glories, are pictures to the blind, and music to the deaf.

I should not have entered so much into detail upon this passage, but here seems to be the point, to which all the lines of difference converge as to their source and centre. (I mean, as far as, and in whatever respect, my poetic creed *does* differ from the doctrines promulged in this preface.) I adopt with full faith the principle of Aristotle, that poetry as poetry is essentially[53] *ideal,*

---

[53] Say not that I am recommending abstractions; for these class-characteristics which constitute the instructiveness of a character, are so modified and particularized in each person of the Shakespearean Drama, that life itself does not excite more distinctly that sense of individuality which belongs to real existence. Paradoxical as it may sound, one of the essential properties of Geometry is not less essential

that it avoids and excludes all *accident;* that its apparent in-
dividualities of rank, character, or occupation must be *repre-
sentative* of a class; and that the *persons* of poetry must be
clothed with *generic* attributes, with the *common* attributes of
the class: not with such as one gifted individual might *possibly*
possess, but such as from his situation it is most probable before-
hand that he *would* possess. If my premises are right and my
deductions legitimate, it follows that there can be no *poetic*
medium between the swains of Theocritus and those of an
imaginary golden age.

The characters of the vicar and the shepherd-mariner in the
poem of "THE BROTHERS," that of the shepherd of Greenhead
Ghyll in the "MICHAEL," have all the verisimilitude and repre-
sentative quality, that the purposes of poetry can require. They
are persons of a known and abiding class, and their manners
and sentiments the natural product of circumstances common to
the class. Take "MICHAEL" for instance:

> "An old man stout of heart, and strong of limb:
> His bodily frame had been from youth to age
> Of an unusual strength: his mind was keen,
> Intense, and frugal, apt for all affairs,
> And in his shepherd's calling he was prompt
> And watchful more than ordinary men.

---

to dramatic excellence; and Aristotle has accordingly required of the
poet an involution of the universal in the individual. The chief differ-
ences are, that in Geometry it is the universal truth, which is upper-
most in the consciousness; in poetry the individual form, in which the
truth is clothed. With the ancients, and not less with the elder drama-
tists of England and France, both comedy and tragedy were considered
as kinds of poetry. They neither sought in comedy to make us laugh
merely; much less to make us laugh by wry faces, accidents of jargon,
slang phrases for the day, or the clothing of common-place morals
drawn from the shops or mechanic occupations of their characters. Nor
did they condescend in tragedy to wheedle away the applause of the
spectators, by representing before them facsimiles of their own mean
selves in all their existing meanness, or to work on the sluggish sympa-
thies by a pathos not a whit more respectable than the maudlin tears
of drunkenness. Their tragic scenes were meant to *affect* us indeed;
but yet within the bounds of pleasure, and in union with the activity
both of our understanding and imagination. They wished to transport
the mind to a sense of its possible greatness, and to implant the germs
of that greatness, during the temporary oblivion of the worthless
"thing we are," and of the peculiar state in which each man *happens*
to be, suspending our individual recollections and lulling them to sleep
amid the music of nobler thoughts.

FRIEND, Pages 251, 252.

Hence he had learnt the meaning of all winds,
Of blasts of every tone; and oftentimes
When others heeded not, he heard the South
Make subterraneous music, like the noise
Of bagpipers on distant Highland hills.
The shepherd, at such warning, of his flock
Bethought him, and he to himself would say,
The winds are now devising work for me!
And truly at all times the storm, that drives
The traveller to a shelter, summon'd him
Up to the mountains. He had been alone
Amid the heart of many thousand mists,
That came to him and left him on the heights.
So liv'd he, till his eightieth year was pass'd.
And grossly that man errs, who should suppose
That the green vallies, and the streams and rocks,
Were things indifferent to the shepherd's thoughts.
Fields, where with chearful spirits he had breath'd
The common air; the hills, which he so oft
Had climb'd with vigorous steps; which had impress'd
So many incidents upon his mind
Of hardship, skill or courage, joy or fear,
Which, like a book, preserved the memory
Of the dumb animals, whom he had sav'd,
Had fed or shelter'd, linking to such acts,
So grateful in themselves, the certainty
Of honorable gain; these fields, these hills
Which were his living being, even more
Than his own blood—what could they less? had laid
Strong hold on his affections, were to him
A pleasureable feeling of blind love,
The pleasure which there is in life itself."

On the other hand, in the poems which are pitched at a lower
note, as the "HARRY GILL," "IDIOT BOY," the *feelings* are those
of human nature in general; though the poet has judiciously laid
the *scene* in the country, in order to place *himself* in the vicinity
of interesting images, without the necessity of ascribing a senti-
mental perception of their beauty to the persons of his drama.
In the "Idiot Boy," indeed, the mother's character is not so much
a real and native product of a "situation where the essential
passions of the heart find a better soil, in which they can attain
their maturity and speak a plainer and more emphatic language,"
as it is an impersonation of an instinct abandoned by judgement.
Hence the two following charges seem to me not wholly ground-
less: at least, they are the only plausible objections, which I
have heard to that fine poem. The one is, that the author has
not, in the poem itself, taken sufficient care to preclude from

the reader's fancy the disgusting images of *ordinary morbid idiocy,* which yet it was by no means his intention to represent. He has even by the "burr, burr, burr," uncounteracted by any preceding description of the boy's beauty, assisted in recalling them. The other is, that the idiocy of the *boy* is so evenly balanced by the folly of the *mother,* as to present to the general reader rather a laughable burlesque on the blindness of anile dotage, than an analytic display of maternal affection in its ordinary workings.

In the "Thorn" the poet himself acknowledges in a note the necessity of an introductory poem, in which he should have pourtrayed the character of the person from whom the words of the poem are supposed to proceed: a superstitious man moderately imaginative, of slow faculties and deep feelings, "a captain of a small trading vessel, for example, who, being past the middle age of life, had retired upon an annuity, or small independent income, to some village or country town of which he was not a native, or in which he had not been accustomed to live. Such men having nothing to do become credulous and talkative from indolence." But in a poem, still more in a lyric poem (and the NURSE in Shakespeare's Romeo and Juliet alone prevents me from extending the remark even to dramatic *poetry,* if indeed the Nurse itself can be deemed altogether a case in point) it is not possible to imitate truly a dull and garrulous discourser, without repeating the effects of dullness and garrulity. However this may be, I dare assert, that the parts (and these form the far larger portion of the whole) which might as well or still better have proceeded from the poet's own imagination, and have been spoken in his own character, are those which have given, and which will continue to give, universal delight; and that the passages exclusively appropriate to the supposed narrator, such as the last couplet of the third stanza;[54] the seven last lines of the tenth; and the five following stanzas,[55] with

[54] "I've measured it from side to side;
'Tis three feet long, and two feet wide."
[55] "Nay, rack your brain—'tis all in vain,
I'll tell you every thing I know;
But to the Thorn, and to the Pond
Which is a little step beyond,
I wish that you would go:
Perhaps when you are at the place,
You something of her tale may trace.

I'll give you the best help I can:
Before you up the mountain go,

the exception of the four admirable lines at the commencement of the fourteenth, are felt by many unprejudiced and unsophisticated hearts, as sudden and unpleasant sinkings from the height to which the poet had previously lifted them, and to which he again re-elevates both himself and his reader.

If then I am compelled to doubt the theory, by which the

> Up to the dreary mountain-top,
> I'll tell you all I know.
> 'Tis now some two-and-twenty years
> Since she (her name is Martha Ray)
> Gave, with a maiden's true good will,
> Her company to Stephen Hill;
> And she was blithe and gay,
> And she was happy, happy still
> Whene'er she thought of Stephen Hill.
>
> And they had fix'd the wedding-day,
> The morning that must wed them both;
> But Stephen to another maid
> Had sworn another oath;
> And, with this other maid, to church
> Unthinking Stephen went—
> Poor Martha! on that woeful day
> A pang of pitiless dismay
> Into her soul was sent;
> A fire was kindled in her breast,
> Which might not burn itself to rest.
>
> They say, full six months after this,
> While yet the summer leaves were green,
> She to the mountain-top would go,
> And there was often seen.
> 'Tis said a child was in her womb,
> As now to any eye was plain;
> She was with child, and she was mad;
> Yet often she was sober sad
> From her exceeding pain.
> Oh me! ten thousand times I'd rather
> That he had died, that cruel father!
> ❋   ❋   ❋   ❋   ❋   ❋
> ❋   ❋   ❋   ❋   ❋   ❋
> ❋   ❋   ❋   ❋   ❋   ❋
> ❋   ❋   ❋   ❋   ❋   ❋
>
> Last Christmas when we talked of this,
> Old farmer Simpson did maintain,
> That in her womb the infant wrought
> About its mother's heart, and brought
> Her senses back again:

choice of *characters* was to be directed, not only *à priori*, from grounds of reason, but both from the few instances in which the poet himself *need* be supposed to have been governed by it, and from the comparative inferiority of those instances; still more must I hesitate in my assent to the sentence which immediately follows the former citation; and which I can neither admit as particular fact, or as general rule. "The language too of these men is adopted (purified indeed from what appear to be its real defects, from all lasting and rational causes of dislike or disgust) because such men hourly communicate with the best objects from which the best part of language is originally derived; and because, from their rank in society and the sameness and narrow circle of their intercourse, being less under the action of social vanity, they convey their feelings and notions in simple and unelaborated expressions." To this I reply; that a rustic's language, purified from all provincialism and grossness, and so far reconstructed as to be made consistent with the rules of grammar (which are in essence no other than the laws of universal logic, applied to psychological materials) will not differ from the language of any other man of common-sense, however learned or refined he may be, except as far as the notions, which the rustic has to convey, are fewer and more indiscriminate. This will become still clearer, if we add the consideration (equally important though less obvious) that the rustic, from the more imperfect developement of his faculties, and from the lower state of their cultivation, aims almost solely to convey *insulated facts*, either those of his scanty experience or his traditional belief; while the educated man chiefly seeks to discover and express those *connections* of things, or those relative *bearings* of fact to fact, from which some more or less general law is deducible. For *facts* are valuable to a wise man, chiefly as

---

> And, when at last her time drew near,
> Her looks were calm, her senses clear.
>
> No more I know, I wish I did,
> And I would tell it all to you:
> For what became of this poor child
> There's none that ever knew:
> And if a child was born or no,
> There's no one that could ever tell;
> And if 'twas born alive or dead,
> There's no one knows, as I have said:
> But some remember well.
> That Martha Ray about this time
> Would up the mountain often climb."

they lead to the discovery of the indwelling *law,* which is the true *being* of things, the sole solution of their modes of existence, and in the knowledge of which consists our dignity and our power.

As little can I agree with the assertion, that from the objects with which the rustic hourly communicates the best part of language is formed. For first, if to communicate with an object implies such an acquaintance with it, as renders it capable of being discriminately reflected on; the distinct knowledge of an uneducated rustic would furnish a very scanty vocabulary. The few things, and modes of action, requisite for his bodily conveniences, would alone be individualized; while all the rest of nature would be expressed by a small number of confused general terms. Secondly, I deny that the words and combinations of words derived from the objects, with which the rustic is familiar, whether with distinct or confused knowledge, can be justly said to form the *best* part of language. It is more than probable, that many classes of the brute creation possess discriminating sounds, by which they can convey to each other notices of such objects as concern their food, shelter, or safety. Yet we hesitate to call the aggregate of such sounds a language, otherwise than metaphorically. The best part of human language, properly so called, is derived from reflection on the acts of the mind itself. It is formed by a voluntary appropriation of fixed symbols to internal acts, to processes and results of imagination, the greater part of which have no place in the consciousness of uneducated man; though in civilized society, by imitation and passive remembrance of what they hear from their religious instructors and other superiors, the most uneducated share in the harvest which they neither sowed or reaped. If the history of the phrases in hourly currency among our peasants were traced, a person not previously aware of the fact would be surprised at finding so large a number, which three or four centuries ago were the exclusive property of the universities and the schools; and, at the commencement of the Reformation, had been transferred from the school to the pulpit, and thus gradually passed into common life. The extreme difficulty, and often the impossibility, of finding words for the simplest moral and intellectual processes of the languages of uncivilized tribes has proved perhaps the weightiest obstacle to the progress of our most zealous and adroit missionaries. Yet these tribes are surrounded by the same nature as our peasants are; but in still more impressive forms; and they are, moreover, obliged to *particularize* many more of them. When, therefore, Mr. Wordsworth adds, "accordingly, such a language" (meaning, as before, the language of rustic life purified from provincialism) "arising out of repeated experience and regular feelings, is a more permanent, and a far more philosophical language, than that which is frequently substituted for it by poets, who think they are conferring honor upon themselves and their art in proportion as they indulge in arbitrary and capricious habits of expression:" it may be answered, that the language, which he has in view, can be attributed to rustics with no greater right, than the style of Hooker or Bacon to Tom Brown or Sir Roger L'Estrange. Doubtless, if what is peculiar to each were omitted in each, the result must needs be the same. Further, that the poet, who uses an illogical diction, or a style fitted to excite only the low and changeable pleasure of wonder by means of groundless novelty, substitutes a language of *folly* and *vanity,* not for that of the *rustic,* but for that of *good sense* and *natural feeling.*

Here let me be permitted to remind the reader, that the positions, which I controvert, are contained in the sentences— "*a selection of the* REAL *language of men;*"—"*the language of these men*" (i.e. men in low and rustic life) "*I propose to myself to imitate, and, as far as is possible, to adopt the very language of men.*" "*Between the language of prose and that of metrical composition, there neither is, nor can be any essential difference.*" It is against these exclusively that my opposition is directed.

I object, in the very first instance, to an equivocation in the use of the word "real." Every man's language varies, according to the extent of his knowledge, the activity of his faculties, and the depth or quickness of his feelings. Every man's language has, first, its *individualities;* secondly, the common properties of the *class* to which he belongs; and thirdly, words and phrases of *universal* use. The language of Hooker, Bacon, Bishop Taylor, and Burke differs from the common language of the learned class only by the superior number and novelty of the thoughts and relations which they had to convey. The language of Algernon Sidney differs not at all from that, which every well-educated gentleman would wish to write, and (with due allowances for the undeliberateness, and less connected train, of thinking natural and proper to conversation) such as he would wish to talk. Neither one nor the other differ half so much from the general language of cultivated society, as the language of Mr. Wordsworth's homeliest composition differs from that of a common peasant. For "real" therefore, we must substitute *ordinary,* or *lingua communis.* And this, we have proved, is no more to be found in the phraseology of low and rustic life than in that of any other class. Omit the peculiarities of each, and the result of course must be common to all. And assuredly the omissions and changes to be made in the language of rustics, before it could be transferred to any species of poem, except the drama or other professed imitation, are at least as numerous and weighty, as would be required in adapting to the same purpose the ordinary language of tradesmen and manufacturers. Not to mention, that the language so highly extolled by Mr. Wordsworth varies in every county, nay in every village, according to the accidental character of the clergyman, the existence or non-existence of schools; or even, perhaps, as the exciseman, publican, or barber, happen to be, or not to be, zealous politicians, and readers of the weekly newspaper *pro bono publico.* Anterior to cultivation, the lingua communis of every country, as Dante has well observed, exists every where in parts, and no where as a whole.

Neither is the case rendered at all more tenable by the addition of the words, *in a state of excitement.* For the nature of a man's words, where he is strongly affected by joy, grief, or anger, must necessarily depend on the number and quality of the general truths, conceptions and images, and of the words expressing them, with which his mind had been previously stored. For the property of passion is not to *create;* but to set in increased activity. At least, whatever new connections of thoughts or images, or (which is equally, if not more than equally, the appropriate effect of strong excitement) whatever generalizations of truth or experience, the heat of passion may produce; yet the terms of their conveyance must have pre-existed in his former conversations, and are only collected and crowded together by the unusual stimulation. It is indeed very possible to adopt in a poem the unmeaning repetitions, habitual phrases, and other blank counters, which an unfurnished or confused understanding interposes at short intervals, in order to keep hold of his subject, which is still slipping from him, and to give him time for recollection; or in mere aid of vacancy, as in the scanty companies of a country stage the same player pops backwards and forwards, in order to prevent the appearance of empty spaces, in the procession of Macbeth, or Henry VIIIth. But what assistance to the poet, or ornament to the poem, these can supply, I am at a loss to conjecture. Nothing assuredly can differ either in origin or in mode more widely from the *apparent* tautologies of intense and turbulent feeling, in which the passion is greater and of longer endurance than to be exhausted or satisfied by a single representation of the image or incident exciting it. Such repetitions I admit to be a beauty of the highest kind; as illustrated by Mr. Wordsworth himself from the song of Deborah. *"At her feet he bowed, he fell, he lay down; at her feet he bowed, he fell; where he bowed, there he fell down dead."*

CHAPTER XVIII

Language of metrical composition, why and wherein essentially different from that of prose—Origin and elements of metre—Its necessary consequences, and the conditions thereby imposed on the metrical writer in the choice of his diction.

I CONCLUDE, therefore, that the attempt is impracticable; and that, were it not impracticable, it would still be useless. For the very power of making the selection implies the previous possession of the language selected. Or where can the poet have lived? And by what rules could he direct his choice, which would not have enabled him to select and arrange his words by the light of his own judgement? We do not adopt the language of a class by the mere adoption of such words exclusively, as that class would use, or at least understand; but likewise by following the *order,* in which the words of such men are wont to succeed each other. Now this order, in the intercourse of uneducated men, is distinguished from the diction of their superiors in knowledge and power, by the greater *disjunction* and *separation* in the component parts of that, whatever it be, which they wish to communicate. There is a want of that prospectiveness of mind, that *surview,* which enables a man to foresee the whole of what he is to convey, appertaining to any one point; and by this means so to subordinate and arrange the different parts according to their relative importance, as to convey it at once, and as an organized whole.

Now I will take the first stanza, on which I have chanced to open, in the Lyrical Ballads. It is one the most simple and the least peculiar in its language.

> "In distant countries have I been,
> And yet I have not often seen
> A healthy man, a man full grown,
> Weep in the public roads alone.
> But such a one, on English ground,
> And in the broad highway, I met;
> Along the broad highway he came.

> His cheeks with tears were wet:
> Sturdy he seem'd, though he was sad:
> And in his arms a lamb he had."

The words here are doubtless such as are current in all ranks of life; and of course not less so in the hamlet and cottage than in the shop, manufactory, college, or palace. But is this the *order,* in which the rustic would have placed the words? I am grievously deceived, if the following less *compact* mode of commencing the same tale be not a far more faithful copy. "I have been in a many parts, far and near, and I don't know that I ever saw before a man crying by himself in the public road; a grown man I mean, that was neither sick nor hurt," &c., &c. But when I turn to the following stanza in "The Thorn":

> "At all times of the day and night
> This wretched woman thither goes,
> And she is known to every star,
> And every wind that blows:
> And there, beside the thorn, she sits,
> When the blue day-light's in the skies;
> And when the whirlwind's on the hill,
> Or frosty air is keen and still;
> And to herself she cries,
> Oh misery! Oh misery!
> Oh woe is me! Oh misery!"

and compare this with the language of ordinary men; or with that which I can conceive at all likely to proceed, in *real* life, from *such* a narrator, as is supposed in the note to the poem; compare it either in the succession of the images or of the sentences; I am reminded of the sublime prayer and hymn of praise, which MILTON, in opposition to an established liturgy, presents as a fair *specimen* of common extemporary devotion, and such as we might expect to hear from every self-inspired minister of a conventicle! And I reflect with delight, how little a mere theory, though of his own workmanship, interferes with the processes of genuine imagination in a man of true poetic genius, who possesses, as Mr. Wordsworth, if ever man did, most assuredly does possess,

"THE VISION AND THE FACULTY DIVINE."

One point then alone remains, but that the most important; its examination having been, indeed, my chief inducement for the preceding inquisition. *"There neither is or can be any essential difference between the language of prose and metrical com-*

position." Such is Mr. Wordsworth's assertion. Now prose itself, at least in all argumentative and consecutive works, differs, and ought to differ, from the language of conversation; even as[56] reading ought to differ from talking. Unless therefore the difference denied be that of the mere *words*, as materials common to all styles of writing, and not of the *style* itself in the universally admitted sense of the term, it might be naturally presumed that there must exist a still greater between the ordonnance of poetic composition and that of prose, than is expected to distinguish prose from ordinary conversation.

There are not, indeed, examples wanting in the history of literature, of apparent paradoxes that have summoned the public wonder as new and startling truths, but which on examination have shrunk into tame and harmless *truisms;* as the eyes of a cat, seen in the dark, have been mistaken for flames of fire. But Mr. Wordsworth is among the last men, to whom a delusion of this kind would be attributed by anyone, who had enjoyed the slightest opportunity of understanding his mind and character. Where an objection has been anticipated by such an author as

[56] It is no less an error in teachers, than a torment to the poor children, to inforce the necessity of reading as they would talk. In order to cure them of *singing* as it is called, that is, of too great a difference, the child is made to repeat the words with his eyes from off the book; and then, indeed, his tones resemble talking, as far as his fears, tears and trembling will permit. But as soon as his eye is again directed to the printed page, the spell begins anew; for an instinctive sense tells the child's feelings, that to utter its own momentary thoughts, and to recite the written thoughts of another, as of another, and a far wiser than himself, are two widely different things; and as the two acts are accompanied with widely different feelings, so must they justify different modes of enunciation. Joseph Lancaster, among his other sophistications of the excellent Dr. Bell's invaluable system, cures this fault of *singing*, by hanging fetters and chains on the child, to the music of which one of his school-fellows, who walks before, dolefully chaunts out the child's last speech and confession, birth, parentage, and education. And this soul-benumbing ignominy, this unholy and heart-hardening burlesque on the last fearful infliction of outraged law, in pronouncing the sentence to which the stern and familiarized judge not seldom bursts into tears, has been extolled as a happy and ingenious method of remedying—what? and how?—why, one extreme in order to introduce another, scarce less distant from good sense, and certainly likely to have worse moral effects, by enforcing a semblance of petulant ease and self-sufficiency, in repression, and possible after-perversion of the natural feelings. I have to beg Dr. Bell's pardon for this connection of the two names, but he knows that contrast is no less powerful a cause of association than likeness.

natural, his answer to it must needs be interpreted in some
sense which either is, or has been, or is capable of being con-
troverted. My object then must be to discover some other
meaning for the term "*essential difference*" in this place, exclu-
sive of the indistinction and community of the words them-
selves. For whether there ought to exist a class of words in the
English, in any degree resembling the poetic dialect of the
Greek and Italian, is a question of very subordinate impor-
tance. The number of such words would be small indeed, in
our language; and even in the Italian and Greek, they consist not
so much of different words, as of slight differences in the *forms*
of declining and conjugating the same words; forms, doubtless,
which having been, at some period more or less remote, the com-
mon grammatic flexions of some tribe or province, had been
accidentally appropriated to poetry by the general admiration
of certain master intellects, the first established lights of inspira-
tion, to whom that dialect happened to be native.

Essence, in its primary signification, means the principle of
individuation, the inmost principle of the possibility of any thing,
as that particular thing. It is equivalent to the *idea* of a thing,
when ever we use the word, idea, with philosophic precision.
Existence, on the other hand, is distinguished from essence, by
the superinduction of *reality*. Thus we speak of the essence, and
essential properties of a circle; but we do not therefore assert,
that any thing, which really exists, is mathematically circular.
Thus too, without any tautology we contend for the *existence* of
the Supreme Being; that is, for a reality correspondent to the
idea. There is, next, a *secondary* use of the word essence, in
which it signifies the point or ground of contra-distinction be-
tween two modifications of the same substance or subject. Thus
we should be allowed to say, that the style of architecture of
Westminster Abbey is *essentially* different from that of St. Paul's,
even though both had been built with blocks cut into the same
form, and from the same quarry. Only in this latter sense of
the term must it have been *denied* by Mr. Wordsworth (for in
this sense alone is it *affirmed* by the general opinion) that the
language of poetry (i.e. the formal construction, or architecture,
of the words and phrases) is *essentially* different from that of
prose. Now the burthen of the proof lies with the oppugner,
not with the supporters of the common belief. Mr. Wordsworth,
in consequence, assigns as the proof of his position, "that not
only the language of a large portion of every good poem, even of
the most elevated character, must necessarily, except with ref-
erence to the metre, in no respect differ from that of good prose,

but likewise that some of the most interesting parts of the best poems will be found to be strictly the language of prose, when prose is well written. The truth of this assertion might be demonstrated by innumerable passages from almost all the poetical writings even of Milton himself." He then quotes Gray's sonnet—

> "In vain to me the smiling mornings shine,
> And reddening Phœbus lifts his golden fire;
> The birds in vain their amorous descant join,
> Or chearful fields resume their green attire.
> These ears, alas! for other notes repine;
> *A different object do these eyes require;*
> *My lonely anguish melts no heart but mine;*
> *And in my breast the imperfect joys expire.*
> Yet morning smiles the busy race to cheer,
> And newborn pleasure brings to happier men:
> The fields to all their wonted tribute bear,
> To warm their little loves the birds complain.
> *I fruitless mourn to him that cannot hear,*
> *And weep the more because I weep in vain,"*

and adds the following remark:—"It will easily be perceived, that the only part of this Sonnet, which is of any value, is the lines printed in italics. It is equally obvious, that, except in the rhyme, and in the use of the single word 'fruitless' for 'fruitlessly,' which is so far a defect, the language of these lines does in no respect differ from that of prose."

An idealist defending his system by the fact, that when asleep we often believe ourselves awake, was well answered by his plain neighbour, "Ah, but when awake do we ever believe ourselves asleep?"—Things identical must be convertible. The preceding passage seems to rest on a similar sophism. For the question is not, whether there may not occur in prose an order of words, which would be equally proper in a poem; nor whether there are not beautiful lines and sentences of frequent occurrence in good poems, which would be equally becoming as well as beautiful in good prose; for neither the one nor the other has ever been either denied or doubted by any one. The true question must be, whether there are not modes of expression, a *construction*, and an *order* of sentences, which are in their fit and natural place in a serious prose composition, but would be disproportionate and heterogeneous in metrical poetry; and, vice versa, whether in the language of a serious poem there may not be an arrangement both of words and sentences, and a use and selection of (what are called) *figures of speech*, both as to their kind, their frequency, and their occasions, which on a subject of equal weight would be vicious and alien in correct and manly prose. I contend that in both cases this unfitness of each for the place of the other frequently will and ought to exist.

And first from the *origin* of metre. This I would trace to the balance in the mind effected by that spontaneous effort which strives to hold in check the workings of passion. It might be easily explained likewise in what manner this salutary antagonism is assisted by the very state, which it counteracts; and how this balance of antagonists became organized into *metre* (in the usual acceptation of that term) by a supervening act of the will and judgement, consciously and for the foreseen purpose of pleasure. Assuming these principles, as the data of our argument, we deduce from them two legitimate conditions, which the critic is entitled to expect in every metrical work. First, that, as the *elements* of metre owe their existence to a state of increased excitement, so the metre itself should be accompanied by the natural language of excitement. Secondly, that as these elements are formed into metre *artificially*, by a *voluntary* act, with the design and for the purpose of blending *delight* with emotion, so the traces of present *volition* should throughout the metrical language be proportionately discernible. Now these two conditions must be reconciled and co-present. There must be not only a partnership, but a union; an interpenetration of passion and of will, of *spontaneous* impulse and of *voluntary* purpose. Again, this union can be manifested only in a frequency of forms and figures of speech (originally the offspring of passion, but now the adopted children of power) greater than would be desired or endured, where the emotion is not voluntarily encouraged and kept up for the sake of that pleasure, which such emotion, so tempered and mastered by the will, is found capable of communicating. It not only dictates, but of itself tends to produce, a more frequent employment of picturesque and vivifying language, than would be natural in any other case, in which there did not exist, as there does in the present, a previous and well understood, though tacit, *compact* between the poet and his reader, that the latter is entitled to expect, and the former bound to supply, this species and degree of pleasureable excitement. We may in some measure apply to this union the answer of POLIXENES, in the Winter's Tale, to PERDITA's neglect of the streaked gilly-flowers, because she had heard it said,

"There is an art which, in their piedness, shares
    With great creating nature.
                    Pol: Say there be;
Yet nature is made better by no mean,

But nature makes that mean; so, ev'n that art,
Which, you say, adds to nature, is an art,
That nature makes. You see, sweet maid, we marry
A gentler scyon to the wildest stock;
And make conceive a bark of ruder kind
By bud of nobler race. This is an art,
Which does mend nature—change it rather; but
The art itself is nature."

Secondly, I argue from the EFFECTS of metre. As far as metre acts in and for itself, it tends to increase the vivacity and susceptibility both of the general feelings and of the attention. This effect it produces by the continued excitement of surprize, and by the quick reciprocations of curiosity still gratified and still re-excited, which are too slight indeed to be at any one moment objects of distinct consciousness, yet become considerable in their aggregate influence. As a medicated atmosphere, or as wine during animated conversation; they act powerfully, though themselves unnoticed. Where, therefore, correspondent food and appropriate matter are not provided for the attention and feelings thus roused, there must needs be a disappointment felt; like that of leaping in the dark from the last step of a stair-case, when we had prepared our muscles for a leap of three or four.

The discussion on the powers of metre in the preface is highly ingenious and touches at all points on truth. But I cannot find any statement of its powers considered abstractly and separately. On the contrary Mr. Wordsworth seems always to estimate metre by the powers, which it exerts during (and, as I think, in *consequence of*) its combination with other elements of poetry. Thus the previous difficulty is left unanswered, *what* the elements are, with which it must be combined in order to produce its own effects to any pleasureable purpose. Double and tri-syllable rhymes, indeed, form a lower species of wit, and, attended to exclusively for their own sake, may become a source of momentary amusement; as in poor Smart's distich to the Welsh 'Squire who had promised him a hare:

"Tell me, thou son of great Cadwallader!
Hast sent the hare? or hast thou swallow'd her?"

But for any *poetic* purposes, metre resembles (if the aptness of the simile may excuse its meanness) yeast, worthless or disagreeable by itself, but giving vivacity and spirit to the liquor with which it is proportionally combined.

The reference to the "Children in the Wood," by no means satisfies my judgement. We all willingly throw ourselves back for awhile into the feelings of our childhood. This ballad, there-fore, we read under such recollections of our own childish feel-ings, as would equally endear to us poems, which Mr. Words-worth himself would regard as faulty in the opposite extreme of gaudy and technical ornament. Before the invention of print-ing, and in a still greater degree, before the introduction of writ-ing, metre, especially *alliterative* metre (whether alliterative at the beginning of the words, as in "Pierce Plouman," or at the end as in rhymes) possessed an independent value as assisting the recollection, and consequently the preservation, of *any* series of truths or incidents. But I am not convinced by the collation of facts, that the "Children in the Wood" owes either its preserva-tion, or its popularity, to its metrical form. Mr. Marshal's reposi-tory affords a number of tales in prose inferior in pathos and general merit, some of as old a date, and many as widely popular. "TOM HICKATHRIFT," "JACK THE GIANT-KILLER," "GOODY TWO-SHOES," and "LITTLE RED RIDING-HOOD" are formidable rivals. And that they have continued in prose, cannot be fairly explained by the assumption, that the comparative meanness of their thoughts and images precluded even the humblest forms of metre. The scene of GOODY TWO-SHOES in the church is perfectly susceptible of metrical narration; and, among the Θαύματα θαυμαστότατα even of the present age, I do not recollect a more astonishing image than that of the *"whole rookery, that flew out of the giant's beard,"* scared by the tremendous voice, with which this monster answered the challenge of the heroic TOM HICKATHRIFT!

If from these we turn to compositions universally and inde-pendently of all early associations, beloved and admired; would "THE MARIA," "THE MONK," or "THE POOR MAN'S ASS" of Sterne, be read with more delight, or have a better chance of immortality, had they without any change in the diction been composed in rhyme, than in their present state? If I am not grossly mistaken, the general reply would be in the negative. Nay, I will confess, that, in Mr. Wordsworth's own volumes, the "ANECDOTE FOR FATHERS," "SIMON LEE," "ALICE FELL," "THE BEGGARS," and "THE SAILOR'S MOTHER," notwithstanding the beauties which are to be found in each of them where the poet interposes the music of his own thoughts, would have been more delightful to me in prose, told and managed, as by Mr. Wordsworth they would have been, in a moral essay, or pedestrian tour.

Metre in itself is simply a stimulant of the attention, and there-fore excites the question: Why is the attention to be thus stimu-lated? Now the question cannot be answered by the pleasure of the metre itself: for this we have shown to be *conditional,* and dependent on the appropriateness of the thoughts and expressions, to which the metrical form is superadded. Neither can I conceive any other answer that can be rationally given, short of this: I write in metre, because I am about to use a language different from that of prose. Besides, where the language is not such, how interesting soever the reflections are, that are capable of being drawn by a philosophic mind from the thoughts or incidents of the poem, the metre itself must often become feeble. Take the last three stanzas of "THE SAILOR'S MOTHER," for instance. If I could for a moment abstract from the effect produced on the author's feelings, as a man, by the incident at the time of its real occurrence, I would dare appeal to his own judgement, whether in the *metre* itself he found a sufficient reason for *their* being written *metrically?*

"And, thus continuing, she said,
   I had a son, who many a day
Sailed on the seas; but he is dead;
   In Denmark he was cast away:
And I have travelled far as Hull, to see
What clothes he might have left, or other property.

The bird and cage they both were his:
   'Twas my son's bird; and neat and trim
He kept it: many voyages
   This singing-bird hath gone with him,
When last he sailed he left the bird behind;
As it might be, perhaps, from bodings of his mind:

He to a fellow-lodger's care
   Had left it, to be watched and fed,
Till he came back again; and there
   I found it when my son was dead;
And now, God help me for my little wit!
I trail it with me, Sir! he took so much delight in it."

If disproportioning the emphasis we read these stanzas so as to make the rhymes perceptible, even *tri-syllable* rhymes could scarcely produce an equal sense of oddity and strangeness, as we feel here in finding *rhymes at all* in sentences so exclusively colloquial. I would further ask whether, but for that visionary state, into which the figure of the woman and the susceptibility of his own genius had placed the poet's imagination, (a state, which spreads its influence and coloring over all, that co-exists with the exciting cause, and in which

> "The simplest, and the most familiar things
> Gain a strange power of spreading awe around [57] them,")

I would ask the poet whether he would not have felt an abrupt downfall in these verses from the preceding stanza?

> "The ancient spirit is not dead;
> Old times, thought I, are breathing there;
> Proud was I that my country bred
> Such strength, a dignity so fair:
> She begged an alms, like one in poor estate;
> I looked at her again, nor did my pride abate."

It must not be omitted, and is besides worthy of notice, that those stanzas furnish the only fair instance that I have been able to discover in all Mr. Wordsworth's writings, of an *actual* adoption, or true imitation, of the *real* and *very* language of *low and rustic life,* freed from provincialisms.

Thirdly, I deduce the position from all the causes elsewhere assigned, which render metre the proper form of poetry, and poetry imperfect and defective without metre. Metre therefore having been connected with *poetry* most often and by a peculiar fitness, whatever else is combined with *metre* must, though it be not itself *essentially* poetic, have nevertheless some property in common with poetry, as an intermedium of affinity, a sort (if I may dare borrow a well-known phrase from technical chemistry) of *mordaunt* between it and the superadded metre. Now poetry, Mr. Wordsworth truly affirms, does always imply PASSION: which word must be here understood in its general sense, as an excited state of the feelings and faculties. And as every passion has its proper pulse, so will it likewise have its characteristic modes of expression. But where there exists that degree of genius and talent which entitles a writer to aim at the honors of a poet, the very *act* of poetic composition *itself* is, and is al-

---

[57] Altered from the description of Night-Mair in the "Remorse."

> "Oh Heaven! 'twas frightful! Now run down and stared at
> By hideous shapes that cannot be remembered;
> Now seeing nothing and imagining nothing;
> But only being afraid—stifled with fear!
> While every goodly or familiar form
> Had a strange power of spreading terror round me!"

N.B. Though Shakespeare has, for his own *all-justifying* purposes, introduced the Night-*Mare* with her own foals, yet Mair means a Sister, or perhaps a Hag.

lowed to imply and to produce, an unusual state of excitement, which of course justifies and demands a correspondent difference of language, as truly, though not perhaps in as marked a degree, as the excitement of love, fear, rage, or jealousy. The vividness of the descriptions or declamations in DONNE or DRYDEN is as much and as often derived from the force and fervor of the describer, as from the reflections, forms or incidents, which constitute their subject and materials. The wheels take fire from the mere rapidity of their motion. To what extent, and under what modifications, this may be admitted to act, I shall attempt to define in an after remark on Mr. Wordsworth's reply to this objection, or rather on his objection to this reply, as already anticipated in his preface.

Fourthly, and as intimately connected with this, if not the same argument in a more general form, I adduce the high spiritual instinct of the human being impelling us to seek unity by harmonious adjustment, and thus establishing the principle, that *all* the parts of an organized whole must be assimilated to the more *important* and *essential* parts. This and the preceding arguments may be strengthened by the reflection, that the composition of a poem is among the *imitative* arts; and that imitation, as opposed to copying, consists either in the interfusion of the SAME throughout the radically DIFFERENT, or of the different throughout a base radically the same.

Lastly, I appeal to the practice of the best poets, of all countries and in all ages, as *authorizing* the opinion (*deduced* from all the foregoing) that in every import of the word ESSENTIAL, which would not here involve a mere truism, there may be, is, and ought to be an *essential* difference between the language of prose and of metrical composition.

In Mr. Wordsworth's criticism of GRAY's Sonnet, the readers' sympathy with his praise or blame of the different parts is taken for granted rather perhaps too easily. He has not, at least, attempted to win or compel it by argumentative analysis. In *my* conception at least, the lines rejected as of no value do, with the exception of the two first, differ as much and as little from the language of common life, as those which he has printed in italics as possessing genuine excellence. Of the five lines thus honourably distinguished, two of them differ from prose, even more widely than the lines which either precede or follow, in the *position* of the words.

> "A *different object do these eyes require;*
> My lonely anguish melts no heart but mine;
> *And in my breast the imperfect joys expire.*"

But were it otherwise, what would this prove, but a truth, of which no man ever doubted? Videlicet, that there are sentences, which would be equally in their place both in verse and prose. Assuredly it does not prove the point, which alone requires proof; namely, that there are not passages, which would suit the one and not suit the other. The first line of this sonnet is distinguished from the ordinary language of men by the epithet to morning. (For we will set aside, at present, the consideration, that the particular word *"smiling"* is hackneyed and (as it involves a sort of personification) not quite congruous with the common and material attribute of *shining*.) And, doubtless, this adjunction of epithets for the purpose of additional description, where no particular attention is demanded for the quality of the thing, would be noticed as giving a poetic cast to a man's conversation. Should the sportsman exclaim, *"Come boys! the rosy morning calls you up,"* he will be supposed to have some song in his head. But no one suspects this, when he says, "A wet morning shall not confine us to our beds." This then is either a defect in poetry, or it is not. Whoever should decide in the *affirmative*, I would request him to re-peruse any one poem of any confessedly great poet from Homer to Milton, or from Æschylus to Shakespeare; and to strike out (in thought I mean) every instance of this kind. If the number of these fancied erasures did not startle him; or if he continued to deem the work improved by their total omission; he must advance reasons of no ordinary strength and evidence, reasons grounded in the essence of human nature. Otherwise, I should not hesitate to consider him as a man not so much *proof against* all authority, as *dead to* it.

The second line,

"And reddening Phœbus lifts his golden fire;"

has indeed almost as many faults as words. But then it is a bad line, not because the language is distinct from that of prose; but because it conveys incongruous images, because it confounds the cause and the effect, the real *thing* with the personified *representative* of the thing; in short, because it differs from the language of GOOD SENSE! That the "Phœbus" is hackneyed, and a schoolboy image, is an *accidental* fault, dependent on the age in which the author wrote, and not deduced from the nature of the thing. That it is part of an exploded mythology, is an objection more deeply grounded. Yet when the torch of ancient learning was re-kindled, so cheering were its beams, that our eldest poets, cut off by Christianity from all *accredited* machinery, and deprived of all *acknowledged* guardians and symbols of the great objects of nature, were naturally induced to adopt, as a *poetic* language, those fabulous personages, those forms of the[58] supernatural in nature, which had given them such dear delight in the poems of their great masters. Nay, even at this day what scholar of genial taste will not so far sympathize with them, as to read with pleasure in PETRARCH, CHAUCER, or SPENSER, what he would perhaps condemn as puerile in a modern poet?

I remember no poet, whose writings would safelier stand the test of Mr. Wordsworth's theory, than SPENSER. Yet will Mr. Wordsworth say, that the style of the following stanza is either undistinguished from prose, and the language of ordinary life? Or that it is vicious, and that the stanzas are *blots* in the "Faery Queen"?

> "By this the northern waggoner had set
> His sevenfold teme behind the steadfast starre,
> That was in ocean waves yet never wet,
> But firme is fixt, and sendeth light from farre
> To all that in the wild deep wandering are:
> And chearful chanticleer with his note shrill
> Had warned once that Phœbus' fiery carre
> In haste was climbing up the easterne hill,
> Full envious that night so long his roome did fill."
>
>   *Book I. Can. 2. St. 2.*

> "At last the golden orientall gate
> Of greatest heaven gan to open fayre,
> And Phœbus fresh, as brydegrome to his mate,
> Came dauncing forth, shaking his deawie hayre,
> And hurl'd his glist'ring beams through gloomy ayre:
> Which when the wakeful elfe perceived, streightway
> He started up, and did him selfe prepayre
> In sun-bright armes and battailous array;
> For with that pagan proud he combat will that day."
>
>   *B. I. Can. 5. St. 2.*

On the contrary to how many passages, both in hymn books and in blank verse poems, could I, (were it not invidious), direct the reader's attention, the style of which is most *unpoetic, because,* and only because, it is the style of *prose?* He will not suppose me capable of having in my mind such verses, as

[58] But still more by the mechanical system of philosophy which has needlessly infected our theological opinions, and teaching us to consider the world in its relation to God, as of a building to its mason, leaves the idea of omnipresence a mere abstract notion in the state-room of our reason.

> "I put my hat upon my head
> And walk'd into the Strand;
> And there I met another man,
> Whose hat was in his hand."

To such specimens it would indeed be a fair and full reply, that these lines are not bad, because they are *unpoetic;* but because they are empty of all sense and feeling; and that it were an idle attempt to prove that an ape is not a Newton, when it is evident that he is not a man. But the sense shall be good and weighty, the language correct and dignified, the subject interesting and treated with feeling; and yet the style shall, notwithstanding all these merits, be justly blamable as *prosaic,* and solely because the words and the order of the words would find their appropriate place in prose, but are not suitable to *metrical* composition. The "Civil Wars" of Daniel is an instructive, and even interesting work; but take the following stanzas (and from the hundred instances which abound I might probably have selected others far more striking):

> "And to the end we may with better ease
> Discern the true discourse, vouchsafe to shew
> What were the times foregoing near to these,
> That these we may with better profit know.
> Tell how the world fell into this disease;
> And how so great distemperature did grow;
> So shall we see with what degrees it came;
> How things at full do soon wax out of frame."

> "Ten kings had from the Norman conqu'ror reign'd
> With intermixt and variable fate,
> When England to her greatest height attain'd
> Of power, dominion, glory, wealth, and state;
> After it had with much ado sustain'd
> The violence of princes, with debate
> For titles and the often mutinies
> Of nobles for their ancient liberties."

> "For first, the Norman, conqu'ring all by might,
> By might was forc'd to keep what he had got;
> Mixing our customs and the form of right
> With foreign constitutions he had brought;
> Mast'ring the mighty, humbling the poorer wight,
> By all severest means that could be wrought;
> And, making the succession doubtful, rent
> His new-got state, and left it turbulent."

B. I. St. VII. VIII. & IX.

Will it be contended on the one side, that these lines are mean and senseless? Or on the other, that they are not prosaic, and for *that* reason unpoetic? This poet's well-merited epithet is that of the *"well-languaged Daniel;"* but likewise, and by the consent of his contemporaries no less than of all succeeding critics, the "prosaic Daniel." Yet those, who thus designate this wise and amiable writer, from the frequent incorrespondency of his diction to his metre in the majority of his compositions, not only deem them valuable and interesting on other accounts; but willingly admit, that there are to be found throughout his poems, and especially in his *Epistles* and in his *Hymen's Triumph,* many and exquisite specimens of that style which, as the *neutral ground* of prose and verse, is common to both. A fine and almost faultless extract, eminent, as for other beauties, so for its perfection in this species of diction, may be seen in LAMB's Dramatic Specimens, &c., a work of various interest from the nature of the selections themselves, (all from the plays of Shakespeare's contemporaries), and deriving a high additional value from the notes, which are full of just and original criticism, expressed with all the freshness of originality.

Among the possible effects of practical adherence to a theory, that aims to *identify* the style of prose and verse, (if it does not indeed claim for the latter a yet nearer resemblance to the average style of men in the vivâ voce intercourse of real life) we might anticipate the following as not the least likely to occur. It will happen, as I have indeed before observed, that the metre itself, the sole acknowledged difference, will occasionally become metre to the eye only. The existence of *prosaisms,* and that they detract from the merit of a poem, *must* at length be conceded, when a number of successive lines can be rendered, even to the most delicate ear, unrecognizable as verse, or as having even been intended for verse, by simply transcribing them as prose; when, if the poem be in blank verse, this can be effected without any alteration, or at most by merely restoring one or two words to their proper places, from which they have been[59] transplanted

---

[59] As the ingenious gentleman under the influence of the Tragic Muse contrived to dislocate, "I wish you a good morning, Sir! Thank you, Sir, and I wish you the same," into two blank-verse heroics:—

> To you a morning good, good Sir! I wish.
> You, Sir! I thank: to you the same wish I.

In those parts of Mr. Wordsworth's works which I have thoroughly studied, I find fewer instances in which this would be practicable than I have met in many poems, where an approximation of prose has

for no assignable cause or reason but that of the author's convenience; but, if it be in rhyme, by the mere exchange of the final word of each line for some other of the same meaning, equally appropriate, dignified, and euphonic.

The answer or objection in the preface to the anticipated remark "that metre paves the way to other distinctions," is contained in the following words. "The distinction of rhyme and metre is voluntary and uniform, and not, like that produced by (what is called) poetic diction, arbitrary, and subject to infinite caprices, upon which no calculation whatever can be made. In the one case the reader is utterly at the mercy of the poet respecting what imagery or diction he may choose to connect with the passion." But is this a *poet*, of whom a poet is speaking? No surely! rather of a fool or madman: or at best of a vain or ignorant phantast! And might not brains so wild and so deficient make just the same havock with rhymes and metres, as they are supposed to effect with modes and figures of speech? How is the reader at the *mercy* of such men? If he continue to read their nonsense, is it not his own fault? The ultimate end of criticism is much more to establish the principles of writing, than to furnish *rules* how to pass judgement on what has been written by others; if indeed it were possible that the two could be separated. But if it be asked, by what principles the poet is to regu-

---

been sedulously and on system guarded against. Indeed excepting the stanzas already quoted from "THE SAILOR'S MOTHER," I can recollect but one instance: viz. a short passage of four or five lines in "THE BROTHERS," that model of English pastoral, which I have never yet read with unclouded eye.—"James, pointing to its summit, over which they had all purposed to return together, informed them that he would wait for them there. They parted, and his comrades passed that way some two hours after, but they did not find him at the appointed place, *a circumstance of which they took no heed:* but one of them, going by chance into the house, which at this time was James's house, learnt *there*, that nobody had seen him all that day." The only change which has been made is in the position of the little word *there* in two instances, the position in the original being clearly such as is not adopted in ordinary conversation. The other words printed in *italics* were so marked because, though good and genuine English, they are not the phraseology of common conversation either in the word put in apposition, or in the connection by the genitive pronoun. Men in general would have said, "but that was a circumstance they paid no attention to, or took no notice of," and the language is, on the theory of the preface, justified only by the narrator's being the *Vicar*. Yet if any ear *could* suspect, that these sentences were ever printed as metre, on these very words alone could the suspicion have been grounded.

late his own style, if he do not adhere closely to the sort and order of words which he hears in the market, wake, high-road, or plough-field? I reply; by principles, the ignorance or neglect of which would convict him of being no *poet*, but a silly or presumptuous usurper of the name! By the principles of grammar, logic, psychology! In one word by such a knowledge of the facts, material and spiritual, that most appertain to his art, as, if it have been governed and applied by *good sense*, and rendered instinctive by habit, becomes the representative and reward of our past conscious reasonings, insights, and conclusions, and acquires the name of TASTE. By what *rule* that does not leave the reader at the poet's mercy, and the poet at his own, is the latter to distinguish between the language suitable to *suppressed*, and the language, which is characteristic of *indulged*, anger? Or between that of rage and that of jealousy? Is it obtained by wandering about in search of angry or jealous people in uncultivated society, in order to copy their words? Or not far rather by the power of imagination proceeding upon the *all in each* of human nature? By *meditation*, rather than by *observation*? And by the latter in consequence only of the former? As eyes, for which the former has pre-determined their field of vision, and to which, as to *its* organ, it communicates a microscopic power? There is not, I firmly believe, a man now living, who has, from his own inward experience, a clearer intuition, than Mr. Wordsworth himself, that the last mentioned are the true sources of *genial* discrimination. Through the same process and by the same creative agency will the poet distinguish the degree and kind of the excitement produced by the very act of poetic composition. As intuitively will he know, what differences of style it at once inspires and justifies; what intermixture of conscious volition is natural to that state; and in what instances such figures and colors of speech degenerate into mere creatures of an arbitrary purpose, cold technical artifices of ornament or connection. For, even as truth is its own light and evidence, discovering at once itself and falsehood, so is it the prerogative of poetic genius to distinguish by parental instinct its proper offspring from the changelings, which the gnomes of vanity or the fairies of fashion may have laid in its cradle or called by its names. Could a rule be given from *without*, poetry would cease to be poetry, and sink into a mechanical art. It would be μόρφωσις, not ποίησις. The *rules* of the IMAGINATION are themselves the very powers of growth and production. The *words*, to which they are reducible, present only the outlines and external appearance of the fruit. A deceptive counterfeit of the superficial form and colors may be elaborated;

ɔut the marble peach feels cold and heavy, and *children* only put it to their mouths. We find no difficulty in admitting as excellent, and the legitimate language of poetic fervor self-impassioned, DONNE's apostrophe to the Sun in the second stanza of his "Progress of the Soul:"

> "Thee, eye of heaven! this great soul envies not:
> By thy male force is all, we have, begot.
> In the first East thou now beginn'st to shine,
> Suck'st early balm and island spices there,
> And wilt anon in thy loose-rein'd career
> At Tagus, Po, Seine, Thames, and Danow dine,
> And see at night this western world of mine:
> Yet hast thou not more nations seen than she,
> Who before thee one day began to be,
> And, thy frail light being quench'd, shall long, long outlive thee!"

Or the next stanza but one:

> "Great destiny, the commissary of God,
> That hast mark'd out a path and period
> For ev'ry thing! Who, where we offspring took,
> Our ways and ends see'st at one instant: thou
> Knot of all causes! Thou, whose changeless brow
> Ne'er smiles or frowns! O! vouchsafe thou to look,
> And shew my story in thy eternal book, &c."

As little difficulty do we find in excluding from the honors of unaffected warmth and elevation the madness prepense of pseudo-poesy, or the startling *hysteric* of weakness over-exerting itself, which bursts on the unprepared reader in sundry odes and apostrophes to abstract terms. Such are the Odes to Jealousy, to Hope, to Oblivion, and the like, in Dodsley's collection and the magazines of that day, which seldom fail to remind me of an Oxford copy of verses on the two SUTTONS, commencing with

"INOCULATION, heavenly maid! descend!"

It is not to be denied that men of undoubted talents, and even poets of true, though not of first-rate, genius, have from a mistaken theory deluded both themselves and others in the opposite extremè. I once read to a company of sensible and well-educated women the introductory period of Cowley's preface to his *"Pindaric Odes, written in imitation of the style and manner of the odes of Pindar."* "If, (says Cowley), a man should undertake to translate Pindar, word for word, it would be thought that one madman had translated another; as may appear, when he, that understands not the original, reads the verbal traduction of him

into Latin prose, than which nothing seems more raving." I then
proceeded with his own free version of the second Olympic,
composed for the charitable purpose of *rationalizing* the Theban
Eagle.

> "Queen of all harmonious things,
>   Dancing words and speaking strings,
> What God, what hero, wilt thou sing?
> What happy man to equal glories bring?
>   Begin, begin thy noble choice,
> And let the hills around reflect the image of thy voice.
> Pisa does to Jove belong,
> Jove and Pisa claim thy song.
> The fair first-fruits of war, th' Olympic games,
> Alcides offer'd up to Jove;
> Alcides too thy strings may move!
> But, oh! what man to join with these can worthy prove?
> Join Theron boldly to their sacred names;
> Theron the next honor claims;
> Theron to no man gives place,
> Is first in Pisa's and in Virtue's race;
> Theron there, and he alone,
> Ev'n his own swift forefathers has outgone."

One of the company exclaimed, with the full assent of the rest,
that if the original were madder than this, it must be incurably
mad. I then translated the ode from the Greek, and as nearly as
possible, word for word; and the impression was, that in the
general movement of the periods, in the form of the connections
and transitions, and in the sober majesty of lofty sense, it ap-
peared to them to approach more nearly, than any other poetry
they had heard, to the style of our Bible in the prophetic books.
The first strophe will suffice as a specimen:

> Ye harp-controuling hymns! (or) ye hymns the sovereigns of harps!
> What God? what Hero?
> What Man shall we celebrate?
> Truly Pisa indeed is of Jove,
> But the Olympiad (or the Olympic games) did Hercules establish,
> The first-fruits of the spoils of war.
> But Theron for the four-horsed car,
> That bore victory to him,
> It behoves us now to voice aloud:
> The Just, the Hospitable,
> The Bulwark of Agrigentum,
> Of renowned fathers
> The Flower, even him
> Who preserves his native city erect and safe."

But are such rhetorical caprices condemnable only for their deviation from the language of real life? and are they by no other means to be precluded, but by the rejection of all distinctions between prose and verse, save that of metre? Surely good sense, and a moderate insight into the constitution of the human mind, would be amply sufficient to prove, that such language and such combinations are the native produce neither of the fancy nor of the imagination; that their operation consists in the excitement of surprise by the juxta-position and *apparent* reconciliation of widely different or incompatible things. As when, for instance, the hills are made to reflect the image of a *voice*. Surely, no unusual taste is requisite to see clearly, that this compulsory juxta-position is not produced by the presentation of impressive or delightful forms to the inward vision, nor by any sympathy with the modifying powers with which the genius of the poet had united and inspirited all the objects of his thought; that it is therefore a species of *wit*, a pure work of the *will*, and implies a leisure and self-possession both of thought and of feeling, incompatible with the steady fervor of a mind possessed and filled with the grandeur of its subject. To sum up the whole in one sentence. When a poem, or a part of a poem, shall be adduced, which is evidently vicious in the figures and contexture of its style, yet for the condemnation of which no reason can be assigned, except that it differs from the style in which men actually converse, then, and not till then, can I hold this theory to be either plausible, or practicable, or capable of furnishing either rule, guidance, or precaution, that might not, more easily and more safely, as well as more naturally, have been deduced in the author's own mind from considerations of grammar, logic, and the truth and nature of things, confirmed by the authority of works, whose fame is not of ONE country nor of ONE age.

CHAPTER XIX

Continuation—Concerning the real object which, it is probable, Mr. Wordsworth had before him in his critical preface—Elucidation and application of this—The neutral style, or that common to Prose and Poetry, exemplified by specimens from Chaucer, Herbert, and others.

IT MIGHT appear from some passages in the former part of Mr. Wordsworth's preface, that he meant to confine his theory of style, and the necessity of a close accordance with the actual language of men, to those particular subjects from low and rustic life, which by way of experiment he had purposed to naturalize as a new species in our English poetry. But from the train of argument that follows; from the reference to Milton; and from the spirit of his critique on Gray's sonnet; those sentences appear to have been rather courtesies of modesty, than actual limitations of his system. Yet so groundless does this system appear on a close examination; and so strange and [60] over-whelming in its consequences, that I cannot, and I do not, believe that the poet did ever himself adopt it in the unqualified sense, in which his expressions have been understood by others, and which, indeed, according to all the common laws of interpretation they seem to bear. What then did he mean? I apprehend, that in the clear perception, not unaccompanied with disgust or contempt, of the gaudy affections of a style which passed current with too many for poetic diction, (though in truth it had as little pretensions to poetry, as to logic or common sense), he narrowed his view for the time; and feeling a justifiable preference for the language of nature and of good sense, even in its humblest and least ornamented forms, he suffered himself to express, in terms at once too large and too exclusive, his predilection for a style the most remote possible from the false and showy splendour which he wished to explode. It is possible, that this predilection, at first merely comparative, deviated for a time into direct partiality. But the real object which he had in view, was, I doubt not, a species of excellence which had been long before most happily characterized by the judicious and amiable GARVE, whose works are so justly beloved and esteemed by the Germans, in his remarks on GELLERT, (see Sammlung einiger Abhandlungen von Christian Garve), from which the following is literally translated. "The talent, that is required to make excellent verses, is perhaps greater than the philosopher is ready to admit, or would find it in his power to acquire: the talent to seek only the apt expression of the thought, and yet to find at the same time with it the rhyme and the metre. Gellert possessed this happy

[60] I had in my mind the striking but untranslatable epithet, which the celebrated Mendelssohn applied to the great founder of the Critical Philosophy "Der alleszermalmende KANT," i.e. the all-becrushing, or rather the all-to-nothing-crushing KANT. In the facility and force of compound epithets, the German from the number of its cases and inflections approaches to the Greek: that language so

"Bless'd in the happy marriage of sweet words."

It is in the woeful harshness of its sounds alone that the German need shrink from the comparison.

gift, if ever any one of our poets possessed it; and nothing perhaps contributed more to the great and universal impression which his fables made on their first publication, or conduces more to their continued popularity. It was a strange and curious phenomenon, and such as in Germany had been previously unheard of, to read verses in which everything was expressed just as one would wish to talk, and yet all dignified, attractive, and interesting; and all at the same time perfectly correct as to the measure of the syllables and the rhyme. It is certain, that poetry when it has attained this excellence makes a far greater impression than prose. So much so indeed, that even the gratification which the very rhymes afford, becomes then no longer a contemptible or trifling gratification."

However novel this phenomenon may have been in Germany at the time of Gellert, it is by no means new, nor yet of recent existence in our language. Spite of the licentiousness with which Spenser occasionally compels the orthography of his words into a subservience to his rhymes, the whole "Faery Queen" is an almost continued instance of this beauty. Waller's song "Go, lovely Rose," is doubtless familiar to most of my readers; but if I had happened to have had by me the Poems of COTTON, more but far less deservedly celebrated as the author of the "Virgil travestied," I should have indulged myself, and I think have gratified many, who are not acquainted with his serious works, by selecting some admirable specimens of this style. There are not a few poems in that volume, replete with every excellence of thought, image, and passion, which we expect or desire in the poetry of the milder muse; and yet so worded, that the reader sees no one reason either in the selection or the order of the words, why he might not have said the very same in an appropriate conversation, and cannot conceive how indeed he could have expressed such thoughts otherwise, without loss or injury to his meaning.

But in truth our language is, and from the first dawn of poetry ever has been, particularly rich in compositions distinguished by this excellence. The final e, which is now mute, in Chaucer's age was either sounded or dropt indifferently. We ourselves still use either *beloved* or *belov'd* according as the rhyme, or measure, or the purpose of more or less solemnity may require. Let the reader then only adopt the pronunciation of the poet and of the court, at which he lived, both with respect to the final e and to the accentuation of the last syllable; I would then venture to ask, what even in the colloquial language of elegant and unaffected women. (who are the peculiar mistresses of "pure English and undefiled,") what could we hear more natural, or seemingly more unstudied, than the following stanzas from Chaucer's "Troilus and Creseide"?

"And after this forth to the gate he wente,
Ther as Creseide out rode a full gode paas,
And up and doun there made he many a wente,
And to himselfe ful oft he said, Alas!
Fro hennis rode my blisse and my solas:
As wouldè blisful God now for his joie,
I might her sene agen come in to Troie!
    And to the yondir hil I gan her guide,
Alas! and there I toke of her my leve:
And yond I saw her to her fathir ride;
For sorrow of which mine hearte shall to-cleve;
And hithir home I came whan it was eve,
And here I dwel, out-cast from allè joie,
And shal, til I maie sene her efte in Troie.
    And of himselfe imaginid he ofte
To ben defaitid, pale and waxen lesse
Than he was wonte, and that men saidin softe,
What may it be? who can the sothè gesse,
Why Troilus hath al this hevinesse?
And al this n' as but his melancolie,
That he had of himselfe suche fantasie.
    Another time imaginin he would
That every wight, that past him by the wey,
Had of him routhe, and that they saien should,
I am right sorry, Troilus wol dey!
And thus he drove a daie yet forth or twey,
As ye have herde: suche life gan he to lede
As he that stode betwixin hope and drede:
    For which him likid in his songis shewe
Th' encheson of his wo as he best might,
And made a songe of wordis but a fewe,
Somwhat his woful hertè for to light,
And whan he was from every mannis sight,
With softé voice he of his lady dere,
That absent was, gan sing as ye may hear:

*   *   *   *   *   *

This song when he thus songin had, ful soon
He fell agen into his sighis olde:
And every night, as was his wonte to done,
He stodè the bright moonè to beholde
And all his sorrowe to the moone he tolde,
And said: I wis, whan thou art hornid newe,
I shall be glad, if al the world be trewe!"

Another exquisite master of this species of style, where the scholar and the poet supplies the material, but the perfect well-bred gentleman the expressions and the arrangement, is George Herbert. As from the nature of the subject, and the too frequent quaintness of the thoughts, his "Temple: or Sacred Poems and Private Ejaculations" are comparatively but little known, I shall extract two poems. The first is a Sonnet, equally admirable for the weight, number, and expression of the thoughts, and for the simple dignity of the language. (Unless indeed a fastidious taste should object to the latter half of the sixth line.) The second is a poem of greater length, which I have chosen not only for the present purpose, but likewise as a striking example and illustration of an assertion hazarded in a former page of these sketches: namely, that the characteristic fault of our elder poets is the reverse of that, which distinguishes too many of our more recent versifiers; the one conveying the most fantastic thoughts in the most correct and natural language; the other in the most fantastic language conveying the most trivial thoughts. The latter is a riddle of words; the former an enigma of thoughts. The one reminds me of an odd passage in Drayton's IDEA:

SONNET IX.

"As other men, so I myself do muse,
Why in this sort I wrest invention so;
And why these *giddy metaphors* I use,
Leaving the path the greater part do go!
I will resolve you: *I am lunatic!*"

The other recalls a still odder passage in the "SYNAGOGUE: *or The Shadow of the Temple*," a connected series of poems in imitation of Herbert's "TEMPLE," and, in some editions, annexed to it.

"O how my mind
Is gravell'd!
Not a thought,
That I can find,
But's ravell'd
All to nought!
Short ends of threds,
And narrow shreds
Of lists,
Knots, snarled ruffs,
Loose broken tufts
Of twists,
Are my torn meditation's ragged clothing,
Which, wound and woven, shape a sute for nothing:

One while I think, and then I am in pain
To think how to unthink that thought again!"

immediately after these burlesque passages I cannot proceed
to the extracts promised, without changing the ludicrous tone of
feeling by the interposition of the three following stanzas of
Herbert's.

VIRTUE.

"Sweet day, so cool, so calm, so bright,
The bridal of the earth and sky,
The dew shall weep thy fall to-night;
For thou must dye.

Sweet rose, whose hue angry and brave
Bids the rash gazer wipe his eye:
Thy root is ever in its grave,
And thou must dye.

Sweet spring, full of sweet days and roses,
A nest, where sweets compacted lie
My musick shews, ye have your closes,
And all must dye."

THE BOSOM SIN:
A SONNET BY GEORGE HERBERT.

"Lord, with what care hast thou begirt us round,
Parents first season us; then schoolmasters
Deliver us to laws; they send us bound
To rules of reason, holy messengers,
Pulpits and Sundays, sorrow dogging sin,
Afflictions sorted, anguish of all sizes,
Fine nets and stratagems to catch us in,
Bibles laid open, millions of surprizes;
Blessings beforehand, ties of gratefulness,
The sound of glory ringing in our ears:
Without, our shame; within, our consciences;
Angels and grace, eternal hopes and fears!
Yet all these fences and their whole array
One cunning BOSOM-SIN blows quite away."

LOVE UNKNOWN.

'Dear friend, sit down, the tale is long and sad:
And in my faintings, I presume, your love
Will more comply than help. A Lord I had,
And have, of whom some grounds, which may improve,
I hold for two lives, and both lives in me.
To him I brought a dish of fruit one day,
And in the middle placed my HEART. But he
(I sigh to say)

Look't on a servant, who did know his eye,
Better than you knew me, or (which is one)
Than I myself. The servant instantly,
Quitting the fruit, seiz'd on my *heart* alone,
And threw it in a font, wherein did fall
A stream of blood, which issued from the side
Of a great rock: I well remember all
And have good cause: there it was dipt and dyed,
And washt, and wrung! the very wringing yet
Enforceth tears. *Your heart was foul, I fear.*
Indeed 'tis true. I did and do commit
Many a fault, more than my lease will bear;
Yet still ask'd pardon, and was not deny'd.
But you shall hear. After my heart was well,
And clean and fair, as I one eventide

(I sigh to tell)

Walk'd by myself abroad, I saw a large
And spacious furnace flaming, and thereon
A boiling caldron, round about whose verge
Was in great letters set AFFLICTION.
The greatness shew'd the owner. So I went
To fetch a sacrifice out of my fold,
Thinking with that, which I did thus present,
To warm his love, which, I did fear, grew cold
But as my heart did tender it, the man
Who was to take it from me, slipt his hand,
And threw my *heart* into the scalding pan;
My heart that brought it (do you understand?)
The *offerer's* heart. *Your heart was hard, I fear.*
Indeed 'tis true. I found a callous matter
Began to spread and to expatiate there:
But with a richer drug than scalding water
I bath'd it often, ev'n with holy blood,
Which at a board, while many drank bare wine,
A friend did steal into my cup for good,
Ev'n taken inwardly, and most divine
To supple hardnesses. But at the length
Out of the caldron getting, soon I fled
Unto my house, where to repair the strength
Which I had lost, I hasted to my bed:
But when I thought to sleep out all these faults,

(I sigh to speak)

I found that some had stuffed the bed with thoughts,
I would say *thorns.* Dear, could my heart not break,
When with my pleasures ev'n my rest was gone?
Full well I understood who had been there:
For I had given the key to none but one:
It must be he. *Your heart was dull, I fear.*
Indeed a slack and sleepy state of mind

Did oft possess me; so that when I pray'd,
Though my lips went, my heart did stay behind.
But all my scores were by another paid,
Who took my guilt upon him. *Truly, friend,*
?or aught I hear, your master shews to you
More favor than you wot of. Mark the end!
The font did only what was old renew:
The caldron suppled what was grown too hard:
The thorns did quicken what was grown too dull:
All did but strive to mend what you had marr'd.
Wherefore be cheer'd, and praise him to the full
Each day, each hour, each moment of the week
Who fain would have you be new, tender, quick!"

CHAPTER XX

The former subject continued.

I HAVE no fear in declaring my conviction, that the excellence
defined and exemplified in the preceding Chapter is not the
characteristic excellence of Mr. Wordsworth's style; because I
can add with equal sincerity, that it is precluded by higher
powers. The praise of uniform adherence to genuine, logical
English is undoubtedly his; nay, laying the main emphasis on the
word *uniform,* I will dare add that, of all contemporary poets,
it is *his alone.* For in a less absolute sense of the word, I should
certainly include Mr. BOWLES, LORD BYRON, and, as to all his
later writings, Mr. SOUTHEY, the exceptions in their work being
so few and unimportant. But of the specific excellence described
in the quotation from Garve, I appear to find more, and more
undoubted specimens in the works of others; for instance, among
the minor poems of Mr. Thomas Moore, and of our illustrious
Laureate. To me it will always remain a singular and noticeable
fact; that a theory which would establish this *lingua communis,*
not only as the best, but as the only commendable style, should
have proceeded from a poet, whose diction, next to that of
Shakespeare and Milton, appears to me of all others the most
individualized and characteristic. And let it be remembered too,
that I am now interpreting the controverted passages of Mr. W.'s
critical preface by the purpose and object, which he may be
supposed to have intended, rather than by the sense which the
words themselves must convey, if they are taken without this
allowance.

A person of any taste, who had but studied three or four of
Shakespeare's principal plays, would without the name affixed

scarcely fail to recognize as Shakespeare's a quotation from any other play, though but of a few lines. A similar peculiarity, though in a less degree, attends Mr. Wordsworth's style, whenever he speaks in his own person; or whenever, though under a feigned name, it is clear that he himself is still speaking, as in the different dramatis personæ of the "Recluse." Even in the other poems, in which he purposes to be most dramatic, there are few in which it does not occasionally burst forth. The reader might often address the poet in his own words with reference to the persons introduced:

> "It seems, as I retrace the ballad line by line,
> That but half of it is theirs, and the better half is thine."

Who, having been previously acquainted with any considerable portion of Mr. Wordsworth's publications, and having studied them with a full feeling of the author's genius, would not at once claim as Wordsworthian the little poem on the rainbow?

> "The child is father of the man, &c."

Or in the "Lucy Gray"?

> "No mate, no comrade Lucy knew;
> She dwelt on a wide moor;
> *The sweetest thing that ever grew*
> *Beside a human door.*"

Or in the "Idle Shepherd-boys"?

> "Along the river's stony marge
> The sand-lark chaunts a joyous song;
> The thrush is busy in the wood,
> And carols loud and strong.
> A thousand lambs are on the rocks,
> All newly born! both earth and sky
> Keep jubilee, and more than all,
> Those boys with their green coronal;
> They never hear the cry,
> That plaintive cry! which up the hill
> Comes from the depth of Dungeon Gill."

Need I mention the exquisite description of the Sea Loch in the "Blind Highland Boy"? Who but a poet tells a tale in such language to the little ones by the fire-side as—

> "Yet had he many a restless dream
> Both when he heard the eagle's scream,

And when he heard the torrents roar,
And heard the water beat the shore
   Near where their cottage stood.

Beside a lake their cottage stood,
Not small like ours, a peaceful flood,
But one of mighty size, and strange,
That, rough or smooth, is full of change,
   And stirring in its bed.

For to this lake, by night and day,
The great sea-water finds its way
Through long, long windings of the hills,
And drinks up all the pretty rills
   And rivers large and strong:

Then hurries back the road it came—
Returns on errand still the same;
This did it when the earth was new;
And this for evermore will do,
   As long as earth shall last.

And with the coming of the tide,
Come boats and ships that sweetly ride,
Between the woods and lofty rocks;
And to the shepherds with their flocks
   Bring tales of distant lands."

I might quote almost the whole of his "RUTH," but take the
following stanzas:

"But, as you have before been told,
This stripling, sportive, gay, and bold,
And with his dancing crest,
So beautiful, through savage lands
Had roamed about with vagrant bands
   Of Indians in the West.

The wind, the tempest roaring high,
The tumult of a tropic sky,
Might well be dangerous food
For him, a youth to whom was given
So much of earth, so much of heaven,
   And such impetuous blood.

Whatever in those climes he found
Irregular in sight or sound,
Did to his mind impart
A kindred impulse, seemed allied
To his own powers, and justified
   The workings of his heart.

> Nor less, to feed voluptuous thought,
> The beauteous forms of nature wrought,
> Fair trees and lovely flowers;
> The breezes their own languor lent;
> The stars had feelings, which they sent
> Into those magic bowers.
>
> Yet, in his worst pursuits, I ween
> That sometimes there did intervene
> Pure hopes of high intent:
> For passions, linked to forms so fair
> And stately, needs must have their share
> Of noble sentiment."

But from Mr. Wordsworth's more elevated compositions, which already form three-fourths of his works; and will, I trust, constitute hereafter a still larger proportion;—from these, whether in rhyme or blank-verse, it would be difficult and almost superfluous to select instances of a diction peculiarly his own, of a style which cannot be imitated, without its being at once recognised as originating in Mr. Wordsworth. It would not be easy to open on any one of his loftier strains, that does not contain examples of this; and more in proportion as the lines are more excellent, and most like the author. For those, who may happen to have been less familiar with his writings, I will give three specimens taken with little choice. The first from the lines on the "BOY OF WINANDERMERE,"—who

> "Blew mimic hootings to the silent owls,
> That they might answer him. And they would shout
> Across the watery vale, and shout again,
> With long halloos and screams, and echoes loud
> Redoubled and redoubled; concourse wild
> Of mirth and jocund din. And when it chanced,
> That pauses of deep silence mock'd his skill,
> *Then sometimes in that silence, while he hung*
> *Listening, a gentle shock of mild surprize*
> *Has carried far into his heart the voice*
> *Of mountain-torrents; or the visible scene*[81]

[81] Mr. Wordsworth's having judiciously adopted *"concourse wild"* in this passage for *"a wild scene"* as it stood in the former edition, encourages me to hazard a remark, which I certainly should not have made in the works of a poet less austerely accurate in the use of the words, than he is, to his own great honor. It respects the propriety of the word *"scene,"* even in the sentence in which it is retained. DRYDEN, and he only in his more careless verses, was the first, as far as my researches have discovered, who for the convenience of rhyme used this word in the vague sense, which has been since too current even in

> *Would enter unawares into his mind*
> *With all its solemn imagery, its rocks,*
> *Its woods, and that uncertain heaven, received*
> *Into the bosom of the steady lake."*

The second shall be that noble imitation of Drayton[62] (if it
was not rather a coincidence) in the "JOANNA."

> "When I had gazed perhaps two minutes' space,
> Joanna, looking in my eyes, beheld
> That ravishment of mine, and laughed aloud.
> The rock, like something starting from a sleep,
> Took up the lady's voice, and laughed again!
> That ancient woman seated on HELM-CRAG
> Was ready with her cavern; HAMMAR-SCAR
> And the tall steep of SILVER-How sent forth
> A noise of laughter; southern LOUGHRIGG heard,
> And FAIRFIELD answered with a mountain tone.
> HELVELLYN far into the clear blue sky

our best writers, and which (unfortunately, I think) is given as its
first-explanation in Dr. Johnson's Dictionary, and therefore would be
taken by an incautious reader as its proper sense. In Shakespeare and
Milton the word is never used without some clear reference, proper or
metaphorical, to the theatre. Thus Milton:

> "Cedar, and pine, and fir, and branching palm,
> A sylvan *scene;* and, as the ranks ascend,
> Shade above shade, a woody *theatre*
> Of stateliest view."

I object to any extension of its meaning, because the word is already
more equivocal than might be wished; inasmuch as in the limited use,
which I recommend, it may still signify two different things; namely,
the scenery, and the characters and actions presented on the stage
during the presence of particular scenes. It can therefore be preserved
from *obscurity* only by keeping the original signification full in mind.
Thus Milton again:

> "Prepare thou for another scene."

[62] "Which COPLAND scarce had spoke, but quickly every hill,
Upon her verge that stands, the neighbouring vallies fill;
HELVILLON from his height it through the mountains threw,
From whom as soon again the sound DUNBALRASE drew,
From whose stone-trophied head it on the WENDROSS went,
Which tow'rds the sea again resounded it to DENT.
That BROADWATER, therewith within her banks astound,
In sailing to the sea, told it to EGREMOUND,
Whose buildings, walks, and streets, with echoes loud and long,
Did mightily commend old COPLAND for her song."
                 DRAYTON'S POLYOLBION: *Song XXX.*

> Carried the lady's voice!—old Skiddaw blew
> His speaking trumpet!—back out of the clouds
> From Glaramara southward came the voice:
> And Kirkstone tossed it from his misty head!"

The third, which is in rhyme, I take from the "Song at the feast of Brougham Castle, upon the restoration of Lord Clifford the shepherd to the estates of his ancestors."

> "Now another day is come,
> Fitter hope, and nobler doom;
> He hath thrown aside his crook,
> And hath buried deep his book;
> *Armour rusting in the halls*
> *On the blood of Clifford calls;*
> *'Quell the Scot,' exclaims the lance!*
> *'Bear me to the heart of France,'*
> *Is the longing of the shield—*
> *Tell thy name, thou trembling field!—*
> *Field of death, where er thou be,*
> *Groan thou with our victory!*
> Happy day, and mighty hour,
> When our shepherd, in his power,
> Mailed and horsed, with lance and sword,
> To his ancestors restored,
> Like a re-appearing star,
> Like a glory from afar,
> *First shall head the flock of war!"*

> "Alas! the fervent harper did not know
> That for a tranquil soul the lay was framed,
> Who, long compelled in humble walks to go,
> Was softened into feeling, soothed, and tamed.

> Love had he found in huts where poor men lie:
> His daily teachers had been woods and rills;
> *The silence that is in the starry sky,*
> *The sleep that is among the lonely hills."*

The words themselves, in the foregoing extracts, are no doubt sufficiently common for the greater part. (But in what poem are they not so, if we except a few misadventurous attempts to translate the arts and sciences into verse?) In the "Excursion" the number of polysyllabic (or what the common people call, *dictionary*) words is more than usually great. And so must it needs be, in proportion to the number and variety of an author's conceptions, and his solicitude to express them with precision. But are those words *in those places* commonly employed in real life to express the same thought or outward thing? Are they the style used in the ordinary intercourse of spoken words? No! nor are the modes of connections; and still less the breaks and transitions. Would any but a poet—at least could any one without being conscious that he had expressed himself with noticeable vivacity —have described a bird singing loud by, "The thrush is *busy* in the wood?"—or have spoken of boys with a string of club-moss round their rusty hats, as the boys *"with their green coronal"*? —or have translated a beautiful May-day into *"Both earth and sky keep jubilee"*? or have brought all the different marks and circumstances of a sea-loch before the mind, as the actions of a living and acting power? Or have represented the reflection of the sky in the water, as *"That uncertain heaven received into the bosom of the steady lake"*? Even the grammatical construction is not unfrequently peculiar; as *"The wind, the tempest roaring high, the tumult of a tropic sky, might well be dangerous food to him, a youth* to whom was given, &c." There is a peculiarity in the frequent use of the ἀσυνάρτητον (i.e. the omission of the connective particle before the last of several words, or several sentences used grammatically as single words, all being in the same case and governing or governed by the same verb) and not less in the construction of words by apposition (*to him, a youth*). In short, were there excluded from Mr. Wordsworth's poetic compositions all, that a literal adherence to the theory of his preface *would* exclude, two-thirds at least of the marked beauties of his poetry must be erased. For a far greater number of lines would be sacrificed than in any other recent poet; because the pleasure received from Wordsworth's poems being less derived either from excitement of curiosity or the rapid flow of narration, the *striking* passages form a larger proportion of their value. I do not adduce it as a fair criterion of comparative excellence, nor do I even think it such; but merely as matter of fact. I affirm, that from no contemporary writer could so many lines be quoted, without reference to the poem in which they are found, for their own independent weight or beauty. From the sphere of my own experience I can bring to my recollection three persons of no every-day powers and acquirements, who had read the poems of others with more, and more unalloyed pleasure, and had thought more highly of their authors, as poets; who yet have confessed to me, that from no modern work had so many passages started up anew in their minds at different times, and as different occasions had awakened a meditative mood.

CHAPTER XXI

Remarks on the present mode of conducting critical journals.

LONG have I wished to see a fair and philosophical inquisition into the character of Wordsworth, as a poet, on the evidence of his published works; and a positive, not a comparative, appreciation of their *characteristic* excellencies, deficiencies, and defects. I know no claim that the mere *opinion* of any individual can have to weigh down the *opinion* of the author himself; against the probability of whose parental partiality we ought to set that of his having thought longer and more deeply on the subject. But I should call that investigation fair and philosophical, in which the critic announces and endeavours to establish the principles, which he holds for the foundation of poetry in general, with the specification of these in their application to the different *classes* of poetry. Having thus prepared his canons of criticism for praise and condemnation, he would proceed to particularize the most striking passages to which he deems them applicable, faithfully noticing the frequent or infrequent recurrence of similar merits or defects, and as faithfully distinguishing what is characteristic from what is accidental, or a mere flagging of the wing. Then if his premises be rational, his deductions legitimate, and his conclusions justly applied, the reader, and possibly the poet himself, may adopt his judgement in the light of judgement and in the independence of free-agency. If he has erred, he presents his errors in a definite place and tangible form, and holds the torch and guides the way to their detection.

I most willingly admit, and estimate at a high value, the services which the EDINBURGH REVIEW, and others formed afterwards on the same plan, have rendered to society in the diffusion of knowledge. I think the commencement of the Edinburgh Review an important epoch in periodical criticism; and that it has a claim upon the gratitude of the literary republic, and indeed of the reading public at large, for having originated the scheme of reviewing those books only, which are susceptible and deserving of argumentative criticism. Not less meritorious, and far more faithfully and in general far more ably executed, is their plan of supplying the vacant place of the trash or mediocrity, wisely left to sink into oblivion by its own weight, with original essays on the most interesting subjects of the time, religious, or political; in which the titles of the books or pamphlets prefixed furnish only the name and occasion of the disquisition. I do not arraign the keenness, or asperity of the damnatory style, in and for itself, as long as the author is addressed or treated as the mere impersonation of the work then under trial. I have no quarrel with them on this account, as long as no personal allusions are admitted, and no re-commitment (for new trial) of juvenile performances, that were published, perhaps forgotten, many years before the commencement of the review: since for the forcing back of such works to public notice no motives are easily assignable, but such as are furnished to the critic by his own personal malignity; or what is still worse, by a *habit* of malignity in the form of mere wantonness.

> "No private grudge they need, no personal spite:
> The *viva sectio* is its own delight!
> All enmity, all envy, they disclaim,
> Disinterested thieves of our good name:
> Cool, sober murderers of their neighbour's fame!"
>
> S. T. C.

Every censure, every sarcasm respecting a publication which the critic, with the criticised work before him, can make good, is the critic's right. The writer is authorised to reply, but not to complain. Neither can anyone prescribe to the critic, how soft or how hard; how friendly, or how bitter; shall be the phrases which he is to select for the expression of such reprehension or ridicule. The critic must know, what effect it is his object to produce; and with a view to this effect must he weigh his words. But as soon as the critic betrays, that he knows more of his author, than the author's publications could have told him; as soon as from this more intimate knowledge, elsewhere obtained, he avails himself of the slightest trait *against* the author; his censure instantly becomes personal injury, his sarcasms personal insults. He ceases to be a CRITIC, and takes on him the most contemptible character to which a rational creature can be degraded, that of a gossip, backbiter, and pasquillant: but with this heavy aggravation, that he steals the unquiet, the deforming passions of the World into the Museum; into the very place which, next to the chapel and oratory, should be our sanctuary, and secure place of refuge; offers abominations on the altar of the muses; and makes its sacred paling the very circle in which he conjures up the lying and profane spirit.

This determination of unlicensed personality, and of permitted and legitimate censure (which I owe in part to the illustrious LESSING, himself a model of acute, spirited, sometimes stinging, but always argumentative and honorable, criticism) is beyond controversy the true one: and though I would not myself exercise all the rights of the latter, yet, let but the former be excluded, I submit myself to its exercise in the hands of others, without complaint and without resentment.

Let a communication be formed between any number of learned men in the various branches of science and literature; and whether the president and central committee be in London, or Edinburgh, if only they previously lay aside their individuality, and pledge themselves inwardly, as well as ostensibly, to administer judgement according to a constitution and code of laws; and if by grounding this code on the two-fold basis of universal morals and philosophic reason, independent of all foreseen application to particular works and authors, they obtain the right to speak each as the representative of their body corporate; they shall have honor and good wishes from me, and I shall accord to them their fair dignities, though self assumed, not less chearfully than if I could inquire concerning them in the heralds' office, or turn to them in the book of peerage. However loud may be the outcries for prevented or subverted reputation, however numerous and impatient the complaints of merciless severity and insupportable despotism, I shall neither feel, nor utter ought but to the defence and justification of the critical machine. Should any literary Quixote find himself provoked by its sounds and regular movements, I should admonish him with Sancho Panza, that it is no giant, but a windmill; there it stands on its own place, and its own hillock, never goes out of its way to attack anyone, and to none and from none either gives or asks assistance. When the public press has poured in any part of its produce between its mill-stones, it grinds it off, one man's sack the same as another, and with whatever wind may happen to be then blowing. All the two and thirty winds are alike its friends. Of the whole wide atmosphere it does not desire a single finger-breadth more than what is necessary for its sails to turn round in. But this space must be left free and unimpeded. Gnats, beetles, wasps, butterflies, and the whole tribe of ephemerals and insignificants, may flit in and out and between; may hum, and buzz, and jarr; may shrill their tiny pipes, and wind their puny horns, unchastised and unnoticed. But idlers and bravadoes of larger size and prouder show must beware, how they place themselves within its sweep. Much less may they presume to lay hands on the sails, the strength of which is neither greater nor less than as the wind is, which drives them round. Whomsoever the remorseless arm slings aloft, or whirls along with it in the air, he has himself alone to blame; though, when the same arm throws him from it, it will more often double than break the force of his fall.

Putting aside the too manifest and too frequent interference of NATIONAL, PARTY, and even PERSONAL predilection or aversion; and reserving for deeper feelings those worse and more criminal intrusions into the sacredness of private life, which not seldom merit legal rather than literary chastisement, the two principal objects and occasions which I find for blame and regret in the conduct of the review in question are: first, its unfaithfulness to its own announced and excellent plan, by subjecting to criticism works neither indecent nor immoral, yet of such trifling importance even in point of size and, according to the critic's own verdict, so devoid of all merit, as must excite in the most candid mind the suspicion, either that dislike or vindictive feelings were at work; or that there was a cold prudential pre-determination to increase the sale of the Review by flattering the malignant passions of human nature. That I may not myself become subject to the charge, which I am bringing against others, by an accusation without proof, I refer to the article on Dr. Rennell's sermons in the very first number of the Edinburgh Review as an illustration of my meaning. If in looking through all the succeeding volumes the reader should find this a solitary instance, I must submit to that painful forfeiture of esteem, which awaits a groundless or exaggerated charge.

The second point of objection belongs to this review only in common with all other works of periodical criticism: at least, it applies in common to the general system of all, whatever exceptions there may be in favor of particular articles. Or if it attaches to the Edinburgh Review, and to its only corrival (the QUARTERLY), with any peculiar force, this results from the superiority of talent, acquirement, and information which both have so undeniably displayed; and which doubtless deepens the regret, though not the blame. I am referring to the substitution of assertion for argument; to the frequency of arbitrary and sometimes petulant verdicts, not seldom unsupported even by a single quotation from the work condemned, which might at least have explained the critic's meaning, if it did not prove the justice of his sentence. Even where this is not the case, the extracts are too often made without reference to any general grounds or rules from which the faultiness or inadmissibility of the qualities attributed may be deduced; and without any attempt to show, that the qualities *are* attributable to the passage extracted. I have met with such extracts from Mr. Wordsworth's poems, annexed to such assertions, as led me to imagine, that the reviewer, having written his critique before he had read the work, had then *pricked with a pin* for passages, wherewith to illustrate the various branches of his preconceived opinions. By what principle of rational choice can we suppose a critic to have been directed (at least in a Christian country, and himself, we hope, a Christian) who gave the following lines, portraying the fervor of solitary devotion excited by the magnificent display of the Almighty's works, as a proof and example of an author's tendency to *downright ravings,* and absolute unintelligibility?

> "O then what soul was his, when on the tops
> Of the high mountains he beheld the sun
> Rise up, and bathe the world in light! He looked—
> Ocean and earth, the solid frame of earth,
> And ocean's liquid mass, beneath him lay
> In gladness and deep joy. The clouds were touched,
> And in their silent faces did he read
> Unutterable love. Sound needed none,
> Nor any *voice* of joy: his spirit drank
> The spectacle! sensation, soul, and form,
> All melted into him; they swallowed up
> His animal being; in them did he live,
> And by them did he live: they were his life."
>
> (EXCURSION.)

Can it be expected, that either the author or his admirers should be induced to pay any serious attention to decisions which prove nothing but the pitiable state of the critic's own taste and sensibility? On opening the Review they see a favorite passage, of the force and truth of which they had an intuitive certainty in their own inward experience, confirmed, if confirmation it could receive, by the sympathy of their most enlightened friends; some of whom, perhaps, even in the world's opinion, hold a higher intellectual rank than the critic himself would presume to claim. And this very passage they find selected, as the characteristic effusion of a mind *deserted by reason;* as furnishing evidence that the writer was raving, or he could not have thus strung words together without sense or purpose! No diversity of taste seems capable of explaining such a contrast in judgement.

That I had *over-rated* the merit of a passage or poem, that I had erred concerning the *degree* of its excellence, I might be easily induced to believe or apprehend. But that lines, the sense of which I had analysed and found consonant with all the best convictions of my understanding; and the imagery and diction of which had collected round these convictions my noblest as well as my most delightful feelings; that I should admit such lines to be mere nonsense or lunacy, is too much for the most ingenious *arguments* to effect. But that such a revolution of taste should be brought about by a few broad assertions, seems little less than impossible. On the contrary, it would require an effort of charity not to dismiss the criticism with the aphorism of the wise man, "in animam malevolam sapientia haud intrare potest."

What then if this very critic should have cited a large number of single lines and even of large paragraphs, which he himself acknowledges to possess eminent and original beauty? What if he himself had owned, that beauties as great are scattered in abundance throughout the whole book? And yet, though under this impression, should have commenced his critique in vulgar exultation with a prophecy meant to secure its own fulfilment? With a "THIS WON'T DO!" What if after such acknowledgements extorted from his own judgement he should proceed from charge to charge of tameness and raving; flights and flatness; and at length, consigning the author to the house of incurables, should conclude with a strain of rudest contempt evidently grounded in the distempered state of his own moral associations? Suppose too all this done without a single leading principle established or even announced, and without any one attempt at argumentative deduction, though the poet had presented a more than usual opportunity for it, by having previously made public his own principles of judgement in poetry, and supported them by a connected train of reasoning!

The office and duty of the poet is to select the most dignified as well as

"The happiest, gayest attitude of things."

The reverse, for in all cases a reverse is possible, is the appropriate business of burlesque and travesty, a predominant taste for which has been always deemed a mark of a low and degraded mind. When I was at Rome, among many other visits to the tomb of Julius II. I went thither once with a Prussian artist, a man of genius and great vivacity of feeling. As we were gazing on Michael Angelo's MOSES, our conversation turned on the horns and beard of that stupendous statue; of the necessity of each to support the other; of the super-human effect of the former, and the necessity of the existence of both to give a harmony and integrity both to the image and the feeling excited by it. Conceive them removed, and the statue would become un-natural, without being super-natural. We called to mind the horns of the rising sun, and I repeated the noble passage from Taylor's Holy Dying. That horns were the emblem of power and sovereignty among the Eastern nations, and are still retained as such in Abyssinia; the Achelous of the ancient Greeks; and the probable ideas and feelings, that originally suggested the mixture of the human and the brute form in the figure, by which they realized the idea of their mysterious Pan, as representing intelligence blended with a darker power, deeper, mightier, and more universal than the conscious intellect of man; than intelligence;—all these thoughts and recollections passed in procession before our minds. My companion who possessed more than his share of the hatred, which his countrymen bore to the French, had just observed to me, "A Frenchman, Sir! is the only animal in the human shape, that by no possibility can lift itself up to religion or poetry:" when, lo! two French officers of distinction and rank entered the church! "Mark you," whispered the Prussian, "the first thing which those scoundrels will notice (for they will begin by instantly noticing the statue in parts, without one moment's pause of admiration impressed by the whole) will be the horns and the beard. And the associations, which they will immediately connect with them will be those of a HE-GOAT and a CUCKOLD." Never did man guess more luckily. Had he inherited a portion of the great legislator's prophetic powers, whose statue we had been contemplating, he could scarcely have uttered words more coincident with the result: for even as he had said, so it came to pass.

In the "EXCURSION" the poet has introduced an old man, born in humble but not abject circumstances, who had enjoyed more than usual advantages of education, both from books and from the more awful discipline of nature. This person he represents, as having been driven by the restlessness of fervid feelings, and from a craving intellect, to an itinerant life; and as having in consequence passed the larger portion of his time, from earliest manhood, in villages and hamlets from door to door,

"A vagrant merchant bent beneath his load."

Now whether this be a character appropriate to a lofty didactick poem, is perhaps questionable. It presents a fair subject for controversy; and the question is to be determined by the congruity or incongruity of such a character with what shall be proved to be the essential constituents of poetry. But surely the critic who, passing by all the opportunities which such a mode of life would present to such a man; all the advantages of the liberty of nature, of solitude, and of solitary thought; all the varieties of places and seasons, through which his track had lain, with all the varying imagery they bring with them; and lastly, all the observations of men,

"Their manners, their enjoyments, and pursuits,
Their passions and their feelings,"

which the memory of these yearly journies must have given and
recalled to such a mind—the critic, I say, who from the multitude
of possible associations should pass by all these in order to fix his
attention exclusively on the *pin-papers,* and *stay-tapes,* which
might have been among the wares of his pack; this critic, in my
opinion, cannot be thought to possess a much higher or much
healthier state of moral feeling, than the FRENCHMEN above
recorded.

CHAPTER XXII

*The characteristic defects of Wordsworth's poetry, with the principles
from which the judgement, that they are defects, is deduced—Their
proportion to the beauties—For the greatest part characteristic of
his theory only.*

IF MR. WORDSWORTH have set forth principles of poetry which his
arguments are insufficient to support, let him and those who have
adopted his sentiments be set right by the confutation of these
arguments, and by the substitution of more philosophical prin-
ciples. And still let the due credit be given to the portion and
importance of the truths, which are blended with his theory;
truths, the too exclusive attention to which had occasioned its
errors, by tempting him to carry those truths beyond their proper
limits. If his mistaken theory have at all influenced his poetic
compositions, let the effects be pointed out, and the instances
given. But let it likewise be shown, how far the influence has
acted; whether diffusively, or only by starts; whether the number
and importance of the poems and passages thus infected be great
or trifling compared with the sound portion; and lastly, whether
they are inwoven into the texture of his works, or are loose and
separable. The result of such a trial would evince beyond a doubt,
what it is high time to announce decisively and aloud, that the
supposed characteristics of Mr. Wordsworth's poetry, whether
admired or reprobated; whether they are simplicity or simple-
ness; faithful adherence to essential nature, or wilful selections
from human nature of its meanest forms and under the least
attractive associations; are as little the *real* characteristics of his
poetry at large, as of his genius and the constitution of his mind.

In a comparatively small number of poems he chose to try an
experiment; and this experiment we will suppose to have failed.
Yet even in these poems it is impossible not to perceive that the

natural *tendency* of the poet's mind is to great objects and elevated conceptions. The poem entitled "Fidelity" is for the greater part written in language, as unraised and naked as any perhaps in the two volumes. Yet take the following stanza and compare it with the preceding stanzas of the same poem.

"There sometimes doth a leaping fish
Send through the tarn a lonely cheer;
The crags repeat the raven's croak,
In symphony austere;
Thither the rainbow comes—the cloud—
And mists that spread the flying shroud;
And sun-beams; and the sounding blast,
That if it could would hurry past;
But that enormous barrier binds it fast."

Or compare the four last lines of the concluding stanza with the former half.

"Yes, proof was plain that since the day
On which the traveller thus had died,
The dog had watched about the spot,
Or by his master's side
How nourish'd there through such long time
He knows, who gave that love sublime,
And gave that strength of feeling, great
Above all human estimate!"

Can any candid and intelligent mind hesitate in determining, which of these best represents the tendency and native character of the poet's genius? Will he not decide that the one was written because the poet *would* so write, and the other because he could not so entirely repress the force and grandeur of his mind, but that he must in some part or other of *every* composition write otherwise? In short, that his only disease is the being out of his element; like the swan, that, having amused himself, for a while, with crushing the weeds on the river's bank, soon returns to his own majestic movements on its reflecting and sustaining surface. Let it be observed that I am here supposing the imagined judge, to whom I appeal, to have already decided against the poet's theory, as far as it is different from the principles of the art, generally acknowledged.

I cannot here enter into a detailed examination of Mr. Wordsworth's works; but I will attempt to give the main results of my own judgement, after an acquaintance of many years, and repeated perusals. And though, to appreciate the defects of a great mind it is necessary to understand previously its characteristic excellences, yet I have already expressed myself with sufficient fulness, to preclude most of the ill effects that might arise from my pursuing a contrary arrangement. I will therefore commence with what I deem the prominent *defects* of his poems hitherto published.

The first *characteristic, though only occasional* defect, which I appear to myself to find in these poems is the INCONSTANCY of the *style*. Under this name I refer to the sudden and unprepared transitions from lines or sentences of peculiar felicity (at all events striking and original) to a style, not only unimpassioned but undistinguished. He sinks too often and too abruptly to that style, which I should place in the second division of language, dividing it into the three species; *first,* that which is peculiar to poetry; *second,* that which is only proper in prose; and *third,* the neutral or common to both. There have been works, such as Cowley's Essay on Cromwell, in which prose and verse are intermixed (not as in the Consolation of Boetius, or the Argenis of Barclay, by the insertion of poems supposed to have been spoken or composed on occasions previously related in prose, but) the poet passing from one to the other, as the nature of the thoughts or his own feelings dictated. Yet this mode of composition does not satisfy a cultivated taste. There is something unpleasant in the being thus obliged to alternate states of feeling so dissimilar, and this too in a species of writing, the pleasure from which is in part derived from the preparation and previous expectation of the reader. A portion of that awkwardness is felt which hangs upon the introduction of songs in our modern comic operas; and to prevent which the judicious Metastasio (as to whose exquisite *taste* there can be no hesitation, whatever doubts may be entertained as to his *poetic genius*) uniformly placed the ARIA at the end of the scene, at the same time that he almost always raises and impassions the style of the recitative immediately preceding. Even in real life, the difference is great and evident between words used as the *arbitrary marks* of thought, our smooth market-coin of intercourse, with the image and superscription worn out by currency; and those which convey pictures either borrowed from *one* outward object to enliven and particularize some *other;* or used allegorically to body forth the inward state of the person speaking; or such as are at least the exponents of his peculiar turn and unusual extent of faculty. So much so indeed, that in the social circles of private life we often find a striking use of the latter put a stop to the general flow of conversation, and by the excitement arising from concentered attention produce a sort of damp and interruption for some minutes after. But in the perusal of works of literary *art*, we *prepare* ourselves for such language; and the business of the writer, like that of a painter whose subject requires unusual splendor and prominence, is so to raise the lower and neutral tints, that what in a different style would be the *commanding* colors, are here used as the means of that gentle *degradation* requisite in order to produce the effect of a *whole*. Where this is not achieved in a poem, the metre merely reminds the reader of his claims in order to disappoint them; and where this defect occurs frequently, his feelings are alternately startled by anticlimax and hyperclimax.

I refer the reader to the exquisite stanzas cited for another purpose from the blind Highland Boy; and then annex, as being in my opinion instances of this *disharmony* in style, the two following:

> "And one, the rarest, was a shell,
> Which he, poor child, had studied well:
> The shell of a green turtle, thin
> And hollow;—you might sit therein,
>   It was so wide, and deep."

> "Our Highland Boy oft visited
> The house which held this prize; and, led
> By choice or chance, did thither come
> One day, when no one was at home,
>   And found the door unbarred."

Or page 172, vol. I.

> " 'Tis gone—forgotten—*let me do*
> *My best*. There was a smile or two—
> I can remember them, I see
> The smiles worth all the world to me.
> Dear Baby, I must lay thee down:
> Thou troublest me with strange alarms;
> Smiles hast thou, sweet ones of thine own:
> I cannot keep thee in my arms;
> For they confound me: *as it is,*
> I have forgot those smiles of his!"

Or page 269, vol. I.

> "Thou hast a nest, for thy love and thy rest,
> And though little troubled with sloth
> Drunken lark! thou would'st be loth
> To be such a traveller as I.
>   Happy, happy liver!
> *With a soul as strong as a mountain river*
> *Pouring out praise to th'Almighty giver!*

> Joy and jollity be with us both!
> Hearing thee or else some other,
>   As merry a brother
> I on the earth will go plodding on
> By myself chearfully till the day is done."

The incongruity, which I appear to find in this passage, is that of the two noble lines in italics with the preceding and following. So vol. II. page 30.

> "Close by a pond, upon the further side,
> He stood alone; a minute's space, I guess,
> I watch'd him, he continuing motionless:
> To the pool's further margin then I drew,
> He being all the while before me full in view."

Compare this with the repetition of the same image, in the next stanza but two.

> "And, still as I drew near with gentle pace,
> Beside the little pond or moorish flood
> Motionless as a cloud the old man stood,
> That heareth not the loud winds as they call,
> And moveth altogether, if it move at all."

Or lastly, the second of the three following stanzas, compared both with the first and the third.

> "My former thoughts returned; the fear that kills;
> And hope that is unwilling to be fed;
> Cold, pain, and labour, and all fleshly ills;
> And mighty poets in their misery dead.
> But now, perplex'd by what the old man had said,
> My question eagerly did I renew,
> 'How is it that you live, and what is it you do?'
>
> He with a smile did then his words repeat;
> And said, that gathering leeches far and wide
> He travell'd; stirring thus about his feet
> The waters of the ponds where they abide.
> 'Once I could meet with them on every side,
> But they have dwindled long by slow decay;
> Yet still I persevere, and find them where I may.'
>
> While he was talking thus, the lonely place,
> The old man's shape, and speech, all troubled me:
> In my mind's eye I seemed to see him pace
> About the weary moors continually,
> Wandering about alone and silently."

Indeed this fine poem is *especially* characteristic of the author. There is scarce a defect or excellence in his writings of which it would not present a specimen. But it would be unjust not to repeat that this defect is only occasional. From a careful reperusal of the two volumes of poems, I doubt whether the objectionable passages would amount in the whole to one hundred lines; not the eighth part of the number of pages. In the "Excursion" the feeling of incongruity is seldom excited by the diction of any passage considered in itself, but by the sudden superiority of some other passage forming the context.

The second defect I can generalize with tolerable accuracy, if the reader will pardon an uncouth and new-coined word. There is, I should say, not seldom a *matter-of-factness* in certain poems. This may be divided into, *first*, a laborious minuteness and fidelity in the representation of objects, and their positions, as they appeared to the poet himself; *secondly*, the insertion of accidental circumstances, in order to the full explanation of his living characters, their dispositions and actions; which circumstances might be necessary to establish the probability of a statement in real life, where nothing is taken for granted by the hearer; but appear superfluous in poetry, where the reader is willing to believe for his own sake. To this *accidentality* I object, as contravening the essence of poetry, which Aristotle pronounces to be σπουδαιότατον καὶ φιλοσοφώτατον γένος, the most intense, weighty and philosophical product of human art; adding, as the *reason*, that it is the most catholic and abstract. The following passage from Davenant's prefatory letter to Hobbes well expresses this truth. "When I considered the actions which I meant to describe, (those inferring the persons), I was again persuaded rather to choose those of a former age, than the present; and in a century so far removed, as might preserve me from their improper examinations, who know not the requisites of a poem, nor how much pleasure they lose, (and even the pleasures of heroic poesy are not unprofitable), who take away the liberty of a poet, and fetter his feet in the shackles of an historian. For why should a poet doubt in story to mend the intrigues of fortune by more delightful conveyances of probable fictions, because austere historians have entered into bond to truth? An obligation, which were in poets as foolish and unnecessary, as in the bondage of false martyrs, who lie in chains for a mistaken opinion. *But by this I would imply, that truth narrative and past is the idol of historians, (who worship a dead thing), and truth operative, and by effects continually alive, is the mistress of poets, who hath not her existence in matter, but in reason."*

For this minute accuracy in the painting of local imagery, the lines in the EXCURSION, pp. 96, 97, and 98, may be taken, if not as a striking instance, yet as an illustration of my meaning. It must be some strong motive (as, for instance, that the description was necessary to the intelligibility of the tale) which could induce me to describe in a number of verses what a draughtsman could present to the eye with incomparably greater satisfaction by half a dozen strokes of his pencil, or the painter with as many touches of his brush. Such descriptions too often occasion in the mind of a reader, who is determined to understand his author, a feeling of labor, not very dissimilar to that, with which he would construct a diagram, line by line, for a long geometrical proposition. It seems to be like taking the pieces of a dissected map out of its box. We first look at one part, and then at another, then join and dove-tail them; and when the successive acts of attention have been completed, there is a retrogressive effort of mind to behold it as a whole. The poet should paint to the imagination, not to the fancy; and I know no happier case to exemplify the distinction between these two faculties. Masterpieces of the former mode of poetic painting abound in the writings of Milton, ex. gr.

> "The fig-tree; not that kind for fruit renown'd,
> But such as at this day, to Indians known,
> In Malabar or Decan spreads her arms
> Branching so broad and long, that in the ground
> The bended twigs take root, *and daughters grow*
> *About the mother tree, a pillar'd shade*
> *High over-arch'd, and* ECHOING WALKS BETWEEN:
> *There oft the Indian Herdsman, shunning heat,*
> *Shelters in cool, and tends his pasturing herds*
> *At loop holes cut through thickest shade."*
>
>   MILTON *P. L.* 9. 1100.

This is *creation* rather than *painting*, or if painting, yet such, and with such co-presence of the whole picture flash'd at once upon the eye, as the sun paints in a camera obscura. But the poet must likewise understand and command what Bacon calls the *vestigia communia* of the senses, the latency of all in each, and more especially as by a magical *penna duplex*, the excitement of vision by sound and the exponents of sound. Thus "THE ECHOING WALKS BETWEEN," may be almost said to reverse the fable in tradition of the head of Memnon, in the Egyptian statue.

Such may be deservedly entitled the *creative words* in the world of imagination.

The second division respects an apparent minute adherence to *matter-of-fact* in characters and incidents; *a biographical* attention to probability, and an *anxiety* of explanation and retrospect. Under this head I shall deliver, with no feigned diffidence, the results of my best reflection on the great point of controversy between Mr. Wordsworth and his objectors; namely, on THE CHOICE OF HIS CHARACTERS. I have already declared and, I trust, justified, my utter dissent from the mode of argument which his critics have hitherto employed. To *their* question, Why did you chuse such a character, or a character from such a rank of life? the poet might in my opinion fairly retort: why with the conception of my character did you make wilful choice of mean or ludicrous associations not furnished by me, but supplied from your own sickly and fastidious feelings? How was it, indeed, probable, that such arguments could have any weight with an author, whose plan, whose guiding principle, and main object it was to attack and subdue that state of association, which leads us to place the chief value on those things in which man DIFFERS from man, and to forget or disregard the high dignities, which belong to HUMAN NATURE, the sense and the feeling, which *may* be, and *ought* to be, found in *all* ranks? The feelings with which, as Christians, we contemplate a mixed congregation rising or kneeling before their common Maker: Mr. Wordsworth would have us entertain at *all* times, as men, and as readers; and by the excitement of this lofty, yet prideless impartiality in *poetry*, he might hope to have encouraged its continuance in *real life*. The praise of good men be his! In real life, and, I trust, even in my imagination, I honor a virtuous and wise man, without reference to the presence or absence of artificial advantages. Whether in the person of an armed baron, a laurel'd bard, &c., or of an old pedlar, or still older leech-gatherer, the same qualities of head and heart must claim the same reverence. And even in poetry I am not conscious, that I have ever suffered my feelings to be disturbed or offended by any thoughts or images, which the poet himself has not presented.

But yet I object nevertheless and for the following reasons. First, because the object in view, as an *immediate* object, belongs to the moral philosopher, and would be pursued, not only more appropriately, but in my opinion with far greater probability of success, in sermons or moral essays, than in an elevated poem. It seems, indeed, to destroy the main fundamental distinction, not only between a poem and prose, but even between philosophy and works of fiction, inasmuch as it proposes *truth* for its immediate object, instead of *pleasure*. Now till the blessed time shall come, when truth itself shall be pleasure, and both shall be so united, as to be distinguishable in words only, not in feeling, it will remain the poet's office to proceed upon that state of association, which actually exists as *general;* instead of attempting first to *make* it what it ought to be, and then to let the pleasure follow. But here is unfortunately a small *Hysteron-Proteron*. For the communication of pleasure is the introductory means by which alone the poet must expect to moralize his readers. Secondly: though I were to admit, for a moment, *this* argument to be groundless: yet how is the moral effect to be produced, by merely attaching the name of some low profession to powers which are *least* likely, and to qualities which are assuredly not *more* likely, to be found in it? The poet, speaking in his own person, may at once delight and improve us by sentiments, which teach us the independence of goodness, of wisdom, and even of genius, on the favors of fortune. And having made a due reverence before the throne of Antonine, he may bow with equal awe before Epictetus among his fellow-slaves—

> ——————————"and rejoice
> In the plain presence of his dignity."

Who is not at once delighted and improved, when the POET Wordsworth himself exclaims,

> "O many are the poets that are sown
> By Nature; man endowed with highest gifts,
> The vision and the faculty divine,
> Yet wanting the accomplishment of verse,
> Nor having e'er, as life advanced, been led
> By circumstance to take unto the height
> The measure of themselves, these favor'd beings,
> All but a scatter'd few, live out their time
> Husbanding that which they possess within,
> And go to the grave unthought of. Strongest minds
> Are often those of whom the noisy world
> Hears least."

EXCURSION, B. I.

To use a colloquial phrase, such sentiments, in such language, do one's heart good; though I for my part, have not the fullest faith in the *truth* of the observation. On the contrary I believe the instances to be exceedingly rare; and should feel almost as strong an objection to introduce such a character in a poetic riction, as a pair of black swans on a lake in a fancy-landscape. When I think how many, and how much better books than Homer, or even than Herodotus, Pindar or Æschylus, could have read, are in the power of almost every man, in a country where almost every man is instructed to read and write; and how restless, how difficultly hidden, the powers of genius are; and yet find even in situations the most favorable, according to Mr. Wordsworth, for the formation of a pure and poetic language; in situations which ensure familiarity with the grandest objects of the imagination; but *one* BURNS, among the shepherds of *Scotland,* and not a single poet of humble life among those of *English* lakes and mountains; I conclude, that POETIC GENIUS is not only a very delicate but a very rare plant.

But be this as it may, the feelings with which

> "I think of CHATTERTON, the marvellous boy,
> The sleepless soul, that perished in his pride;
> Of BURNS, that walk'd in glory and in joy
> Behind his plough upon the mountain-side"—

are widely different from those with which I should read a *poem,* where the author, having occasion for the character of a poet and a philosopher in the fable of his narration, had chosen to make him a *chimney-sweeper;* and then, in order to remove all doubts on the subject, had *invented* an account of his birth, parentage and education, with all the strange and fortunate accidents which had concurred in making him at once poet, philosopher, and sweep! Nothing but biography can justify this. If it be admissible even in a *Novel,* it must be one in the manner of De Foe's, that were meant to pass for histories, not in the manner of Fielding's: in the life of Moll Flanders, or Colonel Jack, not in a Tom Jones, or even a Joseph Andrews. Much less then can it be legitimately introduced in a *poem,* the characters of which, amid the strongest individualization, must still remain representative. The precepts of Horace, on this point, are grounded on the nature both of poetry and of the human mind. They are not more peremptory, than wise and prudent. For in the first place a deviation from them perplexes the reader's feelings, and all the circumstances, which are feigned in order to make such accidents less improbable, divide and disquiet his faith, rather than aid and support it. Spite of all attempts, the fiction *will* appear, and unfortunately not as *fictitious* but as *false.* The reader not only *knows,* that the sentiments and language are the poet's own, and his own too in his *artificial* character, *as poet;* but by the fruitless endeavours to make him think the contrary, he is not even suffered to *forget* it. The effect is similar to that produced by an epic poet, when the fable and the characters are *derived* from Scripture history, as in the *Messiah* of *Klopstock,* or in *Cumberland's Calvary;* and not merely *suggested* by it, as in the Paradise Lost of Milton. That *illusion,* contra-distinguished from *delusion,* that *negative* faith, which simply permits the images presented to work by their own force, without either denial or affirmation of their real existence by the judgement, is rendered impossible by their immediate neighbourhood to words and facts of known and absolute truth. A faith, which transcends even historic belief, must absolutely *put out* this mere poetic Analogon of faith, as the summer sun is said to extinguish our household fires, when it shines full upon them. What would otherwise have been yielded to as pleasing fiction, is repelled as revolting falsehood. The effect produced in this latter case by the solemn belief of the reader, is in a less degree brought about in the instances, to which I have been objecting, by the baffled attempts of the author to *make* him believe.

Add to all the foregoing the seeming uselessness both of the project and of the anecdotes from which it is to derive support. Is there one word, for instance, attributed to the pedlar in the "EXCURSION," characteristic of a *pedlar?* One sentiment, that might not more plausibly, even without the aid of any previous explanation, have proceeded from any wise and beneficent old man, of a rank or profession in which the language of learning and refinement are natural and to be expected? Need the rank have been at all particularized, where nothing follows which the knowledge of that rank is to explain or illustrate? When on the contrary this information renders the man's language, feelings, sentiments, and information a riddle, which must itself be solved by episodes of anecdote? Finally when this, and this alone, could have induced a genuine *poet* to inweave in a poem of the loftiest style, and on subjects the loftiest and of most universal interest, such minute matters of fact, (not unlike those furnished for the obituary of a magazine by the friends of some obscure *ornament of society lately deceased* in some obscure town), as

> "Among the hills of Athol he was born:
> There, on a small hereditary farm,
> An unproductive slip of rugged ground,
> His Father dwelt; and died in poverty;
> While he, whose lowly fortune I retrace,
> The youngest of three sons, was yet a babe,
> A little one—unconscious of their loss.
> But, ere he had outgrown his infant days,

His widowed mother, for a second mate,
Espoused the teacher of the Village School;
Who on her offspring zealously bestowed
Needful instruction."

"From his sixth year, the Boy of whom I speak,
In summer tended cattle on the hills;
But, through the inclement and the perilous days
Of long-continuing winter, he repaired
To his step-father's school,"—&c.

For all the admirable passages interposed in this narration,
might, with trifling alterations, have been far more appropriately,
and with far greater verisimilitude, told of a poet in the char-
acter of a poet; and without incurring another defect which I
shall now mention, and a sufficient illustration of which will
have been here anticipated.

Third; an undue predilection for the *dramatic* form in certain
poems, from which one or other of two evils result. Either the
thoughts and diction are different from that of the poet, and
then there arises an incongruity of style; or they are the same
and indistinguishable, and then it presents a species of ventrilo-
quism, where two are represented as talking, while in truth one
man only speaks.

The fourth class of defects is closely connected with the
former; but yet are such as arise likewise from an intensity of
feeling disproportionate to *such* knowledge and value of the
objects described, as can be fairly anticipated of men in general,
even of the most cultivated classes; and with which therefore few
only, and those few particularly circumstanced, can be supposed
to sympathize. In this class, I comprise occasional prolixity,
repetition, and an eddying, instead of progression, of thought.
As instances, see pages 27, 28, and 62 of the Poems, Vol. I. and
the first eighty lines of the Sixth Book of the Excursion.

Fifth and last; thoughts and images too great for the subject.
This is an approximation to what might be called *mental* bom-
bast, as distinguished from verbal: for, as in the latter there is
a disproportion of the expressions to the thoughts, so in this
there is a disproportion of thought to the circumstance and
occasion. This, by the bye, is a fault of which none but a man
of genius is capable. It is the awkwardness and strength of
Hercules with the distaff of Omphale.

It is a well-known fact, that bright colors in motion both make
and leave the strongest impressions on the eye. Nothing is more
likely too, than that a vivid image or visual spectrum, thus

originated, may become the link of association in recalling the feelings and images that had accompanied the original impression. But if we describe this in such lines, as

> "They flash upon that inward eye,
> Which is the bliss of solitude!"

in what words shall we describe the joy of retrospection, when the images and virtuous actions of a whole well-spent life, pass before that conscience which is indeed the *inward* eye: which is indeed *"the bliss of solitude"*? Assuredly we seem to sink most abruptly, not to say burlesquely, and almost as in a *medly,* from this couplet to—

> "And then my heart with pleasure fills,
> And dances with the *daffodils.*"
>
> Vol. I. p. 320.

The second instance is from Vol. II. page 12, where the poet, having gone out for a day's tour of pleasure, meets early in the morning with a knot of *gypsies,* who had pitched their blanket-tents and straw-beds, together with their children and asses, in some field by the road-side. At the close of the day on his return our tourist found them in the same place. "Twelve hours," says he,

> "Twelve hours, twelve bounteous hours are gone, while I
> Have been a traveller under open sky,
> Much witnessing of change and cheer,
> Yet as I left I find them here!"

Whereat the poet, without seeming to reflect that the poor tawny wanderers might probably have been tramping for weeks together through road and lane, over moor and mountain, and consequently must have been right glad to rest themselves, their children and cattle, for one whole day; and overlooking the obvious truth, that such repose might be quite as necessary for *them,* as a walk of the same continuance was pleasing or healthful for the more fortunate poet; expresses his indignation in a series of lines, the diction and imagery of which would have been rather above, than below the mark, had they been applied to the immense empire of China improgressive for thirty centuries:

> "The weary SUN betook himself to rest:—
> —Then issued VESPER from the fulgent west,
> Outshining, like a visible God,

The glorious path in which he trod!
And now, ascending, after one dark hour,
And one night's diminution of her power,
Behold the mighty MOON! this way
She looks, as if at them—but they
Regard not her:—oh, better wrong and strife,
Better vain deeds or evil than such life!
The silent HEAVENS have goings on:
The STARS have tasks!—but *these* have none!"

The last instance of this defect (for I know no other than these already cited) is from the Ode, page 351, Vol. II., where, speaking of a child, "a six years' darling of a pigmy size," he thus addresses him:

"Thou best philosopher, who yet dost keep
Thy heritage! Thou eye among the blind,
That, deaf and silent, read'st the eternal deep,
Haunted for ever by the Eternal Mind,—
Mighty Prophet! Seer blest!
On whom those truths do rest,
Which we are toiling all our lives to find!
Thou, over whom thy immortality
Broods like the day, a master o'er the slave,
A presence that is not to be put by!"

Now here, not to stop at the daring spirit of metaphor which connects the epithets "deaf and silent," with the apostrophized *eye:* or (if we are to refer it to the preceding word, philosopher) the faulty and equivocal syntax of the passage; and without examining the propriety of making a "master *brood* o'er a slave," or the *day* brood *at all;* we will merely ask, what does all this mean? In what sense is a child of that age a *philosopher?* In what sense does he *read* "the eternal deep"? In what sense is he declared to be *"for ever haunted"* by the Supreme Being? or so inspired as to deserve the splendid titles of a *mighty prophet,* a *blessed seer?* By reflection? by knowledge? by conscious intuition? or by *any* form or modification of consciousness? These would be tidings indeed; but such as would presuppose an immediate revelation to the inspired communicator, and require miracles to authenticate his inspiration. Children at this age give us no such information of themselves; and at what time were we dipped in the Lethe, which has produced such utter oblivion of a state so godlike? There are many of us that still possess some remembrances, more or less distinct, respecting themselves at six years old; pity that the worthless straws only should float, while treasures, compared with which all the mines of Golconda and Mexico were but straws, should be absorbed by some unknown gulf into some unknown abyss.

But if this be too wild and exorbitant to be suspected as having been the poet's meaning; if these mysterious gifts, faculties, and operations, are *not* accompanied with consciousness; who *else* is conscious of them? or how can it be called the child, if it be no part of the child's conscious being? For aught I know, the thinking Spirit within me may be *substantially* one with the principle of life, and of vital operation. For aught I know, it might be employed as a secondary agent in the marvellous organization and organic movements of my body. But, surely, it would be strange language to say, that *I* construct my *heart!* or that *I* propel the finer influences through my *nerves!* or that *I* compress my brain, and draw the curtains of sleep round my own eyes! SPINOZA and BEHMEN were, on different systems, both Pantheists; and among the ancients there were philosophers, teachers of the ΕΝ ΚΑΙ ΠΑΝ, who not only taught that God was All, but that this All constituted God. Yet not even these would confound the *part, as* a part, with the Whole, *as* the whole. Nay, in no system is the distinction between the individual and God, between the Modification, and the one only Substance, more sharply drawn, than in that of SPINOZA. JACOBI indeed relates of LESSING, that, after a conversation with him at the house of the poet, GLEIM (the Tyrtæus and Anacreon of the German Parnassus) in which conversation L. had avowed privately to Jacobi his reluctance to admit any *personal* existence of the Supreme Being, or the *possibility* of personality except in a finite Intellect, and while they were sitting at table, a shower of rain came on unexpectedly. Gleim expressed his regret at the circumstance, because they had meant to drink their wine in the garden: upon which Lessing in one of his half-earnest half-joking moods, nodded to Jacobi, and said, "It is *I,* perhaps, that am doing *that,*" i.e. *raining!* and J. answered, "or perhaps I"; Gleim contented himself with staring at them both, without asking for any explanation.

So with regard to this passage. In what sense can the magnificent attributes, above quoted, be appropriated to a *child,* which would not make them equally suitable to a *bee,* or a *dog,* or a *field of corn:* or even to a ship, or to the wind and waves that propel it? The omnipresent Spirit works equally in them, as in the child; and the child is equally unconscious of it as they. It cannot surely be, that the four lines, immediately following, are to contain the explanation?

> "To whom the grave
> Is but a lonely bed without the sense or sight
> Of day or the warm light,
> A place of thought where we in waiting lie."

Surely, it cannot be that this wonder-rousing apostrophe is but a comment on the little poem, "We are seven"? that the whole meaning of the passage is reducible to the assertion, that a *child*, who by the bye at six years old would have been better instructed in most Christian families, has no other notion of death than that of lying in a dark, cold place? And still, I hope, not as in a *place of thought!* not the frightful notion of lying *awake* in his grave! The analogy between death and sleep is too simple, too natural, to render so horrid a belief possible for children; even had they not been in the habit, as all Christian children are, of hearing the latter term used to express the former. But if the child's belief be only, that "he is not dead, but sleepeth:" wherein does it differ from that of his father and mother, or any other adult and instructed person? To form an idea of a thing's becoming nothing; or of nothing becoming a thing; is impossible to all finite beings alike, of whatever age, and however educated or uneducated. Thus it is with splendid paradoxes in general. If the words are taken in the common sense, they convey an absurdity; and if, in contempt of dictionaries and custom, they are so interpreted as to avoid the absurdity, the meaning dwindles into some bald truism. Thus you must at once understand the words *contrary* to their common import, in order to arrive at any *sense;* and *according* to their common import, if you are to receive from them any feeling of *sublimity* or *admiration.*

Though the instances of this defect in Mr. Wordsworth's poems are so few, that for themselves it would have been scarce just to attract the reader's attention toward them; yet I have dwelt on it, and perhaps the more for this very reason. For being so very few, they cannot sensibly detract from the reputation of an author, who is even characterized by the number of profound truths in his writings, which will stand the severest analysis; and yet few as they are, they are exactly those passages which his *blind* admirers would be most likely, and best able, to imitate. But WORDSWORTH, where he is indeed Wordsworth, may be mimicked by Copyists, he may be plundered by Plagiarists; but he can not be imitated, except by those who are not born to be imitators. For without his depth of feeling and his imaginative power his *sense* would want its vital warmth and peculiarity; and without his strong sense, his *mysticism* would become *sickly*—mere fog, and dimness!

To these defects which, as appears by the extracts, are only occasional, I may oppose, with far less fear of encountering the dissent of any candid and intelligent reader, the following (for the most part correspondent) excellences. First, an austere purity of language both grammatically and logically; in short a perfect appropriateness of the words to the meaning. Of how high value I deem this, and how particularly estimable I hold the example at the present day, has been already stated: and in part too the reasons on which I ground both the moral and intellectual importance of habituating ourselves to a strict accuracy of expression. It is noticeable, how limited an acquaintance with the masterpieces of art will suffice to form a correct and even a sensitive taste, where none but master-pieces have been seen and admired: while on the other hand, the most correct notions, and the widest acquaintance with the works of excellence of all ages and countries, will not perfectly secure us against the contagious familiarity with the far more numerous offspring of tastelessness or of a perverted taste. If this be the case, as it notoriously is, with the arts of music and painting, much more difficult will it be to avoid the infection of multiplied and daily examples in the practice of an art, which uses words, and words only, as its instruments. In poetry, in which every line, every phrase, may pass the ordeal of deliberation and deliberate choice, it is possible, and barely possible, to attain that ultimatum which I have ventured to propose as the infallible test of a blameless style; its *untranslatableness* in words of the same language without injury to the meaning. Be it observed, however, that I include in the *meaning* of a word not only its correspondent object, but likewise all the associations which it recalls. For language is framed to convey not the object alone, but likewise the character, mood and intentions of the person who is representing it. In poetry it *is* practicable to preserve the diction uncorrupted by the affectations and misappropriations, which promiscuous authorship, and reading not promiscuous only because it is disproportionally most conversant with the compositions of the day, have rendered general. Yet even to the poet, composing in his own province, it is an arduous work: and as the result and pledge of a watchful good sense, of fine and luminous distinction, and of complete self-possession, may justly claim all the honor which belongs to an attainment equally difficult and valuable, and the more valuable for being rare. It is at *all* times the proper food of the understanding; but in an age of corrupt eloquence it is both food and antidote.

In prose I doubt whether it be even possible to preserve our style wholly unalloyed by the vicious phraseology which meets us everywhere, from the sermon to the newspaper, from the harangue of the legislator to the speech from the convivial chair, announcing a *toast* or sentiment. Our chains rattle, even while we are complaining of them. The poems of Boetius rise high in our estimation when we compare them with those of his contemporaries, as Sidonius Appollinarius, &c. They might even be referred to a purer age, but that the prose, in which they are set, as jewels in a crown of lead or iron, betrays the true age of the writer. Much however may be effected by education. I believe not only from grounds of reason, but from having in great measure assured myself of the fact by actual though limited experience, that, to a youth led from his first boyhood to investigate the meaning of every word and the reason of its choice and position, Logic presents itself as an old acquaintance under new names.

On some future occasion, more especially demanding such disquisition, I shall attempt to prove the close connection between veracity and habits of mental accuracy; the beneficial after-effects of verbal precision in the preclusion of fanaticism, which masters the feelings more especially by indistinct watchwords; and to display the advantages which language alone, at least which language with incomparably greater ease and certainty than any other means, presents to the instructor of impressing modes of intellectual energy so constantly, so imperceptibly, and as it were by such elements and atoms, as to secure in due time the formation of a second nature. When we reflect, that the cultivation of the judgement is a positive command of the moral law, since the reason can give the *principle* alone, and the conscience bears witness only to the *motive,* while the application and effects must depend on the judgement: when we consider, that the greater part of our success and comfort in life depends on distinguishing the similar from the same, that which is peculiar in each thing from that which it has in common with others, so as still to select the most probable, instead of the merely possible or positively unfit, we shall learn to value earnestly and with a practical seriousness a mean, already prepared for us by nature and society, of teaching the young mind to think well and wisely by the same unremembered process and with the same never forgotten results, as those by which it is taught to speak and converse. Now how much warmer the interest is, now much more genial the feelings of reality and practicability, and thence how much stronger the impulses to imitation are, which a *contemporary* writer, and especially a contemporary *poet,* excites in youth and commencing manhood, has been treated of in the earlier pages of these sketches. I have only to add, that all the praise which is due to the exertion of such influence for a purpose so important, joined with that which must be claimed for the infrequency of the same excellence in the same perfection, belongs in full right to Mr. Wordsworth. I am far however from denying that we have poets whose *general* style possesses the same excellence, as Mr. Moore, Lord Byron, Mr. Bowles, and, in all his later and more important works, our laurel-honoring Laureate. But there are none, in whose works I do not appear to myself to find *more* exceptions, than in those of Wordsworth. Quotations or specimens would here be wholly out of place, and must be left for the critic who doubts and would invalidate the justice of this eulogy so applied.

The second characteristic excellence of Mr. W.'s work is: a correspondent weight and sanity of the Thoughts and Sentiments, won—not from books, but—from the poet's own meditative observation. They are *fresh* and have the dew upon them. His muse, at least when in her strength of wing, and when she hovers aloft in her proper element,

> "Makes audible a linked lay of truth,
> Of truth profound a sweet continuous lay,
> Not learnt, but native, her own natural notes!"
>
> S. T. C.

Even throughout his smaller poems there is scarcely one, which is not rendered valuable by some just and original reflection.

See page 25, vol. 2nd.: or the two following passages in one of his humblest compositions.

> "O Reader! had you in your mind
> Such stores as silent thought can bring,
> O gentle Reader! you would find
> A tale in every thing;"

and

> "I've heard of hearts unkind, kind deeds
> With coldness still returning;
> Alas! the gratitude of men
> Has oftener left me mourning;"

or in a still higher strain the six beautiful quatrains, page 134.

"Thus fares it still in our decay:
        And yet the wiser mind
Mourns less for what age takes away
        Than what it leaves behind.

The Blackbird in the summer trees,
        The Lark upon the hill,
Let loose their carols when they please,
        Are quiet when they will.

With nature never do *they* wage
        A foolish strife; they see
A happy youth, and their old age
        Is beautiful and free!

But we are pressed by heavy laws,
        And often, glad no more,
We wear a face of joy, because
        We have been glad of yore.

If there is one, who need bemoan
        His kindred laid in earth,
The household hearts that were his own,
        It is the man of mirth.

My days, my Friend, are almost gone,
        My life has been approved,
And many love me; but by none
        Am I enough beloved."

or the sonnet on Buonaparte, page 202, vol. 2; or finally (for
a volume would scarce suffice to exhaust the instances) the last
stanza of the poem on the withered Celandine, vol. 2, p. 212.

"To be a prodigal's favorite—then, worse truth,
    A miser's pensioner—behold our lot!
O man! that from thy fair and shining youth
    Age might but take the things youth needed not."

Both in respect of this and of the former excellence, Mr.
Wordsworth strikingly resembles Samuel Daniel, one of the
golden writers of our golden Elizabethan age, now most cause-
lessly neglected: Samuel Daniel, whose diction bears no mark
of time, no distinction of age, which has been, and as long as
our language shall last, will be so far the language of the to-day
and for ever, as that it is more intelligible to us, than the transi-
tory fashions of our own particular age. A similar praise is due
to his sentiments. No frequency of perusal can deprive them
of their freshness. For though they are brought into the full day-
light of every reader's comprehension; yet are they drawn up

rrom depths which few in any age are privileged to visit, into
which few in any age have courage or inclination to descend. If
Mr. Wordsworth is not equally with Daniel alike intelligible to
all readers of average understanding in all passages of his works,
the comparative difficulty does not arise from the greater im-
purity of the ore, but from the nature and uses of the metal. A
poem is not necessarily obscure, because it does not aim to be
popular. It is enough, if a work be perspicuous to those for whom
it is written, and

> "Fit audience find, though few."

To the "Ode on the intimation of immortality from recollec-
tions of early childhood" the poet might have prefixed the lines
which Dante addresses to one of his own Canzoni—

> "Canzon, io credo, che saranno radi
> Che tua ragione intendan bene,
> Tanto lor sei faticoso ed alto."

> "O lyric song, there will be few, think I,
> Who may thy import understand aright:
> Thou art for *them* so arduous and so high!"

But the ode was intended for such readers only as had been
accustomed to watch the flux and reflux of their inmost nature,
to venture at times into the twilight realms of consciousness, and
to feel a deep interest in modes of inmost being, to which they
know that the attributes of time and space are inapplicable and
alien, but which yet can not be conveyed save in symbols of
time and space. For such readers the sense is sufficiently plain,
and they will be as little disposed to charge Mr. Wordsworth with
believing the Platonic pre-existence in the ordinary interpretation
of the words, as I am to believe, that Plato himself ever meant
or taught it.

> Πολλά μοι ὑπ' ἀγκῶ-
> νος ὠκέα βέλη
> ἔνδον ἐντὶ φαρέτρας
> φωνᾶντα συνετοῖσιν· ἐς
> δὲ τὸ πᾶν ἑρμηνέων
> χατίζει. σοφὸς ὁ πολ-
> λὰ εἰδὼς φυᾷ.
> μαθόντες δέ, λάβροι
> παγγλωσσίᾳ, κόρακες ὥς,
> ἄκραντα γαρύετον
> Διὸς πρὸς ὄρνιχα θεῖον.

Third (and wherein he soars far above Daniel) the sinewy
strength and originality of single lines and paragraphs: the fre-

quent curiosa felicitas of his diction, of which I need not here give specimens, having anticipated them in a preceding page. This beauty, and as eminently characteristic of Wordsworth's poetry, his rudest assailants have felt themselves compelled to acknowledge and admire.

Fourth; the perfect truth of nature in his images and descriptions, as taken immediately from nature, and proving a long and genial intimacy with the very spirit which gives the physiognomic expression to all the works of nature. Like a green field reflected in a calm and perfectly transparent lake, the image is distinguished from the reality only by its greater softness and lustre. Like the moisture or the polish on a pebble, genius neither distorts nor false-colours its objects; but on the contrary brings out many a vein and many a tint, which escapes the eye of common observation, thus raising to the rank of gems what had been often kicked away by the hurrying foot of the traveller on the dusty high road of custom.

Let me refer to the whole description of skating, vol. I., page 42 to 47, especially to the lines

> "So through the darkness and the cold we flew,
> And not a voice·was idle: with the din
> Meanwhile the precipices rang aloud;
> The leafless trees and every icy crag
> Tinkled like iron; while the distant hills
> Into the tumult sent an alien sound
> Of melancholy, not unnoticed, while the stars
> Eastward were sparkling clear, and in the west
> The orange sky of evening died away."

Or to the poem on the green linnet, vol. I. page 244. What can be more accurate yet more lovely than the two concluding stanzas?

> "Upon yon tuft of hazel trees,
> That twinkle to the gusty breeze,
> Behold him perched in ecstasies,
>   Yet seeming still to hover;
> There! where the flutter of his wings
> Upon his back and body flings
> Shadows and sunny glimmerings,
>   That cover him all over.
>
> While thus before my eyes he gleams,
> A brother of the leaves he seems;
> When in a moment forth he teems
>   His little song in gushes:
> As if it pleased him to disdain
> And mock the form which he did feign,

> While he was dancing with the train
> Of leaves among the bushes."

Or the description of the blue-cap, and of the noon-tide silence, page 284; or the poem to the cuckoo, page 299; or, lastly, though I might multiply the references to ten times the number, to the poem, so completely Wordsworth's, commencing

> "Three years she grew in sun and shower," &c.

Fifth: a meditative pathos, a union of deep and subtle thought with sensibility; a sympathy with man as man; the sympathy indeed of a contemplator, rather than a fellow-sufferer or co-mate, (spectator, haud particeps) but of a contemplator, from whose view no difference of rank conceals the sameness of the nature; no injuries of wind or weather, or toil, or even of ignorance, wholly disguise the human face divine. The superscription and the image of the Creator still remain legible to *him* under the dark lines, with which guilt or calamity had cancelled or cross-barred it. Here the man and the poet lose and find themselves in each other, the one as glorified, the latter as substantiated. In this mild and philosophic pathos, Wordsworth appears to me without a compeer. Such he *is*: so he *writes*. See vol. I. page 134 to 136, or that most affecting composition, the "Affliction of Margaret —— of ——," page 165 to 168, which no mother, and, if I may judge by my own experience, no parent can read without a tear. Or turn to that genuine lyric, in the former edition, entitled "The Mad Mother," page 174 to 178, of which I cannot refrain from quoting two of the stanzas, both of them for their pathos, and the former for the fine transition in the two concluding lines of the stanza, so expressive of that deranged state, in which from the increased sensibility the sufferer's attention is abruptly drawn off by every trifle, and in the same instant plucked back again by the one despotic 'hought, bringing home with it, by the blending, *fusing* power of Imagination and Passion, the alien object to which it had been so abruptly diverted, no longer an alien but an ally and an inmate.

> "Suck, little babe, oh suck again!
> It cools my blood; it cools my brain:
> Thy lips, I feel them, baby! they
> Draw from my heart the pain away.
> Oh! press me with thy little hand;
> It loosens something at my chest:
> About that tight and deadly band
> I feel thy little fingers prest.

The breeze I see is in the tree!
It comes to cool my babe and me."

"Thy father cares not for my breast,
'Tis thine, sweet baby, there to rest,
'Tis all thine own!—and, if its hue
Be changed, that was so fair to view,
'Tis fair enough for thee, my dove!
My beauty, little child, is flown,
But thou wilt live with me in love;
And what if my poor cheek be brown?
'Tis well for me, thou canst not see
How pale and wan it else would be."

Last, and pre-eminently, I challenge for this poet the gift of IMAGINATION in the highest and strictest sense of the word. In the play of *Fancy*, Wordsworth, to my feelings, is not always graceful, and sometimes *recondite*. The *likeness* is occasionally too strange, or demands too peculiar a point of view, or is such as appears the creature of pre-determined research, rather than spontaneous presentation. Indeed his fancy seldom displays itself, as mere and unmodified fancy. But in imaginative power, he stands nearest of all modern writers to Shakespeare and Milton; and yet in a kind perfectly unborrowed and his own. To employ his own words, which are at once an instance and an illustration, he does indeed to all thoughts and to all objects

"————————add the gleam,
The light that never was, on sea or land,
The consecration, and the poet's dream."

I shall select a few examples as most obviously manifesting this faculty; but if I should ever be fortunate enough to render my analysis of imagination, its origin and characters, thoroughly intelligible to the reader, he will scarcely open on a page of this poet's works without recognising, more or less, the presence and the influences of this faculty.

From the poem on the Yew Trees, vol. I. page 303, 304.

"But worthier still of note
Are those fraternal four of Borrowdale,
Joined in one solemn and capacious grove:
Huge trunks!—and each particular trunk a growth
Of intertwisted fibres serpentine
Up-coiling, and inveterately convolved,—
Not uninformed with phantasy, and looks
That threaten the profane;—a pillared shade,
Upon whose grassless floor of red-brown hue,

By sheddings from the pinal umbrage tinged
Perennially—beneath whose sable roof
Of boughs, as if for festal purpose decked
With unrejoicing berries, ghostly shapes
May meet at noontide—FEAR and trembling HOPE,
SILENCE and FORESIGHT—DEATH, the skeleton,
And TIME, the shadow—there to celebrate,
As in a natural temple scattered o'er
With altars undisturbed of mossy stone,
United worship; or in mute repose
To lie, and listen to the mountain flood
Murmuring from Glaramara's inmost caves."

The effect of the old man's figure in the poem of Resignation
and Independence, vol. II. page 33.

"While he was talking thus, the lonely place,
The old man's shape, and speech, all troubled me:
In my mind's eye I seemed to see him pace
About the weary moors continually,
Wandering about alone and silently."

Or the 8th, 9th, 19th, 26th, 31st, and 33d, in the collection
of miscellaneous sonnets—the sonnet on the subjugation of Switz-
erland, page 210, or the last ode, from which I especially select
the two following stanzas or paragraphs, page 349 to 350.

"Our birth is but a sleep and a forgetting;
The soul that rises with us, our life's star,
Hath had elsewhere its setting,
        And cometh from afar.
Not in entire forgetfulness,
And not in utter nakedness,
But trailing clouds of glory do we come
From God, who is our home:
Heaven lies about us in our infancy!
Shades of the prison-house begin to close
        Upon the growing boy;
But he beholds the light, and whence it flows,
        He sees it in his joy!
The youth who daily further from the East
Must travel, still is nature's priest,
        And by the splendid vision
        Is on his way attended;
At length the man perceives it die away,
And fade into the light of common day."

And page 352 to 354 of the same ode.

"O joy that in our embers
Is something that doth live,

That nature yet remembers
What was so fugitive!
The thought of our past years in me doth breed
Perpetual benedictions: not indeed
For that which is most worthy to be blest;
Delight and liberty, the simple creed
Of childhood, whether busy or at rest,
With new-fledged hope still fluttering in his breast:—
Not for these I raise
The song of thanks and praise;
But for those obstinate questionings
Of sense and outward things,
Fallings from us, vanishings;
Blank misgivings of a creature
Moving about in worlds not realized,
High instincts, before which our mortal nature
Did tremble like a guilty thing surprised!
But for those first affections,
Those shadowy recollections,
Which, be they what they may,
Are yet the fountain light of all our day,
Are yet a master light of all our seeing;
Uphold us—cherish—and have power to make
Our noisy years seem moments in the being
Of the eternal silence; truths that wake
      To perish never:
Which neither listlessness, nor mad endeavour,
Nor man nor boy,
Nor all that is at enmity with joy,
Can utterly abolish or destroy!
Hence, in a season of calm weather,
Though inland far we be,
Our souls have sight of that immortal sea
Which brought us hither;
Can in a moment travel thither—
And see the children sport upon the shore,
And hear the mighty waters rolling evermore."

And since it would be unfair to conclude with an extract,
which, though highly characteristic, must yet, from the nature
of the thoughts and the subject, be interesting, or perhaps intel
ligible, to but a limited number of readers; I will add, from the
poet's last published work. a passage equally Wordsworthian; of
the beauty of which, and of the imaginative power displayed
therein, there can be but one opinion, and one feeling. See
"White Doe," page 5.

      "Fast the church-yard fills;—anon
      Look again and they are gone;

The cluster round the porch, and the folk
Who sate in the shade of the prior's oak!
And scarcely have they disappear'd,
Ere the prelusive hymn is heard;—
With one consent the people rejoice,
Filling the church with a lofty voice!
They sing a service which they feel,
For 'tis the sun-rise of their zeal;
And faith and hope are in their prime
In great Eliza's golden time.

"A moment ends the fervent din,
And all is hushed, without and within;
For though the priest, more tranquilly,
Recites the holy liturgy,
The only voice which you can hear
Is the river murmuring near.
When soft!—the dusky trees between,
And down the path through the open green,
Where is no living thing to be seen;
And through yon gateway, where is found,
Beneath the arch with ivy bound,
Free entrance to the church-yard ground;
And right across the verdant sod,
Towards the very house of God;
Comes gliding in with lovely gleam,
Comes gliding in serene and slow,
Soft and silent as a dream,
A solitary doe!
White she is as lily of June,
And beauteous as the silver moon
When out of sight the clouds are driven
And she is left alone in heaven!
Or like a ship some gentle day
In sunshine sailing far away—
A glittering ship, that hath the plain
Of ocean for her own domain.

    ❋   ❋   ❋   ❋   ❋   ❋

"What harmonious pensive changes
Wait upon her as she ranges
Round and through this pile of state
Overthrown and desolate!
Now a step or two her way
Is through space of open day,
Where the enamoured sunny light
Brightens her that was so bright;
Now doth a delicate shadow fall,
Falls upon her like a breath,

From some lofty arch or wall,
As she passes underneath."

The following analogy will, I am apprehensive, appear dim and fantastic, but in reading Bartram's Travels I could not help transcribing the following lines as a sort of allegory, or connected simile and metaphor of Wordsworth's intellect and genius.—"The soil is a deep, rich, dark mould, on a deep stratum of tenacious clay; and that on a foundation of rocks, which often break through both strata, lifting their back above the surface. The trees which chiefly grow here are the gigantic black oak; magnolia magni-floria; fraxinus excelsior; platane; and a few stately tulip trees." What Mr. Wordsworth *will* produce, it is not for me to prophecy: but I could pronounce with the liveliest convictions what he is capable of producing. It is the FIRST GENUINE PHILO-SOPHIC POEM.

The preceding criticism will not, I am aware, avail to overcome the prejudices of those, who have made it a business to attack and ridicule Mr. Wordsworth's compositions.

Truth and prudence might be imaged as concentric circles. The poet may perhaps have passed beyond the latter, but he has con-fined himself far within the bounds of the former, in designating these critics, as too petulant to be passive to a genuine poet, and too feeble to grapple with him;—"men of palsied imaginations, in whose minds all healthy action is languid;—who, therefore, feed as the many direct them, or with the many are greedy after vicious provocatives."

Let not Mr. Wordsworth be charged with having expressed himself too indignantly, till the wantonness and the systematic and malignant perseverance of the aggressions have been taken into fair consideration. I myself heard the commander in chief of this unmanly warfare make a boast of his private admiration of Wordsworth's genius. I have heard him declare, that whoever came into his room would probably find the Lyrical Ballads lying open on his table, and that (speaking exclusively of those written by Mr. Wordsworth himself) he could nearly repeat the whole of them by heart. *But* a Review, in order to be a saleable article, must be *personal, sharp,* and *pointed:* and, *since then,* the poet has made himself, and with himself all who were, or were sup-posed to be, his friends and admirers, the object of the critic's revenge—how? by having spoken of a work so conducted in the terms which it deserved! I once heard a clergyman in boots and buckskin avow, that he would cheat his own father *in a horse*. A moral system of a similar nature seems to have been adopted by too many anonymous critics. As we used to say at school, in reviewing they *make* being rogues: and he, who complains, is to be laughed at for his ignorance of *the game*. With the pen out of their hand they are *honorable men*. They exert indeed power (which is to that of the injured party who should attempt to expose their glaring perversions and misstatements, as twenty to one) to write down, and (where the author's circumstances permit) to *impoverish* the man, whose learning and genius they themselves in private have repeatedly admitted. They knowingly strive to make it impossible for the man even to publish[63] any future work without exposing himself to all the wretchedness of debt and embarrassment. But this is all *in their vocation:* and, bating what they do in their *vocation*, *"who can say that black is the white of their eye?"*

So much for the detractors from Wordsworth's merits. On the other hand, much as I might wish for their fuller sympathy, I dare not flatter myself, that the freedom with which I have declared my opinions concerning both his theory and his defects, most of which are more or less connected with his theory, either as cause or effect, will be satisfactory or pleasing to *all* the poet's admirers and advocates. More indiscriminate than mine their admiration may be: deeper and more sincere it can not be. But I have advanced no opinion either for praise or censure, other than as texts introductory to the reasons which compel me to form it. Above all, I was fully convinced that such a criticism was not only wanted; but that, if executed with adequate ability, it must conduce, in no mean degree, to Mr. Wordsworth's *reputation*. His *fame* belongs to another age, and can neither be accelerated nor retarded. How small the proportion of the defects are to the beauties, I have repeatedly declared; and that no one of them originates in deficiency of poetic genius. Had they been more and greater, I should still, as a friend to his literary character in the present age, consider an analytic display of them as *pure gain;* if only it removed, as surely to all reflecting minds even the foregoing analysis must have removed, the strange mistake, so slightly grounded, yet so widely and industriously propagated, of Mr. Wordsworth's turn for SIMPLICITY! I am not half so much irritated by hearing his enemies abuse him for vulgarity of style, subject, and conception; as I am disgusted with

[63] Not many months ago an eminent bookseller was asked what he thought of ——? The answer was: "I have heard his powers very highly spoken of by some of our first-rate men; but I would not have a work of his if any one would give it me: for he is spoken but slightly of, or not at all, in the Quarterly Review: and the Edinburgh, you know, is decided to cut him up!"

the gilded side of the same meaning, as displayed by some affected admirers, with whom he is, forsooth, a *sweet, simple poet!* and *so* natural, that little master Charles and his younger sister are *so* charmed with them, that they play at "Goody Blake," or at "Johnny and Betty Foy"!

Were the collection of poems, published with these biographical sketches, important enough, (which I am not vain enough to believe), to deserve such a distinction; EVEN AS I HAVE DONE, SO WOULD I BE DONE UNTO.

For more than eighteen months have the volume of Poems, entitled SIBYLLINE LEAVES, and the present volumes, up to this page, been printed, and ready for publication. But, ere I speak of myself in the tones, which are alone natural to me under the circumstances of late years, I would fain present myself to the Reader as I was in the first dawn of my literary life:

> "When Hope grew round me, like the climbing vine,
> And fruits and foliage, not my own, seem'd mine!"

For this purpose I have selected from the letters, which I wrote home from Germany, those which appeared likely to be most interesting, and at the same time most pertinent to the title of this work.

SATYRANE'S LETTERS

LETTER I

ON SUNDAY morning, September 16, 1798, the Hamburg Pacquet set sail from Yarmouth; and I, for the first time in my life, beheld my native land retiring from me. At the moment of its disappearance—in all the kirks, churches, chapels, and meeting-houses, in which the greater number, I hope, of my countrymen were at that time assembled, I will dare question whether there was one more ardent prayer offered up to heaven, than that which I then preferred for my country. "Now, then," (said I to a gentleman who was standing near me), "we are out of our country." "Not yet, not yet!" he replied, and pointed to the sea; "This, too, is a Briton's country." This bon mot gave a fillip to my spirits, I rose and looked round on my fellow-passengers, who were all on the deck. We were eighteen in number, videlicet, five Englishmen, an English lady, a French gentleman and his serv-ant, an Hanoverian and his servant, a Prussian, a Swede, two Danes, and a Mulatto boy, a German tailor and his wife, (the smallest couple I ever beheld), and a Jew. We were all on the deck; but in a short time I observed marks of dismay. The lady retired to the cabin in some confusion, and many of the faces round me assumed a very doleful and frog-coloured appearance; and within an hour the number of those on deck was lessened by one half. I was giddy, but not sick, and the giddiness soon went away, but left a feverishness and want of appetite, which I attributed, in great measure, to the *sæva Mephitis* of the bilge-water; and it was certainly not decreased by the exportations from the cabin. However, I was well enough to join the able-bodied passengers, one of whom observed not inaptly, that Momus might have discovered an easier way to see a man's inside, than by placing a window in his breast. He needed only have taken a salt-water trip in a pacquet-boat.

I am inclined to believe, that a pacquet is far superior to a stage-coach, as a means of making men open out to each other. In the latter the uniformity of posture disposes to dozing, and the definiteness of the period, at which the company will separate, makes each individual think more of those *to* whom he is going, than of those *with* whom he is going. But at sea, more curiosity is excited, if only on this account, that the pleasant or unpleasant qualities of your companions are of greater importance to you, from the uncertainty how long you may be obliged to house with them. Besides, if you are countrymen, that now begins to form a distinction and a bond of brotherhood; and if of different countries, there are new incitements of conversation, more to ask and more to communicate. I found that I had interested the Danes in no common degree. I had crept into the boat on the deck and fallen asleep; but was awaked by one of them, about three o'clock in the afternoon, who told me that they had been seeking me in every hole and corner, and insisted that I should join their party and drink with them. He talked English with such fluency, as left me wholly unable to account for the singular and even ludicrous incorrectness with which he spoke it. I went, and found some excellent wines and a dessert of grapes with a pineapple. The Danes had christened me Doctor Teology, and dressed as I was all in black, with large shoes and black worsted stockings, I might certainly have passed very well for a Methodist missionary. However I disclaimed my title. What then may you be? A man of fortune? No!—A merchant? No! A merchant's traveller? No!—A clerk? No!—Un Philosophe, perhaps? It was at that time in my life, in which of all possible names and characters I had the greatest disgust to that of "un Philosophe." But I was weary of being questioned, and rather than be nothing, or at best only the abstract idea of a man, I submitted by a bow, even to the aspersion implied in the word "un Philosophe."—The Dane then informed me, that all in the present party were philosophers likewise. Certes we were not of the stoic school. For we drank and talked and sung, till we talked and sung all together; and then we rose and danced on the deck a set of dances, which in *one* sense of the word at least, were very intelligibly and appropriately intitled *reels*. The passengers, who lay in the cabin below in all the agonies of sea-sickness, must have found our bacchanalian merriment

> "—————————————————a tune
> Harsh and of dissonant mood from their complaint."

I thought so at the time; and (by way, I suppose, of supporting my newly assumed philosophical character) I thought too, how closely the greater number of our virtues are connected with the fear of death, and how little sympathy we bestow on pain, where there is no danger.

The two Danes were brothers. The one was a man with a clear white complexion, white hair, and white eyebrows; looked silly, and nothing that he uttered gave the lie to his looks. The other, whom by way of eminence I have called THE DANE, had likewise white hair, but was much shorter than his brother, with slender limbs, and a very thin face slightly pock-fretten. This man convinced me of the justice of an old remark. that many a faithful portrait in our novels and farces has been rashly censured for an outrageous caricature, or perhaps nonentity. I had retired to my station in the boat—he came and seated himself by my side, and appeared not a little tipsy. He commenced the conversation in the most magnific style, and, as a sort of pioneering to his own vanity, he flattered me with *such* grossness! The parasites of the old comedy were modest in the comparison. His language and accentuation were so exceedingly singular, that I determined for once in my life to take notes of a conversation. Here it follows, somewhat abridged indeed, but in all other respects as accurately as my memory permitted.

THE DANE. Vat imagination! vat language! vat vast science! and vat eyes! vat a milk-vite forehead! O my heafen! vy, you're a Got!

ANSWER. You do me too much honour, Sir.

THE DANE. O me! if you should dink I is flattering you!—No, no, no! I haf ten tousand a year—yes, ten tousand a year—yes, ten tousand pound a year! Vel—and vat is dhat? a mere trifle! I 'ouldn't gif my sincere heart for ten times dhe money.—Yes, you're a Got! I a mere man! But, my dear friend! dhink of me, as a man! Is, is—I mean to ask you now, my dear friend—is I not very eloquent? Is I not speak English very fine?

Answ. Most admirably! Believe me, Sir! I have seldom heard even a native talk so *fluently*.

The Dane. (*squeezing my hand with great vehemence.*) My *dear* friend! vat an affection and fidelity ve have for each odher! But tell me, do tell me,—Is I not, now and den, speak some fault? Is I not in some wrong?

Answ. Why, Sir! perhaps it might be observed by nice critics in the English language, that you occasionally use the word "Is" instead of "am." In our best companies we generally say I am, and not I is or I'se. Excuse me, Sir! it *is* a mere trifle.

The Dane. O!—is, is, am, am, am. Yes, yes—I know, I know.

Answ. I am, thou art, he is, we are, ye are, they are.

The Dane. Yes, yes,—I know, I know—Am, am, am, is dhe presens, and Is is dhe perfectum—yes, yes—and *are* is dhe plusquam perfectum.

Answ. And "Art," Sir! is——?

The Dane. My dear friend! it is dhe plusquam perfectum, no, no—dhat is a great lie. "Are" is dhe plusquam perfectum—and "art" is dhe plusquam plueperfectum—(*then swinging my hand to and fro, and cocking his little bright hazel eyes at me, that danced with vanity and wine*) You see, my dear friend! that I too have *some* lehrning.

Answ. Learning, Sir? Who dares suspect it? Who can listen to you for a minute, who can even look at you, without perceiving the extent of it?

The Dane. My *dear* friend!—(*then with a would-be humble look, and in a tone of voice as if he was reasoning*) I could not talk so of presens and imperfectum, and futurum and plusquam plueperfectum, and all dhat, my dear friend! without *some* lehrning?

Answ. Sir! a man like you cannot talk on any subject without discovering the depth of his information.

The Dane. Dhe grammatic Greek, my friend! ha! ha! ha! (*laughing, and swinging my hand to and fro—then with a sudden transition to great solemnity*) Now I will tell you, my dear friend! Dhere did happen about me vat de whole historia of Denmark record no instance about nobody else. Dhe bishop did ask me all dhe questions about all dhe religion in dhe Latin grammar.

Answ. The grammar, Sir? The language, I presume—

The Dane. (*A little offended.*) Grammar is language, and language is grammar—

Answ. Ten thousands pardons!

The Dane. Vell, and I was only fourteen years—

Answ. Only fourteen years old?

THE DANE. No more. I vas fourteen years old—and he asked me all questions, religion and philosophy, and all in dhe Latin language—and I answered him all every one, my dear friend! all in dhe Latin language.

ANSW. A prodigy! an absolute prodigy!

THE DANE. No, no, no! he was a bishop, a great superintendent.

ANSW. Yes! a bishop.

THE DANE. A bishop—not a mere predicant, not a prediger—

ANSW. My dear Sir! we have misunderstood each other. I said that your answering in Latin at so early an age was a prodigy, that is, a thing that is wonderful, that does not often happen.

THE DANE. Often! Dhere is not von instance recorded in dhe whole historia of Denmark.

ANSW. And since then Sir——?

THE DANE. I was sent ofer to dhe Vest Indies—to our Island, and dhere I had no more to do vid books. No! no! I put my genius anodher way—and I haf made ten tousand pound a year. Is not dhat *ghenius,* my dear friend?—But vat is money? I dhink dhe poorest man alive my equal. Yes, my dear friend; my little fortune is pleasant to my generous heart, because I can do good—no man with so little a fortune ever did so much generosity—no person, no man person, no woman person ever denies it. But we are all Got's children.

Here the Hanoverian interrupted him, and the other Dane, the Swede, and the Prussian, joined us, together with a young Englishman who spoke the German fluently, and interpreted to me many of the Prussian's jokes. The Prussian was a travelling merchant, turned of threescore, a hale man, tall, strong, and stout, full of stories, gesticulations, and buffoonery, with the soul as well as the look of a mountebank, who, while he is making you laugh, picks your pocket. Amid all his droll looks and droll gestures, there remained one look untouched by laughter; and that one look was the true face, the others were but its mask. The Hanoverian was a pale, fat, bloated young man, whose father had made a large fortune in London, as an army-contractor. He seemed to emulate the manners of young Englishmen of fortune. He was a good-natured fellow, not without information or literature; but a most egregious coxcomb. He had been in the habit of attending the House of Commons, and had once spoken, as he informed me, with great applause in a debating society. For this he appeared to have qualified himself with laudable industry: for he was perfect in Walker's Pronouncing Dictionary, and with an accent which forcibly reminded me of the Scotchman in

Roderic Random, who professed to teach the English pronunciation, he was constantly *deferring* to my superior judgement, whether or no I had pronounced this or that word with propriety, or "the true delicacy." When he spoke, though it were only half a dozen sentences, he always rose; for which I could detect no other motive, than his partiality to that elegant phrase so liberally introduced in the orations of our British legislators, "While I am on my legs." The Swede, whom for reasons that will soon appear, I shall distinguish by the name of "Nobility," was a strong-featured, scurvy-faced man, his complexion resembling in color a red hot poker beginning to cool. He appeared miserably dependent on the Dane; but was, however, incomparably the best informed and most rational of the party. Indeed his manners and conversation discovered him to be both a man of the world and a gentleman. The Jew was in the hold: the French gentleman was lying on the deck so ill, that I could observe nothing concerning him, except the affectionate attentions of his servant to him. The poor fellow was very sick himself, and every now and then ran to the side of the vessel, still keeping his eye on his master, but returned in a moment and seated himself again by him, now supporting his head, now wiping his forehead and talking to him all the while in the most soothing tones. There had been a matrimonial squabble of a very ludicrous kind in the cabin, between the little German tailor and his little wife. He had secured two beds, one for himself and one for her. This had struck the little woman as a very cruel action; she insisted upon their having but one, and assured the mate in the most piteous tones, that she was his lawful wife. The mate and the cabin boy decided in her favor, abused the little man for his want of tenderness with much humor, and hoisted him into the same compartment with his sea-sick wife. This quarrel was interesting to me, as it procured me a bed, which I otherwise should not have had.

In the evening, at 7 o'clock, the sea rolled higher, and the Dane, by means of the greater agitation, eliminated enough of what he had been swallowing to make room for a great deal more. His favorite potation was sugar and brandy, i.e. a very little warm water with a large quantity of brandy, sugar, and nut-meg. His servant boy, a black-eyed Mulatto, had a good-natured round face, exactly the color of the skin of the walnut-kernel. The Dane and I were again seated, tête-à-tête, in the ship's boat. The conversation, which was now indeed rather an oration than a dialogue, became extravagant beyond all that I ever heard. He told me that he had made a large fortune in the island of Santa Cruz, and was now returning to Denmark to enjoy it. He expatiated on

the style in which he meant to live, and the great undertakings
which he proposed to himself to commence, till, the brandy aid-
ing his vanity, and his vanity and garrulity aiding the brandy,
he talked like a madman—entreated me to accompany him to
Denmark—there I should see his influence with the government,
and he would introduce me to the king, &c., &c. Thus he went
on dreaming aloud, and then passing with a very lyrical transition
to the subject of general politics, he declaimed, like a member
of the Corresponding Society, *about* (not concerning) the Rights
of Man, and assured me that, notwithstanding his fortune, he
thought the poorest man alive his equal. "All are equal, my dear
friend! all are equal! Ve are all Got's children. The poorest man
haf the same rights with me. Jack! Jack! some more sugar and
brandy. Dhere is dhat fellow now! He is a Mulatto—but he is
my equal.—That's right, Jack! (*taking the sugar and brandy*).
Here you Sir! shake hands with dhis gentleman! Shake hands
with me, you dog! Dhere, dhere!—We are all equal, my dear
friend!—Do I not speak like Socrates, and Plato, and Cato—they
were all philosophers, my dear philosophe! all very great men!—
and so was Homer and Virgil—but they were poets, yes, yes! I
know all about it!—But what can anybody say more than this?
We are all equal, all Got's children. I haf ten tousand a year,
but I am no more dhan de meanest man alive. I haf no pride;
and yet, my dear friend! I can say, do! and it is done. Ha! ha! ha!
my dear friend! Now dhere is dhat gentleman (*pointing to Nobil-
ity*) he is a Swedish baron—you shall see. Ho! (*calling to the
Swede*) get me, will you, a bottle of wine from the cabin. SWEDE.
—Here, Jack! go and get your master a bottle of wine from the
cabin. DANE. No, no, no! do *you* go now—you go yourself—*you*
go now! SWEDE. Pah!—DANE. Now go! Go, I pray you. AND THE
SWEDE WENT!!

After this the Dane commenced an harangue on religion, and
mistaking me for "un philosophe" in the continental sense of the
word, he talked of Deity in a declamatory style, very much re-
sembling the devotional rants of that rude blunderer, Mr. Thomas
Paine, in his Age of Reason, and whispered in my ear, what
damned *hypocrism* all Jesus Christ's business was. I dare aver,
that few men have less reason to charge themselves with indulg-
ing in *persiflage* than myself. I should hate it, if it were only that
it is a Frenchman's vice, and feel a pride in avoiding it, because
our own language is too honest to have a word to express it by.
But in this instance the temptation had been too powerful, and
I have placed it on the list of my offences. Pericles answered one
of his dearest friends, who had solicited him on a case of life and

death, to take an equivocal oath, for his preservation: *Debeo amicis opitulari, sed usque ad Deos.*[64] Friendship herself must place her last and boldest step on this side the altar. What Pericles would not do to save a friend's life, you may be assured, I would not hazard merely to mill the chocolate-pot of a drunken fool's vanity till it frothed over. Assuming a serious look, I professed myself a believer, and sunk at once an hundred fathoms in his good graces. He retired to his cabin, and I wrapped myself up in my great coat, and looked at the water. A beautiful white cloud of foam at momently intervals coursed by the side of the vessel with a roar, and little stars of flame danced and sparkled and went out in it: and every now and then light detachments of this white cloud-like foam darted off from the vessel's side, each with its own small constellation, over the sea, and scoured out of sight like a Tartar troop over a wilderness.

It was cold, the cabin was at open war with my olfactories, and I found reason to rejoice in my great coat, a weighty high-caped, respectable rug, the collar of which turned over, and played the part of a night-cap very passably. In looking up at two or three bright stars, which oscillated with the motion of the sails, I fell asleep, but was awakened at one o'clock, Monday morning, by a shower of rain. I found myself compelled to go down into the cabin, where I slept very soundly, and awoke with a very good appetite at breakfast time, my nostrils, the most placable of all the senses, reconciled to or indeed insensible of the mephitis.

Monday, September 17th, I had a long conversation with the Swede, who spoke with the most poignant contempt of the Dane, whom he described as a fool, purse-mad; but he confirmed the boasts of the Dane respecting the largeness of his fortune, which he had acquired in the first instance as an advocate, and afterwards as a planter. From the Dane and from himself I collected that he was indeed a Swedish nobleman, who had squandered a fortune, that was never very large, and had made over his property to the Dane, on whom he was now utterly dependent. He seemed to suffer very little pain from the Dane's insolence. He was in a high degree humane and attentive to the English lady, who suffered most fearfully, and for whom he performed many little offices with a tenderness and delicacy which seemed to prove real goodness of heart. Indeed his general manners and conversation were not only pleasing, but even interesting; and I struggled to believe his insensibility respecting the Dane philo-

[64] TRANSLATION: It behoves me to side with my friends, but only as far as the gods.

sophical fortitude. For though the Dane was now quite sober, his character oozed out of him at every pore. And after dinner, when he was again flushed with wine, every quarter of an hour or perhaps oftener he would shout out to the Swede, "Ho! Nobility, go—do such a thing! Mr. Nobility!—tell the gentlemen such a story, and so forth;" with an insolence which must have excited disgust and detestation, if his vulgar rants on the sacred rights of equality, joined to his wild havoc of general grammar, no less than of the English language, had not rendered it so irresistibly laughable.

At four o'clock I observed a wild duck swimming on the waves, a single solitary wild duck. It is not easy to conceive, how inter-esting a thing it looked in that round objectless desert of waters. I had associated such a feeling of immensity with the ocean, that I felt exceedingly disappointed, when I was out of sight of all land, at the narrowness and *nearness*, as it were, of the circle of the horizon. So little are images capable of satisfying the obscure feelings connected with words. In the evening the sails were lowered, lest we should run foul of the land, which can be seen only at a small distance. And at four o'clock, on Tuesday morning, I was awakened by the cry of land! land! It was an ugly island rock at a distance on our left, called Heiligeland, well known to many passengers from Yarmouth to Hamburg, who have been obliged by stormy weather to pass weeks and weeks in weary captivity on it, stripped of all their money by the exorbitant demands of the wretches who inhabit it. So at least the sailors informed me.—About nine o'clock we saw the main land, which seemed scarcely able to hold its head above water, low, flat, and dreary, with lighthouses and land-marks which seemed to give a character and language to the dreariness. We entered the mouth of the Elbe, passing Neu-werk; though as yet the right bank only of the river was visible to us. On this I saw a church, and thanked God for my safe voyage, not without affectionate thoughts of those I had left in England. At eleven o'clock on the same morning we arrived at Cuxhaven, the ship dropped anchor, and the boat was hoisted out, to carry the Hanoverian and a few others on shore. The captain agreed to take us, who remained, to Hamburg for ten guineas, to which the Dane contributed so largely, that the other passengers paid but half a guinea each. Accordingly we hauled anchor, and passed gently up the river. At Cuxhaven both sides of the river may be seen in clear weather; we could now see the right bank only. We passed a multitude of English traders that had been waiting many weeks for a wind. In a short time both banks became visible, both flat and evidenc

ing the labor of human hands by their extreme neatness. On the
left bank I saw a church or two in the distance; on the right bank
we passed by steeple and windmill and cottage, and windmill and
single house, windmill and windmill, and neat single house, and
steeple. These were the objects and in this succession. The shores
were very green and planted with trees not inelegantly. Thirty-
five miles from Cuxhaven the night came on us, and, as the navi-
gation of the Elbe is perilous, we dropped anchor.

Over what place, thought I, does the moon hang to *your* eye,
my dearest friend? To me it hung over the left bank of the Elbe.
Close above the moon was a huge volume of deep black cloud,
while a very thin fillet crossed the middle of the orb, as narrow
and thin and black as a ribbon of crape. The long trembling road
of moonlight, which lay on the water and reached to the stern
of our vessel, glimmered dimly and obscurely. We saw two or
three lights from the right bank, probably from bed-rooms. I
felt the striking contrast between the silence of this majestic
stream, whose banks are populous with men and women and
children, and flocks and herds—between the silence by night of
this peopled river, and the ceaseless noise, and uproar, and loud
agitations of the desolate solitude of the ocean. The passengers
below had all retired to their beds; and I felt the interest of this
quiet scene the more deeply from the circumstance of having just
quitted them. For the Prussian had during the whole of the eve-
ning displayed all his talents to captivate the Dane, who had
admitted him into the train of his dependents. The young Eng-
lishman continued to interpret the Prussian's jokes to me. They
were all without exception profane and abominable, but some
sufficiently witty, and a few incidents, which he related in his
own person, were valuable as illustrating the manners of the
countries in which they had taken place.

Five o'clock on Wednesday morning we hauled the anchor, but
were soon obliged to drop it again in consequence of a thick fog,
which our captain feared would continue the whole day; but
about nine it cleared off, and we sailed slowly along, close by
the shore of a very beautiful island, forty miles from Cuxhaven,
the wind continuing slack. This holme or island is about a mile
and a half in length, wedge-shaped, well wooded, with glades of
the liveliest green, and rendered more interesting by the remark-
ably neat farm house on it. It seemed made for retirement with-
out solitude—a place that would allure one's friends, while it pre-
cluded the impertinent calls of mere visitors. The shores of the
Elbe now became more beautiful, with rich meadows and trees
running like a low wall along the river's edge; and peering over

them, neat houses and (especially on the right bank) a profusion of steeple-spires, white, black, or red. An instinctive taste teaches men to build their churches in flat countries with spire-steeples, which, as they cannot be referred to any other object, point as with silent finger to the sky and stars, and sometimes, when they reflect the brazen light of a rich though rainy sun-set, appear like a pyramid of flame burning heavenward. I remember once, and once only, to have seen a spire in a narrow valley of a mountainous country. The effect was not only mean but ludicrous, and reminded me against my will of an *extinguisher;* the close neighbourhood of the high mountain, at the foot of which it stood, had so completely dwarfed it, and deprived it of all connection with the clouds or sky. Forty-six English miles from Cuxhaven, and sixteen from Hamburg, the Danish village Veder ornaments the left bank with its black steeple, and close by it the wild and pastoral hamlet of Schulau. Hitherto both the right and left bank, green to the very brink, and level with the river, resembled the shores of a park canal. The trees and houses were alike low, sometimes the low trees overtopping the yet lower houses, sometimes the low houses rising above the yet lower trees. But at Schulau the left bank rises at once forty or fifty feet, and stares on the river with its perpendicular fassade of sand, thinly patched with tufts of green. The Elbe continued to present a more and more lively spectacle from the multitude of fishing boats and the flocks of sea gulls wheeling round them, the clamorous rivals and companions of the fishermen; till we come to Blankaness, a most interesting village scattered amid scattered trees, over three hills in three divisions. Each of the three hills stares upon the river, with faces of bare sand, with which the boats with their bare poles, standing in files along the banks, made a sort of fantastic harmony. Between each fassade lies a green and woody dell, each deeper than the other. In short it is a large village made up of individual cottages, each cottage in the centre of its own little wood or orchard, and each with its own separate path: a village with a labyrinth of paths, or rather a *neighbourhood* of houses! It is inhabited by fishermen and boat-makers, the Blankaness boats being in great request through the whole navigation of the Elbe. Here first we saw the spires of Hamburg, and from hence as far as Altona the left bank of the Elbe is uncommonly pleasing, considered as the vicinity of an industrious and republican city—in that style of beauty, or rather prettiness, that might tempt the citizen into the country, and yet gratify the taste which he had acquired in the town. Summer-houses and Chinese show-work are every where scattered along the high and green banks;

the boards of the farm-houses left unplaistered and gaily painted with green and yellow; and scarcely a tree not cut into shapes and made to remind the human being of his own power and intelligence instead of the wisdom of nature. Still, however, these are links of connection between town and country, and far better than the affectation of tastes and enjoyments for which men's habits have disqualified them. Pass them by on Saturdays and Sundays with the burgers of Hamburg smoking their pipes, the women and children feasting in the alcoves of box and yew, and it becomes a nature of its own. On Wednesday, four o'clock, we left the vessel, and passing with trouble through the huge masses of shipping that seemed to choke the wide Elbe from Altona upward, we were at length landed at the Boom House, Hamburg.

LETTER II (To a Lady)

RATZEBURG.

Meine liebe Freundin,

See how natural the German comes from me, though I have not yet been six weeks in the country!—almost as fluently as English from my neighbour the Amptschreiber, (or public secretary), who as often as we meet, though it should be half a dozen times in the same day, never fails to greet me with—" * * *ddam your ploot unt eyes, my dearest Englander! vhee goes it!"*—which is certainly a proof of great generosity on his part, these words being his whole stock of English. I had, however, a better reason than the desire of displaying my proficiency: for I wished to put you in good humour with a language, from the acquirement of which I have promised myself much edification and the means too of communicating a new pleasure to you and your sister, during our winter readings. And how can I do this better than by pointing out its gallant attention to the ladies? Our English affix *ess* is, I believe, confined either to words derived from the Latin, as *actress, directress,* &c., or from the French, as *mistress, duchess,* and the like. But the German *in* enables us to designate the sex in every possible relation of life. Thus the Amptman's lady is the *Frau* Amptman*in*—the secretary's wife, (by the bye, the handsomest woman I have yet seen in Germany) is die allerliebste Frau Amptschreiber*in*—the colonel's lady, die Frau Obrist*in* or Colonel*in*—and even the parson's wife, die Frau Pastor*in*. But I am especially pleased with their *freundin,* which, unlike the *amica* of the Romans, is seldom used but in its best and purest sense. Now I know it will be said, that a friend is already something more than a friend, when a man feels an anxiety to express to himself that this friend is a female; but this I deny—in that sense at least in which the objection will be made. I would hazard the impeachment of heresy, rather than abandon my belief that there is a sex in our souls as well as in their perishable garments; and he who does not feel it, never truly loved a sister—nay, is not capable even of loving a wife as she deserves to be loved, if she indeed be worthy of that holy name.

Now I know, my gentle friend, what you are murmuring to yourself—"This is so like him! running away after the first bubble, that chance had blown off from the surface of his fancy; when me is anxious to learn where he is and what he has seen." Well then! that I am settled at Ratzeburg, with my motives and the particulars of my journey hither, —— will inform you. My first letter to him, with which, doubtless, he has edified your whole fireside, left me safely landed at Hamburg on the Elbe Stairs, at the Boom House. While standing on the stairs, I was amused by the contents of the passage-boat, which crosses the river once or twice a day from Hamburg to Haarburg. It was stowed close with all people of all nations, in all sorts of dresses; the men all with pipes in their mouths, and these pipes of all shapes and fancies— straight and wreathed, simple and complex, long and short, cane, clay, porcelain, wood, tin, silver, and ivory; most of them with silver chains and silver bowl-covers. Pipes and boots are the first universal characteristic of the male Hamburgers that would strike the eye of a raw traveller. But I forgot my promise of journalizing as much as possible.—Therefore, *Septr.* 19 *Afternoon.* My companion, who, you recollect, speaks the French language with unusual propriety, had formed a kind of confidential acquaintance with the emigrant, who appeared to be a man of sense, and whose manners were those of a perfect gentleman. He seemed about fifty or rather more. Whatever is unpleasant in French manners from excess in the *degree,* had been softened down by age or affliction; and all that is delightful in the *kind,* alacrity and delicacy in little attentions, &c., remained, and without bustle, gesticulation, or disproportionate eagerness. His demeanour exhibited the minute philanthropy of a polished Frenchman, tempered by the sobriety of the English character disunited from its reserve. There is something strangely attractive in the character of a *gentleman* when you apply the word emphatically, and yet in that sense of the term which it is more easy to *feel* than to define. It neither includes the possession of high moral excellence, nor of necessity even the ornamental graces of manner. I have now in my mind's eye a person whose life would scarcely stand scrutiny even in the court of honor, much less in that of conscience; and his manners, if nicely observed, would of the two excite an idea of awkwardness rather than of elegance: and yet every one who conversed with him felt and acknowledged *the gentleman.* The secret of the matter, I believe to be this—we feel the gentlemanly character present to us, whenever, under all the circumstances of social intercourse, the trivial not less than the important, through the whole *detail* of his manners and deportment, and with the ease of a habit, a person shows respect to others in *such a way,* as at the same time implies in his own feelings an habitual and assured anticipation of reciprocal respect from them to himself. In short, the *gentlemanly* character arises out of the feeling of Equality, acting as a Habit, yet flexible to the varieties of Rank, and modified without being disturbed or superseded by them. This description will perhaps explain to you the ground of one of your own remarks, as I was englishing to you the interesting dialogue concerning the causes of the corruption of eloquence. "What perfect gentlemen these old Romans must have been! I was impressed, I remember, with the same feeling at the time I was reading a translation of Cicero's philosophical dialogues and of his epistolary correspondence: while in Pliny's Letters I seemed to have a different feeling—he gave me the notion of a very *fine* gentleman." You uttered the words as if you had felt that the adjunct had injured the substance and the encreased degree altered the kind. Pliny was the courtier of an absolute monarch—Cicero an aristocratic republican. For this reason the character of gentleman, in the sense to which I have confined it, is frequent in England, rare in France, and found, where it is found, in age or the latest period of manhood; while in Germany the character is almost unknown. But the proper *antipodes* of a gentleman is to be sought for among the Anglo-American democrats.

I owe this digression, as an act of justice to this amiable Frenchman, and of humiliation for myself. For in a little controversy between us on the subject of French poetry, he made me feel my own ill behaviour by the silent reproof of contrast, and when I afterwards apologized to him for the warmth of my language, he answered me with a chearful expression of surprize, and an immediate compliment, which a gentleman might both make with dignity and receive with pleasure. I was pleased, therefore to find it agreed on, that we should, if possible, take up our quarters in the same house. My friend went with him in search of an hotel, and I to deliver my letters of recommendation.

I walked onward at a brisk pace, enlivened not so much by anything I actually saw, as by the confused sense that I was for the first time in my life on the *continent* of our planet. I seemed to myself like a liberated bird that had been hatched in an aviary.

who now after his first soar of freedom poises himself in the upper air. Very naturally I began to wonder at *all* things, some for being so like and some for being so unlike the things in England—Dutch women with large umbrella hats shooting out half a yard before them, with a prodigal plumpness of petticoat behind—the women of Hamburg with caps plaited on the caul with silver, or gold, or both, bordered round with stiffened lace, which *stood out* before their eyes, but not lower, so that the eyes sparkled through it—the Hanoverian women with the fore part of the head bare, then a stiff lace standing up like a wall perpendicular on the cap, and the cap behind *tailed* with an enormous quantity of ribbon which lies or tosses on the back:

> "Their visnomies seem'd like a goodly banner
> Spread in defiance of all enemies."
>
> SPENSER.

—The ladies all in English dresses, all *rouged,* and all with bad teeth: which you notice instantly from their contrast to the almost *animal, too* glossy mother-of-pearl whiteness and the regularity of the teeth of the laughing, loud-talking country-women and servant-girls, who with their clean white stockings and with slippers without heel-quarters tripped along the dirty streets, as if they were secured by a charm from the dirt: with a lightness, too, which surprised me, who had always considered it as one of the annoyances of sleeping *in an Inn,* that I had to clatter up stairs in a pair of them. The streets narrow; to my English nose sufficiently offensive, and explaining at first sight the universal use of boots; without any appropriate path for the foot-passengers; the gable ends of the houses all towards the street, some in the ordinary triangular form, and *entire,* as the botanists say, but the greater number notched and scolloped with more than Chinese grotesqueness. Above all, I was struck with the profusion of windows, so large and so many, that the houses look all glass. Mr. Pitt's Window Tax, with its pretty little *additionals* sprouting out from it like young toadlets on the back of a Surinam toad, would certainly improve the appearance of the Hamburg houses, which have a slight summer look, not *in keeping* with their size, incongruous with the climate, and precluding that feeling of retirement and self-content, which one wishes to associate with a house in a noisy city. But a conflagration would, I fear, be the previous requisite to the production of any architectural beauty in Hamburg: for verily it is a filthy town. I moved on and crossed a multitude of ugly bridges, with huge black deformities of water wheels close by them. The water intersects the city every where, and would have furnished to the genius of Italy the capabilities of all that is most beautiful and magnificent in architecture. It might have been the rival of Venice, and it is huddle and ugliness, stench and stagnation. The Jungfer Stieg (i.e., Young Ladies' Walk), to which my letters directed me, made an exception. It was a walk or promenade planted with treble rows of elm trees, which, being yearly pruned and cropped, remain slim and dwarf-like. This walk occupies one side of a square piece of water, with many swans on it perfectly tame, and, moving among the swans, shewy pleasure boats with ladies in them, rowed by their husbands or lovers. **********

(*Some paragraphs have been here omitted.*)

Thus embarrassed by sad and solemn politeness, still more than by broken English, it sounded like the voice of an old friend when I heard the emigrant's servant inquiring after me. He had come for the purpose of guiding me to our hotel. Through streets and streets I pressed on as happy as a child, and, I doubt not, with a childish expression of wonderment in my busy eyes, amused by the wicker waggons with moveable benches across them, one behind the other, (these were the hackney coaches); amused by the sign-boards of the shops, on which all the articles sold within are painted, and that too very exactly, though in a grotesque confusion, (a useful substitute for language in this great mart of nations); amused with the incessant tinkling of the shop and house door bells, the bell hanging over each door and struck with a small iron rod at every entrance and exit;—and finally, amused by looking in at the windows, as I passed along; the ladies and gentlemen drinking coffee or playing cards, and the gentlemen all smoking. I wished myself a painter, that I might have sent you a sketch of one of the card parties. The long pipe of one gentleman rested on the table, its bowl half a yard from his mouth, fuming like a censer by the fish-pool—the other gentleman, who was dealing the cards, and of course had both hands employed, held his pipe in his teeth, which, hanging down be-- tween his knees, smoked beside his ancles. Hogarth himself never drew a more ludicrous distortion both of attitude and physiognomy, than this effort occasioned: nor was there wanting beside it one of those beautiful female faces which the same Hogarth, in whom the satirist never extinguished that love of beauty which belonged to him as a poet, so often and so gladly introduces, as the central figure in a crowd of humorous deformities, which figure (such is the power of true genius!) neither acts, nor is *meant* to act as a contrast; but diffuses through all, and over each of the group, a spirit of reconciliation and human kindness; and, even when the attention is no longer consciously directed to the cause of this feeling, still blends its tenderness with our laughter: and thus prevents the instructive merriment at the whims of nature or the foibles or humours of our fellow-men from degenerating into the heart-poison of contempt or hatred.

Our hotel DER WILDE MAN, (the sign of which was no bad likeness of the landlord, who had ingrafted on a very grim face a restless grin, that was at every man's service, and which, indeed, like an actor rehearsing to himself, he kept playing in *expectation* of an occasion for it) neither our hotel, I say, nor its landlord were of the genteelest class. But it has one great advantage for a stranger, by being in the market place, and the next neighbour of the huge church of St. Nicholas: a church with shops and houses built up against it, out of which *wens* and *warts* its high massy steeple rises, *necklaced* near the top with a round of large gilt balls. A better pole-star could scarcely be desired. Long shall I retain the impression made on my mind by the awful echo, so loud and long and tremulous, of the deep-toned clock within this church, which awoke me at two in the morning from a distressful dream, occasioned, I believe, by the feather bed, which is used here instead of bed-clothes. I will rather carry my blanket about with me like a wild Indian, than submit to this abominable custom. Our emigrant acquaintance was, we found, an intimate friend of the celebrated Abbé de Lisle: and from the large fortune, which he possessed under the monarchy, had rescued sufficient not only for independence, but for respectability. He had offended some of his fellow-emigrants in London, whom he had obliged with considerable sums, by a refusal to make further advances, and in consequence of their intrigues had received an order to quit the kingdom. I thought it one proof of his innocence, that he attached no blame either to the alien act, or to the minister who had exerted it against him; and a still greater, that he spoke of London with rapture, and of his favorite niece, who had married and settled in England, with all the fervor and all the pride of a fond parent. A man sent by force out of a country, obliged to sell out of the stocks at a great loss, and exiled from those pleasures and that style of society which habit had rendered essential to his happiness, whose predominant feelings were yet all of a private nature, resentment for friendship outraged, and anguish for domestic affections interrupted—such a man, I think, I could dare warrant guiltless of *espionage* in any service, most of all in that of the present French Directory. He spoke with extacy of Paris under the Monarchy: and yet the particular facts, which made up his description, left as deep a conviction on my mind of French worthlessness, as his own tale had done of emigrant ingratitude. Since my arrival in Germany, I have not met a single person, even among those who abhor the Revolution, that spoke with favor, or even charity, of the French emigrants. Though the belief of their influence in the origination of this disastrous war (from the horrors of which North Germany deems itself only reprieved, not secured) may have some share in the general aversion with which they are regarded: yet I am deeply persuaded that the far greater part is owing to their own profligacy, to their treachery and hardheartedness to each other, and the domestic misery or corrupt principles which so many of them have carried into the families of their protectors. My heart dilated with honest pride, as I recalled to mind the stern yet amiable characters of the English patriots, who sought refuge on the Continent at the Restoration! O let not our civil war under the first Charles be parallelled with the French revolution! In the former, the chalice overflowed from excess of principle; in the latter, from the fermentation of the dregs! The former was a civil war between the virtues and virtuous prejudices of the two parties; the latter, between the vices. The Venetian glass of the French monarchy shivered and flew asunder with the working of a double poison.

Sept. 20th. I was introduced to Mr. Klopstock, the brother of the poet, who again introduced me to Professor Ebeling, an intelligent and lively man, though deaf: so deaf, indeed, that it was a painful effort to talk with him, as we were obliged to drop all our pearls into a huge ear-trumpet. From this courteous and kind-hearted man of letters (I hope the German literati in general may resemble this first specimen) I heard a tolerable Italian pun, and an interesting anecdote. When Buonaparte was in Italy, having been irritated by some instance of perfidy, he said in a loud and vehement tone, in a public company—"'tis a true proverb, *gli Italiani tutti ladroni*"—(i.e. *the Italians all plunderers.*) A lady had the courage to reply, "Non tutti; ma BUONA PARTE," (*not all, but a good part,* or *Buonaparte.*) This, I confess, sounded to *my* ears, as one of the many good things that *might have been* said. The anecdote is more valuable; for it instances the ways and means of French insinuation. Hoche had received much information concerning the face of the country from a map of unusual fulness and accuracy, the maker of which, he heard, resided at Düsseldorf. At the storming of Düsseldorf by the French army, Hoche previously ordered, that the house and property of this man should be preserved, and intrusted the performance of the order to an officer on whose troop he could rely. Finding afterwards, that the man had escaped before the storming commenced, Hoche exclaimed, "HE had no reason to flee! It is *for* such men, not *against* them, that the French nation makes war, and consents to shed the blood of its children." You remember Milton's sonnet—

> "The great Emathian conqueror bid spare
> The house of Pindarus when temple and tower
> Went to the ground"————————

Now though the Düsseldorf map-maker may stand in the same relation to the Theban bard, as the snail that marks its path by lines of film on the wall it creeps over, to the eagle that soars sunward and beats the tempest with its wings; it does not therefore follow, that the Jacobin of France may not be as valiant a general and as good a politician as the madman of Macedon.

From Professor Ebeling's Mr. Klopstock accompanied my friend and me to his own house where I saw a fine bust of his brother. There was a solemn and heavy greatness in his countenance, which corresponded to my preconceptions of his style and genius.—I saw there, likewise, a very fine portrait of Lessing, whose works are at present the chief object of my admiration. His eyes were uncommonly like mine; if any thing, rather larger and more prominent. But the lower part of his face, and his nose —O what an exquisite expression of elegance and sensibility!— There appeared no depth, weight, or comprehensiveness in the forehead.—The whole face seemed to say, that Lessing was a man of quick and voluptuous feelings; of an active but light fancy; acute; yet acute not in the observation of actual life, but in the arrangements and management of the ideal world, i.e. in taste and in metaphysics. I assure you that I wrote these very words in my memorandum-book with the portrait before my eyes, and when I knew nothing of Lessing but his name, and that he was a German writer of eminence.

We consumed two hours and more over a bad dinner, at the table d'Hôte. "PATIENCE *at a German ordinary, smiling at time.*" The Germans are the worst cooks in Europe. There is placed for every two persons a bottle of common wine—Rhenish and Claret alternately; but in the houses of the opulent, during the many and long intervals of the dinner, the servants hand round glasses of richer wines. At the Lord of Culpin's they came in this order. Burgundy — Madeira — Port — Frontiniac — Pacchiaretti — Old Hock — Mountain — Champagne — Hock again — Bishop, and lastly, Punch. A tolerable quantum, methinks! The last dish at the ordinary, viz. slices of roast pork (for all the larger dishes are brought in, cut up, and first handed round and then set on the table) with stewed prunes and other sweet fruits, and this followed by cheese and butter, with plates of apples, reminded me of Shakespeare,[65] and Shakespeare put it in my head to go to the French comedy.

*   *   *

Bless me! why it is worse than our modern English plays! The first act informed me, that a court martial is to be held on a Count Vatron, who had drawn his sword on the Colonel, his brother-in-law. The officers plead in his behalf—in vain! His wife, the Colonel's sister, pleads with most tempestuous agonies —in vain! She falls into hysterics and faints away, to the dropping of the inner curtain! In the second act sentence of death is passed on the Count—his wife, as frantic and hysterical as before: more so (good industrious creature!) she could not be. The third and last act, the wife still frantic, very frantic indeed! the soldiers just about to fire, the handkerchief actually dropped; when reprieve! reprieve! is heard from behind the scenes: and in comes Prince somebody, pardons the Count, and the wife is still frantic, only with joy; that was all!

O dear lady! this is one of the cases, in which laughter is followed by melancholy: for such is the *kind* of drama, which is now substituted every where for Shakespeare and Racine. You well know, that I offer violence to my own feelings in joining these names. But however meanly I may think of the French serious drama, even in its most perfect specimens; and with whatever right I may complain of its perpetual falsification of the language, and of the connections and transitions of thought, which Nature has appropriated to states of passion; still, however, the French tragedies are consistent works of art, and the offspring of great intellectual power. Preserving a fitness in the parts, and a harmony in the whole, they form a nature of their own, though a false nature. Still, they excite the minds of the spectators to active thought, to a striving after ideal excellence. The soul is not stupefied into mere sensations by a worthless sympathy with our own ordinary sufferings, or an empty curiosity for the surprising, undignified by the language or the situations which awe and delight the imagination. What (I would ask of the crowd, that press forward to the pantomimic tragedies and

[65] "*Slender.* I bruised my shin with playing with sword and dagger for a dish of stewed prunes, and by my troth I cannot abide the smell of hot meat since." So again, *Evans.* "I will make an end of my dinner: there's pippins and cheese yet to come."

weeping comedies of Kotzebue and his imitators) what are you seeking? Is it comedy? But in the comedy of Shakespeare and Molière the more accurate my knowledge, and the more profoundly I think, the greater is the satisfaction that mingles with my laughter. For though the qualities which these writers pourtray are ludicrous indeed, either from the kind or the excess, and exquisitely ludicrous, yet are they the natural growth of the human mind and such as, with more or less change in the drapery, I can apply to my own heart, or at least to whole classes of my fellow-creatures. How often are not the moralist and the metaphysician obliged for the happiest illustrations of general truths and the subordinate laws of human thought and action to quotations, not only from the tragic characters, but equally from the Jaques, Falstaff, and even from the fools and clowns of Shakespeare, or from the Miser, Hypochondriast, and Hypocrite, of Molière! Say not, that I am recommending abstractions: for these class-characteristics, which constitute the instructiveness of a character, are so modified and particularized in each person of the Shakespearean Drama, that life itself does not excite more distinctly that sense of individuality which belongs to real existence. Paradoxical as it may sound, one of the essential properties of geometry is not less essential to dramatic excellence, and, (if I may mention his name without pedantry to a lady,) Aristotle has accordingly required of the poet an involution of the universal in the individual. The chief differences are, that in geometry it is the universal truth itself, which is uppermost in the consciousness, in poetry the individual form in which the Truth is clothed. With the ancients, and not less with the elder dramatists of England and France, both comedy and tragedy were considered as kinds of *poetry*. They neither sought in comedy to make us laugh merely, much less to make us laugh by wry faces, accidents of jargon, slang phrases for the day, or the clothing of commonplace morals in metaphors drawn from the shops or mechanic occupations of their characters; nor did they condescend in tragedy to wheedle away the applause of the spectators, by representing before them fac-similes of their own mean selves in all their existing meanness, or to work on their sluggish sympathies by a pathos not a whit more respectable than the maudlin tears of drunkenness. Their tragic scenes were meant to affect us indeed, but within the bounds of pleasure, and in union with the activity both of our understanding and imagination. They wished to transport the mind to a sense of its possible greatness, and to implant the germs of that greatness during the temporary oblivion of the worthless "thing we are" and of the peculiar state, in which each man *happens* to be; suspending our individual recollections and lulling them to sleep amid the music of nobler thoughts.

Hold! (methinks I hear the spokesman of the crowd reply, and we will listen to him. I am the plaintiff, and be he the defendant.)

DEFENDANT. Hold! are not our modern sentimental plays filled with the best Christian morality?

PLAINTIFF. Yes! just as much of it, and just that part of it, which you can exercise without a single Christian virtue—without a single sacrifice that is really painful to you!—just as much as *flatters* you, sends you away pleased with your own hearts, and quite reconciled to your vices, which can never be thought very ill of, when they keep such good company, and walk hand in hand with so much compassion and generosity; adulation so loathsome, that you would spit in the man's face who dared offer it to you in a private company, unless you interpreted it as insulting irony, you appropriate with infinite satisfaction, when you share the garbage with the whole stye, and gobble it out of a common trough. No Cæsar must pace your boards—no Antony, no royal Dane, no Orestes, no Andromache!—

D. No: or as few of them as possible. What has a plain citizen of London, or Hamburg, to do with your kings and queens, and your old school-boy Pagan heroes? Besides, every body knows the *stories;* and what curiosity can we feel——

P. What, Sir, not for the *manner?* not for the delightful language of the poet? not for the situations, the action and reaction of the passions?

D. You are hasty, Sir! the only curiosity, we feel, is in the story: and how can we be anxious concerning the end of a play, or be surprized by it, when we know how it will turn out?

P. Your pardon, for having interrupted you! we now understand each other. You seek then, in a tragedy, which wise men of old held for the highest effort of human genius, the same gratification, as that you receive from a new novel, the last German romance, and other dainties of the day, which *can* be enjoyed but once. If you carry these feelings to the sister art of Painting, Michael Angelo's Sistine Chapel, and the Scripture Gallery of Raphael can expect no favor from you. *You know all about them beforehand;* and are, doubtless, more familiar with the subjects of those paintings, than with the tragic tales of the historic or heroic ages. There is a consistency, therefore, in your preference of contemporary writers: for the great men of former times, those at least who were deemed great by our ancestors, sought so little to gratify *this kind* of curiosity, that they seemed to have regarded the *story* in a not much higher light, than the painter regards his canvass: as that *on*, not *by*, which they were to display their appropriate excellence. No work, resembling a tale or romance, can well show less variety of invention in the incidents, or less anxiety in weaving them together, than the Don Quixote of Cervantes. Its admirers feel the disposition to go back and reperuse some preceding chapter at least ten times for once that they find any eagerness to hurry forwards: or open the book on those parts which they best recollect, even as we visit those friends oftenest whom we love most, and with whose characters and actions we are the most intimately acquainted. In the divine Ariosto, (as his countrymen call this, their darling poet,) I question whether there be a single *tale* of his own invention, or the elements of which were not familiar to the readers of "old romance." I will pass by the ancient Greeks, who thought it even necessary to the fable of a tragedy, that its substance should be previously known. That there had been at least fifty tragedies with the same title, would be one of the motives which determined Sophocles and Euripides in the choice of Electra as a subject. But Milton—

D. Aye Milton, indeed!—but do not Dr. Johnson and other great men tell us, that nobody now reads Milton but as a task?

P. So much the worse for them, of whom this can be truly said! But why then do you pretend to admire *Shakespeare?* The greater part, if not all, of *his* dramas were, as far as the names and the main incidents are concerned, already stock plays. All the *stories*, at least, on which they are built, pre-existed in the chronicles, ballads, or translations of contemporary or preceding English writers. Why, I repeat, do you pretend to admire *Shakespeare?* Is it, perhaps, that you only *pretend* to admire him? However, as once for all you have dismissed the well-known events and personages of history, or the epic muse, what have you taken in their stead? Whom has *your* tragic muse armed with her bowl and dagger? the sentimental muse I should have said, whom you have seated in the throne of tragedy? What heroes has *she* reared on her buskins?

D. O! our good friends and next-door neighbours—honest tradesmen, valiant tars, high-spirited half-pay officers, philanthropic Jews, virtuous courtezans, tender-hearted braziers, and sentimental rat-catchers! (a little bluff or so, but all our very generous, tender-hearted characters *are* a little rude or misanthropic, and all our misanthropes very tender-hearted).

P. But I pray you, friend, in what actions great or interesting, can such men be engaged?

D. They give away a great deal of money; find rich dowries

for young men and maidens who have all other good qualities; they brow-beat lords, baronets, and justices of the peace, (for they are as bold as Hector!)—they rescue stage coaches at the instant they are falling down precipices; carry away infants in the sight of opposing armies; and some of our performers act a muscular able-bodied man to such perfection, that our dramatic poets, who always have the actors in their eye, seldom fail to make their favorite male character as strong as Samson. And then they take such prodigious leaps!! and what is *done* on the stage is more striking even than what is acted. I once remember such a deafening explosion, that I could not hear a word of the play for half an act after it: and a little real gun-powder being set fire to at the same time, and smelt by all the spectators, the naturalness of the scene was quite astonishing!

P. But how can you connect with such men and such actions that dependence of thousands on the fate of one, which gives so lofty an interest to the personages of Shakespeare, and the Greek Tragedians? How can you connect with them that sublimest of all feelings, the power of destiny and the controlling might of heaven, which seems to elevate the characters which sink beneath its irresistible blow?

D. O mere fancies! We seek and find on the present stage our own wants and passions, our own vexations, losses, and embarrassments.

P. It is your own poor pettifogging nature then, which you desire to have represented before you? not human nature in its height and vigor? But surely you might find the former with all its joys and sorrows, more conveniently in your own houses and parishes.

D. True! but here comes a difference. Fortune is blind, but the poet has his eyes open, and is besides as complaisant as fortune is capricious. He makes every thing turn out exactly as we would wish it. He gratifies us by representing those as hateful or contemptible whom we hate and wish to despise.

P. (*aside.*) That is, he gratifies your envy by libelling your superiors.

D. He makes all those precise moralists, who affect to be better than their neighbours, turn out at last abject hypocrites, traitors, and hard-hearted villains; and your men of spirit, who take their girl and their glass with equal freedom, prove the true men of honor, and (that no part of the audience may remain unsatisfied) reform in the last scene, and leave no doubt on the minds of the ladies, that they will make most faithful and excellent husbands: though it does seem a pity, that they should

be obliged to get rid of qualities which had made them so in-
teresting! Besides, the poor become rich all at once; and in the
final matrimonial choice the opulent and high-born themselves
are made to confess, that VIRTURE IS THE ONLY TRUE NOBILITY,
AND THAT A LOVELY WOMAN IS A DOWRY OF HERSELF!!

P. Excellent! But you have forgotten those brilliant flashes of
loyalty, those patriotic praises of the king and old England,
which, especially if conveyed in a metaphor from the ship or
the shop, so often solicit and so unfailingly receive the public
plaudit; I give your prudence credit for the omission. For the
whole system of your drama is a moral and intellectual *Jacobin-
ism* of the most dangerous kind, and those common-place rants
of loyalty are no better than hypocrisy in your playwrights, and
your own sympathy with them a gross self-delusion. For the
whole secret of dramatic popularity consists with you in the
confusion and subversion of the natural order of things, their
causes and their effects; in the excitement of surprise, by repre-
senting the qualities of liberality, refined feeling, and a nice
sense of honor (those things rather which pass among you for
such) in persons and in classes of life where experience teaches
us least to expect them; and in rewarding with all the sym-
pathies, that are the dues of virtue, those criminals whom law,
reason, and religion have excommunicated from our esteem!

And now good night! Truly! I might have written this last
sheet without having gone to Germany; but I fancied myself
talking to you by your own fireside, and can you think it a
small pleasure to me to forget now and then, that I am *not*
there? Besides, you and my other good friends have made up
your minds to me as I am, and from whatever place I write you
will expect that part of my "Travels" will consist of the excur-
sions in my own mind.

LETTER III

RATZEBURG.

No LITTLE fish thrown back again into the water, no fly unim-
prisoned from a child's hand, could more buoyantly enjoy its
element, than I this clean and peaceful house, with this lovely
view of the town, groves, and lake of Ratzeburg, from the win-
dow at which I am writing. My spirits certainly, and my health
I fancied, were beginning to sink under the noise, dirt, and un-
wholesome air of our Hamburg hotel. I left it on Sunday, Sept.
23rd, with a letter of introduction from the poet Klopstock, to
the Amptman of Ratzeburg. The Amptman received me with

kindness, and introduced me to the worthy pastor, who agreȝ
to board and lodge me for any length of time not less than a
month. The vehicle, in which I took my place, was considerably
larger than an English stage coach, to which it bore much the
same proportion and rude resemblance, that an elephant's ear
does to the human. Its top was composed of naked boards of
different colours, and seeming to have been parts of different
wainscots. Instead of windows there were leathern curtains with
a little eye of glass in each; they perfectly answered the purpose
of keeping out the prospect and letting in the cold. I could
observe little therefore, but the inns and farm houses at which
we stopped. They were all alike, except in size: one great room,
like a barn, with a hay-loft over it, the straw and hay dangling
in tufts through the boards which formed the ceiling of the room,
and the floor of the loft. From this room, which is paved like
a street, sometimes one, sometimes two smaller ones, are en-
closed at one end. These are commonly floored. In the large
room, the cattle, pigs, poultry, men, women, and children, live
in amicable community; yet there was an appearance of cleanli-
ness and rustic comfort. One of these houses I measured. It was
an hundred feet in length. The apartments were taken off from
one corner. Between these and the stalls there was a small inter-
space, and here the breadth was forty-eight feet, but thirty-two
where the stalls were; of course, the stalls were on each side
eight feet in depth. The faces of the cows, &c. were turned
towards the room; indeed they were in it, so that they had at
least the comfort of seeing each other's faces. Stall-feeding is
universal in this part of Germany, a practice concerning which
the agriculturist and the poet are likely to entertain opposite
opinions—or at least, to have very different feelings. The wood-
work of these buildings on the outside is left unplastered, as in
old houses among us, and, being painted red and green, it cuts
and tesselates the buildings very gaily. From within three miles
of Hamburg almost to Molln, which is thirty miles from it, the
country, as far as I could see it, was a dead flat, only varied by
woods. At Molln it became more beautiful. I observed a small
lake nearly surrounded with groves, and a palace in view be-
longing to the King of Great Britain, and inhabited by the In-
spector of the Forests. We were nearly the same time in travelling
the thirty-five miles from Hamburg to Ratzeburg, as we had been
in going from London to Yarmouth, one hundred and twenty-six
miles.

The lake of Ratzeburg runs from south to north, about nine
miles in length, and varying in breadth from three miles to half

a mile. About a mile from the southernmost point it is divided into two, of course very unequal, parts by an island, which, being connected by a bridge and a narrow slip of land, with the one shore, and by another bridge of immense length with the other shore, forms a complete isthmus. On this island the town of Ratzeburg is built. The pastor's house or vicarage, together with the Amptman's, Amptschreiber's, and the church, stands near the summit of a hill, which slopes down to the slip of land and the little bridge, from which, through a superb military gate, you step into the island town of Ratzeburg. This again is itself a little hill, by ascending and descending which, you arrive at the long bridge, and so to the other shore. The water to the south of the town is called the Little Lake, which however almost engrosses the beauties of the whole: the shores being just often enough green and bare to give the proper effect to the magnificent groves which occupy the greater part of their circumference. From the turnings, windings, and indentations of the shore, the views vary almost every ten steps, and the whole has a sort of majestic beauty, a feminine grandeur. At the north of the Great Lake, and peeping over it, I see the seven church towers of Lubec, at the distance of twelve or thirteen miles, yet as distinctly as if they were not three. The only defect in the view is, that Ratzeburg is built entirely of red bricks, and all the houses roofed with red tiles. To the eye, therefore, it presents a clump of brick-dust red. Yet this evening, Oct. 10th, twenty minutes past five, I saw the town perfectly beautiful, and the whole softened down into *complete keeping*, if I may borrow a term from the painters. The sky over Ratzeburg and all the east was a pure evening blue, while over the west it was covered with light sandy clouds. Hence a deep red light spread over the whole prospect, in undisturbed harmony with the red town, the brown-red woods, and the yellow-red reeds on the skirts of the lake. Two or three boats, with single persons paddling them, floated up and down in the rich light, which not only was itself in harmony with all, but brought all into harmony.

I should have told you that I went back to Hamburg on Thursday (Sept. 27th) to take leave of my friend, who travels southward, and returned hither on the Monday following. From Empfelde, a village half way from Ratzeburg, I walked to Hamburg through deep sandy roads and a dreary flat: the soil everywhere white, hungry, and excessively pulverised; but the approach to the city is pleasing. Light cool country houses, which you can look through and see the gardens behind them, with arbours and trellis work, and thick vegetable walls, and trees in cloisters and piazzas, each house with neat rails before it, and green seats within the rails. Every object, whether the growth of nature or the work of man, was neat and artificial. It pleased me far better, than if the houses and gardens, and pleasure fields, had been in a nobler taste: for this nobler taste would have been mere apery. The busy, anxious, money-loving merchant of Hamburg could only have *adopted,* he could not have *enjoyed* the simplicity of nature. The mind begins to love nature by imitating human conveniences in nature; but this is a step in intellect, though a low one—and were it not so, yet all around me spoke of innocent enjoyment and sensitive comforts, and I entered with unscrupulous sympathy into the enjoyments and comforts even of the busy, anxious, money-loving merchants of Hamburg. In this charitable and *catholic* mood I reached the vast ramparts of the city. These are huge green cushions, one rising above the other, with trees growing in the interspaces, pledges and symbols of a long peace. Of my return I have nothing worth communicating, except that I took extra post, which answers to posting in England. These north German post chaises are uncovered wicker carts. An English dust-cart is a piece of finery, a chef d'œuvre of mechanism, compared with them: and the horses! a savage might use their ribs instead of his fingers for a numeration table. Wherever we stopped, the postilion fed his cattle with the brown rye bread of which he eat himself, all breakfasting together; only the horses had no gin to their water, and the postilion no water to his gin. Now and henceforward for subjects of more interest to you, and to the objects in search of which I left you: namely, the literati and literature of Germany.

Believe me, I walked with an impression of awe on my spirits, as W—— and myself accompanied Mr. Klopstock to the house of his brother, the poet, which stands about a quarter of a mile from the city gate. It is one of a row of little common-place summer-houses (for so they looked) with four or five rows of young meagre elm trees before the windows, beyond which is a green, and then a dead flat intersected with several roads. Whatever beauty (thought I) may be before the poet's eyes at present, it must certainly be purely of his own creation. We waited a few minutes in a neat little parlour, ornamented with the figures of two of the Muses and with prints, the subjects of which were from Klopstock's odes. The poet entered. I was much disappointed in his countenance, and recognised in it no likeness to the bust. There was no comprehension in the forehead, no weight over the eye-brows, no expression of peculiarity, moral or intellectual, on the eyes, no massiveness in the general countenance. He is, if anything, rather below the middle size. He wore very large half-boots, which his legs filled, so fearfully were they swoln. However, though neither W—— nor myself could discover any indications of sublimity or enthusiasm in his physiognomy, we were both equally impressed with his liveliness, and his kind and ready courtesy. He talked in French with my friend, and with difficulty spoke a few sentences to me in English. His enunciation was not in the least affected by the entire want of his upper teeth. The conversation began on his part by the expression of his rapture at the surrender of the detachment of French troops under General Humbert. Their proceedings in Ireland with regard to the committee which they had appointed, with the rest of their organizing system, seemed to have given the poet great entertainment. He then declared his sanguine belief in Nelson's victory, and anticipated its confirmation with a keen and triumphant pleasure. His words, tones, looks, implied the most vehement Anti-Gallicanism. The subject changed to literature, and I inquired in Latin concerning the history of German poetry and the elder German poets. To my great astonishment he confessed that he knew very little on the subject. He had indeed occasionally read one or two of their elder writers, but not so as to enable him to speak of their merits. Professor Ebeling, he said, would probably give me every information of this kind: the subject had not particularly excited his curiosity. He then talked of Milton and Glover, and thought Glover's blank verse superior to Milton's. W—— and myself expressed our surprise: and my friend gave his definition and notion of harmonious verse, that it consisted (the English iambic blank verse above all) in the apt arrangement of pauses and cadences, and the sweep of whole paragraphs,

> ——————"with many a winding bout
> Of linked sweetness long drawn out,"

and not in the even flow, much less in the prominence or antithetic vigour, of single lines, which were indeed injurious to the total effect, except where they were introduced for some specific purpose. Klopstock assented, and said that he meant to confine Glover's superiority to single lines. He told us that he had read Milton, in a prose translation, when he was fourteen.[66]

[66] This was accidentally confirmed to me by an old German gentleman at Helmstadt, who had been Klopstock's school and bed-fellow. Among other boyish anecdotes, he related that the young poet set a particular value on a translation of the Paradise Lost, and always slept with it under his pillow.

I understood him thus myself, and W—— interpreted Klopstock's French as I had already construed it. He appeared to know very little of Milton—or indeed of our poets in general. He spoke with great indignation of the English prose translation of his Messiah. All the translations had been bad, very bad—but the English was *no* translation—there were pages on pages not in the original:—and half the original was not to be found in the translation. W—— told him that I intended to translate a few of his odes as specimens of German lyrics—he then said to me in English, "I wish you would render into English some select passages of the Messiah, and *revenge* me of your countryman!" It was the liveliest thing which he produced in the whole conversation. He told us, that his first ode was fifty years older than his last. I looked at him with much emotion—I considered him as the venerable father of German poetry; as a good man; as a Christian; seventy-four years old; with legs enormously swoln; yet active, lively, chearful, and kind, and communicative. My eyes felt as if a tear were swelling into them. In the portrait of Lessing there was a toupee perriwig, which enormously injured the effect of his physiognomy—Klopstock wore the same, powdered and frizzled. By the bye, old men ought never to wear powder—the contrast between a large snow-white wig and the colour of an old man's skin is disgusting, and wrinkles in such a neighbourhood appear only channels for dirt. It is an honor to poets and great men, that you think of them as parts of nature; and anything of trick and fashion wounds you in them, as much as when you see venerable yews clipped into miserable peacocks.—The author of the Messiah should have worn his own grey hair.—His powder and perriwig were to the eye what Mr. Virgil would be to the ear.

Klopstock dwelt much on the superior power which the German language possessed of concentrating meaning. He said, he had often translated parts of Homer and Virgil, line by line, and a German line proved always sufficient for a Greek or Latin one. In English you cannot do this. I answered, that in English we could commonly render one Greek heroic line in a line and a half of our common heroic metre, and I conjectured that this line and a half would be found to contain no more syllables than one German or Greek hexameter. He did not understand me:[67]

[67] Klopstock's observation was partly true and partly erroneous. In the literal sense of his words, and, if we confine the comparison to the average of space required for the expression of the same thought in the two languages, it is erroneous. I have translated some German hexameters into English hexameters, and find, that on the average

and, I, who wished to hear his opinions, not to correct them, was glad that he did not.

We now took our leave. At the beginning of the French Revolution Klopstock wrote odes of congratulation. He received some honorary presents from the French Republic, (a golden crown I believe), and, like our Priestley, was invited to a seat in the legislature, which he declined. But when French liberty metamorphosed herself into a fury, he sent back these presents with a palinodia, declaring his abhorrence of their proceedings: and since then he has been perhaps more than enough an Anti-Gallican. I mean, that in his just contempt and detestation of

---

three English lines will express four lines German. The reason is evident: our language abounds in monosyllables and dissyllables. The German, not less than the Greek, is a polysyllable language. But in another point of view the remark was not without foundation. For the German possessing the same unlimited privilege of forming compounds, both with prepositions and with epithets, as the Greek, it can express the richest single Greek word in a single German one, and is thus freed from the necessity of weak or ungraceful paraphrases. I will content myself with one example at present, viz. the use of the prefixed participles *ver, zer, ent,* and *weg:* thus reissen to rend, verreissen to rend away, zerreissen to rend to pieces, entreissen to rend off or out of a thing, in the active sense: or schmelzen to melt—*ver, zer, ent, schmelzen*—and in the like manner through all the verbs neuter and active. If you consider only how much we should feel the loss of the prefix *be,* as in bedropt, besprinkle, besot, especially in our poetical language, and then think that this same mode of composition is carried through all their simple and compound prepositions, and many of their adverbs; and that with most of these the Germans have the same privilege as we have of dividing them from the verb and placing them at the end of the sentence; you will have no difficulty in comprehending the reality and the cause of this superior power in the German of condensing meaning, in which its great poet exulted. It is impossible to read half a dozen pages of Wieland without perceiving that in this respect the German has no rival but the Greek. And yet I feel, that concentration or condensation is not the happiest mode of expressing this excellence, which seems to consist not so much in the less time required for conveying an impression, as in the unity and simultaneousness with which the impression is conveyed. It tends to make their language more picturesque: it *depictures* images better. We have obtained this power in part by our compound verbs derived from the Latin: and the sense of its great effect no doubt induced our Milton both to the use and the abuse of Latin derivatives. But still these prefixed particles, conveying no separate or separable meaning to the mere English reader, cannot possibly act on the mind with the force or liveliness of an original and homogeneous language such as the German is, and besides are confined to certain words.

the crimes and follies of the Revolutionists, he suffers himself to forget that the Revolution itself is a process of the Divine Providence; and that as the folly of men is the wisdom of God, so are their iniquities instruments of his goodness. From Klopstock's house we walked to the ramparts, discoursing together on the poet and his conversation, till our attention was diverted to the beauty and singularity of the sunset and its effects on the objects around us. There were woods in the distance. A rich sandy light (nay, of a much deeper colour than sandy) lay over these woods, that blackened in the blaze. Over that part of the woods, which lay immediately under the intenser light, a brassy mist floated. The trees on the ramparts, and the people moving to and fro between them, were cut or divided into equal segments of deep shade and brassy light. Had the trees, and the bodies of the men and women, been divided into equal segments by a rule or pair of compasses, the portions could not have been more regular. All else was obscure. It was a fairy scene! and to encrease its romantic character, among the moving objects, thus divided into alternate shade and brightness, was a beautiful child, dressed with the elegant simplicity of an English child, riding on a stately goat, the saddle, bridle, and other accoutrements of which were in a high degree costly and splendid. Before I quit the subject of Hamburg, let me say, that I remained a day or two longer than I otherwise should have done, in order to be present at the feast of St. Michael, the patron saint of Hamburg, expecting to see the civic pomp of this commercial Republic. I was however disappointed. There were no processions, two or three sermons were preached to two or three old women in two or three churches, and St. Michael and his patronage wished elsewhere by the higher classes, all places of entertainment, theatre, &c. being shut up on this day. In Hamburg, there seems to be no religion at all; in Lubec it is confined to the women. The men seemed determined to be divorced from their wives in the other world, if they cannot in this. You will not easily conceive a more singular sight, than is presented by the vast aisle of the principal church at Lubec, seen from the organ loft: for being filled with female servants and persons in the same class of life, and all their caps having gold and silver cauls, it appears like a rich pavement of gold and silver.

I will conclude this letter with the mere transcription of notes, which my friend W—— made of his conversations with Klopstock, during the interviews that took place after my departure. On these I shall make but one remark at present, and that will appear a presumptuous one, namely, that Klopstock's

remarks on the venerable sage of Koenigsberg are to my own
knowledge injurious and mistaken; and so far is it from being
true, that his system is now given up, that throughout the
Universities of Germany there is not a single professor who is
not either a Kantean, or a disciple of Fichte, whose system is
built on the Kantean, and pre-supposes its truth; or lastly, who,
though an antagonist of Kant, as to his theoretical work, has not
embraced wholly or in part his moral system, and adopted part
of his nomenclature. "Klopstock having wished to see the Calvary
of Cumberland, and asked what was thought of it in England,
I went to Remnant's (the English bookseller) where I procured
the Analytical Review, in which is contained the review of
Cumberland's Calvary. I remembered to have read there some
specimens of a blank verse translation of the Messiah. I had
mentioned this to Klopstock, and he had a great desire to see
them. I walked over to his house and put the book into his hands.
On adverting to his own poem, he told me he began the Messiah
when he was seventeen: he devoted three entire years to the
plan without composing a single line. He was greatly at a loss
in what manner to execute his work. There were no successful
specimens of versification in the German language before this
time. The first three cantos he wrote in a species of measured
or numerous prose. This, though done with much labor and some
success, was far from satisfying him. He had composed hexam-
eters both Latin and Greek as a school exercise, and there had
been also in the German language attempts in that style of
versification. These were only of very moderate merit.—One day
he was struck with the idea of what could be done in this way—
he kept his room a whole day, even went without his dinner, and
found that in the evening he had written twenty-three hexam-
eters, versifying a part of what he had before written in prose.
From that time, pleased with his efforts, he composed no more in
prose. To-day he informed me that he had finished his plan
before he read Milton. He was enchanted to see an author who
before him had trod the same path. This is a contradiction of
what he said before. He did not wish to speak of his poem to
any one till it was finished: but some of his friends who had seen
what he had finished, tormented him till he had consented to
publish a few books in a journal. He was then, I believe, very
young, about twenty-five. The rest was printed at different pe-
riods, four books at a time. The reception given to the first
specimens was highly flattering. He was nearly thirty years in
finishing the whole poem, but of these thirty years not more
than two were employed in the composition. He only composed

in favorable moments; besides he had other occupations. He values himself upon the plan of his odes, and accuses the modern lyrical writers of gross deficiency in this respect. I laid the same accusation against Horace: he would not hear of it— but waived the discussion. He called Rousseau's Ode to Fortune a moral dissertation in stanzas. I spoke of Dryden's St. Cecilia; but he did not seem familiar with our writers. He wished to know the distinctions between our dramatic and epic blank verse. He recommended me to read his Hermann before I read either The Messiah or the odes. He flattered himself that some time or other his dramatic poems would be known in England. He had not heard of Cowper. He thought that Voss in his translation of the Iliad had done violence to the idiom of the Germans, and had sacrificed it to the Greeks, not remembering sufficiently that each language has its particular spirit and genius. He said Lessing was the first of their dramatic writers. I complained of Nathan as tedious. He said there was not enough of action in it; but that Lessing was the most chaste of their writers. He spoke favourably of Goethe; but said that his 'Sorrows of Werter' was his best work, better than any of his dramas: he preferred the first written to the rest of Goethe's dramas. Schiller's 'Robbers' he found so extravagant, that he could not read it. I spoke of the scene of the setting sun. He did not know it. He said Schiller could not live. He thought Don Carlos the best of his dramas; but said that the plot was inextricable.—It was evident he knew little of Schiller's works: indeed, he said, he could not read them. Bürger, he said, was a true poet, and would live; that Schiller, on the contrary, must soon be forgotten; that he gave himself up to the imitation of Shakespeare, who often was extravagant, but that Schiller was ten thousand times more so. He spoke very slightingly of Kotzebue, as an immoral author in the first place, and next, as deficient in power. At Vienna, said he, they are transported with him; but we do not reckon the people of Vienna either the wisest or the wittiest people of Germany. He said Wieland was a charming author, and a sovereign master of his own language: that in this respect Goethe could not be compared to him, nor indeed could any body else. He said that his fault was to be fertile to exuberance. I told him the Oberon had just been translated into English. He asked me if I was not delighted with the poem. I answered, that I thought the story began to flag about the seventh or eighth book; and observed, that it was unworthy of a man of genius to make the interest of a long poem turn entirely upon animal gratification. He seemed at first disposed to excuse this by saying, that there are different subjects for poetry, and that poets are not willing to be restricted in their choice. I answered, that I thought the *passion* of love as well suited to the purposes of poetry as any other passion; but that it was a cheap way of pleasing to fix the attention of the reader through a long poem on the mere *appetite*. Well! but, said he, you see, that such poems please every body. I answered, that it was the province of a great poet to raise people up to his own level, not to descend to theirs. He agreed, and confessed, that on no account whatsoever would he have written a work like the Oberon. He spoke in raptures of Wieland's style, and pointed out the passage where Retzia is delivered of her child, as exquisitely beautiful. I said that I did not perceive any very striking passages; but that I made allowance for the imperfections of a translation. Of the thefts of Wieland, he said, they were so exquisitely managed, that the greatest writers might be proud to steal as he did. He considered the books and fables of old romance writers in the light of the ancient mythology, as a sort of common property, from which a man was free to take whatever he could make a good use of. An Englishman had presented him with the Odes of Collins, which he had read with pleasure. He knew little or nothing of Gray, except his Elegy in the Churchyard. He complained of the fool in Lear. I observed that he seemed to give a terrible wildness to the distress; but still he complained. He asked whether it was not allowed, that Pope had written rhymed poetry with more skill than any of our writers— I said I preferred Dryden, because his couplets had greater variety in their movement. He thought my reason a good one; but asked whether the rhymes of Pope were not more exact. This question I understood as applying to the final terminations, and observed to him that I believed it was the case; but that I thought it was easy to excuse some inaccuracy in the final sounds, if the general sweep of the verse was superior. I told him that we were not so exact with regard to the final endings of the lines as the French. He did not seem to know that we made no distinction between masculine and feminine (i.e. single or double) rhymes: at least he put inquiries to me on this subject. He seemed to think that no language could ever be so far formed as that it might not be enriched by idioms borrowed from another tongue. I said this was a very dangerous practice; and added, that I thought Milton had often injured both his prose and verse by taking this liberty too frequently. I recommended to him the prose works of Dryden as models of pure and native English. I was treading upon tender ground, as I have reason to suppose that he has himself liberally indulged in the practice.

The same day I dined at Mr. Klopstock's, where I had the pleasure of a third interview with the poet. We talked principally about indifferent things. I asked him what he thought of Kant. He said that his reputation was much on the decline in Germany. That for his own part he was not surprised to find it so, as the works of Kant were to him utterly incomprehensible—that he had· often been pestered by the Kanteans, but was rarely in the practice of arguing with them. His custom was to produce the book, open it and point to a passage, and beg they would explain it. This they ordinarily attempted to do by substituting their own ideas. I do not want, I say, an explanation of your own ideas, but of the passage which is before us. In this way I generally bring the dispute to an immediate conclusion. He spoke of Wolf as the first Metaphysician they had in Germany. Wolf had followers; but they could hardly be called a sect, and luckily till the appearance of Kant, about fifteen years ago, Germany had not been pestered by any sect of philosophers whatsoever; but that each man had separately pursued his enquiries uncontrolled by the dogmas of a Master. Kant had appeared ambitious to be the founder of a sect; that he had succeeded: but that the Germans were now coming to their senses again. That Nicolai and Engel had in different ways contributed to disenchant the nation; but above all the incomprehensibility of the philosopher and his philosophy. He seemed pleased to hear, that as yet Kant's doctrines had not met with many admirers in England—did not doubt but that we had too much wisdom to be duped by a writer who set at defiance the common sense and common understandings of men. We talked of tragedy. He seemed to rate highly the power of exciting tears—I said that nothing was more easy than to deluge an audience, that it was done every day by the meanest writers."

I must remind you, my friend, first, that these notes are not intended as specimens of Klopstock's intellectual power, or even "*colloquial prowess*," to judge of which by an accidental conversation, and this with strangers, and those too foreigners, would be not only unreasonable, but calumnious. Secondly, I attribute little other interest to the remarks than what is derived from the celebrity of the person who made them. Lastly, if you ask me, whether I have read the Messiah, and what I think of it? I answer —as yet the first four books only: and as to my opinion (the reasons of which hereafter) you may guess it from what I could not help muttering to myself, when the good pastor this morning ωλu me, that Klopstock was the German Milton——"a very *German* Milton indeed!!!"——Heaven preserve you, and

S. T. Coleridge.

CHAPTER XXIII

"Quid quod præfatione præmunierim libellum, quâ conor omnem offendiculi ansam præcidere? Neque quicquam addubito, quin ea candidis omnibus faciat satis. Quid autem facias istis, qui vel ob ingenii pertinaciam sibi satisfieri nolint, vel stupidiores sint, quam ut satisfactionem intelligant? Nam quemadmodum Simonides dixit, Thessalos hebetiores esse, quam ut possint a se decipi, ita quosdam videas stupidiores, quam ut placari queant. Adhæc, non mirum est, invenire quod calumnietur, qui nihil aliud quærit, nisi quod calumnietur."

Erasmus ad Dorpium Theologum.

In the rifacciamento of The Friend, I have inserted extracts from the Conciones ad Populum, printed, though scarcely published, in the year 1795, in the very heat and height of my anti-ministerial enthusiasm: these in proof that my principles of *politics* have sustained no change.—In the present chapter, I have annexed to my Letters from Germany, with particular reference to that, which contains a disquisition on the modern drama, a critique on the Tragedy of Bertram, written within the last twelve months: in proof, that I have been as falsely charged with any fickleness in my principles of *taste*.—The letter was written to a friend: and the apparent abruptness with which it begins, is owing to the omission of the introductory sentences.

You remember, my dear Sir, that Mr. Whitbread, shortly before his death, proposed to the assembled subscribers of Drury-Lane Theatre, that the concern should be farmed to some responsible individual under certain conditions and limitations: and that his proposal was rejected, not without indignation, as subversive of the main object, for the attainment of which the enlightened and patriotic assemblage of philo-dramatists had been induced to risk their subscriptions. Now this object was avowed to be no less than the redemption of the British stage not only from horses, dogs, elephants, and the like zoological rarities, but also from the more pernicious barbarisms and Kotzebuisms in morals and taste. Drury Lane was to be restored to its former classical renown; Shakespeare, Jonson, and Otway, with the expurgated muses of Vanbrugh, Congreve, and Wycherley, were to be reinaugurated in their rightful dominion over British audiences; and the Herculean process was to commence, by exterminating the speaking monsters imported from the banks of the Danube, compared with which their mute relations, the emigrants from Exeter 'Change, and Polito's (late Pidcock's) show-carts, were tame and inoffensive. Could an heroic project, at once so refined and so arduous, be consistently entrusted to, could its success be rationally expected from, a mercenary manager, at whose critical quarantine the *lucri bonus odor* would conciliate a bill of health to the plague in person? No! As the work proposed, such must be the work-masters. Rank, fortune, liberal education, and (their natural accompaniments, or consequences) critical discernment, delicate tact, disinterestedness, unsuspected morals, notorious patriotism, and tried Mæcenasship, these were the recommendations that influenced the votes of the proprietary subscribers of Drury Lane Theatre, these the motives that occasioned the election of its Supreme Committee of Management. This circumstance alone would have excited a strong interest in the public mind, respecting the first production of the Tragic Muse which had been announced under such auspices, and had passed the ordeal of such judgements; and the Tragedy, on which you have requested my judgement, was the work on which the great expectations, justified by so many causes, were doomed at length to settle.

But before I enter on the examination of *Bertram, or the Castle of St. Aldobrand,* I shall interpose a few words, on the phrase *German Drama,* which I hold to be altogether a misnomer. At the time of Lessing, the German stage, such as it was, appears to have been a flat and servile copy of the French. It was Lessing who first introduced the name and the works of Shakespeare to the admiration of the Germans; and I should not perhaps go too far, if I add, that it was Lessing who first proved to all thinking men, even to Shakespeare's own countrymen, the true nature of his apparent irregularities. These, he demonstrated, were deviations only from the *accidents* of the Greek tragedy; and from such accidents as hung a heavy weight on the wings of the Greek poets, and narrowed their flight within the limits of what we may call the *Heroic Opera.* He proved that in all the essentials of art, no less than in the truth of nature, the plays of Shakespeare were incomparably more coincident with the principles of Aristotle, than the productions of Corneille and Racine, notwithstanding the boasted regularity of the latter. Under these convictions were Lessing's own dramatic works composed. Their deficiency is in depth and imagination; their excellence is in the construction of the plot; the good sense of the sentiments; the sobriety of the morals; and the high polish of the diction and dialogue. In short, his dramas are the very antipodes of all those which it has been the fashion of late years at once to abuse and enjoy, under the name of the German Drama. Of this latter, Schiller's *Robbers* was the earliest specimen; the first fruits of his youth (I had almost said of his boyhood) and, as such, the pledge and promise of no ordinary genius. Only as *such* did the mature judgement of the author tolerate the Play. During his whole life he expressed himself concerning this production with more than needful asperity, as a monster not less offensive to good taste, than to sound morals; and, in his latter years, his indignation at the unwonted popularity of the *Robbers* seduced him into the *contrary* extremes, viz. a studied feebleness of interest, (as far as the interest was to be derived from incidents and the excitement of curiosity); a diction elaborately metrical; the affectation of rhymes; and the pedantry of the chorus.

But to understand the true character of the ROBBERS, and of the countless imitations which were its spawn, I must inform you, or at least call to your recollection, that, about that time, and for some years before it, three of the most popular books in the German language were the translations of *Young's Night Thoughts, Hervey's Meditations,* and *Richardson's Clarissa Harlow.* Now we have only to combine the bloated style and peculiar rhythm of Hervey, which is poetic only on account of its utter unfitness for prose, and might as appropriately be called prosaic, from its utter unfitness for poetry; we have only, I repeat, to combine these Herveyisms with the strained thoughts, the figurative metaphysics, and solemn epigrams of Young on the one hand; and with the loaded sensibility, the minute detail, the morbid consciousness of every thought and feeling in the whole flux and reflux of the mind, in short the self-involution and dreamlike continuity of Richardson on the other hand; and then to add the horrific incidents, and mysterious villains (geniuses of supernatural intellect, if you will take the author's word for it, but on a level with the meanest ruffians of the condemned cells, if we are to judge by their actions and contrivances) to add the ruined castles, the dungeons, the trap-doors, the skeletons, the flesh-and-blood ghosts, and the perpetual moonshine of a modern author (themselves the literary brood of the *Castle of Otranto,* the translations of which, with the imitations and improvements aforesaid, were about that time beginning to make as much noise in Germany as their originals were making in England) and, as the compound of these ingredients duly mixed, you will recognize the so called *German* drama. The *Olla Podrida* thus cooked up was denounced by the best critics in Germany as the mere cramps of weakness and orgasms of a sickly imagination on the part of the author, and the lowest provocation of torpid feeling on that of the readers. The old blunder, however, concerning the irregularity and wildness of Shakespeare, in which the German did but echo the French, who again were but the echoes of our own critics, was still in vogue, and Shakespeare was quoted as authority for the most anti-Shakespearean drama. We have indeed two poets who wrote as one, near the age of Shakespeare, to whom, (as the worst characteristic of their writings) the Coryphæus of the present drama may challenge the honor of being a poor relation, or impoverished descendant. For if we would charitably consent to forget the comic humour, the wit, the felicities of style, in other words, *all* the poetry, and nine-tenths of all the genius of Beaumont and Fletcher, that which would remain becomes a Kotzebue.

The so called *German* drama, therefore, is *English* in its *origin*, *English* in its *materials*, and *English* by re-adoption; and till we can prove that Kotzebue, or any of the whole breed of Kotzebues, whether dramatists, or romantic writers, or writers of romantic dramas, were ever admitted to any other shelf in the libraries of well-educated Germans than were occupied by their originals and apes' apes in their mother country, we should submit to carry our own brat on our own shoulders; or rather consider it as a lack-grace returned from transportation with such improvements only in growth and manners as young transported convicts usually come home with.

I know nothing that contributes more to a clearer insight into the true nature of any literary phenomenon, than the comparison of it with some elder production, the *likeness* of which is *striking*, yet only *apparent*, while the *difference* is *real*. In the present case this opportunity is furnished us, by the old Spanish play, entitled *Atheista Fulminato*, formerly, and perhaps still, acted in the churches and monasteries of Spain, and which, under various names (*Don Juan, the Libertine, &c.*) has had its day of favor in every country throughout Europe. A popularity so extensive, and of a work so grotesque and extravagant, claims and merits philosophical attention and investigation. The first point to be noticed is, that the play is throughout *imaginative*. Nothing of it belongs to the real world, but the names of the places and persons. The comic parts, equally with the tragic; the living, equally with the defunct characters, are creatures of the brain; as little amenable to the rules of ordinary probability, as the *Satan* of *Paradise Lost*, or the *Caliban* of *the Tempest*, and therefore to be understood and judged of as impersonated *abstractions.* Rank, fortune, wit, talent, acquired knowledge, and liberal accomplishments, with beauty of person, vigorous health, and constitutional hardihood,—all these advantages, elevated by the habits and sympathies of noble birth and national character, are supposed to have combined in *Don Juan,* so as to give him the means of carrying into all its *practical* consequences the doctrine of a godless nature, as the sole ground and efficient cause not only of all things, events, and appearances, but likewise of all our thoughts, sensations, impulses and actions. Obedience to nature is the only virtue: the gratification of the passions and appetites her only dictate: each individual's self-will the sole organ through which nature utters her commands, and

> "Self-contradiction is the only wrong!
> For, by the laws of spirit, in the right
> Is every individual character
> That acts in strict consistence with itself."

That speculative opinions, however impious and daring they may be, are not always followed by correspondent conduct, is most true, as well as that they can scarcely in any instance be *systematically* realized, on account of their unsuitableness to human nature and to the institutions of society. It can be hell, only where it is *all* hell; and a separate world of devils is necessary for the existence of any one complete devil. But on the other hand it is no less clear, nor, with the biography of Carrier and his fellow-atheists before us, can it be denied without wilful blindness, that the (so called) *system of nature* (i.e. materialism, with the utter rejection of moral responsibility, of a present providence, and of both present and future retribution) may influence the characters and actions of individuals, and even of communities, to a degree that almost does away the distinction between men and devils, and will make the page of the future historian resemble the narration of a madman's dreams. It is not the *wickedness* of *Don Juan,* therefore, which constitutes the character an *abstraction,* and removes it from the rules of probability; but the rapid succession of the correspondent acts and incidents, his intellectual superiority, and the splendid accumulation of his gifts and desireable qualities, as co-existent with entire wickedness in one and the same person. But this likewise is the very circumstance which gives to this strange play its charm and universal interest. *Don Juan* is, from beginning to end, an *intelligible* character: as much so as the *Satan* of Milton. The poet asks only of the reader, what, as a poet, he is privileged to ask: namely, that sort of negative faith in the existence of such a being, which we willingly give to productions *professedly ideal*, and a disposition to the same state of feeling, as that with which we contemplate the *idealized* figures of the Apollo Belvedere, and the Farnese Hercules. What the Hercules is to the *eye* in *corporeal* strength, *Don Juan* is to the *mind* in strength of *character*. The ideal consists in the happy balance of the generic with the individual. The former makes the character representative and symbolical, therefore instructive; because, *mutatis mutandis*, it *is* applicable to whole classes of men. The latter gives it *living* interest; for nothing *lives* or is *real*, but as definite and individual. To understand this completely, the reader need only recollect the specific state of his feelings, when in looking at a picture of the historic (more properly of the poetic or heroic) class, he objects to a particular figure as being too much of a *portrait;* and this interruption of his complacency he feels without the least reference to, or the least acquaintance with, any person in real life whom he might recognise in this figure. It is enough that such a figure is not ideal: and therefore not ideal, because one of the two factors or elements of the ideal is in excess. A similar and more powerful objection he would feel towards a set of figures which were *mere* abstractions, like those of Cipriani, and what have been called Greek forms and faces, i.e. outlines drawn according to a recipe. *These* again are not *ideal;* because in these the other element is in excess. *"Forma formans per formam formatam translucens,"* is the definition and perfection of *ideal* art.

This excellence is so happily achieved in the *Don Juan*, that it is capable of interesting without poetry, nay, even without words, as in our pantomime of that name. We see clearly how the character is formed; and the very extravagance of the incidents, and the super-human *entireness* of *Don Juan's* agency, prevents the wickedness from shocking our minds to any painful degree. (We do not *believe* it enough for this effect; no, not even with that kind of temporary and negative belief or acquiescence which I have described above.) Meantime the qualities of his character are too desireable, too flattering to our pride and our wishes, not to make up on this side as much additional faith as was lost on the other. There is no danger (thinks the spectator or reader) of *my* becoming such a monster of iniquity as *Don Juan! I* never shall be an atheist! *I* shall never disallow all distinction between right and wrong! *I* have not the least inclination to be so outrageous a drawcansir in my love affairs! But to possess such a power of captivating and enchanting the affections of the other sex!—to be capable of inspiring in a charming and even a virtuous woman, a love so deep, and so entirely personal to *me!*—that even my worst vices (if I *were* vicious), even my cruelty and perfidy (if I *were* cruel and perfidious), could not eradicate the passion! to be so loved for my *own self*, that even with a distinct knowledge of my character, she yet died to save me! this, sir, takes hold of two sides of our nature, the better and the worse. For the heroic disinterestedness, to which love can transport a woman, can not be contemplated without an honourable emotion of reverence towards womanhood: and, on the other hand, it is among the miseries, and abides in the dark ground-work of our nature, to crave an outward confirmation of that *something* within us, which is our *very self*, that something, not *made up* of our qualities and relations, but itself the supporter and substantial basis of all these. Love *me,* and not my qualities, may be a vicious and an insane wish, but it is not a wish wholly without a meaning.

Without power, virtue would be insufficient and incapable of revealing its being. It would resemble the magic transformation of Tasso's heroine into a tree, in which she could only groan and bleed. Hence power is necessarily an object of our desire and of our admiration. But of all power, that of the mind is, on every account, the grand desideratum of human ambition. We shall be as Gods in knowledge, was and must have been the *first* temptation: and the co-existence of great intellectual lordship with guilt has never been adequately represented without exciting the strongest interest, and for this reason, that in this bad and heterogeneous co-ordination we can contemplate the intellect of man more exclusively as a separate self-subsistence, than in its proper state of subordination to his own conscience, or to the will of an infinitely superior being.

This is the sacred charm of Shakespeare's male characters in general. They are all cast in the mould of Shakespeare's own gigantic intellect; and this is the open attraction of his *Richard, Iago, Edmund,* &c. in particular. But again; of all intellectual power, that of superiority to the fear of the invisible world is the most dazzling. Its influence is abundantly proved by the one circumstance, that it can bribe us into a voluntary submission of our better knowledge, into suspension of all our judgement derived from constant experience, and enable us to peruse with the liveliest interest the wildest tales of ghosts, wizards, genii, and secret talismans. On this propensity, so deeply rooted in our nature, a specific *dramatic* probability may be raised by a true poet, if the whole of his work be in harmony: a *dramatic* probability, sufficient for dramatic pleasure, even when the component characters and incidents border on impossibility. The poet does not require us to be awake and believe; he solicits us only to yield ourselves to a dream; and this too with our eyes open, and with our judgement *perdue* behind the curtain, ready to awaken us at the first motion of our will: and meantime, only, not to *dis-believe*. And in such a state of mind, who but must be impressed with the cool intrepidity of *Don John* on the appearance of his father's ghost:

GHOST.—Monster! behold these wounds!

D. JOHN.—I do! They were well meant, and well performed, I see.

GHOST.——Repent, repent of all thy villanies.
My clamorous blood to heaven for vengeance cries,
Heaven will pour out his judgements on you all.
Hell gapes for you, for you each fiend doth call,
And hourly waits your unrepenting fall.
You with eternal horrors they'll torment,
Except of all your crimes you suddenly repent.   (Ghost sinks.)

D. JOHN.—Farewell, thou art a foolish ghost. Repent, quoth he! what could this mean? Our senses are all in a mist, sure.

D. ANTONIO.—(one of D. Juan's reprobate companions.) They are not! 'Twas a ghost.

D. LOPEZ.—(another reprobate.) I ne'er believed those foolish tales before.

D. JOHN.—Come! 'Tis no matter. Let it be what it will, it must be natural.

D. ANT.—And nature is unalterable in us too.

D. JOHN.—'Tis true! The nature of a ghost can not change ours.

Who also can deny a portion of sublimity to the tremendous consistency with which he stands out the last fearful trial, like a second Prometheus?

Chorus of Devils.

STATUE-GHOST.—Will you not relent and feel remorse?

D. JOHN.—Could'st thou bestow another heart on me I might. But with this heart I have, I can not.

D. LOPEZ.—These things are prodigious.

D. ANTON.—I have a sort of grudging to relent, but something holds me back.

D. LOP.—If we could, 'tis now too late. I will not.

D. ANT.—We defy thee!

GHOST.—Perish, ye impious wretches, go and find the punishments laid up in store for you!
     (Thunder and lightning. D. LOP. and D. ANT. are swallowed up.)

GHOST TO D. JOHN.—Behold their dreadful fates, and know that thy last moment's come!

D. JOHN.—Think not to fright me, foolish ghost; I'll break your marble body in pieces and pull down your horse.
        (Thunder and lightning—chorus of devils, &c.)

D. JOHN.—These things I see with wonder, but no fear.

Were all the elements to be confounded,
And shuffled all into their former chaos;
Were seas of sulphur flaming round about me,
And all mankind roaring within those fires,
I could not fear, or feel the least remorse.
To the last instant I would dare thy power.
Here I stand firm, and all thy threats contemn.
Thy murderer (*to the ghost of one whom he had murdered*) stands
here! Now do thy worst! (*He is swallowed up in a cloud of fire.*)

In fine the character of *Don John* consists in the union of
every thing desireable to human nature, as *means,* and which
therefore by the well known law of association become at length
desireable on their own account. On their own account, and,
in their own dignity, they are here displayed, as being employed
to *ends* so *un*human, that in the effect they appear almost as
means without an *end.* The ingredients too are mixed in the
happiest proportion, so as to uphold and relieve each other—
more especially in that constant interpoise of wit, gaiety, and
social generosity, which prevents the criminal, even in his most
atrocious moments, from sinking into the mere ruffian, as far,
at least, as our *imagination* sits in judgement. Above all, the fine
suffusion, through the whole, with the characteristic manners and
feelings of a highly-bred gentleman gives life to the drama. Thus
having invited the *statue-ghost* of the governor, whom he had
murdered, to supper, which invitation the marble ghost accepted
by a nod of the head, *Don John* has prepared a banquet.

D. JOHN.—Some wine, sirrah! Here's to Don Pedro's ghost—he
should have been welcome.
D. LOP.—The rascal is afraid of you after death.
(*One knocks hard at the door.*)
D. JOHN.—(*to the servant*)—Rise and do your duty.
SERV.—Oh the devil, the devil! (*marble ghost enters.*)
D. JOHN.—Ha! 'tis the ghost! Let's rise and receive him!
Come, Governor, you are welcome, sit there; if we had thought you
would have come, we would have staid for you.

    ❋   ❋   ❋   ❋   ❋   ❋

Here, Governor, your health! Friends, put it about! Here's excellent
meat, taste of this ragout. Come, I'll help you, come, eat, and let old
quarrels be forgotten. (*The ghost threatens him with vengeance.*)
D. JOHN.—We are too much confirmed—curse on this dry dis-
course. Come, here's to your mistress, you had one when you were
living: not forgetting your sweet sister. (*devils enter.*)
D. JOHN.—Are these some of your retinue? Devils, say you? I'm
sorry I have no burnt brandy to treat 'em with, that's drink fit for
devils, &c.

Nor is the scene, from which we quote, interesting in *dramatic* probability alone; it is susceptible likewise of a sound moral; of a moral that has more than common claims on the notice of a too numerous class, who are ready to receive the qualities of gentlemanly courage, and scrupulous honor (in all the recognised laws of honor) as the *substitutes* of virtue, instead of its *ornaments.* This, indeed, is the moral value of the play at large, and that which places it at a world's distance from the spirit of modern Jacobinism. The latter introduces to us clumsy copies of these showy instrumental qualities, in order to *reconcile* us to vice and want of principle; while the *Atheista Fulminato* presents an exquisite portraiture of the same qualities, in all their gloss and glow, but presents them for the sole purpose of displaying their hollowness, and in order to put us on our guard by demonstrating their utter indifference to vice and virtue, whenever these and the like accomplishments are contemplated for themselves alone.

Eighteen years ago I observed, that the whole secret of the modern Jacobinical drama (which, and not the German, is its appropriate designation) and of all its popularity, consists in the confusion and subversion of the natural order of things in their causes and effects: namely, in the excitement of surprise by representing the qualities of liberality, refined feeling, and a nice sense of honor (those things rather which pass amongst us for such) in persons and in classes where experience teaches us least to expect them; and by rewarding with all the sympathies which are the due of virtue, those criminals whom law, reason, and religion have excommunicated from our esteem.

This of itself would lead me back to *Bertram,* or the *Castle of St. Aldobrand;* but, in my own mind, this tragedy was brought into connection with the *Libertine* (Shadwell's adaptation of the *Atheista Fulminato* to the English stage in the reign of Charles the Second) by the fact, that our modern drama is taken, in the substance of it, from the first scene of the third act of the *Libertine.* But with what palpable superiority of judgement in the original! Earth and hell, men and spirits, are up in arms against Don John; the two former acts of the play have not only prepared us for the supernatural, but accustomed us to the prodigious. It is, therefore, neither more nor less than we anticipate, when the Captain exclaims: "In all the dangers I have been, such horrors I never knew. I am quite unmanned:" and when the Hermit says, that he had "beheld the ocean in wildest rage, yet ne'er before saw a storm so dreadful; such horrid flashes of lightning, and such claps of thunder, were never in my remembrance." And

Don John's burst of startling impiety is equally intelligible in its motive, as dramatic in its effect.

But what is there to account for the prodigy of the tempest at *Bertram's* shipwreck? It is a mere supernatural effect, without even a hint of any supernatural agency; a prodigy, without any circumstance mentioned that is prodigious; and a miracle introduced without a ground, and ending without a result. Every event and every scene of the play might have taken place as well if Bertram and his vessel had been driven in by a common hard gale, or from want of provisions. The first act would have indeed lost its greatest and most *sonorous* picture; a scene for the sake of a scene, without a word spoken; as *such,* therefore (a rarity without a precedent) we must take it, and be thankful! In the opinion of not a few, it was, in every sense of the word, the best scene in the play. I am quite certain it was the most *innocent:* and the steady, quiet uprightness of the flame of the wax-candles, which the monks held over the roaring billows amid the storm of wind and rain, was *really* miraculous.

The Sicilian sea coast: a convent of monks: night: a most por· tentous, unearthly storm: a vessel is wrecked: contrary to all human expectation, one man saves himself by his prodigious powers as a swimmer, aided by the peculiarity of his destination—

PRIOR.———All, all did perish—
FIRST MONK.—Change, change those drenched weeds—
PRIOR.—I wist not of them—every soul did perish—

Enter 3d Monk hastily.

3D MONK.—No, there was one did battle with the storm
With careless desperate force; full many times
His life was won and lost, as tho' he recked not—
No hand did aid him, and he aided none—
Alone he breasted the broad wave, alone
That man was saved.

Well! This man is led in by the monks, supposed dripping wet, and to very natural inquiries he either remains silent, or gives most brief and surly answers, and after three or four of these half-line courtesies, *"dashing off the monks"* who had saved him, he exclaims in the true sublimity of our modern misanthropic heroism—

Off! ye are men—there's poison in your touch.
But I must yield, for this (*What?*) hath left me strengthless.

So end the first three scenes. In the next (the Castle of St. Aldobrand) we find the servants there equally frightened with

this unearthly storm, though wherein it differed from other
·violent storms we are not told, except that Hugo informs us,
page 9—

PIET.—Hugo, well met. Does e'en thy age bear
Memory of so terrible a storm?
HUGO.—They have been frequent lately.
PIET.—They are ever so in Sicily.
HUGO.—So it is said. But storms when I was young
Would still pass o'er like Nature's fitful fevers,
And rendered all more wholesome. Now their rage,
Sent thus unseasonable and profitless,
Speaks like the threats of heaven.

A most perplexing theory of Sicilian storms is this of old Hugo!
and what is very remarkable, not apparently founded on any
great familiarity of his own with this troublesome article. For
when Pietro asserts the *"ever more frequency"* of tempests in
Sicily, the old man professes to know nothing more of the fact,
but by hearsay. "So it is said."—But why he assumed this storm
to be unseasonable, and on what he grounded his prophecy (for
the storm is still in full fury), that it would be profitless, and
without the physical powers common to all other violent sea-
winds in purifying the atmosphere, we are left in the dark; as
well concerning the particular points in which he knew it, during
its continuance, to differ from those that he had been acquainted
with in his youth. We are at length introduced to the Lady Imo-
gine, who, we learn, had not rested *"through"* the night; not on
account of the tempest, for

"Long ere the storm arose, her restless gestures
    Forbade all hope to see her blest with sleep."

Sitting at a table, and looking at a portrait, she informs us—First,
that portrait-painters may make a portrait from memory,

"The limner's art may trace the absent feature."

For surely these words could never mean, that a painter may
have a person sit to him who afterwards may leave the room
or perhaps the country? Secondly, that a portrait-painter can
enable a mourning lady to possess a good likeness of her absent
lover, but that the portrait-painter cannot, and who shall—

"Restore the *scenes* in which they met and parted?"

The natural answer would have been—Why the scene-painter to
be sure! But this unreasonable lady requires in addition sundry
things to be painted that have neither lines nor colours—

> "The thoughts, the recollections, sweet and bitter,
> Or the Elysian dreams of lovers when they loved."

Which last sentence must be supposed to mean; *when they were present, and* making love to each other.—Then, if this portrait could speak, it would "acquit the faith of woman-kind." How? Had she remained constant? No, she has been married to another man, whose wife she now is. How then? Why, that, in spite of her marriage vow, she had continued to yearn and crave for her former lover—

> "This has her body, that her mind:
> Which has the better bargain?"

The lover, however, was not contented with this precious arrangement, as we shall soon find. The lady proceeds to inform us that, during the many years of their separation, there have happened in the different parts of the world, a number of "*such things;*" even such, as in a course of years always have, and till the Millennium, doubtless always will happen somewhere or other. Yet this passage, both in language and in metre, is perhaps amongst the best parts of the play. The lady's loved companion and most esteemed attendant, Clotilda, now enters and explains this love and esteem by proving herself a most passive and dispassionate listener, as well as a brief and lucky querist, who asks, by *chance,* questions that we should have thought made for the very sake of the answers. In short, she very much reminds us of those puppet-heroines, for whom the showman contrives to dialogue without any skill in ventriloquism. This, notwithstanding, is the best scene in the Play, and though crowded with solecisms, corrupt diction, and offences against metre, would possess merits sufficient to out-weigh them, if we could suspend the moral sense during the perusal. It tells well and passionately the preliminary circumstances, and thus overcomes the main difficulty of most first acts, viz. that of retrospective narration. It tells us of her having been honorably addressed by a noble youth, of rank and fortune vastly superior to her own: of their mutual love, heightened on her part by gratitude; of his loss of his sovereign's favor; his disgrace; attainder; and flight; that he (thus degraded) sank into a vile ruffian, the chieftain of a murderous banditti; and that from the habitual indulgence of the most reprobate habits and ferocious passions, he had become so changed, even in appearance, and features,

> "That she who bore him had recoiled from him,
> Nor known the alien visage of her child.
> Yet still *she* (Imogine) lov'd him."

She is compelled by the silent entreaties of a father, perishing with "bitter shameful want on the cold earth," to give her hand, with a heart thus irrevocably pre-engaged, to Lord Aldobrand, the enemy of her lover, even to the very man who had baffled his ambitious schemes, and was, at the present time, entrusted with the execution of the sentence of death which had been passed on Bertram. Now, the proof of "woman's love," so industriously held forth for the sympathy, if not for the esteem of the audience, consists in this, that, though Bertram had become a robber and a murderer by trade, a ruffian in manners, yea, with form and features at which his *own mother* could not but "recoil," yet she (Lady Imogine) "the wife of a most noble, honored Lord," estimable as a man, exemplary and affectionate as a husband, and the fond father of her only child—that she, notwithstanding all this, striking her heart, dares to say to it—

> "But thou art Bertram's still, and Bertram's ever."

A Monk now enters, and entreats in his Prior's name for the wonted hospitality, and "free *noble usage*" of the Castle of St. Aldobrand for some wretched ship-wrecked souls, and from this we learn, for the first time, to our infinite surprise, that notwithstanding the supernaturalness of the storm aforesaid, not only Bertram, but the whole of his gang, had been saved, by what means we are left to conjecture, and can only conclude that they had all the same desperate swimming powers, and the same saving destiny as the Hero, Bertram himself. So ends the first act, and with it the tale of the events, both those with which the Tragedy begins, and those which had occurred previous to the date of its commencement. The second displays Bertram in disturbed sleep, which the Prior, who hangs over him, prefers calling a "starting trance," and with a strained voice, that would have awakened one of the seven sleepers, observes to the audience—

> "How the lip works! How the bare teeth *do* grind!
> And beaded drops course[68] down his writhen brow!"

---

[68] ————————"The big round tears
Cours'd one another down his innocent nose
In piteous chase,"

says Shakespeare of a wounded stag hanging its head over a stream: naturally, from the position of the head, and most beautifully, from the association of the preceding image of the chase, in which "the poor sequester'd stag from the hunter's aim had ta'en hurt." In the supposed position of Bertram, the metaphor, if not false, loses all the propriety of the original.

The dramatic effect of which passage we not only concede to the admirers of this tragedy, but acknowledge the further advantages of preparing the audience for the most surprising series of wry faces, proflated mouths, and lunatic gestures that were ever "*launched*" on an audience to "*sear*[69] *the sense.*"

PRIOR.—I will awake him from this *horrid trance.*
This is no natural sleep! Ho, *wake thee,* stranger!

This is rather a whimsical application of the verb reflex, we must confess, though we remember a similar transfer of the agent to the patient in a manuscript tragedy, in which the Bertram of the piece, prostrating a man with a single blow of his fist, exclaims—"Knock me thee down, then ask thee if thou liv'st."— Well; the stranger obeys, and whatever his sleep might have been, his waking was perfectly natural; for lethargy itself could not withstand the scolding stentorship of Mr. Holland, the Prior. We next learn from the best authority, his own confession, that the misanthropic hero, whose destiny was incompatible with drowning, is Count Bertram, who not only reveals his past fortunes, but avows with open atrocity, his Satanic hatred of Imogine's Lord, and his frantic thirst of revenge; and so the raving character raves, and the scolding character scolds—and what else? Does not the Prior *act*? Does he not send for a posse of constables or thief-takers to handcuff the villain, or take·him either to Bedlam or Newgate? Nothing of the kind; the author preserves the unity of character, and the scolding Prior from first to last does nothing but scold, with the exception indeed of the last scene of the last act, in which, with a most surprizing revolution, he whines, weeps, and kneels to the condemned blaspheming assassin out of pure affection to the high-hearted man, the sublimity of whose angel-sin rivals the star-bright apostate (i.e. who was as proud as Lucifer, and as wicked as the Devil), and, "had thrilled him" (Prior Holland aforesaid), with wild admiration.

[69] Among a number of other instances of words chosen without reason, Imogine in the first act declares, that thunder-storms were not able to intercept her prayers for "the desperate man, in desperate *ways* who *dealt*"———

"Yea, when the launched bolt did sear her sense,
    Her soul's deep orisons were breathed for him;"

i.e. when a red-hot bolt, launched at her from a thunder-cloud, had cauterized her sense, in plain English, burnt her eyes out of her head, she kept still praying on.

"Was not *this* love? Yea. thus doth woman love!"

Accordingly, in the very next scene, we have this tragic Macheath, with his whole gang, in the Castle of St. Aldobrand, without any attempt on the Prior's part either to prevent him, or to put the mistress and servants of the Castle on their guard against their new inmates; though he (the Prior) knew, and confesses that he knew, that Bertram's "fearful mates" were assassins so habituated and naturalized to guilt, that—

> "When their *drenched hold* forsook both gold and gear,
> They griped their daggers with a murderer's instinct;"

and though he also knew, that Bertram was the leader of a band whose trade was blood. To the Castle however he goes thus, with the holy Prior's consent, if not with his assistance; and thither let us follow him.

No soooner is our hero safely housed in the Castle of St. Aldobrand, than he attracts the notice of the lady and her confidante, by his "wild and terrible dark eyes," "muffled form," "fearful form," [70] "darkly wild," "proudly stern," and the like commonplace indefinites, seasoned by merely verbal antitheses, and at best, copied, with very slight change, from the CONRADE of Southey's Joan of Arc. The lady Imogine, who has been (as is the case, she tells us, with all soft and solemn spirits) *worshipping* the moon on a terrace or rampart within view of the Castle, insists on having an interview with our hero, and this too tête-à-tête. Would the reader learn why and wherefore the confidante is excluded, who very properly remonstrates against such "conference, alone, at night, with one who bears such fearful form;" the reason follows—"why, *therefore* send him:" I say, *follows*, because the next line, "all things of fear have lost their power over me," is separated from the former by a break or pause, and, besides that it is a very poor answer to the danger, is no answer at all to the gross indelicacy of this wilful exposure. We must

---

[70] This sort of repetition is one of this writer's peculiarities, and there is scarce a page which does not furnish one or more instances— Ex. gr. in the first page or two. Act I, line 7, "and *deemed* that I might sleep."—Line 10, "Did rock and quiver in the bickering *glare.*" —Lines 14, 15, 16, &c., "But by the momently *gleams* of sheeted blue, Did the pale marbles *glare* so *sternly* on me, I almost *deemed* they lived."—Line 37, "The *glare* of Hell."—Line 35, "O holy Prior, this is no *earthly storm.*"—Line 38, "This is no *earthly storm.*"—Line 42, "*Dealing* with us."—Line 43, "*Deal* thus sternly."—Line 44, "Speak! thou hast *something seen?*"—"A *fearful sight!*"—Line 45, "What hast thou *seen?* A piteous, *fearful sight.*"—Line 48, "*quivering gleams.*"— Line 50, "In the hollow *pauses of the storm.*"—Line 61, "The *pauses of the storm*, &c."

therefore regard it as a mere after-thought, that a little softens the rudeness, but adds nothing to the weight, of that exquisite woman's reason aforesaid. And so exit Clotilda and enter Bertram, who "stands without looking at her," that is, with his lower limbs forked, his arms akimbo, his side to the lady's front, the whole figure resembling an inverted Y. He is soon however roused from the state surly to the state frantic, and then follow raving, yelling, cursing, she fainting, he relenting, in runs Imogine's child, squeaks "mother!" He snatches it up, and with a "God bless thee, child! Bertram has kissed thy child,"—the curtain drops. The third act is short, and short be our account of it. It introduces Lord St. Aldobrand on his road homeward, and next Imogine in the convent, confessing the foulness of her heart to the Prior, who first indulges his old humour with a fit of senseless scolding, then leaves her alone with her ruffian paramour, with whom she makes at once an infamous appointment, and the curtain drops, that it may be carried into act and consummation.

I want words to describe the mingled horror and disgust with which I witnessed the opening of the fourth act, considering it as a melancholy proof of the depravation of the public mind. The shocking spirit of Jacobinism seemed no longer confined to politics. The familiarity with atrocious events and characters appeared to have poisoned the taste, even where it had not directly disorganized the moral principles, and left the feelings callous to all the mild appeals, and craving alone for the grossest and most outrageous stimulants. The very fact then present to our senses, that a British audience could remain passive under such an insult to common decency, nay, receive with a thunder of applause, a human being supposed to have come reeking from the consummation of this complex foulness and baseness, these and the like reflections so pressed as with the weight of lead upon my heart, that actor, author, and tragedy would have been forgotten, had it not been for a plain elderly man sitting beside me, who, with a very serious face, that at once expressed surprize and aversion, touched my elbow, and, pointing to the actor, said to me in a half-whisper—"Do you see that little fellow there? he has just been committing adultery!" Somewhat relieved by the laugh which this droll address occasioned, I forced back my attention to the stage sufficiently to learn, that Bertram is recovered from a transient fit of remorse by the information, that St. Aldobrand was commissioned (to do, what every honest man must have done without commission, if he did his duty) to seize him and deliver him to the just vengeance of the law; an information which (as he had long known himself to be an attainted traitor and proclaimed outlaw, and not only a trader in blood himself, but notoriously the *Captain* of a gang of thieves, pirates, and assassins) assuredly could not have been new to him. It is this, however, which alone and instantly restores him to his accustomed state of raving, blasphemy, and nonsense. Next follows Imogine's constrained interview with her injured husband, and his sudden departure again, all in love and kindness, in order to attend the feast of St. Anselm at the convent. This was, it must be owned, a very strange engagement for so tender a husband to make within a few minutes after so long an absence. But first his lady has told him that she has "a vow on her," and wishes "that black perdition may gulf her perjured soul"—(Note: she is lying at the very time)—if she ascends his bed, till her penance is accomplished. How, therefore, is the poor husband to amuse himself in this interval of her penance? But do not be distressed, reader, on account of St. Aldobrand's absence! As the author has contrived to send him out of the house, when a husband would be in his, and the lover's way, so he will doubtless not be at a loss to bring him back again as soon as he is wanted. Well! the husband gone in on the one side, out pops the lover from the other, and for the fiendish purpose of harrowing up the soul of his wretched accomplice in guilt, by announcing to her, with most brutal and blasphemous execrations, his fixed and deliberate resolve to assassinate her husband; all this too is for no discoverable purpose on the part of the author, but that of introducing a series of super-tragic starts, pauses, screams, struggling, dagger-throwing, falling on the ground, starting up again wildly, swearing, outcries for help, falling again on the ground, rising again, faintly tottering towards the door, and, to end the scene, a most convenient fainting fit of our lady's, just in time to give Bertram an opportunity of seeking the object of his hatred, before she alarms the house, which indeed she has had full time to have done before, but that the author rather chose she should amuse herself and the audience by the above-described ravings and startings. She recovers slowly, and to her enter Clotilda, the confidante, and mother confessor; then commences, what in theatrical language is called the madness, but which the author more accurately entitles delirium, it appearing indeed a sort of intermittent fever with fits of light-headedness off and on, whenever occasion and stage effect happen to call for it. A convenient return of the storm (we told the reader beforehand how it would be) had changed—

> "The rivulet, that bathed the convent walls,
> Into a foaming flood: upon its brink

The Lord and his small train *do* stand appalled.
With torch and bell from their high battlements
The monks *do* summon to the pass in vain;
He must return to-night."—

Talk of the devil, and his horns appear, says the proverb:
and sure enough, within ten lines of the exit of the messenger,
sent to stop him, the arrival of Lord St. Aldobrand is an-
nounced. Bertram's ruffian band now enter, and range them-
selves across the stage, giving fresh cause for Imogine's screams
and madness. St. Aldobrand, having received his mortal wound
behind the scenes, totters in to welter in his blood, and to die
at the feet of this double-damned adultress.

Of her, as far as she is concerned in this 4th act, we have
two additional points to notice: first, the low cunning and Jesu-
itical trick with which she deludes her husband into *words* of
forgiveness, which he himself does not understand; and secondly,
that everywhere she is made the object of interest and sympathy,
and it is not the author's fault, if, at any moment, she excites
feelings less gentle, than those we are accustomed to associate
with the self-accusations of a sincere religious penitent. And did
a British audience endure all this?—They received it with plau-
dits, which, but for the rivalry of the carts and hackney coaches,
might have disturbed the evening-prayers of the scanty week
day congregation at St. Paul's cathedral.

Tempora mutantur, nos et mutamur in illis.

Of the fifth act, the only thing noticeable (for rant and non-
sense, though abundant as ever, have long before the last act
become things of course), is the profane representation of the
high altar in a chapel, with all the vessels and other prepara-
tions for the holy sacrament. A hymn is actually sung on the
stage by the chorister boys! For the rest, Imogine, who now
and then *talks* deliriously, but who is always light-headed as
far as her *gown* and *hair* can make her so, wanders about in
dark woods with cavern-rocks and precipices in the back-scene;
and a number of mute dramatis personæ move in and out con-
tinually, for whose presence there is always at least this reason,
that they afford something to be *seen*, by that very large part
of a Drury Lane audience who have small chance of *hearing*
a word. She had, it appears, taken her child with her, but what
becomes of the child, whether she murdered it or not, nobody
can tell, nobody can learn; it was a riddle at the *representa-
tion*, and after a most attentive *perusal* of the play, a riddle
it remains.

"No more I know, I wish I did,
And I would tell it all to you;
For what became of this poor child
There's none that ever knew."
                    WORDSWORTH'S THORN.

Our whole information[71] is derived from the following words—

PRIOR.—Where is thy child?
CLOTIL.—(Pointing to the cavern into which she has looked)
Oh, he lies cold within his cavern-tomb!
Why dost thou urge her with the horrid theme?
    PRIOR.—(who will not, the reader may observe, be disappointed of
    his dose of scolding)
It was to make (quere wake) one living cord o' th' heart,
And I will try, tho' my own breaks at it.
Where is thy child?
    IMOG.—(with a frantic laugh)
The forest fiend hath snatched him—
He (who? the fiend or the child?) rides the night-mare thro' the wiz-
    zard woods.

Now these two lines consist in a senseless plagiarism from the
counterfeited madness of Edgar in Lear, who, in imitation of
the gipsey incantations, puns on the old word Mair, a Hag; and
the no less senseless adoption of Dryden's forest-fiend, and the
wizzard-stream by which Milton, in his Lycidas, so finely char-
acterizes the spreading Deva, fabulosus Amnis. Observe too these
images stand unique in the speeches of Imogine, without the
slightest resemblance to anything she says before or after. But
we are weary. The characters in this act frisk about, here, there,
and every where, as teasingly as the Jack o' Lanthorn-lights
which mischievous boys, from across a narrow street, throw with
a looking glass on the faces of their opposite neighbours. Bertram
disarmed, out-heroding Charles de Moor in the Robbers, befaces
the collected knights of St. Anselm (all in complete armour),
and so, by pure dint of black looks, he outdares them into passive
poltroons. The sudden revolution in the Prior's manners we have
before noticed, and it is indeed so outré, that a number of the
audience imagined a great secret was to come out, viz.: that the
Prior was one of the many instances of a youthful sinner meta-
morphosed into an old scold, and that this Bertram would appear
at last to be his son. Imogine re-appears at the convent, and dies

[71] The child is an important personage, for I see not by what pos-
sible means the author could have ended the second and third acts
but for its timely appearance. How ungrateful then not further to no-
tice its fate!

of her own accord. Bertram stabs himself, and dies by her side, and that the play may conclude as it began, viz. in a superfetation of blasphemy upon nonsense, because he had snatched a sword from a despicable coward, who retreats in terror when it is pointed towards him in sport; this *felo de se,* and thief-captain, this loathsome and leprous confluence of robbery, adultery, murder, and cowardly assassination, this monster, whose best deed is, the having saved his betters from the degradation of hanging him, by turning jack ketch to himself; first recommends the charitable Monks and holy Prior to pray for his soul, and then has the folly and impudence to exclaim—

"I die no felon's death,
A warrior's weapon freed a warrior's soul!"

CHAPTER XXIV

CONCLUSION

IT SOMETIMES happens that we are punished for our faults by incidents, in the causation of which these faults had no share: and this I have always felt the severest punishment. The wound indeed is of the same dimensions; but the edges are jagged, and there is a dull underpain that survives the smart which it had aggravated. For there is always a consolatory feeling that accompanies the sense of a proportion between antecedents and consequents. The sense of Before and After becomes both intelligible and intellectual when, and *only* when, we contemplate the succession in the relations of Cause and Effect, which, like the two poles of the magnet manifest the being and unity of the one power by relative opposites, and give, as it were, a substratum of permanence, of identity, and therefore of reality, to the shadowy flux of Time. It is Eternity revealing itself in the phenomena of Time: and the perception and acknowledgment of the proportionality and appropriateness of the Present to the Past, prove to the afflicted Soul, that it has not yet been deprived of the sight of God, that it can still recognise the effective presence of a Father, though through a darkened glass and a turbid atmosphere, though of a Father that is chastising it. And for this cause, doubtless, are we so framed in mind, and even so organized in brain and nerve, that all confusion is painful.—It is within the experience of many medical practitioners, that a patient, with strange and unusual symptoms of disease, has been more distressed, in mind, more wretched, from the fact of being unintelligible to himself and others, than from the pain or danger of the disease: nay, that the patient has received the most solid comfort, and resumed a genial and enduring chearfulness, from some new symptom or product, that had at once determined the name and nature of his complaint, and rendered it an intelligible effect of an intelligible cause: even though the discovery did at the same moment preclude all hope of restoration. Hence the mystic theologians, whose delusions we may more confidently hope to separate from their actual intuitions, when we condescend to read their works without the presumption that whatever our fancy (always the ape, and too often the adulterator and counterfeit of our memory) has not made or cannot make a picture of, must be nonsense,—hence, I say, the Mystics have joined in representing the state of the reprobate spirits as a dreadful dream in which there is no sense of reality, not even of the pangs they are enduring—an eternity without time, and as it were below it—God present without manifestation of his presence. But these are depths, which we dare not linger over. Let us turn to an instance more on a level with the ordinary sympathies of mankind. Here then, and in this same healing influence of *Light* and distinct Beholding, we may detect the final cause of that instinct which, in the great majority of instances, leads, and almost compels the Afflicted to communicate their sorrows. Hence too flows the alleviation that results from *"opening out* our griefs:" which are thus presented in distinguishable forms instead of the mist, through which whatever is shapeless becomes magnified and (literally) *enormous.* Casimir, in the fifth Ode of his third Book, has happily[72] expressed this thought.

> "Me longus silendi
> Edit amor, facilesque luctus
> Hausit medullas. Fugerit ocius,

[72] *Classically* too, as far as consists with the allegorizing fancy of the *modern,* that still *striving to project* the inward, contradistinguishes itself from the seeming ease with which the poetry of the ancients *reflects* the world without. Casimir affords, perhaps, the most striking instance of this characteristic difference.—For his *style* and *diction* are really classical: while Cowley, who resembles Casimir in many respects, compleatly barbarizes *his* Latinity, and even his metre, by the heterogeneous nature of his thoughts. That Dr. Johnson should have passed a contrary judgement, and have even preferred Cowley's Latin Poems to Milton's, is a caprice that has, if I mistake not, excited the surprise of all scholars. I was much amused last summer with the laughable *affright,* with which an Italian poet perused a page of Cowley's Davideis, contrasted with the enthusiasm with which he first ran through, and then read aloud, Milton's Mansus and Ad Patrem.

Simul negantem visere jusseris
    Aures amicorum, et loquacem
    Questibus evacuâris iram.

Olim querendo desinimus queri,
Ipsoque fletu lacryma perditur:
    Nec fortis æque, si per omnes
    Cura volat residetque ramos.

Vires amicis perdit in auribus,
Minorque semper dividitur dolor
    Per multa permissus vagari
        Pectora."—   Id. Lib. iii. Od. 5.

I shall not make this an excuse, however, for troubling my
Readers with any complaints or explanations, with which, as
Readers, they have little or no concern. It may suffice (for the
present at least) to declare, that the causes that have delayed
the publication of these volumes for so long a period after they
have been printed off, were not connected with any neglect of
my own; and that they would form an instructive comment on
the Chapter concerning Authorship as a Trade, addressed to
young men of genius in the first volume of this work. I remem-
ber the ludicrous effect of the first sentence of an autobiography,
which, happily for the writer, was as meagre in incidents as it
is well possible for the Life of an Individual to be—"The *eventful*
Life which I am about to record, from the hour in which I rose
into existence on this Planet, &c." Yet when, notwithstanding this
warning example of Self-importance before me, I review my own
life, I cannot refrain from applying the same epithet to it, and
with more than ordinary emphasis—and no private feeling, that
affected myself only, should prevent me from *publishing* the
same (for *write* it I assuredly shall, should life and leisure be
granted me), if continued reflection should strengthen my pres-
ent belief, that my history would add its contingent to the en-
forcement of one important truth, viz. that we must not only
love our neighbours as ourselves, but ourselves likewise as our
neighbours; and that we can do neither unless we love God
above both.

"Who lives, that's not
Depraved or depraves? Who dies, *that bears
Not one spurn to the grave—of their friends' gift?*"

Strange as the delusion may appear, yet it is most true that
three years ago I did not know or believe that I had an enemy in
the world: and now even my strongest sensations of gratitude

are mingled with fear, and I reproach myself for being too often disposed to ask,—Have I one friend?—During the many years which intervened between the composition and the publication of the CHRISTABEL, it became almost as well known among literary men as if it had been on common sale, the same references were made to it, and the same liberties taken with it, even to the very names of the imaginary persons in the poem. From almost all of our most celebrated Poets, and from some with whom I had no personal acquaintance, I either received or heard of expressions of admiration that (I can truly say) appeared to myself utterly disproportionate to a work, that pretended to be nothing more than a common Faery Tale. Many, who had allowed no merit to my other poems, whether printed or manuscript, and who had frankly told me as much, uniformly made an exception in favour of the CHRISTABEL and the Poem entitled LOVE. Year after year, and in societies of the most different kinds, I had been entreated to recite it: and the result was still the same in all, and altogether different in this respect from the effect produced by the occasional recitation of any other poems I had composed.—This before the publication. And since then, with very few exceptions, I have heard nothing but abuse, and this too in a spirit of bitterness at least as disproportionate to the pretensions of the poem, had it been the most pitiably below mediocrity, as the previous eulogies, and far more inexplicable. In the Edinburgh Review it was assailed with a malignity and a spirit of personal hatred that ought to have injured only the work in which such a tirade appeared: and this review was generally attributed (whether rightly or no I know not) to a man, who both in my presence and in my absence has repeatedly pronounced it the finest poem in the language.— This may serve as a warning to authors, that in their calculations on the probable reception of a poem, they must subtract to a large amount from the panegyric, which may have encouraged them to publish it, however unsuspicious and however various the sources of this panegyric may have been. And, first, allowances must be made for private enmity, of the very existence of which they had perhaps entertained no suspicion—for personal enmity behind the mask of anonymous criticism: secondly for the necessity of a certain proportion of abuse and ridicule in a Review, in order to make it saleable, in consequence of which, if they have no friends behind the scenes, the chances must needs be against them; but lastly and chiefly, for the excitement and temporary sympathy of feeling, which the recitation of the poem by an admirer, especially if he be at once a warm admirer, and a man of acknowledged celebrity, calls forth in the audience. For this is really a species of Animal Magnetism, in which the enkindling reciter, by perpetual comment of looks and tones, lends his own will and apprehensive faculty to his auditors. They *live* for the time within the dilated sphere of his intellectual being. It is equally possible, though not equally common, that a reader left to himself should sink below the poem, as that the poem left to itself should flag beneath the feelings of the reader. —But, in my own instance, I had the additional misfortune of having been gossiped about, as devoted to metaphysics, and worse than all, to a system incomparably nearer to the visionary flights of Plato, and even to the jargon of the Mystics, than to the established tenets of Locke. Whatever therefore appeared with my name was condemned beforehand, as predestined metaphysics. In a dramatic poem, which had been submitted by me to a gentleman of great influence in the theatrical world, occurred the following passage:—

> "O we are querulous creatures! Little less
> Than all things can suffice to make us happy:
> And little more than nothing is enough
> To make us wretched."

Aye, here now! (exclaimed the Critic) here comes Coleridge's *Metaphysics!* And the very same motive (that is, not that the lines were unfit for the present state of our immense Theatres; but that they were *Metaphysics*[73]) was assigned elsewhere for the rejection of the two following passages. The first is spoken in answer to a usurper, who had rested his plea on the circumstances, that he had been chosen by the acclamations of the people:—

> "What people? How conven'd? or, if conven'd,
> Must not the magic power that charms together
> Millions of men in council, needs have power
> To win or wield them? Rather, O far rather,
> Shout forth thy titles to yon circling mountains,
> And with a thousand-fold reverberation
> Make the rocks flatter thee, and the volleying air,
> Unbribed, shout back to thee, King Emerich!
> By wholesome laws to embank the Sovereign Power,

[73] Poor unlucky Metaphysics! and what are they? A single sentence expresses the object and thereby the contents of this science. Γνῶθι σεαυτόν: et Deum quantum licet, et in Deo omnia scibis. Know thyself: and so shalt thou know God, as far as is permitted to a creature, and in God all things.—Surely, there is a strange—nay, rather a too natural—aversion in many to know themselves.

> To deepen by restraint, and by prevention
> Of lawless will to amass and guide the flood
> In its majestic channel, is man's task
> And the true patriot's glory! In all else
> Men safelier trust to heaven, than to themselves
> When least themselves: even in those whirling crowds
> Where folly is contagious, and too oft
> Even wise men leave their better sense at home,
> To chide and wonder at them, when return'd."

The second passage is in the mouth of an old and experienced Courtier, betrayed by the man in whom he had most trusted:—

> "And yet Sarolta, simple, inexperienced,
> Could see him as he was, and oft has warn'd me.
> Whence learned she this? O she was innocent!
> And to be innocent is Nature's wisdom!
> The fledge-dove knows the prowlers of the air,
> Fear'd soon as seen, and flutters back to shelter.
> And the young steed recoils upon his haunches,
> The never-yet-seen adder's hiss first heard!
> Ah! surer than suspicion's hundred eyes
> Is that fine sense, which to the pure in heart,
> By mere oppugnancy of their own goodness,
> Reveals the approach of evil."

As therefore my character as a writer could not easily be more injured by an overt act than it was already in consequence of the report, I published a work, a large portion of which was professedly metaphysical. A long delay occurred between its first annunciation and its appearance; it was reviewed therefore by anticipation with a malignity so avowedly and exclusively personal, as is, I believe, unprecedented even in the present contempt of all common humanity that disgraces and endangers the liberty of the press. After its appearance, the author of this lampoon was chosen to review it in the Edinburgh Review; and under the single condition, that he should have written what he himself really thought, and have criticised the work as he would have done had its author been indifferent to him, I should have chosen that man myself, both from the vigor and the originality of his mind, and from his particular acuteness in speculative reasoning, before all others.—I remembered Catullus's lines:—

> "Desine de quoquam quicquam bene velle mereri,
>   Aut aliquem fieri posse putare pium.
> Omnia sunt ingrata: nihil fecisse benigne est:
>   Immo etiam tædet, tædet obestque magis;
> Ut mihi, quem nemo gravius nec acerbius urget,
>   Quam modo qui me unum atque unicum amicum habuit."

But I can truly say, that the grief with which I read this rhapsody of predetermined insult, had the rhapsodist himself for its whole and sole object: and that the indignant contempt which it excited in me, was as exclusively confined to his employer and suborner. I refer to this review at present, in consequence of information having been given me, that the innuendo of my "potential infidelity," grounded on one passage of my first Lay Sermon, has been received and propagated with a degree of *credence*, of which I can safely acquit the originator of the calumny. I give the sentences, as they stand in the sermon, premising only that I was speaking exclusively of miracles worked for the outward senses of men. "It was only to overthrow the usurpation exercised in and through the senses, that the senses were miraculously appealed to. REASON AND RELIGION ARE THEIR OWN EVIDENCE. The natural sun is in this respect a symbol of the spiritual. Ere he is fully arisen, and while his glories are still under veil, he calls up the breeze to chase away the usurping vapours of the night-season, and thus converts the air itself into the minister of its own purification: not surely in proof or elucidation of the light from heaven, but to prevent its interception."

"Wherever, therefore, similar circumstances co-exist with the same moral causes, the principles revealed, and the examples recorded, in the inspired writings, render miracles superfluous: and if we neglect to apply truths in expectation of wonders, or under pretext of the cessation of the latter, we tempt God, and merit the same reply which our Lord gave to the Pharisees on a like occasion."

In the sermon and the notes both the historical truth and the necessity of the miracles are strongly and frequently asserted. "The testimony of books of history (i.e. relatively to the signs and wonders, with which Christ came) is one of the strong and stately *pillars* of the church: but it is not the *foundation!*" Instead, therefore, of defending myself, which I could easily effect by a series of passages, expressing the same opinion, from the Fathers and the most eminent Protestant Divines, from the Reformation to the Revolution, I shall merely state what my belief is, concerning the true evidences of Christianity. 1. Its consistency with right Reason, I consider as the outer Court of the Temple—the common area, within which it stands. 2. The miracles, with and through which the Religion was first revealed and attested, I regard as the steps, the vestibule, and the portal of the Temple. 3. The sense, the inward feeling, in the soul of each Believer of its exceeding *desireableness*—the experience, that he *needs* some-

thing, joined with the strong foretokening, that the Redemption and the Graces propounded to us in Christ are *what* he needs—this I hold to be the true FOUNDATION of the spiritual Edifice. With the strong *a priori* probability that flows in from 1 and 3 on the correspondent historical evidence of 2, no man can refuse or neglect to make the experiment without guilt. But, 4, it is the experience derived from a practical conformity to the conditions of the Gospel—it is the opening Eye; the dawning Light: the terrors and the promises of spiritual Growth; the blessedness of loving God as God, the nascent sense of Sin hated as Sin, and of the incapability of attaining to either without Christ; it is the sorrow that still rises up from beneath and the consolation that meets it from above; the bosom treacheries of the Principal in the warfare and the exceeding faithfulness and long-suffering of the uninterested Ally;—in a word, it is the actual *Trial* of the Faith in Christ, with its accompaniments and results, that must form the arched ROOF, and the Faith itself is the completing KEYSTONE. In order to an efficient belief in Christianity, a man must have been a Christian, and this is the seeming argumentum in circulo, incident to all spiritual Truths, to every subject not presentable under the forms of Time and Space, as long as we attempt to master by the reflex acts of the Understanding what we can only *know* by the act of *becoming*. "Do the will of my Father, and ye shall KNOW whether I am of God." These four evidences I believe to have been and still to be, for the world, for the whole Church, all necessary, all equally necessary: but at present, and for the majority of Christians born in Christian countries, I believe the third and the fourth evidences to be the most operative, not as superseding but as involving a glad undoubting faith in the two former. Credidi, ideóque intellexi, appears to me the dictate equally of Philosophy and Religion, even as I believe Redemption to be the antecedent of Sanctification and not its consequent. All spiritual predicates may be construed indifferently as modes of Action or as states of Being. Thus Holiness and Blessedness are the same idea, now seen in relation to act and now to existence. The ready belief which has been yielded to the slander of my "potential infidelity," I attribute in part to the openness with which I have avowed my doubts, whether the heavy interdict, under which the name of BENEDICT SPINOZA lies, is merited on the whole or to the whole extent. Be this as it may, I wish, however, that I could find in the books of philosophy, theoretical or moral, which are alone recommended to the present students of Theology in our established schools, a few passages as thoroughly *Pauline*, as compleatly accordant with the doctrines of

the Established Church, as the following sentences in the concluding page of Spinoza's Ethics. "Deinde quó mens hoc amore divino seu beatitudine magis gaudet, eó plus *intelligit*, hoc est, eó majorem in affectus habet potentiam, et eó minus ab affectibus, qui mali sunt, patitur; atque adeó ex eo, quod mens hoc amore divino seu beatitudine gaudet, potestatem habet libidines coërcendi, nemo beatitudine gaudet quia affectus coërcuit; sed contra potestas libidines coërcendi ex ipsâ beatitudine oritur."

With regard to the Unitarians, it has been shamelessly asserted, that I have denied them to be Christians. God forbid! For how should I know, what the piety of the Heart may be, or what Quantum of Error in the Understanding may consist with a saving faith in the intentions and actual dispositions of the whole moral Being in any one Individual? Never will God reject a soul that sincerely loves him: be his speculative opinions what they may: and whether in any given instance certain opinions, be they Unbelief, or Misbelief, are compatible with a sincere Love of God, God can only know.—But this I have said, and shall continue to say: that if the doctrines, the sum of which I *believe* to constitute the Truth in Christ, *be* Christianity, then Unitarian*ism* is not, and vice versa: and that, in speaking theologically and *impersonally,* i.e. of PSILANTHROPISM and THEANTHROPISM as schemes of Belief, without reference to Individuals who profess either the one or the other, it will be absurd to use a different language as long as it is the dictate of common sense, that two opposites cannot properly be called by the same name. I should feel no offence if a Unitarian applied the same to me, any more 'han if he were to say, that 2 and 2 being 4, 4 and 4 must be 8.

> ἀλλὰ βροτῶν
> τὸν μὲν κενεόφρονες αὖχαι
> ἐξ ἀγαθῶν ἔβαλον·
> τὸν δ' αὖ καταμεμφθέντ' ἄγαν
> ἰσχὺν οἰκείων παρέσφαλεν καλῶν,
> χειρὸς ἕλκων ὀπίσσω, θυμὸς ἄτολμος.
> PINDAR, Nem. Ode xi.

This has been my Object, and this alone can be my Defence—. and O! that with this my personal as well as my LITERARY LIFE might conclude! the unquenched desire I mean, not without the consciousness of having earnestly endeavoured, to kindle young minds, and to guard them against the temptations of Scorners, by showing that the Scheme of Christianity, as taught in the Liturgy and Homilies of our Church, though not discoverable by human Reason, is yet in accordance with it; that link follows link by necessary consequence; that Religion passes out of the ken of Reason only where the eye of Reason has reached its own Horizon; and that Faith is then but its continuation: even as the Day softens away into the sweet Twilight, and Twilight, hushed and breathless, steals into the Darkness. It is Night, sacred Night! the upraised Eye views only the starry Heaven which manifests itself alone: and the outward Beholding is fixed on the sparks twinkling in the aweful depth, though Suns of other Worlds, only to preserve the Soul steady and collected in its pure *Act* of inward adoration to the great I AM, and to the filial WORD that re-affirmeth it from Eternity to Eternity, whose choral Echo is the universe.

ΘΕΩι ΜΟΝΩι ΔΟΞΑ.

FINIS.

LITERARY CRITICISM

SHAKESPEARE'S JUDGMENT EQUAL TO HIS GENIUS

THUS then Shakespeare appears, from his Venus and Adonis and Rape of Lucrece alone, apart from all his great works, to have possessed all the conditions of the true poet. Let me now proceed to destroy, as far as may be in my power, the popular notion that he was a great dramatist by mere instinct, that he grew immortal in his own despite, and sank below men of second or third-rate power, when he attempted aught beside the drama—even as bees construct their cells and manufacture their honey to admirable perfection; but would in vain attempt to build a nest. Now this mode of reconciling a compelled sense of inferiority with a feeling of pride, began in a few pedants, who having read that Sophocles was the great model of tragedy, and Aristotle the infallible dictator of its rules, and finding that the Lear, Hamlet, Othello, and other master-pieces were neither in imitation of Sophocles, nor in obedience to Aristotle,—and not having (with one or two exceptions) the courage to affirm, that the delight which their country received from generation to generation, in defiance of the alterations of circumstances and habits, was wholly groundless,—took upon them, as a happy medium and refuge, to talk of Shakespeare as a sort of beautiful *lusus naturæ,* a delightful monster,—wild, indeed, and without taste or judgment, but like the inspired idiots so much venerated in the East, uttering, amid the strangest follies, the sublimest truths. In nine places out of ten in which I find his awful name mentioned, it is with some epithet of "wild," "irregular," "pure child of nature," &c. If all this be true, we must submit to it; though to a thinking mind it can not but be painful to find any excellence, merely human, thrown out of all human analogy, and thereby leaving us neither rules for imitation, nor motives to imitate;—but if false, it is a dangerous falsehood;—for it affords a refuge to secret self-conceit,—enables a vain man at once to escape his reader's indignation by general swoln panegyrics, and merely by his *ipse dixit* to treat, as contemptible, what he has not intellect enough to comprehend, or soul to feel, without assigning any reason, or referring his opinion to any demonstrative principle; thus leaving

Shakespeare as a sort of grand Lama, adored indeed, and his very excrements prized as relics, but with no authority or real influence. I grieve that every late voluminous edition of his works would enable me to substantiate the present charge with a variety of facts, one tenth of which would of themselves exhaust the time allotted to me. Every critic, who has or has not made a collection of black-letter books—in itself a useful and respectable amusement,—puts on the seven-league boots of self-opinion, and strides at once from an illustrator into a supreme judge, and blind and deaf, fills his three-ounce phial at the waters of Niagara; and determines positively the greatness of the cataract to be neither more nor less than his three-ounce phial has been able to receive.

I think this a very serious subject. It is my earnest desire—my passionate endeavor,—to enforce at various times, and by various arguments and instances, the close and reciprocal connection of just taste with pure morality. Without that acquaintance with the heart of man, or that docility and childlike gladness to be made acquainted with it, which those only can have, who dare look at their own hearts—and that with a steadiness which religion only has the power of reconciling with sincere humility; —without this, and the modesty produced by it, I am deeply convinced that no man, however wide his erudition, however patient his antiquarian researches, can possibly understand, or be worthy of understanding, the writings of Shakespeare.

Assuredly that criticism of Shakespeare will alone be genial which is reverential. The Englishman, who, without reverence, a proud and affectionate reverence, can utter the name of William Shakespeare, stands disqualified for the office of critic. He wants one at least of the very senses, the language of which he is to employ, and will discourse at best, but as a blind man, while the whole harmonious creation of light and shade with all its subtle interchange of deepening and dissolving colors rises in silence to the silent *fiat* of the uprising Apollo. However inferior in ability I may be to some who have followed me, I own I am proud that I was the first in time who publicly demonstrated to the full extent of the position, that the supposed irregularity and extravagances of Shakespeare were the mere dreams of a pedantry that arraigned the eagle because it had not the dimensions of the swan. In all the successive courses of lectures delivered by me, since my first attempt at the Royal Institution, it has been, and it still remains, my object, to prove that in all points from the most important to the most minute, the judgment of Shakespeare is commensurate with his genius—nay, that his genius reveals itself in his judgment, as in its most exalted form. And the more gladly do I recur to this subject from the clear conviction, that to judge aright, and with distinct consciousness of the grounds of our judgment, concerning the works of Shakespeare, implies the power and the means of judging rightly of all other works of intellect, those of abstract science alone excepted.

It is a painful truth that not only individuals, but even whole nations, are ofttimes so enslaved to the habits of their education and immediate circumstances, as not to judge disinterestedly even on those subjects, the very pleasure arising from which consists in its disinterestedness, namely, on subjects of taste and polite literature. Instead of deciding concerning their own modes and customs by any rule of reason, nothing appears rational, becoming, or beautiful to them, but what coincides with the peculiarities of their education. In this narrow circle, individuals may attain to exquisite discrimination, as the French critics have done in their own literature; but a true critic can no more be such without placing himself on some central point, from which he may command the whole, that is, some general rule, which, founded in reason, or the faculties common to all men, must therefore apply to each—than an astronomer can explain the movements of the solar system without taking his stand in the sun. And let me remark, that this will not tend to produce despotism, but, on the contrary, true tolerance, in the critic. He will, indeed, require, as the spirit and substance of a work, something true in human nature itself, and independent of all circumstances; but in the mode of applying it, he will estimate genius and judgment according to the felicity with which the imperishable soul of intellect, shall have adapted itself to the age, the place, and the existing manners. The error he will expose, lies in reversing this, and holding up the mere circumstances as perpetual to the utter neglect of the power which can alone animate them. For art can not exist without, or apart from, nature; and what has man of his own to give to his fellow-man, but his own thoughts and feelings, and his observations, so far as they are modified by his own thoughts or feelings?

Let me, then, once more submit this question to minds emancipated alike from national, or party, or sectarian prejudice:— Are the plays of Shakespeare works of rude uncultivated genius, in which the splendor of the parts compensates, if aught can compensate, for the barbarous shapelessness and irregularity of the whole? Or is the form equally admirable with the matter, and the judgment of the great poet, not less deserving our wonder than his genius?—Or, again, to repeat the question in other words:—Is Shakespeare a great dramatic poet on account only of those beauties and excellences which he possesses in common with the ancients, but with diminished claims to our love and honor to the full extent of his differences from them?—Or are these very differences additional proofs of poetic wisdom, at once results and symbols of living power as contrasted with lifeless mechanism—of free and rival originality as contra-distinguished from servile imitation, or, more accurately, a blind copying of effects, instead of a true imitation of the essential principles?—Imagine not that I am about to oppose genius to rules. No! the comparative value of these rules is the very cause to be tried. The spirit of poetry, like all other living powers, must of necessity circumscribe itself by rules, were it only to unite power with beauty. It must embody in order to reveal itself; but a living body is of necessity an organized one; and what is organization but the connection of parts in and for a whole, so that each part is at once end and means?—This is no discovery of criticism;—it is a necessity of the human mind; and all nations have felt and obeyed it, in the invention of metre, and measured sounds, as the vehicle and *involucrum* of poetry—itself a fellow-growth from the same life —even as the bark is to the tree!

No work of true genius dares want its appropriate form, neither indeed is there any danger of this. As it must not, so genius can not, be lawless; for it is even this that constitutes it genius—the power of acting creatively under laws of its own origination. How then comes it that not only single *Zoili,* but whole nations have combined in unhesitating condemnation of our great dramatist, as a sort of African nature, rich in beautiful monsters—as a wild heath where islands of fertility look the greener from the surrounding waste, where the loveliest plants now shine out among unsightly weeds, and now are choked by their parasitic growth, so intertwined that we can not disentangle the weed without snapping the flower?—In this statement I have had no reference to the vulgar abuse of Voltaire, save as far as his charges are coincident with the decisions of Shakespeare's own commentators and (so they would tell you) almost idolatrous admirers. The true ground of the mistake lies in the confounding mechanical regularity with organic form. The form is mechanic, when on any given material we impress a pre-determined form, not necessarily arising out of the properties of the material;—as when to a mass of wet clay we give whatever shape we wish it to retain when hardened. The organic form, on the other hand, is innate; it shapes, as it develops, itself from within, and the fulness of its development is one and the same with the perfection of its outward form. Such as the life is, such is the form. Nature, the prime genial artist, inexhaustible in diverse powers, is equally inexhaustible in forms;—each exterior is the physiognomy of the being within—its true image reflected and thrown out from the concave mirror;—and even such is the appropriate excellence of her chosen poet, of our own Shakespeare—himself a nature humanized, a genial understanding directing self-consciously a power and an implicit wisdom deeper even than our consciousness.

I greatly dislike beauties and selections in general; but as proof positive of his unrivalled excellence, I should like to try Shakespeare by this criterion. Make out your amplest catalogue of all the human faculties, as reason or the moral law, the will, the feeling of the coincidence of the two (a feeling *sui generis et demonstratio demonstrationum*) called the conscience, the understanding or prudence, wit, fancy, imagination, judgment—and then of the objects on which these are to be employed, as the beauties, the terrors, and the seeming caprices of nature, the realities and the capabilities, that is, the actual and the ideal, of the human mind, conceived as an individual or as a social being, as in innocence or in guilt, in a play-paradise, or in a war-field of temptation;—and then compare with Shakespeare under each of these heads all or any of the writers in prose and verse that have ever lived! Who, that is competent to judge, doubts the result? —And ask your own hearts—ask your own common-sense—to conceive the possibility of this man being—I say not, the drunken savage of that wretched socialist, whom Frenchmen, to their shame, have honored before their elder and better worthies—but the anomalous, the wild, the irregular, genius of our daily criticism! What! are we to have miracles in sport?—Or, I speak reverently, does God choose idiots by whom to convey divine truths to man?

SUMMARY OF THE CHARACTERISTICS OF SHAKESPEARE'S DRAMAS

IT SEEMS to me that his plays are distinguished from those of all other dramatic poets by the following characteristics:

1. Expectation in preference to surprise. It is like the true reading of the passage—'God said, Let there be light, and there was *light*;'—not there *was* light. As the feeling with which we startle at a shooting star compared with that of watching the sunrise at the pre-established moment, such and so low is surprise compared with expectation.

2. Signal adherence to the great law of nature, that all opposites tend to attract and temper each other. Passion in Shakespeare generally displays libertinism, but involves morality; and if there are exceptions to this, they are, independently of their intrinsic value, all of them indicative of individual character, and, like the farewell admonitions of the parent, have an end beyond the parental relation. Thus the Countess's beautiful precepts to Bertram, by elevating her character, raise that of Helena her favorite, and soften down the point in her which Shakespeare does not mean us not to see, but to see and to forgive, and at length to justify. And so it is in Polonius, who is the personified memory of wisdom no longer actually possessed. This admirable character is always misrepresented on the stage. Shakespeare never intended to exhibit him as a buffoon; for although it was natural that Hamlet,—a young man of fire and genius, detesting formality, and disliking Polonius on political grounds, as imagining that he had assisted his uncle in his usurpation,—should express himself satirically,—yet this must not be taken as exactly the poet's conception of him. In Polonius a certain induration of character had arisen from long habits of business; but take his advice to Laertes, and Ophelia's reverence for his memory, and we shall see that he was meant to be represented as a statesman somewhat past his faculties—his recollections of life all full of wisdom, and showing a knowledge of human nature, whilst what immediately takes place before him, and escapes from him, is indicative of weakness.

But as in Homer all the deities are in armor, even Venus; so in Shakespeare all the characters are strong. Hence real folly and dulness are made by him the vehicles of wisdom. There is no difficulty for one being a fool to imitate a fool; but to be, remain, and speak like a wise man and a great wit, and yet so as to give a vivid representation of a veritable fool,—*hic labor, hoc opus est*. A drunken constable is not uncommon, nor hard to draw; but see and examine what goes to make up a Dogberry.

3. Keeping at all times in the high road of life. Shakespeare has no innocent adulteries, no interesting incests, no virtuous vice;—he never renders that amiable which religion and reason alike teach us to detest, or clothes impurity in the garb of virtue, like Beaumont and Fletcher, the Kotzebues of the day. Shakespeare's fathers are roused by ingratitude, his husbands stung by unfaithfulness; in him, in short, the affections are wounded in those points in which all may, nay, must, feel. Let the morality of Shakespeare be contrasted with that of the writers of his own, or the succeeding age, or of those of the present day, who boast

their superiority in this respect. No one can dispute that the result of such a comparison is altogether in favor of Shakespeare; —even the letters of women of high rank in his age were often coarser than his writings. If he occasionally disgusts a keen sense of delicacy, he never injures the mind; he neither excites, nor flatters passion, in order to degrade the subject of it; he does not use the faulty thing for a faulty purpose, nor carries on warfare against virtue, by causing wickedness to appear as no wickedness, through the medium of a morbid sympathy with the unfortunate. In Shakespeare vice never walks as in twilight; nothing is purposely out of its place;—he inverts not the order of nature and propriety,—does not make every magistrate a drunkard or glutton, nor every poor man meek, humane, and temperate; he has no benevolent butchers, nor any sentimental rat-catchers.

4. Independence of the dramatic interest on the plot. The interest in the plot is always in fact on account of the characters, not *vice versa*, as in almost all other writers; the plot is a mere canvass and no more. Hence arises the true justification of the same stratagem being used in regard to Benedict and Beatrice,— the vanity in each being alike. Take away from the Much Ado About Nothing all that which is not indispensable to the plot, either as having little to do with it, or, at best, like Dogberry and his comrades, forced into the service, when any other less ingeniously absurd watchmen and night-constables would have answered the mere necessities of the action;—take away Benedict, Beatrice, Dogberry, and the reaction of the former on the character of Hero,—and what will remain? In other writers the main agent of the plot is always the prominent character; in Shakespeare it is so, or is not so, as the character is in itself calculated, or not calculated, to form the plot. Don John is the mainspring of the plot of this play; but he is merely shown and then withdrawn.

5. Independence of the interest on the story as the groundwork of the plot. Hence Shakespeare never took the trouble of inventing stories. It was enough for him to select from those that had been already invented or recorded such as had one or other, or both, of two recommendations, namely, suitableness to his particular purpose, and their being parts of popular tradition,—names of which we had often heard, and of their fortunes, and as to which all we wanted was, to see the man himself. So it is just the man himself, the Lear, the Shylock, the Richard, that Shakespeare makes us for the first time acquainted with. Omit the first scene in Lear, and yet every thing will remain; so the first and second scenes in the Merchant of Venice. Indeed it is universally true.

6. Interfusion of the lyrical—that which in its very essence is poetical—not only with the dramatic, as in the plays of Metastasio, where at the end of the scene comes the *aria* as the *exit* speech of the character,—but also in and through the dramatic. Songs in Shakespeare are introduced as songs only, just as songs are in real life, beautifully as some of them are characteristic of the person who has sung or called for them, as Desdemona's 'Willow,' and Ophelia's wild snatches, and the sweet carollings in As You Like It. But the whole of the Midsummer Night's Dream is one continued specimen of the dramatized lyrical. And observe how exquisitely the dramatic of Hotspur;—

> Marry, and I'm glad on't with all my heart;
> I'd rather be a kitten and cry—mew, &c.

melts away into the lyric of Mortimer;—

> I understand thy looks: that pretty Welsh
> Which thou pourest down from these swelling heavens,
> I am too perfect in, &c.
>
> Henry IV. part i. act iii. sc. i.

7. The characters of the *dramatis personæ*, like those in real life, are to be inferred by the reader;—they are not told to him. And it is well worth remarking that Shakespeare's characters, like those in real life, are very commonly misunderstood, and almost always understood by different persons in different ways. The causes are the same in either case. If you take only what the friends of the character say, you may be deceived, and still more so, if that which his enemies say; nay, even the character himself sees himself through the medium of his character, and not exactly as he is. Take all together, not omitting a shrewd hint from the clown or the fool, and perhaps your impression will be right; and you may know whether you have in fact discovered the poet's own idea, by all the speeches receiving light from it, and attesting its reality by reflecting it.

Lastly, in Shakespeare the heterogeneous is united, as it is in nature. You must not suppose a pressure or passion always acting on or in the character!—passion in Shakespeare is that by which the individual is distinguished from others, not that which makes a different kind of him. Shakespeare followed the main march of the human affections. He entered into no analysis of the passions or faiths of men, but assured himself that such and such passions and faiths were grounded in our common nature, and not in the mere accidents of ignorance or disease. This is an important consideration and constitutes our Shakespeare the morning star, the guide and the pioneer, of true philosophy.

ROMEO AND JULIET

IN A former lecture I endeavoured to point out the union of the Poet and the Philosopher, or rather the warm embrace between them, in the "Venus and Adonis" and "Lucrece" of Shakespeare. From thence I passed on to "Love's Labours Lost," as the link between his character as a Poet, and his art as a Dramatist; and I shewed that, although in that work the former was still predominant, yet that the germs of his subsequent dramatic power were easily discernible.

I will now, as I promised in my last, proceed to "Romeo and Juliet," not because it is the earliest, or among the earliest of Shakespeare's works of that kind, but because in it are to be found specimens, in degree, of all the excellences which he afterwards displayed in his more perfect dramas, but differing from them in being less forcibly evidenced, and less happily combined: all the parts are more or less present, but they are not united with the same harmony.

There are, however, in "Romeo and Juliet" passages where the poet's whole excellence is evinced, so that nothing superior to them can be met with in the productions of his after years. The main distinction between this play and others is, as I said, that the parts are less happily combined, or to borrow a phrase from the painter, the whole work is less in keeping. Grand portions are produced: we have limbs of giant growth; but the production, as a whole, in which each part gives delight for itself, and the whole, consisting of these delightful parts, communicates the highest intellectual pleasure and satisfaction, is the result of the application of judgment and taste. These are not to be attained but by painful study, and to the sacrifice of the stronger pleasures derived from the dazzling light which a man of genius throws over every circumstance, and where we are chiefly struck by vivid and distinct images. Taste is an attainment after a poet has been disciplined by experience, and has added to genius that talent by which he knows what part of his genius he can make acceptable, and intelligible to the portion of mankind for which he writes.

In my mind it would be a hopeless symptom, as regards genius, if I found a young man with anything like perfect taste. In the earlier works of Shakespeare we have a profusion of double epithets, and sometimes even the coarsest terms are employed, if they convey a more vivid image; but by degrees the associations are connected with the image they are designed to impress, and the poet descends from the ideal into the real world so far as to conjoin both—to give a sphere of active operations to the ideal, and to elevate and refine the real.

In "Romeo and Juliet" the principal characters may be divided into two classes: in one class passion—the passion of love—is drawn and drawn truly, as well as beautifully; but the persons are not individualised farther than as the actor appears on the stage. It is a very just description and development of love, without giving, if I may so express myself, the philosophical history of it—without shewing how the man became acted upon by that particular passion, but leading it through all the incidents of the drama, and rendering it predominant.

Tybalt is, in himself, a common-place personage. And here allow me to remark upon a great distinction between Shakespeare, and all who have written in imitation of him. I know no character in his plays, (unless indeed Pistol be an exception) which can be called the mere portrait of an individual: while the reader feels all the satisfaction arising from individuality, yet that very individual is a sort of class character, and this circumstance renders Shakespeare the poet of all ages.

Tybalt is a man abandoned to his passions—with all the pride of family, only because he thought it belonged to him as a member of that family, and valuing himself highly, simply because he does not care for death. This indifference to death is perhaps more common than any other feeling: men are apt to flatter themselves extravagantly, merely because they possess a quality which it is a disgrace not to have, but which a wise man never puts forward, but when it is necessary.

Jeremy Taylor in one part of his voluminous works, speaking of a great man, says that he was naturally a coward, as indeed most men are, knowing the value of life, but the power of his reason enabled him, when required, to conduct himself with uniform courage and hardihood. The good bishop, perhaps, had in his mind a story, told by one of the ancients, of a Philosopher and a Coxcomb, on board the same ship during a storm: the Coxcomb reviled the Philosopher for betraying marks of fear: "Why are you so frightened? I am not afraid of being drowned: I do not care a farthing for my life."—"You are perfectly right," said the Philosopher, "for your life is not worth a farthing."

Shakespeare never takes pains to make his characters win

your esteem, but leaves it to the general command of the passions, and to poetic justice. It is most beautiful to observe, in "Romeo and Juliet," that the characters principally engaged in the incidents are preserved innocent from all that could lower them in our opinion, while the rest of the personages, deserving little interest in themselves, derive it from being instrumental in those situations in which the more important personages develope their thoughts and passions.

Look at Capulet—a worthy, noble-minded old man of high rank, with all the impatience that is likely to accompany it. It is delightful to see all the sensibilities of our nature so exquisitely called forth; as if the poet had the hundred arms of the polypus, and had thrown them out in all directions to catch the predominant feeling. We may see in Capulet the manner in which anger seizes hold of everything that comes in its way, in order to express itself, as in the lines where he reproves Tybalt for his fierceness of behaviour, which led him to wish to insult a Montague, and disturb the merriment.—

> "Go to, go to;
> You are a saucy boy. Is't so, indeed?
> This trick may chance to scath you;—I know what.
> You must contrary me! marry, 'tis time.—
> Well said, my hearts!—You are a princox: go:
> Be quiet or—More light, more light!—For shame!
> I'll make you quiet.—What! cheerly, my hearts!"
>
> *Act I., Scene 5.*

The line

> "This trick may chance to scath you;—I know what,"

was an allusion to the legacy Tybalt might expect; and then, seeing the lights burn dimly, Capulet turns his anger against the servants. Thus we see that no one passion is so predominant, but that it includes all the parts of the character, and the reader never has a mere abstract of a passion, as of wrath or ambition, but the whole man is presented to him—the one predominant passion acting, if I may so say, as the leader of the band to the rest.

It could not be expected that the poet should introduce such a character as Hamlet into every play; but even in those personages, which are subordinate to a hero so eminently philosophical, the passion is at least rendered instructive, and induces the reader to look with a keener eye, and a finer judgment into human nature.

Shakespeare has this advantage over all other dramatists—

that he has availed himself of his psychological genius to de-
velope all the minutiæ of the human heart: shewing us the thing
that, to common observers, he seems solely intent upon, he makes
visible what we should not otherwise have seen: just as, after
looking at distant objects through a telescope, when we behold
them subsequently with the naked eye, we see them with greater
distinctness, and in more detail, than we should otherwise have
done.

Mercutio is one of our poet's truly Shakespearean characters;
for throughout his plays, but especially in those of the highest
order, it is plain that the personages were drawn rather from
meditation than from observation, or to speak correctly, more
from observation, the child of meditation. It is comparatively
easy for a man to go about the world, as if with a pocket-book
in his hand, carefully noting down what he sees and hears: by
practice he acquires considerable facility in representing what
he has observed, himself frequently unconscious of its worth, or
its bearings. This is entirely different from the observation of
a mind, which, having formed a theory and a system upon its
own nature, remarks all things that are examples of its truth, con-
firming it in that truth, and, above all, enabling it to convey the
truths of philosophy, as mere effects derived from, what we may
call, the outward watchings of life.

Hence it is that Shakespeare's favourite characters are full of
such lively intellect. Mercutio is a man possessing all the elements
of a poet: the whole world was, as it were, subject to his law of
association. Whenever he wishes to impress anything, all things
become his servants for the purpose: all things tell the same tale,
and sound in unison. This faculty, moreover, is combined with
the manners and feelings of a perfect gentleman, himself utterly
unconscious of his powers. By his loss it was contrived that the
whole catastrophe of the tragedy should be brought about: it
endears him to Romeo, and gives to the death of Mercutio an
importance which it could not otherwise have acquired.

I say this in answer to an observation, I think by Dryden, (to
which indeed Dr. Johnson has fully replied) that Shakespeare
having carried the part of Mercutio as far as he could, till his
genius was exhausted, had killed him in the third Act, to get him
out of the way. What shallow nonesense! As I have remarked,
upon the death of Mercutio the whole catastrophe depends; it is
produced by it. The scene in which it occurs serves to show how
indifference to any subject but one, and aversion to activity on
the part of Romeo, may be overcome and roused to the most reso-
lute and determined conduct. Had not Mercutio been rendered

so amiable and so interesting, we could not have felt so strongly the necessity for Romeo's interference, connecting it immediately, and passionately, with the future fortunes of the lover and his mistress.

But what am I to say of the Nurse? We have been told that her character is the mere fruit of observation—that it is like Swift's "Polite Conversation," certainly the most stupendous work of human memory, and of unceasingly active attention to what passes around us, upon record. The Nurse in "Romeo and Juliet" has sometimes been compared to a portrait by Gerard Dow, in which every hair was so exquisitely painted, that it would bear the test of the microscope. Now, I appeal confidently to my hearers whether the closest observation of the manners of one or two old nurses would have enabled Shakespeare to draw this character of admirable generalisation? Surely not. Let any man conjure up in his mind all the qualities and peculiarities that can possibly belong to a nurse, and he will find them in Shakespeare's picture of the old woman: nothing is omitted. This effect is not produced by mere observation. The great prerogative of genius (and Shakespeare felt and availed himself of it) is now to swell itself to the dignity of a god, and now to subdue and keep dormant some part of that lofty nature, and to descend even to the lowest character—to become everything, in fact, but the vicious.

Thus, in the Nurse you have all the garrulity of old age, and all its fondness; for the affection of old age is one of the greatest consolations of humanity. I have often thought what a melancholy world this would be without children, and what an inhuman world without the aged.

You have also in the Nurse the arrogance of ignorance, with the pride of meanness at being connected with a great family. You have the grossness, too, which that situation never removes, though it sometimes suspends it; and, arising from that grossness, the little low vices attendant upon it, which, indeed, in such minds are scarcely vices.—Romeo at one time was the most delightful and excellent young man, and the Nurse all willingness to assist him; but her disposition soon turns in favour of Paris, for whom she professes precisely the same admiration. How wonderfully are these low peculiarities contrasted with a young and pure mind, educated under different circumstances!

Another point ought to be mentioned as characteristic of the ignorance of the Nurse:—it is, that in all her recollections, she assists herself by the remembrance of visual circumstances. The great difference, in this respect, between the cultivated and the uncultivated mind is this—that the cultivated mind will be found to recal the past by certain regular trains of cause and effect; whereas, with the uncultivated mind, the past is recalled wholly by coincident images, or facts which happened at the same time. This position is fully exemplified in the following passages put into the mouth of the Nurse:—

> "Even or odd, of all days in the year,
> Come Lammas eve at night shall she be fourteen.
> Susan and she—God rest all Christian souls!—
> Were of an age.—Well, Susan is with God;
> She was too good for me. But, as I said,
> On Lammas eve at night shall she be fourteen;
> That shall she, marry: I remember it well.
> 'Tis since the earthquake now eleven years;
> And she was wean'd,—I never shall forget it,—
> Of all the days of the year, upon that day;
> For I had then laid wormwood to my dug,
> Sitting in the sun under the dove-house wall:
> My lord and you were then at Mantua.—
> Nay, I do bear a brain:—but, as I said,
> When it did taste the wormwood on the nipple
> Of my dug, and felt it bitter, pretty fool,
> To see it tetchy, and fall out with the dug!
> Shake, quoth the dove-house: 'twas no need, I trow,
> To bid me trudge.
> And since that time it is eleven years;
> For then she could stand alone."
>
> *Act I., Scene 3.*

She afterwards goes on with similar visual impressions, so true to the character.—More is here brought into one portrait than could have been ascertained by one man's mere observation, and without the introduction of a single incongruous point.

I honour, I love, the works of Fielding as much, or perhaps more, than those of any other writer of fiction of that kind: take Fielding in his characters of postillions, landlords, and landladies, waiters, or indeed, of any-body who had come before his eye, and nothing can be more true, more happy, or more humorous; but in all his chief personages, Tom Jones for instance, where Fielding was not directed by observation, where he could not assist himself by the close copying of what he saw, where it is necessary that something should take place, some words be spoken, or some object described, which he could not have witnessed, (his soliloquies for example, or the interview between the hero and Sophia Western before the reconciliation) and I will venture to say. loving and honouring the man and his productions as I do, that nothing can be more forced and unnatural: the language is without vivacity or spirit, the whole matter is incongruous, and totally destitute of psychological truth.

On the other hand, look at Shakespeare: where can any character be produced that does not speak the language of nature? where does he not put into the mouths of his *dramatis personæ*, be they high or low, Kings or Constables, precisely what they must have said? Where, from observation, could he learn the language proper to Sovereigns, Queens, Noblemen or Generals? yet he invariably uses it.—Where, from observation, could he have learned such lines as these, which are put into the mouth of Othello, when he is talking to Iago of Brabantio?

> "Let him do his spite:
> My services, which I have done the signiory,
> Shall out-tongue his complaints. 'Tis yet to know,
> Which, when I know that boasting is an honour,
> I shall promulgate, I fetch my life and being
> From men of royal siege; and my demerits
> May speak, unbonneted, to as proud a fortune
> As this that I have reach'd: for know, Iago,
> But that I love the gentle Desdemona,
> I would not my unhoused free condition
> Put into circumscription and confine
> For the sea's worth."

Act I., Scene 2.

I ask where was Shakespeare to observe such language as this? If he did observe it, it was with the inward eye of meditation upon his own nature: for the time, he became Othello, and spoke as Othello, in such circumstances, must have spoken.

Another remark I may make upon "Romeo and Juliet" is, that in this tragedy the poet is not, as I have hinted, entirely blended with the dramatist,—at least, not in the degree to be afterwards noticed in "Lear," "Hamlet," "Othello," or "Macbeth." Capulet and Montague not unfrequently talk a language only belonging to the poet, and not so characteristic of, and peculiar to, the passions of persons in the situations in which they are placed—a mistake, or rather an indistinctness, which many of our later dramatists have carried through the whole of their productions.

When I read the song of Deborah, I never think that she is a poet, although I think the song itself a sublime poem: it is as simple a dithyrambic production as exists in any language; but it is the proper and characteristic effusion of a woman highly elevated by triumph, by the natural hatred of oppressors, and resulting from a bitter sense of wrong: it is a song of exultation on deliverance from these evils, a deliverance accomplished by herself. When she exclaims, "The inhabitants of the villages ceased, they ceased in Israel, until that I, Deborah, arose, that I arose a mother in Israel," it is poetry in the highest sense: we have no reason, however, to suppose that if she had not been agitated by passion, and animated by victory, she would have been able so to express herself; or that if she had been placed in different circumstances, she would have used such language of truth and passion. We are to remember that Shakespeare, not placed under circumstances of excitement, and only wrought upon by his own vivid and vigorous imagination, writes a language that invariably, and intuitively becomes the condition and position of each character.

On the other hand, there is a language not descriptive of passion, not uttered under the influence of it, which is at the same time poetic, and shows a high and active fancy, as when Capulet says to Paris,—

> "Such comfort as do lusty young men feel,
> When well-apparell'd April on the heel
> Of limping winter treads, even such delight
> Among fresh female buds, shall you this night
> Inherit at my house."
>
> *Act I., Scene 2.*

Here the poet may be said to speak, rather than the dramatist; and it would be easy to adduce other passages from this play, where Shakespeare, for a moment forgetting the character, utters his own words in his own person.

In my mind, what have often been censured as Shakespeare's conceits are completely justifiable, as belonging to the state, age, or feeling of the individual. Sometimes, when they cannot be vindicated on these grounds, they may well be excused by the taste of his own and of the preceding age; as for instance, in Romeo's speech,

> "Here's much to do with hate, but more with love:—
> Why then, O brawling love! O loving hate!
> O anything, of nothing first created!
> O heavy lightness! serious vanity!
> Misshapen chaos of well-seeming forms!
> Feather of lead, bright smoke, cold fire, sick health!
> Still-waking sleep, that is not what it is!"
>
> *Act I., Scene 1.*

I dare not pronounce such passages as these to be absolutely unnatural, not merely because I consider the author a much better judge than I can be, but because I can understand and allow for an effort of the mind, when it would describe what it cannot satisfy itself with the description of, to reconcile opposites and qualify contradictions, leaving a middle state of mind more strictly appropriate to the imagination than any other, when it is, as it were, hovering between images. As soon as it is fixed on one image, it becomes understanding; but while it is unfixed and wavering between them, attaching itself permanently to none, it is imagination. Such is the fine description of Death in Milton:—

> "The other shape,
> If shape it might be call'd, that shape had none
> Distinguishable in member, joint, or limb,
> Or substance might be call'd, that shadow seem'd,
> For each seem'd either: black it stood as night;
> Fierce as ten furies, terrible as hell,
> And shook a dreadful dart: what seem'd his head
> The likeness of a kingly crown had on."
> *Paradise Lost,* Book II.

The grandest efforts of poetry are where the imagination is called forth, not to produce a distinct form, but a strong working of the mind, still offering what is still repelled, and again creating what is again rejected; the result being what the poet wishes to impress, namely, the substitution of a sublime feeling of the unimaginable for a mere image. I have sometimes thought that the passage just read might be quoted as exhibiting the narrow limit of painting, as compared with the boundless power of poetry: painting cannot go beyond a certain point; poetry rejects all control, all confinement. Yet we know that sundry painters have attempted pictures of the meeting between Satan and Death at the gates of Hell; and how was Death represented? Not as Milton has described him, but by the most defined thing that can be imagined—a skeleton, the dryest and hardest image that it is possible to discover; which, instead of keeping the mind in a state of activity, reduces it to the merest passivity,—an image, compared with which a square, a triangle, or any other mathematical figure, is a luxuriant fancy.

It is a general but mistaken notion that, because some forms of writing, and some combinations of thought, are not usual, they are not natural; but we are to recollect that the dramatist represents his characters in every situation of life and in every state of mind, and there is no form of language that may not be introduced with effect by a great and judicious poet, and yet be most strictly according to nature. Take punning, for instance, which may be the lowest, but at all events is the most harmless, kind of wit, because it never excites envy. A pun may be a necessary consequence of association: one man, attempting to prove something that was resisted by another, might when agitated by strong feeling, employ a term used by his adversary with a directly contrary meaning to that for which that adversary had resorted to it: it might come into his mind as one way, and sometimes the best, of replying to that adversary. This form of speech is generally produced by a mixture of anger and contempt, and punning is a natural mode of expressing them.

It is my intention to pass over none of the important so-called conceits of Shakespeare, not a few of which are introduced into his later productions with great propriety and effect. We are not to forget, that at the time he lived there was an attempt at, and an affectation of, quaintness and adornment, which emanated from the Court, and against which satire was directed by Shakespeare in the character of Osrick in Hamlet. Among the schoolmen of that age, and earlier, nothing was more common than the use of conceits: it began with the revival of letters, and the bias thus given was very generally felt and acknowledged.

I have in my possession a dictionary of phrases, in which the epithets applied to love, hate, jealousy, and such abstract terms, are arranged; and they consist almost entirely of words taken from Seneca and his imitators, or from the schoolmen, showing perpetual antithesis, and describing the passions by the conjunction and combination of things absolutely irreconcileable. In treating the matter thus, I am aware that I am only palliating the practice in Shakespeare: he ought to have had nothing to do with merely temporary peculiarities: he wrote not for his own only, but for all ages, and so far I admit the use of some of his conceits to be a defect. They detract sometimes from his universality as to time, person, and situation.

If we were able to discover, and to point out the peculiar faults, as well as the peculiar beauties of Shakespeare, it would materially assist us in deciding what authority ought to be attached to certain portions of what are generally called his works. If we met with a play, or certain scenes of a play, in which we could trace neither his defects nor his excellences, we should have the strongest reason for believing that he had had no hand in it. In the case of scenes so circumstanced we might come to the conclusion that they were taken from the older plays, which, in some instances, he reformed or altered, or that they were inserted afterwards by some underhand, in order to please the mob. If a drama by Shakespeare turned out to be too heavy for popular audiences, the clown might be called in to lighten the representation; and if it appeared that what was added was not in Shakespeare's manner, the conclusion would be inevitable, that it was not from Shakespeare's pen.

It remains for me to speak of the hero and heroine, of Romeo and Juliet themselves; and I shall do so with unaffected diffidence, not merely on account of the delicacy, but of the great importance of the subject. I feel that it is impossible to defend Shakespeare from the most cruel of all charges,—that he is an immoral writer—without entering fully into his mode of pourtraying female characters, and of displaying the passion of love. It seems to me, that he has done both with greater perfection than any other writer of the known world, perhaps with the single exception of Milton in his delineation of Eve.

When I have heard it said, or seen it stated, that Shakespeare wrote for man, but the gentle Fletcher for woman, it has always given me something like acute pain, because to me it seems to do the greatest injustice to Shakespeare: when, too, I remember how much character is formed by what we read, I cannot look upon it as a light question, to be passed over as a mere amusement, like a game of cards or chess. I never have been able to tame down my mind to think poetry a sport, or an occupation for idle hours.

Perhaps there is no more sure criterion of refinement in moral character, of the purity of intellectual intention, and of the deep conviction and perfect sense of what our own nature really is in all its combinations, than the different definitions different men would give of love. I will not detain you by stating the various known definitions, some of which it may be better not to repeat: I will rather give you one of my own, which, I apprehend, is equally free from the extravagance of pretended Platonism (which, like other things which super-moralise, is sure to demoralise) and from its grosser opposite.

Consider myself and my fellow-men as a sort of link between heaven and earth, being composed of body and soul, with power to reason and to will, and with that perpetual aspiration which tells us that this is ours for a while, but it is not ourselves; considering man, I say, in this two-fold character, yet united in one person, I conceive that there can be no correct definition of love which does not correspond with our being, and with that subordination of one part to another which constitutes our perfection. I would say therefore that—

"Love is a desire of the whole being to be united to some thing, or some being, felt necessary to its completeness, by the most perfect means that nature permits, and reason dictates."

It is inevitable to every noble mind, whether man or woman, to feel itself, of itself, imperfect and insufficient, not as an animal only, but as a moral being. How wonderfully, then, has Providence contrived for us, by making that which is necessary to us a step in our exaltation to a higher and nobler state! The Creator has ordained that one should possess qualities which the other has not, and the union of both is the most complete ideal of human character. In everything the blending of the similar with the dissimilar is the secret of all pure delight. Who shall dare to stand alone, and vaunt himself, in himself, sufficient? In poetry it is the blending of passion with order that constitutes perfection: this is still more the case in morals, and more than all in the exclusive attachment of the sexes.

True it is, that the world and its business may be carried on without marriage; but it is so evident that Providence intended man (the only animal of all climates, and whose reason is pre-eminent over instinct) to be the master of the world, that marriage, or the knitting together of society by the tenderest, yet firmest ties, seems ordained to render him capable of maintaining his superiority over the brute creation. Man alone has been privileged to clothe himself, and to do all things so as to make him, as it were, a secondary creator of himself, and of his own happiness or misery: in this, as in all, the image of the Deity is impressed upon him.

Providence, then, has not left us to prudence only; for the power of calculation, which prudence implies, cannot have existed, but in a state which pre-supposes marriage. If God has done this, shall we suppose that he has given us no moral sense, no yearning, which is something more than animal, to secure that, without which man might form a herd, but could not be a society? The very idea seems to breathe absurdity.

From this union arise the paternal, filial, brotherly and sisterly relations of life; and every state is but a family magnified. All the operations of mind, in short, all that distinguishes us from brutes, originate in the more perfect state of domestic life. —One infallible criterion in forming an opinion of a man is the reverence in which he holds women. Plato has said, that in this way we rise from sensuality to affection, from affection to love, and from love to the pure intellectual delight by which we become worthy to conceive that infinite in ourselves, without which it is impossible for man to believe in a God. In a word, the grandest and most delightful of all promises has been expressed to us by this practical state—our marriage with the Redeemer of mankind.

I might safely appeal to every man who hears me, who in youth has been accustomed to abandon himself to his animal passions, whether when he first really fell in love, the earliest symptom was not a complete change in his manners, a contempt and a hatred of himself for having excused his conduct by asserting, that he acted according to the dictates of nature, that his vices were the inevitable consequences of youth, and that his passions at that period of life could not be conquered? The surest friend of chastity is love: it leads us, not to sink the mind in the body, but to draw up the body to the mind—the immortal part of our nature. See how contrasted in this respect are some portions of the works of writers, whom I need not name, with other portions of the same works: the ebullitions of comic humour have at times, by a lamentable confusion, been made the means of debasing our nature, while at other times, even in the same volume, we are happy to notice the utmost purity, such as the purity of love, which above all other qualities renders us most pure and lovely.

Love is not, like hunger, a mere selfish appetite: it is an associative quality. The hungry savage is nothing but an animal, thinking only of the satisfaction of his stomach: what is the first effect of love, but to associate the feeling with every object in nature? the trees whisper, the roses exhale their perfumes, the nightingales sing, nay the very skies smile in unison with the feeling of true and pure love. It gives to every object in nature a power of the heart, without which it would indeed be spiritless.

Shakespeare has described this passion in various states and stages, beginning, as was most natural, with love in the young. Does he open his play by making Romeo and Juliet in love at first sight—at the first glimpse, as any ordinary thinker would do? Certainly not: he knew what he was about, and how he was to accomplish what he was about: he was to develope the whole passion, and he commences with the first elements—that sense of imperfection, that yearning to combine itself with something lovely. Romeo became enamoured of the idea he had formed in his own mind, and then, as it were, christened the first real being of the contrary sex as endowed with the perfections he desired. He appears to be in love with Rosaline; but, in truth, he is in love only with his own idea. He felt that necessity of being beloved which no noble mind can be without. Then our poet, our poet who so well knew human nature, introduces Romeo to Juliet, and makes it not only a violent, but a permanent love—a point for which Shakespeare has been ridiculed by the ignorant and unthinking. Romeo is first represented in a state most susceptible of love, and then, seeing Juliet, he took and retained the infection.

This brings me to observe upon a characteristic of Shakespeare, which belongs to a man of profound thought and high genius. It has been too much the custom, when anything that happened in his dramas could not easily be explained by the few words the poet has employed, to pass it idly over, and to say that it is beyond our reach, and beyond the power of philosophy—a sort of terra incognita for discoverers—a great ocean to be hereafter explored. Others have treated such passages as hints and glimpses of something now nonexistent, as the sacred fragments of an ancient and ruined temple, all the portions of which are beautiful, although their particular relation to each other is unknown. Shakespeare knew the human mind, and its most minute and intimate workings, and he never introduces a word, or a thought, in vain or out of place: if we do not understand him, it is our own fault or the fault of copyists and typographers; but study, and the possession of some small stock of the knowledge by which he worked, will enable us often to detect and explain his meaning. He never wrote at random, or hit upon points of character and conduct by chance; and the smallest fragment of his mind not unfrequently gives a clue to a most perfect, regular, and consistent whole.

As I may not have another opportunity, the introduction of Friar Laurence into this tragedy enables me to remark upon the different manner in which Shakespeare has treated the priestly character, as compared with other writers. In Beaumont and Fletcher priests are represented as a vulgar mockery; and, as in others of their dramatic personages, the errors of a few are mistaken for the demeanour of the many: but in Shakespeare they always carry with them our love and respect. He made no injurious abstracts: he took no copies from the worst parts of our nature; and, like the rest, his characters of priests are truly drawn from the general body.

It may strike some as singular, that throughout all his productions he has never introduced the passion of avarice. The truth is, that it belongs only to particular parts of our nature, and is prevalent only in particular states of society; hence it could not, and cannot, be permanent. The Miser of Molière and Plautus is now looked upon as a species of madman, and avarice as a species of madness. Elwes, of whom everybody has heard, was an individual influenced by an insane condition of mind; but, as a passion, avarice has disappeared. How admirably, then, did Shakespeare foresee, that if he drew such a character it could not be permanent! he drew characters which would always be natural, and therefore permanent, inasmuch as they were not dependent upon accidental circumstances.

There is not one of the plays of Shakespeare that is built upon anything but the best and surest foundation; the characters must be permanent—permanent while men continue men,—because they stand upon what is absolutely necessary to our existence. This cannot be said even of some of the most famous authors of antiquity. Take the capital tragedies of Orestes, or of the husband of Jocasta: great as was the genius of the writers, these dramas have an obvious fault, and the fault lies at the very root of the action. In Œdipus a man is represented oppressed by fate for a crime of which he was not morally guilty; and while we read we are obliged to say to ourselves, that in those days they considered actions without reference to the real guilt of the persons.

There is no character in Shakespeare in which envy is pourtrayed, with one solitary exception—Cassius, in "Julius Cæsar"; yet even there the vice is not hateful, inasmuch as it is counterbalanced by a number of excellent qualities and virtues. The poet leads the reader to suppose that it is rather something constitutional, something derived from his parents, something that he cannot avoid, and not something that he has himself acquired; thus throwing the blame from the will of man to some inevitable circumstance, and leading us to suppose that it is hardly to be looked upon as one of those passions that actually debase the mind.

Whenever love is described as of a serious nature, and much more when it is to lead to a tragical result, it depends upon a law of the mind, which, I believe, I shall hereafter be able to make intelligible, and which would not only justify Shakespeare, but show an analogy to all his other characters.

HAMLET, 1813

SHAKESPEARE'S mode of conceiving characters out of his own intellectual and moral faculties, by conceiving any one intellectual or moral faculty in morbid excess and then placing himself, thus mutilated and diseased, under given circumstances. This we shall have repeated occasion to re-state and enforce. In Hamlet I conceive him to have wished to exemplify the moral necessity of a due balance between our attention to outward objects and our meditation on inward thoughts—a due balance between the real and the imaginary world. In Hamlet this balance does not exist—his thoughts, images, and fancy [being] far more vivid than his perceptions, and his very perceptions instantly passing thro' the medium of his contemplations, and acquiring as they pass a form and color not naturally their own. Hence great, enormous, intellectual activity, and a consequent proportionate aversion to real action, with all its symptoms and accompanying qualities.

> Action is transitory, a step, a blow, etc.

Then as in the first instance proceed with a cursory survey thro' the play, with comments, etc.

(1) The easy language of ordinary life, contrasted with the direful music and wild rhythm of the opening of *Macbeth*. Yet the armour, the cold, the dead silence, all placing the mind in the state congruous with tragedy.

(2) The admirable judgement and yet confidence in his own marvellous powers in introducing the ghost twice, each rising in solemnity and awfulness before its third appearance to Hamlet himself.

(3) Shakespeare's tenderness with regard to all innocent superstition: no Tom Paine declarations and pompous philosophy.

(4) The first words that Hamlet speaks—

> A little more than kin, and less than kind.

He begins with that play of words, the complete absence of which characterizes *Macbeth* . . . [?]. No one can have heard quarrels among the vulgar but must have noticed the close connection of punning with angry contempt. Add too what is highly characteristic of superfluous activity of mind, a sort of playing with a thread or watch chain or snuff box.

(5) And [note] how the character develops itself in the next speech—the aversion to externals, the betrayed habit of brooding over the world within him, and the prodigality of beautiful words, which are, as it were, the half embodyings of thoughts, that make them more than thoughts, give them an outness, a reality *sui generis*, and yet retain their correspondence and shadowy approach to the images and movements within.

(6) The first soliloquy [I. ii.

O, that this too too solid flesh would melt.]

.The] reasons why *taedium vitae* oppresses minds like Hamlet's: the exhaustion of bodily feeling from perpetual exertion of mind; that all mental form being indefinite and ideal, realities must needs become cold, and hence it is the indefinite that combines with passion.

(7) And in this mood the relation is made [by Horatio, who tells Hamlet of his father's ghost], of which no more than [that] it is a perfect model of dramatic narration and dramatic style, the purest poetry and yet the most natural language, equally distant from the inkhorn and the provincial plough.

(8) Hamlet's running into long reasonings [while waiting for the ghost], carrying off the impatience and uneasy feelings of expectation by running away from the *particular* in[to] the *general*. This aversion to personal, individual concerns, and escape to generalizations and general reasonings a most important characteristic.

Besides that, it does away with surprizing all the ill effects that the two former appearances of the ghost would have produced by rendering the ghost an expected phenomenon, and restores to it all the suddenness essential to the effect.

(9) The ghost [is] a superstition connected with the most [sacred?] truths of revealed religion and, therefore, O how contrasted from the withering and wild language of the [witches in] *Macbeth.*

(10) The instant and over violent resolve of Hamlet—how he wastes in the efforts of resolving the energies of action. Compare this with the . . . [?] of Medea; and [note] his quick relapse into the satirical and ironical vein [after the ghost disappears].

(11) Now comes the difficult task, [interpreting the jests of Hamlet when his companions overtake him].

The familiarity, comparative at least, of a brooding mind with shadows is something. Still more the necessary alternation when one muscle long strained is relaxed; the antagonist comes into action of itself. Terror [is] closely connected with the ludicrous; the latter [is] the common mode by which the mind tries to emancipate itself from terror. The laugh is rendered by nature itself the language of extremes, even as tears are. Add too, Hamlet's wildness is but *half-false.* O that subtle trick to pretend the *acting* only when we are very near *being* what we act. And this explanation of the same with Ophelia's vivid images [describing Hamlet's desperation when he visits her]; nigh akin to, and productive of, temporary mania. [See II. i. 75-100, the speeches of] Ophelia, [which were just mentioned,] proved by [Hamlet's wildness at Ophelia's grave, V. i. 248-78].

(12) Hamlet's character, as I have conceived [it, is] described by himself [in the soliloquy after the players leave him—

O, what a rogue and peasant slave am I, etc.]

But previous to this, speak of the exquisite judgement in the diction of the introduced play. Absurd to suppose it extracted in order to be ridiculed from [an] old play. It is in thought and even in the separate parts of the diction highly poetical, so that this is its fault, that it is too poetical, the language of lyric vehemence and epic pomp, not of the drama. But what if Shakespeare had made the language truly dramatic? Where would have been the contrast between *Hamlet* and the play of *Hamlet?*

(13) And then conclude with the objections; see the cover and first page of this book. Schlegel, III, 67, 69.

(14) After this whether it will not do to speak of the honest pride of our Englishmen—Milton, Shakespeare, Bacon, Newton, and now Wellington—and how the glorious events of the day all are [?] deducible from the attack on England.

＊　　＊　　＊　　＊　　＊

The significancy of the names of Shakespeare's plays, the "Twelfth Night," "Midsummer Night's Dream," "As You Like It," "Winter's Tale," when the total effect is produced by a co-ordination of the characters, by a wreath of flowers: but "Coriolanus," "Lear," "Romeo and Juliet," "Hamlet," "Othello, Moor of Venice," when the effect arises from the subordination of all to one, either as the prominent person or the principal object. "Cymbeline" is the only exception and even that has its advantages and prepares the audience for the chaos of time, place, and costume by throwing the date back into a [legendary] king's . . . [?] reign.

But as of more importance, so more striking is the judgement displayed by our truly *dramatic* poet as well as *poet* of the drama in the management of his first scenes. With the single exception of *Cymbeline* they either place before us in one glance both the past and the future in some effect which implies the continuance and full agency of its cause, as in the feuds and party spirit of the servants of the two houses in the first scene of *Romeo and Juliet,* or in the degrading passion for shews and public spectacles, and the overwhelming attachment for the newest successful war-chief in the Roman people, already become a populace, contrasted with the jealousy of the nobles, in *Julius Caesar;* or they at once commence the action so as to excite a curiosity for the explanation in the following [scenes], as in the storm of the wind, the waves, and the boatswain in the *Tempest,* instead of anticipating our curiosity, as in most other first scenes and in too many other first *acts;* or they act, by contrast of diction suited to the characters, at once to heighten the effect and yet to give a naturalness to the language and rhythm of the principal characters, either as that of Prospero and Miranda, in the last instance, by the appropriate lowness of the style, or as in *King John* by the equally appropriate stateliness of state harangue or official narration, so that the after blank verse seems to belong to the rank and quality of the speakers and not to the poet; or they strike at once the key-note, give the predominant spirit of the play, as in the *Twelfth Night* and in *Macbeth;* or the first scene comprizes all these advantages at once, as in *Hamlet.*

In all the best attested stories of ghosts and visions, as in that of Brutus, of Archbishop Cranmer, that of Benvenuto Cellini recorded by himself, and the vision of Galileo communicated by him to his favorite pupil Torricelli, the ghost-seers were in a state of cold or chilling damp from without, and of anxiety inwardly. It has been with all of them as with Francisco on his guard—alone, in the depth and silence of the night—"'twas bitter cold and they were sick at heart"—and "not a mouse stirring." The attention to minute sounds,—naturally associated with the recollection of minute objects, and the more familiar and trifling, the more impressive from the unusualness of their producing any impression at all—gives a philosophic pertinency to this last image, but it has likewise its dramatic use and purpose, for its commonness in ordinary conversation tends to produce the sense of *reality,* and at once hides the poet and yet approximates the reader or spectator to that state in which the highest poetry will appear, and in its component parts, tho' not in whole composition, really is the language of nature. If I should not speak it, I feel that I should be thinking it; the voice only is the poet's, the words are my own. That Shakespeare meant to put an *effect* in the actor's power in the very first words, *"Who's there?"* is evident from the impatience expressed in the words that follow. "Nay, answer me: stand and unfold yourself." A brave man is never so peremptory, as when he fears that he is afraid.

The gradual transition from the silence and the recent habit of listening in Francisco's "I think I hear them," and the more cheerful call out, which a good actor would observe, in the "Stand ho! Who is there?" Bernardo's enquiry after Horatio, and the repetition of his name, and in his own presence, [indicate] *respect* or eagerness . . . [?] that implies him as one of the persons who are to appear in the foreground; and the scepticism attributed to him—

> Horatio says, 'tis but our phantasy;
> And will not let belief take hold of him—

preparing us for Hamlet's after eulogy on him as one whose blood and judgement were happily commingled. The indefiniteness of the first opening out of the occasion of this anxiety: "Welcome, Horatio!" (gladness); "welcome, good Marcellus" (courtesy).

> *M.* What has *this thing* [appear'd again to-night?]

rising with the next speech into

> Touching this dreaded sight twice seen of us.

Horatio's confirmation of his disbelief—

> [Tush, tush, 'twill not appear]—

and the silence with which the scene opened again restored by the narration. The solemnity of it and the exquisite proof of the narrator's deep feeling of what he is himself about to relate, [shown] by his turning off from it, as from a something that is forcing him too deep into himself, to the outward objects, the realities of nature that had accompanied it—

> [*Ber.*] Last night of all,
> [When yond same star that's westward from the pole
> Had made his course to illume that part of heaven
> Where now it burns, Marcellus and myself,
> The bell then beating one,—]

seem to contradict the critical law that what is told makes a faint impression compared with what is beheld, and do indeed convey to the mind more than the eye can see; and [note] the interruption of the narration at the very moment when we are most intensely listening for the sequel, and have our thoughts diverted from the dreaded sight in expectation of the desired, yet almost dreaded, tale, thus giving all the suddenness and surprize of the original appearance—

> Peace, break thee off! look where it comes again!

The judgement in having two of the persons present as having seen it twice before, hence naturally confirming their former opinions, while the sceptic is silent, and after [he has] twice been addressed by his friends, answers with two hasty syllables, "Most like," and confession of horror—

[it harrows me with fear and wonder.]

HAMLET

THE seeming inconsistencies in the conduct and character of Hamlet have long exercised the conjectural ingenuity of critics; and, as we are always loth to suppose that the cause of defective apprehension is in ourselves, the mystery has been too commonly explained by the very easy process of setting it down as in fact inexplicable, and by resolving the phenomenon into a misgrowth or *lusus* of the capricious and irregular genius of Shakespeare. The shallow and stupid arrogance of these vulgar and indolent decisions I would fain do my best to expose. I believe the character of Hamlet may be traced to Shakespeare's deep and accurate science in mental philosophy. Indeed, that this character must have some connection with the common fundamental laws of our nature may be assumed from the fact, that Hamlet has been the darling of every country in which the literature of England has been fostered. In order to understand him, it is essential that we should reflect on the constitution of our own minds. Man is distinguished from the brute animals in proportion as thought prevails over sense: but in the healthy processes of the mind, a balance is constantly maintained between the impressions from outward objects and the inward operations of the intellect:—for if there be an overbalance in the contemplative faculty, man thereby becomes the creature of mere meditation, and loses his natural power of action. Now one of Shakespeare's modes of creating characters is, to conceive any one intellectual or moral faculty in morbid excess, and then to place himself, Shakespeare, thus mutilated or diseased, under given circumstances. In Hamlet he seems to have wished to exemplify the moral necessity of a due balance between our attention to the objects of our senses, and our meditation on the workings of our minds,—an *equilibrium* between the real and the imaginary worlds. In Hamlet this balance is disturbed: his thoughts, and the images of his fancy, are far more vivid than his actual perceptions, and his very perceptions, instantly passing through the *medium* of his contemplations, acquire, as they pass, a form and a color not naturally their own. Hence we see a great, an almost enormous, intellectual activity, and a proportionate aversion to real action, consequent upon it, with all its symptoms and accompanying qualities. This character Shakespeare places in circumstances, under which it is obliged to act on the spur of the moment:— Hamlet is brave and careless of death; but he vacillates from sensibility, and procrastinates from thought, and loses the power of action in the energy of resolve. Thus it is that this tragedy presents a direct contrast to that of Macbeth; the one proceeds with the utmost slowness, the other with a crowded and breathless rapidity.

The effect of this overbalance of the imaginative power is beautifully illustrated in the everlasting broodings and superfluous activities of Hamlet's mind, which, unseated from its healthy relation, is constantly occupied with the world within, and abstracted from the world without,—giving substance to shadows, and throwing a mist over all common-place actualities. It is the nature of thought to be indefinite;—definiteness belongs to external imagery alone. Hence it is that the sense of sublimity arises, not from the sight of an outward object, but from the beholder's reflection upon it;—not from the sensuous impression, but from the imaginative reflex. Few have seen a celebrated waterfall without feeling something akin to disappointment: it is only subsequently that the image comes back full into the mind, and brings with it a train of grand or beautiful associations. Hamlet feels this; his senses are in a state of trance, and he looks upon external things as hieroglyphics. His soliloquy—

> Oh! that this too, too solid flesh would melt, &c.

springs from that craving after the indefinite—for that which is not—which most easily besets men of genius; and the self-delusion common to this temper of mind is finely exemplified in the character which Hamlet gives of himself:—

> —It can not be
> But I am pigeon-livered, and lack gall
> To make oppression bitter.

He mistakes the seeing his chains for the breaking of them, delays action till action is of no use, and dies the victim of mere circumstance and accident.

There is a great significancy in the names of Shakespeare's plays. In the Twelfth Night, Midsummer Night's Dream, As You Like It, and Winter's Tale, the total effect is produced by a co-ordination of the characters as in a wreath of flowers. But in Coriolanus, Lear, Romeo and Juliet, Hamlet, Othello, &c., the effect arises from the subordination of all to one, either as the prominent person, or the principal object. Cymbeline is the only exception; and even that has its advantages in preparing the audience for the chaos of time, place, and costume, by throwing the date back into a fabulous king's reign.

But as of more importance, so more striking, is the judgment displayed by our truly dramatic poet, as well as poet of the drama, in the management of his first scenes. With the single exception of Cymbeline, they either place before us at one glance both the past and the future in some effect, which implies the continuance and full agency of its cause, as in the feuds and party-spirit of the servants of the two houses in the first scene of Romeo and Juliet; or in the degrading passion for shows and public spectacles, and the overwhelming attachment for the newest successful war-chief in the Roman people, already become a populace, contrasted with the jealousy of the nobles in Julius Cæsar;—or they at once commence the action so as to excite a curiosity for the explanation in the following scenes, as in the storm of wind and waves, and the boatswain in the Tempest, instead of anticipating our curiosity, as in most other first scenes, and in too many other first acts;—or they act, by contrast of diction suited to the characters, at once to heighten the effect, and yet to give a naturalness to the language and rhythm of the principal personages, either as that of Prospero and Miranda by the appropriate lowness of the style,—or as in King John, by the equally appropriate stateliness of official harangues or narratives, so that the after blank verse seems to belong to the rank and quality of the speakers, and not to the poet;—or they strike at once the key-note, and give the predominant spirit of the play, as in the Twelfth Night and in Macbeth;—or finally, the first scene comprises all these advantages at once, as in Hamlet.

Compare the easy language of common life, in which this drama commences, with the direful music and wild wayward rhythm and abrupt lyrics of the opening of Macbeth. The tone is quite familiar;—there is no poetic description of night, no elaborate information conveyed by one speaker to another of what both had immediately before their senses—(such as the first distich in Addison's Cato, which is a translation into poetry of 'Past four o'clock and a dark morning!');—and yet nothing bordering on the comic on the one hand, nor any striving of the intellect on the other. It is precisely the language of sensation among men who feared no charge of effeminacy for feeling what they had no want of resolution to bear. Yet the armor, the dead silence, the watchfulness that first interrupts it, the welcome relief of the guard, the cold, the broken expressions of compelled attention to bodily feelings still under control—all excellently accord with, and prepare for, the after gradual rise into tragedy;—but, above all, into a tragedy, the interest of which is as eminently *ad et apud intra*, as that of Macbeth is directly *ad extra*.

In all the best attested stories of ghosts and visions, as in that of Brutus, of Archbishop Cranmer, that of Benvenuto Cellini recorded by himself, and the vision of Galileo communicated by him to his favorite pupil Torricelli, the ghost-seers were in a state of cold or chilling damp from without, and of anxiety inwardly. It has been with all of them as with Francisco on his guard,—alone, in the depth and silence of the night;—' 'twas bitter cold, and they were sick at heart, and *not a mouse stirring.*' The attention to minute sounds,—naturally associated with the recollection of minute objects, and the more familiar and trifling, the more impressive from the unusualness of their producing any impression at all—gives a philosophic pertinency to this last image; but it has likewise its dramatic use and purpose. For its commonness in ordinary conversation tends to produce the sense of reality, and at once hides the poet, and yet approximates the reader or spectator to that state in which the highest poetry will appear, and in its component parts, though not in the whole composition, really is, the language of nature. If I should not speak it, I feel that I should be thinking it;—the voice only is the poet's,—the words are my own. That Shakespeare meant to put an effect in the actor's power in the very first words—'Who's there?'—is evident from the impatience expressed by the startled Francisco in the words that follow—'Nay, answer me: stand and unfold yourself.' A brave man is never so peremptory, as when he fears that he is afraid. Observe the gradual transition from the silence and the still recent habit of listening in Francisco's—'I think I hear them'—to the more cheerful call out, which a good actor would observe, in the—'Stand ho! Who is there?' Bernardo's inquiry after Horatio, and the repetition of his name and in his own presence indicate a respect or an eagerness that implies him as one of the persons who are in the foreground; and the skepticism attributed to him,—

> Horatio says, 'tis but our fantasy;
> And will not let belief take hold of him—

prepares us for Hamlet's after-eulogy on him as one whose blood and judgment were happily commingled. The actor should also be careful to distinguish the expectation and gladness of Bernardo's 'Welcome, Horatio!' from the mere courtesy of his 'Welcome, good Marcellus!'

Now observe the admirable indefiniteness of the first opening out of the occasion of all this anxiety. The preparation informative of the audience is just as much as was precisely necessary, and no more;—it begins with the uncertainty appertaining to a question:—

Mar. What! has *this thing* appeared again to-night?—

Even the word 'again' has its *credibilizing* effect. Then Horatio, the representative of the ignorance of the audience, not himself, but by Marcellus to Bernardo, anticipates the common solution— ''tis but our fantasy!' upon which Marcellus rises into

This dreaded sight, twice seen of us—

which immediately afterwards becomes 'this apparition,' and that, too, an intelligent spirit, that is, to be spoken to! Then comes the confirmation of Horatio's disbelief;—

Tush! tush! 'twill not appear!—

and the silence, with which the scene opened, is again restored in the shivering feeling of Horatio sitting down, at such a time, and with the two eye-witnesses, to hear a story of a ghost, and that, too, of a ghost which had appeared twice before at the very same hour. In the deep feeling which Bernardo has of the solemn nature of what he is about to relate, he makes an effort to master his own imaginative terrors by an elevation of style,— itself a continuation of the effort,—and by turning off from the apparition, as from something which would force him too deeply into himself, to the outward objects, the realities of nature, which had accompanied it:—

> *Ber.* Last night of all,
> When yon same star, that's westward from the pole,
> Had made his course to illume that part of heaven
> Where now it burns, Marcellus and myself,
> The bell then beating one—

This passage seems to contradict the critical law that what is told, makes a faint impression compared with what is beholden; for it does indeed convey to the mind more than the eye can see; whilst the interruption of the narrative at the very moment when we are most intensely listening for the sequel, and have our thoughts diverted from the dreaded sight in expectation of the desired, yet almost dreaded, tale—this gives all the suddenness and surprise of the original appearance;—

> *Mar.* Peace, break thee off; look, where it comes again!—

Note the judgment displayed in having the two persons present, who, as having seen the Ghost before, are naturally eager in confirming their former opinions,—whilst the skeptic is silent, and after having been twice addressed by his friends, answers with two hasty syllables—'Most like,'—and a confession of horror:—

> It harrows me with fear and wonder.

O heaven! words are wasted on those who feel, and to those who do not feel the exquisite judgment of Shakespeare in this scene, what can be said?—Hume himself could not but have had faith in this Ghost dramatically, let his anti-ghostism have been as strong as Samson against other ghosts less powerfully raised. Act i. sc. 1.

> *Mar.* Good now, sit down, and tell me, he that knows
> Why this same strict and most observant watch, &c.

How delightfully natural is the transition to the retrospective narrative! And observe, upon the Ghost's reappearance, how much Horatio's courage is increased by having translated the late individual spectator into general thought and past experience,— and the sympathy of Marcellus and Bernardo with his patriotic surmises in daring to strike at the Ghost; whilst in a moment, upon its vanishing the former solemn awe-stricken feeling returns upon them:—

> We do it wrong, being so majestical,
> To offer it the show of violence.—

Ib. Horatio's speech:—

> I have heard,
> The cock, that is the trumpet to the morn,
> Doth with his lofty and shrill sounding throat
> Awake the god of day, &c.

No Addison could be more careful to be poetical in diction than Shakespeare in providing the grounds and sources of its propriety. But how to elevate a thing almost mean by its familiarity, young poets may learn in this treatment of the cock-crow.

Ib. Horatio's speech:—

And, by my advice,
Let us impart what we have seen to-night
Unto young Hamlet; for, upon my life,
The spirit, dumb to us, will speak to him.

Note the unobtrusive and yet fully adequate mode of introducing the main character, 'young Hamlet,' upon whom is transferred all the interest excited for the acts and concerns of the king his father.

Ib. sc. 2. The audience are now relieved by a change of scene to the royal court, in order that Hamlet may not have to take up the leavings of exhaustion. In the king's speech, observe the set and pedantically antithetic form of the sentences when touching that which galled the heels of conscience,—the strain of undignified rhetoric,—and yet in what follows concerning the public weal, a certain appropriate majesty. Indeed was he not a royal brother?—

Ib. King's speech:—

And now, Laertes, what's the news with you? &c.

Thus with great art Shakespeare introduces a most important, but still subordinate character first, Laertes, who is yet thus graciously treated in consequence of the assistance given to the election of the late king's brother instead of his son by Polonius.

Ib.

Ham. A little more than kin, and less than kind.
King. How is it that the clouds still hang on you?
Ham. Not so, my lord, I am too much i' the sun.

Hamlet opens his mouth with a playing on words, the complete absence of which throughout characterizes Macbeth. This playing on words may be attributed to many causes or motives, as either to an exuberant activity of mind, as in the higher comedy of Shakespeare generally;—or to an imitation of it as a mere fashion, as if it were said—'Is not this better than groaning?' —or to a contemptuous exultation in minds vulgarized and overset by their success, as in the poetic instance of Milton's Devils in the battle;—or it is the language of resentment, as is familiar to every one who has witnessed the quarrels of the lower orders, where there is invariably a profusion of punning invective, whence, perhaps, nicknames have in a considerable degree sprung up;—or it is the language of suppressed passion, and especially of a hardly smothered personal dislike. The first and last of these combine in Hamlet's case; and I have little doubt that Farmer is right in supposing the equivocation carried on in the expression 'too much i' the sun,' or son.

Ib.

> *Ham.* Ay, madam, it is common.

Here observe Hamlet's delicacy to his mother, and how the suppression prepares him for the overflow in the next speech, in which his character is more developed by bringing forward his aversion to externals, and which betrays his habit of brooding over the world within him, coupled with a prodigality of beautiful words, which are the half-embodyings of thought, and are more than thought, and have an outness, a reality *sui generis,* and yet contain their correspondence and shadowy affinity to the images and movements within. Note also Hamlet's silence to the long speech of the king which follows, and his respectful, but general, answer to his mother.

Ib. Hamlet's first soliloquy:—

> O, that this too too solid flesh would melt,
> Thaw, and resolve itself into a dew! &c.

This *tædium vitæ* is a common oppression on minds cast in the Hamlet mould, and is caused by disproportionate mental exertion, which necessitates exhaustion of bodily feeling. Where there is a just coincidence of external and internal action, pleasure is always the result; but where the former is deficient, and the mind's appetency of the ideal is unchecked, realities will seem cold and unmoving. In such cases, passion combines itself with the indefinite alone. In this mood of his mind the relation of the appearance of his father's spirit in arms is made all at once to Hamlet:—it is—Horatio's speech, in particular—a perfect model of the true style of dramatic narrative;—the purest poetry, and yet in the most natural language, equally remote from the ink-horn and the plough.

Ib. sc. 3. This scene must be regarded as one of Shakespeare's lyric movements in the play, and the skill with which it is interwoven with the dramatic parts is peculiarly an excellence of our poet. You experience the sensation of a pause without the sense of a stop. You will observe in Ophelia's short and general answer to the long speech of Laertes the natural carelessness of innocence, which can not think such a code of cautions and prudences necessary to its own preservation.

Ib. Speech of Polonius:—(in Stockdale's edition.)

> Or (not to crack the wind of the poor phrase)
> Wronging it thus, you'll tender me a fool.

I suspect this 'wronging' is here used much in the same sense as 'wringing' or 'wrenching;' and that the parenthesis should be extended to, 'thus.'

Ib. Speech of Polonius:—

———How prodigal the soul
Lends the tongue vows:—these blazes, daughter, &c.

A spondee has, I doubt not, dropped out of the text. Either insert 'Go to' after 'vows;'—

Lends the tongue vows: Go to, these blazes, daughter—

or read

Lends the tongue vows:—These blazes, daughter, mark you—

Shakespeare never introduces a catalectic line without intending an equivalent to the foot omitted in the pauses, or the dwelling emphasis, or the diffused retardation. I do not, however, deny that a good actor might by employing the last-mentioned means, namely, the retardation, or solemn knowing drawl, supply the missing spondee with good effect. But I do not believe that in this or any other of the foregoing speeches of Polonius, Shakespeare meant to bring out the senility or weakness of that personage's mind. In the great ever-recurring dangers and duties of life, where to distinguish the fit objects for the application of the maxims collected by the experience of a long life, requires no fineness of tact, as in the admonitions to his son and daughter, Polonius is uniformly made respectable. But if an actor were even capable of catching these shades in the character, the pit and the gallery would be malcontent at their exhibition. It is to Hamlet that Polonius is, and is meant to be, contemptible, because in inwardness and uncontrollable activity of movement, Hamlet's mind is the logical contrary to that of Polonius, and besides, as I have observed before, Hamlet dislikes the man as false to his true allegiance in the matter of the succession to the crown.

Ib. sc. 4. The unimportant conversation with which this scene opens is a proof of Shakespeare's minute knowledge of human nature. It is a well-established fact, that on the brink of any serious enterprise, or event of moment, men almost invariably endeavor to elude the pressure of their own thoughts by turning aside to trivial objects and familiar circumstances: thus this dialogue on the platform begins with remarks on the coldness of the air, and inquiries, obliquely connected, indeed, with the expected hour of the visitation, but thrown out in a seeming vacuity of

topics, as to the striking of the clock and so forth. The same
desire to escape from the impending thought is carried on in
Hamlet's account of, and moralizing on, the Danish custom of
wassailing: he runs off from the particular to the universal, and
in his repugnance to personal and individual concerns, escapes,
as it were, from himself in generalizations, and smothers the im-
patience and uneasy feelings of the moment in abstract reasoning.
Besides this, another purpose is answered;—for by thus entan-
gling the attention of the audience in the nice distinctions and
parenthetical sentences of this speech of Hamlet's, Shakespeare
takes them completely by surprise on the appearance of the
Ghost, which comes upon them in all the suddenness of its vi-
sionary character. Indeed, no modern writer would have dared,
like Shakespeare, to have preceded this last visitation by two dis-
tinct appearances,—or could have contrived that the third should
rise upon the former two in impressiveness and solemnity of in-
terest.

But in addition to all the other excellences of Hamlet's speech
concerning the wassel-music—so finely revealing the predomi-
nant idealism, the ratiocinative meditativeness, of his character—
it has the advantage of giving nature and probability to the
impassioned continuity of the speech instantly directed to the
Ghost. The *momentum* had been given to his mental activity;
the full current of the thoughts and words had set in, and the
very forgetfulness, in the fervor of his augmentation, of the pur-
pose for which he was there, aided in preventing the appearance
from benumbing the mind. Consequently, it acted as a new im-
pulse,—a sudden stroke which increased the velocity of the body
already in motion, whilst it altered the direction. The co-presence
of Horatio, Marcellus, and Bernardo is most judiciously contrived;
for it renders the courage of Hamlet and his impetuous eloquence
perfectly intelligible. The knowledge,—the unthought of con-
sciousness,—the sensation,—of human auditors—of flesh and
blood sympathists—acts as a support and a stimulation *a tergo,*
while the front of the mind, the whole consciousness of the
speaker, is filled, yea, absorbed, by the apparition. Add too, that
the apparition itself has by its previous appearances been brought
nearer to a thing of this world. This accrescence of objectivity
in a Ghost that yet retains all its ghostly attributes and fearful
subjectivity, is truly wonderful.

Ib. sc. 5. Hamlet's speech:—

> O all you host of heaven! O earth! What else?
> And shall I couple hell?—

I remember nothing equal to this burst unless it be the first speech of Prometheus in the Greek Drama, after the exit of Vulcan and the two Afrites. But Shakespeare alone could have produced the vow of Hamlet to make his memory a blank of all maxims and generalized truths, that 'observation had copied there,'—followed immediately by the speaker noting down the generalized fact,

> That one may smile, and smile, and be a villain!

Ib.

> *Mar.* Hillo, ho, ho, my lord!
> *Ham.* Hillo, ho, ho, boy! come bird, come, &c.

This part of the scene after Hamlet's interview with the Ghost has been charged with an improbable eccentricity. But the truth is, that after the mind has been stretched beyond its usual pitch and tone, it must either sink into exhaustion and inanity, or seek relief by change. It is thus well known, that persons conversant in deeds of cruelty contrive to escape from conscience by connecting something of the ludicrous with them, and by inventing grotesque terms and a certain technical phraseology to disguise the horror of their practices. Indeed, paradoxical as it may appear, the terrible by a law of the human mind always touches on the verge of the ludicrous. Both arise from the perception of something out of the common order of things—something, in fact, out of its place; and if from this we can abstract danger, the uncommonness will alone remain, and the sense of the ridiculous be excited. The close alliance of these opposites—they are not contraries—appears from the circumstance, that laughter is equally the expression of extreme anguish and horror as of joy: as there are tears of sorrow and tears of joy, so is there a laugh of terror and a laugh of merriment. These complex causes will naturally have produced in Hamlet the disposition to escape from his own feelings of the overwhelming and supernatural by a wild transition to the ludicrous,—a sort of cunning bravado, bordering on the flights of delirium. For you may, perhaps, observe that Hamlet's wildness is but half false; he plays that subtle trick of pretending to act only when he is very near really being what he acts.

The subterraneous speeches of the Ghost are hardly defensible:—but I would call your attention to the characteristic difference between this Ghost, as a superstition connected with the most mysterious truths of revealed religion,—and Shakespeare's consequent reverence in his treatment of it,—and the foul earthly witcheries and wild language in Macbeth.

Act ii. sc. 1. Polonius and Reynaldo.

In all things dependent on, or rather made up of, fine address, the manner is no more or otherwise rememberable than the light motions, steps, and gestures of youth and health. But this is almost everything:—no wonder, therefore, if that which can be put down by rule in the memory should appear to us as mere poring, maudlin, cunning,—slyness blinking through the watery eye of superannuation. So in this admirable scene, Polonius, who is throughout the skeleton of his own former skill and statecraft, hunts the trail of policy at a dead scent, supplied by the weak fever-smell in his own nostrils.

Ib. sc. 2. Speech of Polonius:—

> My liege, and madam, to expostulate, &c.

Warburton's note.

> Then as to the jingles, and play on words, let us but look into the sermons of Dr. Donne (the wittiest man of that age), and we shall find them full of this vein.

I have, and that most carefully, read Dr. Donne's sermons, and find none of these jingles. The great art of an orator—to make whatever he talks of appear of importance—this, indeed, Donne has effected with consummate skill.

Ib.

> *Ham.* Excellent well;
> You are a fishmonger.

That is, you are sent to fish out this secret. This is Hamlet's own meaning.

Ib.

> *Ham.* For if the sun breeds maggots in a dead dog,
> Being a god, kissing carrion—

These purposely obscure lines, I rather think, refer to some thought in Hamlet's mind, contrasting the lovely daughter with such a tedious old fool, her father, as he, Hamlet, represents Polonius to himself:—'Why, fool as he is, he is some degrees in rank above a dead dog's carcass; and if the sun, being a god that kisses carrion, can raise life out of a dead dog,—why may not good fortune, that favors fools, have raised a lovely girl out of this dead-alive old fool?' Warburton is often led astray, in his interpretations, by his attention to general positions without the due Shakespearean reference to what is probably passing in the mind of his speaker, characteristic, and expository of his particular character and present mood. The subsequent passage,—

O Jephtha, judge of Israel! what a treasure hadst thou!

is confirmatory of my view of these lines.

Ib.

Ham. You can not, Sir, take from me any thing that I will more willingly part withal; except my life, except my life, except my life.

This repetition strikes me as most admirable.

Ib.

Ham. Then are our beggars, bodies; and our monarchs, and out-stretched heroes, the beggars' shadows.

I do not understand this; and Shakespeare seems to have intended the meaning not to be more than snatched at:—'By my fay, I can not reason!'

Ib.

The rugged Pyrrhus—he whose sable arms, &c.

This admirable substitution of the epic for the dramatic, giving such a reality to the impassioned dramatic diction of Shakespeare's own dialogue, and authorized too, by the actual style of the tragedies before his time (Porrex and Ferrex, Titus Andronicus, &c.), is well worthy of notice. The fancy, that a burlesque was intended, sinks below criticism: the lines, as epic narrative, are superb.

In the thoughts, and even in the separate parts of the diction, this description is highly poetical: in truth, taken by itself, that is its fault that it is too poetical!—the language of lyric vehemence and epic pomp, and not of the drama. But if Shakespeare had made the diction truly dramatic, where would have been the contrast between Hamlet and the play in Hamlet?

Ib.

———had seen the *mobled* queen, &c.

A mob-cap is still a word in common use for a morning-cap, which conceals the whole head of hair, and passes under the chin. It is nearly the same as the night-cap, that is, it is an imitation of it, so as to answer the purpose ('I am not drest for company'), and yet reconciling it with neatness and perfect purity.

Ib. Hamlet's soliloquy:—

O, what a rogue and peasant slave am I! &c.

This is Shakespeare's own attestation to the truth of the idea of Hamlet which I have before put forth.

Ib.

> The spirit that I have seen,
> May be a devil: and the devil hath power
> To assume a pleasing shape; yea, and, perhaps
> Out of my weakness, and my melancholy,
> (As he is very potent with such spirits)
> Abuses me to damn me.

See Sir Thomas Brown:—

I believe —— that those apparitions and ghosts of departed persons are not the wandering souls of men, but the unquiet walks of devils, prompting and suggesting us unto mischief, blood, and villany, instilling and stealing into our hearts, that the blessed spirits are not at rest in their graves, but wander solicitous of the affairs of the world. *Relig. Med.* pt. i. sec. 37.

Act iii. sc. 1. Hamlet's soliloquy:—

> To be, or not to be, that is the question, &c.

This speech is of absolutely universal interest,—and yet to which of all Shakespeare's characters could it have been appropriately given but to Hamlet? For Jaques it would have been too deep, and for Iago too habitual a communion with the heart; which in every man belongs, or ought to belong, to all mankind.

Ib.

> That undiscover'd country, from whose bourne
> No traveller returns.—

Theobald's note in defence of the supposed contradiction of this in the apparition of the Ghost.

O miserable defender! If it be necessary to remove the apparent contradiction,—if it be not rather a great beauty,—surely it were easy to say, that no traveller returns to this world, as to his home or abiding-place.

Ib.

> *Ham.* Ha, ha! are you honest?
> *Oph.* My lord?
> *Ham.* Are you fair?

Here it is evident that the penetrating Hamlet perceives, from the strange and forced manner of Ophelia, that the sweet girl was not acting a part of her own, but was a decoy; and his after-speeches are not so much directed to her as to the listeners and spies. Such a discovery in a mood so anxious and irritable accounts for a certain harshness in him;—and yet a wild up-working of love, sporting with opposites in a wilful self-torment-ing strain of irony, is perceptible throughout. 'I did love you once;'—'I lov'd you not;'—and particularly in his enumeration of the faults of the sex from which Ophelia is so free, that the mere freedom therefrom constitutes her character. Note Shakespeare's charm of composing the female character by the absence of characters, that is, marks and out-jottings.

Ib. Hamlet's speech:—

I say, we will have no more marriages: those that are married already, all but one, shall live: the rest shall keep as they are.

Observe this dallying with the inward purpose, characteristic of one who had not brought his mind to the steady acting point. He would fain sting the uncle's mind;—but to stab his body!— The soliloquy of Ophelia, which follows, is the perfection of love —so exquisitely unselfish!

Ib. sc. 2. This dialogue of Hamlet with the players is one of the happiest instances of Shakespeare's power of diversifying the scene while he is carrying on the plot.

Ib.

Ham. My lord, you play'd once i' the university, you say? (*To Polonius.*)

To have kept Hamlet's love for Ophelia before the audience in any direct form, would have made a breach in the unity of the interest;—but yet to the thoughtful reader it is suggested by his spite to poor Polonius, whom he can not let rest.

Ib. The style of the interlude here is distinguished from the real dialogue by rhyme, as in the first interview with the players by epic verse.

Ib.

Ros. My lord, you once did love me.
Ham. So I do still, by these pickers and stealers.

I never heard an actor give this word 'so' its proper emphasis. Shakespeare's meaning is—'lov'd you? Hum!—*so* I do still,' &c. There has been no change in my opinion:—I think as ill of you as I did. Else Hamlet tells an ignoble falsehood, and a useless one, as the last speech to Guildenstern—'Why, look you now,' &c.—proves.

Ib. Hamlet's soliloquy:—

Now could I drink hot blood,
And do such business as the bitter day
Would quake to look on.

The utmost at which Hamlet arrives, is a disposition, a mood, to do something;—but what to do, is still left undecided, while every word he utters tends to betray his disguise. Yet observe how perfectly equal to any call of the moment is Hamlet, let it only not be for the future.

Ib. sc. 4. Speech of Polonius. Polonius's volunteer obtrusion of himself into this business, while it is appropriate to his character, still itching after former importance, removes all likelihood that Hamlet should suspect his presence, and prevents us from making his death injure Hamlet in our opinion.

Ib. The king's speech:—

> O, my offence is rank, it smells to heaven, &c.

This speech well marks the difference between crime and guilt of habit. The conscience here is still admitted to audience. Nay, even as an audible soliloquy, it is far less improbable than is supposed by such as have watched men only in the beaten road of their feelings. But the final—'all may be well!' is remarkable; —the degree of merit attributed by the self-flattering soul to its own struggle, though baffled, and to the indefinite half-promise, half-command, to persevere in religious duties. The solution is in the divine *medium* of the Christian doctrine of expiation:— not what you have done, but what you are, must determine.

Ib. Hamlet's speech:—

> Now might I do it, pat, now he is praying:
> And now I'll do it:—And so he goes to heaven:
> And so am I revenged? That would be scann'd, &c.

Dr. Johnson's mistaking of the marks of reluctance and procrastination for impetuous, horror-striking fiendishness!—Of such importance is it to understand the germ of a character. But the interval taken by Hamlet's speech is truly awful! And then—

> My words fly up, my thoughts remain below:
> Words, without thoughts, never to heaven go,—

O what a lesson concerning the essential difference between wishing and willing, and the folly of all motive-mongering, while the individual self remains!

Ib. sc. 4.

> *Ham.* A bloody deed;—almost as bad, good mother,
> As kill a king, and marry with his brother.
> *Queen.* As kill a king?

I confess that Shakespeare has left the character of the Queen in an unpleasant perplexity. Was she, or was she not, conscious of the fratricide?

Act iv. sc. 2.

Ros. Take you me for a sponge, my lord?
Ham. Ay, Sir; that soaks up the King's countenance, his rewards, his authorities, &c.

Hamlet's madness is made to consist in the free utterance of all the thoughts that had passed through his mind before;—in fact, in telling home-truths.

Act iv. sc. 5. Ophelia's singing. O, note the conjunction here of these two thoughts that had never subsisted in disjunction, the love for Hamlet, and her filial love, with the guileless floating on the surface of her pure imagination of the cautions so lately expressed, and the fears not too delicately avowed, by her father and brother, concerning the dangers to which her honor lay exposed. Thought, affliction, passion, murder itself—she turns to favor and prettiness. This play of association is instanced in the close:—

My brother shall know of it, and I thank you for your good counsel.

Ib. Gentleman's speech:—

> And as the world were now but to begin
> Antiquity forgot, custom not known,
> The ratifiers and props of every ward—
> They cry, &c.

Fearful and self-suspicious as I always feel, when I seem to see an error of judgment in Shakespeare, yet I can not reconcile the cool, and, as Warburton calls it, 'rational and consequential,' reflection in these lines with the anonymousness, or the alarm, of this Gentleman or Messenger, as he is called in other editions.

Ib. King's speech:—

> There's such divinity doth hedge a king,
> That treason can but peep to what it would,
> Acts little of his will.

Proof, as indeed all else is, that Shakespeare never intended us to see the King with Hamlet's eyes; though, I suspect, the managers have long done so.

Ib. Speech of Laertes:—

> To hell, allegiance! vows, to the blackest devil!

Laertes is a *good* character, but, &c.   WARBURTON.

Mercy on Warburton's notion of goodness! Please to refer to the seventh scene of this act:—

> 1 will do it;
> And for this purpose I'll anoint my sword, &c.

uttered by Laertes after the King's description of Hamlet;—

> He being remiss,
> Most generous, and free from all contriving,
> Will not peruse the foils.

Yet I acknowledge that Shakespeare evidently wishes, as much as possible, to spare the character of Laertes,—to break the extreme turpitude of his consent to become an agent and accomplice of the King's treachery;—and to this end he re-introduces Ophelia at the close of this scene to afford a probable stimulus of passion in her brother.

Ib. sc. 6. Hamlet's capture by the pirates. This is almost the only play of Shakespeare, in which mere accidents, independent of all will, form an essential part of the plot;—but here how judiciously in keeping with the character of the over-meditative Hamlet, ever at last determined by accident or by a fit of passion?

Ib. sc. 7. Note how the King first awakens Laertes's vanity by praising the reporter, and then gratifies it by the report itself and finally points it by—

> Sir, this report of his
> Did Hamlet so envenom with his envy!—

Ib. King's speech:—

> For goodness, growing to a *pleurisy,*
> Dies in his own too much.

Theobald's note from Warburton, who conjectures 'plethory.' I rather think that Shakespeare meant 'pleurisy,' but involved in it the thought of *plethora,* as supposing pleurisy to arise from too much blood; otherwise I can not explain the following line—

> And then this *should* is like a spendthrift sigh,
> That hurts by easing.

In a stitch in the side every one must have heaved a sigh that 'hurt by easing.'

Since writing the above I feel confirmed that 'pleurisy' is the right word; for I find that in the old medical dictionaries the pleurisy is often called the 'plethory.'

> *Queen.* Your sister's drown'd, Laertes.
> *Laer.* Drown'd! O, where?

'That Laertes might be excused in some degree for not cooling, the Act concludes with the affecting death of Ophelia,—who in the beginning lay like a little projection of land into a lake or stream, covered with spray-flowers, quietly reflected in the quiet waters, but at length is undermined or loosened, and becomes a fairy isle, and after a brief vagrancy sinks almost without an eddy!

Act v. sc. 1. O, the rich contrast between the Clowns and Hamlet, as two extremes! You see in the former the mockery of logic, and a traditional wit valued, like truth, for its antiquity, and treasured up, like a tune, for use.

Ib. sc. 1 and 2. Shakespeare seems to mean all Hamlet's character to be brought together before his final disappearance from the scene;—his meditative excess in the grave-digging, his yielding to passion with Laertes, his love for Ophelia blazing out, his tendency to generalize on all occasions in the dialogue with Horatio, his fine gentlemanly manners with Osrick, and his and Shakespeare's own fondness for presentiment:

> But thou would'st not think, how ill all's here about my heart: but It is no matter.

MILTON

Born in London, 1608.—Died, 1674.

IF WE divide the period from the accession of Elizabeth to the Protectorate of Cromwell into two unequal portions, the first ending with the death of James I., the other comprehending the reign of Charles and the brief glories of the Republic, we are forcibly struck with a difference in the character of the illustrious actors, by whom each period is rendered severally memorable. Or rather, the difference in the characters of the great men in each period, leads us to make this division. Eminent as the intellectual powers were that were displayed in both; yet in the number of great men, in the various sorts of excellence, and not merely in the variety but almost diversity of talents united in the same individual, the age of Charles falls short of its predecessor; and the stars of the Parliament, keen as their radiance was, in fulness and richness of lustre, yield to the constellation at the court of Elizabeth;—which can only be paralleled by Greece in her brightest moment, when the titles of the poet, the philosopher, the historian, the statesman, and the general not seldom formed a garland round the same head, as in the instances of our

Sidneys and Raleighs. But then, on the other hand, there was a vehemence of will, an enthusiasm of principle, a depth and an earnestness of spirit, which the charms of individual fame and personal aggrandizement could not pacify,—an aspiration after reality, permanence, and general good,—in short, a moral grandeur in the latter period, with which the low intrigues, Machiavellic maxims, and selfish and servile ambition of the former, stand in painful contrast.

The causes of this it belongs not to the present occasion to detail at length; but a mere allusion to the quick succession of revolutions in religion, breeding a political indifference in the mass of men to religion itself, the enormous increase of the royal power in consequence of the humiliation of the nobility and the clergy—the transference of the papal authority to the crown,—the unfixed state of Elizabeth's own opinions, whose inclinations were as popish as her interests were protestant—the controversial extravagance and practical imbecility of her successor—will help to explain the former period; and the persecutions that had given a life-and-soul interest to the disputes so imprudently fostered by James,—the ardor of a conscious increase of power in the commons, and the greater austerity of manners and maxims, the natural product and most formidable weapon of religious disputation, not merely in conjunction, but in closest combination, with newly-awakened political and republican zeal, these perhaps account for the character of the latter æra.

In the close of the former period, and during the bloom of the latter, the poet Milton was educated and formed; and he survived the latter, and all the fond hopes and aspirations which had been its life; and so in evil days, standing as the representative of the combined excellence of both periods, he produced the Paradise Lost as by an after-throe of nature. "There are some persons" (observes a divine, a contemporary of Milton's), "of whom the grace of God takes early hold, and the good spirit inhabiting them, carries them on in an even constancy through innocence into virtue, their Christianity bearing equal date with their manhood, and reason and religion, like warp and woof, running together, make up one web of a wise and exemplary life. This (he adds) is a most happy case, wherever it happens; for, besides that there is no sweeter or more lovely thing on earth than the early buds of piety, which drew from our Saviour signal affection to the beloved disciple, it is better to have no wound than to experience the most sovereign balsam, which, if it work a cure, yet usually leaves a scar behind." Although it was and is my intention to defer the consideration of Milton's own character to the conclusion of this Lecture, yet I could not prevail on myself to approach the Paradise Lost without impressing on your minds the conditions under which such a work was in fact producible at all, the original genius having been assumed as the immediate agent and efficient cause; and these conditions I find in the character of the times and in his own character. The age in which the foundations of his mind were laid, was congenial to it as one golden æra of profound erudition and individual genius;—that in which the superstructure was carried up, was no less favorable to it by a sternness of discipline and a show of self-control, highly flattering to the imaginative dignity of an heir of fame, and which won Milton over from the dear-loved delights of academic groves and cathedral aisles to the anti-prelatic party. It acted on him too, no doubt, and modified his studies by a characteristic controversial spirit (his presentation of God is tinted with it)—a spirit not less busy indeed in political than in theological and ecclesiastical dispute, but carrying on the former almost always, more or less, in the guise of the latter. And so far as Pope's censure of our poet—that he makes God the Father a school divine—is just, we must attribute it to the character of his age, from which the men of genius, who escaped, escaped by a worse disease, the licentious indifference of a Frenchified court.

Such was the *nidus* or soil which constituted, in the strict sense of the word, the circumstances of Milton's mind. In his mind itself there were purity and piety absolute; an imagination to which neither the past nor the present were interesting, except as far as they called forth and enlivened the great ideal, in which and for which he lived; a keen love of truth, which, after many weary pursuits, found a harbor in the sublime listening to the still voice in his own spirit, and as keen a love of his country, which, after a disappointment still more depressive, expanded and soared into a love of man as a probationer of immortality. These were, these alone could be, the conditions under which such a work as the Paradise Lost could be conceived and accomplished. By a life-long study Milton had known—

> What was of use to know,
> What best to say could say, to do had done.
> His actions to his words agreed, his words
> To his large heart gave utterance due, his heart
> Contain'd of good, wise, fair, the perfect shape;

And he left the imperishable total, as a bequest to the ages coming, in the PARADISE LOST.

Difficult as I shall find it to turn over these leaves without catching some passage, which would tempt me to stop, I propose to consider, 1st, the general plan and arrangement of the work; 2dly, the subject with its difficulties and advantages;—3dly, the poet's object, the spirit in the letter, the ἐνθύμιον ἐν μύθῳ, the true school-divinity: and lastly, the characteristic excellencies of the poem, in what they consist, and by what means they were produced.

1. As to the plan and ordonnance of the Poem.

Compare it with the Iliad, many of the books of which might change places without any injury to the thread of the story. Indeed, I doubt the original existence of the Iliad as one poem; it seems more probable that it was put together about the time of the Pisistratidæ. The Iliad—and, more or less, all epic poems, the subjects of which are taken from history—have no rounded conclusion; they remain, after all, but single chapters from the volume of history, although they are ornamental chapters. Consider the exquisite simplicity of the Paradise Lost. It and it alone really possesses a beginning, a middle, and an end; it has the totality of the poem as distinguished from the *ab ovo* birth and parentage, or straight line, of history.

2. As to the subject.

In Homer, the supposed importance of the subject, as the first effort of confederated Greece, is an after-thought of the critics; and the interest, such as it is, derived from the events themselves, as distinguished from the manner of representing them, is very languid to all but Greeks. It is a Greek poem. The superiority of the Paradise Lost is obvious in this respect, that the interest transcends the limits of a nation. But we do not generally dwell on this excellence of the Paradise Lost, because it seems attributable to Christianity itself;—yet in fact the interest is wider than Christendom, and comprehends the Jewish and Mohammedan worlds;—nay, still further, inasmuch as it represents the origin of evil, and the combat of evil and good, it contains matter of deep interest to all mankind, as forming the basis of all religion, and the true occasion of all philosophy whatsoever.

The FALL of man is the subject; Satan is the cause; man's blissful state the immediate object of his enmity and attack; man is warned by an angel who gives him an account of all that was requisite to be known, to make the warning at once intelligible and awful, then the temptation ensues, and the Fall; then the immediate sensible consequence; then the consolation, wherein an angel presents a vision of the history of man with the ultimate triumph of the Redeemer. Nothing is touched in this vision but what is of general interest in religion; any thing else would have been improper.

The inferiority of Klopstock's Messiah is inexpressible. I admit the prerogative of poetic feeling, and poetic faith; but I can not suspend the judgment even for a moment. A poem may in one sense be a dream, but it must be a waking dream. In Milton you have a religious faith combined with the moral nature; it is an efflux; you go along with it. In Klopstock there is a wilfulness; he makes things so and so. The feigned speeches and events in the Messiah shock us like falsehoods; but nothing of that sort is felt in the Paradise Lost, in which no particulars, at least very few indeed, are touched which can come into collision or juxtaposition with recorded matter.

But notwithstanding the advantages in Milton's subject, there were concomitant insuperable difficulties, and Milton has exhibited marvellous skill in keeping most of them out of sight. High poetry is the translation of reality into the ideal under the predicament of succession of time only. The poet is an historian, upon condition of moral power being the only force in the universe. The very grandeur of his subject ministered a difficulty to Milton. The statement of a being of high intellect, warring against the supreme Being, seems to contradict the idea of a supreme Being. Milton precludes our feeling this, as much as possible, by keeping the peculiar attributes of divinity less in sight, making them to a certain extent allegorical only. Again poetry implies the language of excitement; yet how to reconcile such language with God! Hence Milton confines the poetic passion in God's speeches to the language of Scripture; and once only allows the *passio vera*, or *quasi humana* to appear, in the passage, where the Father contemplates his own likeness in the Son before the battle:—

> Go then, thou Mightiest, in thy Father's might,
> Ascend my chariot, guide the rapid wheels
> That shake Heaven's basis, bring forth all my war,
> My bow and thunder; my almighty arms
> Gird on, and sword upon thy puissant thigh;
> Pursue these sons of darkness, drive them out
> From all Heaven's bounds into the utter deep:
> There let them learn, as likes them, to despise
> God and Messiah his anointed king.
>
> B. vi. v. 710.

3. As to Milton's object:

It was to justify the ways of God to man! The controversial spirit observable in many parts of the poem, especially in God's speeches, is immediately attributable to the great controversy of that age, the origination of evil. The Arminians considered it a mere calamity. The Calvinists took away all human will. Milton asserted the will, but declared for the enslavement of the will out of an act of the will itself. There are three powers in us, which distinguish us from the beasts that perish:—1, reason; 2, the power of viewing universal truth; and 3, the power of contracting universal truth into particulars. Religion is the will in the reason, and love in the will.

The character of Satan is pride and sensual indulgence, finding in self the sole motive of action. It is the character so often seen *in little* on the political stage. It exhibits all the restlessness, temerity, and cunning which have marked the mighty hunters of mankind from Nimrod to Napoleon. The common fascination of men is, that these great men, as they are called, must act from some great motive. Milton has carefully marked in his Satan the intense selfishness, the alcohol of egotism, which would rather reign in hell than serve in heaven. To place this lust of self in opposition to denial of self or duty, and to show what exertions it would make, and what pains endure to accomplish its end, is Milton's particular object in the character of Satan. But around this character he has thrown a singularity of daring, a grandeur of sufferance, and a ruined splendor, which constitute the very height of poetic sublimity.

Lastly, as to the execution:—

The language and versification of the Paradise Lost are peculiar in being so much more necessarily correspondent to each than those in any other poem or poet. The connection of the sentences and the position of the words are exquisitely artificial; but the position is rather according to the logic of passion or universal logic, than to the logic of grammar. Milton attempted to make the English language obey the logic of passion, as perfectly as the Greek and Latin. Hence the occasional harshness in the construction.

Sublimity is the pre-eminent characteristic of the Paradise Lost. It is not an arithmetical sublime like Klopstock's, whose rule always is to treat what we might think large as contemptibly small. Klopstock mistakes bigness for greatness. There is a greatness arising from images of effort and daring, and also from those of moral endurance; in Milton both are united. The fallen angels are human passions, invested with a dramatic reality.

The apostrophe to light at the commencement of the third book is particularly beautiful as an intermediate link between Hell and Heaven; and observe, how the second and third book support the subjective character of the poem. In all modern poetry in Christendom there is an under consciousness of a sinful nature, a fleeting away of external things, the mind or subject greater than the object, the reflective character predominant. In the Paradise Lost the sublimest parts are the revelations of Milton's own mind, producing itself and evolving its own greatness; and this is so truly so, that when that which is merely entertaining for its objective beauty is introduced, it at first seems a discord.

In the description of Paradise itself, you have Milton's sunny side as a man; here his descriptive powers are exercised to the utmost, and he draws deep upon his Italian resources. In the description of Eve, and throughout this part of the poem, the poet is predominant over the theologian. Dress is the symbol of the Fall, but the mark of intellect; and the metaphysics of dress are, the hiding what is not symbolic and displaying by discrimination what is. The love of Adam and Eve in Paradise is of the highest merit—not phantomatic, and yet removed from every thing degrading. It is the sentiment of one rational being towards another made tender by a specific difference in that which is essentially the same in both; it is a union of opposites, a giving and receiving mutually of the permanent in either, a completion of each in the other.

Milton is not a picturesque, but a musical, poet; although he has this merit, that the object chosen by him for any particular foreground always remains prominent to the end, enriched, but not encumbered, by the opulence of descriptive details furnished by an exhaustless imagination. I wish the Paradise Lost were more carefully read and studied than I can see any ground for believing it is, especially those parts which, from the habit of always looking for a story in poetry, are scarcely read at all,—as for example, Adam's vision of future events in the 11th and 12th books. No one can rise from the perusal of this immortal poem without a deep sense of the grandeur and the purity of Milton's soul, or without feeling how susceptible of domestic enjoyments he really was, notwithstanding the discomforts which actually resulted from an apparently unhappy choice in marriage. He was, as every truly great poet has ever been, a good man; but finding it impossible to realize his own aspirations, either in religion or politics, or society, he gave up his heart to the living spirit and light within him, and avenged himself on the world by enriching it with this record of his own transcendent ideal.

[1818]

ON THE PRINCIPLES OF POLITICAL KNOWLEDGE:

ESSAY XIII

ON THE LAW OF NATIONS

Πρὸς πόλεως εὐδαιμονίαν καὶ δικαιοσύνην πάντα ἰδιώτον ἔμπροσθεν τέτακ-
ται φύσει· τούτων δὲ τὰ μὲν ἀνθρώπινα εἰς τὰ θεῖα, τὰ δὲ θεῖα εἰς τὸν ἡγεμόνα
νοῦν ξύμπαντα δεῖ βλέπειν, οὐχ ὡς πρὸς ἀρετῆς τὶ μόριον, ἀλλὰ πρὸς ἀρετὴν
ἐν ἀρεταῖς ἀεὶ ὑπομενοῦσαν, ὡς πρὸς νόμον τίνα νομοθετοῦντα.   PLATO.

For all things that regard the well-being and justice of a state are
pre-ordained and established in the nature of the individual. Of these
it behooves that the merely human (the temporal and fluxional) should
be referred and subordinated to the divine in man, and the divine in
like manner to the Supreme Mind, so however that the state is not to
regulate its actions by reference to any particular form and fragments
of virtue, but must fix its eye on that virtue, which is the abiding spirit
and (as it were) *substratum* in all the virtues, as on a law that is itself
legislative.

IT WERE absurd to suppose, that individuals should be under a
law of moral obligation, and yet that a million of the same in-
dividuals acting collectively or through representatives, should
be exempt from all law: for morality is no accident of human
nature, but its essential characteristic. A being altogether with-
out morality is either a beast or a fiend, accordingly as we con-
ceive this want of conscience to be natural or self-produced; a
mere negation of goodness, or the consequence of rebellion to it.
Yet were it possible to conceive a man wholly immoral, it would
remain impossible to conceive him without a moral obligation to
be otherwise; and none, but a madman, will imagine that the
essential qualities of any thing can be altered by its becoming
part of an aggregate; that a grain of corn, for instance, shall cease
to contain flour, as soon as it is part of a peck or bushel. It is,
therefore, grounded in the nature of the thing, and not by a mere
fiction of the mind, that wise men, who have written on the law
of nations, contemplate the several states of the civilized world,
as so many individuals, and equally with the latter under a
moral obligation to exercise their free agency within such bounds,

as render it compatible with the existence of free agency in oth-
ers. We may represent to ourselves this original free agency, as a
right of common, the formation of separate states as an inclosure
of this common, the allotments awarded severally to the co-pro-
prietors as constituting national rights, and the law of nations as
the common register-office of their title-deeds. But in all mo-
rality, though the principle, which is the abiding spirit of the
law, remains perpetual and unaltered, even as that Supreme
Reason in whom and from whom it has its being, yet the letter
of the law, that is, the application of it to particular instances,
and the mode of realizing it in actual practice, must be modified
by the existing circumstances. What we should desire to do,
the conscience alone will inform us; but how and when we are
to make the attempt, and to what extent it is in our power to
accomplish it, are questions for the judgment, and require an ac-
quaintance with facts, and their bearings on each other. Thence
the improvement of our judgment, and the increase of our
knowledge, on all subjects included within our sphere of action,
are not merely advantages recommended by prudence, but abso-
lute duties imposed on us by conscience.

As the circumstances, then, under which men act as states-
men, are different from those under which they act as individuals,
a proportionate difference must be expected in the practical rules
by which their public conduct is to be determined. Let me not
be misunderstood: I speak of a difference in the practical rules,
not in the moral law itself, the means of administering in par-
ticular cases, and under given circumstances, which it is the sole
object of these rules to point out. The spirit continues one and
the same, though it may vary its form according to the element
into which it is transported. This difference, with its grounds
and consequences, it is the province of the philosophical publicist
to discover and display: and exactly in this point (I speak with
unfeigned diffidence) it appears to me that the writers on the law
of nations,* whose works I have had the opportunity of studying,
have been least successful.

* Grotius, Bynkerschoek, Puffendorf, Wolfe, and Vattel; to whose
works I must add, as comprising whatever is most valuable in the
preceding authors, with many important improvements and additions,
Robinson's Reports of Cases in the Admiralty Court, under Sir W.
Scott: to whom international law is under no less obligation than the
law of commercial proceeding was to the late Lord Mansfield. As I
have never seen Sir W. Scott, nor either by myself or my connections
enjoy the honor of the remotest acquaintance with him, I trust that
even by those who may think my opinion erroneous, I shall not at least
be suspected of intentional flattery. 1817.

In what does the law of nations differ from the laws enacted by a particular state for its own subjects? The solution is evident. The law of nations, considered apart from the common principle of all morality, is not fixed or positive in itself, nor supplied with any regular means of being enforced. Like those duties in private life which, for the same reasons, moralists have entitled imperfect duties (though the most atrocious guilt may be involved in the omission or violation of them), the law of nations appeals only to the conscience and prudence of the parties concerned. Wherein then does it differ from the moral laws which the reason, considered as conscience, dictates for the conduct of individuals? This is a more difficult question; but my answer would be determined by, and grounded on, the obvious differences of the circumstances in the two cases. Remember then, that we are now reasoning, not as sophists or system-mongers, but as men anxious to discover what is right in order that we may practise it, or at least give our suffrage and the influence of our opinion in recommending its practice. We must therefore confine the question to those cases, in which honest men and real patriots can suppose any controversy to exist between real patriotism and common honesty. The objects of the patriot are, that his countrymen should, as far as circumstances permit, enjoy what the Creator designed for the enjoyment of animals endowed with reason, and of course that they should have it in their power to develop those faculties which were given them to be developed. He would do his best that every one of his countrymen should possess whatever all men may and should possess, and that a sufficient number should be enabled and encouraged to acquire those excellencies which, though not necessary or possible for all men, are yet to all men useful and honorable. He knows that patriotism itself is a necessary link in the golden chain of our affections and virtues, and turns away with indignant scorn from the false philosophy or mistaken religion, which would persuade him that cosmopolitism is nobler than nationality, the human race a sublimer object of love than a people; and that Plato, Luther, Newton, and their equals, formed themselves neither in the market nor the senate, but in the world, and for all men of all ages. True! But where, and among whom are these giant exceptions produced? In the wide empires of Asia, where millions of human beings acknowledge no other bond but that of a common slavery, and are distinguished on the map but by a name which themselves perhaps never heard, or bearing abhor? No! in a circle defined by human affections, the first firm sod within which becomes sacred beneath the quickened step of the returning citizen;—here, where the powers and interests of men spread without confusion through a common sphere, like the vibrations propagated in the air by a single voice, distinct yet coherent, and all uniting to express one thought and the same feeling;—here, where even the common soldier dares force a passage for his comrades by gathering up the bayonets of the enemy into his own breast, because his country expected every man to do his duty, and this not after he has been hardened by habit, but, as probably in his first battle; not reckless or hopeless, but braving death from a keener sensibility to those blessings which make life dear, to those qualities which render himself worthy to enjoy them;—here, where the royal crown is loved and worshiped as a glory around the sainted head of freedom;—where the rustic at his plough whistles with equal enthusiasm, "God save the King," and "Britons never shall be slaves," or, perhaps, leaves one thistle unweeded in his garden, because it is the symbol of his dear native land;*—here, from within this circle defined, as light by shade, or rather as light within light, by its intensity,—here alone, and only within these magic circles, rise up the awful spirits, whose words are oracles for mankind, whose love embraces all countries, and whose voice sounds through all ages! Here, and here only, may we confidently expect those mighty minds to be reared and ripened, whose names are naturalized in foreign lands, the sure fellow-travellers of civilization, and yet render their own country dearer and more proudly dear to their own countrymen. This is indeed cosmopolitism, at once the nurseling and the nurse of patriotic affection. This, and this alone, is genuine philanthropy, which like the olive-tree, sacred to concord and to wisdom, fattens not exhausts the soil, from which it sprang, and in which it remains rooted. It is feebleness only which can not be generous without injustice, or just

* I can not here refuse myself the pleasure of recording a speech of the poet Burns, related to me by the lady to whom it was addressed. Having been asked by her, why in his more serious poems he had not changed the two or three Scotch words which seemed only to disturb the purity of the style,—the poet with great sweetness, and his usual happiness in reply, answered that in truth it would have been better, but—

> The rough bur-thistle spreading wide
>   Amang the bearded bear,
> I turn'd the weeder-clips aside
>   An' spar'd the symbol dear.

An author may be allowed to quote from his own poems, when he does it with as much modesty and felicity as Burns did in this instance.

without ceasing to be generous. Is the morning star less brilliant, or does a ray less fall on the golden fruitage of the earth, because the moons of Saturn too feed their lamps from the same sun? Even Germany,—though curst with a base and hateful brood of nobles and princelings, cowardly and ravenous jackals to the very flocks intrusted to them as to shepherds, who hunt for the tiger and whine and wag their tails for his bloody offal—even Germany, the ever-changing boundaries of which superannuate the last year's map, and are altered as easily as the hurdles of a temporary sheep-fold, is still remembered with filial love and a patriot's pride, when the thoughtful German hears the names of Luther and Leibnitz. Ah! why, he sighs, why for herself in vain should my country have produced such a host of immortal minds! Yea, even the poor enslaved, degraded, and barbarized Greek can still point to the harbor of Tenedos, and say,—"There lay our fleet when we were besieging Troy."

Reflect a moment on the past history of this wonderful people. What were they while they remained free and independent,— when Greece resembled a collection of mirrors set in a single frame, each having its own focus of patriotism, yet all capable, as at Marathon and Platea, of converging to one point and of consuming a common foe? What were they then? The fountains of light and civilization, of truth and of beauty, to all mankind! they were the thinking head, the beating heart, of the whole world! They lost their independence, and with their independence their patriotism; and became the cosmopolites of antiquity. It has been truly observed by the author of the work for which Palm was murdered, that, after the first acts of severity, the Romans treated the Greeks not only more mildly than their other slaves and dependents, but behaved to them even affectionately and with munificence. The victor nation felt reverentially the presence of the visible and invisible deities that gave sanctity to every grove, every fountain, and every forum. "Think," (writes Pliny to one of his friends) "that you are sent into the province of Achaia, that true and genuine Greece, where civilization, letters, even corn, are believed to have been discovered; that you are sent to administer the affairs of free states, that is, to men eminently free, who have retained their natural right by valor, by services, by friendship, lastly by treaty and by religion. Revere the gods their founders, the sacred influences represented in those gods; revere their ancient glory and this very old age which in man is venerable, in cities sacred. Cherish in thyself a reverence of antiquity, a reverence for their great exploits, a reverence even for their fables. Detract nothing from the liberty, or the dignity, or even the pretensions of any state; keep before thine eyes that this is the land which sent us our institutions, which gave us our laws, not after it was subjugated, but in compliance with our petition." And what came out of these men, who were eminently free without patriotism, because without national independence? (which eminent freedom, however, Pliny himself, in the very next sentence, styles the shadow and *residuum* of liberty.) While they were intense patriots, they were the benefactors of all mankind, legislators for the very nation that afterwards subdued and enslaved them. When, therefore, they became pure cosmopolites, and no partial affections interrupted their philanthropy, and when yet they retained their country, their language, and their arts, what noble works, what mighty discoveries may we not expect from them? If the applause of a little city, the first-rate town of a country not much larger than Yorkshire, and the encouragement of a Pericles, produced a Phidias, a Sophocles, and a constellation of other stars scarcely inferior in glory, what will not the applause of the world effect, and the boundless munificence of the world's imperial masters? Alas! no Sophocles appeared, no Phidias was born; individual genius fled with national independence, and the best products were cold and laborious copies of what their fathers had thought and invented in grandeur and majesty. At length nothing remained, but dastardly and cunning slaves, who avenged their own ruin and degradation by assisting to degrade and ruin their conquerors; and the golden harp of their divine language remained only as the frame on which priests and monks spun their dirty cobwebs of sophistry and superstition!

If then in order to be men we must be patriots, and patriotism can not exist without national independence, we need no new or particular code of morals to justify us in placing and preserving our country in that relative situation which is most favorable to its independence. But the true patriot is aware that this object is not to be accomplished by a system of general conquest, such as was pursued by Philip of Macedon and his son, nor yet by the political annihilation of the one state, which happens to be its most formidable rival;—the unwise measure recommended by Cato, and carried into effect by the Romans in the instance of Carthage. Not by the latter;—for rivalry between two nations conduces to the independence of both, calls forth or fosters all the virtues by which national security is maintained;—and still less by the former; for the victor nation itself must at length, by the very extension of its own conquests, sink into a mere province; nay, it will most probably become the most abject portion of the empire, and the most cruelly oppressed, both because it will be more feared and suspected by the common tyrant, and because it will be the sink and centre of his luxury and corruption. Even in cases of actual injury and just alarm the patriot sets bounds to the reprisal of national vengeance, and contents himself with such securities as are compatible with the welfare, though not with the ambitious projects of the nation, the aggressions of which had given the provocation: for as patriotism inspires no superhuman faculties, neither can it dictate any conduct which would require such. He is too conscious of his own ignorance of the future, to dare extend his calculations into remote periods; nor, because he is a statesman, arrogates to himself the cares of Providence and the government of the world. How does he know, but that the very independence and consequent virtues of the nation, which in the anger of cowardice he would fain reduce to absolute insignificance, and rob even of its ancient name, may in some future emergence be the destined guardians of his own country; and that the power which now alarms, may hereafter protect and preserve it? The experience of history authorizes to believe not only in the possibility, but even the probability, of such an event. An American commander, who has deserved and received the highest honors which his grateful country, through her assembled representatives, could bestow upon him, once said to me with a sigh: In an evil hour for my country did the French and Spaniards abandon Louisiana to the United States. We were not sufficiently a country before: and should we ever be mad enough to drive the English from Canada and her other North American provinces, we shall soon cease to be a country at all. Without local attachment, without national honor, we shall resemble a swarm of insects that settle on the fruits of the earth to corrupt and consume them, rather than men who love and cleave to the land of their forefathers. After a shapeless anarchy and a series of civil wars, we shall at last be formed into many countries; unless the vices engendered in the process should demand further punishment, and we should previously fall beneath the despotism of some military adventurer, like a lion consumed by an inward disease, prostrate and helpless beneath the beak and talons of a vulture, or yet meaner bird of prey.

ON THE GROUNDS OF MORALS AND RELIGION, AND THE DISCIPLINE OF THE MIND REQUISITE FOR A TRUE UNDERSTANDING OF THE SAME:

ESSAY IV

METHOD

Ὁ δὲ μετὰ ταῦτα δίκαιόν ἐςι ποιεῖν, ἄκουε, ἵνα σοι καὶ ἀποκρίνωμαι ὃ σὺ ἐρωτᾷς, πῶς χρὴ ἔχειν ἐμὲ καὶ σὲ πρὸς ἀλλήλους. Εἰ μὲν ὅλως φιλοσοφίας καταπεφρόνηκας, ἔαν χαίρειν· εἰ δὲ παρ' ἑτέρου ἀκήκοας ἤ αὐτὸς βελτίονε εὕρηκας τῶν παρ' ἐμοί, ἐκεῖνα τίμα· εἰ δ' ἄρα τὰ παρ' ἡμῶν σοι ἀρέσκει, τιμη-τέον καὶ ἐμὲ μάλιζα. PLATO.

Hear then what are the terms on which you and I ought to stand toward each other. If you hold philosophy altogether in contempt, bid it farewell. Or if you have heard from any other person, or have your-self found out a better than mine, then give honor to that, whichever it be. But if the doctrine taught in these our works please you, then it is but just that you should honor me too in the same proportion.

WHAT is that which first strikes us, and strikes us at once, in a man of education, and which, among educated men, so instantly distinguishes the man of superior mind, that (as was observed with eminent propriety of the late Edmund Burke) "we can not stand under the same archway during a shower of rain, without finding him out"? Not the weight or novelty of his remarks; not any unusual interest of facts communicated by him; for we may suppose both the one and the other precluded by the shortness of our intercourse, and the triviality of the subjects. The difference will be impressed and felt, though the conversation should be confined to the state of the weather or the pavement. Still less will it arise from any peculiarity in his words and phrases. For if he be, as we now assume, a well-educated man as well as a man of superior powers, he will not fail to follow the golden rule of Julius Cæsar, *insolens verbum, tanquam scopulum, evitare.* Unless where new things necessitate new terms, he will avoid an unusual word as a rock. It must have been among the earliest lessons of his youth, that the breach of this precept, at all times hazardous, becomes ridiculous in the topics of ordinary conversation. There remains but one other point of distinction possible; and this must be, and in fact is, the true cause of the impression made on us. It is the unpremeditated and evidently habitual arrangement of his words, grounded on the habit of foreseeing, in each integral part, or (more plainly) in every sentence, the whole that he then intends to communicate. However irregular and desultory his talk, there is method in the fragments.

Listen, on the other hand, to an ignorant man, though perhaps shrewd and able in his particular calling, whether he be describing or relating. We immediately perceive, that his memory alone is called into action; and that the objects and events recur in the narration in the same order, and with the same accompaniments, however accidental or impertinent, in which they had first occurred to the narrator. The necessity of taking breath, the efforts of recollection, and the abrupt rectification of its failures, produce all his pauses; and with exception of the "and then," the "and there," and the still less significant, "and so," they constitute likewise all his connections.

Our discussion, however, is confined to method as employed in the formation of the understanding, and in the constructions of science and literature. It would indeed be superfluous to attempt a proof of its importance in the business and economy of active or domestic life. From the cotter's hearth or the work shop of the artisan to the palace or the arsenal, the first merit, that which admits neither substitute nor equivalent, is, that everything be in its place. Where this charm is wanting, every other merit either loses its name, or becomes an additional ground of accusation and regret: Of one, by whom it is eminently possessed, we say proverbially, he is like clock-work. The resemblance extends beyond the point of regularity, and yet falls short of the truth. Both do, indeed, at once divide and announce the silent and otherwise indistinguishable lapse of time. But the man of methodical industry and honorable pursuits does more; he realizes its ideal divisions, and gives a character and individuality to its moments. If the idle are described as killing time, he may be justly said to call it into life and moral being, while he makes it the distinct object not only of the consciousness, but of the conscience. He organizes the hours, and gives them a soul; and that, the very essence of which is to fleet away, and evermore to have been, he takes up into his own permanence, and communicates to it the imperishableness of a spiritual nature. Of the *good and faithful servant*, whose energies, thus directed, are thus methodized, it is less truly affirmed, that he lives in time, than that time lives in him. His days, months, and years, as the stops and punctual marks in the records of duties performed, will survive the wreck of worlds, and remain extant when time itself shall be no more.

But as the importance of method in the duties of social life is incomparably greater, so are its practical elements proportionably obvious, and such as relate to the will far more than to the understanding. Henceforward, therefore, we contemplate its bearings on the latter.

The difference between the products of a well-disciplined and those of an uncultivated understanding, in relation to what we will now venture to call the science of method, is often and admirably exhibited by our great dramatist. I scarcely need refer my readers to the Clown's evidence, in the first scene of the second act of Measure for Measure, or to the Nurse in Romeo and Juliet. But not to leave the position, without an instance to illustrate it, I will take the easy-yielding Mrs. Quickly's relation of the circumstances of Sir John Falstaff's debt to her:—

FALSTAFF. What is the gross sum that I owe thee?

HOST. Marry, if thou wert an honest man, thyself and the money too Thou didst swear to me upon a parcel-gilt goblet, sitting in my Dolphin chamber, at the round table, by a sea-coal fire, upon Wednesday in Whitsun week, when the prince broke thy head for liking his father to a singing-man of Windsor; thou didst swear to me then, as I was washing thy wound, to marry me and make me my lady thy wife. Canst thou deny it? Did not goodwife Keech, the butcher's wife, come in then and call me gossip Quickly?—coming in to borrow a mess of vinegar; telling us she had a good dish of prawns; whereby thou didst desire to eat some; whereby I told thee they were ill for a green wound, &c.

And this, be it observed, is so far from being carried beyond the bounds of a fair imitation, that the poor soul's thoughts and sentences are more closely interlinked than the truth of nature would have required, but that the connections and sequence, which the habit of method can alone give, have in this instance a substitute in the fusion of passion. For the absence of method, which characterizes the uneducated, is occasioned by an habitual submission of the understanding to mere events and images as such, and independent of any power in the mind to classify or appropriate them. The general accompaniments of time and place are the only relations which persons of his class appear to regard in their statements. As this constitutes their leading feature, the contrary excellence, as distinguishing the well-educated man, must be referred to the contrary habit. Method, therefore, becomes natural to the mind which has been accustomed to contemplate not things only, or for their own sake alone, but likewise and chiefly the relations of things, either their relations to each other, or to the observer, or to the state and apprehension of the hearers. To enumerate and analyze these relations, with the conditions under which alone they are discoverable, is to teach the science of method.

The enviable results of this science, when knowledge has been ripened into those habits which at once secure and evince its possession, can scarcely be exhibited more forcibly as well as more pleasingly, than by contrasting with the former extract from Shakespeare the narration given by Hamlet to Horatio of the occurrences during his proposed transportation to England, and the events that interrupted his voyage:—

> HAM. Sir, in my heart there was a kind of fighting
> That would not let me sleep: methought, I lay
> Worse than the mutines in the bilboes. Rashly,
> And praised be rashness for it—— Let us know,
> Our indiscretion sometimes serve us well,
> When our deep plots do fail: and that should teach us,
> There's a divinity that shapes our ends,
> Rough-hew them how we will.
> HOR. That is most certain.
> HAM. Up from my cabin,
> My sea-gown scarf'd about me, in the dark
> Grop'd I to find out them; had my desire;
> Finger'd their packet; and, in fine, withdrew
> To my own room again: making so bold,
> My fears forgetting manners, to unseal
> Their grand commission; where I found, Horatio,
> A royal knavery; an exact command—
> Larded with many several sorts of reasons,
> Importing Denmark's health, and England's too,
> With, ho! such bugs and goblins in my life—
> That on the supervise, no leisure bated,
> No, not to stay the grinding of the axe,
> My head should be struck off!
> HOR. Is't possible?
> HAM. Here's the commission;—read it at more leisure.[1]

Here the events, with the circumstances of time and place, are all stated with equal compression and rapidity, not one introduced which could have been omitted without injury to the intelligibility of the whole process. If any tendency is discoverable, as far as the mere facts are in question, it is the tendency to omission: and, accordingly, the reader will observe in the following quotation that the attention of the narrator is called back to one material circumstance, which he was hurrying by, by a direct question from the friend to whom the story is communicated,

[1] Act v. sc. 2.

"How was this sealed?" But by a trait which is indeed peculiarly characteristic of Hamlet's mind, ever disposed to generalize, and meditative if to excess (but which, with due abatement and reduction, is distinctive of every powerful and methodizing intellect), all the digressions and enlargements consist of reflections, truths, and principles of general and permanent interest, either directly expressed or disguised in playful satire.

> —————————— I sat me down;
> Devis'd a new commission; wrote it fair.
> I once did hold it, as our statists do,
> A baseness to write fair, and labored much
> How to forget that learning; but, sir, now
> It did me yeoman's service. Wilt thou know
> The effect of what I wrote?
>   HOR. Ay, good my lord.
>   HAM. An earnest conjuration from the king,—
> As England was his faithful tributary;
> As love between them, like the palm, might flourish,
> As peace should still her wheaten garland wear,
> And stand a comma 'tween their amities,
> And many such like ases of great charge—
> That on the view and knowing of their contents,
> Without debatement further, more or less,
> He should the bearers put to sudden death,
> No shriving time allowed.
>   HOR. How was this seal'd?
>   HAM. Why, even in that was heaven ordinant
> I had my father's signet in my purse,
> Which was the model of that Danish seal:
> Folded the writ up in the form of the other;
> Subscribed it; gave't the impression; placed it safely,
> The changeling never known. Now, the next day
> Was our sea-fight; and what to this was sequent,
> Thou know'st already.
>   HOR. So Guildenstern and Rosencrantz go to't?
>   HAM. Why, man, they did make love to this employment.
> They are not near my conscience: their defeat
> Doth by their own insinuation grow.
> 'Tis dangerous when the baser nature comes
> Between the pass and fell incensed points
> Of mighty opposites.[2]

It would, perhaps, be sufficient to remark of the preceding passage, in connection with the humorous specimen of narration,

> Fermenting o'er with frothy circumstance,

[2] Act v. sc. 2.

in Henry IV., that if, overlooking the different value of the matter in each, we considered the form alone, we should find both immethodical,—Hamlet from the excess, Mrs. Quickly from the want, of reflection and generalization; and that method, therefore, must result from the due mean or balance between our passive impressions and the mind's own re-action on the same. Whether this re-action do not suppose or imply a primary act positively originating in the mind itself, and prior to the object in order of nature, though co-instantaneous with it in its manifestation, will be hereafter discussed. But I had a further purpose in thus contrasting these extracts from our myriad-minded bard, μυριονοῦς ἀνήρ. I wished to bring forward, each for itself, these two elements of method, or, to adopt an arithmetical term, its two main factors.

Instances of the want of generalization are of no rare occurrence in real life: and the narrations of Shakespeare's Hostess and the Tapster differ from those of the ignorant and unthinking in general by their superior humor, the poet's own gift and infusion, not by their want of method, which is not greater than we often meet with in that class, of which they are the dramatic representatives. Instances of the opposite fault, arising from the excess of generalization and reflection in minds of the opposite class, will, like the minds themselves, occur less frequently in the course of our own personal experience. Yet they will not have been wanting to our readers, nor will they have passed unobserved, though the great poet himself (ὁ τὴν ἑαυτοῦ ψυχὴν ὧσει ὕλην τίνα ἀσώματον μορφαῖς ποικιλαῖς μορφώσας[3]) has more conveniently supplied the illustrations. To complete, therefore, the purpose aforementioned, that of presenting each of the two components as separately as possible, I chose an instance in which, by the surplus of its own activity, Hamlet's mind disturbs the arrangement, of which that very activity had been the cause and impulse.

Thus exuberance of mind, on the one hand, interferes with the forms of method; but sterility of mind, on the other, wanting the spring and impulse to mental action, is wholly destructive of method itself. For in attending too exclusively to the relations which the past or passing events and objects bear to general truth, and the moods of his own thought, the most intelligent man is sometimes in danger of overlooking that other relation, in

---

[3] He that moulded his own soul, as some incorporeal material, into various forms.—THEMISTIUS.

which they are likewise to be placed to the apprehension and sympathies of his hearers. His discourse appears like soliloquy intermixed with dialogue. But the uneducated and unreflecting talker overlooks all mental relations, both logical and psychological; and consequently precludes all method which is not purely accidental. Hence the nearer the things and incidents in time and place, the more distant, disjointed, and impertinent to each other, and to any common purpose, will they appear in his narration: and this from the want of a staple, or starting-post, in the narrator himself; from the absence of the leading thought, which, borrowing a phrase from the nomenclature of legislation, I may not inaptly call the initiative. On the contrary, where the habit of method is present and effective, things the most remote and diverse in time, place, and outward circumstance, are brought into mental contiguity and succession, the more striking as the less expected. But while I would impress the necessity of this habit, the illustrations adduced give proof that in undue preponderance, and when the prerogative of the mind is stretched into despotism, the discourse may degenerate into the grotesque or the fantastical.

With what a profound insight into the constitution of the human soul is this exhibited to us in the character of the Prince of Denmark, where flying from the sense of reality, and seeking a reprieve from the pressure of its duties in that ideal activity, the overbalance of which, with the consequent indisposition to action, is his disease, he compels the reluctant good sense of the high yet healthful-minded Horatio to follow him in his wayward meditation amid the graves!

HAM. To what base uses we may return, Horatio! Why may not imagination trace the noble dust of Alexander till he find it stopping a bunghole?

HOR. 'Twere to consider too curiously, to consider so.

HAM. No, 'faith, not a jot; but to follow him thither with modesty enough, and likelihood to lead it: As thus; Alexander died, Alexander was buried, Alexander returneth to dust; the dust is earth; of earth we make loam: and why of that loam whereto he was converted, might they not stop a beer-barrel?

> Imperious Cæsar, dead, and turn'd to clay,
> Might stop a hole to keep the wind away! [a]

But let it not escape our recollection, that when the objects thus connected are proportionate to the connecting energy, relatively to the real, or at least to the desirable, sympathies of man-

[a] Act v. sc. 1.

kind; it is from the same character that we derive the genial method in the famous soliloquy, "To be, or not to be" [5]—which, admired as it is, and has been, has yet received only the first-fruits of the admiration due to it.

We have seen that from the confluence of innumerable impressions in each moment of time the mere passive memory must needs tend to confusion; a rule, the seeming exceptions to which (the thunder-bursts in Lear, for instance) are really confirmations of its truth. For, in many instances, the predominance of some mighty passion takes the place of the guiding thought, and the result presents the method of nature, rather than the habit of the individual. For thought, imagination (and I may add, passion), are, in their very essence, the first, connective, the latter coadunative: and it has been shown, that if the excess lead to method misapplied, and to connections of the moment, the absence, or marked deficiency, either precludes method altogether, both form and substance; or (as the following extract will exemplify) retains the outward form only.

> My liege and Madam, to expostulate
> What majesty should be, what duty is,
> Why day is day, night night, and time is time,
> Were nothing but to waste night, day and time.
> Therefore—since brevity is the soul of wit,
> And tediousness the limbs and outward flourishes,—
> I will be brief. Your noble son is mad:
> Mad call I it; for to define true madness,
> What is't, but to be nothing else but mad!
> But let that go.
>
>   QUEEN. More matter with less art.
>
>   POL. Madam, I swear, I use no art at all.
> That he is mad, 'tis true: 'tis true, 'tis pity:
> And pity 'tis, 'tis true: a foolish figure;
> But farewell it, for I will use no art.
> Mad let us grant him then: and now remains,
> That we find out the cause of this effect,
> Or rather say the cause of this defect:
> For this effect defective comes by cause.
> Thus it remains, and the remainder thus
> Perpend.[6]

Does not the irresistible sense of the ludicrous in this flourish of the soul-surviving body of old Polonius's intellect, not less than in the endless confirmations and most undeniable matters of fact

[5] Act iii. sc. 1.
[6] Act ii. sc. 2.

of Tapster Pompey or the hostess of the tavern prove to our feelings, even before the word is found which presents the truth to our understandings, that confusion and formality are but the opposite poles of the same null-point?

It is Shakespeare's peculiar excellence, that throughout the whole of his splendid picture-gallery (the reader will excuse the acknowledged inadequacy of this metaphor), we find individuality everywhere, mere portrait nowhere. In all his various characters, we still feel ourselves communing with the same nature, which is everywhere present as the vegetable sap in the branches, sprays, leaves, buds, blossoms, and fruits, their shapes, tastes, and odors. Speaking of the effect, that is, his works themselves, we may define the excellence of their method as consisting in that just proportion, that union and interpenetration, of the universal and the particular, which must ever pervade all works of decided genius and true science. For method implies a progressive transition, and it is the meaning of the word in the original language. The Greek μέθοδος is literally a way or path of transit. Thus we extol the Elements of Euclid, or Socrates' discourse with the slave in the Menon of Plato, as methodical, a term which no one who holds himself bound to think or speak correctly, would apply to the alphabetical order or arrangement of a common dictionary. But as without continuous transition there can be no method, so without a preconception there can be no transition with continuity. The term, method, can not therefore, otherwise than by abuse, be applied to a mere dead arrangement, containing in itself no principle of progression.

ESSAY VII

THE NECESSITY OF IDEAS TO SCIENTIFIC METHOD

Ταυτῇ τοινῦν διαίρω χῶρις μὲν, οὓς νῦν δὴ ἔλεγες φιλοθεάμονάς τε, καὶ φιλοτέχνους, καὶ πρακτίκους, καὶ χῶρις αὖ περὶ ὧν ὁ λόγος, οὓς μόνους ἄν τὶς ὀρθῶς προσείποι φιλοσόφους, ὡς μὲν γιγνώσκοντας, τίνος ἔξιν ἐπιζήμμι ἐκάξη τούτων τῶν ἐπιζήμων, ὁ τυγχάνει ὂν ἄλλο αὐτῆς τῆς ἐπιζήμης.

PLATO.

In the following then I distinguish, first, those whom you indeed may call philotheorists, or philotechnists, or practicians, and secondly those whom alone you may rightly denominate philosophers, as knowing what the science of all these branches of science is, which may prove to be something more than the mere aggregate of the knowledge in any particular science.

FROM Shakespeare to Plato, from the philosophic poet to the poetic philosopher, the transition is easy, and the road is crowded with illustrations of our present subject. For of Plato's works, the larger and more valuable portion have all one common end, which comprehends and shines through the particular purpose of each several dialogue; and this is to establish the sources, to evolve the principles, and exemplify the art of method. This is the clue, without which it would be difficult to exculpate the noblest productions of the divine philosopher from the charge of being tortuous and labyrinthine in their progress, and unsatisfactory in their ostensible results. The latter indeed appear not seldom to have been drawn for the purpose of starting a new problem, rather than that of solving the one proposed as the subject of the previous discussion. But with the clear insight that the purpose of the writer is not so much to establish any particular truth, as to remove the obstacles, the continuance of which is preclusive of all truth, the whole scheme assumes a different aspect, and justifies itself in all its dimensions. We see, that to open anew a well of springing water, not to cleanse the stagnant tank, or fill, bucket by bucket, the leaden cistern; that the education of the intellect, by awakening the principle and method of self-development, was his proposed object, not any specific information that can be conveyed into it from without;—not to assist in storing the passive mind with the various sorts of knowledge most in request, as if the human soul were a mere repository or banqueting-room, but to place it in such relations of circumstance as should gradually excite the germinal power that craves no knowledge but what it can take up into itself, what it can appropriate, and reproduce in fruits of its own. To shape, to dye, to paint over, and to mechanize the mind, he resigned, as their proper trade, to the sophists, against whom he waged open and unremitting war. For the ancients, as well as the moderns, had their machinery for the extemporaneous mintage of intellects, by means of which, off-hand, as it were, the scholar was enabled to make a figure on any and all subjects, on any and all occasions. They too had their glittering vapors, which (as the comic poet tells us) fed a host of sophists—

> μεγάλαι θεαὶ ἀνδράσιν ἀργοῖς,
> αἵπερ γνώμην, καὶ διάλεξιν, καὶ νοῦν ἡμῖν παρέχουσι,
> καὶ τερατείαν, καὶ περίλεξιν, καὶ κροῦσιν, καὶ κατάληψιν.

> Great goddesses are they to lazy folks,
> Who pour down on us gifts of fluent speech,
> Sense most sententious, wonderful fine effect,

And how to talk about it and about it,
Thoughts brisk as bees, and pathos soft and thawy.

In fine, as improgressive arrangement is not method, so neither is a mere mode or set fashion of doing a thing. Are further facts required? I appeal to the notorious fact that zoology, soon after the commencement of the latter half of the last century, was falling abroad, weighed down and crushed, as it were, by the inordinate number and manifoldness of facts and *phænomena* apparently separate, without evincing the least promise of systematizing itself by any inward combination, any vital interdependence, of its parts. John Hunter, who appeared at times almost a stranger to the grand conception, which yet never ceased to work in him as his genius and governing spirit, rose at length in the horizon of physiology and comparative anatomy. In his printed works, the one directing thought seems evermore to flit before him, twice or thrice only to have been seized, and after a momentary detention to have been again let go: as if the words of the charm had been incomplete, and it had appeared at its own will only to mock his calling. At length, in the astonishing preparations for his museum, he constructed it for the scientific apprehension out of the unspoken alphabet of nature. Yet notwithstanding the imperfection in the annunciation of the idea, how exhilarating have been the results! I dare appeal to[1] Abernethy, to Everard Home, to Hatchett, whose communcation to Sir Everard on the egg and its analogies, in a recent paper of the latter (itself of high excellence) in the Philosophical Transactions, I may point out as being, in the proper sense of the term, the development of a fact in the history of physiology, and to which I refer as exhibiting a luminous instance of what I mean by the discovery of a central *phænomenon*. To these I appeal, whether whatever is grandest in the views of Cuvier be not either a reflection of this light or a continuation of its rays, well and wisely directed through fit *media* to the appropriate object.[2]

[1] Since this was written, Mr. Abernethy has realized this anticipation, dictated solely by my wishes, and at the time justified only by my general admiration of Mr. A.'s talents and principles, and composed without the least knowledge that he was then actually engaged in proving the assertion here hazarded, at large and in detail. See his eminent Treatise on Physiology, 1821.

[2] Nor should it be wholly unnoticed, that Cuvier, who, I understand, was not born in France, and is not of unmixed French extraction, had prepared himself for his illustrious labors (as I learn from a reference in the first chapter of his great work, and should have concluded from the general style of thinking, though the language betrays

We have seen that a previous act and conception of the mind is indispensable even to the mere semblances of method; that neither fashion, mode, nor orderly arrangement can be produced without a prior purpose, and a pre-cogitation *ad intentionem ejus quod quæritur,* though this purpose may have been itself excited, and this pre-cogitation itself abstracted from the perceived like-nesses and differences of the objects to be arranged. But it has likewise been shown, that fashion, mode, ordonnance, are not method, inasmuch as all method supposes a principle of unity with progression; in other words, progressive transition without breach of continuity. But such a principle, it has been proved, can never in the science of experiment or in those of observation be adequately supplied by a theory built on generalization. For what shall determine the mind to abstract and generalize one common point rather than another;—and within what limits, from what number of individual objects, shall the generalization be made? The theory must still require a prior theory for its own legitimate construction. With the mathematician the defi-nition makes the object, and pre-establishes the terms which, and which alone, can occur in the after-reasoning. If a circle be found not to have the *radii* from the centre to the circumfer-ence perfectly equal, which in fact it would be absurd to expect of any material circle, it follows only that it was not a circle; and the tranquil geometrician would content himself with smil-ing at the *quid pro quo* of the simple objector. A mathemat-ical *theoria seu contemplatio* may therefore be perfect. For the mathematician can be certain that he has contemplated all that appertains to his proposition. The celebrated Euler, treating on some point respecting arches, makes this curious remark:—"All experience is in contradiction to this; *sed potius fidendum est analysi;* but this is no reason for doubting the analysis." The words sound paradoxical; but in truth mean no more than this, that the properties of space are not less certainly the properties of space because they can never be entirely transferred to mate-rial bodies. But in physics, that is, in all the sciences which have for their objects the things of nature, and not the *entia ra-tionis*—more philosophically, intellectual acts and the products of those acts, existing exclusively in and for the intellect itself—the definition must follow, and not precede, the reasoning. It is representative not constitutive, and is indeed little more than an abbreviature of the preceding observation, and the deductions

suppression, as of one who doubted the sympathy of his readers or audience) in a very different school of methodology and philosophy than any which Paris could have afforded.

therefrom. But as the observation, though aided by experiment, is necessarily limited and imperfect, the definition must be equally so. The history of theories, and the frequency of their subversion by the discovery of a single new fact, supply the best illustrations of this truth.[3]

As little can a true scientific method be grounded on an hypothesis, unless where the hypothesis is an exponential image or picture-language of an idea which is contained in it more or less clearly; or the symbol of an undiscovered law, like the characters of unknown quantities in algebra, for the purpose of submitting the *phænomena* to a scientific *calculus*. In all other instances, it is itself a real or supposed *phænomenon*, and therefore a part of the problem which it is to solve. It may be among the foundation-stones of the edifice, but can never be the ground.

[3] The following extract from a most respectable scientific Journal contains an exposition of the impossibility of a perfect theory in physics, the more striking because it is directly against the purpose and intention of the writer. I content myself with one question,—what if Kepler, what if Newton in his investigations concerning the tides, had holden themselves bound to this canon, and, instead of propounding a law, had employed themselves exclusively in collecting materials for a theory?

"The magnetic influence has long been known to have a variation which is constantly changing; but that change is so slow, and at the same time so different in various parts of the world, that it would be in vain to seek for the means of reducing it to established rules, until all its local and particular circumstances are clearly ascertained and recorded by accurate observations made in various parts of the globe. The necessity and importance of such observations are now pretty generally understood, and they have been actually carrying on for some years past; but these (and by parity of reason the incomparably greater number that remain to be made) must be collected, collated, proved, and afterwards brought together into one focus before ever a foundation can be formed upon which any thing like a sound and stable theory can be constituted for the explanation of such changes." *Journal of Science and the Arts,* No. vii. p. 103.

An intelligent friend, on reading the words "into one focus," observed: "But what and where is the lens?" I however fully agree with the writer. All this and much more must have been achieved before "a sound and stable theory" could be "constituted;"—which even then (except as far as it might occasion the discovery of a law) might possibly explain (*ex plicis plana reddere*), but never account for, the facts in question. But the most satisfactory comment on these and similar assertions would be afforded by a matter of fact history of the rise and progress, the accelerating and retarding *momenta,* of science in the civilized world.

But in experimental philosophy, it may be said how much do we not owe to accident? Doubtless: but let it not be forgotten, that if the discoveries so made stop there; if they do not excite some master idea; if they do not lead to some law (in whatever dress of theory or hypothesis the fashions and prejudices of the time may disguise or disfigure it);—the discoveries may remain for ages limited in their uses, insecure and unproductive. How many centuries, we might have said *millennia*, have passed, since the first accidental discovery of the attraction and repulsion of light bodies by rubbed amber! Compare the interval with the progress made within less than a century, after the discovery of the *phænomena* that led immediately to a theory of electricity. That here as in many other instances, the theory was supported by insecure hypotheses; that by one theorist two heterogeneous fluids are assumed, the vitreous and the resinous; by another, a *plus* and *minus* of the same fluid; that a third considers it a mere modification of light; while a fourth composes the electrical *aura* of oxygen, hydrogen, and caloric;—this does but place the truth we have been evolving in a stronger and clearer light. For abstract from all these suppositions, or rather imaginations, that which is common to, and involved in, them all; and we shall have neither notional fluid or fluids, nor chemical compounds, nor elementary matter,—but the idea of two—opposite—forces, tending to rest by *equilibrium.* These are the sole factors of the *calculus,* alike in all the theories. These give the law, and in it the method, both of arranging the *phænomena* and of substantiating appearances into facts of science; with a success proportionate to the clearness or confusedness of the insight into the law. For this reason, I anticipate the greatest improvements in the method, the nearest approaches to a system of electricity, from these philosophers, who have presented the law most purely, and the correlative idea as an idea;—those, namely, who, since the year 1798, in the true spirit of experimental dynamics, rejecting the imagination of any material substrate, simple or compound, contemplate in the *phænomena* of electricity the operation of a law which reigns through all nature, the law of polarity, or the manifestation of one power by opposite forces;—who trace in these appearances, as the most obvious and striking of its innumerable forms, the agency of the positive and negative poles of a power essential to all material construction; the second, namely, of the three primary principles, for which the beautiful and most appropriate symbols are given by the mind in the three ideal dimensions of space.

The time is, perhaps, nigh at hand, when the same comparison between the results of two unequal periods,—the interval between the knowledge of a fact, and that from the discovery of the law,—will be applicable to the sister science of magnetism. But how great the contrast between magnetism and electricity at the present moment! From remotest antiquity, the attraction of iron by the magnet was known and noticed; but, century after century, it remained the undisturbed property of poets and orators. The fact of the magnet and the fable of the phœnix stood on the same scale of utility. In the thirteenth century, or perhaps earlier, the polarity of the magnet, and its communicability to iron, were discovered; and soon suggested a purpose so grand and important, that it may well be deemed the proudest trophy ever raised by accident in the service of mankind,—the invention of the compass. But it led to no idea, to no law, and consequently to no method: though a variety of *phænomena*, as startling as they are mysterious, have forced on us a presentiment of its intimate connection with all the great agencies of nature; of a revelation, in ciphers, the key to which is still wanting. I can recall no event of human history that impresses the imagination more deeply than the moment when Columbus,[4] on an un-

---

[4] It can not be deemed alien from the purposes of this disquisition, if I am anxious to attract the attention of my readers to the importance of speculative meditation, even for the worldly interests of mankind; and to that concurrence of nature and historic event with the great revolutionary movements of individual genius, of which so many instances occur in the study of history;—to point out how nature, or that which in nature itself is more than nature, seems to come forward in order to meet, to aid, and to reward every idea excited by a contemplation of her methods in the spirit of filial care, and with the humility of love. It is with this view that I extract the following lines from an ode of Chiabrera's, which, in the strength of the thought and the lofty majesty of the poetry, has but "few peers in ancient or in modern song."

> Certo da cor, ch' alto destin non scelse,
> Son l' imprese magnanime neglette;
> Ma le bell' alme alle bell' opre elette
> Sanno gioir nelle fatiche eccelse;
> Nè biasmo popolar frale catena,
> Spirto d' onore, il suo cammin raffrena.
> Cosi lunga stagion per modi indegni
> Europa disprezzò l'inclita speme,
> Schernendo il vulgo e seco i regi insieme,
> Nudo nocchier promettitor di regni;
> Ma per le sconosciute onde marine
> L' invitta prora ei pur sospinse al fine.
> Qual uom, che torni alla gentil consorte,

known ocean, first perceived one of these startling facts, the change of the magnetic needle.

In what shall we seek the cause of this contrast between the rapid progress of electricity and the stationary condition of magnetism? As many theories, as many hypotheses, have been advanced in the latter science as in the former. But the theories and fictions of the electricians contained an idea, and all the same idea, which has necessarily led to method; implicit indeed, and only regulative hitherto, but which requires little more than the dismission of the imagery to become constitutive like the ideas of the geometrician. On the contrary, the assumptions of the magnetists (as for instance, the hypothesis that the planet itself is one vast magnet, or that an immense magnet is concealed within it, or that of a concentric globe within the earth, revolving on its own independent axis), are but repetitions of the same fact or *phænomenon* looked at through a magnifying glass; the reiteration of the problem, not its solution. The naturalist, who can not or will not see, that one fact is often worth a thousand, as including them all in itself, and that it first makes all the other facts,—who has not the head to comprehend, the soul to reverence, a central experiment or observation (what the Greeks would perhaps have called a *protophænomenon*),—will never receive an auspicious answer from the oracle of nature.

ESSAY IX

THE BACONIAN METHOD ESSENTIALLY ONE WITH THE PLATONIC

A great authority may be a poor proof, but it is an excellent presumption: and few things give a wise man a truer delight than to reconcile two great authorities, that had been commonly but falsely held to be dissonant.   STAPZLTON.

> Tal ei da sua magion spiegò l'antenne;
> L' ocean corse, e i turbini sostenne,
> Vinse le crude immagini di morte;
> Poscia, dell' ampio mar spenta la guerra,
> Scorse la dianzi favolosa terra.
> Allor dal cavo pin scende veloce,
>   E di grand' orma il nuovo mondo imprime;
> Nè men ratto per l'aria erge sublime,
> Segno del ciel, l'insuperabil croce;
> E porge umile esempio, onde adorarla
> Debba sua gente.   CHIABRERA, P. I. 12.

UNDER a deep impression of the importance of the truths I have essayed to develop, I would fain remove every prejudice that does not originate in the heart rather than in the understanding. For truth, says the wise man, will not enter a malevolent spirit.

To offer or to receive names in lieu of sound arguments, is only less reprehensible than an ostentatious contempt of the great men of former ages; but we may well and wisely avail ourselves of authorities, in confirmation of truth, and above all, in the removal of prejudices founded on imperfect information. I do not see, therefore, how I can more appropriately conclude this first, explanatory and controversial section of the inquiry, than by a brief statement of our renowned countryman's own principles of method, conveyed for the greater part in his own words. Nor do I see, in what more precise form I can recapitulate the substance of the doctrines asserted and vindicated in the preceding pages. For I rest my strongest pretensions to a calm and respectful perusal, in the first instance, on the fact, that I have only reproclaimed the coinciding prescripts of the Athenian Verulam, and the British Plato—*genuinam scilicet Platonis dialecticem, et methodologiam principialem.*

FRANCISCI DE VERULAMIO

In the first instance, Lord Bacon equally with myself demands what I have ventured to call the intellectual or mental initiative, as the motive and guide of every philosophical experiment; some well-grounded purpose, some distinct impression of the probable results, some self-consistent anticipation as the ground of the *prudens quæstio,* the forethoughtful query, which he affirms to be the prior half of the knowledge sought, *dimidium scientiæ.* With him, therefore, as with me, an idea is an experiment proposed, an experiment is an idea realized. For so, though in other words, he himself informs us: *neque id molimur tam instrumentis quam experimentis; etenim experimentorum longe major est subtilitas quam sensus ipsius, licet instrumentis exquisitis adjuti. De iis loquimur experimentis, quæ ad intentionem ejus quod quæritur perite et secundum artem excogitata et apposita sunt. Itaque perceptioni sensus immediatæ ac propriæ non multum tribuimus: sed eo rem deducimus, ut sensus tantum de experimento, experimentum de re, judicet.* This last sentence is, as the attentive reader will have himself detected, one of those faulty verbal antitheses not unfrequent in Lord Bacon's writings. Pungent antitheses, and the analogies of wit in which the resemblance is too often more indebted to the double or equivocal sense of a word, than to any real conformity[1] in the thing or image, form the *dulcia vitia* of his style, the Dalilahs of our philosophical Samson. But in this instance, as indeed throughout all his works, the meaning is clear and evident;—namely, that the sense can apprehend, through the organs of sense, only the *phænomena* evoked by the experiment: *vis vero mentis ea, quæ experimentum excogitaverat, de re judicet:* that is, that power, which out of its own conceptions had shaped the experiment, must alone determine the true import of the *phænomena.* If again we ask, what it is which gives birth to the question, and then *ad intentionem quæstionis suæ experimentum excogitat, unde de re judicet,* the answer is,—*lux intellectus, lumen siccum,* the pure and impersonal reason, freed from all the various idols enumerated by our great legislator of science (*idola tribus, specus, fori, theatri*); that is, freed from the limits, the passions, the prejudices, the peculiar habits of the human understanding, natural or acquired; but above all, pure from the arrogance, which leads man to take the forms and mechanism of his own mere reflective faculty, as the measure of nature and of Deity. In this indeed we find the great object both of Plato's and of Lord Bacon's labors. They both saw that there could be no hope of any fruitful and secure method, while forms, merely subjective, were presumed as the true and proper moulds of objective truth. This is the sense in which Lord Bacon uses the phrases, *intellectus humanus, mens hominis,* so profoundly and justly characterized in the preliminary essay to the *Novum Organum.* And with all right and propriety did he so apply them: for this was, in fact, the sense in which the phrases were applied by the teachers, whom he is controverting; by the doctors of the schools, and the visionaries of the laboratory. To adopt the bold but happy phrase of a late ingenious French writer, it is the *homme particulier,* as contrasted with *l'homme général,* against which, Heraclitus and Plato, among the ancients, and among the moderns, Bacon and Stewart (rightly understood), warn and preadmonish the sincere inquirer. Most truly, and in strict consonance with his two great predecessors, does our immortal Verulam teach, that the human understanding, even independently of the causes that always, previously to its purification by philosophy, render it more or less turbid or uneven, *sicut speculum inæquale rerum radios ex figura et sectione propria immutat:*

---

[1] Thus (to take the first instance that occurs), Bacon says, that some knowledges, like the stars, are so high that they give no light. Where the word, "high," means "deep or sublime," in the one case, and "distant" in the other.

that our understanding not only reflects the objects subjectively, that is, substitutes for the inherent laws and properties of the objects the relations which the objects bear to its own particular constitution; but that in all its conscious presentations and reflexes, it is itself only a *phænomenon* of the inner sense, and requires the same corrections as the appearances transmitted by the outward senses. But that there is potentially, if not actually, in every rational being, a somewhat, call it what you will, the pure reason, the spirit, *lumen siccum,* νοῦς, φῶς νοερὸν, intellectual intuition, or the like,—and that in this are to be found the indispensable conditions of all science, and scientific research, whether meditative, contemplative, or experimental,—is often expressed and everywhere supposed, by Lord Bacon. And that this is not only the right but the possible nature of the human mind, to which it is capable of being restored, is implied in the various remedies prescribed by him for its diseases, and in the various means of neutralizing or converting into useful instrumentality the imperfections which can not be removed. There is a sublime truth contained in his favorite phrase, *idola intellectus.* He thus tells us, that the mind of man is an edifice not built with human hands, which needs only be purged of its idols and idolatrous services to become the temple of the true and living Light. Nay, he has shown and established the true criterion between the ideas and the *idola* of the mind; namely, that the former are manifested by their adequacy to those ideas in nature, which in and through them are contemplated. *Non leve quiddam interest inter humanæ mentis idola et divinæ mentis ideas, hoc est, inter placita quædam inania et veras signaturas atque impressiones factas in creaturis, prout inveniuntur.* Thus the difference, or rather distinction, between Plato and Lord Bacon is simply this: that philosophy being necessarily bipolar, Plato treats principally of the truth, as it manifests itself at the ideal pole, as the science of intellect (*de mundo intelligibili*); while Bacon confines himself, for the most part, to the same truth, as it is manifested at the other or material pole, as the science of nature (*de mundo sensibili*). It is as necessary, therefore, that Plato should direct his inquiries chiefly to those objective truths that exist in and for the intellect alone, the images and representatives of which we construct for ourselves by figure, number, and word; as that Lord Bacon should attach his main concern to the truths which have their signatures in nature, and which (as he himself plainly and often asserts) may indeed be revealed to us through and with, but never by the senses, or the faculty of sense. Otherwise, indeed, instead of being more objective than the former (which they are not in any sense, both being in this respect the same), they would be less so, and, in fact, incapable of being insulated from the *idola tribus* (*quæ*) *sunt fundata in ipsa natura humana, atque in ipsa tribu seu gente hominum. Falso enim asseritur sensum humanum esse mensuram rerum; quin contra, omnes perceptiones tam sensus quam mentis, sunt ex analogia hominis, non ex analogia universi.* Hence too, it will not surprise us, that Plato so often calls ideas living laws, in which the mind has its whole true being and permanence; or that Bacon, *vice versa*, names the laws of nature ideas; and represents what I have in a former part of this disquisition called facts of science and central *phænomena*, as signatures, impressions, and symbols of ideas. A distinguishable power self-affirmed, and seen in its unity with the Eternal Essence, is, according to Plato, an idea: and the discipline, by which the human mind is purified from its idols (εἴδωλα), and raised to the contemplation of ideas, and thence to the secure and ever-progressive, though never-ending, investigation of truth and reality by scientific method, comprehends what the same philosopher so highly extols under the title of dialectic. According to Lord Bacon, as describing the same truth seen from the opposite point, and applied to natural philosophy, an idea would be defined as— *intuitio sive inventio, quæ in perceptione sensus non est* (*ut quæ puræ et sicci luminis intellectioni est propria*) *idearum divinæ mentis, prout in creaturis per signaturas suas sese patefaciant.* "That (saith the judicious Hooker) which doth assign unto each thing the kind, that which doth moderate the force and power, that which doth appoint the form and measure, of working, the same we term a law."

We can now, as men furnished with fit and respectable credentials, proceed to the historic importance and practical application of method, under the deep and solemn conviction, that without this guiding light neither can the sciences attain to their full evolution, as the organs of one vital and harmonious body, nor that most weighty and concerning of all sciences, the science of education, be understood in its first elements, much less display its powers, as the *nisus formativus*[2] of social man, as the

---

[2] So our medical writers commonly translate Professor Blumenbach's *Bildungstrieb*, the *vis plastica*, or *vis vitæ formatrix*, of the elder physiologists, and the life or living principle of John Hunter, the profoundest, I had almost said the only, physiological philosopher of the latter half of the preceding century. For in what other sense can we understand his assertion, that this principle or agent is indepedent of organization, which yet it animates, sustains, and repairs, or the pur-

appointed protoplast of true humanity. Never can society comprehend fully, and in its whole practical extent, the permanent distinction, and the occasional contrast, between cultivation and civilization; never can it attain to a due insight into the momentous fact, fearfully as it has been, and even now is, exemplified in a neighbor country, that a nation can never be a too

---

port of that magnificent commentary on his system, the Hunterian Museum? The Hunterian idea of a life or vital principle independent of the organization, yet in each organ working instinctively towards its preservation, as the ants or termites in repairing the nests of their own fabrication, demonstrates that John Hunter did not, as Stahl and others had done, individualize, or make an *hypostasis* of the principles of life, as a something manifestable *per se,* and consequently itself a *phænomenon;* the latency of which was to be attributed to accidental, or at least contingent causes, as for example, the limits or imperfection of our senses, or the inaptness of the *media;* but that herein he philosophized in the spirit of the purest Newtonians, who in like manner refused to hypostasize the law of gravitation into an ether, which even if its existence were conceded, would need another gravitation for itself. The Hunterian position is a genuine philosophic idea, the negative test of which, as of all ideas is, that it is equi-distant from an *ens logicum* or abstraction, an *ens repræsentativum* or generalization, and an *ens phantasticum* or imaginary thing or *phænomenon.*

Is not the progressive enlargement, the boldness without temerity, of chirurgical views and chirurgical practice since Hunter's time to the present day, attributable, in almost every instance, to his substitution of what may perhaps be called experimental dynamics, for the mechanical notions, or the less injurious traditional empiricism, of his predecessors? And this, too, though the light is still struggling through a cloud, and though it is shed on many who see either dimly or not at all the idea from which it is eradiated? Willingly would I designate, what I have elsewhere called the mental initiative, by some term less obnoxious to the anti-Platonic reader, than this of idea—obnoxious, I mean, as soon as any precise and peculiar sense is attached to the sound. Willingly would I exchange the term, might it be done without sacrifice of the import: and did I not see, too, clearly, that it is the meaning, not the word, which is the object of that aversion, which, fleeing from inward alarm, tries to shelter itself in outward contempt; which is at once folly and a stumbling-block to the partisans of a crass and sensual materialism, the advocates of the *nihil nisi ab extra:*—

> They shrink in, as moles,
> Nature's mute monks, live mandrakes of the ground,
> Creep back from light, then listen for its sound;
> See but to dread, and dread they know not why,
> The natural alien of their negative eye!

Poet. Works, VII. p. 196.

cultivated, but may easily become an over-civilized race: never, I repeat, can this sanative and preventive knowledge take up its abode among us, while we oppose ourselves voluntarily to that grand prerogative of our nature, a hungering and thirsting after truth, as the appropriate end of our intelligential, and its point of union with our moral nature; but therefore after truth, that must be found within us before it can be intelligibly reflected back on the mind from without, and a religious regard to which is indispensable, both as guide and object to the just formation of the human being, poor and rich: while, in a word, we are blind to the master-light, which I have already presented in various points of view, and recommended by whatever is of highest authority with the venerators of the ancient, and the adherents of modern philosophy.

ESSAY X

EXISTENCE OF A SELF-ORGANIZING PURPOSE
IN NATURE AND MAN

Πολυμαθίη νόον οὐ διδάσκει.—Εἶναι γὰρ ἓν τὸ σοφὸν, ἐπίζασθαι γνώμην ἥτε ἐγκυβερνήσει πάντα διὰ πάντων.   HERACLITUS.

The effective education of the reason is not to be supplied by multifarious acquirements: for there is but one knowledge that merits to be called wisdom, a knowledge that is one with a law which shall govern all in and through all.

HISTORICAL AND ILLUSTRATIVE

THERE is still preserved in the Royal Observatory at Richmond the model of a bridge, constructed by the late justly celebrated Mr. Atwood (at that time, however, in the decline of life), in the confidence that he had explained the wonderful properties of the arch as resulting from the compound action of simple wedges, or of the rectilinear solids of which the material arch was composed; and of which supposed discovery, his model was to exhibit ocular proof. Accordingly, he took a sufficient number of wedges of brass highly polished. Arranging these at first on a skeleton arch of wood, he then removed this scaffolding or support; and the bridge not only stood firm, without any cement between the squares, but he could take away any given portion of them, as a third or a half, and appending a correspondent weight, at either side, the remaining part stood as before. Our venerable sovereign, who is known to have had a particular interest and pleasure in all works and discoveries of mechanic science or ingenuity, looked at it for awhile steadfastly, and, as his manner was, with quick and broken expressions of praise and courteous approbation, in the form of answers to his own questions. At length, turning to the constructor, he said, "But, Mr. Atwood, you have presumed the figure. You have put the arch first in this wooden skeleton. Can you build a bridge of the same wedges in any other figure? A strait bridge, or with two lines touching at the apex? If not, is it not evident, that the bits of brass derive their continuance in the present position from the property of the arch, and not the arch from the property of the wedge?" The objection was fatal, the justice of the remark not to be resisted; and I have ever deemed it a forcible illustration of the Aristotelian axiom, with respect to all just reasoning, that the whole is of necessity prior to its parts; nor can I conceive a more apt illustration of the scientific principles I have already laid down.

All method supposes a union of several things to a common end, either by disposition, as in the works of man; or by convergence, as in the operations and products of nature. That we acknowledge a method, even in the latter, results from the religious instinct which bids us "find tongues in trees; books in the running streams; sermons in stones; and good (that is, some useful end answering to some good purpose) in every thing." In a self-conscious and thence reflecting being, no instinct can exist without engendering the belief of an object corresponding to it, either present or future, real or capable of being realized; much less the instinct, in which humanity itself is grounded;—that by which, in every act of conscious perception, we at once identify our being with that of the world without us, and yet place ourselves in contra-distinction to that world. Least of all can this mysterious pre-disposition exist without evolving a belief that the productive power,[1] which in nature acts as nature, is essentially one (that

[1] Obscure from too great compression. The sense is, that the productive power, or *vis naturans,* which in the sensible world, or *natura naturata,* is what we mean by the word, nature, when we speak of the same as an agent, is essentially one, &c. In other words, idea and law are the subjective and objective poles of the same magnet, that is, of the same living and energizing reason. What an idea is in the subject, that is, in the mind, is a law in the object, that is, in nature. But throughout these essays, the want of illustrative examples, and varied exposition is, I am conscious, the main defect, and it was occasioned by the haunting dread of being tedious. But O! the cold water that was thrown on me, chiefly from those from whom I ought to have received warmth and encouragement! "Who, do you expect, will read

is, of one kind) with the intelligence, which is in the human mind above nature; however disfigured this belief may become by accidental forms or accompaniments, and though like heat in the thawing of ice, it may appear only in its effects. So universally has this conviction leavened the very substance of all discourse, that there is no language on earth in which a man can abjure it as a prejudice, without employing terms and conjunctions that suppose its reality, with a feeling very different from that which accompanies a figurative or metaphorical use of words. In all aggregates of construction therefore, which we contemplate as wholes, whether as integral parts or as a system, we assume an intention, as the initiative, of which the end is the correlative.

Hence proceeds the introduction of final causes in the works of nature equally as in those of man. Hence their assumption, as constitutive and explanatory, by the mass of mankind; and the employment of the presumption, as an auxiliary and regulative principle, by the enlightened naturalist, whose office it is·to seek, discover, and investigate the efficient causes. Without denying, that to resolve the efficient into the final may be the ultimate aim of philosophy, he, of good right, resists the substitution of the latter for the former, as premature, presumptuous, and preclusive of all science; well aware, that those sciences have been most progressive, in which this confusion has been either precluded by the nature of the science itself, as in pure mathematics, or avoided by the good sense of its cultivator. Yet even he admits a teleological ground in physics and physiology; that is, the presumption of a something analogous to the casualty of the human will, by which, without assigning to nature, as nature, a conscious purpose, he may yet distinguish her agency from a blind and lifeless mechanism. Even he admits its use, and, in many instances, its necessity, as a regulative principle; as a ground of anticipation, for the guidance of his judgment and for the direction of his observation and experiment;—briefly in all that preparatory process, which the French language so happily expresses by s'orienter, to find out the east for one's self. When the naturalist contemplates the structure of a bird, for instance, the hollow cavity of the bones, the position of the wings for motion, and of the tail for steering its course, and the like, he knows indeed that there must be a correspondent mechanism, as

this," &c.—But, vanity as it may appear, it is nevertheless true, and uttered with feelings the most unlike those of self-conceit, that it has been my mistake through life to be looking up to those whom I ought to have been looking at, nay (in some instances) down upon.—June 23d, 1829.

the *nexus effectivus;* but he knows, likewise, that this will no more explain the particular existence of the bird, than the principles of cohesion could inform him why of two buildings one is a palace and the other a church. Nay, it must not be overlooked, that the assumption of the *nexus effectivus* itself originates in the mind, as one of the laws under which alone it can reduce the manifold of the impression from without into unity, and thus contemplate it as one thing; and could never (as hath been clearly proved by Mr. Hume) have been derived from outward experience, in which it is indeed presupposed as a necessary condition. *Notio nexus causalis non oritur, sed supponitur, a sensibus.* Between the purpose and the end the component parts are included, and thence receive their position and character as means, that is, parts contemplated as parts. It is in this sense, that I will affirm that the parts, as means to an end, derive their position, and therein their qualities (or character)—nay, I dare add, their very existence, as particular things,—from the antecedent method, or self-organizing purpose; upon which therefore i have dwelt so long.

I am aware that it is with our cognitions as with our children. There is a period in which the method of nature is working for them; a period of aimless activity and unregulated accumulation, during which it is enough if we can preserve them in health and out of harm's way. Again, there is a period of orderliness, of circumspection, of discipline, in which we purify, separate, define, select, arrange, and settle the nomenclature of communication. There is also a period of dawning and twilight, a period of anticipation, affording trials of strength. And all these, both in the growth of the sciences and in the mind of a rightly-educated individual, will precede the attainment of a scientific method. But, notwithstanding this, unless the importance of the latter be felt and acknowledged, unless its attainment be looked forward to and from the very beginning prepared for, there is little hope and small chance that any education will be conducted aright; or will ever prove in reality worth the name.

Much labor, much wealth may have been expended, yet the final result will too probably warrant the sarcasm of the Scythian traveller: *Væ! quantum nihili!* and draw from a wise man the earnest recommendation of a full draught from Lethe, as the first and indispensable preparative for the waters of the true Helicon. Alas! how many examples are now present to my memory, of young men the most anxiously and expensively be-school-mastered, be-tutored, be-lectured, any thing but educated; who have received arms and ammunition, instead of skill, strength, and courage; varnished rather than polished; perilously over-civilized, and most pitiably uncultivated! And all from inattention to the method dictated by nature herself, to the simple truth, that as the forms in all organized existence, so must all true and living knowledge proceed from within; that it may be trained, supported, fed, excited, but can never be infused, or impressed.

Look back on the history of the sciences. Review the method in which providence has brought the more favored portion of mankind to their present state. Lord Bacon has justly remarked, *antiquitas sæculi juventus mundi*—antiquity of time is the youth of the world and of science. In the childhood of the human race, its education commenced with the cultivation of the moral sense; the object proposed being such as the mind only could apprehend, and the principle of obedience being placed in the will. The appeal in both was made to the inward man. *Through faith we understand that the worlds were framed by the word of God; so that things which are seen were not made of things which do appear*. The solution of *phænomena* can never be derived from *phænomena*. Upon this ground the writer of the epistle to the Hebrews (c. xi.) is not less philosophical than eloquent. The aim, the method throughout was, in the first place, to awaken, to cultivate, and to mature the truly human in human nature, in and through itself, or as independently as possible of the notices derived from sense, and of the motives that had reference to the sensations; till the time should arrive when the senses themselves might be allowed to present symbols and attestations of truths, learnt previously from deeper and inner sources. Thus the first period of the education of our race was evidently assigned to the cultivation of humanity itself, or of that in man, which of all known embodied creatures he alone possesses, the pure reason, as designed to regulate the will. And by what method was this done? First, by the excitement of the idea of their Creator as a spirit, of an idea which they were strictly forbidden to realize to themselves under any image; and secondly, by the injunction of obedience to the will of a super-sensual Being. Nor did the method stop here. For, unless we are equally to contradict Moses and the New Testament, in compliment to the paradox of a Warburton, the rewards of their obedience were placed at a distance. For the time present they equally with us were to endure, as seeing him who is invisible. Their bodies they were taught to consider as fleshly tents, which as pilgrims they were bound to pitch wherever the invisible Director of their route should appoint, however barren or thorny ᴜᴇ spot might appear. *Few and evil have the days of the years of my life been,*[2] says the aged Israel. But that life was but his pilgrimage, and he trusted in the promises.

Thus were the very first lessons in the divine school assigned to the cultivation of the reason and of the will; or rather of both as united in faith. The common and ultimate object of the will and of the reason was purely spiritual, and to be present in the mind of the disciple—μόνον ἐν ἰδέᾳ, μηδαμῆ εἰδωλικῶς, that is, in the idea alone, and never as an image or imagination. The means too, by which the idea was to be excited, as well as the symbols by which it was to be communicated, were to be, as far as possible, intellectual.

Those, on the contrary, who wilfully chose a mode opposite to this method, who determined to shape their convictions and deduce their knowledge from without, by exclusive observation of outward and sensible things as the only realities, became, it appears, rapidly civilized. They built cities, invented musical instruments, were artificers in brass and in iron, and refined on the means of sensual gratification, and the conveniencies of courtly intercourse. They became the great masters of the agreeable, which fraternized readily with cruelty and rapacity; these being, indeed, but alternate moods of the same sensual selfishness. Thus, both before and after the flood, the vicious of mankind receded from all true cultivation, as they hurried towards civilization. Finally, as it was not in their power to make themselves wholly beasts, or to remain without a semblance of religion; and yet continuing faithful to their original maxim, and determined to receive nothing as true, but what they derived, or believed themselves to derive from their senses, or (in modern phrase) what they could prove *à posteriori,* they became idolaters of the heavens and the material elements. From the harmony of operation they concluded a certain unity of nature and design, but were incapable of finding in the facts any proof of a unity of person. They did not, in this respect, pretend to find what they must themselves have first assumed. Having thrown away the clusters, which had grown in the vineyard of revelation, they could not, as later reasoners, by being born in a Christian country, have been enabled to do, hang the grapes on thorns, and then pluck them as the native growth of the bushes. But the men of sense of the patriarchal times, neglecting reason and having rejected faith, adopted what the facts seemed to involve and the most obvious analogies to suggest. They acknowledged a whole beᴇ

[2] Gen. xlvii. 9

hive of natural gods: but while they were employed in building a temple[3] consecrated to the material heavens, it pleased divine wisdom to send on them a confusion of lip accompanied with the usual embitterment of controversy, where all parties are in the wrong, and the grounds of quarrel are equally plausible on all sides. As the modes of error are endless, the hundred forms of polytheism had each its group of partisans who, hostile or alienated, thenceforward formed separate tribes kept aloof from each other by their ambitious leaders. Hence arose, in the course of a few centuries, the diversity of languages, which has sometimes been confounded with the miraculous event that was indeed its first and principal, though remote, cause.

Following next, and as the representative of the youth and approaching manhood of the human intellect, we have ancient Greece, from Orpheus, Linus, Musæus, and the other mythological bards, or perhaps the brotherhoods impersonated under those names, to the time when the republics lost their independence, and their learned men sank into copyists and commentators of the works of their forefathers. That I include these as educated under a distinct providential, though not miraculous, dispensation, will surprise no one, who reflects that in whatever has a permanent operation on the destinies and intellectual condition of mankind at large—that in all which has been manifestly employed as a co-agent in the mightiest revolution of the moral world, the propagation of the gospel; and in the intellectual progress of mankind, in the restoration of philosophy, science, and the ingenuous arts—it were irreligion not to acknowledge the hand of Divine providence. The periods, too, join on to each other. The earliest Greeks took up the religious and lyrical poetry of the Hebrews; and the schools of the prophets were,

[3] I am far from being a Hutchinsonian, nor have I found much to respect in the twelve volumes of Hutchinson's works, either as biblical comment or natural philosophy; though I give him credit for orthodoxy and good intentions. But his interpretation of the first nine verses of Genesis xi. seems not only rational in itself, and consistent with after accounts of the sacred historian, but proved to be the literal sense of the Hebrew text. His explanation of the cherubim is pleasing and plausible: I dare not say more. Those who would wish to learn the most important points of the Hutchinsonian doctrine in the most favorable form, and in the shortest possible space, I can refer to Duncan Forbes's Letter to a Bishop. If my own judgment did not withhold my assent, I should never be ashamed of a conviction holden, professed, and advocated by so good and wise a man as Duncan Forbes.

however partially and imperfectly, represented by the mysteries, derived through the corrupt channel of the Phœnicians. With these secret schools of physiological theology the mythical poets were doubtless in connection; and it was these schools, which prevented polytheism from producing all its natural barbarizing effects. The mysteries and the mythical hymns and pæans shaped themselves gradually into epic poetry and history on the one hand, and into the ethical tragedy and philosophy on the other. Under their protection, and that of a youthful liberty secretly controlled by a species of internal theocracy, the sciences and the sterner kinds of the fine arts, namely, architecture and statuary, grew up together;—followed, indeed, by painting, but a statuesque and austerely idealized painting, which did not degenerate into mere copies of the sense, till the process, for which Greece existed, had been completed. Contrast the rapid progress and perfection of all the products, which owe their existence and character to the mind's own acts, intellectual or imaginative, with the rudeness of their application to the investigation of physical laws and *phænomena*: then contemplate the Greeks (Γραῖοι ἀεὶ παῖδες) as representing a portion only of the education of man; and the conclusion is inevitable.

In the education of the mind of the race, as in that of the individual, each different age and purpose requires different objects and different means; though all dictated by the same principle, tending toward the same end, and forming consecutive parts of the same method. But if the scale taken be sufficiently large to neutralize or render insignificant the disturbing forces of accident, the degree of success is the best criterion by which to appreciate both the wisdom of the general principle, and the fitness of the particular objects to the given epoch or period. Now it is a fact, for the greater part of universal acceptance, and attested as to the remainder by all that is of highest fame and authority, by the great, wise, and good, during a space of at least seventeen centuries—weighed against whom the opinions of a few distinguished individuals, or the fashion of a single age, must be holden light in the balance,—it is a fact, I say, that whatever could be educed by the mind out of its own essence, by attention to its own acts and laws of action, or as the products of the same; and whatever likewise could be reflected from material masses transformed as it were into mirrors, the excellence of which is to reveal, in the least possible degree, their own original forms and natures;—all these, whether arts or sciences, the ancient Greeks carried to an almost ideal perfection: while in the application of their skill and science to the investigation of the laws of the sensible world, and the qualities and composition of material concretes, chemical, mechanical, or organic, their essays were crude and improsperous, compared with those of the moderns during the early morning of their strength, and even at the first reascension of the light. But still more striking will the difference appear, if we contrast the physiological schemes and fancies of the Greeks with their own discoveries in the region of the pure intellect, and with their still unrivalled success in the arts of imagination. In the aversion of their great men from any practical use of their philosophic discoveries, as in the well-known instance of Archimedes, the soul of the world was at work; and the few exceptions were but a rush of billows driven shoreward by some chance gust before the hour of tide, instantly retracted, and leaving the sands bare and soundless long after the momentary glitter had been lost in evaporation.

The third period, that of the Romans, was devoted to the preparations for preserving, propagating, and realizing the labors of the preceding; to war, empire, law. To this we may refer the defect of all originality in the Latin poets and philosophers, on the one hand, and on the other, the predilection of the Romans for astrology, magic, divination in all its forms. It was the Roman instinct to appropriate by conquest and to give fixure by legislation. And it was the bewilderment and prematurity of the same instinct which restlessly impelled them to materialize the ideas of the Greek philosophers, and to render them practical by superstitious uses.

Thus the Hebrews may be regarded as the fixed mid point of the living line, toward which the Greeks as the ideal pole, and the Romans as the material, were ever approximating; till the coincidence and final synthesis took place in Christianity, of which the Bible is the law, and Christendom the *phænomenon.* So little confirmation from history, from the process of education planned and conducted by unerring Providence, do those theorists receive, who would at least begin (too many, alas! both begin and end) with the objects of the senses; as if nature herself had not abundantly performed this part of the task, by continuous, irresistible enforcements of attention to her presence, to the direct beholding, to the apprehension and observation, of the objects that stimulate the senses;—as if the cultivation of the mental powers, by methodical exercise of their own forces, were not the securest means of forming the true correspondents to them in the functions of comparison, judgment, and interpretation.

From ESSAY XI

THE MEANING OF EXISTENCE

Sapimus animo, fruimur anima: sine animo anima est debilis.
L. Accii Fragmenta.

I HAVE thus delineated the two great directions of man and so-
ciety with their several objects and ends. Concerning the con-
ditions and principles of method appertaining to each, I have
affirmed (for the facts hitherto adduced have been rather for
illustration than for evidence, to make the position distinctly un-
derstood rather than to enforce the conviction of its truth); that
in both there must be a mental antecedent; but that in the one
it may be an image or conception received through the senses,
and originating from without, the inspiriting passion or desire be-
ing alone the immediate and proper offspring of the mind; while
in the other the initiative thought, the intellectual seed, must it-
self have its birth-place within, whatever excitement from without
may be necessary for its germination. Will the soul thus awak-
ened neglect or undervalue the outward and conditional causes
of her growth? Far rather, might I dare borrow a wild fancy
from the Mantuan bard, or the poet of Arno, will it be with
her, as if a stem or trunk, suddenly endued with sense and reflec-
tion, should contemplate its green shoots, their leafits and bud-
ding blossoms, wondered at as then first noticed, but welcomed
nevertheless as its own growth: while yet with undiminished
gratitude, and a deepened sense of dependency, it would bless
the dews and the sunshine from without, deprived of the awaken-
ing and fostering excitement of which, its own productivity would
have remained forever hidden from itself, or felt only as the
obscure trouble of a baffled instinct.

Hast thou ever raised thy mind to the consideration of exist-
ence, in and by itself, as the mere act of existing? Hast thou
ever said to thyself thoughtfully, It is! heedless in that moment,
whether it were a man before thee, or a flower, or a grain of
sand,—without reference, in short, to this or that particular mode
or form of existence? If thou hast indeed attained to this, thou
wilt have felt the presence of a mystery, which must have fixed
thy spirit in awe and wonder. The very words,—there is noth-
ing! or,—There was a time, when there was nothing! are self-
contradictory. There is that within us which repels the propo-

sition with as full and instantaneous a light, as if it bore evidence against the fact in the right of its own eternity.

Not to be, then, is impossible: to be, incomprehensible. If thou hast mastered this intuition of absolute existence, thou wilt have learnt likewise, that it was this, and no other, which in the earlier ages seized the nobler minds, the elect among men, with a sort of sacred horror. This it was which first caused them to feel within themselves a something ineffably greater than their own individual nature. It was this which, raising them aloft, and projecting them to an ideal distance from themselves, prepared them to become the lights and awakening voices of other men, the founders of law and religion, the educators and foster-gods of mankind. The power, which evolved this idea of being, being in its essence, being limitless, comprehending its own limits in its dilatation, and condensing itself into its own apparent mounds—how shall we name it? The idea itself, which like a mighty billow at once overwhelms and bears aloft—what is it? Whence did it come? In vain would we derive it from the organs of sense: for these supply only surfaces, undulations, phantoms. In vain from the instruments of sensation: for these furnish only the chaos, the shapeless elements of sense. And least of all may we hope to find its origin, or sufficient cause, in the moulds and mechanism of the understanding, the whole purport and functions of which consist in individualization, in outlines and differencings by quantity and relation. It were wiser to seek substance in shadow, than absolute fulness in mere negation.

I have asked then for its birth-place in all that constitutes our relative individuality, in all that each man calls exclusively himself. It is an alien of which they know not: and for them the question itself is purposeless, and the very words that convey it are as sounds in an unknown language, or as the vision of heaven and earth expanded by the rising sun, which falls but as warmth on the eyelids of the blind. To no class of *phænomena* or particulars can it be referred, itself being none; therefore, to no faculty by which these alone are apprehended. As little dare we refer it to any form of abstraction or generalization; for it has neither co-ordinate nor *analogon;* it is absolutely one; and that it is, and affirms itself to be, is its only predicate. And yet this power, nevertheless, is;—in supremacy of being it is;[1]—and he for

---

[1] To affirm that reason is, is the same as to affirm that reason is being, or that the true being is reason, 'O Λόγος.—Hence, the reason or law of a thing constitutes its actual being, the ground of its reality. —1829.

whom it manifests itself in its adequate idea, dare as little arrogate it to himself as his own, can as little appropriate it either totally or by partition, as he can claim ownership in the breathing air, or make an inclosure in the cope of heaven.[2] He bears witness of it to his own mind, even as he describes life and light: and, with the silence of light, it describes itself and dwells in us only as far as we dwell in it. The truths which it manifests are such as it alone can manifest, and in all truth it manifests itself. By what name then canst thou call a truth so manifested? Is it not revelation? Ask thyself whether thou canst attach to that latter word any consistent meaning not included in the idea of the former. And the manifesting power, the source and the correlative of the idea thus manifested—is it not God? Either thou knowest it to be God, or thou hast called an idol by that awful name. Therefore in the most appropriate, no less than in the highest, sense of the word were the earliest teachers of humanity inspired. They alone were the true seers of God, and therefore prophets of the human race.

Look round you, and you behold everywhere an adaptation of means to ends. Meditate on the nature of a being whose ideas are creative, and consequently more real, more substantial than the things that, at the height of their creaturely state, are but their dim reflexes;[3] and the intuitive conviction will arise that

[2] And yet this same is, is the essential predicate of the correspondent object of this power. What must we infer? Even this;—that the object and subject are one;—that the reason is being;—the supreme reason the supreme Being; and that the antithesis of truth and being is but the result of the polarizing property of all finite mind, for which unity is manifested only by correspondent opposites. Here do we stop? Woe to us, if we do! Better that we had never begun. A deeper yet must be sought for,—even the absolute Will, the Good, the superessential source of being, and in the eternal act of self-affirmation, the I Am, the Father—who with the only-begotten *Logos* (word, idea, supreme mind, *pleroma*, the word containing every word that proceedeth from the mouth of the Most Highest) and with the Spirit proceeding, is the one only God from everlasting to everlasting.—1829.

[3] If I may not rather resemble them to the resurgent ashes, with which (according to the tales of the later alchemists) the substantial forms of bird and flower made themselves visible as,

τὰ κακῆς ὕλης βλαζήματα χρηζὰ καὶ ἐσθλά.

And let me be permitted to add, in especial reference to this passage, a premonition quoted from the same work (*Zoroastris Oracula Magica*),

Ἃ Νοῦς λέγει, τῷ νοοῦντι δὴ π8 λέγει.

Of the flower apparitions so solemnly affirmed by Sir K. Digby,

in such a being there could exist no motive to the creation of a machine for its own sake; that, therefore, the material world must have been made for the sake of man, at once the high-priest and representative of the Creator, as far as he partakes of that reason in which the essences of all things co-exist in all their distinctions yet as one and indivisible. But I speak of man in his idea, and as subsumed in the divine humanity, in whom alone God loved the world.

In all inferior things from the grass on the house-top to the giant tree of the forest; from the gnats that swarm in its shade, and the mole that burrows amid its roots to the eagle which builds in its summit, and the elephant which browses on its branches, we behold—first, a subjection to universal laws by which each thing belongs to the whole, as interpenetrated by the powers of the whole; and, secondly, the intervention of particular laws by which the universal laws are suspended or tempered for the weal and sustenance of each particular class. Hence and thus we see too that each species, and each individual of every species, becomes a system, a world of its own. If then we behold this economy everywhere in the irrational creation, shall we not hold it probable that by some analogous intervention a similar temperament will have been effected for the rational and moral? Are we not entitled to expect some appropriate agency in behalf of the presiding and alone progressive creature? To presume some especial provision for the permanent interest of the creature destined to move and grow towards that divine humanity which we have learnt to contemplate as the final cause of all creation, and the centre in which all its lines converge?

To discover the mode of intervention requisite for man's development and progression, we must seek then for some general law, by the untempered and uncounteracted action of which man's development and progression would be prevented and endangered. But this we shall find in that law of his understanding and fancy, by which he is impelled to abstract the changes and outward relations of matter and to arrange them under the form of causes and effects. And this was necessary, as the condition under which alone experience and intellectual growth are possible. But, on the other hand, by the same law he is inevitably tempted to misinterpret a constant precedence into positive causation, and thus to break and scatter the one divine and invisible life

---

Kercher, Helmont, and others, see a full and most interesting account in Southey's Omniana, with a probable solution of this chemical marvel.

of nature into countless idols of the sense; and falling prostrate before lifeless images, the creatures of his own abstraction, is himself sensualized, and becomes a slave to the things of which he was formed to be the conqueror and sovereign. From the fetisch of the imbruted African to the soul-debasing errors of the proud fact-hunting materialist we may trace the various ceremonials of the same idolatry, and shall find selfishness, hate, and servitude as the results. If therefore by the overruling and suspension of the phantom-cause of this superstition; if by separating effects from their natural antecedents; if by presenting the *phænomena* of time (as far as is possible) in the absolute forms of eternity; the nursling of experience should, in the early period of his pupilage, be compelled by a more impressive experience to seek in the invisible life alone for the true cause and invisible *nexus* of the things that are seen, we shall not demand the evidences of ordinary experience for that which, if it ever existed, existed as its antithesis and for its counteraction. Was it an appropriate mean to a necessary end? Has it been attested by lovers of truth; has it been believed by lovers of wisdom? Do we see throughout all nature the occasional intervention of particular agencies in counter-check of universal laws? (And of what other definition is a miracle susceptible?) These are the questions: and if to these our answers must be affirmative, then we too will acquiesce in the traditions of humanity, and yielding as to a high interest of our own being, will discipline ourselves to the reverential and kindly faith, that the guides and teachers of mankind were the hands of power, no less than the voices of inspiration: and little anxious concerning the particular forms, proofs, and circumstances of each manifestation we will give an historic credence to the historic fact, that men sent by God have come with signs and wonders on the earth.

If it be objected, that in nature, as distinguished from man, this intervention of particular laws is, or with the increase of science will be, resolvable into the universal laws which they had appeared to counterbalance, we will reply: Even so it may be in the case of miracles; but wisdom forbids her children to antedate their knowledge, or to act and feel otherwise or further than they know. But should that time arrive, the sole difference, that could result from such an enlargement of our view, would be this;—that what we now consider as miracles in opposition to ordinary experience, we should then reverence with a yet higher devotion as harmonious parts of one great complex miracle, when the antithesis between experience and belief would itself be taken up into unity of intuitive reason.

And what purpose of philosophy can this acquiescence answer? A gracious purpose, a most valuable end; if it prevent the energies of philosophy from being idly wasted, by removing the contrariety without confounding the distinction between philosophy and faith. The philosopher will remain a man in sympathy with his fellow-men. The head will not be disjoined from the heart, nor will speculative truth be alienated from practical wisdom. And vainly without the union of both shall we expect an opening of the inward eye to the glorious vision of that existence which admits of no question out of itself, acknowledges no predicate but the I AM IN THAT I AM! Θαυμάζοντες φιλοσοφοῦμεν· φιλοσοφήσαντες θαμβοῦμεν. In wonder (τῷ θαυμάζειν) says Aristotle, does philosophy begin; and in astoundment (τῷ θαμβεῖν) says Plato, does all true philosophy finish. As every faculty, with every the minutest organ of our nature, owes its whole reality and comprehensibility to an existence incomprehensible and groundless, because the ground of all comprehension; not without the union of all that is essential in all the functions of our spirit, not without an emotion tranquil from its very intensity, shall we worthily contemplate in the magnitude and integrity of the world that life-ebullient stream which breaks through every momentary embankment, again, indeed, and evermore to embank itself, but within no banks to stagnate or be imprisoned.

But here it behooves us to bear in mind, that all true reality has both its ground and its evidence in the will, without which as its complement science itself is but an elaborate game of shadows, begins in abstractions and ends in perplexity. For considered merely intellectually, individuality, as individuality, is only conceivable as with and in the universal and infinite, neither before nor after it. No transition is possible from one to the other, as from the architect to the house, or the watch to its maker. The finite form can neither be laid hold of by, nor can it appear to, the mere speculative intellect as any thing of itself real, but merely as an apprehension, a frame-work which the human imagination forms by its own limits, as the foot measures itself on the snow; and the sole truth of which we must again refer to the divine imagination, in virtue of its omniformity. For even as thou art capable of beholding the transparent air as little during the absence as during the presence of light, so canst thou behold the finite things as actually existing neither with nor without the substance. Not without,—for then the forms cease to be, and are lost in night: not with it,—for it is the light, the substance shining through it, which thou canst alone really see.

The ground-work, therefore, of all pure speculation is the full apprehension of the difference between the contemplation of reason, namely, that intuition of things which arises when we possess ourselves, as one with the whole, which is substantial knowledge, and that which presents itself when transferring reality to the negations of reality, to the ever-varying frame-work of the uniform life, we think of ourselves as separated beings, and place nature in antithesis to the mind, as object to subject, thing to thought, death to life. This is abstract knowledge, or the science of the mere understanding. By the former, we know that existence is its own predicate, self-affirmation, the one attribute in which all others are contained, not as parts, but as manifestations. It is an eternal and infinite self-rejoicing, self-loving, with a joy unfathomable, with a love all-comprehensive. It is absolute; and the absolute is neither singly that which affirms, nor that which is affirmed; but the identity and living *copula* of both.

On the other hand, by the abstract knowledge which belongs to us as finite beings, and which leads to a science of delusion, then only, when it would exist for itself instead of being the instrument of the former—(even as the former is equally hollow and yet more perilously delusive, where it is not radicated in a deeper ground) when it would itself, I say, be its own life and verity, instead of being, as it were, a translation of the living word into a dead language, for the purposes of memory, arrangement, and general communication,—it is by this abstract knowledge that the understanding distinguishes the affirmed from the affirming. Well if it distinguish without dividing! Well if by distinction it add clearness to fulness, and prepare for the intellectual re-union of the all in one in that eternal Reason whose fulness hath no opacity, whose transparency hath no *vacuum.*

If we thoughtfully review the three preceding paragraphs, we shall find the conclusion to be;—that the dialectic intellect by the exertion of its own powers exclusively can lead us to a general affirmation of the supreme reality of an absolute being. But here it stops. It is utterly incapable of communicating insight or conviction concerning the existence or possibility of the world, as different from Deity. It finds itself constrained to identify, more truly to confound, the Creator with the aggregate of his creature, and, cutting the knot which it can not untwist. to deny altogether the reality of all finite existence, and then to shelter itself from its own dissatisfaction, its own importunate queries, in the wretched evasion that of nothings, no solution can be required; till pain haply, and anguish, and remorse, with bitter scoff and moody laughter inquire;—Are we then indeed nothings?—

till through every organ of sense nature herself asks;—How and whence did this sterile and pertinacious nothing acquire its plural number?—*Unde quæso, hæc nihili in nihila tam portentosa transnihilatio?*—and lastly;—What is that inward mirror, in which these nothings have at least relative existence? The inevitable result of all consequent reasoning, in which the intellect refuses to acknowledge a higher or deeper ground than it can itself supply, and weens to possess within itself the centre of its own system, is—and from Zeno the Eleatic to Spinosa, and from Spinosa to the Schellings, Okens and their adherents, of the present day, ever has been—pantheism under one or other of its modes, the least repulsive of which differs from the rest, not in its consequences, which are one and the same in all, and in all alike are practically atheistic, but only as it may express the striving of the philosopher himself to hide these consequences from his own mind. This, therefore, I repeat, is the final conclusion. All speculative disquisition must begin with postulates, which the conscience alone can at once authorize and substantiate: and from whichever point the reason may start, from the things which are seen to the one invisible, or from the idea of the absolute one to the things that are seen, it will find a chasm, which the moral being only, which the spirit and religion of man alone, can fill up.

Thus I prefaced my inquiry into the science of method with a principle deeper than science, more certain than demonstration. For that the very ground, saith Aristotle, is groundless or self-grounded, is an identical proposition. From the indemonstrable flows the sap that circulates through every branch and spray of the demonstration. To this principle I referred the choice of the final object, the control over time, or, to comprise all in one, the method of the will. From this I started, or rather seemed to start; for it still moved before me, as an invisible guardian and guide, and it is this the re-appearance of which announces the conclusion of the circuit, and welcomes me at the goal. Yea (saith an enlightened physician), there is but one principle, which alone reconciles the man with himself, with others, and with the world; which regulates all relations, tempers all passions, gives power to overcome or support all suffering, and which is not to be shaken by aught earthly, for it belongs not to the earth; namely, the principle of religion, the living and substantial faith *which passeth all understanding,* as the cloud-piercing rock, which overhangs the stronghold of which it had been the quarry and remains the foundation. This elevation of the spirit above the semblances of custom and the senses to a world of spirit, this life in the idea, even in the supreme and godlike, which alone merits the name of life, and without which our organic life is but a state of somnambulism; this it is which affords the sole sure anchorage in the storm, and at the same time the substantiating principle of all true wisdom, the satisfactory solution of all the contradictions of human nature, of the whole riddle of the world. This alone belongs to and speaks intelligibly to all alike, the learned and the ignorant, if but the heart listens. For alike present in all, it may be awakened, but it can not be given. But let it not be supposed, that it is a sort of knowledge: no! it is a form of BEING, or indeed it is the only knowledge that truly *is*, and all other science is real only so far as it is symbolical of this. The material universe, saith a Greek philosopher, is but one vast complex *mythus*, that is, symbolical representation, and mythology the *apex* and complement of all genuine physiology. But as this principle can not be implanted by the discipline of logic, so neither can it be excited or evolved by the arts of rhetoric. For it is an immutable truth, that what comes from the heart, that alone goes to the heart; what proceeds from a divine impulse, that the godlike alone can awaken.

FROM *AIDS TO REFLECTION*

PRUDENTIAL APHORISM I

Leighton and Coleridge.

WITH respect to any final aim or end, the greater part of mankind live at hazard. They have no certain harbor in view, nor direct their course by any fixed star. But to him that knoweth not the port to which he is bound, no wind can be favorable; neither can he, who has not yet determined at what mark he is to shoot, direct his arrow aright.

It is not, however, the less true that there is a proper object to aim at; and if this object be meant by the term happiness (though I think that not the most appropriate term for a state, the perfection of which consists in the exclusion of all hap, that is, chance), I assert that there is such a thing as human happiness, a *summum bonum*, or ultimate good. What this is, the Bible alone shows clearly and certainly, and points out the way that leads to the attainment of it. This is that which prevailed with St. Augustine to study the Scriptures, and engaged his affection to them. 'In Cicero, and Flato, and other such writers,' says he, 'I meet with many things acutely said, and things that excite a certain warmth of emotion, but in none of them do I find these words, *Come unto me, all ye that labor, and are heavy laden, and I will give you rest.*

COMMENT

Felicity, in its proper sense, is but another word for fortunateness, or happiness; and I can see no advantage in the improper use of words, when proper terms are to be found, but, on the contrary, much mischief. For, by familiarizing the mind to equivocal expressions, that is, such as may be taken in two or more different meanings, we introduce confusion of thought, and furnish the sophist with his best and handiest tools. For the juggle of sophistry consists, for the greater part, in using a word in one sense in the premiss, and in another sense in the conclusion. We should accustom ourselves to think, and reason in precise and steadfast terms, even when custom, or the deficiency, or the corruption of the language will not permit the same strictness in speaking. The mathematician finds this so necessary to the truths which he is seeking, that his science begins with, and is founded on, the definition of his terms. The botanist, the chemists, the anatomist, feel and submit to this necessity at all costs, even at the risk of exposing their several pursuits to the ridicule of the many, by technical terms, hard to be remembered, and alike quarrelsome to the ear and the tongue. In the business of moral and religious reflection, in the acquisition of clear and distinct conceptions of our duties, and of the relations in which we stand to God, our neighbor, and ourselves, no such difficulties occur. At the utmost we have only to rescue words, already existing and familiar, from the false or vague meanings imposed on them by carelessness, or by the clipping and debasing misusage of the market. And surely happiness, duty, faith, truth, and final blessedness, are matters of deeper and dearer interest for all men, than circles to the geometrician, or the characters of plants to the botanist, or the affinities and combining principle of the elements of bodies to the chemist, or even than the mechanism (fearful and wonderful though it be!) of the perishable tabernacle of the soul can be to the anatomist. Among the aids to reflection, place the following maxim prominent: let distinctness in expression advance side by side with distinction in thought. For one useless subtlety in our elder divines and moralists, I will produce ten sophisms of equivocation in the writings of our modern preceptors: and for one error resulting from excess in distinguishing the indifferent, I could show ten mischievous delusions from the habit of confounding the diverse.

Whether you are reflecting for yourself, or reasoning with another, make it a rule to ask yourself the precise meaning of the word, on which the point in question appears to turn; and if it may be (that is, by writers of authority has been) used in several senses, then ask which of these the word is at present intended to convey. By this mean, and scarcely without it, you will at length acquire a facility in detecting the *quid pro quo*. And believe me, in so doing you will enable yourself to disarm and expose four-fifths of the main arguments of our most renowned irreligious philosophers, ancient and modern. For the *quid pro quo* is at once the rock and quarry, on and with which the strongholds of disbelief, materialism, and (more pernicious still) Epicurean morality, are built.

APHORISMS ON THAT WHICH IS INDEED SPIRITUAL RELIGION:

APHORISM IV

THE CHARACTERISTIC DIFFERENCE BETWEEN THE DISCIPLINE OF THE ANCIENT PHILOSOPHERS AND THE DISPENSATION OF THE GOSPEL.

BY UNDECEIVING, enlarging, and informing the intellect, Philosophy sought to purify and to elevate the moral character. Of course, those alone could receive the latter and incomparably greater benefit, who by natural capacity and favorable contingencies of fortune were fit recipients of the former. How small the number, we scarcely need the evidence of history to assure us. Across the night of Paganism, Philosophy flitted on, like the lantern-fly of the Tropics, a light to itself, and an ornament, but alas! no more than an ornament, of the surrounding darkness.

Christianity reversed the order. By means accessible to all, by inducements operative on all, and by convictions, the grounds and materials of which all men might find in themselves, her first step was to cleanse the heart. But the benefit did not stop here. In preventing the rank vapors that steam up from the corrupt heart, Christianity restores the intellect likewise to its natural clearness. By relieving the mind from the distractions and importunities of the unruly passions, she improves the quality of the understanding: while at the same time she presents for its contemplations objects so great and so bright as can not but enlarge the organ, by which they are contemplated. The fears, the hopes, the remembrances, the anticipations, the inward and outward experience, the belief and the faith, of a Christian, form of themselves a philosophy and a sum of knowledge, which a life spent in the Grove of Academus, or the painted Porch, could not have attained or collected. The result is contained in the fact of a wide and still widening Christendom.

Yet I dare not say that the effects have been proportionate to the divine wisdom of the scheme. Too soon did the Doctors of the Church forget that the heart, the moral nature, was the beginning and the end: and that truth, knowledge, and insight were comprehended in its expansion. This was the true and first apostasy—when in council and synod the divine humanities of the Gospel gave way to speculative systems, and religion became a science of shadows under the name of theology, or at best a bare skeleton of truth, without life or interest, alike inaccessible and unintelligible to the majority of Christians. For these therefore there remained only rites and ceremonies and spectacles, shows and semblances. Thus among the learned *the substance of things hoped for* (Heb. xi. 1) passed off into notions; and for the unlearned the surfaces of things became substance. The Christian world was for centuries divided into the many, that did not think at all, and the few who did nothing but think—both alike unreflecting, the one from defect of the act, the other from the absence of an object.

FAITH, REASON, AND UNDERSTANDING:
APHORISM VIII

Leighton.

FAITH elevates the soul not only above sense and sensible things, but above reason itself. As reason corrects the errors which sense might occasion, so supernatural faith corrects the errors of natural reason judging according to sense.

COMMENT

My remarks on this Aphorism from Leighton can not be better introduced, or their purport more distinctly announced, than by the following sentence from Harrington, with no other change than is necessary to make the words express, without aid of the context, what from the context it is evident was the writer's meaning. "The definition and proper character of man—that, namely, which should contra-distinguish him from other animals —is to be taken from his reason rather than from his understanding: in regard that in other creatures there may be something of understanding, but there is nothing of reason."

Sir Thomas Browne, in his *Religio Medici,* complains, that there are not impossibilities enough in religion for his active faith; and adopts by choice and in free preference such interpretations of certain texts and declarations of Holy Writ, as place them in irreconcilable contradiction to the demonstrations of science and the experience of mankind, because (says he) "I love to lose myself in a mystery, and 'tis my solitary recreation to pose my apprehension with those involved enigmas and riddles of the Trinity and Incarnation;"—and because he delights (as thinking it no vulgar part of faith) to believe a thing not only above but contrary to reason, and against the evidence of our proper senses.

For the worthy knight could answer all the objections of the Devil and reason "with the old resolution he had learnt of Tertullian: *Certum est quia impossibile est*. It is certainly true because it is quite impossible!" Now this I call Ultrafidianism.[1]

[1] There is this advantage in the occasional use of a newly minted term or title, expressing the doctrinal schemes of particular sects or parties, that it avoids the inconvenience that presses on either side, whether we adopt the name which the party itself has taken up by which to express its peculiar tenets, or that by which the same party is designated by its opponents. If we take the latter, it most often happens that either the persons are invidiously aimed at in the designation of the principles, or that the name implies some consequence or occasional accompaniment of the principles denied by the parties themselves, as applicable to them collectively. On the other hand, convinced as I am, that current appellations are never wholly indifferent or inert: and that, when employed to express the characteristic belief or object of a religious confederacy, they exert on the many a great and constant, though insensible, influence; I can not but fear that in adopting the former I may be sacrificing the interests of truth beyond what the duties of courtesy can demand or justify. I have elsewhere stated my objections to the word Unitarians, as a name which in its proper sense can belong only to the maintainers of the truth impugned by the persons, who have chosen it as their designation. For *unity* or unition, and indistinguishable *unicity* or sameness, are incompatible terms. We never speak of the unity of attraction, or the unity of repulsion; but of the unity of attraction and repulsion in each corpuscle. Indeed, the essential diversity of the conceptions, unity and sameness, was among the elementary principles of the old logicians; and Leibnitz, in his critique on Wissowatius, has ably exposed the sophisms grounded on the confusion of the two terms. But in the exclusive sense, in which the name, Unitarian, is appropriated by the Sect, and in which they mean it to be understood, it is a presumptuous boast and an uncharitable calumny. No one of the Churches to which they on this article of the Christian Faith stand opposed, Greek or Latin, ever adopted the term, Trini—or Tri-uni-tarians as their ordinary and proper name: and had it been otherwise, yet unity is assuredly no logical opposite to Tri-unity, which expressly includes it. The triple alliance is *à fortiori* an alliance. The true designation of their characteristic tenet, and which would simply and inoffensively express a fact admitted on all sides, is Psilanthropism, or the assertion of the mere humanity of Christ.

I dare not hesitate to avow my regret that any scheme of doctrines or tenets should be the subject of penal law: though I can easily conceive, that any scheme, however excellent in itself, may be propagated, and however false or injurious, may be assailed, in a manner and by means that would make the advocate or assailant justly punishable. But then it is the manner, the means, that constitute the crime. The merit or demerit of the opinions themselves depends on their originating and determining causes, which may differ in every different believer, and are certainly known to Him alone, who commanded us, *Judge not, lest ye be judged.* At all events, in the present state of the law, I do not see where we can begin, or where we can stop, without inconsistency and consequent hardship. Judging by all that we can pretend to know or are entitled to infer, who among us will take on himself to deny that the late Dr. Priestley was a good and benevolent man, as sincere in his love, as he was intrepid and indefatigable in his pursuit, of truth? Now let us construct three parallel tables, the first containing the articles of belief, moral and theological, maintained by the venerable Hooker, as the representative of the Established Church, each article being distinctly lined and numbered; the second the tenets and persuasions of Lord Herbert, as the representative of the Platonizing Deists; and the third, those of Dr. Priestley. Let the points, in which the second and third agree with or differ from the first, be considered as to the comparative number modified by the comparative weight and importance of the several points—and let any competent and upright man be appointed the arbiter, to decide according to his best judgment, without any reference to the truth of the opinions, which of the two differed from the first more widely. I say this, well aware that it would be abundantly more prudent to leave it unsaid. But I say it in the conviction, that the adoption of admitted misnomers in the naming of doctrinal systems, if only they have been negatively legalized, is but an equivocal proof of liberality towards the persons who dissent from us. On the contrary, I more than suspect that the former liberality does in too many men arise from a latent pre-disposition to transfer their reprobation and intolerance from the doctrines to the doctors, from the belief to the believers. Indecency, abuse, scoffing on subjects dear and awful to a multitude of our fellow-citizens, appeals to the vanity, appetites, and malignant passions of ignorant and incompetent judges—these are flagrant over-acts, condemned by the law written in the heart of every honest man, Jew, Turk, and Christian. These are points respecting which the humblest honest man feels it his duty to hold himself infallible, and dares not hesitate in giving utterance to the verdict of his conscience in the jury-box as fearlessly as by his fire-side. It is far otherwise with respect to matters of faith and inward conviction: and with respect to these I say— Tolerate no belief that you judge false and of injurious tendency: and arraign no believer. The man is more and other than his belief: and God only knows, how small or how large a part of him the belief in question may be, for good or for evil. Resist every false doctrine: and call no man heretic. The false doctrine does not necessarily make the man a heretic; but an evil heart can make any doctrine heretical.

Actuated by these principles, I have objected to a false and deceptive designation in the case of one system. Persuaded that the doctrines, enumerated in pp. 229, 230 are not only essential to the Christian religion, but those which contra-distinguish the religion as Christian, I merely repeat this persuasion in another form, when I assert, that (in my sense of the word, Christian) Unitarianism is not

Christianity. But do I say, that those who call themselves Unitarians are not Christians? God forbid! I would not think, much less promulgate, a judgment at once so presumptuous and so uncharitable. Let a friendly antagonist retort on my scheme of faith in the like manner: I shall respect him all the more for his consistency as a reasoner, and not confide the less in his kindness towards me as his neighbor and fellow-Christian. This latter and most endearing name I scarcely know how to withhold even from my friend, Hyman Hurwitz, as often as I read what every reverer of Holy Writ and of the English Bible ought to read, his admirable *Vindiciæ Hebraicæ*. It has trembled on the verge, as it were, of my lips, every time I have conversed with that pious, learned, strong-minded, and single-hearted Jew, an Israelite indeed, and without guile—

> *Cujus cura sequi naturam, legibus uti,*
> *Et mentem vitiis, ora negare dolis;*
> *Virtutes opibus, verum præponere falso,*
> *Nil vacuum sensu dicere, nil facere.*
> *Post obitum vivam secum,* secum requiescam,*
> *Nec fiat melior sors mea sorte sua!*
> > *From a poem of Hildebert on his Master, the*
> > *persecuted Berengarius.*

* I do not answer for the corrupt Latin.

Under the same feelings I conclude this aid to reflection by applying the principle to another misnomer not less inappropriate and far more influential. Of those, whom I have found most reason to respect and value, many have been members of the Church of Rome: and certainly I did not honor those the least, who scrupled even in common parlance to call our Church a reformed Church. A similar scruple would not, methinks, disgrace a Protestant as to the use of the words, Catholic or Roman Catholic; and if (tacitly at least, and in thought) he remembered that the Romish anti-Catholic Church would more truly express the fact. *Romish*, to mark that the corruptions in discipline, doctrine, and practice do, for the larger part, owe both their origin and perpetuation to the Romish Court, and the local tribunals of the City of Rome; and neither are nor ever have been Catholic, that is, universal, throughout the Roman Empire, or even in the whole Latin or Western Church—and anti-Catholic, because no other Church acts on so narrow and excommunicative a principle, or is characterized by such a jealous spirit of monopoly. Instead of a Catholic (universal) spirit, it may be truly described as a spirit of particularism counterfeiting Catholicity by a negative totality, and heretical self-circumscription—in the first instances cutting off, and since then cutting herself off from, all the other members of Christ's body. For the rest, I think as that man of true catholic spirit and apostolic zeal, Richard Baxter, thought; and my readers will thank me for conveying my reflections in his own words, in the following golden passage from his

Again, there is a scheme constructed on the principle of retaining the social sympathies, that attend on the name of believer, at the least possible expenditure of belief; a scheme of picking and choosing Scripture texts for the support of doctrines, that have been learned beforehand from the higher oracle of common sense; which, as applied to the truths of religion, means the popular part of the philosophy in fashion. Of course, the scheme differs at different times and in different individuals in the number of articles excluded; but, it may always be recognized by this permanent character, that its object is to draw religion down to the believer's intellect, instead of raising his intellect up to religion. And this extreme I call Minimi-fidianism.

Now if there be one preventive of both these extremes more efficacious than another, and preliminary to all the rest, it is the being made fully aware of the diversity of Reason and the Understanding. And this is the more expedient, because, though there is no want of authorities ancient and modern for the distinction of the faculties, and the distinct appropriation of the terms, yet our best writers too often confound the one with the

---

Life, "faithfully published from his own original MSS. by Matthew Silvester, 1696."

"My censures of the Papists do much differ from what they were at first. I then thought that their errors in the doctrines of faith were their most dangerous mistakes. But now I am assured that their mis-expressions and misunderstanding of us, with our mistakings of them, and inconvenient expressing of our own opinions, have made the difference in most points appear much greater than it is; and that in some it is next to none at all. But the great and unreconcilable differences lie in their Church tyranny; in the usurpations of their hierarchy, and priesthood, under the name of spiritual authority exercising a temporal lordship; in their corruptions and abasement of God's worship; but above all in their systematic befriending of ignorance and vice.

"At first I thought that Mr. Perkins well proved that a Papist can not go beyond a reprobate; but now I doubt not that God hath many sanctified ones among them, who have received the true doctrine of Christianity so practically, that their contradictory errors prevail not against them, to hinder their love of God and their salvation: but that their errors are like a conquerable dose of poison, which a healthful nature doth overcome. *And I can never believe that a man may not be saved by that religion, which doth but bring him to a true love of God and to a heavenly mind and life: nor that God will ever cast a soul into hell that truly loveth him.* Also at first it would disgrace any doctrine with me, if I did but hear it called Popery and anti-Christian; but I have long learned to be more impartial, and to know that Satan can use even the names of Popery and Antichrist, to bring a truth into suspicion and discredit."—Baxter's *Life*, Part I. p. 131.

other. Even Lord Bacon himself, who in his *Novum Organum* has so incomparably set forth the nature of the difference, and the unfitness of the latter faculty for the objects of the former, does nevertheless in sundry places use the term reason where he means the understanding, and sometimes, though less frequently, understanding for reason. In consequence of thus confounding the two terms, or rather of wasting both words for the expression of one and the same faculty, he left himself no appropriate term for the other and higher gift of reason, and was thus under the necessity of adopting fantastical and mystical phrases, for example, the dry light (*lumen siccum*), the lucific vision, and the like, meaning thereby nothing more than reason in contradistinction from the understanding. Thus too in the preceding Aphorism, by reason Leighton means the human understanding, the explanation annexed to it being (by a noticeable coincidence) word for word, the very definition which the founder of the Critical Philosophy gives of the understanding—namely, "the faculty judging according to sense."

ON THE DIFFERENCE IN KIND OF REASON AND THE UNDERSTANDING

SCHEME OF THE ARGUMENT

ON THE contrary, Reason is the power of universal and necessary convictions, the source and substance of truths above sense, and having their evidence in themselves. Its presence is always marked by the necessity of the position affirmed: this necessity being conditional, when a truth of reason is applied to facts of experience, or to the rules and maxims of the understanding; but absolute, when the subject matter is itself the growth or offspring of reason. Hence arises a distinction in reason itself, derived from the different mode of applying it, and from the objects to which it is directed: accordingly as we consider one and the same gift, now as the ground of formal principles, and now as the origin of ideas. Contemplated distinctively in reference to formal (or abstract) truth, it is the Speculative Reason; but in reference to actual (or moral) truth, as the fountain of ideas and the light of the conscience, we name it the Practical Reason. Whenever by self-subjection to this universal light, the will of the individual, the particular will, has become a will of reason, the man is regenerate: and reason is then the spirit of the regenerated man, whereby the person is capable of a quickening intercommunion with the Divine Spirit. And herein consists the mystery of Redemption, that this has been rendered possible for us. *And so it is written; the first man Adam was made a living soul, the last Adam a quickening Spirit.* (1 Cor. xv. 45.) We need only compare the passages in the writings of the Apostles Paul and John, concerning the Spirit and spiritual gifts, with those in the Proverbs and in the Wisdom of Solomon respecting Reason, to be convinced that the terms are synonymous. In this at once most comprehensive and most appropriate acceptation of the word, Reason is pre-eminently spiritual, and a spirit, even our spirit, through an effluence of the same grace by which we are privileged to say, Our Father!

On the other hand, the judgments of the Understanding are binding only in relation to the objects of our senses, which we reflect under the forms of the understanding. It is, as Leighton rightly defines it, "the faculty judging according to sense." Hence we add the epithet human without tautology: and speak of the human understanding in disjunction from that of beings higher or lower than man. But there is, in this sense, no human reason. There neither is nor can be but one reason, one and the same; even the light that lighteth every man's individual understanding (*discursus*), and thus maketh it a reasonable understanding, discourse of reason—*one only,* yet *manifold: it goeth through all understanding, and remaining in itself regenerateth all other powers.* The same writer calls it likewise *an influence from the Glory of the Almighty,* this being one of the names of the Messiah, as the *Logos,* or co-eternal Filial Word. And most noticeable for its coincidence is a fragment of Heraclitus, as I have indeed already noticed elsewhere;—"To discourse rationally it behooves us to derive strength from that which is common to all men: for all human understandings are nourished by the one Divine Word."

Beasts, I have said, partake of understanding. If any man deny this, there is a ready way of settling the question. Let him give a careful perusal to Hüber's two small volumes on bees and ants (especially the latter), and to Kirby and Spence's Introduction to Entomology; and one or other of two things must follow. He will either change his opinion as irreconcilable with the facts; or he must deny the facts; which yet I can not suppose, inasmuch as the denial would be tantamount to the no less extravagant than uncharitable assertion, that Hüber, and the several eminent naturalists, French and English, Swiss, German, and Italian, by whom Hüber's observations and experiments have been repeated and confirmed, have all conspired to impose a series of falsehoods and fairy-tales on the world. I see no way, at least, by which he can get out of this dilemma, but by over-leaping the admitted rules and fences of all legitimate discussion, and either transferring to the word, Understanding, the definition already appropriated to Reason, or defining understanding *in genere* by the specific and accessional perfections which the human understanding derives from its co-existence with reason and free-will in the same individual person; in plainer words, from its being exercised by a self-conscious and responsible creature. And, after all, the supporter of Harrington's position would have a right to ask him, by what other name he would designate the faculty in the instances referred to? If it be not understanding what is it?

In no former part of this Volume have I felt the same anxiety to obtain a patient attention. For I do not hesitate to avow, that on my success in establishing the validity and importance of the distinction between Reason and the Understanding, rest my hopes of carrying the Reader along with me through all that is to follow. Let the student but clearly see and comprehend the diversity in the things themselves, and the expediency of a correspondent distinction and appropriation of the words will follow of itself. Turn back for a moment to the Aphorism, and having re-perused the first paragraph of this Comment thereon, regard the two following narratives as the illustration. I do not say proof: for I take these from a multitude of facts equally striking for the one only purpose of placing my meaning out of all doubt.

I. Hüber put a dozen humble-bees under a bell-glass along with a comb of about ten silken cocoons so unequal in height as not to be capable of standing steadily. To remedy this two or three of the humble-bees got upon the comb, stretched themselves over its edge, and with their heads downwards fixed their forefeet on the table on which the comb stood, and so with their hind feet kept the comb from falling. When these were weary others took their places. In this constrained and painful posture, fresh bees relieving their comrades at intervals, and each working in its turn, did these affectionate little insects support the comb for nearly three days: at the end of which they had prepared sufficient wax to build pillars with. But these pillars having accidentally got displaced, the bees had recourse again to the same manœuvre, till Hüber pitying their hard case, &c.

II. "I shall at present describe the operations of a single ant that I observed sufficiently long to satisfy my curiosity.

"One rainy day I observed a laborer digging the ground near the aperture which gave entrance to the ant-hill. It placed in a heap the several fragments it had scraped up, and formed them into small pellets, which it deposited here and there upon the nest. It returned constantly to the same place, and appeared to have a marked design, for it labored with ardor and perseverance. I remarked a slight furrow, excavated in the ground in a straight line, representing the plan of a path or gallery. The laborer, the whole of whose movements fell under my immediate observation, gave it greater depth and breadth, and cleared out its borders: and I saw at length, in which I could not be deceived, that it had the intention of establishing an avenue which was to lead from one of the stories to the underground chambers. This path, which was about two or three inches in length, and formed by a single ant, was opened above and bordered on each side by a buttress of earth; its concavity *en forme de goutière* was of the most perfect regularity, for the architect had not left an atom too much. The work of this ant was so well followed and understood, that I could almost to a certainty guess its next proceeding, and the very fragment it was about to remove. At the side of the opening where this path terminated, was a second opening to which it was necessary to arrive by some road. The same ant engaged in and executed alone this undertaking. It furrowed out and opened another path, parallel to the first, leaving between each a little wall of three or four lines in height. Those ants who lay the foundation of a wall, chamber, or gallery, from working separately occasion, now and then, a want of coincidence in the parts of the same or different objects. Such examples are of no unfrequent occurrence, but they by no means embarrass them. What follows proves that the workman, on discovering his error, knew how to rectify it. A wall had been erected with the view of sustaining a vaulted ceiling, still incomplete, that had been projected from the wall of the opposite chamber. The workman who began constructing it, had given it too little elevation to meet the opposite partition upon which it was to rest. Had it been continued on the original plan, it must infallibly have met the wall at about one half of its height, and this it was necessary to avoid. This state of things very forcibly claimed my attention, when one of the ants arriving at the place, and visiting the works, appeared to be struck by the difficulty which presented itself; but this it as soon obviated, by taking down the ceiling and raising the wall upon which it reposed. It then, in my presence, constructed a new ceiling with the fragments of the former one."—*Hüber's Natural History of Ants,* pp. 38-41.

Now I assert, that the faculty manifested in the acts here narrated does not differ *in kind* from understanding, and that it *does* so differ from reason. What I conceive the former to be, physiologically considered, will be shown hereafter. In this place I take the understanding as it exists in men, and in exclusive reference to its *intelligential* functions; and it is in this sense of the word that I am to prove the necessity of contra-distinguishing it from reason.

Premising then, that two or more subjects having the same essential characters are said to fall under the same general definition, I lay it down, as a self-evident truth—(it is, in fact, an identical proposition)—that whatever subjects fall under one and the same general definition are of one and the same kind: consequently, that which does *not* fall under this definition, must differ in kind from each and all of those that *do*. Difference in degree does indeed suppose sameness in kind; and difference in kind precludes distinction from difference of degree. *Heterogenea non comparari, ergo nec distingui, possunt.* The inattention to this rule gives rise to the numerous sophisms comprised by Aristotle under the head of μετάβασις εἰς ἄλλο γένος, that is, transition into a new kind, or the falsely applying to X what had been truly asserted of A, and might have been true of X, had it differed from A in its degree only. The sophistry consists in the omission to notice what not being noticed will be supposed not to exist; and where the silence respecting the difference in kind is tantamount to an assertion that the difference is merely in degree. But the fraud is especially gross, where the heterogeneous subject, thus clandestinely slipt in, is in its own nature insusceptible of degree: such as, for instance, certainty or circularity, contrasted with strength, or magnitude.

To apply these remarks for our present purpose, we have only to describe Understanding and Reason, each by its characteristic qualities. The comparison will show the difference.

UNDERSTANDING	REASON
1. Understanding is discursive.	1. Reason is fixed.
2. The Understanding in all its judgments refers to some other faculty as its ultimate authority.	2. The Reason in all its decisions appeals to itself as the ground and *substance* of their truth. (*Heb.* vi. 13.)

UNDERSTANDING	REASON
3. Understanding is the faculty of reflection.	3. Reason of contemplation. Reason indeed is much nearer to Sense than to Understanding: for Reason (says our great Hooker) is a direct aspect of truth, an inward beholding, having a similar relation to the intelligible or spiritual, as Sense has to the material or phenomenal.

The result is, that neither falls under the definition of the other. They differ *in kind:* and had my object been confined to the establishment of this fact, the preceding columns would have superseded all further disquisition. But I have ever in view the especial interest of my youthful readers, whose reflective power is to be cultivated, as well as their particular reflections to be called forth and guided. Now the main chance of their reflecting on religious subjects aright, and of their attaining to the contemplation of spiritual truths at all, rests on their insight into the nature of this disparity still more than on their conviction of its existence. I now, therefore, proceed to a brief analysis of the Understanding, in elucidation of the definitions already given.

The Understanding then, considered exclusively as an organ of human intelligence, is the faculty by which we reflect and generalize. Take, for instance, any object consisting of many parts, a house, or a group of houses: and if it be contemplated, as a whole, that is, as many constituting a one, it forms what, in the technical language of psychology, is called a total impression. Among the various component parts of this, we direct our attention especially to such as we recollect to have noticed in other total impressions. Then, by a voluntary act, we withhold our attention from all the rest to reflect exclusively on these; and these we henceforward use as common characters, by virtue of which the several objects are referred to one and the same sort.[2] Thus, the whole process may be reduced to three acts, all de-

---

[2] Accordingly as we attend more or less to the differences, the sort becomes, of course, more or less comprehensive. Hence there arises for the systematic naturalist the necessity of subdividing the sorts into orders, classes, families, &c.: all which, however, resolve themselves for the mere logician into the conception of *genus* and *species,* that is, the comprehending and the comprehended.

pending on and supposing a previous impression on the senses: first, the appropriation of our attention; second (and in order to the continuance of the first) abstraction, or the voluntary withholding of the attention; and, third, generalization. And these are the proper functions of the Understanding: and the power of so doing, is what we mean, when we say we possess understanding, or are created with the faculty of understanding.[3]

[3] It is obvious, that the third function includes the act of comparing one object with another. The act of comparing supposes in the comparing faculty certain inherent forms, that is, modes of reflecting not referable to the objects reflected on, but pre-determined by the constitution and mechanism of the understanding itself. And under some one or other of these forms, the resemblances and differences must be subsumed in order to be conceivable, and à fortiori therefore in order to be comparable. The senses do not compare, but merely furnish the materials for comparison.

Were it not so, how could the first comparison have been possible? It would involve the absurdity of measuring a thing by itself. But if we think on some one thing, the length of our own foot, or of our hand and arm from the elbow-joint, it is evident that in order to do this, we must have the conception of measure. Now these antecedent and most general conceptions are what is meant by the constituent forms of the understanding: we call them constituent because they are not acquired by the understanding, but are implied in its constitution. As rationally might a circle be said to acquire a centre and circumference, as the understanding to acquire these its inherent forms or ways of conceiving. This is what Leibnitz meant, when to the old adage of the Peripatetics, Nihil in intellectu quod non prius in sensu—there is nothing in the understanding not derived from the senses, or —there is nothing conceived that was not previously perceived,—he replied—præter intellectum ipsum, except the understanding itself.

And here let me remark for once and all: whoever would reflect to any purpose—whoever is in earnest in his pursuit of self-knowledge, and of one of the principal means to this, an insight into the meaning of the words he uses, and the different meanings properly or improperly conveyed by one and the same word, accordingly as it is used in the schools or the market,—accordingly as the kind or a high degree is intended (for example, heat, weight, and the like, as employed scientifically, compared with the same word used popularly)—whoever, I say, seriously, proposes this as his object, must so far overcome his dislike of pedantry, and his dread of being sneered at as a pedant, as not to quarrel with an uncouth word or phrase, till he is quite sure that some other and more familiar one would not only have expressed the precise meaning with equal clearness, but have been as likely to draw attention to this meaning exclusively. The ordinary language of a philosopher in conversation or popular writings, compared with the language he uses in strict reasoning, is as his watch compared with the chronometer in his observatory. He sets the former by the town-clock, or even, perhaps, by the Dutch clock in his kitchen, not because he believes it right, but because his neighbors and his cook go by it. To afford the reader an opportunity for exercising the forbearance here recommended, I turn back to the phrase, "most general conceptions," and observe, that in strict and severe propriety of language, I should have said *generalific* or *generific* rather than general, and concipiences or conceptive acts rather than conceptions.

It is an old complaint, that a man of genius no sooner appears, but the host of dunces are up in arms to repel the invading alien. This observation would have made more converts to its truth, I suspect, had it been worded more dispassionately and with a less contemptuous antithesis. For "dunces," let us substitute "the many," or the "*οὖτος κόσμος*" (*this world*) of the Apostle, and we shall perhaps find no great difficulty in accounting for the fact. To arrive at the root, indeed, and last ground of the problem, it would be necessary to investigate the nature and effects of the sense of difference on the human mind where it is not holden in check by reason and reflection. We need not go to the savage tribes of North America, or the yet ruder natives of the Indian Isles, to learn how slight a degree of difference will, in un-cultivated minds, call up a sense of diversity, and inward perplexity and contradiction, as if the strangers were, and yet were not, of the same kind with themselves. Who has not had occasion to observe the effect which the gesticulations and nasal tones of a Frenchman pro-duce on our own vulgar? Here we may see the origin and primary import of our *unkindness*. It is a sense of *un*kind, and not the mere negation but the positive opposite of the sense of *kind*. Alienation, aggravated now by fear, now by contempt, and not seldom by a mix-ture of both, aversion, hatred, enmity, are so many successive shapes of its growth and *metamorphosis*. In application to the present case, it is sufficient to say, that Pindar's remark on sweet music holds equally true of genius: as many as are not delighted by it are disturbed, per-plexed, irritated. The beholder either recognizes it as a projected form of his own being, that moves before him with a glory round its head, or recoils from it as from a spectre. But this speculation would lead me too far; I must be content with having referred to it as the ultimate ground of the fact, and pass to the more obvious and proximate causes. And as the first, I would rank the person's not understanding what yet he expects to understand, and as if he had a right to do so. An original mathematical work, or any other that requires peculiar and technical marks and symbols, will excite no uneasy feelings—not in the mind of a competent reader, for he understands it; and not with others, be-cause they neither expect nor are expected to understand it. The sec-ond place we may assign to the misunderstanding, which is almost sure to follow in cases where the incompetent person, finding no out-ward marks (diagrams, arbitrary signs, and the like) to inform him at first sight, that the subject is one which he does not pretend to understand, and to be ignorant of which does not detract from his estimation as a man of abilities generally, will attach some meaning to what he hears or reads; and as he is out of humor with the author, it will most often be such a meaning as he can quarrel with and exhibit in a ridiculous or offensive point of view.

But above all, the whole world almost of minds, as far as we regard intellectual efforts, may be divided into two classes of the busy-indolent and lazy-indolent. To both alike all thinking is painful, and all attempts to rouse them to think, whether in the re-examination of their existing convictions, or for the reception of new light, are irritating. "It *may* all be very deep and clever; but really one ought to be quite sure of it before one wrenches one's brain to find out what it is. I take up a book as a companion, with whom I can have an easy cheerful chitchat on what we both know beforehand, or else matters of fact. In our leisure hours we have a right to relaxation and amusement."

Well! but in their *studious* hours, when their bow is to be bent, when they are *apud Musas*, or amidst the Muses? Alas! it is just the same. The same craving for *amusement*, that is, to be away from the Muses; for relaxation, that is, the unbending of a bow which in fact had never been strung? There are two ways of obtaining their applause. The first is: enable them to reconcile in one and the same occupation the love of sloth and the hatred of vacancy. Gratify indolence, and yet save them from *ennui*—in plain English, from themselves. For, spite of their antipathy to dry reading, the keeping company with themselves is, after all, the insufferable annoyance: and the true secret of their dislike to a work of thought and inquiry lies in its tendency to make them acquainted with their own permanent being. The other road to their favor is, to introduce to them their own thoughts and predilections, tricked out in the fine language, in which it would gratify their vanity to express them in their own conversation, and with which they can imagine themselves showing off: and this (as has been elsewhere remarked) is the characteristic difference between the second-rate writers of the last two or three generations, and the same class under Elizabeth and the Stuarts. In the latter we find the most far-fetched and singular thoughts in the simplest and most native language; in the former, the most obvious and commonplace thoughts in the most far-fetched and motley language. But lastly, and as the *sine qua non* of their patronage, a sufficient arc must be left for the reader's mind to oscillate in—freedom of choice,

To make the shifting cloud be what you please,

save only where the attraction of curiosity determines the line of motion. The attention must not be fastened down: and this every work of genius, not simply narrative, must do before it can be justly appreciated.

In former times a popular work meant one that adapted the results of studious meditation or scientific research to the capacity of the people, presenting in the concrete, by instances and examples, what had been ascertained in the abstract and by discovery of the law. Now, on the other hand, that is a popular work which gives back to the people

Now when a person speaking to us of any particular object or appearance refers it by means of some common character to a known class (which he does in giving it a name), we say, that we understand him; that is, we understand his words. The name of a thing, in the original sense of the word name (*nomen*, νούμενον, τὸ *intelligible, id quod intelligitur*), expresses that which is *understood* in an appearance, that which we place (or make to *stand*) *under* it, as the condition of its real existence, and in proof that it is not an accident of the senses, or affection of the individual, not a phantom or apparition, that is, an appearance which is *only* an appearance. (See *Gen.* ii. 19, 20, and in *Psalm* xx. 1, and in many other places of the Bible, the identity of *nomen* with *numen,* that is, invisible power and presence, the *nomen substantivum* of all real objects, and the ground of their reality, independently of the affections of sense in the percipient). In like manner, in a connected succession of names, as the speaker passes from one to the other, we say that we understand his *discourse, discursio intellectus, discursus,* his passing from one thing to another. Thus, in all instances, it is words, names, or, if images, yet images used as words or names, that are the only and exclusive subjects of understanding. In no instance do we understand a thing in itself; but only the name to which it is referred. Sometimes indeed, when several classes are recalled conjointly, we identify the words with the object—though by courtesy of idiom rather than in strict propriety of language. Thus we may say that we *understand* a rainbow, when recalling successively the several names for the several sorts of colors, we know that they are to be applied to one and the same *phæ-nomenon,* at once distinctly and simultaneously; but even in common speech we should not say this of a single color. No one would say he understands red or blue. He *sees* the color, and had seen it before in a vast number and variety of objects; and he understands the *word* red, as referring his fancy or memory to this his collective experience.

If this be so, and so it most assuredly is—if the proper functions of the understanding be that of generalizing the notices re-

---

their own errors and prejudices, and flatters the many by creating them under the title of THE PUBLIC, into a supreme and inappellable tribunal of intellectual excellence.

P.S. In a continuous work, the frequent insertion and length of notes would need an apology: in a book like this, of aphorisms and detached comments, none is necessary, it being understood beforehand that the sauce and the garnish are to occupy the greater part of the dish.

ceived from the senses in order to the construction of names: of
referring particular notices, that is, impressions or sensations, to
their proper names; and, *vice versa*, names to their correspondent
class or kind of notices—then it follows of necessity, that the
Understanding is truly and accurately defined in the words of
Leighton and Kant, a faculty judging according to sense.

Now whether in defining the speculative Reason,—(that is,
the reason considered abstractedly as an intellective power)—we
call it "the source of necessary and universal principles, according
to which the notices of the senses are either affirmed or denied;"
or describe it as "the power by which we are enabled to draw
from particular and contingent appearances universal and neces-
sary conclusions:" [4] it is equally evident that the two definitions

[4] Take a familiar illustration. My sight and touch convey to me a
certain impression, to which my understanding applies its pre-concep-
tions (*conceptus antecedentes et generalissimi*) of quantity and re-
lation, and thus refers it to the class and name of three-cornered
bodies—we will suppose it the iron of a turf-spade. It compares the
sides, and finds that any two measured as one are greater than the
third; and according to a law of the imagination, there arises a pre-
sumption that in all other bodies of the same figure (that is, three-
cornered and equilateral) the same proportion exists. After this, the
senses have been directed successively to a number of three-cornered
bodies of unequal sides—and in these too the same proportion has been
found without exception, till at length it becomes a fact of experience,
that in all triangles hitherto seen, the two sides together are greater
than the third: and there will exist no ground or analogy for antici-
pating an exception to a rule, generalized from so vast a number of
particular instances. So far and no farther could the understanding
carry us: and as far as this "the faculty, judging according to sense,"
conducts many of the inferior animals, if not in the same, yet in in-
stances analogous and fully equivalent.

The reason supersedes the whole process, and on the first conception
presented by the understanding in consequence of the first sight of a
triangular figure, of whatever sort it might chance to be, it affirms with
an assurance incapable of future increase, with a perfect certainty,
that in all possible triangles any two of the inclosing lines will and
must be greater than the third. In short, understanding in its highest
form of experience remains commensurate with the experimental no-
tices of the senses from which it is generalized. Reason, on the other
hand, either predetermines experience, or avails itself of a past expe-
rience to supersede its necessity in all future time; and affirms truths
which no sense could perceive, nor experiment verify, nor experience
confirm.

Yea, this is the test and character of a truth so affirmed, that in its
own proper form it is inconceivable. For to conceive is a function of
the understanding, which can be exercised only on subjects subordi-

nate thereto. And yet to the forms of the understanding, all truth must be reduced, that is to be fixed as an object of reflection, and to be rendered expressible. And here we have a second test and sign of a truth so affirmed, that it can come forth out of the moulds of the understanding only in the disguise of two contradictory conceptions, each of which is partially true, and the conjunction of both conceptions becomes the representative or expression (the exponent) of a truth beyond conception and inexpressible. Examples: Before Abraham *was*, I *am*.—God is a circle, the centre of which is everywhere, and circumference nowhere. The soul is all in every part.

If this appear extravagant, it is an extravagance which no man can indeed learn from another, but which, (were this possible,) I might have learnt from Plato, Kepler, and Bacon; from Luther, Hooker, Pascal, Leibnitz, and Fénelon. But in this last paragraph I have, I see, unwittingly overstepped my purpose, according to which we were to take reason as a simply intellectual power. Yet even as such, and with all the disadvantage of a technical and arbitrary abstraction, it has been made evident:—1. that there is an intuition or *im*mediate beholding, accompanied by a conviction of the necessity and universality of the truth so beholden, not derived from the senses, which intuition, when it is construed by pure sense, gives birth to the science of mathematics, and when applied to objects supersensuous or spiritual is the organ of theology and philosophy⊢—and 2. that there is likewise a reflective and discursive faculty, or mediate apprehension which, taken by itself and uninfluenced by the former, depends on the senses for the materials on which it is exercised, and is contained within the sphere of the senses. And this faculty it is, which in generalizing the notices of the senses constitutes sensible experience, and gives rise to maxims or rules which may become more and more general, but can never be raised into universal verities, or beget a consciousness of absolute certainty; though they may be sufficient to extinguish all doubt. (Putting revelation out of view, take our first progenitor in the 50th or 100th year of his existence. His experience would probably have freed him from all doubt, as the sun sank in the horizon, that it would re-appear the next morning. But compare this state of assurance with that which the same man would have had of the 47th proposition of Euclid, supposing him like Pythagoras to have discovered the demonstration.) Now is it expedient, I ask, or conformable to the laws and purposes of language, to call two so altogether disparate subjects by one and the same name? Or, having two names in our language, should we call each of the two diverse subjects by both—that is, by either name, as caprice might dictate? If not, then as we have the two words, reason and understanding (as indeed what language of cultivated man has not?)—what should prevent us from appropriating the former to the power distinctive of humanity? We need only place the derivatives from the two terms in opposition (for example, "A and B are both rational beings; but there is no comparison between them in point of intelligence," or "She always concludes rationally, though not a woman of much understanding") to see that we can not reverse the

differ in their essential characters, and consequently the subjects differ in *kind.*

The dependence of the Understanding on the representations of the senses, and its consequent posteriority thereto, as contrasted with the independence and antecedency of Reason, are strikingly exemplified in the Ptolemaic system—that truly wonderful product and highest boast of the faculty, judging according to the senses—compared with the Newtonian, as the offspring of a yet higher power, arranging, correcting, and annulling the representations of the senses according to its own inherent laws and constitutive ideas.

---

order—that is, call the higher gift understanding, and the lower reason. What should prevent us? I asked. Alas! that which has prevented us—the cause of this confusion in the terms—is only too obvious; namely, inattention to the momentous distinction in the things, and generally, to the duty and habit recommended in the fifth introductory Aphorism of this Volume. But the cause of this, and of all its lamentable effects and subcauses, *false doctrine, blindness of heart, and contempt of the word,* is best declared by the philosophic Apostle: *they did not like to retain God in their knowledge* (Rom. i. 28), and though they could not extinguish *the light that lighteth every man,* and which *shone in the darkness:* yet because the darkness could not comprehend the light, they refused to bear witness of it and worshiped, instead, the shaping mist, which the light had drawn upward from the ground (that is, from the mere animal nature and instinct), and which that light alone had made visible, that is, by superinducing on the animal instinct the principle of self-consciousness.

FROM *LITERARY REMAINS*

CONFESSIO FIDEI. Nov. 3, 1816

I.—I

I BELIEVE that I am a free agent, inasmuch as, and so far as, I have a will, which renders me justly responsible for my actions, omissive as well as commissive. Likewise that I possess reason, or a law of right and wrong, which, uniting with my sense of moral responsibility, constitutes the voice of conscience.

II. Hence it becomes my absolute duty to believe, and I do believe, that there is a God, that is, a Being, in whom supreme reason and a most holy will are one with an infinite power; and that all holy will is coincident with the will of God, and therefore secure in its ultimate consequences by His omnipotence;—having, if such similitude be not unlawful, such a relation to the goodness of the Almighty, as a perfect time-piece will have to the sun.

COROLLARY

The wonderful works of God in the sensible world are a perpetual discourse, reminding me of his existence, and shadowing out to me his perfections. But as all language presupposes in the intelligent hearer or reader those primary notions, which it symbolizes; as well as the power of making those combinations of these primary notions, which it represents and excites us to combine,—even so I believe, that the notion of God is essential to the human mind; that it is called forth into distinct consciousness principally by the conscience, and auxiliarly by the manifest adaptation of means to ends in the outward creation. It is, therefore, evident to my reason, that the existence of God is absolutely and necessarily insusceptible of a scientific demonstration, and that Scripture has so represented it. For it commands us to believe in one God. *I am the Lord thy God: thou shalt have none other gods but me.* Now all commandment necessarily relates to the will; whereas all scientific demonstration is independent of the will, and is apodictic or demonstrative only as far as it is compulsory on the mind, *volentem, nolentem.*

III. My conscience forbids me to propose to myself the pains and pleasures of this life, as the primary motive, or ultimate end, of my actions;—on the contrary, it makes me perceive an utter disproportionateness and heterogeneity between the acts of the spirit, as virtue and vice, and the things of the sense, such as all earthly rewards and punishments must be. Its hopes and fears, therefore, refer me to a different and spiritual state of being: and I believe in the life to come, not through arguments acquired by my understanding or discursive faculty, but chiefly and effectively, because so to believe is my duty, and in obedience to the commands of my conscience.

Here ends the first table of my creed, which would have been my creed, had I been born with Adam; and which, therefore, constitutes what may in this sense be called natural religion, that is, the religion of all finite rational beings. The second table contains the creed of revealed religion, my belief as a Christian.

II

IV. I BELIEVE, and hold it as the fundamental article of Christianity, that I am a fallen creature; that I am of myself capable of moral evil, but not of myself capable of moral good, and that an evil ground existed in my will, previously to any given act, or assignable moment of time, in my consciousness. I am born a child of wrath. This fearful mystery I pretend not to understand. I can not even conceive the possibility of it,—but I know that it is so. My conscience the sole fountain of certainty, commands me to believe it, and would itself be a contradiction, were it not so—and what is real must be possible.

V. I receive with full and grateful faith the assurance of revelation, that the Word, which is from all eternity with God, and is God, assumed our human nature in order to redeem me, and all mankind from this our connate corruption. My reason convinces me, that no other mode of redemption is conceivable, and, as did Socrates, would have yearned after the Redeemer, though it would not dare expect so wonderful an act of divine love, except only as an effort of my mind to conceive the utmost of the infinite greatness of that love.

VI. I believe, that this assumption of humanity by the Son of God was revealed and realized to us by the Word made flesh, and manifested to us in Christ Jesus; and that his miraculous birth, his agony, his crucifixion, death, resurrection, and ascension, were all both symbols of our redemption (φαινόμενα τῶν νουμένων) and necessary parts of the awful process.

VII. I believe in the descent and sending of the Holy Spirit, by whose free grace obtained for me by the merits of my Redeemer,

I can alone be sanctified and restored from my natural inheritance of sin and condemnation, be a child of God, and an inheritor of the kingdom of God.

COROLLARY

The Trinity of persons in the Unity of the God would have been a necessary idea of my speculative reason, deduced from the necessary postulate of an intelligent creator, whose ideas being anterior to the things, must be more actual than those things, even as those things are more actual than our images derived from them; and who, as intelligent, must have had co-eternally an adequate idea of himself, in and through which he created all things both in heaven and earth. But this would only have been a speculative idea, like those of circles and other mathematical figures, to which we are not authorized by the practical reason to attribute reality. Solely in consequence of our Redemption does the Trinity become a doctrine, the belief of which as real is commanded by our conscience. But to Christians it is commanded, and it is false candor in a Christian, believing in original sin and redemption therefrom, to admit that any man denying the divinity of Christ can be a Christian. The true language of a Christian, which reconciles humility with truth would be;—God and not man is the judge of man: which of the two is the Christian, he will determine; but this is evident, that if the theanthropist is a Christian, the psilanthropist can not be so; and *vice versa*. Suppose, that two tribes used the same written characters, but attached different and opposite meanings to them, so that *niger*, for instance, was used by one tribe to convey the notion *black*, by the other, *white*;—could they, without absurdity, be said to have the same language? Even so, in the instance of the crucifixion, the same image is present to the theanthropist and to the psilanthropist or Socinian—but to the latter it represents a mere man, a good man indeed and divinely inspired, but still a mere man, even as Moses or Paul, dying in attestation of the truth of his preaching, and in order by his resurrection to give a proof of his mission, and inclusively of the resurrection of all men:—to the former it represents God incarnate taking upon himself the sins of the world, and himself thereby redeeming us, and giving us life everlasting, not merely teaching it. The same difference, that exists between God and man, between giving and the declaration of a gift, exists between the Trinitarian and the Unitarian. This might be proved in a few moments, if we would only conceive a Greek or Roman, to whom two persons relate their belief, each calling Christ by a different name. It would be impossible for the Greek even to guess, that they both meant the same person, or referred to the same facts.

A NIGHTLY PRAYER. 1831

ALMIGHTY GOD, by thy eternal Word my Creator, Redeemer and Preserver! who hast in thy free communicative goodness glorified me with the capability of knowing thee, the one only absolute Good, the eternal I Am, as the author of my being, and of desiring and seeking thee as its ultimate end; who, when I fell from thee into the mystery of the false and evil will, didst not abandon me, poor self-lost creature, but in thy condescending mercy didst provide an access and a return to thyself, even to thee the Holy One, in thine only-begotten Son, the way and the truth from everlasting, and who took on himself humanity, yea, became flesh, even the man Christ Jesus, that for man he might be the life and the resurrection!—O Giver of all good gifts, who art thyself the one only absolute Good, from whom I have received whatever good I have, whatever capability of good there is in me, and from thee good alone,—from myself and my own corrupted will all evil and the consequences of evil,—with inward prostration of will, mind, and affections I adore thy infinite majesty; I aspire to love thy transcendent goodness!—In a deep sense of my unworthiness, and my unfitness to present myself before thee, of eyes too pure to behold iniquity, and whose light, the beatitude of spirits conformed to thy will, is a consuming fire to all vanity and corruption; but in the name of the Lord Jesus, of the dear Son of thy love, in whose perfect obedience thou deignest to behold as many as have received the seed of Christ into the body of his death;—I offer this my bounden nightly sacrifice of praise and thanksgiving, in humble trust, that the fragrance of my Saviour's righteousness may remove from it the taint of my mortal corruption. Thy mercies have followed me through all the hours and moments of my life; and now I lift up my heart in awe and thankfulness for the preservation of my life through the past day, for the alleviation of my bodily sufferings and languors, for the manifold comforts which thou hast reserved for me, yea, in thy fatherly compassion hast rescued from the wreck of my own sins or sinful infirmities;—for the kind and affectionate friends thou hast raised up for me, especially for those of this household, for the mother and mistress of this family whose love to me hath been great and faithful, and for the dear friend, the supporter and sharer of my studies and researches; but above all, for the heavenly Friend, the crucified Saviour, the glorified Mediator, Christ Jesus, and for the heavenly Comforter, source cf all abiding comforts, thy Holy Spirit! O grant me the aid of thy Spirit, that I may with a deeper faith, a more enkindled love, bless thee, who through thy Son hast privileged me to call thee Abba, Father! O, thou who hast revealed thyself in thy holy word as a God that hearest prayer; before whose infinitude all differences cease of great and small; who like a tender parent foreknowest all our wants, yet listenest well-pleased to the humble petitions of thy children; who hast not alone permitted, but taught us, to call on thee in all our needs,—earnestly I implore the continuance of thy free mercy, of thy protecting providence, through the coming night. Thou hearest every prayer offered to thee believingly with a penitent and sincere heart. For thou in withholding grantest, healest in inflicting the wound, yea turnest all to good for as many as truly seek thee through Christ, the Mediator! Thy will be done! But if it be according to thy wise and righteous ordinances, O shield me this night from the assaults of disease, grant me refreshment of sleep unvexed by evil and distempered dreams; and if the purpose and aspiration of my heart be upright before thee who alone knowest the heart of man, O in thy mercy vouchsafe me yet in this my decay of life an interval of ease and strength; if so (thy grace disposing and assisting) I may make compensation to thy church for the unused talents thou hast intrusted to me, for the neglected opportunities, which thy loving-kindness had provided. O let me be found a laborer in the vineyard, though of the late hour, when the Lord and Heir of the vintage, Christ Jesus, calleth for his servant.

Our Father, &c.

To thee, great omnipresent Spirit, whose mercy is over all thy works, who now beholdest me, who hearest me, who hast framed my heart to seek and trust in thee, in the name of my Lord and Saviour Christ Jesus, I humbly commit and commend my body, soul, and spirit.

Glory be to thee, O God!

NOTES ON THE BOOK OF COMMON PRAYER

PRAYER

A MAN may pray night and day, and yet deceive himself; but no man can be assured of his sincerity, who does not pray. Prayer is faith passing into act; a union of the will and the intellect realizing in an intellectual act. It is the whole man that prays. Less than this is wishing, or lip-work; a charm or a mummery. *Pray always,* says the Apostle;—that is, have the habit of prayer, turning your thoughts into acts by connecting them with the idea of the redeeming God, and even so reconverting your actions into thoughts.

HENRY MORE'S THEOLOGICAL WORKS

THERE are three principal causes to which the imperfections and errors in the theological schemes and works of our elder divines, the glories of our Church,—men of almost unparalleled learning and genius, the rich and robust intellects from the reign of Elizabeth to the death of Charles II.,—may, I think, be reasonably attributed. And striking, unusually striking, instances of all three abound in this volume; and in the works of no other divine are they more worthy of being regretted: for hence has arisen a depreciation of Henry More's theological writings, which yet contain more original, enlarged, and elevating views of the Christian dispensation than I have met with in any other single volume. For More had both the philosophic and the poetic genius, supported by immense erudition. But unfortunately the two did not amalgamate. It was not his good fortune to discover, as in the preceding generation William Shakespeare discovered, a *mordaunt* or common base of both, and in which both the poetic and the philosophical power blended in one.

These causes are,—

First, and foremost,—the want of that logical προπαιδεία δοκιμαστική, that critique of the human intellect, which, previously to the weighing and measuring of this or that, begins by assaying the weights, measures, and scales themselves; that fulfilment of the heaven-descended *nosce teipsum,* in respect to the intellective part of man, which was commenced in a sort of tentative broadcast way by Lord Bacon in his *Novum Organum,* and brought to a systematic completion by Immanuel Kant in his *Kritik der reinen Vernunft, der Urtheilskraft, und der metaphysiche Anfangsgründe der Naturwissenschaft.*

From the want of this searching logic, there is a perpetual confusion of the subjective with the objective in the arguments of our divines, together with a childish or anile overrating of human testimony, and an ignorance in the art of sifting it, which necessarily engendered credulity.

Second,—the ignorance of natural science, their physiography scant in fact, and stuffed out with fables; their physiology imbrangled with an inapplicable logic and a misgrowth of *entia rationalia,* that is, substantiated abstractions; and their physiogony a blank or dreams of tradition, and such "intentional colors" as occupy space but can not fill it. Yet if Christianity is to be the religion of the world, if Christ be that Logos or Word that *was in the beginning,* by whom all things *became;* if it was the same Christ who said, *Let there be light;* who in and by the creation commenced that great redemptive process, the history of life which begins in its detachment from nature, and is to end in its union with God;—if this be true, so true must it be that the book of nature and the book of revelation, with the whole history of man as the intermediate link, must be the integral and coherent parts of one great work: and the conclusion is, that a scheme of the Christian faith which does not arise out of, and shoot its beams downward into, the scheme of nature, but stands aloof as an insulated afterthought, must be false or distorted in all its particulars. In confirmation of this position, I may challenge any opponent to adduce a single instance in which the now exploded falsities of physical science, through all its revolutions from the second to the seventeenth century of the Christian æra, did not produce some corresponding warps in the theological systems and dogmas of the several periods.

The third and last cause, and especially operative in the writings of this author, is the presence and regnancy of a false and fantastic philosophy, yet shot through with refracted light from the not risen but rising truth,—a scheme of physics and physiology compounded of Cartesian mechanics and empiricism (for it was the credulous childhood of experimentalism), and a corrupt, mystical, theurgical, pseudo-Platonism, which infected the rarest minds under the Stuart dynasty. The only not universal belief in witchcraft and apparitions, and the vindication of such monster follies by such men as Sir M. Hale, Glanville, Baxter, Henry More, and a host of others, are melancholy proofs of my position. Hence, in the first chapters of this volume, the most idle inventions of the ancients are sought to be made credible by the most fantastic hypotheses and analogies.

To the man who has habitually contemplated Christianity as interesting all rational finite beings, as the very *spirit of truth,* the application of the prophecies as so many fortune-tellings and soothsayings to particular events and persons, must needs be felt as childish—like faces seen in the moon, or the sediments of a teacup. But reverse this, and a Pope and a Bonaparte can never be wanting,—the molehill becomes an Andes. On the other hand, there are few writers whose works could be so easily defecated as More's. Mere omission would suffice; and perhaps one half (an unusually large proportion) would come forth from the furnace pure gold; if but a fourth, how great a gain!

DEFINITION OF MIRACLE

A PHÆNOMENON in no connection with any other phænomenon, as its immediate cause, is a miracle; and what is believed to have been such, is miraculous for the person so believing. When it is strange and surprising, that is, without any analogy in our former experience, it is called a miracle. The kind defines the thing:—the circumstances the word.[1]

To stretch out my arm is a miracle, unless the materialists should be more cunning than they have proved themselves hitherto. To reanimate a dead man by an act of the will, no intermediate agency employed, not only is, but is called, a miracle. A Scripture miracle, therefore, must be so defined, as to express, not only its miraculous essence, but likewise the condition of its appearing miraculous; add therefore to the preceding, the words *præter omnem priorem experientiam.*

It might be defined likewise an effect, not having its cause in any thing congenerous. That thought calls up thought is no more miraculous than that a billiard ball moves a billiard ball; but that a billiard ball should excite a thought, that is, be perceived, is a miracle, and, were it strange, would be called such. For take the converse, that a thought should call up a billiard ball! Yet where is the difference, but that the one is a common experience, the other never yet experiencd?

It is not strictly accurate to affirm, that every thing would appear a miracle, if we were wholly uninfluenced by custom, and saw things as they are:—for then the very ground of all miracles would probably vanish, namely, the heterogeneity of spirit and matter. For the *quid ulterius?* of wonder, we should have the *ne plus ultra* of adoration.

Again—the word miracle has an objective, a subjective, and a popular meaning; as objective,—the essence of a miracle consists in the heterogeneity of the consequent and its causative antecedent:—as subjective,—in the assumption of the heterogeneity. Add the wonder and surprise excited, when the conse-

---

[1] A reader of this definition compared it with the following saying of Doctor Johnson: "There is undoubtedly a sense in which all life is miraculous, as it is an union of powers of which we can image no connection, a succession of motions of which the first cause must be supernatural."—*Life of Sir Thomas Browne.*—S. C.

quent is out of the course of experience, and we know the popular sense and ordinary use of the word.

DEATH, AND GROUNDS OF BELIEF IN A FUTURE STATE

IT IS an important thought, that death, judged of by corporeal analogies, certainly implies discerption or dissolution of parts; but pain and pleasure do not; nay, they seem inconceivable except under the idea of concentration. Therefore the influence of the body on the soul will not prove the common destiny of both. I feel myself not the slave of nature (nature used here as the *mundus sensibilis*) in the sense in which animals are. Not only my thoughts and affections extend to objects transnatural, as truth, virtue, God; not only do my powers extend vastly beyond all those, which I could have derived from the instruments and organs, with which nature has furnished me; but I can do what nature *per se* can not. I ingraft, I raise heavy bodies above the clouds, and guide my course over ocean and through air. I alone am lord of fire and light; other creatures are but their alms-folk, and of all the so-called elements, water, earth, air, and all their compounds (to speak in the ever-enduring language of the senses, to which nothing can be revealed, but as compact, or fluid, or aerial), I not merely subserve myself of them, but I employ them. *Ergo*, there is in me, or rather I am, a præter-natural, that is, a supersensuous thing: but what is not nature, why should it perish with nature? why lose the faculty of vision, because my spectacles are broken?

Now to this it will be objected, and very forcibly too;—that the soul or self is acted upon by nature through the body, and water or caloric, diffused through or collected in the brain, will derange the faculties of the soul by deranging the organization of the brain; the sword can not touch the soul; but by rending the flesh it will rend the feelings. Therefore the violence of nature may, in destroying the body, mediately destroy the soul! It is to this objection that my first sentence applies; and is an important, and, I believe, a new, and the only satisfactory reply I have ever heard.

The one great and binding ground of the belief of God and a hereafter, is the law of conscience: but as the aptitudes and beauty, and grandeur, of the world, are a sweet and beneficent inducement to this belief, a constant fuel to our faith, so here we seek these arguments, not as dissatisfied with the one main ground, not as *of little* faith, but because, believing it to be, it is natural we should expect to find traces of it, and as a noble way of employing and developing, and enlarging the faculties of the soul, and this, not by way of motive, but of assimilation, producing virtue. 2d April, 1811.

FORMATION OF A MORE COMPREHENSIVE THEORY OF LIFE

WHEN we stand before the bust of John Hunter, or as we enter the magnificent museum furnished by his labors, and pass slowly, with meditative observation, through this august temple, which the genius of one great man has raised and dedicated to the wisdom and uniform working of the Creator, we perceive at every step the guidance, we had almost said, the inspiration, of those profound ideas concerning Life, which dawn upon us indeed, through his written works, but which he has here presented to us in a more perfect language than that of words—the language of God himself, as uttered by Nature.

That the true idea of Life existed in the mind of John Hunter I do not entertain the least doubt; but it may, perhaps, be doubted whether his incessant occupation, and his stupendous industry in the service, both of his contemporaries and of posterity, added to his comparatively slight acquaintance with the arts and aids of logical arrangement, permitted him fully to unfold and arrange it in distinct, clear, and communicable conceptions. Assuredly, however, I may, without incurring the charge of arrogance or detraction, venture to assert that, in his writings the light which occasionally flashes upon us seems at other times, and more frequently, to struggle through an unfriendly medium, and even sometimes to suffer a temporary occultation. At least, in order to dissipate the undeniable obscurities, and to reconcile the apparent contradictions found in his works,—to distinguish, in short, the numerous passages in which without, perhaps, losing sight internally of his own peculiar belief, he yet falls into the phraseology and mechanical solutions of his age,—we must distinguish such passages from those in which the form corresponds to the substance, and in which, therefore, the nature and essential laws of vital action are expressed, as far as his researches had unveiled them to his own mind, without disguise. To effect this, we must, as it were, climb up on his shoulders, and look at the same objects in a distincter form, because seen from the more commanding point of view furnished by himself. This has, indeed, been more than once attempted already, and, in one instance, with so evident a display of power and insight as announces in the assertor and vindicator of the Hunterian Theory a congenial intellect, and a disciple in whom Hunter himself would have exulted. Would that this attempt had been made on a larger scale, that the writer to whom I refer[1] had in consequence developed his opinions systematically, and carried them yet further back, even to their ultimate principle!

But this the scientific world has yet to expect; or it is more than probable that the present humble endeavor would have been superseded, or confined, at least, to the task of restating the opinion of my predecessor with such modifications as the differences that will always exist between men who have thought independently, and each for himself, have never failed to introduce, even on problems of far easier and more obvious solution.

Without further preface or apology, therefore, I shall state at once my objections to all the definitions that have hitherto been given of Life, as meaning too much or too little, with an exception, however, in favor of those which mean nothing at all; and even these last must, in certain cases, receive an honor they do not merit, and be confuted, or rather detected, on account of their too general acceptance, and the incalculable power of words over the minds of men in proportion to the remoteness of the subject from the cognizance of the senses.

It would be equally presumptuous and unreasonable should I, with a late writer on this subject, "exhort the reader to be particularly on his guard against loose and indefinite expressions;" but I perfectly agree with him that they are the bane of all science, and have been remarkably injurious in the different departments of physiology.

The attempts to explain the nature of Life, which have fallen within my knowledge, presuppose the arbitrary division of all that surrounds us into things with life, and things without life— a division grounded on a mere assumption. At the best, it can be regarded only as a hasty deduction from the first superficial notices of the objects that surround us, sufficient, perhaps, for the purpose of ordinary discrimination, but far too indeterminate and diffluent to be taken unexamined by the philosophic inquirer. The positions of science must be tried in the jeweller's scales, not like the mixed commodities of the market, on the weigh-bridge of common opinion and vulgar usage. Such, however, has been

[1] Mr. Abernethy.

the procedure in the present instance, and the result has been answerable to the coarseness of the process. By a comprisal of the *petitio principii* with the *argumentum in circulo*,—in plain English, by an easy logic, which begins with begging the question, and then moving in a circle, comes round to the point where it began,—each of the two divisions has been made to define the other by a mere reassertion of their assumed contrariety. The physiologist has luminously explained Y plus x by informing us that it is a somewhat that is the antithesis of Y minus x; and if we ask, what then is Y — x? the answer is, the antithesis of Y + x, a reciprocation of great service, that may remind us of the twin sisters in the fable of the Lamiæ, with but one eye between them both, which each borrowed from the other as either happened to want it; but with this additional disadvantage, that in the present case it is after all but an eye of glass. The definitions themselves will best illustrate our meaning. I will begin with that given by Bichat. "Life is the sum of all the functions by which death is resisted," in which I have in vain endeavored to discover any other meaning than that life consists in being able to live. This author, with a whimsical gravity, prefaces his definition with the remark, that the nature of life has hitherto been sought for in *abstract* considerations; as if it were possible that four more inveterate abstractions could be brought together in one sentence than are here assembled in the words, life, death, function, and resistance. Similar instances might be cited from Richerand and others. The word Life is translated into other more learned words; and this *paraphrase* of the *term* is substituted for the *definition* of the *thing*, and therefore (as is always the case in every *real* definition as contra-distinguished from a *verbal* definition), for at least a partial *solution* of the *fact*. Such as these form the *first* class.—The second class takes some one particular function of Life common to all living objects,—nutrition, for instance; or, to adopt the phrase most in vogue at present, assimilation, for the purposes of reproduction and growth. Now this, it is evident, can be an appropriate definition only of the very lowest species, as of a Fungus or a Mollusca; and just as comprehensive an idea of the mystery of Life, as a Mollusca might give, can this definition afford. But this is not the only objection. For, *first,* it is not pretended that we begin with seeking for an organ evidently appropriated to nutrition, and then infer that the substance in which such an organ is found *lives*. On the contrary, in a number of cases among the obscurer animals and vegetables we infer the organ from the pre-established fact of its life. *Secondly,* it identifies the process itself with a

certain range of its forms, those, namely, by which it is mani-
fested in animals and vegetables. For this, too, no less than the
former, presupposes the arbitrary division of all things into the
living and lifeless, on which, as I before observed, all these defini-
tions are grounded. But it is sorry logic to take the proof of an
affirmative in one thing as the proof of the negative in another.
All animals that have lungs breathe, but it would be a childish
oversight to deduce the converse, viz. all animals that breathe
have lungs. The theory in which the French chemists organized
the discoveries of Black, Cavendish, Priestley, Scheele, and other
English and German philosophers, is still, indeed, the reigning
theory, but rather, it should seem, from the absence of a rival
sufficiently popular to fill the throne in its stead, than from the
continuance of an implicit belief in its own stability. We no
longer at least cherish that intensity of faith which, before Davy
commenced his brilliant career, had not only identified it with
chemistry itself, but had substituted its nomenclature, even in
common conversation, for the far more philosophic language
which the human race had abstracted from the laboratory of
Nature. I may venture to prophesy that no future Beddoes will
make it the corrival of the mathematical sciences in demonstrative
evidence. I think it a matter of doubt whether, during the period
of its supposed infallibility, physiology derived more benefit from
the extension, or injury from the misdirection, of its views.
Enough of the latter is fresh in recollection to make it but an
equivocal compliment to a physiological position, that it must
stand or fall with the corpuscular philosophy, as modified by the
French theory of chemistry. Yet should it happen (and the event
is not impossible, nor the supposition altogether absurd), that
more and more decisive facts should present themselves in con-
firmation of the metamorphosis of elements, the position that life
consists in assimilation would either cease to be distinctive, or
fall back into the former class as an identical proposition, namely,
that Life, meaning by the word that sort of growth which takes
place by means of a peculiar organization, consists in that sort
of growth which is peculiar to organized life. *Thirdly,* the defini-
tion involves a still more egregious flaw in the reasoning, namely,
that of *cum hoc, ergo propter hoc* (or the assumption of causa-
tion from mere coexistence); and this, too, in its very worst form.
For it is not *cum hoc solo, ergo propter hoc,* which would in many
cases supply a presumptive proof by induction, but *cum hoc, et
plurimis aliis, ergo propter hoc!* Shell, of some kind or other, is
common to the whole order of testacea, but it would be absurd to
define the *vis vitæ* of testaceous animals as existing in the shell,

though we know it to be the constant accompaniment, and have every reason to believe the constant effect, of the specific life that acts in those animals. Were we (*argumenti causâ*) to imagine shell coextensive with the organized creation, this would produce no abatement in the falsity of the reasoning. Nor does the flaw stop here; for a physiological, that is, a real, definition, as distinguished from the verbal definitions of lexicography, must consist neither in any single property or function of the thing to be defined, nor yet in all collectively, which latter, indeed, would be a history, not a definition. It must consist, therefore, in the *law*, of the thing, or in such an *idea* of it, as being admitted, all the properties and functions are admitted by implication. It must likewise be so far *causal*, that a full insight having been obtained of the law, we derive from it a progressive insight into the necessity and *generation* of the phenomena of which it is the law. Suppose a disease in question, which appeared always accompanied with certain symptoms in certain stages, and with some one or more symptoms in all stages—say deranged digestion, capricious alternation of vivacity and languor, headache, dilated pupil, diminished sensibility to light, &c.—Neither the men who selected the one constant symptom, nor he who enumerated all the symptoms, would give the scientific definition *talem scilicet, quali scientia fit vel datur,* but the man who at once named and defined the disease hydrocephalus, producing pressure on the brain. For it is the essence of a scientific definition to be causative, not by introduction of imaginary somewhats, natural or supernatural, under the name of causes, but by announcing the law of action in the particular case, in subordination to the common law of which all the phenomena are modifications or results.

Now in the definition on which, as the representative of a whole class, we are *now* animadverting, a single effect is given as constituting the cause. For nutrition by digestion is certainly necessary to life, only under certain circumstances, but that life is previously necessary to digestion is absolutely certain under all circumstances. Besides, what other phenomenon of Life would the conception of assimilation, *per se,* or as it exists in the lowest order of animals, involve or explain? How, for instance, does it include sensation, locomotion, or habit? or if the two former should be taken as distinct from life, *toto genere,* and supervenient to it, we then ask what conception is given of *vital* assimilation as contra-distinguished from that of the nucleus of a crystal?

Lastly, this definition confounds the Law of Life, or the primary and universal form of vital agency, with the conception,

Animals. For the kind, it substitutes the representative of its degrees and modifications. But the first and most important office of science, physical, or physiological, is to contemplate the power in kind, abstracted from the degree. The ideas of caloric, whether as substance or property, and the conception of latent heat, the heat in ice, &c., that excite the wonder or the laughter of the vulgar, though susceptible of the most important practical applications, are the result of this abstraction; while the only purpose to which a definition like the preceding could become subservient, would be in supplying a nomenclature with the character of the most common species of a genus—its *genus generalissimum,* and even this would be useless in the present instance, inasmuch as it presupposes the knowledge of the things characterized.

The third class, and far superior to the two former, selects some property characteristic of all living bodies, not merely found in all *animals* alike, but existing equally in all parts of all living things, both animals and plants. Such, for instance, is the definition of Life, as consisting in anti-putrescence, or the power of resisting putrefaction. Like all the others, however, even this confines the idea of Life to those degrees or concentrations of it, which manifest themselves in organized beings, or rather in those the organization of which is apparent to us. Consequently, it substitutes an abstract term, or generalization of effects, for the idea, or superior form of causative agency. At best, it describes the *vis vitæ* by one only of its many influences. It is however, as we have said before, preferable to the former, because it is not, as they are, altogether unfruitful, inasmuch as it attests, less equivocally than any other sign, the presence or absence of that degree of the *vis vitæ* which is the necessary condition of organic or self-renewing power. It throws no light, however, on the law or principle of action; it does not increase our insight into the other phenomena; it presents to us no *inclusive* form, out of which the other forms may be developed, and finally, its defect as a definition may be detected by generalizing it into a higher formula, as a power which, during its continuance, resists or subordinates heterogeneous and adverse powers. Now this holds equally true of chemical relatively to the mechanical powers; and really affirms no more of Life than may be equally affirmed of every form of being, namely, that it tends to preserve itself, and resists, to a certain extent, whatever is incompatible with the laws that constitute its particular state for the time being. For it is not true only of the great divisions or classes into which we have found it expedient to distinguish, while we generalize, the powers acting in nature, as into intellectual, vital, chemical, mechanical; but it holds equally true of the degrees, or species of each of these genera relatively to each other: as in the decomposition of the alkalies by heat, or the galvanic spark. Like the combining power of Life, the copula here resists for awhile the attempts to dissolve it, and then yields, to reappear in new phenomena.

It is a wonderful property of the human mind, that when once a momentum has been given to it in a fresh direction, it pursues the new path with obstinate perseverance, in all conceivable bearings, to its utmost extremes. And by the startling consequences which arise out of these extremes, it is first awakened to its error, and either recalled to some former track, or receives some fresh impulse, which it follows with the same eagerness, and admits to the same monopoly. Thus in the 13th century the first science which roused the intellects of men from the torpor of barbarism, was, as in all countries ever has been, and ever must be the case, the science of *Metaphysics* and *Ontology*. We first seek what can be found at home, and what wonder if truths, that appeared to reveal the secret depths of our own souls, should take possession of the whole mind, and all truths appear trivial which could not either be evolved out of similar principles, by the same process, or at least brought under the same forms of thought, by perceived or imagined analogies? And so it was. For more than a century men continued to invoke the oracle of their own spirits, not only concerning its own forms and modes of being, but likewise concerning the laws of external nature. All attempts at philosophical explication were commenced by a mere effort of the understanding, as the power of abstraction; or by the imagination, transferring its own experiences to every object presented from without. By the former, a class of phenomena were in the first place abstracted, and fixed in some general term: of course this could designate only the impressions made by the outward objects, and so far, therefore, having been thus metamorphosed, they were effects of these objects; but then made to supply the place of their own causes, under the name of occult qualities. Thus the properties peculiar to gold, were abstracted from those it possessed in common with other bodies, and then generalized in the term *Aureity*: and the inquirer was instructed that the Essence of Gold, or the cause which constituted the peculiar modification of matter called gold, was the power of aureity. By the latter, *i.e.* by the imagination, thought and will were superadded to the occult quality, and every form of nature had its appropriate Spirit, to be controlled or conciliated by an appropriate ceremonial. This was entitled its SUBSTANTIAL FORM. Thus, physic became a sort of dull poetry, and the art of medicine (for physiology could scarcely be said to exist) was a system of magic, blended with traditional empiricism. Thus the forms of thought proceeded to act in their own emptiness, with no attempt to fill or substantiate them by the information of the senses, and all the branches of science formed so many sections of logic and metaphysics. And so it continued, even to the time that the Reformation sounded the second trumpet, and the authority of the schools sank with that of the hierarchy, under the intellectual courage and activity which this great revolution had inspired. Power, once awakened, cannot rest in one object. All the sciences partook of the new influences. The world of experimental philosophy was soon mapped out for posterity by the comprehensive and enterprising genius of Bacon, and the laws explained by which experiment could be dignified into experience.[2] But no sooner was the impulse given, than the same propensity was made manifest of looking at all things in the one point of view which chanced to be of predominant attraction. Our Gilbert, a man of genuine philosophical genius, had no sooner multiplied the facts of magnetism, and extended our knowledge concerning the property of magnetic bodies, but all things in heaven, and earth, and in the waters beneath the earth, were resolved into *magnetic* influences.

Shortly after a new light was struck by Harriott and Descartes, with their contemporaries, or immediate predecessors, and the restoration of ancient geometry, aided by the modern invention of algebra, placed the science of mechanism on the philosophic throne. How widely this domination spread, and how long it continued, if, indeed, even now it can be said to have abdicated its pretensions, the reader need not be reminded. The sublime discoveries of Newton, and, together with these, his not less fruitful than wonderful application, of the higher mathesis to the movements of the celestial bodies, and to the laws of light, gave almost a religious sanction to the corpuscular system and mechanical theory. It became synonymous with philosophy itself It was the sole portal at which truth was permitted to enter. The human body was treated of as an hydraulic machine, the operations of medicine were solved, and alas! even directed by reference partly to gravitation and the laws of motion, and partly by chemistry, which itself, however, as far as its theory was concerned, was but a branch of mechanics working exclusively by

[2] Experiment, as an organ of reason, not less distinguished from the blind or dreaming industry of the alchemists, than it was successfully opposed to the barren subtleties of the schoolmen.

imaginary wedges, angles, and spheres. Should the reader chance to put his hand on the 'Principles of Philosophy,' by La Forge, an immediate disciple of Descartes, he may see the phenomena of sleep solved in a copper-plate engraving, with all the figures into which the globules of the blood shaped themselves, and the results demonstrated by mathematical calculations. In short, from the time of Kepler[3] to that of Newton, and from Newton to Hartley, not only all things in external nature, but the subtlest mysteries of life and organization, and even of the intellect and moral being, were conjured within the magic circle of mathematical formulæ. And now a new light was struck by the discovery of electricity, and, in every sense of the word, both playful and serious, both for good and for evil, it may be affirmed to have electrified the whole frame of natural philosophy. Close on its heels followed the momentous discovery of the principal gases by Scheele and Priestley, the composition of water by Cavendish, and the doctrine of latent heat by Black. The scientific world was prepared for a new dynasty; accordingly, as soon as Lavoisier had reduced the infinite variety of chemical phenomena to the actions, reactions, and interchanges of a few elementary substances, or at least excited the expectation that this would speedily be effected, the hope shot up, almost instantly, into full faith, that it had been effected. Henceforward the new path, thus brilliantly opened, became the common road to all departments of knowledge: and, to this moment, it has been pursued with an eagerness and almost epidemic enthusiasm which, scarcely less than its political revolutions, characterize the spirit of the age. Many and inauspicious have been the invasions and inroads of this new conqueror into the rightful territories of other sciences; and strange alterations have been made in less harmless points than those of terminology, in homage to an art unsettled, in the very ferment of imperfect discoveries, and either without a theory, or with a theory maintained only by composition and compromise. Yet this very circumstance has favored its encroachments, by the gratifications which its novelty affords to our curiosity, and by the keener interest and higher excitement which an unsettled and revolutionary state is sure to inspire. He who supposes that science possesses an immunity from such influences knows little of human nature. How, otherwise, could men of strong minds and sound judgments have attempted to penetrate by the clue of chemical experiment, the

[3] Whose own mind, however, was not comprehended in the vortex; where Kepler erred it was in the other extreme.

secret recesses, the sacred adyta of organic life, without being aware that chemistry must needs be at its extreme limits, when it has approached the threshold of a higher power? Its own transgressions, however, and the failure of its enterprises will become the means of defining its absolute boundary, and we shall have to guard against the opposite error of rejecting its aid altogether as analogy, because we have repelled its ambitious claims to an identity with the vital powers.

Previously to the submitting my own ideas on the subject of life, and the powers into which it resolves itself, or rather in which it is manifested to *us,* I have hazarded this apparent digression from the anxiety to *preclude certain suspicions,* which the subject itself is so fitted to awaken, and while I anticipate the charges, to plead in answer to each a full and unequivocal —not guilty!

In the first place, therefore, I distinctly disclaim all intention of explaining life into an occult quality; and retort the charge on those who can satisfy themselves with defining it as the peculiar power by which death is resisted.

Secondly. Convinced—by revelation, by the consenting authority of all countries, and of all ages, by the imperative voice of my own conscience, and by that wide chasm between man and the noblest animals of the brute creation, which no perceivable or conceivable difference of organization is sufficient to overbridge—that I have a rational and responsible soul, I think far too reverentially of the same to degrade it into an hypothesis, and cannot be blind to the contradiction I must incur, if I assign that soul which I believe to constitute the peculiar nature of man as the cause of functions and properties, which man possesses in common with the oyster and the mushroom.[4]

Thirdly, while I disclaim the error of Stahl in deriving the phenomena of life from the unconscious actions of the rational soul, I repel with still greater earnestness the assertion and even

---

[4] But still less would I avail myself of its acknowledged inappropriateness to the purposes of physiology, in order to cast a self-complacent sneer on the soul itself, and on all who believe in its existence. First, because in my opinion it would be impertinent; secondly, because it would be imprudent and injurious to the character of my profession; and, lastly, because it would argue an irreverence to the feelings of mankind, which I deem scarcely compatible with a good heart, and a degree of arrogance and presumption which I have never found, except in company with a corrupt taste and a shallow capacity

the supposition that the functions are the offspring of the structure, and "Life[5] the result of organization," connected with it as effect with cause. Nay, the position seems to me little less strange, than as if a man should say, that building with all the included handicraft, of plastering, sawing, planing, &c. were the offspring of the house; and that the mason and carpenter were the result of a suite of chambers, with the passages and staircases that lead to them. To make A the offspring of B, when the very existence of B as B presupposes the existence of A, is preposterous in the *literal* sense of the word, and a consummate instance of the *hysteron proteron* in logic. But if I reject the organ as the *cause* of that, of which it is the organ, though I might admit it among the *conditions* of its actual functions; for the same reason I must reject *fluids* and *ethers* of all kinds, magnetical, electrical, and universal, to whatever quintessential thinness they may be treble distilled, and (as it were) super-substantiated. With these, I abjure likewise all *chemical* agencies, compositions, and decompositions, were it only that as stimulants they suppose a stimulability *sui generis*, which is but another paraphrase for life. Or if they are themselves at once both the excitant and the excitability, I miss the connecting link between this imaginary ether and the visible body, which then becomes no otherwise distinguished from inanimate matter, than by its juxtaposition in mere space, with an heterogeneous inmate, the cycle of whose actions revolves within itself. Besides which I should think that I was confounding metaphors and realities most absurdly, if I imagined that I had a greater insight into the meaning and possibility of a living alcohol, than of a living quicksilver. In short, visible SURFACE and *power* of any kind, much more the *power* of life, are ideas which the very forms of the human understanding make it impossible to identify. But whether the powers which manifest themselves to us under certain conditions in the forms of electricity, or chemical attraction, have any analogy to the power which manifests itself in growth and organization, is altogether a different question, and demands altogether a different chain of reasoning: if it be indeed a tree of knowledge, it will be known by its fruits, and these will depend not on the mere assertion, but on the inductions by which the position is supported, and by the additions which it makes to our insight into the nature of the facts it is meant to illustrate.

To *account* for Life is one thing: to explain Life another. In the first we are supposed to state something prior (if not in time,

---

[5] Vide Lawrence's Lecture.

yet in the order of Nature) to the thing accounted for, as the ground or cause of that thing, or (which comprises the meaning and force of both words) as its *sufficient cause, quæ et facit, et subest.* And to this, in the question of Life, I know no possible answer, but GOD. To account for a thing is to see into the principle of its possibility, and from that principle to evolve its being. Thus the mathematician demonstrates the truths of geometry by constructing them. It is an admirable remark of Joh. Bapt. a Vico, in a Tract published at Naples, 1710,[6] "Geometrica ideò demonstramus, quia facimus; physica si demonstrare possimus, faceremus. Metaphysici veri claritas eadem ac lucis, quam non nisi per opaca cognoscimus; nam non lucem sed lucidas res videmus. Physica sunt opaca, nempe formata et finita, in quibus Metaphysici veri lumen videmus." The reasoner who assigns structure or organization as the antecedent of Life, who names the former a cause, and the *latter* its effect, *he* it is who pretends to account for life. Now Euclid would, with great right, demand of such a philosopher to *make* Life; in the same sense, I mean, in which Euclid makes an Icosaedron, or a figure of twenty sides, namely, in the understanding or by an intellectual construction. An argument which, of itself, is sufficient to prove the untenable nature of Materialism.

To explain a power, on the other hand, is (the power itself being assumed, though not comprehended, *ut qui datur, non intelligitur*) to unfold or spread it out: *ex implicito planum facere.* In the present instance, such an explanation would consist in the reduction of the idea of Life to its simplest and most comprehensive form or mode of action; that is, to some characteristic *instinct* or *tendency,* evident in all its manifestations, and involved in the idea itself. This assumed as existing in *kind,* it will be required to present an ascending series of corresponding phenomena as involved *in,* proceeding *from,* and so far therefore explained *by,* the supposition of its progressive intensity and of the gradual enlargement of its sphere, the necessity of which again must be contained in the idea of the tendency itself. In other words, the tendency having been given in *kind,* it is required to render the phenomena intelligible as its different degrees and modifications. Still more perfect will the explanation be, should the necessity of this progression and of these ascending gradations be contained in the assumed idea of life, as thus defined by the general form and common purport of all its vari-

[6] Joh. Bapt. a Vico, Neapol. Reg. eloq. Professor, de antiquissima Itallorum sapientia ex lingua Latina originibus eruendâ: libri tres. Neap., 1710.

ous tendencies. This done, we have only to add the conditions common to all its phenomena, and those appropriate to each place and rank, in the scale of ascent, and then proceed to determine the primary and constitutive forms, *i.e.* the elementary powers in which this tendency realizes itself under different degrees and conditions.[7]

[7] The object I have proposed to myself, and wherein its distinction exists, may be thus illustrated. A complex machine is presented to the common view, the moving power of which is hidden. Of those who are studying and examining it, *one* man fixes his attention on some one application of that power, on certain effects produced by that particular application, and on a certain part of the structure evidently appropriated to the production of these effects, neither the one or other of which he had discovered in a neighboring machine, which he at the same time asserts to be quite distinct from the former, and to be moved by a power altogether different, though many of the works and operations are, he admits. common to both machines. In this supposed peculiarity he places the essential character of the former machine, and defines it by the presence of that which is, or which he supposes to be, absent in the latter. Supposing that a stranger to both were about to visit the two machines, this peculiarity would be so far useful as that it might enable him to distinguish the one from the other, and thus to look in the proper place for whatever else he had heard remarkable concerning either; not that he or his informant would understand the machine any better or otherwise, than the common character of a whole class in the nomenclature of botany would enable a person to understand all, or any one of the plants contained in that class. But if, on the other hand, the machine in question were such as no man was a stranger to, if even the supposed peculiarity, either by its effects, or by the construction of that portion of the works which produced them, were equally well known to all men, in this case we can conceive no use at all of such a definition; for at the best it could only be admitted as a definition for the purposes of nomenclature, which never adds to knowledge, although it may often facilitate its communication. But in this instance it would be nomenclature misplaced, and without an object. Such appears to me to be the case with all those definitions which place the essence of Life in nutrition, contractility, &c. As the second instance, I will take the inventor and maker of the machine himself, who knows its moving power, or perhaps himself constitutes it, who is, as it were, the soul of the work, and in whose mind all its parts, with all their bearings and relations, had pre-existed long before the machine itself had been put together. In him therefore there would reside, what it would be presumption to attempt to acquire, or to pretend to communicate, the most perfect insight not only of the machine itself, and of all its various operations, but of its ultimate principle and its essential causes. The mysterious ground, the efficient causes of vitality, and whether different lives differ absolutely or only in degree, He alone can know who not only said,

What is Life? Were such a question proposed, we should be tempted to answer, what is *not* Life that really *is?* Our reason convinces us that the quantities of things, taken abstractedly as quantity, exist only in the relations they bear to the percipient; in plainer words, they exist only in our minds, *ut quorum esse est percipi.* For if the definite quantities have a ground, and therefore a reality, in the external world, and independent of the mind that perceives them, this ground is *ipso facto* a quality; the very etymon of this word showing that a quality, not taken in its own nature but in relation to another thing, is to be defined *causa sufficiens, entia, de quibus loquimur; esse talia, qualia sunt.* Either the quantities perceived exist only in the perception, or they have likewise a real existence. In the former case, the quality (the word is here used in an active sense) that determines them belongs to Life, *per ipsam hypothesin;* and in the other case, since by the agreement of all parties Life may exist in other forms than those of consciousness, or even of sensibility, the *onus probandi* falls on those who assert of any quality that it is *not* Life. For the analogy of all that we know is clearly in favor of the contrary supposition, and if a man would analyze the meaning of his own words, and carefully distinguish his perceptions and sensations from the external cause exciting them, and at the same time from the quantity or superficies under which that cause is acting, he would instantly find himself, if we mistake not, involuntarily identifying the ideas of Quality and Life. Life, it is admitted on all hands, does not necessarily imply consciousness or sensibility; and we, for our parts, can not see that the irritability which metals manifest to galvanism, can be more remote

---

"Let the earth bring forth the living creature, the beast of the earth after his kind, and it was so;" but who said, "Let us make man in our image, who himself breathed into his nostrils the breath of Life, and *man* became a living soul."

The third case which I would apply to my own attempt would be that of the inquirer, who, presuming to know nothing of the power that moves the whole machine, takes those parts of it which are presented to his view, seeks to reduce its various movements to as few and simple laws of motion as possible, and out of their separate and conjoint action proceeds to explain and appropriate the structure and relative positions of the works. In obedience to the canon,—"Principia non esse multiplicanda præter summam necessitatem cui suffragamur non ideo quia causalem in mundo unitatem vel ratione vel experientiâ perspiciamus, sed illam ipsam indagamus impulsu intellectûs, qui tantundem sibi in explicatione phænomenorum profecisse videtur quantum ab eodem principio ad plurima rationata descendere ipsi concessum est."

from that which may be supposed to exist in the tribe of lichens, or in the helvellæ, pezizee, &c., than the latter is from the phenomena of excitability in the human body, whatever name it may be called by, or in whatever way it may modify itself.[8] That the mere act of growth does not constitute the idea of Life, or the absence of that act exclude it, we have a proof in every egg before it is placed under the hen, and in every grain of corn before it is put into the soil. All that could be deduced by fair reasoning would amount to this only, that the life of metals, as the power which affects and determines their comparative cohesion, ductility, &c., was yet lower on the scale than the Life which produces the first attempts of organization, in the almost shapeless tremella, or in such fungi as grow in the dark recesses of the mine.

If it were asked, to what purpose or with what view we should generalize the idea of Life thus broadly, I should not hesitate to reply that, were there no other use conceivable, there would be *some* advantage in merely destroying an arbitrary assumption in natural philosophy, and in reminding the physiologists that they could not hear the life of metals asserted with a more contemptuous surprise than they themselves incur from the vulgar, when they speak of the Life in mould or mucor. But this is not the case. This wider view not only precludes a groundless assumption, it likewise fills up the arbitrary chasm between physics and physiology, and justifies us in using the former as means of insight into the latter, which would be contrary to all sound rules of ratiocination if the powers working in the objects of the two sciences were absolutely and essentially diverse. For as to abstract the idea of *kind* from that of *degrees,* which are alone designated in the language of common use, is the first and indispensable step in philosophy, so are we the better enabled to form a notion of the *kind,* the lower the *degree* and the simpler the form is in which it appears to us. We study the complex in the simple; and only from the intuition of the lower can we safely proceed to the intellection of the higher degrees. The only danger lies in the leaping from low to high, with the neglect of the intervening gradations. But the same error would introduce discord into the gamut, *et ab abusu contra usum non valet consequentia.* That these degrees will themselves bring forth secondary kinds sufficiently distinct for all the purposes of science, and even for common sense, will be seen in the course of this inquisition: for this is one proof of the essential vitality of nature,

---

[8] The arborescent forms on a frosty morning, to be seen on the window and pavement, must have *some* relation to the more perfect forms developed in the vegetable world.

that she does not ascend as links in a suspended chain, but as the steps in a ladder; or rather she at one and the same time *ascends* as by a climax, and expands as the concentric circles on the lake from the point to which the stone in its fall had given the first impulse. At all events, a contemptuous rejection of this mode of reasoning would come with an ill grace from a medical philosopher, who cannot combine any three phenomena of health or of disease without the assumption of powers, which he is compelled to deduce without being able to demonstrate; nay, even of material substances as the *vehicles* of these powers, which he can never expect to exhibit before the senses.

From the preceding it should appear, that the most comprehensive formula to which life is reducible, would be that of the internal copula of bodies, or (if we may venture to borrow a phrase from the Platonic school) the *power* which discloses itself from within as a principle of *unity* in the *many*. But that there is a physiognomy in words, which, without reference to their fitness or necessity, make unfavorable as well as favorable impressions, and that every unusual term in an abstruse research incurs the risk of being denominated jargon, I should at the same time have borrowed a scholastic *term*, and defined life *absolutely*, as the principle of unity in *multeity*, as far as the former, the unity to wit, is produced *ab intra*; but *eminently* (*sensu eminenti*), I define life as *the principle of individuation*, or the power which unites a given *all* into a *whole* that is presupposed by all its parts. The link that combines the two, and acts throughout both, will, of course, be defined by the *tendency* to *individuation*. Thus, from its utmost *latency*, in which life is one with the elementary powers of mechanism, that is, with the powers of mechanism considered as qualitative and actually synthetic, to its highest manifestation (in which, as the *vis vitæ vivida*, or life *as* life, it subordinates and modifies these powers, becoming contradistinguished from mechanism,[9] *ab extra*, under the form of organization), there is an ascending series of intermediate classes, and of analogous gradations in each class. To a reflecting mind, indeed, the very fact that the powers peculiar to life in living animals *include* cohesion, elasticity, &c. (or, in the words of a late publication, "that living matter exhibits these physical properties,"[10]) would demonstrate that, in the truth of things, they

[9] Thus we may say that whatever is organized from without, is a product of mechanism; whatever is mechanized from within, is a production of organization.

[10] "The matter that surrounds us is divided into two great classes, living and dead; the latter is governed by physical laws, such as at-

are homogeneous, and that both the classes are but degrees and different dignities of one and the same tendency. For the latter are not subjected to the former as a lever, or walking-stick to the muscles; the more intense the life is, the less does *elasticity*, for instance, appear *as* elasticity. It sinks down into the nearest approach to its *physical* form by a series of degrees from the contraction and elongation of the irritable muscle to the physical hardness of the insensitive nail. The lower powers are *assimilated*, not merely *employed*, and assimilation presupposes the homogeneous nature of the thing assimilated; else it is a miracle, only not the same as that of a *creation*, because it would imply that additional and equal miracle of annihilation. In short, all the impossibilities which the acutest of the reformed Divines have detected in the hypothesis of transubstantiation would apply, *totidem verbis et syllabis*, to that of assimilation, if the objects and the agents were really heterogeneous. Unless, therefore, a thing can exhibit properties which do not belong to it, the very admission that living matter exhibits *physical* properties, includes the further admission, that those physical or dead properties are themselves vital in essence, really *distinct* but in appearance only *different*; or in absolute contrast with each other.

In all cases that which, *abstractly* taken, is the definition of the *kind*, will, when applied *absolutely*, or in its fullest sense, be the definition of the highest *degree* of that kind. If life, in general, be defined *vis ab intra, cujus proprium est coadunare plura in rem unicam, quantùm est res unica;* the unity will be more intense in proportion as it constitutes each particular thing a whole of itself; and yet more, again, in proportion to the number and interdependence of the parts, which it unites as a whole. But a whole composed, *ab intra*, of different parts, so far interdependent that each is reciprocally means and end, is an individual, and the individuality is most intense where the greatest dependence of the parts on the whole is combined with the greatest dependence of the whole on its parts; the first (namely, the dependence of the parts on the whole) being absolute; the second (namely, the dependence of the whole on its parts) being proportional to the importance of the relation which the parts have to the whole, that is, as their action extends more or less

---

traction, gravitation, chemical affinity; and it exhibits physical properties, such as cohesion, elasticity, divisibility, &c. Living matter also exhibits these properties, and is subject, in great measure, to physical laws. But living bodies are endowed moreover with a set of properties altogether different from these, and contrasting with them very remarkably." (Vide Lawrence's Lectures, p. 121.)

beyond themselves. For this spirit of the whole is most expressed in that part which derives its importance as an End from its importance as a Mean, relatively to all the parts under the same copula.

Finally, of individuals, the living power will be most intense in that individual which, as a whole, has the greatest number of integral parts presupposed in it; when, moreover, these integral parts, together with a proportional increase of their interdependence, as *parts*, have themselves most the character of wholes in the sphere occupied by them. A mathematical point, line, or surface, is an *ens rationis*, for it expresses an intellectual act; but a physical atom is *ens fictitium*, which may be made subservient, as ciphers are in arithmetic, to the purposes of hypothetical construction, *per regulam falsi;* but transferred to *Nature*, it is in the strictest sense an *absurd* quantity; for extension, and consequently divisibility, or *multeity*[11] (for space can not be divided), is the indispensable condition, under which alone any thing can *appear* to us, or even be *thought* of, as a *thing*. But if it should be replied, that the elementary particles are atoms not positively, but by such a hardness communicated to them as is relatively invincible, I should remind the asserter that *temeraria citatio supernaturalium est pulvinar intellectûs pigri*, and that he who requires me to believe a miracle of his own dreaming, must first work a miracle to convince me that he had dreamt by inspiration. Add too, the gross inconsistency of resorting to an immaterial influence in order to complete a system of materialism, by the exclusion of all modes of existence which the theorist cannot in imagination, at least, *finger* and *peer* at! Each of the preceding gradations, as above defined, might be represented as they exist, and are realized in Nature. But each would require a work for itself, co-extensive with the science of metals, and that of fossils (both as geologically applied); of crystallization; and of vegetable and animal physiology, in all its distinct branches. The nature of the present essay scarcely permits the space sufficient to illustrate our meaning. The proof of its probability (for to that only can we arrive by so partial an application of the hy-

---

[11] Much against my will I repeat this scholastic term, *multeity*, but I have sought in vain for an unequivocal word of a less repulsive character, that would convey the notion in a positive and not comparative sense in kind, as opposed to the *unum et simplex*, not in degree, as contracted with the *few*. We can conceive no reason that can be adduced in justification of the word *caloric*, as invented to distinguish the external cause of the sensation heat, which would not equally authorize the introduction of a technical term in this instance.

pothesis), is to be found in its powers of solving the particular class of phenomena, that form the subjects of the present inquisition, more satisfactorily and profitably than has been done, or even attempted before.

Exclusively, therefore, for the purposes of *illustration*, I would take as an instance of the first step, the metals, those, namely, that are capable of permanent reduction. For, by the established laws of nomenclature, the others (as sodium, potassium, calcium, silicium, &c.) would be entitled to a class of their own, under the name of *bases*. It is long since the chemists have despaired of decomposing this class of bodies. They still remain, one and all, as elements or simple bodies, though, on the principles of the corpuscularian philosophy, nothing can be more improbable than that they really are such; and no reason has or can be assigned on the grounds of that system, why, in no one instance, the contrary has not been proved. But this is at once explained, if we assume them as the simplest form of unity, namely, the unity of powers and properties. For these, it is evident, may be endlessly modified, but can never be decomposed. If I were asked by a philosopher who had previously extended the attribute of Life to the *Byssus speciosa*, and even to the crustaceous matter, or outward bones of a lobster, &c., whether the ingot of gold expressed *life*, I should answer without hesitation, as the *ingot* of gold assuredly not, for its form is accidental and *ab extra*. It may be added to or detracted from without in the least affecting the nature, state, or properties in the specific matter of which the ingot consists. But as *gold*, as that special union of absolute and of relative gravity, ductility, and hardness, which, wherever they are found, constitute *gold*, I should answer no less fearlessly, in the affirmative. But I should further add, that of the two counteracting tendencies of nature, namely, that of *detachment* from the universal life, which universality is represented to us by gravitation, and that of *attachment* or reduction into it, this and the other noble metals represented the units in which the latter tendency, namely, that of identity with the life of nature, subsisted in the greatest overbalance over the former. It is the form of unity with the least degree of tendency to individuation.

Rising in the ascent, I should take, as illustrative of the second step, the various forms of crystals as a union, not of powers only, but of parts, and as the simplest forms of composition in the next narrowest sphere of affinity. Here the form, or apparent *quantity*, is manifestly the result of the *quality*, and the chemist himself not seldom admits them as infallible characters of the substances united in the whole of a given crystal.

In the first step, we had Life, as the mere *unity* of powers; in the second we have the simplest forms of *totality* evolved. The third step is presented to us in those vast formations, the tracing of which generically would form the science of Geology, or its history in the strict sense of the word, even as their description and diagnostics constitute its preliminaries.

Their claim to this rank I cannot here even attempt to support. It will be sufficient to explain my reason for having assigned it to them, by the avowal, that I regard them in a twofold point of view: 1st, as the residue and product of vegetable and animal life; 2d, as manifesting the tendencies of the Life of Nature to vegetation or animalization. And this process I believe—in one instance by the peat morasses of the northern, and in the other instance by the coral banks of the southern hemisphere—to be still connected with the present order of vegetable and animal Life, which constitutes the fourth and last step in these wide and comprehensive divisions.

In the lowest forms of the vegetable and animal world we perceive totality dawning into *individuation,* while in man, as the highest of the class, the individuality is not only perfected in its corporeal sense, but begins a new series beyond the appropriate limits of physiology. The tendency to individuation, more or less obscure, more or less obvious, constitutes the common character of all classes, as far as they maintain for themselves a distinction from the universal life of the planet; while the degrees, both of intensity and extension, to which this tendency is realized, form the species, and their ranks in the great scale of ascent and expansion.

In the treatment of a subject so vast and complex, within the limits prescribed for an essay like the present, where it is impossible not to say either too much or too little (and too much because too little), an author is entitled to make large claims on the candor of his judges. Many things he must express inaccurately, not from ignorance or oversight, but because the more precise expression would have involved the necessity of a further explanation, and this another, even to the first elements of the science This is an inconvenience which presses on the analytic method, on however large a scale it may be conducted, compared with the synthetic; and it must bear with a tenfold weight in the present instance, where we are not permitted to avail ourselves of its usual advantages as a counterbalance to its inherent defects. I shall have done all that I dared propose to myself, or that can be justly demanded of me by others, if I have succeeded in conveying a sufficiently clear, though indistinct and inadequate notion, so as of its many results to render intelligible that one which I am to apply to my particular subject, not as a truth already demonstrated, but as an hypothesis, which pretends to no higher merit than that of explaining the particular class of phenomena to which it is applied, and ask no other reward than a presumption in favor of the general system of which it affirms itself to be a dependent though integral part. By Life I everywhere mean the true Idea of Life, or that most general form under which Life manifests itself to us, which includes all its other forms. This I have stated to be the *tendency to individuation,* and the degrees or intensities of Life to consist in the progressive realization of this tendency. The power which is ackowledged to exist, wherever the realization is found, must subsist wherever the tendency is manifested. The power which comes forth and stirs abroad in the bird, must be latent in the egg. I have shown, moreover, that this tendency to individuate can not be conceived without the opposite tendency to connect, even as the centrifugal power supposes the centripetal, or as the two opposite poles constitute each other, and are the constituent acts of one and the same power in the magnet. We might say that the life of the magnet subsists in their union, but that it lives (acts or manifests itself) in their strife. Again, if the tendency be at once to individuate and to connect, to detach, but so as either to retain or to reproduce attachment, the individuation itself must be a tendency to the ultimate production of the highest and most comprehensive individuality. This must be the one great end of Nature, her ultimate production of the highest and most comprehensive individuality. This must be the one great end of Nature, her ultimate object, or by whatever other word we may designate that something which bears to a final cause the same relation that Nature herself bears to the Supreme Intelligence.

According to the plan I have prescribed for this inquisition, we are now to seek for the highest law, or most general form, under which this tendency acts, and then to pursue the same process with this, as we have already done with the tendency itself, namely, having stated the law in its highest abstraction, to present it in the different forms in which it appears and reappears in higher and higher dignities. I restate the question. The tendency having been ascertained, what is its most general law? I answer—*polarity,* or the essential dualism of Nature, arising out of its productive unity, and still tending to reaffirm it, either as equilibrium, indifference, or identity. In its *productive* power, of which the product is the only measure, consists its incompatibility with mathematical calculus. For the full applicability of an abstract science ceases, the moment reality begins.[12] Life, then, we consider as the copula, or the unity of thesis and antithesis, position and counterposition,—Life itself being the positive of both; as, on the other hand, the two counterpoints are the nec-

---

[12] For abstractions are the conditions and only subject of all abstract sciences. Thus the theorist (vide Dalton's Theory), who reduces the chemical process to the positions of atoms, would doubtless thereby render chemistry calculable, but that he commences by destroying the chemical process itself, and substitutes for it a *mote dance* of abstractions; for even the powers which he appears to leave real, those of attraction and repulsion, he immediately unrealizes by representing them as diverse and separable properties. We can abstract the quantities and the quantitative motion from masses, passing over or leaving for other sciences the question of what constitutes the masses, and thus apply not to the masses themselves, but to the abstractions therefrom,—the laws of geometry and universal arithmetic. And where the quantities are the infallible signs of real powers, and our chief concern with the masses is as SIGNS, sciences may be founded thereon of the highest use and dignity. Such, for instance, is the sublime science of astronomy, having for its objects the vast masses which "God placed in the firmament of the heaven to be for *signs* and for seasons, for days and years." For the whole doctrine of physics may be reduced to three great divisions: First, *quantitative motion*, which is proportioned to the quantity of matter exclusively. This is the science of weight or statics. Secondly, *relative motion*, as communicated to bodies externally by impact. This is the science of mechanics. Thirdly, *qualitative motion*, or that which is accordant to properties of matter. And this is chemistry. Now it is evident that the first two sciences presuppose that which forms the exclusive object of the third, namely, quality; for all quantity in nature is either itself derived, or at least derives its powers from some *quality*, as that of weight, specific cohesion, hardness, &c.; and therefore the attempt to reduce to the distances or impacts of atoms, under the assumptions of two powers, which are themselves declared to be no more than mere general terms for those quantities of motion and impact (the atom itself being a fiction formed by abstraction, and in truth a third occult quality for the purpose of explaining hardness and density), amounts to an attempt to destroy chemistry itself, and at the same time to exclude the sole reality and only positive contents of the very science into which that of chemistry is to be degraded. Now what qualities are to chemistry, *productiveness* is to the science of Life; and this being excluded, physiology or zoonomy would sink into chemistry, chemistry by the same process into mechanics, while mechanics themselves would lose the substantial principle, which, bending the lower extreme towards its apex, produces the organic circle of the sciences, and elevates them all into different arcs or stations of the one absolute science of Life.

essary conditions of the *manifestations* of Life. These, by the same necessity, unite in a synthesis; which again, by the law of dualism, essential to all actual existence, expands, or *produces* itself, from the point into the *line*, in order again to converge, as the initiation of the same productive process in some intenser form of reality. Thus, in the identity of the two counter-powers, Life *sub*sists; in their strife it *con*sists: and in their reconciliation it at once dies and is born again into a new form, either falling back into the life of the whole, or starting anew in the process of individuation.

Whence shall we take our beginning? From Space, *istud litigium philosophorum*, which leaves the mind equally dissatisfied, whether we deny or assert its real existence. To make it wholly ideal, would be at the same time to idealize all phenomena, and to undermine the very conception of an external world. To make it real, would be to assert the existence of something, with the properties of nothing. It would far transcend the height to which a physiologist must confine his flights, should we attempt to reconcile this apparent contradiction. It is the duty and the privilege of the theologian to demonstrate, that *space* is the ideal organ by which the soul of man perceives the *omnipresence* of the Supreme Reality, as distinct from the works, which in him move, and live, and have their being; while the equal mystery of *Time* bears the same relation to his *Eternity*, or what is fully equivalent, his Unity.

Physiologically contemplated, Nature begins, proceeds, and ends in a contradiction; for the moment of absolute solution would be that in which Nature would cease to be Nature, *i.e.* a scheme of ever-varying relations; and physiology, in the ambitious attempt to solve phenomena into absolute realities, would itself become a mere web of verbal abstractions.

But it is in strict connection with our subject, that we should make the universal FORMS as well as the not less universal LAW of Life, clear and intelligible in the example of *Time* and *Space*, these being both the first specification of the principle, and ever after its indispensable symbols. First, a single act of self-inquiry will show the impossibility of distinctly conceiving the one without some involution of the other; either time expressed in space, in the form of the mathematical line, or space within time, as in the circle. But to form the first conception of a *real* thing,

---

This explanation, which in appearance only is a digression, was indispensably requisite to prevent the idea of polarity, which has been given as the universal law of Life, from being misunderstood as a mere refinement on those mechanical systems of physiology, which it has been my main object to explode.

we state both as one in the idea, *duration*. The formula is: $\widehat{A = B + B = A.} = \widehat{A = A}$, or the oneness of space and time, is the predicate of all *real* being.

But as little can we conceive the oneness, except as the mid-point producing itself on each side; that is, manifesting itself on two opposite poles. Thus, from identity we derive duality, and from both together we obtain polarity, synthesis, indifference, predominance. The line is Time + Space, under the predominance of Time: Surface is Space + Time, under the predominance of Space, while Line + Surface as the synthesis of units, is the circle in the first dignity; to the sphere in the second; and to the globe in the third. In short, neither can the antagonists appear but as two forces of one power, nor can the power be conceived by us but as the equatorial point of the two counteracting forces; of which the *hypomochlion* of the lever is as good an illustration as any thing can be that is thought of *mechanically* only, and exclusively of life. To make it adequate, we must substitute the idea of positive production for that of rest, or mere neutralization. To the fancy alone it is the null-point, or zero, but to the reason it is the *punctum saliens*, and the power itself in its eminence. Even in these, the most abstract and universal forms of all thought and perception—even in the ideas of time and space, we slip under them, as it were, a *substratum;* for we can not think of them but as far as they are co-inherent, and therefore as reciprocally the measures of each other. Nor, again, can we finish the process without having the idea of *motion* as its immediate product. Thus we say, that time has one dimension, and imagine it to ourselves as a line. But the line we have already proved to be the productive synthesis of time, with space under the predominance of time. If we exclude space by an abstract assumption, the time remains as a spaceless point, and represents the concentered power of unity and active negation, *i.e.* retraction, determination, and limit, *ab intra*. But if we assume the time as excluded, the line vanishes, and we leave space dimensionless, and indistinguishable ALL, and therefore the representative of absolute weakness and formlessness, but, for that very reason, of infinite capacity and formability.

We have been thus full and express on this subject, because these simple ideas of time, space, and motion; of length, breadth, and depth, are not only the simplest and universal, but the necessary symbols of all philosophic construction. They will be found the primary factors and elementary forms of every calculus and of every diagram in the algebra and geometry of a scientific physiology. Accordingly, we shall recognize the same forms under other names; but at each return more specific and intense; and the whole process repeated with ascending gradations of reality, *exempli gratiâ:* Time + space = motion; Tm + space = line + breadth = depth; depth + motion = force; Lf + Bf = Df; LDf + BDf = attraction + repulsion = gravitation; and so on, even till they pass into outward phenomena, and form the intermediate link between productive powers and fixed products in light, heat, and electricity. If we pass to the construction of matter, we find it as the product, or *tertium aliud,* of antagonist powers of repulsion and attraction. Remove these powers, and the conception of matter vanishes into space—conceive repulsion only, and you have the same result. For infinite repulsion, uncounteracted and alone, is tantamount to infinite, dimensionless diffusion, and this again to infinite weakness; viz., to space. Conceive attraction alone, and as an infinite contraction, its product amounts to the absolute point, viz., to time. Conceive the synthesis of both, and you have matter as a fluxional antecedent, which, in the very act of formation, passes into body by its gravity, and yet in all bodies it still remains as their mass, which, being exclusively calculable under the law of gravitation, gives rise, as we before observed, to the science of statics, most improperly called celestial mechanics.

In strict consistence with the same philosophy which, instead of considering the powers of bodies to have been miraculously stuck into a prepared and pre-existing matter, as pins into a pincushion, conceives the powers as the productive factors, and the body or phenomenon as the fact, product, or fixture; we revert again to potentiated length in the power of magnetism; to surface in the power of electricity; and to the synthesis of both, or potentiated depth, in constructive, that is, chemical affinity. But while the two factors are as poles to each other, each factor has likewise its own poles, and thus in the simple cross—

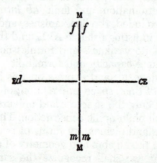

M M being the magnetic line, with ff its northern pole, or pole of attraction; and mm its south, or pole of repulsion, E E one of the lines that spring from each point of M M, with its east, or pole of contraction, and d its west, or pole of diffluence and expansion—we have presented to us the universal quadruplicity, or four elemental forms of power; in the endless proportions and modifications of which, the innumerable offspring of all-bearing Nature consist. Wisely docile to the suggestions of Nature herself, the ancients significantly expressed these forces under the names of earth, water, air, and fire; not meaning any tangible or visible substance so generalized, but the powers predominant, and, as it were, the living basis of each, which no chemical decomposition can ever present to the senses, were it only that their interpenetration and co-inherence first constitutes them sensible, and is the condition and meaning of a—*thing*. Already our more truly philosophical naturalists (Ritter, for instance) have begun to generalize the four great elements of chemical nomenclature, carbon, azote, oxygen, and hydrogen: the two former as the positive and negative pole of the magnetic axis, or as the power of fixity and mobility; and the two latter as the opposite poles, or plus and minus states of cosmical electricity, as the powers of contraction and dilatation, or of comburence and combustibility. These powers are to each other as longitude to latitude, and the poles of each relatively as north to south, and as east to west. For surely the reader will find no distrust in a system only because Nature, ever consistent with herself, presents us everywhere with harmonious and accordant symbols of her consistent doctrines. Nothing would be more easy than, by the ordinary principles of sound logic and common sense, to demonstrate the impossibility and expose the absurdity of the corpuscularian or mechanic system, or than to prove the untenable nature of any intermediate system. But we can not force any man into an insight or intuitive possession of the true philosophy, because we can not give him abstraction, intellectual intuition, or constructive imagination; because we can not organize for him an eye that can see, an ear that can listen to, or a heart that can feel, the harmonies of Nature, or recognize in her endless forms, the thousandfold realization of those simple and majestic laws, which yet in their absoluteness can be discovered only in the recesses of his own spirit,—not by that man, therefore, whose imaginative powers have been *ossified* by the continual reaction and assimilating influences of mere *objects* on his mind, and who is a prisoner to his own eye and its reflex, the passive fancy!—not by him in whom an unbroken familiarity with the organic world, as if it were mechanical, with the sensitive, but as if it were insensate, has engendered the coarse and hard spirit of a sorcerer. The former is unable, the latter unwilling, to master the absolute prerequisites. There is neither hope nor occasion for him "to cudgel his brains about it, he has no feeling of the business." If he do not see the necessity from without, if he have not learned the possibility from within, of interpenetration, of total intussusception, of the existence of all in each as the condition of Nature's unity and substantiality, and of the latency under the predominance of some one power, wherein subsists her life and its endless variety, as he must be, by habitual slavery to the eye, or its reflex, the passive fancy, under the influences of the corpuscularian philosophy, he has so paralyzed his imaginative powers as to be unable—or by that hardness and heart-hardening spirit of contempt, which is sure to result from a perpetual commune with the lifeless, he has so far debased his inward being—as to be unwilling to comprehend the prerequisite, he must be content, while standing thus at the threshold of philosophy, to receive the results, though he can not be admitted to the deliberation—in other words, to act upon *rules* which he is incapable of understanding as LAWS, and to reap the harvest with the sharpened iron for which others have delved for him in the mine.

It is not improbable that there may exist, and even be discovered, higher forms and more akin to Life than those of magnetism, electricity, and constructive (or chemical) affinity appear to be, even in their finest known influences. It is not improbable that we may hereafter find ourselves justified in revoking certain of the latter, and unappropriating them to a yet unnamed triplicity; or that, being thus assisted, we may obtain a qualitative instead of a quantitative insight into vegetable animation, as distinct from animal, and that of the insect world from both. But in the present state of science, the magnetic, electric, and chemical powers are the last and highest of inorganic nature. These, therefore, we assume as presenting themselves again to us, in their next metamorphosis, as reproduction (*i.e.* growth and identity of the whole, amid the change or flux of all the parts), irritability and sensibility; reproduction corresponding to magnetism, irritability to electricity, and sensibility to constructive chemical affinity.

But before we proceed further, it behooves us to answer the objections contained in the following passage, or withdraw ourselves in time from the bitter contempt in which it would involve us. Acting under such a necessity, we need not apologize for the length of the quotation.

1. "If," says Mr. Lawrence, "the properties of living matter are to be explained in this way, why should not we adopt the same plan with physical properties, and account for gravitation, or chemical affinity, by the supposition of appropriate subtle fluids? Why does the irritability of a muscle need such an explanation, if explanation it can be called, more than the elective attraction of a salt?"

2. "To make the matter more intelligible, this vital principle is compared to magnetism, to electricity, and to galvanism; or it is roundly stated to be oxygen. 'Tis like a camel, or like a whale, or like what you please."

3. "You have only to grant that the phenomena of the sciences just alluded to depend on extremely fine and invisible fluids, superadded to the matters in which they are exhibited, and to allow further that Life, and magnetic, galvanic, and electric phenomena correspond perfectly; the existence of a subtile matter of Life will then be a very probable inference."

4. "On this illustration you will naturally remark, that the existence of the magnetic, electric, and galvanic fluids, which is offered as a proof of the existence of a vital fluid, is as much a matter of doubt as that of the vital fluid itself."

5. "It is singular, also, that the vital principle should be like both magnetism and electricity, when these two are not like each other."

6. "It would have been interesting to have had this illustration prosecuted a little further. We should have been pleased to learn whether the human body is more like a loadstone, a voltaic pile, or an electrical machine; whether the organs are to be regarded as Leyden jars, magnetic needles, or batteries."

7. "The truth is, there is no resemblance, no analogy, between Electricity and Life; the two orders of phenomena are completely distinct; they are incommensurable. Electricity illustrates life no more than life illustrates electricity." [13]

---

[13] I apprehend that by men of a certain school it would be deemed no demerit, even though they should never have condescended to look into any system of Aristotelian logic. It is enough for these gentlemen that they are experimentalists! Let it not, however, be supposed that they make more experiments than their neighbors, who consider induction as a means and not an end; or have stronger motives for making them, unless it can be believed that Tycho Brähe must have been urged to repeat his sweeps of the heavens with greater accuracy and

To avoid unnecessary description, I shall refer to the passages by the numbers affixed to them, for that purpose, in the margin.

In reply to No. 1, I ask whether, in the nature of the mind, illustration and explanation must not of necessity proceed from the lower to the higher? or whether a boy is to be taught his addition, subtraction, multiplication, and division, by the highest branches of algebraic analysis? Is there any better way of systematic teaching, than that of illustrating each new step, or having each new step illustrated to him by its identity in kind with the step the next below it? though it be the only mode in which this objection can be answered, yet it seems affronting to remind the objector, of rules so simple as that the complex must even be illustrated by the more simple, or the less scrutible by that which is more subject to our examination.

In reply to No. 2, I first refer to the author's eulogy on Mr. Hunter, p. 163, in which he is justly extolled for having "surveyed the whole *system* of organized beings, from plants to man:" of course, therefore, *as a system;* and therefore under some *one common law.* Now in the very same sense, and no other, than that in which the writer himself by implication compares himself as a man to the *dermestes typographicus,* or the *fucus scorpioides,* do I compare the principle of Life to magnetism, electricity, and constructive affinity,—or rather to that power to which the two former are the thesis and antithesis, the latter the synthesis. But if to compare involve the sense of its etymon, and involve the sense of parity, I utterly deny that I do at all compare them; and, in truth, in no conceivable sense of the word is it applicable, any more than a geometrician can be affirmed to compare a polygon to a point, because he generates the line out of the point. The writer attributes to a philosophy essentially vital the barrenness of the mechanic system, with which alone

---

industry than Herschel, for no better reason than that the former flourished before the theory of gravitation was perfected. No, but they have the honor of being mere experimentalists! If, however, we may not refer to logic, we may to common sense and common experience. It is not improbable, however, that they have both read and studied a book of hypothetical psychology on the assumptions of the crudest materialism, stolen too without acknowledgment from our David Hartley's Essay on Man, which is well known under the whimsical name of Condillac's Logic. But, as Mr. Brand has lately observed, "The French are a queer people," and we should not be at all surprised to hear of a book of fresh importation from Paris, on determinate proportions in chemistry, announced by the author in his title-page as a new and improved system either of arithmetic or geometry.

his imagination has been familiarized, and which, as hath been justly observed by a contemporary writer, is contra-distinguished from the former principally in this respect; that demanding for every mode and act of existence real or possible visibility, it knows only of distance and nearness, composition (or rather compaction) and decomposition, in short, the relations of unproductive particles to each other; so that in every instance the result is the exact sum of the component qualities, as in arithmetical addition. This is the philosophy of Death, and only of a dead nature can it hold good. In Life, and in the view of a vital philosophy, the two component counter-powers actually interpenetrate each other, and generate a higher third, including both the former, "ita tamen ut sit alia et major."

As a complete answer to No. 3, I refer the reader to many passages in the preceding and following pages, in which, on far higher and more demonstrative grounds than the mechanic system can furnish, I have exposed the unmeaningness and absurdity of these finer fluids, as applied even to electricity itself; unless, indeed, they are assumed as its product. But in addition I beg leave to remind the author, that it is incomparably more agreeable to all experience to originate the formative process in the *fluid*, whether fine or gross, than in corporeal *atoms*, in which we are not only deserted by all experience, but contradicted by the primary conception of body itself.

Equally inapplicable is No. 4: and of No. 5 I can only repeat, first, that I do not make Life *like* magnetism, or *like* electricity; that the difference between magnetism and electricity, and the powers illustrated by them, is an essential part of my system, but that the animal Life of man is the identity of all three. To whatever other system this objection may apply, it is utterly irrelevant to that which I have here propounded: though from the narrow limits prescribed to me, it has been propounded with an inadequacy painful to my own feelings.

The ridicule in No. 6 might be easily retorted; but as it could prove nothing, I will leave it where I found it, in a page where nothing is proved.

A similar remark might be sufficient for the bold and blank assertion (No. 7) with which the extract concludes; but that I feel some curiosity to discover what meaning the author attaches to the term analogy. Analogy implies a difference in sort, and not merely in degree; and it is the sameness of the end, with the difference of the means, which constitutes analogy. No one would say the lungs of a man were analogous to the lungs of a monkey, but any one might say that the gills of fish and the spiracula of insects are analogous to lungs. Now if there be any philosophers who have asserted that electricity as electricity is the *same* as Life, for that reason they can not be *analogous* to each other; and as no man in his senses, philosopher or not, is capable of imagining that the lightning which destroys a sheep, was a means to the same end with the principle of its organization; for this reason, too, the two powers can not be represented as analogous. Indeed I know of no system in which the word, as thus applied, would admit of an endurable meaning, but that which teaches us, that a mass of marrow in the skull is analogous to the rational soul, which Plato and Bacon, equally with the "poor Indian," believe themselves to have received from the Supreme Reason.

It would be blindness not to see, or affectation to pretend not to see, the work at which these sarcasms were levelled. The author of that work is abundantly able to defend his own opinions; yet I should be ambitious to address *him* at the close of the contest in the lines of the great Roman poet:

> "Et nos tela, Pater, ferrumque haud debile dextrâ
> Spargimus, et nostro sequitur, de vulnere sanguis."

In Mr. Abernethy's Lecture on the Theory of Life, it is impossible not to see a presentiment of a great truth. He has, if I may so express myself, caught it in the breeze: and we seem to hear the first glad opening and shout with which he springs forward to the pursuit. But it is equally evident that the prey has not been followed through its doublings and windings, or driven out from its brakes and covers into full and open view. Many of the least tenable phrases may be fairly interpreted as illustrations, rather than precise exponents of the author's meaning; at least, while they remain as a mere suggestion or annunciation of his ideas, and till he has expanded them over a larger sphere, it would be unjust to infer the contrary. But it is not with men, however strongly their professional merits may entitle them to reverence, that my concern is at present. If the opinions here supported are the same with those of Mr. Abernethy, I rejoice in his authority. If they are different, I shall wait with an anxious interest for an exposition of that difference.

Having reasserted that I no more confound magnetism with electricity, or the chemical process, than the mathematician confounds length with breadth, or either with depth; I think it sufficient to add that there are two views of the subject, the former of which I do not believe attributable to any philosopher, while both are alike disclaimed by me as forming any part of my views.

The first is that which is supposed to consider electricity identical with life, as it subsists in organized bodies. The other considers electricity as everywhere present, and penetrating all bodies under the image of a subtile fluid or substance, which, in Mr. Abernethy's inquiry, I regard as little morē than a mere diagram on his slate, for the purpose of fixing the attention on the intellectual conception, or as a possible *product* (in which case electricity must be a composite power), or at worst, as words *quæ humana incuria fudit*. This which, in inanimate Nature, is manifested now as magnetism, now as electricity, and now as chemical agency, is supposed, on entering an organized body, to constitute its vital *principle,* something in the same manner as the steam becomes the *mechanic* power of the steam-engine, in *consequence* of its compression by the steam-engine; or as the breeze that murmurs indistinguishably in the forest becomes the element, the substratum, of melody in the Æolian harp, and of consummate harmony in the organ. Now this hypothesis is as directly opposed to my view as supervention is to evolution, inasmuch as I hold the organized body itself, in all its marvellous contexture, to be the PRODUCT and representant of the power which is here supposed to have supervened to it. So far from admitting a *transfer,* I do not admit it even in electricity itself, or in the phenomena universally called electrical; among other points I ground my explanation of remote sympathy on the directly contrary supposition.

But my opinions will be best explained by a rapid exemplification in the processes of Nature, from the first rudiments of individualized life in the lowest classes of its two great poles, the vegetable and animal creation, to its crown and consummation in the human body; thus illustrating at once the unceasing *polarity of life, as the form of its process, and its tendency to progressive individuation as the law of its direction.*

Among the conceptions, of the mere ideal character of which the philosopher is well aware, and which yet become necessary from the necessity of assuming a beginning; the original fluidity of the planet is the chief. Under some form or other it is expressed or implied in every system of cosmogony and even of geology, from Moses to Thales, and from Thales to Werner. This assumption originates in the same law of mind that gave rise to the *prima materia* of the Peripatetic school. In order to *comprehend* and *explain* the *forms* of things, we must imagine a state *antecedent* to form. A chaos of heterogeneous substances, such as our Milton has described, is not only an *impossible* state (for this may be equally true of every other attempt), but it is *palpably* impossible. It presupposes, moreover, the thing it is intended to solve; and makes *that* an *effect* which had been called in as the explanatory *cause.* The requisite and only serviceable fiction, therefore, is the representation of CHAOS as one vast homogeneous drop! In this sense it may be even justified, as an appropriate symbol of the great fundamental truth that all things spring from, and subsist in, the endless strife between indifference and difference. The whole history of Nature is comprised in the specification of the transitional states from the one to the other. The symbol only is fictitious: the thing signified is not only grounded in truth—it is the law and actuating principle of all other truths, whether physical or intellectual.

Now, by magnetism in its widest sense, I mean the first and simplest *differential* act of Nature, as the power which works in *length,* and produces the first distinction between the indistinguishable by the generation of a *line.* Relatively, therefore, to fluidity, that is, to matter, the parts of which can not be distinguished from each other by figure, magnetism is the power of fixity; but, relatively to itself, magnetism, like every other power in Nature, is designated by its opposite poles, and must be represented as the magnetic axis, the northern pole of which signifies rest, attraction, fixity, coherence, or hardness; the element of EARTH in the nomenclature of *observation* and the CARBONIC principle in that of *experiment;* while the southern pole, as its antithesis, represents mobility, repulsion, incoherence, and fusibility; the element of air in the nomenclature of observation (that is, of Nature as it appears to us when unquestioned by art), and azote or nitrogen in the nomenclature of experiment (that is, of Nature in the state so beautifully allegorized in the Homeric fable of Proteus bound down, and forced to answer by Ulysses, after having been pursued through all his metamorphoses into his ultimate form[14]). That nothing real does or can exist corresponding to either pole *exclusively,* is involved in the very definition of a THING as the synthesis of opposing energies. That a thing *is,* is owing to the co-inherence therein of any two powers; but that it is *that* particular thing arises from the proportions in which these powers are co-present, either as predominance or as reciprocal neutralization; but under the modification of twofold power to which magnetism itself is, as the thesis to its antithesis.

[14] Such is the interpretation given by Lord Bacon. To which of the two gigantic intellects, the poet's or philosophic commentator's, the allegory belongs, I shall not presume to decide. Its extraordinary beauty and appropriateness remains the same in either case.

The correspondent, in the world of the senses, to the magnetic axis, exists in the series of metals. The metalleity, as the universal base of the planet, is a necessary deduction from the principles of the system. From the infusible, though evaporable, diamond to nitrogen itself, the metallic nature of which has been long suspected by chemists, though still under the mistaken notion of an oxyde, we trace a series of metals from the maximum of coherence to positive fluidity, in all ordinary temperatures, we mean. Though, in point of fact, cold itself is but a superinduction of the one pole, or, what amounts to the same thing, the subtraction of the other, under the modifications afore described; and therefore are the metals indecomposible, because they are themselves the decompositions of the metallic axis, in all its degrees of longitude and latitude. Thus the substance of the planet from which it *is*, is metallic; while that which is ever *becoming*, is in like manner produced through the perpetual modification of the first by the opposite forces of the second; that is, by the principle of contraction and difference at the eastern extreme—the element of fire, or the oxygen of the chemists; and by the elementary power of dilatation, or universality at its western extreme—the ὕδωρ ἐν ὕδατι of the ancients, and the hydrogen of the laboratory.

It has been before noticed that the progress of Nature is more truly represented by the ladder, than by the suspended chain, and that she expands as by concentric circles. This is, indeed, involved in the very conception of individuation, whether it be applied to the different species or to the individuals. In what manner the evident interspace is reconciled with the equally evident continuity of the life of Nature, is a problem that can be solved by those minds alone, which have intuitively learnt that the whole *actual* life of Nature originates in the existence, and consists in the perpetual reconciliation, and as perpetual resurgency of the primary contradiction, of which universal polarity is the result and the exponent. From the first moment of the differential impulse—(the primæval chemical epoch of the Wernerian school)—when Nature, by the tranquil deposition of crystals, prepared, as it were, the fulcrum of her after-efforts, from this, her first, and in part *irrevocable*, self-contraction, we find, in each ensuing production, more and more tendency to independent existence in the increasing multitude of strata, and in the relics of the lowest orders, first of vegetable and then of animal life. In the schistous formations, which we must here assume as in great measure the residue of vegetable creations, that have sunk back into the universal life, and in the later predominant calcareous masses, which are the *caput mortuum* of animalized existence, we ascend from the laws of attraction and repulsion, as united in gravity, to magnetism, electricity, and constructive power, till we arrive at the point representative of a new and far higher intensity. For from this point flow, as in opposite directions, the two streams of vegetation and animalization, the former characterized by the predominance of magnetism in its highest power, as reproduction, the other by electricity intensified—as irritability, in like manner. The vegetable and animal world are the thesis and antithesis, or the opposite poles of organic life. We are not, therefore, to seek in either for analogies to the other, but for counterpoints. On the same account, the nearer the common source, the greater the likeness; the farther the remove, the greater the opposition. At the extreme limits of inorganic Nature, we may detect a dim and obscure prophecy of her ensuing process in the twigs and rude semblances that occur in crystallization of some of the copper ores, and in the well-known *arbor Dianæ*, and *arbor Veneris*. These latter Ritter has already ably explained by considering the oblique branches and their acute angles as the result of magnetic repulsion, from the presentation of the same poles, &c. In the CORALS and CONCHYLIA, the whole act and purpose of their existence seems to be that of connecting the animal with the inorganic world by the perpetual formation of calcareous earth. For the corals are nothing but polypi, which are characterized by still passing away and dissolving into the earth, which they had previously excreted, as if they were the first feeble effort of detachment. The power seems to step forward from out the inorganic world only to fall back again upon it, still, however, under a new form, and under the predominance of the more active pole of magnetism. The product must have the same connection, therefore, with azote, which the first rudiments of vegetation have with carbon: the one and the other exist not for their own sakes, but in order to produce the conditions best fitted for the production of higher forms. In the polypi, corallines, &c., individuality is in its first dawn; there is the same shape in them all, and a multitude of animals form, as it were, a common animal. And as the individuals run into each other, so do the different genera. They likewise pass into each other so indistinguishably, that the whole order forms a very network.

As the corals approach the conchylia, this interramification decreases. The tubipora forms the transition to the serpula; for the characteristic of all zoophytes, namely, the star shape of their openings, here disappears, and the tubiporæ are distinguished from the rest of the corals by this very circumstance, that the hollow calcareous pipes are placed side by side, without inter-branching. In the serpula they have already become separate. How feeble this attempt is to individuate, is most clearly shown in their mode of generation. Notwithstanding the report of Professor Pallas, it still remains doubtful whether there exists any actual copulation among the polypi. The mere existence of a polypus suffices for its endless multiplication. They may be indefinitely propagated by cuttings, so languid is the power of individuation, so boundless that of reproduction. But the delicate jelly dissolves, as lightly as it was formed, into its own product, and it is probable that the Polynesia, as a future continent, will be the gigantic monument, not so much of their life, as of the life of Nature in them. Here we may observe the first instance of that general law, according to which Nature still assimilates her extreme points. In these, her first and feeblest attempts to animalize organization, it is latent, because undeveloped, and merely potential; while, in the human brain, the last and most consummate of her combined energies, it is again lost or disguised in the subtlety[15] and multiplicity of its evolution.

In the class immediately above (Mollusca) we find the individuals separate, a more determinate form, and in the higher species, the rudiment of nerves, as the first scarce distinguishable impress and exponent of sensibility; still, however, the vegetative reproduction is the predominant form; and even the nerves "which float in the same cavity with the other viscera," are probably subservient to it, and extend their power in the increased intensity of the reproductive force. Still prevails the transitional state from the fluid to the solid; and the jelly, that rudiment in which all animals, even the noblest, have their commencement; constitutes the whole sphere of these rudimental animals.

In the snail and muscle, the residuum of the coral reappears, but refined and ennobled into a part of the animal. The whole class is characterized by the separation of the fluid from the solid. On the one side, a gelatinous semi-fluid; on the other side, an entirely inorganic, though often a most exquisitely mechanized, calcareous excretion! Animalization in general is, we know, contra-distinguished from vegetables in general by the predominance of azote in the chemical composition, and of irritability in the organic process. But in this and the foregoing classes, as being still near the common equator, or the punctum indifferentiæ, the carbonic principle still asserts its claims, and the force of reproduction struggles with that of irritability. In the unrecon-

[15] The Anatomical Demonstrations of the Brain, by Dr. Spurzheim, which I have seen, presented to me the most satisfactory proof of this.

ciled strife of these two forces consists the character of the *Vermes*, which appear to be the preparatory step for the next class. Hence the difficulties which have embarrassed the naturalists, who adopt the Linnæan classification, in their endeavors to discover determinate characters of distinction between the vermes and the insecta.

But no sooner have we passed the borders, than endless variety of form and the bold display of instincts announce, that Nature has succeeded. She has created the intermediate link between the vegetable world, as the product of the reproductive or magnetic power, and the animal as the exponent of sensibility. Those that live and are nourished, on the bodies of other animals, are comparatively few, with little diversity of shape, and almost all of the same natural family. These we may pass by as exceptions. But the insect world, taken at large, appears as an intenser life, that has struggled itself loose and become emancipated from vegetation, *Floræ liberti, et libertini!* If for the sake of a moment's relaxation we might indulge a Darwinian flight, though at the risk of provoking a smile, (not, I hope, a frown,) from sober judgment, we might imagine the life of insects an apotheosis of the petals, stamina, and nectaries, round which they flutter, or of the stems and pedicles, to which they adhere. Beyond and above this step, Nature seems to act with a sort of free agency, and to have formed the classes from choice and bounty. Had she proceeded no further, yet the whole vegetable, together with the whole insect creation, would have formed within themselves an entire and independent system of Life. All plants have insects, most commonly each genus of vegetables its appropriate genera of insects; and so reciprocally interdependent and necessary to each other are they, that we can almost as little think of vegetation without insects, as of insects without vegetation. Though probably the mere likeness of *shape*, in the *papilio*, and the papilionaceous plants, suggested the idea of the former, as the latter in a state of detachment, to our late poetical and theoretical brother; yet a something, that approaches to a graver plausibility, is given to this fancy of a flying blossom; when we reflect how many plants depend upon insects for their fructification. Be it remembered, too, that with few and very obscure exceptions, the irritable power and an analogon of voluntary motion first dawn on us in the vegetable world, in the stamina, and anthers, at the period of impregnation. Then, as if Nature had been encouraged by the success of the first experiment, both the one and the other appear as predominance and general character. THE INSECT WORLD IS THE EXPONENT OF IRRITABILITY, AS THE VEGETABLE IS OF REPRODUCTION.

With the ascent in power, the intensity of individuation keeps even pace; and from this we may explain all the characteristic distinctions between this class and that of the vermes. The almost homogeneous jelly of the animalcula infusoria became, by a vital oxydation, granular in the polypi. This granulation formed itself into distinct organs in the molluscæ; while for the snails, which are the next step, the animalized lime, that seemed the sole final cause of the life of the polypi, assumes all the characters of an ulterior purpose. Refined into a hornlike substance, it becomes to the snails the substitute of an organ, and their outward skeleton. Yet how much more manifold and definite, the organization of an insect, than that of the preceding class, the patient researches of Swammerdam and Lyonnet have evinced, to the delight and admiration of every reflecting mind.

In the insect, for the first time, we find the distinct commencement of a separation between the exponents of sensibility and those of irritability; *i.e.* between the *nervous* and the *muscular* system. The latter, however, asserts its pre-eminence throughout. The prodigal provision of organs for the purposes of respiration, and the marvellous powers which numerous tribes of insects possess, of accommodating the most corrupted airs, for a longer or shorter period, to the support of their excitability, would of itself lead us to presume, that here the *vis irritabilis* is the reigning dynasty. There is here no confluence of nerves into one reservoir, as evidence of the independent existence of sensibility *as* sensibility;—and therefore no counterpoise of a vascular system, as a distinct exponent of the irritable pole. The whole muscularity of these animals is the organ of irritability; and the nerves themselves are probably feeders of the motory power. The petty rills of sensibility flow into the full expanse of irritability, and there lose themselves. The nerves appertaining to the senses, on the other hand, are indistinct, and comparatively unimportant. The multitude of immovable eyes appear not so much conductors of light, as its ultimate recipient. We are almost tempted to believe that they constitute, rather than subserve, their sensorium.

These eye-facets form the sense of light, rather than organs of seeing. Their almost paradoxical number at least, and the singularity of their forms, render it probable that they impel the animal by some modification of its irritability, herein likewise containing a striking analogy to the known influence of light on plants, than as excitements of sensibility. The sense that is near-est akin to irritability, and which alone resides in the muscular system, is that of touch, or feeling. This, therefore, is the first sense that emerges. Being confined to absolute contact, it oc-cupies the lowest rank; but for that very reason it is the ground of all the other senses, which act, according to the ratio of their ascent, at still increasing distances, and become more and more ideal, from the tentacles of the .polypus, to the human eye; which latter might be defined the outward organ of the identity, or at least of the indifference, of the real and ideal. But as the calcareous residuum of the lowest class approaches to the nature of horn in the snail, so the cumbrous shell of the snail has been transformed into polished and movable plates of defensive ar-mor in the insect. Thus, too, the same power of progressive individuation articulates the tentacula of the polypus and holo-thuria into antennæ; thereby manifesting the full emersion and eminency of irritability as a power which acts in, and gives its own character to, that of reproduction. The least observant must have noticed the lightning-like rapidity with which the insect tribes devour and eliminate their food, as by an instinc-tive necessity, and in the least degree for the purposes of the animal's own growth or enlargement. The same predominance of irritability, and at the same time a new start in individuation, is shown in the reproductive power as generation. There is now a regular projection, *ab intra ad extra*, for which neither sprouts nor cuttings can any longer be the substitutes. We have not space for further detail; but there is one point too strikingly illustrative and even confirmative of the proposed system, to be omitted altogether. We mean the curious fact, that the same characteristic tendency, *ad extra*, which in the males and females of certain insect tribes is realized in the functions of generation, conception, and parturiency, manifests and expands itself in the *sexless* individuals (which are always in this case the great ma-jority of the species), as instincts of art, and in the construc-tion of works completely detached and inorganic; while the geometric regularity of these works, which bears an analogy to crystallization, is demonstrably no more than the necessary re-sult of uniform action in a compressed multitude.

Again, as the insect world, averaging the whole, comes near-est to plants (whose very essence is reproduction), in the multi-tude of their germs; so does it resemble plants in the sufficiency of a single impregnation for the evolution of myriads of detached lives. Even so, the metamorphoses of insects, from the egg to the maggot and caterpillar, and from these, through the nympha and aurelia into the perfect insect, are but a more individuated and intenser form of a similar transformation of the plant from the seed-leaflets, or cotyledons, through the stalk, the leaves, and the calyx, into the perfect flower, the various colors of which seem made for the reflection of light, as the antecedent grade to the burnished scales, and scale-like eyes of the insect. Nevertheless, with all this seeming prodigality of organic power, the whole tendency is *ad extra*, and the life of insects, as electricity in the quadrate, acts chiefly on the superficies of their bodies, to which we may add the negative proof arising from the absence of sensibility. It is well known, that the two halves of a divided insect have continued to perform, or attempt, each their separate functions, the trunkless head feeding with its accustomed voracity, while the headless trunk has exhibited its appropriate excitability to the sexual influence.

The intropulsive force, that sends the ossification inward as to the centre, is reserved for a yet higher step, and this we find embodied in the class of *fishes*. Even here, however, the process still seems imperfect, and (as it were) initiatory. The skeleton has left the surface, indeed, but the bones approach to the nature of gristle. To feel the truth of this, we need only compare the most perfect bone of a fish with the thigh-bones of the mammalia, and the distinctness with which the latter manifest the co-presence of the *magnetic* power in its solid parietes, of the *electrical* in its branching arteries, and of the third greatest power, viz., the *qualitative* and interior, in its marrow. The senses of fish are more distinct than those of insects. Thus, the intensity of its sense of smell has been placed beyond doubt, and rises in the extent of its sphere far beyond the irritable sense, or the feeling, in insects. I say the *feeling*, not the touch; for the touch seems, as it were, a supervention to the feeling, a perfection *given* to it by the reaction of the higher powers. As the feeling of the insect, in subtlety and virtual distance, rises above the solitary sense of taste[16] in the mollusca, so does the smell of the fish rise above the feeling of the insect. In the fish, likewise, the eyes are single and movable, while it is remarkable that the only insect that possesses this latter privilege, is an inhabitant of the waters. Finally, here first, unequivocally, and on a *large* scale (for I pretend not to control the freedom, in which the necessity of Nature is rooted, by the precise limits of a sys-

[16] The remark on the feeling of the antennæ, compared with the touch of man, or even of the half-reasoning elephant, is yet more applicable to the taste, which in the segelatinous animals might, perhaps not inappropriately, be entitled the gastric sense.

tem),—here first, Nature exhibits, in the power of sensibility, the consummation of those vital forms (the *nisus formativi*) the adequate and the sole measure of which is to be sought for in their several organic products. But as if a weakness of exhaustion had attended this advance in the same moment it was made, Nature seems necessitated to fall back, and re-exert herself on the lower ground which she had before occupied, that of the vital magnetism, or the power of reproduction. The intensity of this latter power in the fishes, is shown both in their voracity and in the number of their eggs, which we are obliged to calculate by *weight,* not by *tale.* There is an equal intensity both of the *immanent* and the *projective* reproduction, in which, if we take in the comparative number of individuals in each species, and likewise the different intervals between the acts, the fish (it is probable) would be found to stand in a similar relation to the insect, as the insect, in the latter point, stands to the system of vegetation. Meantime, the fish sinks a step below the insect, in the mode and circumstances of impregnation. To this we will venture to add, the predominance of *length,* as the *form* of growth in so large a proportion of the known orders of fishes, and not less of their rectilineal path of motion. In all other respects, the correspondence combined with the progress in individuation, is striking in the whole detail. Thus the eye, in addition to its movability, has besides acquired a saline moisture in its higher development, as accordant with the life of its element. Add to these the glittering covering in both, the splendor of the scales in the one answering to the brilliant plates in the other,—the luminous reservoirs of the fire-flies,—the phosphorescence and electricity of many fishes,—the same analoga of moral qualities, in their rapacity, boldness, modes of seizing their prey by surprise,—their gills, as presenting the intermediate state between the spiracula of the grade next below, and the lungs of the step next above, both extremes of which seem combined in the structure of birds and of their quill-feathers; but above all, the convexity of the crystalline lens, so much greater than in birds, quadrupeds, and man, and seeming to collect, in one powerful organ, the hundredfold microscopic facettes of the insect's *light* organs; and it will not be easy to resist the conviction, that the same power is at work in both, and reappears under higher auspices. The intention of Nature is repeated; but, as was to have been expected, with two main differences. First, that in the lower grade the reproductions themselves seem merged in those of irritability, from the very circumstance that the latter constitutes no pole, either to the former, or to sensibility. The force of irritability acts, therefore, in the insect world, in full predominance; while the emergence of sensibility in the fish calls forth the opposite pole of reproduction, as a *distinct* power, and causes therefore the irritability to flow, in part, into the power of reproduction. The second result of this ascent is the direction of the organizing power, *ad intra*, with the consequent greater simplicity of the exterior form, and the substitution of condensed and flexible force, with comparative unity of implements, for that variety of tools, almost as numerous as the several objects to which they are to be applied, which arises from, and characterizes the superficial life of the insect creation. This grade of ascension, however, like the former, is accompanied by an apparent retrograde movement. For from this very accession of vital intensity we must account for the absence in the fishes of all the formative, or rather (if our language will permit it) *fabricative* instincts. How could it be otherwise? These instincts are the surplus and projection of the organizing power in the direction *ad extra*, and could not, therefore, have been expected in the class of animals that represent the first intuitive effort of organization, and are themselves the product of its first movement in the direction *ad intra*. But Nature never loses what she has once learnt, though in the acquirement of each new power she intermits, or performs less energetically, the act immediately preceding. She often drops a faculty, but never fails to pick it up again. She may seem forgetful and absent, but it is only to recollect herself with *additional*, as well as *recruited* vigor, in some after and higher state; as if the sleep of powers, as well as of bodies, were the season and condition of their growth. Accordingly, we find these instincts again, and with them a wonderful synthesis of fish and insect, as a higher third, in the feathered inhabitants of the air. Nay, she seems to have gone yet further back, and having given $B + C = D$ in the birds, so to have sported with one solitary instance of $B + D = A$ in that curious animal the dragon, the anatomy of which has been recently given to the public by Tiedemann; from whose work it appears, that this creature presents itself to us with the wings of the insect, and with the nervous system, the brain, and the cranium of the bird, in their several rudiments.

The synthesis of fish and insect in the birds, might be illustrated equally in detail with the former; but it will be sufficient for our purpose, that as in both the former cases, the insect and the fish, so here in that of the birds, the powers are under the predominance of irritability; the sensibility being dormant in the first, awakening in the second, and awake, but still subordinate, in the third. Of this my limits confine me to a single presumptive proof, viz., the superiority in strength and courage of the female in the birds of prey. For herein, indeed, does the difference of the sexes universally consist, wherever both the forces are developed, that the female is characterized by quicker irritability, and the male by deeper sensibility. How large a stride has been now made by Nature in the progress of individuation, what ornithologist does not know? From a multitude of instances we select the most impressive, the power of sound, with the first rudiments of modulation! That all languages designate the melody of birds as singing (though according to Blumenbach man only sings, while birds do but whistle), demonstrates that it has been felt as, what indeed it is, a tentative and prophetic prelude of something yet to come. With this conjoin the power and the tendency to acquire articulation, and to imitate speech; conjoin the building instinct and the migratory, the monogamy of several species, and the pairing of almost all; and we shall have collected new instances of the usage (I dare not say law) according to which Nature lets fall, in order to resume, and steps backward the furthest, when she means to leap forwards with the greatest concentration of energy.

For lo! in the next step of ascent the power of sensibility has assumed her due place and rank: her minority is at an end, and the complete and universal presence of a nervous system unites absolutely, by instanteity of time what, with the due allowances for the transitional process, had before been either lost in sameness, or perplexed by multiplicity, or compacted by a finer mechanism. But with this, all the analogies with which Nature had delighted us in the preceding step seem lost, and, with the single exception of that more than valuable, that estimable philanthropist, the dog, and, perhaps, of the horse and elephant, the analogies to ourselves, which we can discover in the quadrupeds or quadrumani, are of our vices, our follies, and our imperfections. The facts in confirmation of both the propositions are so numerous and so obvious, the advance of Nature, under the predominance of the third synthetic power, both in the intensity of life and in the intenseness and extension of individuality, is so undeniable, that we may leap forward at once to the highest realization and reconciliation of both her tendencies, that of the most perfect detachment with the greatest possible union, to that last work, in which Nature did not assist as handmaid under the eye of her sovereign Master, who made Man in his own image, by superadding self-consciousness with self-government, and breathed into him a living soul.

The class of *Vermes* deposit a calcareous stuff, as if it had torn loose from the earth a piece of the gross mass which it must still drag about with it. In the insect class this residuum has refined itself. In the fishes and amphibia it is driven back or inward, the organic power begins to be intuitive, and sensibility appears. In the birds the bones have become hollow; while, with apparent proportional recess, but, in truth, by the excitement of the opposite pole, their exterior presents an actual vegetation. The bones of the mammalia are filled up, and their coverings have become more simple. Man possesses the most perfect osseous structure, the least and most insignificant covering. The whole force of organic power has attained an inward and centripetal direction. He has the whole world in counterpoint to him, but he contains an entire world within himself. Now, for the first time at the apex of the living pyramid, it is Man and Nature, but Man himself is a syllepsis, a compendium of Nature—the Microcosm! Naked and helpless cometh man into the world. Such has been the complaint from eldest time; but we complain of our chief privilege, our ornament, and the connate mark of our sovereignty. *Porphyrigeniti sumus!* In Man the centripetal and individualizing tendency of all Nature is itself concentred and individualized—he is a revelation of Nature! Henceforward, he is referred to himself, delivered up to his own charge; and he who stands the most on himself, and stands the firmest, is the truest, because the most individual, Man. In social and political life this acme is inter-dependence; in moral life it is independence; in intellectual life it is genius. Nor does the form of polarity, which has accompanied the law of individuation up its whole ascent, desert it here. As the height, so the depth. The intensities must be at once opposite and equal. As the liberty, so must be the reverence for law. As the independence, so must be the service and the submission to the Supreme Will! As the ideal genius and the originality, in the same proportion must be the resignation to the real world, the sympathy and the inter-communion with Nature. In the conciliating mid-point, or equator, does the Man live, and only by its equal presence in both its poles can that life be manifested!

If it had been possible, within the prescribed limits of this essay, to have deduced the philosophy of Life synthetically, the evidence would have been carried over from section to section, and the *quod erat demonstrandum* at the conclusion of one section would reappear as the principle of the succeeding—the goal of the one would be the starting-post of the other. Positions arranged in my own mind, as intermediate and organic links of administration, must be presented to the reader in the first instance, at least, as a mere hypothesis. Instead of demanding his assent as a right, I must solicit a suspension of his judgment as a courtesy; and, after all, however firmly the hypothesis may support the phenomena piled upon it, we can deduce no more than a practical rule, grounded on a strong presumption. The license of arithmetic, however, furnishes instances that a rule may be usefully applied in practice, and for the particular purpose may be sufficiently authenticated by the result, before it has itself been duly demonstrated. It is enough, if only it hath been rendered fully intelligible.

In a system where every position proceeds from a scientific preconstruction, a power acting exclusively in length, would be magnetism by virtue of our own definition of the term. In like manner, a surface power would be electricity, as far as that system was concerned, whether it accorded or not with the facts ordinarily so called. But it is incumbent on us, who must treat the subject *analytically*, to show by experiment that magnetism does in fact act longitudinally, and electricity superficially; and that, consequently, the former is distinguished from, and yet contained in, the latter, as a straight line is distinguished from, yet contained in, a superficies.

First, that magnetism, in its conductors, seeks and follows length only, and by the length is itself conducted, has been proved by Brugmans, in his philosophical Essay on the Matter of Magnetism, where he relates that a magnet capable of supporting a body four times heavier than itself, and which acted as a magnetic needle at the distance of twenty inches, was so weakened by the interposition of three cast-iron plates of considerable thickness, as scarcely to move the magnetic needle from its place at a distance of only three inches. A similar experiment had been made by Descartes. I concluded, therefore, said Brugmans, that if the iron plates were interposed between the magnet and the needle lengthways, instead of breadthways or right across, the action of the magnet on the magnetic needle would, in consequence of this great increase of resistance, become still weaker, or perhaps evanescent. But not less to my surprise than my admiration, I found that the power of the magnet was so far from being *diminished* by this change in the relative position of the iron plates; that, on the contrary, it now extended to a far greater distance than when no iron at all was interposed. Some time after the same philosopher, out of several iron bars, the sides of which were an inch broad each, composed a single bar of the length of more than ten feet, and observed the magnetism make its way through the whole mass. But, in order to try whether the action could be propagated to any length indefinitely, after several experiments with bars of intermediate lengths, in all of which he had succeeded, he tried a four-cornered iron rod, more than twenty feet long, and it was at this length that the magnetic power first began to be diminished. So far Brugmans.

But the shortest way for anyone to convince himself of this relation of the magnetic power would be, in one and the same experiment, to interpose the same piece of iron between the magnet and the compass needle first *breadthways;* and in this case it will be found that the needle, which had been previously deflected by the magnet from its natural position at one of its poles, will instantly resume the same, either wholly or very nearly so—then to interpose the same piece of iron *lengthways;* in which case the position of the compass needle will be scarcely or not at all affected.

The assertion of Bernoulli and others, that the absolute force of the artificial magnet increases in the ratio of its superficies, stands corrected in the far more accurate experiments of Coulomb (published in his Treatise on Magnetism), which proves that the increase takes place (in a far greater degree) in the ratio of its length. The same naturalist even found means to determine that the directing powers of the needle, which he had measured by help of his *balance de tortion,* stand to the length of the needle in such a ratio as that, provided only the length of the needle is from forty to fifty times its diameter, the momenta of these directing powers will increase in the very same direct proportion as the length is increased. Nor is this all that may be deduced from the experiment last mentioned. If only the magnet be strong enough, it will show likewise that magnetism *seeks* the length. The proof is contained in the remarkable fact, that the iron interposed between the magnet and the magnetic needle *breadthways* constantly acquires its two opposite poles at both ends *lengthways.* Though the preceding experiments are abundantly sufficient to prove the position, yet the following deserves mention for the beautiful clearness of its evidence. If the magnetic power is determined exclusively by length, it is to be expected that it will manifest no force, where the piece of iron is of such a shape that no one dimension predominates. Bring a *cube* of iron near the magnetic needle and it will not exert the slightest degree of power beyond what belongs to it as mere iron. By the perfect equality of the dimension, the magnetism of the earth appears, as it were, perplexed and doubtful. Now, then, attach a second cube of iron to the first, and the instantaneous act of the iron on the magnetic needle will make it manifest that with the length thus given, the magnetic influence is given at the same moment.

That electricity, on the other hand, does not act in length merely, is clear, from the fact that every electric body is electric over its whole surface. But that electricity acts both in length and breadth, and *only* in length and breadth, and not in depth; in short, that the (so-called) electrical fluid in an electrified body spreads over the whole surface of that body without penetrating it, or tending *ad intra*, may be proved by direct experiment. Take a cylinder of wood, and bore an indefinite number of holes in it, each of them four lines in depth and four in diameter. Electrify this cylinder, and present to its superficies a small square of gold-leaf, held to it by an insulating needle of gum lac, and bring this square to an electrometer of great sensibility. The electrometer will instantly show an electricity in the gold-leaf, similar to that of the cylinder which had been brought into contact with it. The square of gold-leaf having thus been discharged of its electricity, put it carefully into one of the holes of the cylinder, *so*, namely, that it shall touch only the bottom of the hole, and present it again to the electrometer. It will be then found that the electrometer will exhibit no signs of electricity whatsoever. From this it follows, that the electricity which had been communicated to the cylinder had confined itself to the *surface*. If the time and the limit prescribed would admit, we could multiply experiments, all tending to prove the same law; but we must be content with the barely sufficient. But that the *chemical process* acts in *depth*, and first, therefore, *realizes* and integrates the fluxional power of magnetism and electricity, is involved in the *term* composition; and this will become still more convincing when we have learnt to regard *decomposition* as a mere co-relative, *i.e.* as decomposition relatively to the body decomposed, but composition *actually* and in respect of the substances, *into* which it was decomposed. The alteration in the specific gravity of metals in their chemical amalgams, interesting as the fact is in all points, is *decisive* in the present; for gravity is the sole *inward* of inorganic bodies—it *constitutes* their depth.

I can now, for the first time, give to my opinions that degree of intelligibility, which is requisite for their introduction as hypotheses; the experiments above related, understood as in the common mode of thinking, prove that the magnetic influence flows in length, the electric fluid by suffusion, and that chemical agency (whatever the main agent may be) is qualitative and *in intimis*. Now my hypothesis demands the converse of all this. I affirm that a power, acting exclusively in length, is (wherever it be found) *magnetism;* that a power which acts *both* in length and in breadth, and *only* in length and breadth, is (wherever it be found) *electricity;* and finally, that a power which, together with length and breadth, includes depth likewise, is (wherever it be found) *constructive agency*. That is but *one* phenomenon of magnetism, to which we have appropriated and confined the term magnetism; because of all the natural bodies at present known, iron, and one or two of its nearest relatives in the family of hard yet coherent metals, are the only ones, in which all the conditions are collected, under which alone the magnetic agency can appear in and during the act itself. When, therefore, I affirm the power of reproduction in organized bodies to be magnetism, I must be understood to mean that this power, as it exists in the magnet, and which we there (to use a strong phrase) catch in the very act, is to the same kind of power, working as reproductive, what the root is to the cube of that root. We no more confound the force in the compass needle with that of reproduction, than a man can be said to confound his liver with a lichen, because he affirms that both of them grow.

The same precautions are to be repeated in the identification of electricity with irritability; and the power of depth, for which we have yet no appropriated term, with sensibility. How great the distance is in all, and that the lowest degrees are adopted as the exponent terms, not for their own sakes, but merely because they may be used with less hazard of diverting the attention from the *kind* by peculiar properties arising out of the degree, is evident from the third instance, unless the theorist can be supposed insane enough to apply sensation in good earnest to the effervescence of an acid or an alkali, or to sympathize with the distresses of a vat of new beer when it is working. In whatever way the subject could be treated, it must have remained unintelligible to men who, if they think of space at all, abstract their notion of it from the contents of an exhausted receiver. With this, and with an ether, such men may work wonders; as what, indeed, can not be done with a plenum and a vacuum, when a theorist has privileged himself to assume the one, or the other, *ad libitum?*—in all innocence of heart, and undisturbed by the reflection that the two things can not both be true. That both time and space are mere abstractions I am well aware; but I know with equal certainty that what is *expressed* by them as the *identity* of both is the highest reality, and the root of all power, the power to suffer, as well as the power to act. However mere an *ens logicum* space may be, the *dimensions* of space are real, and the works of Galileo, in more than one elegant passage, prove with what awe and amazement they fill the mind that worthily contemplates them. Dismissing, therefore, all facts of degrees, as introduced merely for the purposes of illustration, I would make as little reference as possible to the magnet, the charged phial, or the processes of the laboratory, and designate the three powers in the process of our animal life, each by two co-relative terms, the one expressing the *form*, and the other the *object* and *product* of the power. My hypothesis will, therefore, be thus expressed, that the constituent forces of life in the human living body are—first, the power of length, or REPRODUCTION; second, the power of surface (that is, length and breadth), or IRRITABILITY; third, the power of depth, or SENSIBILITY. With this observation I may conclude these remarks, only reminding the reader that Life itself is neither of these separately, but the copula of all three—that Life, *as* Life, supposes a positive or universal principle in Nature, with a negative principle in every particular animal, the latter, or limitative power, constantly acting to individualize, and, as it were, *figure* the former. *Thus*, then, Life itself is not a *thing*—a self-subsistent *hypostasis*—but an *act* and *process;* which, pitiable as the prejudice will appear to the *forts esprits*, is a great deal more than either my reason would authorize or my conscience allow me to assert—concerning the Soul, as the principle both of Reason and Conscience.

INDEX OF TITLES

MODERN LIBRARY COLLEGE EDITIONS

HAWTHORNE, NATHANIEL: *The Scarlet Letter* (30921)
HEGEL, GEORG WILHELM FREIDRICH: *The Philosophy of Hegel* (30976)
HERODOTUS: *The Persian Wars* (30954)
IBSEN, HENRIK: *Eight Plays* (32865)
JAMES, HENRY: *The Bostonians* (30959)
JAMES, HENRY: *The Portrait of a Lady* (30947)
JOHNSON, JAMES WELDON, (Ed.): *Utopian Literature* (30996)
LOOMIS, ROGER SHERMAN AND LOOMIS, LAURA HIBBARD, (Ed.): *Medieval Romances* (30970)
MACHIAVELLI, NICCOLO: *The Prince and the Discourses* (30925)
MALRAUX, ANDRE: *Man's Fate* (30975)
MANN, THOMAS: *Death in Venice* (30999)
MANN, THOMAS: *The Magic Mountain* (30993)
MELVILLE, HERMAN: *Moby Dick* (30926)
MILTON, JOHN: *Paradise Lost* (30994)
OATES, WHITNEY J. AND O'NEILL, EUGENE, JR., (Ed.): *Seven Famous Greek Plays* (30930)
O'NEILL, EUGENE: *The Later Plays* (30991)
PLATO: *The Work of Plato* (30971)
POE, EDGAR ALLAN: *The Selected Poetry and Prose* (30958)
PROUST, MARCEL: *Swann's Way* (30967)
QUINTANA, RICARDO, (Ed.): *Eighteenth-Century Plays* (30980)
SHELLEY, PERCY BYSSHE: *Selected Poetry and Prose* (30950)
SOLOMON, ROBERT C., (Ed.): *Existentialism* (31704)
SWIFT, JONATHAN: *Gulliver's Travels and Other Writings* (30932)
TACITUS: *The Complete Works* (30953)
TENNYSON, ALFRED LORD: *Selected Poetry* (30960)
THOREAU, HENRY DAVID: *Walden and Other Writings* (32666)
THUCYDIDES: *The Peloponnesian War* (32978)
TOCQUEVILLE, ALEXIS DE: *Democracy in America* (32675)
TOLSTOY, LEO: *Anna Karenina* (30936)
TURGENEV, IVAN S.: *Fathers and Sons* (30938)
VOLTAIRE: *Candide and Other Writings* (30964)
WHITMAN, WALT: *Leaves of Grass and Selected Prose* (32661)
WINE, M. L., (Ed.): *Drama of The English Renaissance* (30866)
WORDSWORTH, WILLIAM: *Selected Poetry* (30941)